THE POLITICS OF NUMBERS

THE POLITICS OF NUMBERS

William Alonso
and
Paul Starr

Editors

for the
National Committee for Research
on the 1980 Census

RUSSELL SAGE FOUNDATION / NEW YORK

The Russell Sage Foundation

Library of Congress Cataloging-in-Publication Data

The Politics of numbers.

Chiefly papers prepared for a conference on "The political economy of national statistics," held in Washington, D.C., Oct. 13–15, 1983.
Bibliography: p.
Includes index.
1. United States—Statistical services—Political aspects.   2. United States—Census, 1980.   I. Alonso, William.   II. Starr, Paul, 1949–   .
HA37.U55P65 1986   320'.0723   86-10060
ISBN 0-87154-015-0

10 9 8 7 6 5 4 3 2 1

THE POPULATION OF THE UNITED STATES IN THE 1980s

A Census Monograph Series

The National Committee for Research on the 1980 Census

The committee is sponsored by the Social Science Research Council, the Russell Sage Foundation, and the Alfred P. Sloan Foundation, in collaboration with the U.S. Bureau of the Census. The opinions, findings, and conclusions or recommendations expressed the monographs supported by the committee are those of the author(s) and do not necessarily reflect the views of the committee or its sponsors.

Foreword

"The Population of the United States in the 1980s" is an ambitious series of volumes aimed at converting the vast statistical yield of the 1980 census into authoritative analyses of major changes and trends in American life. *The Politics of Numbers* resembles the other volumes in this series in that its point of departure is the United States census; it differs from the other volumes by going far beyond census data to an examination of the compilation and analysis of other official data as well. It is the only volume in the series devoted to the governmental data system itself, rather than to the information contained in that data. Moreover, unlike the other series volumes, it is not a monograph but a collection of essays on official statistics, the outgrowth of a 1983 conference on the subject sponsored by the National Committee for Research on the 1980 Census.

This series represents an important episode in social science research and revives a long tradition of independent census analysis. First in 1930, and then again in 1950 and 1960, teams of social scientists worked with the U.S. Bureau of the Census to investigate significant social, economic, and demographic developments revealed by the decennial census. These census projects produced three landmark series of studies, providing a firm foundation and setting a high standard for our present undertaking.

There is, in fact, more than a theoretical continuity between those earlier census projects and the present one. Like those previous efforts, this new census project has benefited from close cooperation between the Census Bureau and a distinguished, interdisciplinary group of scholars. Like the 1950 and 1960 research projects, research on the 1980 census was initiated by the Social Science Research Council and the Russell Sage Foundation. In deciding once again to promote a coordinated program of census analysis, Russell Sage and the Council were mindful not only of the severe budgetary restrictions imposed on the Census Bureau's own publishing and dissemination activities in the

THE POLITICS OF NUMBERS

1980s, but also of the extraordinary changes that have occurred in so many dimensions of American life over the past two decades.

The studies constituting "The Population of the United States in the 1980s" were planned, commissioned, and monitored by the National Committee for Research on the 1980 Census, a special committee appointed by the Social Science Research Council and sponsored by the Council, the Russell Sage Foundation, and the Alfred P. Sloan Foundation, with the collaboration of the U.S. Bureau of the Census. This committee includes leading social scientists from a broad range of fields—demography, economics, education, geography, history, political science, sociology, and statistics. It has been the committee's task to select the main topics for research, obtain highly qualified specialists to carry out that research, and provide the structure necessary to facilitate coordination among researchers and with the Census Bureau.

The topics treated in this series span virtually all the major features of American society—ethnic groups (blacks, Hispanics, foreign-born); spatial dimensions (migration, neighborhoods, housing, regional and metropolitan growth and decline); and status groups (income levels, families and households, women). Authors were encouraged to draw not only on the 1980 Census but also on previous censuses and on subsequent national data. Each individual research project was assigned a special advisory panel made up of one committee member, one member nominated by the Census Bureau, one nominated by the National Science Foundation, and one or two other experts. These advisory panels were responsible for project liaison and review and for recommendations to the National Committee regarding the readiness of each manuscript for publication. With the final approval of the chairman of the National Committee, each report was released to the Russell Sage Foundation for publication and distribution.

The debts of gratitude incurred by a project of such scope and organizational complexity are necessarily large and numerous. The committee must thank, first, its sponsors—the Social Science Research Council, headed until recently by Kenneth Prewitt; the Russell Sage Foundation, under the direction of president Marshall Robinson; and the Alfred P. Sloan Foundation, led by Albert Rees. The long-range vision and day-to-day persistence of these organizations and individuals sustained this research program over many years. The active and willing cooperation of the Bureau of the Census was clearly invaluable at all stages of this project, and the extra commitment of time and effort made by Bureau economist James R. Wetzel must be singled out for special recognition. A special tribute is also due to David L. Sills of the Social Science Research Council, staff member of the committee, whose organizational, administrative, and diplomatic skills kept this complicated project running smoothly.

The committee also wishes to thank those organizations that contributed additional funding to the 1980 Census project—the Ford Foundation and its deputy vice president, Louis Winnick, the National Science Foundation, the National Institute on Aging, and the National Institute of Child Health and Human Development. Their support of the research program in general and of several particular studies is gratefully acknowledged.

The ultimate goal of the National Committee and its sponsors has been to produce a definitive, accurate, and comprehensive picture of the U.S. population in the 1980s, a picture that would be primarily descriptive but also enriched by a historial perspective and a sense of the challenges for the future inherent in the trends of today. We hope our readers will agree that the present volume takes a significant step toward achieving that goal.

CHARLES F. WESTOFF
Chairman and Executive Director,
National Committee for Research
on the 1980 Census

Contents

Contributors

William Alonso, *Harvard University*
Paul Starr, *Princeton University*
Margo Conk, *University of Wisconsin*
Judith de Neufville, *University of California, Berkeley*
Joseph Duncan, *Dun & Bradstreet*
Judith Gruber, *University of California, Berkeley*
Christopher Jencks, *Northwestern University*
Steven Kelman, *Harvard University*
Nathan Keyfitz, *Harvard University*
Richard P. Nathan, *Princeton University*
Mark Perlman, *University of Pittsburgh*
William Petersen, *Carmel, California*
Kenneth Prewitt, *Rockefeller Foundation*
Abigail Thernstrom, *Lexington, Massachusetts*
Raymond Vernon, *Harvard University*
Janet Weiss, *University of Michigan*

THE POLITICS OF NUMBERS

INTRODUCTION

WILLIAM ALONSO AND PAUL STARR

EVERY day, from the morning paper to the evening news, Americans are served a steady diet of statistics. We are given the latest figures for consumer prices and the unemployment rate, lagging and leading economic indicators, reading scores, and life expectancies, not to mention data on crime, divorce, and the money supply. Most of these numbers are official in the sense that they are produced by government in what are generally presumed to be impersonal and objective bureaucracies. Of course, in some countries, where the regimes are distrusted, official numbers are also routinely disbelieved. But where the statistical collecting and reporting agencies enjoy a reputation for professionalism (as they generally do in our society), their findings are commonly presented—and accepted—as neutral observations, like a weatherman's report on temperature and atmospheric pressure.

This view, we all know, is too simple. Official statistics do not merely hold a mirror to reality. They reflect presuppositions and theories about the nature of society. They are products of social, political, and economic interests that are often in conflict with each other. And they are sensitive to methodological decisions made by complex organizations with limited resources. Moreover, official numbers, especially those that appear in series, often do not reflect all these factors instantaneously: They echo their past as the surface of a landscape reflects its underlying geology.

Official statistics have always been subject to these influences, but more is now at stake. In the United States, an increased share of federal money is distributed to states and localities according to various statistical formulae and criteria. The making of economic policy as well as private economic decisions hinges on fluctuations in key indicators. Standards for affirmative action in employment and school desegregation depend on official data on ethnic and racial composition. Several states now limit their budgets to a fixed share of projected state income, and a proposed "balanced budget" constitutional amendment would do the same for the federal government, in effect incorporating the inexact science of economic measurement and forecasting into the Constitution.

Official statistics directly affect the everyday lives of millions of Americans. They trigger cost-of-living adjustments of many wages and Social Security payments. They determine who qualifies as poor enough for food stamps, public housing programs, and welfare benefits. They are used to set the rates at which Medicare pays hospitals and to regulate businesses large and small.

It is no wonder, then, that America has become a nation of statistics watchers—from the congressmen concerned about redistricting to the elderly couples on Social Security worried about rising costs; from the bankers following changes in the money supply to the farmers watching the figures on cost-price "parity" for their crops. So well institutionalized are statistics such as the unemployment rate, the money supply, and various price indices that the date and even the hour of their release are regular events in the political and economic calendar, setting off debates on the performance of government policy and influencing both stock markets and elections.

But official statistics also affect society in subtler ways. By the questions asked (and not asked), categories employed, statistical methods used, and tabulations published, the statistical systems change images, perceptions, aspirations. The Census Bureau's methods of classifying and measuring the size of population groups determine how many citizens will be counted as "Hispanic" or "Native American." These decisions direct the flow of various federally mandated "preferments," and they in turn spur various allegiances and antagonisms throughout the population. Such numbers shape society as they measure it.

The absence of numbers may also be telling. For years after World War II Lebanon did not hold an official census, out of fear that a count of the torn country's Christians and Muslims might upset their fragile, negotiated sharing of power (which broke down anyway). Saudi Arabia's census has never been officially released, probably because of the Saudis' worry that publishing an exact count (showing their own population to be smaller than many supposed) might encourage enemics to invade the country or promote subversion. In Britain a few years ago, Scotland Yard created a furor when, for the first time, it broke down its statistics on crime according to race. Some Britons objected that the mere publication of the data was inflammatory.

Statistics are lenses through which we form images of our society. During the early decades of the Republic, Americans saw the rapid growth in population and industry that the census recorded as a confirmation, for all the world to see, of the success of the American experiment. The historian Frederick Jackson Turner announced his famous conclusion about the closing of the American frontier on the basis of an observation in the report of the 1890 census.

Today, our national self-perceptions are regularly confirmed or challenged by statistics on such fundamental matters as the condition of the nuclear family (allegedly still eroding), reading and literacy, the (slight) reversal of rural-to-urban migration, and our industrial productivity and military strength relative to other countries. Whether the meanings that politicians or pundits read into the data are reasonable or fanciful, the numbers provide a basis for popular and specialized discussion. Even when the numbers misrepresent reality, they coordinate our misperceptions of it.

The process is thus recursive. Winston Churchill observed that first we shape our buildings and then they shape us. The same may be said of statistics.

Lest there be any confusion, we should emphasize that to say official statistics are entangled in politics and social life is not to say that they are "politicized" in the sense of being corrupt. In some circumstances, they may indeed be corrupt, but that is not our point. Far from it: In the United States, institutional safeguards for the most part shield the statistical agencies from meddling by politicians and interest groups. These safeguards are a political fact in their own right and a foundation essential for public trust in the numbers. Our point, rather, is that political judgments are implicit in the choice of what to measure, how to measure it, how often to measure it, and how to present and interpret the results. These choices become embedded in the statistical systems of the modern state and the information they routinely produce. The forces that shape those systems and their consequences for politics and society are the subject of this book.

Overview of the Book

Just as the collection of statistics is an act of selection, so is the production of a collection about statistics. We have not tried to cover all the kinds of statistics that governments gather or even the full range of analytical problems raised by the interplay of statistics and politics. In designing this collaborative project, we have brought together authors from different fields—economics, history, politics, sociology, and planning—to write on topics that we thought would be interesting in their own right and of broad intellectual reach. Our aim was not to contribute to statistical policy or methodology but to open up a field that scarcely exists—the political economy and sociology of statistics. We hoped the collection would be suggestive, without pretending that it might be definitive.

In the second part of this introductory section, one of us (Starr) attempts to outline the analytical problems and approaches in this area of inquiry and to review not only what we publish here but also some of the relevant literature in history and the social sciences. This is an effort to sort out the analytical issues in the sociology of statistics and to put them in intellectual context and perspective.

A central tenet of this book, as we have already indicated, is that statistics cannot be constructed on purely technical grounds alone but require choices that ultimately turn on considerations of purpose and policy. The point is well illustrated by the three chapters in Part I, *The Politics of Economic Measurement*. In the first, Raymond Vernon first looks at the competing views of statistics held by professional government statisticians, political leaders and policymakers, and academic social scientists. He then considers three cases—comparative figures on economic growth, productivity, and military expenditures—that illustrate the policy choices that inevitably must be made in constructing statistical information. Christopher Jencks examines the choices in the measurement of income, and asks why official statistics of family income in the United States in the 1970s continued to be reported in a highly misleading fashion when the deficiencies were well known. Mark Perlman examines the development of the national income accounts and finds that the policy interests of Keynesian economists were critical in shaping the structure of the accounts in the United States.

In the United States as well as Western Europe, the census has been the subject of particularly open and strenuous political conflict in the last decade. Part II, *The Politics of Population Measurement*, begins with a chapter by Margo Conk on the historical roots of the controversies that erupted over the 1980 U.S. census. William Petersen takes a broad look at the history and nature of disputes over the definition and measurement of ethnicity, and Nathan Keyfitz examines the political and social aspects of the inexact art of population forecasting.

The constitutional mandate for a census grew primarily out of the need to apportion seats in the House of Representatives and the Electoral College. The functions of government statistics have since expanded, but they continue to be tied closely to the demands of democratic government. Part III, *Statistics and Democratic Politics*, deals with those connections. Kenneth Prewitt puts the problems in the context of democratic theory and argues that, despite its limitations, the nation's number system has become vital to pursuing two essential goals of a democratic polity: accountability and the representation of diverse interests. Steven Kelman takes up similar themes in providing an explanation for an apparent conundrum: why the federal government in the nineteenth century produced elaborate statistics at a time when theories of minimal government prevailed. Why did Americans make an exception of statistical inquiries, some of which involved intrusive questions by government about private activities? Kelman rejects an explanation offered by microeconomic theory, which emphasizes the use of government to overcome problems of market failure, and cites historical evidence to argue that statistics were sought for their use in informing political debate, confirming national identity, and securing group recognition. In the final chapter in Part III, Abigail Thernstrom offers a somewhat darker view of the use of statistics. She also focuses on an issue relevant to democratic practice—the assurance of minority representation—and suggests that statistical tests have served as a form of camouflage for changing political objectives in the enforcement of voting rights over the past two decades.

Among their many functions, statistics also mediate the resolution of conflict. In Part IV, *Statistics and American Federalism*, three chapters deal with the interplay of statistics and the various levels of government in the United States. Richard Nathan analyzes the "politics of printouts": the use of statistical formulae to distribute federal aid and the resulting political burden imposed on the statistics and statistical agencies. Judith de Neufville looks at the effect on local statistical practice of changing federal policy, particularly the shift from categorical programs to revenue-sharing and block grants, which create different demands for data. She emphasizes the difficulties of local governments in coping with statistical needs, in part because of local "dependency in statistical production" and federal cutbacks, but also because of the distinctive problems of statistical politics and policymaking at the local level. Looking in the opposite direction—that is, from center to periphery—Judith Gruber and Janet Weiss identify problems in national statistics that derive, in part, from the fragmentation of power among the states and localities. They argue that the effort to create a Common Core of Data for national education statistics failed because of the difficulties of overcoming the dispersed authority for schooling in the federal system and because of a lack of political consensus about how to measure education. The discouraging result is a public statistical system with limited relevance to the vital problems of public policy.

New technological and political developments are greatly altering the mode of statistical production and distribution. In Part V, *The New Political Economy of Statistics*, Joseph W. Duncan looks at the implications of new computer technology and the changing costs and methods of producing, analyzing, and disseminating data. He defends the increasing role of private industry, which the Reagan administration now encourages as a means of cutting back federal statistical commitments. In the final chapter of the volume, Paul Starr and Ross Corson provide an analysis of the rise of the private statistical services industry and its relation to government. They take a critical view of the privatization of public data, suggesting that it threatens some democratic political values of fundamental importance.

The chapters in this volume were initially prepared for a conference on "The Political Economy of National Statistics," held in Washington on October 13–15, 1983. The conference was sponsored by the Social Science Research Council's Committee for Research on the 1980 Census. We wish to thank David L. Sills, who coordinated the project for the Council; and Kenneth Prewitt, then president of the Council, who took a particular interest in this venture. Ross Corson assisted Paul Starr as a research assistant and Jane Skanderup served as David Sills's assistant throughout. We are of course grateful to the contributors to the volume for their work and their patience.

THE SOCIOLOGY OF
OFFICIAL STATISTICS

PAUL STARR

S OCIAL scientists routinely use statistics from official sources as a *means* of analysis, but less frequently do they take the statistics or their sources as an *object* of analysis. If they do, they generally are interested in knowing whether—or showing how—social or political processes have distorted the results and, therefore, why they may be safely ignored or, if possible, what may be done to adjust the data or to improve official statistical practice. Not surprisingly, social scientists in the academy, business, and government approach statistics primarily with their own practical interests in mind—methodology, commerce, and policy.

Yet statistical systems are worth understanding as social phenomena in their own right. Although the sociology of statistics is not an established field of inquiry, much has been written in scattered places about statistical institutions, statistical policy and politics, the social and cultural history of statistics, the uses of statistics in organizations, and other related topics. From these diverse sources emerge general sociological questions about statistics. In this introductory essay I want to set out some of those questions, the approaches taken to them, and the arguments that seem to me most persuasive and useful in understanding statistics as a social phenomenon.[1]

The concept of "statistical system" lies at the center of this inquiry. By a statistical system I mean a system for the production, distribution, and use of numerical information. A statistical system may be said to have two kinds of structure—social and cognitive. Its social organization consists of the social and economic relations of individual respondents, state agencies, private firms, professions, international organizations, and others involved in producing flows of data from original sources to points of analysis, distribution, and use. Cognitive organization refers to the structuring of the information itself, including the boundaries of inquiry, presuppositions about social reality, systems of classification, methods of measurement, and official rules for interpreting and presenting data.

About any information system—whether for record-keeping, surveillance, news, or statistics—it is possible to raise several kinds of sociological questions, depending on whether the object is to explain (or derive consequences from) the origin or pattern of development of the system, its social or cognitive structure, its uses and effects, or its direction of change.[2] On this basis, it seems convenient to divide the sociology of official statistics into five overlapping sets of questions:

[1]The reader should be alerted to three restrictions in the scope of this analysis. First, it is primarily concerned with descriptive statistics that measure social phenomena rather than with statistical data or techniques that measure the effects of different treatments or agents. In the latter category belong evaluation research and controlled social experimentation. The politics of program evaluation, risk assessment, and cost-benefit analysis do not receive sustained attention here. Second, I do not deal with the development of statistical methods. Although the term "statistics" refers both to numerical information and to a field of knowledge (the subject of statistics as a discipline), this analysis concerns statistics only in the first sense. [For historical and sociological work on the development of statistical methods, see Donald A. MacKenzie, *Statistics in Britain, 1865–1930: The Social Construction of Scientific Knowledge* (Edinburgh: Edinburgh University Press, 1981); Paul F. Lazarsfeld, "Notes on the History of Quantification in Sociology—Trends, Sources and Problems," in Harry Woolf, ed., *Quantification: A History of the Meaning of Measurement in the Natural and Social Sciences* (Indianapolis: Bobbs-Merrill, 1961), pp. 147–203; and Lorraine Dastin, Michael Heidelberger, and Lorenz Krüge, eds., *The Probabilistic Revolution, 1800–1930* (Boston: Bradford Books, 1987).] Third, this analysis deals with official statistics, by which I mean statistics that governments produce, finance, or routinely incorporate into their decisions. Although the term "official" is sometimes used to describe any institutionally certified form (professional sports have their "official statistics"), the state is the main pathway to the distinctive cultural authority that official facts characteristically assume. Part of my interest in this topic derives from my earlier work on cultural authority. See *The Social Transformation of American Medicine* (New York: Basic Books, 1982), esp. chap. 1.

[2]In developing these categories, I benefit from James B. Rule's work on surveillance systems. See his *Private Lives and Public Surveillance: Social Control in the Computer Age* (New York: Schocken, 1974), esp. chap. 1. I owe a more general debt here to a classic essay that helped to organize the sociology of knowledge: Robert K. Merton, "Paradigm for the Sociology of Knowledge" [1945], reprinted in Merton, *The Sociology of Science: Theoretical and Empirical Investigations* (Chicago: University of Chicago Press, 1973), pp. 7–40.

1. *System origins and development:* What causes statistical systems to be established? Why do governments or other actors make a decision to count or to allow themselves to be counted? And what processes govern the systems' general historical evolution?
2. *Social organization of statistical systems:* What are the sources and consequences of different designs or patterns in the social organization of statistical systems?
3. *Cognitive organization of statistical systems:* What are the sources and consequences of elements in the informational structure?
4. *System uses and effects:* What effects do the production and distribution of statistical information have on politics and society? Do statistical systems shape understanding of social and economic reality so that effects are due, not to the phenomena measured, but to the system measuring it?
5. *Contemporary system change:* What processes, such as political changes or technological innovations, are now shaping the current and future development of statistical systems? Like the first group, these questions are historical and developmental, but they concern the future rather than the past.

The last of these sets of questions is partially dealt with in the final two chapters in this volume. Here I take up the first four problem areas and try to outline the sorts of questions raised and approaches taken for each of them.

I. Statistical Systems in the Making: Origins and Development

Social and economic statistics, Otis Dudley Duncan has recently observed, share common features with other forms of measurement.[3] Like standard physical weights and measures, as well as measures of time and even common units of currency, they serve an interest in social coordination and control. In their origins and operation, they also have a specific relation to the state. Other institutions or groups often do not command—and have no reason to invest—the financial resources, organization, and authority required to carry out censuses and large-scale surveys. However, precisely because of the state's power, its inquiries are often especially feared and resisted as invasions of privacy and because of their possible use for assessing taxes or catching suspected criminals and subversives. To the use of statistics for domes-

[3]Otis Dudley Duncan, *Notes on Social Measurement: Historical and Critical* (New York: Russell Sage Foundation, 1984), pp. 12–38.

tic intelligence have been added other complex political functions in the allocation of money and power, the setting of norms, the making of policy, and the evaluation of government performance. All these functions have increased the stakes in official statistics and underlined the importance of understanding their origin and development.

Explaining why governments produce social and economic statistics poses two separate tasks. The first is to explain the foundations of measurement: why governments establish the framework for a statistical system and what preconditions allow them to do so. The second is to explain specific decisions to introduce (or eliminate) a statistical series or undertake a particular survey once an intellectual and bureaucratic framework already exists. The first is a problem in institutional innovation; the second, in policy initiation (or termination). The inauguration of a population census or the advent of labor statistics is an example of the first; the introduction of a statistical series on job vacancies is an instance of the second. I shall concentrate here on the foundational problem.

Social Foundations of Official Statistics

One difficulty in explaining the foundations of official statistics is that they have a somewhat confusing line of historical descent. Census-taking originated as a means, not of gathering quantitative data, but of surveillance, conscription, and tax assessment. Neither did the term statistics originally have its present meaning. When first used in German and English, "statistics" meant facts about states and did not specifically refer to numerical data, much less to an abstract set of analytical principles. But although the earliest censuses and statistical studies do not correspond to modern social forms, the connections as well as the discontinuities between them are helpful in understanding the roots of modern statistical systems.

Censuses, Ancient and Modern

Censuses of population can be traced to ancient societies, but from ancient Greece and Rome to early modern societies a census was a registration of people and property. The term census comes from Latin and in Rome referred to "a register of adult male citizens and their property for purposes of taxation, the distribution of military obligations and the determination of political status."[4] The Roman censor was also charged with the control of manners; hence the etymological associa-

---

[4]Walter F. Willcox, "Census," *Encyclopaedia of the Social Sciences* (New York: Macmillan, 1930), vol. 2, pp. 295–300.

tion with our terms censor and censorship. As late as the sixteenth century, Jean Bodin's classic work on statecraft, *The Six Bookes of a Commonweale*, described a census as "nothing else but a valuation of every mans goods," useful not only for levying taxes but also for determining the number and age of men available for war and public works, the needs of cities in the event of a siege, the resolution of civil disputes, and "the discovery of every mans estate and faculty, and whereby he gets his living, therby to expell all drones out of a commonweale . . . and to banish vagabonds, idle persons, theeves, cooseners, & ruffians, which live and converse among good men, as woolves do among the sheepe. . . ."[5] A census at this stage was unambiguously an instrument of state power and social control.

A modern population census differs in several crucial ways.[6] *First*, a modern census is an enumeration of an entire population in a nation or one of its geographical subdivisions. Premodern censuses, according to Willcox, were often limited to males, particular age groups and classes, or hearths and households, and thus were less inclusive.[7] *Second*, a modern census records and counts individuals and provides data at the individual level. As late as the early nineteenth century, the household typically continued to be the unit of enumeration; minimal information, if any, was recorded about individuals other than the head. *Third*, a modern census is an enumeration at a fixed time, whereas the premodern form was often a continuous register. *Fourth*, statistical data from modern censuses are typically expected to be published; premodern censuses were generally state secrets. *Fifth*, and perhaps most significant, nations today generally distinguish statistical agencies from those charged with tax assessment and law enforcement; no such distinction was made in the premodern form. The modern census has as its primary and manifest function the production of quantitative information, whereas the premodern form was used explicitly for keeping people under surveillance and control.

The primacy of statistical functions and their bureaucratic segregation from police and tax collection influence, or are meant to influence, the social relation between census-takers and respondents. Although some respondents are suspicious of census-takers, many share the understanding that the purpose of an official census is to generate information about aggregates of people, not about individuals. Reports in the

[5]Jean Bodin, *The Six Bookes of a Commonweale* [1576], ed. Kenneth Douglas McRae (Cambridge, Mass.: Harvard University Press, 1962), pp. 637, 641.

[6]The characteristics of modern censuses identified here come from a United Nations list of "essential features" of a population census. This is a statement of normative expectations; not every criterion is realized all the time. See Conrad Taeuber, "Census," *International Encyclopedia of the Social Sciences* (New York: Macmillan, 1968–79), vol. 2, pp. 361–62.

[7]Willcox, "Census," p. 295.

mass media impart a general familiarity with statistical inquiry. In liberal democracies, moreover, citizens are generally guaranteed that their census returns will be held confidential.

In its treatment of information about individuals and populations, therefore, the modern census—at least in the liberal democracies— inverts the premodern pattern. In the premodern census, the state obtained information about persons and kept secret information about its population. The modern census is ideally expected to assure anonymity to persons and publicity to facts about population. Behind this inversion of secrecy lies a more profound change. The modern census presumes a cooperative relation between a state and its citizens rather than a coercive relation between a state and its subjects. The emergence of modern censuses, therefore, involves not only the expansion of statistical functions but also the separation of census-taking from surveillance and a new social understanding of the purpose of censuses and, more generally, of the relation between states and peoples.

The cluster of characteristics that I have identified with modern censuses did not come into existence simultaneously or unambiguously. A municipal census of Nuremberg in 1449 may have been the first to include the entire population, but its results were secret. Claims of the first modern census have been variously made for Canada, which as a French colony had an enumeration in 1665; for Sweden, where a census based on parish registers began to be taken in 1749; and for the United States, which in 1790 became the first nation to inaugurate a periodic census, publish the results, and use them in the organization of government. However, even in the United States it was not until the mid-nineteenth century that confidentiality was assured to respondents and the census began to record every individual by name.[8]

The legacy of the premodern census represented a major barrier to the development of the modern form. In eighteenth-century Europe, many statesmen who were convinced of the value of censuses were also convinced that they were administratively unfeasible because of popular or provincial opposition. In France during the mid-1700s, several inquiries into population and economic output were blocked by refusals of cooperation not only from ordinary people but also from local authorities who feared new tax levies. The *parlement* of Rouen threatened to fine anyone complying with one such survey.[9] A proposal for a census

[8]Willcox, "Census"; August Meitzen, *History, Theory, and Technique of Statistics*, vol. 1., supp. to *Annals of the American Academy of Political and Social Science*, March 1891.

[9]David S. Landes, "Statistics as a Source for the History of Economic Development in Western Europe: The Protostatistical Era," in Val R. Lorwin and Jacob M. Price, eds., *The Dimensions of the Past: Materials, Problems, and Opportunities for Quantitative Work in History* (New Haven, Conn.: Yale University Press, 1972), p. 67.

in Great Britain in 1753 met defeat in Parliament at the hands of opponents who saw it as instrument of central domination.[10]

The use of censuses and surveys for surveillance continues to be a political concern. Studies of both the Chinese and the Soviet statistical systems emphasize the historical links between statistics and state intelligence.[11] Such systems have guaranteed neither confidentiality to facts about persons nor publicity to facts about populations. Fears that censuses may threaten individual rights have also arisen in the West and jeopardized the conduct of statistical inquiries. Since the early 1970s, many Western countries have introduced new measures to protect individual privacy, particularly against the risks posed by computerization.

The separation of censuses from surveillance, therefore, is not simply a theoretical dichotomy or historical accomplishment. It is a distinction that at least democratic governments continually must reassert as an institutional reality if they are to ensure the public trust necessary to carry out reliable statistical inquiries.

The Emergence of the Modern Concept of Statistics

As the modern census differs drastically from its antecedents, so, too, does the modern conception of statistics. The term itself indicates its historical association with knowledge of the state. In seventeenth- and eighteenth-century Germany, a series of university professors, beginning with Hermann Conring (1606–81), developed the field of *Staatenkunde,* the systematic study of states, an early form of what we would today call comparative politics. In their use, statistics were facts about a state, regardless of whether they were numerical. Among eighteenth-century practitioners in this field were exponents of *Tabellenstatistik,* who attempted to arrange the facts about states into rows and columns. Though not necessarily consisting of numbers, tables encouraged their use. Nonetheless, the German tradition of "university statistics" remained predominantly nonquantitative.[12]

In seventeenth-century England, William Petty (1623–76) and others pioneered a quantitative approach to problems of public policy.

---

[10]Peter Buck, "People Who Counted: Political Arithmetic in the Eighteenth Century," *Isis* 73 (1982):28–45.

[11]Choh-Ming Li, *The Statistical System of Communist China* (Berkeley: University of California Press, 1962), p. 4; Gregory Grossman, *Soviet Statistics of Physical Output of Industrial Commodities: Their Compilation and Quality* (Princeton, N.J.: Princeton University Press, 1960).

[12]Harald Westergaard, *Contributions to the History of Statistics* (London: P.S. King, 1932), pp. 4–15; Lazarsfeld, "Notes on the History of Quantification in Sociology," pp. 153–64.

Modern statistical thinking has its roots in this English tradition of *political* arithmetic, a term coined by Petty and understandable in light of the predominantly commercial conception of arithmetic at the time. Working with rudimentary data, Petty creatively used ratios, weighted means, and other techniques to estimate population size, agricultural production, trade, tax revenues, and other variables. A follower of Bacon and Hobbes, Petty argued that the objective knowledge of society had to be founded on a science of number, weight, and measure. But he himself often treated numbers in a cavalier fashion, introducing hypothetical figures into chains of unsupported calculations.[13] Other practitioners of political arithmetic further advanced the art of social measurement. John Graunt's 1662 study of the London bills of mortality is recognized as a landmark in demography and epidemiology.[14] The astronomer Edmund Halley published the first life tables in 1693, and in 1696 Gregory King made the first statistically based calculations of national income.[15]

The central preoccupation of political arithmetic was the application of rational calculation to the understanding, exercise, and enhancement of state power. Petty's study *Political Arithmetick*, for example, is an effort to compare the military and economic resources of England, France, and Holland and to argue for the superiority of English power.[16] (Such comparative arguments are still very much alive: Witness Raymond Vernon's chapter in this volume, which deals with analogous topics in a contemporary context.) Gregory King's work on national income was an effort to estimate potential revenue (in today's terminology, tax capacity). Similarly, the studies of mortality rates were prompted in part by the interest in calculating the cost of government annuities. The main use of political arithmetic, according to one of its practitioners, was to "help any ruler to understand fully that strength which he is to guide and direct."[17]

Although the contribution of Petty and his followers is now recognized as seminal, political arithmetic went into decline and eclipse in the eighteenth century. The political economists, such as Adam Smith,

---

[13]On Petty, see E. Strauss, *Sir William Petty: Portrait of a Genius* (London: The Bodley Head, 1954), and Peter Buck, "Seventeenth-Century Political Arithmetic: Civil Strife and Vital Statistics," *Isis* 68 (1977):67–84.

[14]John Graunt, *Natural and Political Observations Made upon the Bills of Mortality* [1662], ed. Walter F. Willcox (Baltimore: Johns Hopkins University Press, 1939).

[15]Gregory King, "Natural and Political Observations and Conclusions upon the State and Condition of England" [1696], in George E. Barnett, ed., *Two Tracts by Gregory King* (Baltimore: Johns Hopkins University Press, 1936), pp. 12–56. See also Paul Studenski, *The Income of Nations* (New York: New York University Press, 1958).

[16]William Petty, *Political Arithmetick* (London, 1690).

[17]Buck, "People Who Counted," p. 45.

were skeptical of the reliability of available data.[18] They also rejected the underlying assumptions about state guidance of economic life.

In the second half of the eighteenth century, according to Peter Buck, a broad ideological shift transformed political arithmetic from "a scientific prospectus for the exercise of state power" into "a program for reversing the growth of government and reducing its influence on English social and economic life."[19] Instead of conceiving of people as subjects, the new work conceived of them as citizens. Buck writes: "In a society where all manner of government functions were being appropriated by local ruling elites, freeing political arithmetic from the ideological albatross of state power stimulated the development of the science by allowing it to reenter the domain of public controversy on new terms."[20]

The term "statistics" entered the English language in the late eighteenth century, initially with the German meaning of facts about a state. The first book in English to use the term in its title was John Sinclair's *Statistical Account of Scotland*, a comprehensive social and geographical survey based on questionnaires sent to local clergy and published in twenty-one volumes between 1791 and 1799. By the 1820s statistics referred primarily—but still not exclusively—to numerical information. Statistical societies founded in Britain and the United States in the 1830s conceived of their goal as the gathering of objective facts, wherever possible to be numerical; yet many of the studies they supported or published were still nonquantitative. By the end of the nineteenth century, however, the transition to the modern meaning of statistics was virtually complete.

In its modern meaning, statistics has no necessary connection to the state. But that the word statistics comes from the same root as "state" testifies to an important stimulus of development: the demands of the modern state for social and economic intelligence.

Statistics and State Building

State building, as Charles Tilly has emphasized, has historically entailed a series of "extractive and repressive" tasks such as the organization of the military, tax system, and police.[21] The development of statistical systems represents a subordinate, auxiliary task of the same kind. I have already mentioned the historical connection of censuses to

[18]Adam Smith, *An Inquiry into the Nature and Causes of the Wealth of Nations* [1776], ed. Edwin Cannan (New York: Random House, 1937), p. 501.
[19]Buck, "People Who Counted," p. 28.
[20]Ibid., p. 35.
[21]Charles Tilly, ed., *The Formation of National States in Western Europe* (Princeton, N.J.: Princeton University Press, 1975).

conscription and tax assessment. In a sense, all three are extractive—of men, money, and information.

The concerns of political arithmetic also clearly show the close association between statistics and state building. As the work of Petty, Halley, King, and other practitioners of political arithmetic suggests, the development of statistics and statistical thinking had a particularly close link to public finance. In early modern states, "where there are taxes, there are statistics."[22] Not only did fiscal problems stimulate census-taking and political arithmetic; in Britain tax returns provided King with data for his estimates of population and national income.

More generally, state building and state-sponsored economic development prompted the wider collection of statistical information. In the seventeenth and eighteenth centuries, David Landes writes, the "mercantilist and cameralist states of Europe sought to promote economic growth for political ends and thereby were led to seek more precise and complete information than before on the conditions and economic activities of their subjects."[23] In this period, Prussia produced more data than most other European countries because of the extensive involvement of the Prussian monarchy in economic development.[24] For similar reasons, elaborate data are also available on the Spanish colonies in Latin America in this era. As John J. TePashke writes:

> Spanish attempts to exercise tight control over the colonies led to a penchant for scrupulous accounting. Private sectors of economic life such as mining and trade were in many ways part of the public sector as well, scrutinized continually by authorities in Madrid and Seville demanding meticulous records of what was going on in the Indies. The very nature of Spanish imperial control probably makes it easier to reconstruct a statistically based picture for the Spanish empire than for the English colonies, where the private activities of merchants and storekeepers were not as much the business of His Majesty's Government.[25]

As a general hypothesis, it seems reasonable to suggest that the more extensive the scope of state authority over economic and social life, the greater the scope, detail, and volume of statistical inquiry. However, other factors complicate any such generalization.

First, the interests of the state do not, of course, automatically call

---

[22]Gregory Grossman informs me that this is an old axiom of economic history.

[23]Landes, "Statistics as a Source for the History of Economic Development in Western Europe," p. 54.

[24]Ibid.

[25]John J. TePashke, "Quantification in Latin American Colonial History," in Lorwin and Price, eds., *The Dimensions of the Past*, p. 438.

up systems of thought. Before governments undertake to collect statistics, they must have some conception of the methods and uses of statistics. As Schumpeter remarks, the Roman empire, facing staggering problems in trade, money and finance, colonial administration, food supply, and slave labor, could have fully employed "a legion of economists," but the intellectual foundations did not then exist.[26] Furthermore, it is one thing to record and number people and things, but another matter entirely to create bodies of manipulable data. The records and results from early forms of data gathering, such as census-taking, were not used to think statistically. Although the seventeenth-century Spanish empire may have kept more comprehensive accounts than did England or its colonies, the English led in statistical analysis. They gathered less numerical data, but they produced more statistical information.

Second, although more interventionist regimes may have a broader interest in statistical inquiry, they may also arouse more resistance and, therefore, be less able to generate reliable information. Consider the reasons cited by Landes for the less ample statistical output of France in the seventeenth and eighteenth centuries, compared with England, despite the greater involvement of the French state in regulating and promoting economic development. Chronically short of revenue, the French monarchy sold offices and farmed out taxes. The sale of offices, notes Landes, limited the administrative capacity of the government, while tax farming put tax collection in the hands of entrepreneurs who "had every interest in keeping the results secret." The efforts to extract more revenue from a population resentful of tax inequities "imbued the subjects of the king with a mistrust of anything connected with the state and an unwillingness to provide any information that might serve the ends of the fisc." As a result, "the French state found it hard to collect statistical data; was ill-prepared to collate and process such data as it did have; and since it really did not want to know the unpleasant truth, was prepared to tolerate the falsification of these data."[27]

The French example underlines the importance of political legitimacy in generating reliable official statistics. The gathering of much statistical information requires wide cooperation. So long as statistics were associated with taxation and conscription, their potential development was limited, particularly insofar as the tax system itself was felt to be inequitable. Thus there may be some connection between statistical inquiry and the rise of representative government.

[26]Joseph A. Schumpeter, *History of Economic Analysis* (New York: Oxford University Press, 1954), pp. 66 67.

[27]Landes, "Statistics as a Source for the History of Economic Development in Western Europe," p. 61.

Statistics and Representative Government

In this volume, Kenneth Prewitt argues that official statistics make vital contributions to the working of democratic governments. Yet there can be little doubt that nondemocratic governments also find statistical information useful. What effect, then, if any, does democracy have on statistics? Is there any particular link that has encouraged or better enabled democratic governments to produce and distribute more statistical information, or particular kinds, or to use distinctive methods?

Clearly, one reason for the interest of democratic states in statistics may be the use of population data in distributing representation. The constitutional requirement of a decennial census in the United States stemmed from the decision to apportion the House of Representatives and Electoral College on the basis of population. Furthermore, this use of the census encouraged a change in the relation between census-taker and respondent. The traditional coupling of censuses with tax assessment had created a strong incentive for people and localities to under-report their numbers or refuse all cooperation whatsoever. The framers of the American Constitution thought they could overcome this problem by making political representation dependent on the count. As the accuracy of the census would depend on the disposition of the states, wrote Madison in *The Federalist*, No. 54,

> it is of great importance that the States should feel as little bias as possible, to swell or reduce the amount of their numbers. Were their share of representation alone to be governed by this rule, they would have an interest in exaggerating their inhabitants. Were the rule to decide their share of taxation alone, a contrary temptation would prevail. By extending the rule to both objects, the States will have the opposite interests, which will control and balance each other, and produce the requisite impartiality.[28]

Another connection between democracy and modern statistics may lie in the greater willingness of democratic states to make statistics public. Willcox argues that "there is a real connection between democratic forms of government, with their attendant publicity, and the taking of a census. . . . The modern census began in the United States in close association with democratic forms of government, and even at the start the results were immediately made public. Along with the growth of democracy in the nineteenth century there was an attendant spread of census taking."[29]

[28]Alexander Hamilton, John Jay, and James Madison, *The Federalist* (New York: Modern Library, n.d. [orig. 1787–88]), p. 359.
[29]Willcox, "Census," p. 296.

Yet another connection between democracy and statistics is the potential value of statistical information in the presentation and evaluation of competing claims for legislation. In this volume, Steven Kelman criticizes the standard approach of microeconomics, which explains government's role in producing information and other public goods as a response to "market failure." Relying on nineteenth-century U.S. congressional debates, Kelman argues that support for public provision of statistics was based primarily on political purposes, such as the need of legislators themselves for information (even about problems for which social or economic legislation was proposed but rejected).

However, between democratic government and the use of quantitative data lies the mediating variable of political culture. In the early years of the Republic, Congress was divided over whether to extend government statistical inquiries beyond the bare requirement of an enumeration. Supporters of broadened inquiry thought such information valuable in helping legislators serve their constituents. They conceived of society as consisting of diverse and competing groups, and they thought of politics as a sphere of interests. The opponents viewed the object of government as the pursuit of an undifferentiated common good; for them, politics was a sphere of virtue, and empirical investigation was irrelevant. By the mid-nineteenth century, empirical inquiry won increasing support. The growing scope of the census thus reflected the triumph of a liberal and pluralist conception of the democratic state.[30]

Yet another reason why liberal democratic government may be particularly hospitable to statistics is its receptivity to diverse interest groups. As Kelman makes clear, the demands for statistics frequently emanated from the quest of groups for public recognition of their identity and importance. This is also a theme of William Petersen's chapter on the politics of ethnic enumeration.

Statistics measure, disclose, and publicize the accomplishments and problems not only of groups but of the nation as a whole. Kelman argues that nineteenth-century Americans supported the census partly because they saw it as producing evidence of national achievement and the success of American democracy. William Kruskal observes that a national census is a kind of collective self-portrait that serves to reinforce national identity.[31] The connection here is not to democratic government per se but to national integration and nation building. Yet as the example of modern Lebanon indicates, in some circumstances no

[30]Patricia Cline Cohen, *A Calculating People: The Spread of Numeracy in Early America* (Chicago: University of Chicago Press, 1982). Some passages in the text here come from my review of Cohen's book in *The New Republic*, February 13, 1984.

[31]William Kruskal, "Research and the Census," paper presented to the Congressional Research Service, Washington, D.C., January 26–27, 1983.

census is conducted for fear that its results may be destabilizing. Whether statistical information serves an interest in social integration and conflict resolution depends on the nature of political bargains and the relationship between social groups, local authorities, and the state. No fixed relationship should be assumed.

Statistics, Capitalism, and Culture

That capitalism encouraged a calculating mentality and thereby promoted statistical thinking in spheres other than business is an argument with a long heritage. Capitalism, in this view, is not merely an economic system but a civilization with a distinctive culture. The bourgeoisie, Marx and Engels wrote, drowned all sentimentality in "the icy water of egotistical calculation."[32] Schumpeter argued that the economy was the "matrix of logic" and that capitalism could proudly take credit for increasingly quantitative habits of mind. For once "defined and quantified" in the economy, the rational habit of mind started "upon its conqueror's career subjugating—rationalizing—man's tools and philosophies, his medical practice, his picture of the cosmos, his outlook on life, everything in fact including his concepts of beauty and justice and his spiritual ambitions."[33]

At least among the English, commercial bookkeeping was certainly taken as an exemplary lesson for government. This was the premise of political arithmetic. "Arithmetic," wrote John Arbuthnot, a seventeenth-century English mathematician, "is not only the great instrument of private commerce, but by it are (or ought to be) kept the public accounts of a nation. . . ."[34] Commerce provided the chief stimulus for acquiring basic numerical skills. Nonetheless, as Patricia Cline Cohen has pointed out, commerce ironically also impeded the spread of quantitative reasoning. Arithmetic was so widely understood as a commercial skill that it was long considered inappropriate for either general or elite education. Furthermore, texts in arithmetic were so thoroughly dedicated to commercial applications that its fundamental principles were ill understood and ill taught. The same mathematical operation would be presented as one rule for pounds and shillings, another rule for ounces and quarts. Because of the plethora of rules that needed to be memorized, arithmetic was believed to be extremely difficult to learn—and under those circumstances, it was.

The link between capitalism and numeracy relies heavily on a

[32]Karl Marx and Friedrich Engels, "Manifesto of the Communist Party" [1848], in Robert C. Tucker, ed., *The Marx-Engels Reader*, 2nd ed. (New York: W. W. Norton, 1978), p. 475.

[33]Joseph A. Schumpeter, *Capitalism, Socialism, and Democracy* (New York: Harper & Row, 1950), pp. 123–24.

[34]As quoted in Cohen, *A Calculating People*, pp. 28–29.

presumed demand of capitalism for systematic accounting. Weber defined "a rational capitalistic establishment" as "one with capital accounting, that is, an establishment which determines its income yielding power by calculation according to the methods of modern bookkeeping and the striking of a balance."[35] Similarly, Sombart identified systematic accounting as a key characteristic distinguishing the capitalistic entrepreneur.[36] However, research into bookkeeping practices between the fourteenth and mid-nineteenth centuries—particularly the use of the double-entry form thought to be essential to capitalist enterprise—suggests that merchants used bookkeeping primarily as a record of accounts and not to calculate profits. Their main interest was to keep track of credit dealings with customers and suppliers and among partners; for such purposes, a simple form of bookkeeping sufficed. The more demanding double-entry system provides a more systematic analysis of profits and losses, financial condition, and return on capital, but it appears that merchants rarely carried through these calculations. "Description of assets appears to have been much more important than their 'quantification,'" writes B. S. Yamey. According to Yamey, household expenses, money received in dowries, and other domestic transactions were included in profit-and-loss accounts. "There is little evidence of a careful calculation and analysis of profits, and even less of any attention to the separation of business from domestic affairs."[37]

Whatever its real application, double-entry bookkeeping represented an ideal of methodical organization that may have had some normative effect on governmental administration and hence on the development of official statistics. Yet it may be wrong to identify this kind of methodical procedure as originating from a raw economic need. As Weber and others have argued, the same concerns may be found elsewhere in the culture, as in religious life. In her study of the rise of numeracy and the spreading "domain of quantification" in Britain and America from the seventeenth through the mid-nineteenth centuries, Cohen argues that measurement met other than economic interests. "In fact, most seventeenth-century capitalists, traders, and mercantilists got along quite well without using the quantitative techniques—double-entry bookkeeping, geometrical gauging, national account books—that the quantifiers praised."[38] She also rejects a variant of the

[35]Max Weber, *General Economic History* [1919/20] (New Brunswick, N.J.: Transaction Books, 1981), p. 275. See also Max Weber, *Economy and Society* [1922], ed. by Guenther Roth and Claus Wittich (New York: Bedminster, 1968), pp. 90–100.

[36]F. L. Nussbaum, *A History of Economic Institutions of Modern Europe* (An Introduction to Sombart's *Der Moderne Kapitalismus*) (New York: F. S. Crofts, 1933), p. 160.

[37] B. S. Yamey, "Scientific Bookkeeping and the Rise of Capitalism," *Economic History Review*, 2nd ser., 1(1949): 99–113.

[38]Cohen, *A Calculating People*, p. 18.

Weberian argument about Protestantism that links religion to the development of numeracy, and instead suggests, in regard to seventeenth-century Britain, that it might be the "chaos and disorder of a revolutionary situation that directly encouraged a quantitative orientation."[39]

Such unsettling conditions, in and of themselves, clearly cannot produce an interest in quantification, except perhaps in the context of particular intellectual traditions. Many accounts of the emergence of statistical inquiries emphasize the influence of Baconian empiricism. In each of the major Western countries where statistical institutions first developed it is possible to identify a line of intellectual descent, running from figures who provided broad philosophical orientations to those who carried out a program of quantification. In Britain, Bacon and Hobbes prepared the ground for Petty, who in turn prepared it for people like King; in the early nineteenth century, Malthus took part in the founding of the Statistical Society of London.[40] In Germany, Leibniz set out a program for official statistics.[41] In France, some of the eighteenth-century *philosophes*, most notably Condorcet, envisioned a social mathematics.[42] After these conceptual pioneers came the people who worked out the ideas in practice and translated them into institutions: in Britain, men like Rickman, Farr, and Chadwick; in Germany, Engel; in Belgium, Quételet; in France, Guerry and Villermé; in America, Jarvis, Walker, and Wright.[43] These early statisticians did not work in a cultural vacuum. By the early nineteenth century, as Cohen relates, the interest in quantification had become widely diffused in popular culture, political controversy, and the professions. She notes, for example, the growing popularity of gazetteers and almanacs with statistical data and the democratization of arithmetic through its simplification and introduction into the schools.[44]

Throughout the West, capitalism no doubt encouraged quantifi-

[39]Ibid., p. 43.

[40]Michael J. Cullen, *The Statistical Movement in Early Victorian Britain: The Foundations of Empirical Social Research* (New York: Barnes & Noble, 1975), p. 79.

[41]Ian Hacking, "Prussian Numbers," in Dastin, Heidelberger, and Krüge, eds., *The Probabilistic Revolution*; and Ian Hacking, *The Emergence of Probability* (London and New York: Cambridge University Press, 1975).

[42]See Keith Michael Baker, *Condorcet: From Natural Philosophy to Social Mathematics* (Chicago: University of Chicago Press, 1975).

[43]Cullen, *The Statistical Movement in Early Victorian Britain*; Hacking, "Prussian Numbers"; Lazarsfeld, "Notes on the History of Quantification in Sociology"; William Coleman, *Death Is a Social Disease: Public Health and Political Economy in Early Industrial France* (Madison: University of Wisconsin Press, 1982); Bernard Lecuyer and Anthony R. Oberschall, "The Early History of Social Research," in *International Encyclopedia of the Social Sciences*, vol. 15, pp. 36–53; Gerald N. Grob, *Edward Jarvis and the Medical World of Nineteenth-Century America* (Knoxville: University of Tennessee Press, 1978).

[44]Cohen, *A Calculating People*.

cation by sweeping more people into a money economy. However, "needs" of the economy, like "needs" of the state, do not automatically call up systems of thought. Cultural influences and intellectual programs provided an independent stimulus to statistics, not reducible to material interests alone. Economic and political developments—the rise of capitalism, the modern state, and political democracy—reacted on a cultural base that already was disposed toward the methodical, rational outlook of which social and economic statistics were one product and expression.

The Path of Development

The production of official statistics has become more routine and grown in scale and sophistication, spans a wider domain of social life, and penetrates more deeply into the workings of society than it did during the formative, early stages of development. A rough parallel may be observed between the evolution of commercial and state accounting systems. Histories of business accounting suggest that there have been three phases to its development. The earliest, record-keeping, consisted of documenting transactions and can be traced to the first literate societies. Bookkeeping, the long intermediate phase, involved classifying transactions "according to a preconceived plan, as the basis for reporting the financial condition and all operating results of a business enterprise." The third phase, accounting, has seen the elaboration of financial analysis and control functions.[45] Official fact-gathering has followed a similar path. As the ancient censuses illustrate, the earliest inquiries were methods of registering and recording people and things, not of creating manipulable numerical data. Like bookkeeping, social and economic statistics in the West through the early nineteenth century involved relatively simple classification and analysis. The rise of modern national income accounting, economic indicators, and other tools of macroeconomic management and planning parallels the transformation of commercial bookkeeping into modern accounting.

We get a somewhat different framing of periods if we focus on the routinization and scope of official statistics as well as advances in complexity. The development of modern European economic statistics, suggests Landes, may be divided into three eras: (1) the "protostatistical era," running approximately through the eighteenth century, when governments were "desultory and incomplete in their collection and publication" of statistics; (2) the "first statistical era," roughly from the

[45]James Don Edwards, "Early Bookkeeping and Its Development into Accounting," *Business History Review* 34 (1960): 446–58.

early nineteenth to the early twentieth century, when states came to realize numbers were too important to be left to chance and began to adopt a "systematic program of regular and fuller coverage" of certain indicators and to create permanent bureaucratic agencies for producing statistics; and (3) the modern or "second statistical era," signaled by the development of composite indexes of wages and prices and national income accounting, as "new conceptions of the role of the state and the character of economic change have made it desirable to go beyond the collation and arithmetical transformation of simple raw numbers and to create aggregative and analytical indicators of a much more highly processed character."[46]

Landes's "first statistical era" began with what earlier historians sometimes described as an "era of statistical enthusiasm" in the 1820s and 1830s. Those decades saw not only a shift from episodic measurement toward routine monitoring of society but also a broadening of interests in what were then called "moral statistics." Governments began to measure and analyze health, education, and crime. The enthusiasm for these inquiries was stirred by a social movement, or at least a movement of intellectuals and administrators, the "statistical movement" of the nineteenth century, whose members founded the first statistical societies and congresses and propagated an ideology of objective fact-finding.[47] Moral statistics were a characteristic expression of the mid-nineteenth-century phase of genteel professionalism, which identified moral reform with scientific knowledge. Reform is, of course, a continuing theme in the making of statistical systems, but it is hard to say whether reformism led to statistics, or statistics to reform. The inauguration of labor statistics in the late nineteenth century was clearly prompted by industrial unrest. But were they created because of the power of the labor movement or labor reformers, or as a diversion of protest and aid to state policy dominated by employers? It is entirely possible that both may be true—for different actors whose joint action resulted in building labor statistical bureaus.[48]

As I suggested earlier in discussing the effects of state intervention on statistics gathering, easy generalizations about the relation of state intervention to statistics should be resisted. To be sure, state planning does seem to promote an interest in statistics; the Soviet statistical system, according to official pronouncements, was created to support central planning.[49] However, the United States established its elaborate

---

[46]Landes, "Statistics as a Source for the History of Economic Development in Western Europe," pp. 53–54.

[47]Westergaard, *Contributions to the History of Statistics*, 136–71.

[48]James Leiby, *Carroll Wright and Labor Reform: The Origin of Labor Statistics* (Cambridge, Mass.: Harvard University Press, 1960).

[49]Grossman, *Soviet Statistics of Physical Output of Industrial Commodities*, pp. 13–21.

social and economic statistical systems without any commitment to planning. Indeed, statistics such as the modern economic indicators seem to have been introduced in the federal government as a substitute for planning. While planning requires elaborate data, so do Keynesian, welfare state, and even monetarist policies. If monetarists want to manage the money supply and to index wages, interest rates, and tax brackets, they need statistics about money, prices, and other variables. But they may not require or want other kinds of social statistics; more important, they may not organize or conceive the data in the same way.

Changing policy interests and ideologies clearly affect the domain of official statistical inquiry, but here we are in the realm of incremental decision-making mentioned at the outset of this section. Once the foundations and framework for official statistics have been established, the decisions about what to measure belong to the everyday world of political conflict and coalition building.[50] Also at work are cycles of faith and skepticism in the power of rational management and the social sciences. Enthusiasm for statistical enterprises such as social indicators rises—and falls. The inability of such movements to secure political support should not always be interpreted as a sign of the limits of policymaking. Though they may have the patina of rationalism, movements on behalf of statistics are not always rational in strictly relating means and ends. For those with a deep belief in the blessings of information, the means become an end. Political leaders who must raise taxes and voters who must pay them cannot always afford such expensive tastes.

II. The Social Organization of Statistical Systems

No social scientist has yet attempted any systematic, comparative analysis of the organization and politics of the statistical process (in the vein, for example, of Wildavsky's studies of the budgetary process).[51] However, suggestive studies of statistical institutions as well as methodological criticism of official statistics help to identify sociologically relevant issues in the design and workings of statistical systems. These issues may be grouped into two general categories: the politics of organizational structure and the sociology of the statistical process.

[50]For the classic incrementalist view, see Charles E. Lindblom, "The Science of Muddling Through," *Public Administration Review* 19 (1957): 79–88, and Aaron Wildavsky, *The Politics of the Budgetary Process* (Boston: Little, Brown, 1964).

[51]Ibid. and Aaron Wildavsky, *Budgeting: A Comparative Theory of Budgetary Processes* (Boston: Little, Brown, 1975).

The Politics of Organizational Structure

Statistical systems take a variety of organizational forms. The division of statistical labor typically involves different bureaucracies and levels of government, the private as well as public sector, and various professions. Choices in organizational design have a bearing on the functional autonomy of statistical institutions; the ability of different actors to secure statistical information relevant to the decisions they face or useful for the pursuit of their claims; ingrained tendencies toward over- or undercounting or errors of classification; and the control over access to information, including the release of information damaging to individuals, agencies, or governments as a whole. In short, the division of statistical labor affects the social distribution of knowledge and power.

At least four such divisions have been persistent matters of political contention:

1. *Central statistical offices versus statistical branches of operating agencies.* Government at every level faces a choice between concentrating statistical activities and competence in a central professional agency and dispersing statisticians among various operating departments. This is an instance of the general problem of choosing between functional and divisional forms of bureaucratic structure. The choice is not, of course, necessarily either/or, since some statistical functions may be concentrated and others dispersed. Some countries, such as Canada, have chosen to create central statistical offices; others, such as the United States, have not. The U.S. Bureau of the Census does represent a highly professionalized statistical agency, but by no means have all federal statistical activities been centralized in it.

Like other professionals, statisticians often prefer independent organization because it allows them more professional autonomy and collegiality. However, such independence may come at the expense of influence over policy. Policymakers and administrators often prefer to have statisticians dispersed in operating agencies because it gives them more authority to direct the statisticians to produce useful data and perhaps more favorable measures of their own performance. On the other hand, an independent professional agency may have higher technical standing and the ability to recruit more highly qualified statisticians. The political problem is to reconcile the advantages and risks of the alternatives. As Margaret Martin puts it: "If the statistics bureau is too close to policy planning and analysis, it runs the risk of becoming partisan. If it is too insulated from policy considerations, the statistics bureau may be perceived and treated as . . . a mere numbers factory. . . .''[52]

2. *National/local divisions of labor.* A second problem of centralization is the allocation of statistical activities or functions among levels of government. For example, even if a census is carried out on a national scale, some aspects of it may be decentralized: (a) The enumerators may be local officials, local clergy, or paid agents responsible to local authorities, rather than permanent employees of the central government; (b) the census returns themselves may be left in the hands of local or provincial governments, with only summaries sent to the central government, instead of being transmitted in full; (c) analytical capacities may be dispersed in provincial or state governments; and (d) control over public access to information may be given to local authorities.

Conflicts over these choices appear throughout the literature on the history and politics of statistics. Early modern censuses typically relied on parish records or local clergy, the overseers of the poor, or other local officials to gather data. As a result, they embedded the production of statistics in local status relations and religious conflicts.[53] Like the coupling of censuses with taxation, the use of such sources or agents inhibited accurate disclosure and thereby distorted the data. Moreover, if the records or clergy of an established church were the sources of information, the statistics sometimes entirely omitted or provided inadequate coverage of dissenters. The historical shift toward paid, secular agents of central governments represented a key change at the "base" of the social structure of official statistics.

Recent protests against a national census in West Germany stemmed in part from a design that potentially allowed local authorities access to personal information about individuals. The West German system is one of those in which the provincial governments transmit only summaries of data to the federal level, whereas in the United States the federal government controls and processes all census returns.[54] In the United States, according to Judith deNeufville's chapter

[52]Margaret E. Martin, "Statistical Practice in Bureaucracies," *Journal of the American Statistical Association* 76 (March 1981):1–8. See also James T. Bonnen, "Federal Statistical Coordination Today: A Disaster or a Disgrace?" *Milbank Memorial Fund Quarterly/Health and Society* 62 (1984):1–41; Claus Moser, "The Role of the Central Statistical Office in Assisting Public Policy Makers," *The American Statistician* 30 (1976):59–67; and United Nations, "The Organization of National Statistical Services: A Review of Major Issues," Studies in Methods, Series F, No. 21 (New York, 1977), pp. 7–10.

[53]Buck, "People Who Counted."

[54]William P. Butz, "Data Confidentiality and Public Perceptions: The Case of the European Censuses," paper presented to the Population Association of America, Minneapolis, May 3, 1984.

in this volume, "dependency in statistical production" limits the ability of local governments to meet their own, highly particular needs for demographic and economic data. On the other hand, according to the chapter by Janet A. Weiss and Judith E. Gruber, decentralized authority over the schools in the United States has prevented the federal government from obtaining consistent and relevant educational statistics. Federal officials lack the power to compel the states to produce data that might reflect badly on their performance. Even in the same society, therefore, both local and national governments may experience dependency in statistical production in different institutional spheres.

3. *Public/private divisions of labor.* Private-to-public transitions in the production of statistics have been common in the history of statistical systems. Many kinds of statistics have been pioneered by private individuals or reform organizations and then taken over by the state. The private efforts of eighteenth- and nineteenth-century English and American reformers in producing labor, public health, and poverty statistics are good examples.[55] But particularly in recent years, there have also been public-to-private transitions, as some governments have abandoned the collection, analysis, or distribution of data on the grounds that those functions were being—or could be—undertaken in the private sector.

Accounting for such transitions takes us back to the first class of problems—what do governments count?—but with more of an emphasis on the exchanges, relations of interdependence, and potential conflicts between the public and private sectors in the performance of statistical functions. Even if government chooses to count, it may not be the only producer of data. A key difference between American and Soviet economic forecasting, as Leonard Silk observes, is that in the United States "official economic reporting and forecasting are heavily constrained by the competition of private economists, analysts, businessmen and reporters, whereas the Soviet variety can exist in a cloudland of its own."[56] When the Commerce or Treasury Departments make projections of economic growth, unemployment, and budget deficits, their projections compete for influence with those of other public sources, such as the Congressional Budget Office, as well as numerous private forecasters. Pluralism is as important a check on the performance of statistical agencies as it is on other organizations. However, governments even in pluralist societies still have a monopoly in producing much raw statistical data because of the sheer cost of production. Therefore, many governmental decisions in the construction of

[55]See Cullen, *The Statistical Movement in Early Victorian Britain,* and Lecuyer and Oberschall, "The Early History of Social Research."

[56]Leonard Silk, "U.S. vs. Soviet Forecasting," The *New York Times,* January 4, 1984.

the data—such as the categories used in official questionnaires—rule out alternative conceptions. Moreover, because of the unique authority of official statistics, private agencies cannot always compete effectively for attention or credibility. Nonetheless, the presence of private statistical criticism and analysis represents a key difference in the functioning of statistical systems between totalitarian and liberal societies.

4. *Bureaucratic/academic divisions of labor.* Like private companies, the academic social sciences, based in institutions enjoying relative autonomy from the state, constitute a partial check on official statistics. Moreover, the universities are the source of much training for the government's own statisticians and social scientists, and the disciplines constitute a key reference group for bureaucratic analysts. On the other hand, academic professionals often depend on bureaucratic professionals for raw data as well as contracts and grants. The role of academic analysts may be high in the early stages of statistical work (such as the formulation of problems and the design of questionnaires), fall through the middle phases of data collection, and then rise again in the latter stages of analysis, interpretation, and public dissemination.

A key question here is the extent of information processing undertaken by official agencies. The more processing is completed in the deep recesses of the bureaucracies, the less able are independent private and academic analysts to unscramble the categories, change the assumptions, and generate alternative data. However, such tasks may, in effect, be spun off by data producers. In his chapter on population forecasting in this volume, Nathan Keyfitz points out that by offering a range of forecasts instead of a single point, demographers have partially ceded to the users of the data the responsibility for choosing among assumptions. The division of labor here is not between bureaucratic and academic analysts but rather between producers and users (who may themselves be researchers, policymakers, or other information consumers). As computerization becomes more widespread and less costly, it permits more independent processing of statistical data by users further "downstream." Instead of being distributed in the relatively fixed medium of printed tables, the data are increasingly distributed in more manipulable electronic form. In this way, computerization may change the distribution of statistical labor, somewhat reducing centralization.

The Sociology of the Statistical Process

I turn now from structural alternatives in the organization of statistical systems to the social relations of the statistical process. By the statistical process I mean the sequence of activities in the production and dissemination of statistics. In official statistical agencies these activities are organized temporally in a production cycle. For purposes of analysis, the cycle may conveniently be divided into several phases: (a) the design of cognitive instruments (such as questionnaire items, classification systems, coding instructions, etcetera) and the planning and fielding of an administrative apparatus for data production; (b) a primary phase of collection consisting of contact and interaction with respondents and the entry of data by respondents, enumerators, or other officials; (c) intermediate social processes, consisting of the transmission and processing of data through various levels of organization; and (d) the higher levels of analysis, representation, and disclosure of data by official agencies. Many of the questions about the design and analysis of statistics I have deferred until the next section on cognitive organization. Under this heading, I primarily consider the possible effects of social relations on statistics production.

1. *Methods of data collection: census, survey, and administrative data.* A choice of statistical sources or methods is a choice of social processes for the generation of data. Censuses and sample surveys are more structurally differentiated processes of social measurement; the production of data is their specific, manifest function. Hence professional statisticians are more likely to assume a dominant role. Administrative data, on the other hand, are generally by-products of bureaucratic processes conducted for other purposes and not controlled by statisticians. Such data are often used for monitoring bureaucratic and professional performance and may, therefore, be particularly subject to image-conscious manipulation. Administrative data are also particularly sensitive to vagaries of bureaucratic policy or procedure unrelated to the external social phenomenon they may be taken to measure. For example, changes in budgets, personnel, and internal incentives and controls such as quotas for cases opened or closed are likely to influence administrative measures of crime, illness, and other forms of social deviance. Rules of eligibility and other screening mechanisms filter administrative readings of poverty, unemployment, homelessness, and other forms of social distress. The very devices that screen out claims on public revenue may produce lower measured rates of distress than would surveys of the general population—a feature that may lead administrative data to be quoted by those in office and denounced as misleading by their critics. Unemployment data generated by unemployment insurance agencies, crime statistics produced by police, health statistics from hospitals and other medical facilities—all such statistics are deeply embedded in local bureaucratic practice and professional cultures and may, therefore, have limited value for comparisons

across societies or over time. To be sure, some of their limitations may be overcome through surveys of crime victimization, unemployment, and illness in the general population. However, no technical method is free of social process. In a sense, all data are administrative since none can be gathered without an administrative apparatus and without formal rules for classification.

The choice between censuses and sample surveys has political, cultural, and economic aspects. In the United States, the Constitution calls for an enumeration every ten years, a requirement interpreted to demand a complete population census. In the nineteenth century, this specific authority led to the concentration of federal statistical inquiries in the decennial census, since it was disputed whether the government had authority to undertake other forms of social research. In the twentieth century, on other hand, the rise of alternative and cheaper methods of inquiry has raised doubts whether a full census is necessary, but the constitutional language stands as a barrier to change. (Another reason for maintaining a national census is that, unlike surveys, it provides data on small areas, which are required for many allocative purposes.) Whether the constitutional requirement of an enumeration allows any estimation procedures—for example, adjustments for population undercounts—became an important point in the legal disputes over the 1980 census. The Census Bureau held that the Constitution did not allow any adjustment, even though census procedures already call for imputing characteristics to households and individuals who do not return census forms and cannot be located by interviewers. [57]

Despite professional cautions that censuses may be subject to errors as great as, or larger than, errors in surveys, censuses appear to retain greater cultural and political authority. A national census involves general public participation in a collective "self-portrait." A count, furthermore, seems a relatively straightforward task. On the other hand, surveys do not constitute public events in themselves, and the logic of sampling is more difficult to comprehend. When a federal agency in the 1930s first used random sampling for a study of the distribution of wealth, the U.S. Chamber of Commerce, displeased with the findings, dismissed them as based merely on a sample and "a random sample at that"! [58] The gradual acceptance of sampling in the twentieth century constitutes a significant change in our political culture.

[57]David Seidman, "Numbers That Count: The Law and Policy of Population Statistics Used in Formula Grant Allocation Programs," *George Washington Law Review* 48 (January 1980):229–67; Note, "Demography and Distrust: Constitutional Issues of the Federal Census," *Harvard Law Review* 94 (1981):841–63.

[58]Joseph W. Duncan and William C. Shelton, *Revolution in United States Government Statistics, 1926–1976* (Washington, D.C.: U.S. Department of Commerce, 1978), p. 41.

Despite the greater authority of censuses, governments increasingly rely on periodic surveys and administrative data for more frequent information. This pattern reflects not only the demand for more up-to-date information but also the steep rise in the costs of interviews relative to the costs of manipulating computerized records.[59] Nonetheless, the national population census remains the central and archetypal statistical enterprise, and it may well survive, despite expense, because of its broader social functions.

2. *Respondent compliance and disclosure.* Response to official sample surveys is generally voluntary and without financial reward, whereas filling out forms for welfare, police, tax collection, and other agencies is typically mandatory and backed by significant rewards or penalties. This difference may produce higher compliance but less reliable disclosure in administrative statistics and, conversely, lower compliance and more reliable disclosure in surveys. In national censuses responses are legally required, but the sanctions for noncompliance are generally less severe than for failing to turn in, say, income tax returns. As previously indicated, the volume and reliability of response to censuses may reflect the level of public trust of governmental authorities, particularly confidence in the segregation of statistics from surveillance, taxation, and law enforcement.

Noncompliance may be divided into two categories: individual and collective. Individual nonresponse has been a rising problem for social research of all kinds in the postwar era in Western Europe and the United States. One recent study attributes this secular tendency, not to methodological deficiencies, but to growing public anxieties about invasions of privacy.[60] Nonresponse may also take the form of organized collective action: a "statistics strike" in which respondents refuse to complete forms and thereby deny a government statistical information.[61] The cancellation of West German censuses in the early 1980s resulted from a threatened statistics strike by about one fourth of the population, as measured by public opinion polls. Opposition to the census arose from feared invasions of privacy, prompted by the government's decision to use it as an opportunity to fill gaps in official local registers of inhabitants. Since census forms did not separate individuals'

---

[59]Wendy Alvey and Fritz Scheuren, "Background for an Administrative Record Census," in Wendy Alvey and Beth Kilss, eds., *Statistics of Income and Related Administrative Record Research: 1982* (Washington, D.C.: Department of the Treasury, 1982), pp. 47–62.

[60]John Goyder and Jean McKenzie Leiper, "The Decline in Survey Response: A Social Values Interpretation," *Sociology* 19 (1985):55–71.

[61]Government Statisticians' Collective, "How Official Statistics Are Produced: Views from the Inside," in John Irvine, Ian Miles, and Jeff Evans, eds., *Demystifying Social Statistics* (London: Pluto Press, 1979), p. 142.

names from answers to questions about personal matters such as income, many West Germans became concerned that the local authorities might use the returns for tax enforcement or to prosecute people who had given false information to registration authorities. Early opposition from the radical Green Party gradually spread to a broad spectrum of the population, and the West German courts canceled an already postponed census planned for April 1983.[62]

In striking contrast, American protests before and after the 1980 census were directed at the probable undercount of minorities and metropolitan areas and sought legal recognition of a "right to be counted." Cities and minority groups mobilized to get the maximum numbers to fill out returns, as they might mobilize to get out the vote in an election.[63]

The explanation for the difference in collective patterns of response to census plans may lie in the incentives created by the political systems. In America, but not in Germany, the census is the basis for major distributional decisions. The stakes have interested the public in being counted. In the *Federalist Papers*, Madison suggested that by apportioning both representatives and taxes according to population, the Constitution would secure a balance of interests that would lead the states neither to swell nor to reduce their reported population. But the balance no longer exists. Federal aid to states and localities now depends on their population, but tax burdens are not similarly allocated. The Sixteenth Amendment, allowing a federal income tax, exempted it from the requirement that direct taxes be apportioned according to the census. This political factor, rather than objective deficiencies in the census, probably explains why census controversy in the United States now focuses on undercounts rather than other problems, such as possible overcounts.[64]

The controversy over census undercounts, however, underlines the important point that noncompliance has a social distribution. In a sense, the problem is analogous to nonvoting, particularly because statistics are used to allocate representatives and to represent social realities. Thus the campaigns for census compliance, adjustments for minority undercounts, and more intensive sampling of minority popula-

[62]"Standing Up to the Counters," *New Statesman*, April 15, 1983, and Butz, "Data Confidentiality and Public Perceptions: The Case of the European Censuses."

[63]On the conflicts over the 1980 census, see Ian I. Mitroff, Richard O. Mason, and Vincent P. Barabba, *The 1980 Census: Policymaking Amid Turbulence* (Lexington, Mass.: Lexington Books, 1983); Bryant Robey, "Adjusting for Census Undercount: The Statistical Nightmare," *American Demographics* (February 1980):18–23, 46; Myron Magnet, "Behind the Bad-News Census," *Fortune*, February 9, 1981; Seidman, "Numbers That Count."

[64]Daniel Melnick, "The 1980 Census: Recalculating the Federal Equation," *Publius: The Journal of Federalism* 11 (Summer 1981):39–65.

tions may be viewed not only as issues of technical adequacy but also as a kind of statistical counterpart to affirmative action.

3. *The social relations of data collection.* Almost all statistics come from answers to questions, and questioning inevitably entails a social relation. Even if the questions appear impersonally on a form, the "government" is asking for information and the answers may be shaped by the respondents' relation to the government—their interest in cooperating, fear of scrutiny, or differences in language and understanding. If interviewers or governmental functionaries ask the questions, their identity and role may influence the transaction. Changes in the makeup of both groups, questioners and questioned, may have major consequences. Thus the growing proportion of women working outside the home has reduced the available supply of educated, low-paid, unthreatening census enumerators as well as the probability of finding a woman respondent at home during the day. This kind of social change may lie behind the narrower economic calculations that have dictated reliance on mailed census questionnaires.

Several general perspectives are evident in the analysis of the social relations of data collection. One emphasizes the rational calculations of respondents and other agents in the statistical apparatus. In this view, official statistics are a function of the strategic behavior of actors at all levels of a statistical system. This approach may be found in Oskar Morgenstern's classic study *On the Accuracy of Economic Observations.* Morgenstern notes, for example, that one difference between "describing a statistical universe made up of physical events exclusively and one in which social events occur" is that people may lie, be evasive, or misunderstand the questions asked of them. Nature does none of these. As Einstein once said, "The Lord God is sophisticated, but he is not malicious."[65] Misrepresentation in the reporting of social and economic data, on the other hand, may inspire countermeasures by those designing statistical inquiries, creating what Morgenstern refers to as "a non-strictly determined two-person game where both sides have to resort to mixed or 'statistical' strategies."[66]

The opportunity for strategic behavior in data reporting is greatly increased by ambiguities of classification and the sheer complexity of some calculations. Without actually lying, respondents such as corporations being questioned about their financial condition may choose to report to the government figures conveniently different from those they use internally. The story is told of a series of interviews for a job as an auditor in a Soviet factory. "How much is two and two?" asks the

[65]Oskar Morgenstern, *On the Accuracy of Economic Observations,* 2nd ed. (Princeton, N.J.: Princeton University Press, 1963), pp. 17–18.
[66]Ibid., p. 22.

manager. "Four," says the first candidate, who is promptly dismissed. Asked the same question, the second job-seeker says "Five"—and obviously he won't do, either. Finally, the third candidate is asked the question, and he responds, "How much do you need?" That man gets the job.[67] The same story might easily be told of creative accounting in the West. It is a commonplace of accounting that numbers are not absolute; they are a policy decision. As Morgenstern argues, any corporate balance sheet consists of values ranging from precisely known, highly liquid assets to others that are purely speculative estimates, such as the value of trademarks.[68] Even within the limits of standard accounting practices, the opportunity for strategic data reporting is vast.

A second approach, common among sociologists influenced by phenomenology, emphasizes the varying interpretations of categories and evidence by those who enter data used for official statistics. A critical analysis of official suicide data by Jack Douglas exemplifies this perspective.[69] The conventional view, represented in sociological studies of suicide since Durkheim's classic work, is that the identification of suicide is unproblematic; if suicide statistics suffer from any deficiencies, it is underreporting because of concealed cases. Hence the reported rates are generally assumed to be low estimates. Douglas shows that the difficulties are much more serious.

To categorize a death as a suicide, one must resolve several types of ambiguity. In the case of a man found dead, for example, coroners, police, or other officials must decide whether he died of natural causes, killed himself, or was murdered; second, if he killed himself, whether he took the action that killed him accidentally or intentionally; and third, if intentionally, whether he knew the action would kill him. Labeling a death a suicide clearly involves attributing an intention to the deceased, which means interpreting his state of mind. This interpretation is often highly conjectural. About many deaths, such as drownings and one-car accidents, the evidence is often minimal; suicide is, so to speak, in the eye of the beholder. Counting up such categorizations does not make them any less interpretive, and calling them official does not make them any less problematic.

Although most definitions of suicide include the idea of an intention to die, even the legal definitions in different countries, let alone the local coroners and police, do not agree about the meaning of suicide and how to infer intention. Douglas argues that official rules and practices for identifying cause of death vary in the objective criteria for assigning

[67]The story comes from Gregory Grossman.
[68]Morgenstern, *On the Accuracy of Economic Observations*, pp. 70–87.
[69]Jack D. Douglas, *The Social Meaning of Suicide* (Princeton, N J : Princeton University Press, 1967), esp. pp. 163–231.

cases to categories, the weight given to conflicting evidence for those criteria, and the "search procedures" for discovering evidence or evaluating reports. And since the moral connotations of suicide vary, so does the willingness of family and officials to categorize deaths as suicides.

Durkheim himself dismissed official statistics about the *motives* for suicide on the ground that these "are actually statistics of the opinions concerning such motives of officials, often of lower officials, in charge of the information service." Durkheim continued: "Unfortunately, official establishments of fact are known to be often defective even when applied to obvious material facts comprehensible to any conscientious observer and leaving no room for evaluation. How suspect must they be considered when applied not simply to recording an accomplished fact but to its interpretation and explanation!"[70] Yet, as Douglas argues, Durkheim failed to see that the suicide statistics themselves were records not of simple facts but of interpretations. Moreover, the same forces that Durkheim saw influencing suicides may instead have been influencing the attribution of suicide by official agencies. For example, Douglas suggests that the better integrated a deceased individual was in the community, the less likely is the coroner to conclude that the person committed suicide; and the more highly integrated the family of the deceased, and hence the closer their relationship to doctors, police, and other officials, the less likely those officials may be to impute suicide over the family's objections. Virtually any argument for the relation of a social factor and suicide rates can be plausibly reconstructed as a relation between the same factor and the rate of suicide attributions. Without ascertaining the magnitude of possible effects on attributions, it is difficult to identify the "true" or at least a consistent suicide rate. In other words, suicide cannot be analyzed through the prism of official statistics without also analyzing the sociology of the statistical process.

Like Morgenstern's work, which also emphasizes inconsistencies of interpretation as well as strategic behavior, the phenomenological approach critical of official statistics is deeply threatening to the entire enterprise of official statistics and the research based on it. Economists have generally ignored Morgenstern's cautions, despite his considerable prestige; sociologists have given somewhat more attention to the phenomenological criticism, particularly in the study of deviance.

In a rebuttal from a Marxist perspective, Hindess insists that official statistics are "in no way reducible to the subjective experience

---

[70]Emile Durkheim, *Suicide* [1897] (New York: Free Press, 1966), p. 148, cited by Douglas, *Social Meaning*, p. 174.

of enumerators and other officials," but rather are "the product of a determinate process of production of knowledge governed by a determinate system of concepts." In support of this position, Hindess analyzes an Indian agricultural census of 1950 in which the categories of income seem to have been drawn from classic British texts of political economy. He argues that the grave problems of classification in this census arose not from the subjective orientations of the interviewers but from the structure of official categories, which inadequately represented the categories of Indian land tenure.[71] Whatever the merits of this analysis, the one case scarcely shows that interactive and interpretative factors never come into play in the generation of official data. But it does underline the potential for ambiguity and error arising from a severe mismatch between official categories and patterns of social life.

4. *The social relations of data processing.* The same arguments about the effects of social interaction on data collection have been made about the intermediate social processes of data production. Administrative statistics, as already mentioned, are particularly subject to pressure because of their use in performance monitoring. In an authoritarian regime, the problem of falsification arises not merely because the regime may lie but because subordinate officials in industry and regional government have good reason to lie to their superiors. Hence progressively larger distortions may appear as information travels up the hierarchy. In a paper on Chinese statistics, Orleans wryly suggests "the greater the number of administrative plateaus which serve as resting places for statistics as they are moved up the line, the less accurate are the figures."[72]

Data processing is a form of work—and in modern societies an increasingly important form. The production of statistical data is, among other things, an industrial process, or labor process, in which large numbers of clerical workers perform routine tasks and are supervised by several levels of administrators and professionals. The distribution of knowledge and control over this work repeats the more general industrial pattern—the concentration of conceptual and planning functions among a relatively small class. In the organization of statistical work, a minority of professionals understands the system and can spot errors. For the majority, on the other hand, the work itself is virtually meaningless. Consequently, they are likely to have neither the interest nor

---

[71]Barry Hindess, *The Use of Official Statistics in Sociology: A Critique of Positivism and Ethnomethodology* (London: Macmillan, 1973), p. 56.

[72]Leo Orleans, "Chinese Statistics: The Impossible Dream," *The American Statistician* 28 (May 1974):51.

the capacity to identify mistakes.[73] Computerization may eliminate some routine clerical tasks and increase the demand for employees with statistical competence, but it seems unlikely to change the basic hierarchical structure of data production.

5. *Disclosure and dissemination: government falsification, statistical blackouts, and the social distribution of public data.* Just as respondents and intermediate officials may falsify statistical reports, so may governments. Morgenstern notes that even the Bank of England for years deliberately misreported its gold reserves.[74] The professionalism of statistical agencies is a partial barrier to "political" tampering with official statistics, but there are numerous examples of misrepresentation. Rather than outright falsification, more common techniques include deceptive use of classifications and tolerance of methodological inadequacies that yield data with useful political effect. For example, many countries in Latin America appear to have underreported infant mortality rates by allowing many infant deaths to go unrecorded.[75]

Statistical blackouts are, in some repects, a functional alternative to misrepresentation and tolerated error. By a statistical blackout I mean the reverse of a statistical strike—that is, the refusal by a government to release statistical data to the public. In Communist China, according to Orleans, 1960 marked "the beginning of a virtual blackout of statistical information."[76] At that time, the Chinese published little statistical information compared to the Soviet Union. Since the late 1970s, however, the Chinese have disclosed more statistical information, while the Soviets have published less. These changes seem to reflect more general tendencies toward "closed" and "open" societies. Thus the volume of statistical output may itself be an interesting indicator of political culture. However, statistical blackouts may also be understood in more strategic terms. The Russians stopped publishing data about infant mortality in the early 1970s, when the figures seem to have grown embarrassingly high. They cut off statistics of grain production when the Carter administration imposed its grain embargo. Altogether, about thirty major items disappeared from the Soviet statistical yearbook in the decade after 1974, according to Murray Feshbach.[77]

[73]Government Statisticians' Collective, "How Official Statistics Are Produced: Views from the Inside," pp. 130–51.

[74]Morgenstern, *On the Accuracy of Economic Observations*, p. 20.

[75]José Carlos Escudero, "On Lies and Health Statistics: Some Latin American Examples," *International Journal of Health Services* 10 (1980):421–35.

[76]Orleans, "Chinese Statistics: The Impossible Dream," p. 49.

[77]Cullen Murphy, "Watching the Russians," *Atlantic Monthly*, February 1983, p. 51 (quoting Feshbach); Amity Shlaes, "Soviet Watchers Face Growing Secrecy on Kremlin's Economic, Crop Statistics," *The Wall Street Journal*, February 2, 1984.

Furthermore, even when the Soviets do publish data, they often fail to explain their methods or change definitions without notice. "Such statistical bad manners," observes Walter Laqueur, "have the same effect as outright disinformation."[78]

Ironically, the United States has become the "leading world supplier" of Soviet economic statistics.[79] The Soviets themselves seem to be relying on American figures. Gregory Grossman points out that the Soviet press sometimes quotes Western reports on Soviet economic performance because of the implicit recognition that Western statistics will have more authority even for the Soviet public.[80]

Not all data are made public in the United States. For example, the budget of the Central Intelligence Agency is secret. There have also been charges that some data series in the United States have been discontinued, or never developed despite congressional authorization, because of fears that they might hurt the administration in power.

Other factors besides decisions about disclosure affect the social distribution of statistical information. Governments face politically significant choices among technologies of dissemination (books, computer tapes, online electronic services); methods for setting prices; options for marketing and publicity; and contacts with various groups of data users, such as commercial organizations, local governments, the mass media, universities and schools, and ordinary citizens.

Patterns of choice in the distribution of public data influence the level of information inequality in a society. No doubt public data in a liberal democracy are a resource more equal in their distribution than proprietary information. But the same public data may have immensely greater value to those who have the skills and resources for analysis than to those who do not. The distribution of statistical competence and analytical resources, such as access to computers, varies greatly in society, not only among individuals but also among businesses, local governments, and community organizations. Stronger and more vocal forces are also better able to use channels of influence to secure the kind of data that serve their interests. The distributional patterns, therefore, have a feedback effect on the cognitive organization of statistics. I turn to that topic next.

---

[78]Walter Laqueur, *A World of Secrets: The Uses and Limits of Intelligence* (New York: Basic Books, 1985), p. 42.

[79]*The Wall Street Journal*, February 2, 1984.

[80]Personal conversation, Berkeley, California.

III.   The Cognitive Organization of Statistical Systems

By the cognitive organization of statistical systems, I mean the more or less permanent ways in which statistical instruments and data are structured to produce information.[81] One way to conceive the cognitive function of statistical systems is that they serve to bring about a progressive reduction of complexity. Social conditions and the activities and characteristics of people are myriad and subtly varied; statistical inquiries must be limited to particular items and categories of response. Yet the raw data thereby collected can be combined and analyzed in sundry ways; scarce cognitive as well as economic resources dictate that only some routes of analysis be followed. Even so, the data and analyses churned out by statistical agencies are too much for the political system and media of communication to absorb. Hence yet another reduction of complexity must be performed by a variety of intermediaries who interpret the data for public consumption.

At each stage in this progressive reduction of complexity, some information is lost as other information is created. Technical criteria alone do not dictate the choice. The statistical information sought—and hence the procedures for combining, analyzing, and representing the data—depends on the purposes in view. The professionals and administrators who design official statistics must, therefore, not only apply their technical competence but also interpret political and social objectives for the data. Their choices will also depend on accepted beliefs about the nature of social reality. Once again, even if unconsciously, they are engaged in a kind of interpretation, choosing a language for inquiry and analysis that does not jar cultural or ideological presuppositions. For so long as their choices fall comfortably within the dominant societal consensus, their judgments are likely to be accepted as objective (by all but philosophers and sociologists). It is where political and cultural conflict and ambiguity exist that the designers of statistical information are likely to experience the greatest anxiety and pressure. In those cases, they may face protests over decisions that sacrifice one sort of information in the interests of producing another kind.

Controversy, however, is only a manifest sign of the political choices that otherwise lie latent and obscure in the cognitive organiza-

---

[81]Here—and generally throughout this chapter—I follow a distinction proposed by Daniel Bell. Data, information, and knowledge, he suggests, may be distinguished according to the complexity of organization of their elements: *Data* are the least organized, whereas *information* is "a pattern or design that rearranges data for instrumental purposes" (that is, for decisions), and *knowledge* consists of the "reasoned judgments" that integrate information at a more abstract level. See Daniel Bell, "The Social Framework of the Information Society," in Michael L. Dertouzos and Joel Moses, eds., *The Computer Age: A Twenty-Year View* (Cambridge: MIT Press, 1979), p.171.

tion of statistics. At the root of the politics of statistical information are the limits of technical knowledge, which cannot resolve large questions about the organization of data. Even the identification of information needs and design of instruments require some conception of social and economic relations and often reflect theoretical schemes from the social sciences. Yet the theories have no official status. At least in the liberal democracies, the public and its officials typically subscribe to a radical empiricism that presumes that statistical inquiry can be theoretically as well as ideologically innocent. These expectations mean that professionals must translate political purposes, cultural presuppositions, and formal social science theories into statistical procedures and data while only seeming to apply their technical skills. Indeed, to avoid cognitive dissonance, they may convince themselves that technical skills are all they are exercising. But as each of the following areas illustrate, the structuring of information allows room for discretionary choice and, therefore, necessarily receives direction from broader social and political values and frames of reference.

The Framing of Inquiry

In the phases of design, fundamental decisions need to be made about the focus, priorities, language, and ultimate objectives of statistical inquiries. To ask some questions is to sacrifice others. The boundaries of official inquiry are the statistical counterpart to the boundaries of the political agenda; and it is an elementary point of political analysis that the control of such boundaries is a critical face of power. Just as statistical blackouts testify to deeper processes at work in a society, so do the patterns of statistical blind spots—that is, the anomalous lacunae in official facts. To make an official count of some phenomenon is often to confer recognition that the phenomenon is real and to risk that its measurement will embarrass those in authority. But omissions may stem from many other possible reasons, including cost-benefit judgments that the additional information is simply not worth the expense, interest group opposition, and general principles for limiting the government's cognitive interest. Even democratic societies decide that some subjects are too sensitive or volatile for political discussion—or for official statistics.[82]

Religion is such a topic in the United States. Neither the census nor any federal surveys ask about religious affiliation. In 1957, when the Census Bureau last included an item about religion in a survey, it was

[82]Stephen Holmes, "Gag Rules or the Politics of Omission," in Jan Elster, ed., *Constitutionalism and Democracy* (forthcoming).

forced to bury the data and abandon plans for a religious question on the next decennial census. Some groups, such as Jews and Christian Scientists, objected to the consequences that they anticipated of officially demarcating and inquiring into that domain.[83] So far as official sources go, statistical Americans have no religion.

A fundamental question in the framing of inquiry is the degree of linkage between theory and data. Data cannot be gathered in a conceptual vacuum, but not all data are conceived with a theoretical design that organizes categories and hypothesizes relations among them. Morgenstern distinguishes between data and observations on the grounds that observations are guided by theory. *"Observations* are deliberately *designed;* other *data* are merely *obtained."*[84] Between the earliest tax and foreign trade statistics, which were mere by-products of administration, and modern systems of economic indicators there is a considerable gulf. The twentieth-century forms illustrate Bell's argument about the increasing centrality of theoretical knowledge.[85] Just as technology and science long proceeded on separate paths of development and only in the last century became closely connected, so large-scale social statistics—a kind of social technology—have only in the last century become closely linked to theories in the social sciences.

The development of the American national income accounts, as Mark Perlman shows in chapter 3, exemplifies the simultaneous importance of political purposes and formal theory in the modern design of statistical systems. In that case, the decision to emphasize economic stabilization policy over long-term growth or distributional questions and the influence of Keynesian theory were critical in framing the system, particularly the decision to treat all government expenditures as consumption and none as investment. In other societies where public investment is critical and the state assumes an active and openly acknowledged role in economic development, the national accounts typically treat state expenditures differently. The American system yields information relevant to the management of demand, but it obscures the role of government in the development of the nation's capital stock. For

[83]Charles R. Foster, "A Question of Religion," Inter- University Case Program No. 66 (Indianapolis: Bobbs-Merrill, 1961).

[84]Morgenstern, *On the Accuracy of Economic Observations,* p. 88.

[85]Daniel Bell, *The Coming of Post-Industrial Society* (New York: Basic Books, 1973). For an argument that the lack of a persuasive theory diminishes the value of social indicators as a guide to policy, see Aaron Wildavsky, *Speaking Truth to Power: The Art and Craft of Policy Analysis* (Boston: Little, Brown, 1979), pp. 26–40. On social indicators, see also Raymond A. Bauer, ed., *Social Indicators* (Cambridge, Mass.: MIT Press, 1966); Daniel Bell, "The Idea of a Social Report," *The Public Interest,* 15 (1969):72–97; Judith Innes de Neufville, *Social Indicators and Public Policy* (New York: Elsevier, 1975); and a special issue of *Items,* bulletin of the Social Science Research Council, vol. 37, no. 4 (December 1983).

example, between 1929 and 1948 the American accounts show an increase in real private output of 57 percent but an increase in the private nonresidential capital stock of only 1 percent. As Robert Gordon points out, this economic miracle is a statistical mirage. The accounts ignore or underrepresent the huge federal investments during World War II in government-owned but privately operated factories in such industries as steel, aluminum, and aircraft.[86]

At issue in the design of national accounts are fundamental questions of policy, not just of fact. In the early debate over the accounts, Simon Kuznets repeatedly emphasized the practical impossibility of measuring national product without making philosophical choices about the end-purpose of economic activity. National income estimators, he wrote, might "find it comforting to cling closely to the raw data yielded by the economy," but the results would have no relation to economic concepts and therefore would be meaningless. Useful data inevitably required "considerable adjustment and purification," and in the process the estimators had no choice but to make explicit philosophical choices.[87]

Systems of Classification

By classification[88] I mean "the ordering or arrangement of objects into groups or sets on the basis of their relationships."[89] At issue here is the choice of categories in the design and analysis of statistics.

Classification is sometimes opposed to quantification as an alternative or lesser form of understanding.[90] But there is no counting without categories, and, as Cohen and Nagel write, classifying "really involves, or is a part of, the formation of hypotheses as to the nature of things."[91] However, social classification—that is, the classification of people, their activities, and their attributes—differs from other kinds (say, the classifications of plants) because people typically have their own con-

[86]Robert Gordon, "$45 Billion of U.S. Private Investment Has Been Mislaid," *American Economic Review* 59 (1969):221–38.

[87]Simon Kuznets, *National Product in Wartime* (New York: National Bureau of Economic Research, 1944), p. 3; Kuznets, "Government Product and National Income," in Erik Lundberg, ed., *Income and Wealth*, ser. 1 (Cambridge, Mass.: Bowes & Bowes, 1951), p. 180.

[88]In this section I draw from an unpublished manuscript of mine on social classification.

[89]Robert R. Sokal, "Classification: Purposes, Principles, Progress, Prospects," *Science* 185 (1974):115–23.

[90]See, for example, Cohen, *A Calculating People*, p. 46.

[91]Morris R. Cohen and Ernest Nagel, *An Introduction to Logic and Scientific Method* (New York: Harcourt Brace, 1934), p. 223, cited in Duncan, *Notes on Social Measurement*, p. 137.

ceptions of membership. Whether the state accepts those conceptions or imposes others may depend on cultural and class divisions, the form of government, and the ability of groups to get their self-definitions recognized as official.

The process of social classification can be broken down analytically into a series of decisions: (1) the definition of a domain of classification; (2) the grouping of elements into sets; (3) labeling of the groups; and (4) the articulation or arrangement of categories in the classificatory order (for example, rank in a hierarchy).

1. *Domain definition.* Domains of social classification do not simply exist. They are historically constituted. To classify by occupation makes sense only when the division of labor is sufficiently advanced. In the congressional debate over the first U.S. Census in 1790, Madison proposed to include an item about occupation. Others, however, doubted that their constituents could report a specific occupation. A congressman from New Hampshire was "confident the distinction . . . could not be performed."[92]

Although our official statistics now classify populations by ethnic group, ethnicity is not a self-evident domain. Alternative, related, or overlapping conceptions, such as race, nationality, ancestry, caste, and religion, compete for recognition. Even where a particular grouping may be clear, its domain may not be. Jews have been variously classified as an ethnicity, a race, or a religion. The choice matters. Furthermore, to classify by ethnicity only makes sense if people understand themselves as having one, and even now it is not clear that all Americans do. As Petersen reports in chapter 5, citing NORC data, some 10 to 15 percent of white Americans give no ethnic identity; another 35 to 40 percent cite two or more ethnic strains, and of these, 11 to 12 percent cannot choose between them. If a classificatory system simply puts individuals in classes (without allowing for different kinds of membership in classes), it may impute more structure to the domain than actually exists. In official social classification, domains are, therefore, doubly constituted: first, in social life; and, second, in the formal classificatory systems—the state's mapping of society.

2. *Grouping.* At stake in the groupings established by official statistics is not only the bounding of an analytical category but often the demarcation of political alliances and coalitions, social movements, and interest groups, which may seek official recognition of their common identity. However, official categories of groups may also put together people who have never thought of themselves as being "in the same category." Nonetheless, by virtue of a common administrative and statistical status, their interests may be joined. In this way, official

[92]Cohen, *A Calculating People,* p. 160.

classification may not merely register but redraw the lines of social differentiation.

Racial and ethnic groupings provide clear examples of such changes, such as the recent statistical amalgamation into the category Hispanic of groups as different as Cuban Americans, Puerto Ricans, and Mexican Americans. This consolidation both reflected a political mobilization and advanced it.

Geographical groupings, such as the boundaries of metropolitan statistical areas (MSAs), also are subject to the same kinds of pressure. In 1983, for example, the Federal Committee on Metropolitan Statistical Areas revised the criteria for designation as an MSA. Some cities that had been joined were separated; others that were separated were joined. But the criteria were not entirely technical. Since the MSA designations are used for economic calculations about advertising and other markets, a merged area may appear to be a more attractive market for business. On the other hand, smaller cities in metropolitan areas often believe they are overshadowed by their bigger neighbor. Norfolk and Newport News, Virginia, wanted a marriage to become the biggest MSA between Washington and Alabama, while Fort Worth got divorced from Dallas, and Oakland from San Francisco.[93]

3. *Labeling*. Different names often indicate different groupings, but even when referring to the same group, two names may suggest entirely different attributes. Labeling theory, developed in the sociology of deviance, emphasizes that the social response to a form of behavior without a label may be quite different from the response to the labeled phenomenon.[94] To count "homelessness" rather than "vagrancy" is the statistical counterpart to transforming deviants into victims. Although from a formal taxonomic standpoint a name is just one of many properties of a category, naming is the point of departure for classification—the trigger for the damages and advantages that categories bring.

A special problem that arises in statistics is the lack of consistency between technical and everyday language. Statistics are sometimes deceptive because operational definitions do not correspond to common understanding. For example, in 1970 over 30 percent of the nation's rural population lived in metropolitan areas; over 40 percent of the nonmetropolitan population was classified as urban; and 90 percent of the land in metropolitan areas was classified as rural![95]

---

[93]John Herbers, "Big City Ringed by Suburbs Giving Way to Sprawl of Small Metropolitan Areas," *The New York Times*, July 8, 1983.

[94]See, for example, Howard S. Becker, *Outsiders* (New York: Free Press, 1963), and John I. Kitsuse and Aaron Cicourel, "A Note on the Uses of Official Statistics," *Social Problems* 2 (1963):135–39.

[95]I owe this example to William Alonso.

4. *Ordering.* The problem of order in classifications arises because social life is not only complex but messy. Boundaries between sets are fuzzy, and the sets overlap but not necessarily to the same degree in all regions of a domain. Occupational classification illustrates these problems. Some occupational roles are reasonably well-defined because of what may be called the primary processes of classification that take place in education and the economy. Systems of credentialing, professional qualification, and collective bargaining help to demarcate some occupations by generating job titles, occupational definitions, and barriers to entry. These primary classification processes constitute a subject for sociological analysis in their own right. But in addition, there is a set of secondary processes in which official agencies attempt to get from this partial structuring of occupations to a total, systematic mapping of occupational roles.

At this secondary level, several notable problems arise: *(i)* Reconciliation of inconsistencies: The job classifications in one firm or city may not match those in another; or they may change from one period to another; or what is worse, the names may not change but the occupational roles do, as when a skilled occupation in one census becomes unskilled by the next; *(ii)* Structuring of ill-defined regions: Just as people may vary in the degree of ethnic identity, so do they vary in attachment to occupational roles—hence the problem of classifying when the subject does not have an occupational self-definition; *(iii)* The elaboration of hierarchy—in two senses: first, defining what goes under what (for example, defining the major occupational divisions); and second, rank-ordering individual occupations and the occupational divisions. The primary processes of classification yield hierarchies within firms and among professional occupations but generally do not do so for the occupational domain as a whole. That ordering or arrangement requires the imposition of some conceptual framework by the observing state on a partially structured domain of social reality. The U.S. Census Bureau, as Margo Conk has shown, has used several such frameworks and thereby has shaped the measurement and understanding of social mobility and social structure in America.[96]

Measurement and Weighting

The social phenomena measured by official statistics are often historically unique. Of course, every physical measurement is a discrete event, but not in "historical time." It makes little difference whether

---

[96]Margo Anderson Conk, *The United States Census and the New Jersey Urban Occupational Structure, 1870–1940* (Madison, Wisc.: UMI Research Press, 1980).

the distance to Jupiter is calculated before or after the next presidential election. Most measurements in the physical sciences can be repeated; so can many measurements in the social sciences needed for evaluating the effects of treatments, procedures, or agents. However, the descriptive statistics that primarily concern us here—the taking of censuses and monitoring of the economy—cannot usually be replicated (though comparisons with independent data and other checks on reliability are sometimes available). The inability to replicate is one reason why their official character is so important. In the social and physical sciences, replicability is the basis for the authority of a finding. For descriptive statistics, official status is a functionally equivalent means of legitimation.

Another feature of much social and economic measurement distinguishes it from measurement of natural phenomena. In nature there are no numbers. Observers have had to create them.[97] The measurement of temperature required a leap of human imagination, but it was not thereafter confused by any scales that the gyrating molecules themselves used. Society, on the other hand, generates its own numerical data before the state comes to count. Just as social classification is complicated by conflicts between subjects' self-conceptions and the categories of official statistics, so problems may arise from the mixing of different systems of measurement—those of subjects and those of observers.

For this reason, it is difficult to make any sharp distinction between primitive and processed social data. Much raw data entered into official statistics have already been privately processed, though not necessarily according to the definitions used in official statistics. I have already mentioned some implications for official statistics of creative accounting and other kinds of strategic data reporting. One problem in official measurement, which arises directly because of its official character, is that the state is handicapped in measuring phenomena some or all of which people want to hide from the state. The state cannot easily determine the level of untaxed income, illegal migration, narcotics traffic, or unreported crime. The "dark figure of crime" has long been the bane of crime statistics (along with the "gray figure" of crime reported to the police but disregarded by them or resolved through informal means and therefore kept out of official records).[98] Society's "dark

---

[97]Morgenstern, *On the Accuracy of Economic Observations*, p. 123.
[98]Albert D. Biderman and Albert J. Reiss, Jr., "On Exploring the 'Dark Figure' of Crime," *Annals of the American Academy of Political and Social Science* 374 (1967):1–15; N. H. Avison, "Criminal Statistics as Social Indicators," in Andrew Shonfield and Stella Shaw, eds., *Social Indicators and Social Policy* (London: Heinemann, 1972), pp. 33–52.

side" is not only difficult technically to estimate; it is sometimes politically impossible to acknowledge. Some regimes, such as those in the Communist world, maintain that problems like unemployment or crime to be found in decadent societies simply do not exist in theirs, at least not in significant degree. The Latin American governments that deny that their countries are major sources of cocaine or marijuana are unlikely to publish estimates of earnings from illegal drugs in their foreign trade statistics.

Many of the enduring political conflicts over statistics are conflicts over the rules of measurement. The classic dispute about the national income accounts concerns the practice of not attributing any economic value to nonmarket services, such as those traditionally provided by women within the family. This is offensive to feminists. Cost-benefit analysis typically measures the value of human life by future earnings; this is offensive to groups representing the elderly. Indeed, the application of cost-benefit analysis to medical care for the aged has rather severe political and ethical limitations.[99] In the determination of the poverty rate, conservatives favor the inclusion of in-kind income, which would bring down the absolute rate by raising the measured income of the poor. On the other hand, advocates of the poor want the income cut-off for poverty raised because the original basis for its computation no longer exists. The index assumes that the poor spend one-third of their income on food; the cut-off is determined, therefore, by multiplying a subsistence food budget by three. However, critics argue that since the poor now spend less than a third of their income on food, the multiple should be higher than three.

In these disputes, the forces arrayed on different sides want their values embodied in the numbers because the numbers influence perceptions of group worth—what women contribute to the economy; what value is to be put on the elderly, and what it is worth spending on them; how many are the poor, and what priority they deserve. To adopt a rule of measurement in these cases is plainly a political choice of great symbolic and practical consequence.

That the political conflicts in these cases concern the underlying *rules* is a critical point. Principles are at issue. Even those who criticize the official figures generally do not suggest that politics enters into particular calculations. The case is somewhat different with the politics of economic and budget forecasting. Perhaps no statistical results are more sensitive to political considerations than are projections and forecasts, for these may be self-fulfilling. A high forecast of economic growth may

---

[99]Jerry Avorn, "Benefit and Cost Analysis in Geriatric Care: Turning Age Discrimination into Health Policy," *New England Journal of Medicine* 310 (May 17, 1984): 1294–1307.

encourage capital spending, whereas a low forecast may crimp investment. A high growth forecast may also bring with it higher projections of government revenues and therefore encourage more government spending; a low forecast may raise projected deficits and thereby disarm advocates of bigger government programs. Projecting "revenue low and expenditure high" is a predictable budget-balancing strategy of ministries of finance, particularly in countries facing severe fiscal problems.[100]

The peculiar problem of official forecasts is that they serve not only to predict future states but also to proclaim present intentions. An administration that intends to "stay the course" is not likely to tolerate forecasts by its own chief economist indicating that current policy will lead to slow growth and high deficits. So it was that Martin Feldstein had to leave his post as chairman of the Council of Economic Advisors in the Reagan administration—and so it was that President Reagan nearly abolished the council. Forecasting may well be a kind of statistical undertaking for which official agencies are structurally disabled.

The Periodicity of Inquiry and Adaptation to Change

Statistical systems have several different kinds of periodicity. Data are gathered and reported at varying intervals; and the questions, categories, and other instruments may be tested and reexamined at other, longer intervals. In the United States, the federal government publishes weekly data on the money supply, monthly data on unemployment, quarterly data on GNP, annual estimates for poverty, and the decennial census of the nation's population. These varying frequencies are almost as much a part of the political system as the election of congressmen every two years, presidents every four, and senators every six.

But obviously different considerations are involved. The frequency of data collection and publication seems to reflect an implicit judgment about the rate of change of the phenomena being measured and the value of up-to-date information. Presumably, slow-moving variables do not require the same frequency of reporting as do those that fluctuate rapidly. This may be the reason that the relatively stable social indicators, such as birth or divorce rates, command less frequent press attention than the more volatile economic indicators. Indeed, the attention given social and economic indicators seems to depend largely on whether and how much they move, or to be more precise, on change in

[100]Wildavsky, *Budgeting: A Comparative Theory of Budgetary Processes*, p. 143.

the rate of change. When the infant mortality rate stopped falling in the early 1980s as rapidly as it had before, that was news.

Statistical information may decline in accuracy not only because measurements get out of date but because the classifications or other underlying principles of cognitive organization lose their validity. For example, changes in the structure of the economy inevitably create new categories of industry and employment. The most rapidly growing industry in New York State at one point was "other." Although statistical systems need continually to be adjusted to take account of such changes, they have powerful inertial forces at work. The more categories and questions are revised, the less comparable are data for different periods. Structural revisions are also costly to undertake. Hence there are strong conservative tendencies that may lead to a lag in the recognition of structural change.

The history of the consumer price index (CPI) illustrates the conservative character of official statistics. The "market basket" of commodities whose prices are included lags behind purchasing patterns. Old product models hang on. Typically new products have been introduced into the index only long after they have been on the market and have already undergone large price declines. Gordon notes:

> The United States became a motorized society in the 1920's and 1930's, when there was an enormous improvement in the performance of automobiles along with a decline in their price—but the automobile was not included in the CPI until 1940. Penicillin entered the CPI in 1951, after it had already experienced a 99 percent decline from its initial price. The pocket calculator entered the CPI in 1978, after it had declined in price about 90 percent from the early 1970-71 models and about 98 percent from the price of a comparable electromechanical desk calculator of the 1960's.[101]

In this particular case, a built-in lag in recognizing change lends an upward bias to the measure of inflation, but there is no definite political pattern to the effects. Statistical systems are conservative in an institutional rather than political sense.

The Presentation of Data in Bureaucratic Life

Neutrality does not fully express the bureaucratic ideal in the presentation of statistical data. It is more like relevance without parti-

---

[101]Robert J. Gordon, "The Consumer Price Index: Measuring Inflation and Causing It," *The Public Interest* 63 (Spring 1981), p. 130. See also Richard W. Wahl, "Is the Consumer Price Index a Fair Measure of Inflation?" *Journal of Policy Analysis and Management* 1 (1982):496–511.

sanship.[102] However, the very fear of appearing partisan, ideological, or sectarian promotes abstention from judgments that express shock or surprise (particularly about the performance of administrations in power!). Nonetheless, official agencies in some societies do quietly produce data that reflect unfavorably on their governments. Even more remarkable is the kind of case that Christopher Jencks discusses in this volume. In reporting changes in real income, federal agencies probably made the performance of the U.S. government and economy in the 1970s seem worse than they actually were. Here again institutional conservativism may chiefly be at work. The methods of reporting did not change; social and economic relations did—but to acknowledge and assimilate those changes in revised statistics might raise more opposition than it would dispel.

The acknowledgment of ambiguity and imprecision in the presentation of data poses a task of considerable delicacy. The appropriate disclaimers may be made in technical appendices, while the basic mode of presentation implicitly says the opposite. In a pattern that Morgenstern calls "specious accuracy," figures are regularly reported to several decimal places even though they cannot possibly be accurate to that degree.[103]

Conceptual ambiguities often suggest the need for more than one indicator, but for political reasons this is rarely done. The U.S. Treasury does produce a series of different numbers for the money supply, each reflecting a different conception. But several other proposals for multiple-number indicators have been rejected. In the debate over the national income accounts in the 1940s, Kuznets argued that rather than producing a single figure for gross national product, the Commerce Department should produce a group of different figures based on varying definitions.[104] Similarly, Eisner has recently suggested that rather than a single number for the federal deficit, the government could justifiably produce a dozen, each with different assumptions and useful for different purposes.[105] However, in the late 1960s, when three different budget figures were in use, the accounting system was revised to yield

[102]Martin, "Statistical Practice in Bureaucracies."

[103]Morgenstern, *On the Accuracy of Economic Observations*, p. 62. Making the same point in another domain of statistics, Tufte writes: "The study of politics, like the study of economics, is usually a one-digit science at best; in fact, we do well to get the sign right more than half the time. How then can anyone be asked to take the third, fourth, and fifth significant digits seriously?" Edward R. Tufte, "Political Statistics for the United States: Observations on Some Major Data Sources," *American Political Science Review* 71 (1977):312.

[104]Simon Kuznets, "National Income: A New Version," *Review of Economics and Statistics* 30 (August 1948), pp. 151–79.

[105]Robert J. Eisner, "Which Budget Deficit: Some Issues of Measurement and Their Implications," *American Economic Association Papers and Proceedings* 74 (May 1984): 138–43.

a single figure for a budget surplus or deficit. The presidential commission that recommended the change claimed that the use of three different numbers had been politically confusing and led to public cynicism about their manipulation.[106] A single number, after all, is the ultimate step in the reduction of complexity that official statistics bring about. If the statistical agencies do not perform that reduction, others will when they translate the data into one-page briefings for policymakers and newspaper headlines for the public.

IV.   Uses and Effects: Do Statistics Count?

The most common metaphors for statistical systems suggest that they passively record and measure social and economic conditions. They are typically called barometers or mirrors, and statistical tables or graphs are described as pictures or photographs. Like photographs, statistics seem to arrest the flow of human activity and fix it for more detached inspection. Numbers seem superior in objective reality to "mere" words for the same reason Susan Sontag cites in suggesting why photography, in contrast to painting, so strongly compels belief: A number, like a photograph, seems a piece of reality, rather than an interpretation of it.[107] However, statistics not only lend themselves to many interpretations; they contain them. And because statistics do not simply reproduce reality, statistical systems represent an independent factor in social life.

Yet to say that statistics count is not to identify (much less measure!) their effects. The effects of information or communication are notoriously difficult to specify. Much research has evaluated the effects of mass communications—radio campaigns, advertising, and violence on television are each the subject of an entire corpus of sociological work[108]—but nothing comparable is available on official statistics. Indeed, the effects are so diffuse and elusive that valid generalizations may be few.

I have already alluded to many uses or functions of official statistics. But use never proves effect. For example, instead of information causing a decision, a decision made for other reasons may cause the in-

---

[106]U.S. President's Commission on Budget Concepts, *Report* (Washington, D.C.: G.P.O, 1967).

[107]Susan Sontag, *On Photography* (New York: Farrar, Strauss & Giroux, 1977), p. 4.

[108]For a review, see Todd Gitlin, "Media Sociology: The Dominant Paradigm," *Theory and Society* 6 (1978):205–52.

formation to be cited. Statistics, as Keyfitz says in chapter 6, are the rhetoric of the age.

While keeping that caution in mind, I shall try to identify a few general effects of official statistical systems. My main concern here is the possible impact on politics and social structure in contemporary society.

Official Statistics as Cognitive Commitments

Although critics often object to the federal government's methods for determining unemployment, inflation, and economic growth, the official figures provide the common point of reference in assessing the condition of the economy and the performance of administrations in office. The official definitions are not the only ones possible; alternatives may be found in academic papers and sometimes in the financial press. But the meanings shared socially in the widest sense are the concepts operationalized in the government's statistical series.

Official statistics thereby become cognitive commitments for a society. We have, in effect, bound ourselves collectively to think of the social phenomenon of unemployment—its magnitude, trends, distribution—in the way that the statistical agencies and commissions have settled upon. The structure of rules (classifications, methods of measurement and weighting) is the cognitive equivalent of a constitution. Just as a constitution binds a polity to rules for elections (a kind of numerical procedure), so the structure of statistics binds it to procedures for resolving potentially divisive questions of fact (how many are unemployed or poor, or whether real income is rising or falling).

The classifications used in official statistics are cognitive commitments of a powerful kind. Once governments decide to use particular categories to count, the terms enter the language of administration and shape both private and governmental decisions. Official categories may help to constitute or divide groups and to illuminate or obscure their problems and achievements. Once the Census Bureau adopted the category Hispanic, American society became cognitively committed to it. In France the use of the category "cadres" in official statistics helped to crystallize the class identity of those in middle-level technical and managerial posts.[109] The groupings for social insurance in Germany, particularly the split between *Arbeiter* and *Angestellten* (wage-workers

---

[109]Luc Boltanski, "Taxinomies sociales et luttes de classes: La mobilisation de 'la classe moyenne' et l'invention des 'cadres,' " *Actes de la recherche en sciences sociales* 29 (September 1979):75–103.

and salaried employees), are said to have helped to shape class consciousness.[110]

Official statistics count even if the methods are faulty and the data incorrect. The axiom of modern computer research—garbage in, garbage out—does not exactly apply when statistics are official. In that case the rule may be *garbage in, consensus out.*

Statistics and the Emergence of Norms

If official statistics affect social perception and cognition, so they also powerfully affect social norms. An average is not just a number; it often becomes a standard. In many contexts, to be average is to be okay. Below an average may lie evidence of failure and possibly presumptions of need, whereas above it may lie evidence of success and claims of merit.

Social norms for public policy tend to keep pace with statistical measures of actual conditions. De Neufville notes that the number of children per classroom influences norms of class size, and the norm varies from one country to another according to the measured ratios.[111] In the United States a 2 percent inflation rate and a 3 or 4 percent unemployment rate were considered normal during the 1950s and 1960s. As measured inflation and unemployment rose in the 1970s, the norms also inched up. By the mid-1980s, normal inflation seems to be about 4 percent, and "full employment" is an unemployment rate of as much as 6 or 7 percent.

Many regularly reported social and economic indicators have instantly recognizable normative content. The numbers do not provide strictly factual information. Since the frameworks of normative judgment are so widely shared, the numbers are tantamount to a verdict. Combining the cognitive commitments of official statistics with shared frameworks of judgment effectively binds our politics to a court in which the statistical agencies pass on the performance of national leaders. And as Kenneth Prewitt points out in these pages, voters seem to base their judgments more on the performance of the national economy than on their own personal experience. Since the statistics are the basis for those readings, their influence on elections may sometimes be critical.

[110]Jurgen Kocka, "Class Formation, Interest Articulation, and Public Policy: The Origins of the German White-Collar Class in the Late Nineteenth and Early Twentieth Centuries," in Suzanne D. Berger, ed., *Organizing Interests in Western Europe* (New York: Cambridge University Press, 1981), pp. 63–82.

[111]De Neufville, *Social Indicators and Public Policy*, p. 4.

Statistical Systems as "Automatic Pilots"

Statistics and statistical formulas have been adopted in a variety of contexts as a device for routinizing decisions. Many of these uses are comparatively recent. Cost of living adjustments (COLAs), typically based on the CPI, first became common in labor contracts in the 1950s and 1960s. In 1972 Congress voted to index Social Security benefits to protect them against inflation, and in 1981 it indexed federal income tax brackets to prevent "bracket creep." In the 1970s the federal government increasingly began to distribute aid to state and local governments according to statistical formulas. And under the Gramm-Rudman plan enacted in 1985, Congress voted to bring down the federal deficit over five years through staged reductions to be made by formula if Congress and the President in any year failed to agree on sufficient spending cuts or tax increases.

In each of these instances, decision makers have used statistical devices to limit the boundaries of discretion. The reasons for the rise of COLAs in collective bargaining may help to identify the general process at work. Sanford M. Jacoby points out that COLAs facilitate contracts of longer duration and, therefore, tend to reduce the "reopening costs" of new negotiations and the risk of strikes. However, before 1950 both unions and management generally opposed COLAs for fear that workers might strike if wages were automatically cut as a result of a fall in prices; employers also did not like guaranteeing wage increases if prices rose. Two principal factors seem to account for the growing use of COLAs in the postwar era: (1) the change in inflationary expectations, which meant that automatic pay cuts were unlikely; and (2) the growing complexity of collective bargaining agreements, which made them more difficult and expensive to renegotiate. The rising cost of contract reopenings led management to accept automatic pay formulas to secure longer and more stable agreements.[112]

The use of automatic formulas for distributing federal aid may reflect similar changes in transaction costs. Just as labor contracts became more complex, so did federal programs. Formulas reduce the need for legislative reopenings and administrative evaluation of specific programs, both of which demand time and potentially increase conflict. The indexing of Social Security may have been directly influenced by the example of COLAs in labor contracts. Just as changed inflationary expectations meant that employees need not fear COLA-induced pay cuts, so, too, Social Security beneficiaries saw a prospect only of upward

---

[112]Sanford M. Jacoby, "Cost-of-Living Escalators Became Prevalent in the 1950's," *Monthly Labor Review* (May 1985):32–33.

adjustments. But in this case, a miscalculation also played a role. The proposal to index Social Security came from Republicans, who erroneously believed it would limit future growth in benefits.[113] In fact, the initial procedure for indexing overcompensated for inflation, and because of the unexpected rise in inflation in the 1970s, the real value of benefits jumped substantially.

As a result of these institutionalized uses in private contracts and public programs, official statistics now affect the distribution of income and other resources. The distributive effects result from both biases in the indexes and variations in their application. If all sources of income and all tax provisions were indexed by one ideal measure of inflation, that measure would have no effect (except presumably to reduce concern about inflation). However, only some sources of income and a few tax provisions are now indexed, and the indexes are far from perfect. Robert Gordon observes that the use of escalator clauses based on the consumer price index has created "a two-class society, separating those who are protected against inflation, legally or by contract, from those who are not."[114] The "class" whose interests are linked to the CPI includes 8 million workers covered by collective bargaining contracts with cost of living adjustments; 31 million Social Security beneficiaries; 2.5 million retired military and federal Civil Services employees and survivors; 20 million food stamp recipients; and 25 million children receiving subsidized school lunches. (The latter two groups' benefits depend not on the CPI as a whole but on one of its components.) Counting dependents, about half the population of the United States is directly affected by the way the CPI measures inflation. The incomes of that class grew at the expense of the unprotected in the late 1970s, when the CPI significantly overstated inflation because of its peculiar treatment of housing costs.

The CPI is an especially clear example of how statistical systems matter. Even though it was widely known that the CPI misrepresented the inflation rate, real political consequences were felt because of the index's behavior. Not only did it redistribute income; it helped to raise inflation and panic the Carter administration into its ill-fated credit controls.

Yet there is another side to this issue. A statistical rule is a device for making a decision impersonal, or at least making it appear to be impersonal. In this regard, statistics represent resources for politics, not only in providing information but in providing a means for reducing the

[113]Paul Light, *Artful Work: The Politics of Social Security Reform* (New York: Random House, 1985), p. 45.

[114]Gordon, "The Consumer Price Index," p. 114.

fear of unchecked power. To be sure, a formula for distributing federal aid may have been designed to benefit the district of an influential congressman. But once the indicators and the formula are established, they resist modification. To subordinate ourselves under an impersonal rule is the fundamental reason why we have laws and constitutions. However imperfect, a rule of law tends to restrain the abuse of power and thereby enlarges liberty. Statistical systems help to accomplish similar purposes, and, despite their imperfections, they may also contribute to our freedom.

A Concluding Note

At the outset I suggested that statistical systems deserved attention as social phenomena in their own right, not just for the practical value of determining whether statistics are distorted by social processes. But, of course, a more thorough understanding of the social and cognitive organization of official statistics may give rise to better ideas about how to produce them—or, for that matter, when to ignore them. Joan Robinson once said that the reason to learn economics is to avoid being deceived by economists. The rationale for sociological inquiry into statistics is partly to avoid being deceived by official statistics. Studies of the development and organization of statistical systems are a journey upstream toward the sources of everyday facts. In that sense, they serve purposes fundamental to sociology and help illuminate a sphere of knowledge that has taken on central importance in our political and economic life. In a small way, this volume may contribute to those larger goals.

PART I
The Politics of Economic Measurement

1

THE POLITICS OF COMPARATIVE ECONOMIC STATISTICS: THREE CULTURES AND THREE CASES

RAYMOND VERNON

I N A WORLD that groans under the weight of the statistics it produces, it would be astonishing if statistical comparisons of different national economies had not worked their way into the political arena. One can hardly make a comparative statement about economic performance without exposing a political nerve in one or another of the countries compared. Almost any such comparison—unemployment, the rate of inflation, the distribution of income, or change in gross national product—provides ammunition in international debates and domestic political struggles.

To explore the interplay between politics and statistics, it may help to recognize from the beginning that three quite different cultures are involved. The first is the culture of professional statisticians and other technical experts, who have devoted themselves to the formidable task of producing national statistics that are comparable across countries and consistent over time. Many of these people work in major international agencies, notably the United Nations secretariat, the World Bank and International Monetary Fund, and the Organization for Economic Cooperation and Development. These experts have long ties with national technicians in the United States and elsewhere. Over the past five or six decades, technical teams from the international agencies and the rich industrialized countries have helped train statistical counter parts in the newer and poorer countries, thereby creating an international group devoted to promoting the comparability and enlarging the scope of their statistical resources.

On first reaction, the goal of promoting the comparability and consistency of national data may be thought of as unequivocally constructive. But as a number of scholars have pointed out, much depends on how that comparability and consistency are achieved.[1] Take, for instance, the efforts of governments to estimate the value of the goods and services produced in a national economy on a basis that is consistent from one government to the next. The conditions encountered in different economies vary enormously. An economic activity in one place may be noneconomic in another; a farmer who fishes in the United States may be engaged in recreation, whereas a farmer who fishes in Pakistan may be engaged in feeding himself. What is a plausible measure of value in one country may be misleading in another; countries that impose official price ceilings may be unable to determine the relative value of their products from such prices. In their efforts to promote comparability, technicians will often find it necessary to suppress such differences rather than to capture them. And there is a risk that the training and conditioning of such technicians will accentuate the desire for a surface uniformity.

The politicians and policymakers with whom the technicians interact are, of course, much more diverse in outlook, varying substantially from one country to the next. What such politicians and policymakers share in common is an interest in using the data—sometimes, too, in suppressing or modifying them—to promote their national or international objectives.

At the national level, the policymakers are ordinarily in command of the technicians; yet there are usually some restraints on the extent to which they can control what the technicians produce. In some countries, such as those in North America and Western Europe, traditions and values may inhibit the politicians from tinkering too overtly with the data; besides, in such countries, experts who are not employed by the government are often sufficiently well informed to raise the alarm with regard to obvious cases of doctoring or suppression. In countries in which public criticism cannot be counted on to act as a restraint on the politicians, however, technicians are ordinarily not in a strong position to resist political pressure to present a favorable statistical picture. One reason is that the data on which the technicians draw are usually incomplete and unreliable; accordingly, whenever the technicians are obliged to put together a complex aggregative measure, such as a GNP

---

[1]See, for instance, Simon Kuznets, *Economic Growth of Nations* (Cambridge, Mass.: Harvard University Press, 1971), pp. 2–10.

series or a consumer price index, they are obliged to make many weak estimates in order to provide some of the missing pieces of the jigsaw. When data of that sort figure prominently in the total, it is difficult for the technicians to defend an unbiased estimate against a biased one.

Once national statistics have been released by a national government to an international agency, it cannot be presumed that international scrutiny will serve as much of a corrective force. The secretariats of international organizations, which are sometimes in an excellent position to know where the bodies are buried, are usually in no position to assist the digging parties; the risk of offending a member state is not one that an international careerist can lightly assume. There are situations, to be sure, in which an international secretariat cannot overlook the fact that the statistics generated by a national government are *prima facie* implausible. The staff reports of the International Monetary Fund and the various international banks commonly carry cautiously phrased references to such implausible data, together with more realistic estimates by the staff. But such documents are ordinarily restricted and the estimates they contain are ordinarily unpublished.

Nor is much critical comment likely to come from other governments. As a rule, diplomats are strongly allergic to the idea of becoming entangled in technical discussions over the merits of complex statistical measures. Inasmuch as national statistics ordinarily originate with national governments, critics would find it hard to take up the cudgels without casting aspersions on the originating government. Besides, sampling methodologies, estimating techniques, and price indexes are not the stuff of which international political debates are made; they capture no loyalties and garner no votes.

The third culture involved in creating the linkages between politics and statistics is, of course, that of the academic world. In contrast to the politicians, the academics see discussions over sampling methodologies, estimating techniques, and the like as the matters of consequence. But academics differ in orientation. Some are principally interested in what the underlying data reveal about such phenomena as economic development, national productivity, and military effort. This group is ordinarily capable of working quite closely with the technicians inasmuch as their principal focus is on applying information rather than questioning its validity. Other academics play a less engaged role, emphasizing the shortcomings of the data and the errors of inference to which the user is exposed. From time to time, the work of the academics impinges on the political process; but in the short run, such work does not appear to penetrate very deeply. The inadequacies and errors that academics profess to see in the data cannot be expected quickly to affect the activities of the technicians or the consciousness of the policymakers. Accordingly, the lessons that academics purport to derive from the data usually take a long time to affect the political process.

These are large generalizations, more in the nature of preliminary hypotheses than of hidebound conclusions. Any adequate test of hypotheses such as these would demand extensive fieldwork, well beyond the scope of this chapter. My objective in the pages that follow is more modest. I hope to sharpen and enrich these hypotheses, thus laying some of the groundwork for more extensive study. And I mean to achieve that limited objective by exploring three cases in which comparisons of the economic performance of a number of countries lie at the center of a political debate.

One of the three cases entails the development of international criteria for distinguishing poor countries from the not-so-poor and from the rich. This is a case in which the role of the international agencies is comparatively strong; although the relevant data are compiled in the first instance by national governments, those governments get plenty of guidance and technical assistance from international agencies. Moreover, the statistical results are important to all the parties concerned because they directly affect the terms on which governments gain access to international credit and foreign markets.

The second case centers on the dispute in the United States over the causes and cures of an alleged decline in the country's productivity. International comparisons are involved in this case because the decline is widely thought to be part of a general deterioration in the performance of the United States relative to that of its principal competitors. In this instance, the political use of the data is largely internal to the United States; the international political process is not directly involved.

The third case involves a long-standing dispute in the United States over the level of its military spending as compared with that of the U.S.S.R. In this case, the validity of the data is at the center of the dispute. Moreover, the disputants have an eye on a number of different audiences: on a domestic U.S. constituency; on the U.S.S.R. itself; and on various allies and antagonists who are listening in on the discussion.

Identifying the Poor Countries
The Issue

Over the past thirty years, distinctions between the rights and duties of poor countries and those of rich countries have been built into international relations in numerous contexts. The World Bank, created at Bretton Woods in the 1940s, was set up with the long-term goal of having the rich countries help finance the development of the poor. In subsequent decades, as the World Bank and its affiliates dispensed funds for development, distinctions between the rich, the poor, and the very poor took on strong operational significance. The Bank's 1982 annual report, for instance, observes that as a general rule "within five years after a country reaches the per capita gross national product (GNP) benchmark of $2,650 at 1980 prices," it will no longer have access to Bank loans.[2] Meanwhile the World Bank's affiliate, the International Development Association, continues to concentrate its resources on the especially poor countries, as it has from the time of its foundation in 1962.[3]

Similar distinctions have developed in the field of international trade. For instance, the Havana Charter for an International Trade Organization, drafted in 1948, acknowledged the special rights of countries in process of development; and in the decades that followed, the successor effort, the General Agreement on Tariffs and Trade (GATT), greatly extended the rights and exemptions of developing countries. Eventually, countries that were classified as developing countries were, in effect, relieved of all the significant obligations of the GATT, while retaining the right of nondiscriminatory treatment in trade matters. Various rich countries also participated in a so-called Generalized System of Preferences, under which specified products from designated poor countries were accorded preferential tariff treatment.

Understandably, governments came to put some value on being classified as poor. To be sure, from the point of view of home politics, governments in such countries usually wished to be able to prove that their economies had been well managed. Nevertheless, from an international viewpoint, it was usually wise not to shed the mantle of poverty too soon. As the incomes of some developing countries expanded, the United States and other rich countries began to speak of exposing those countries to a process of "graduation," of progressively withdrawing the special exemptions and special rights that had previously been bestowed.[4] The hauling and pulling over this issue came to represent a problem of first-class proportions, especially for such fast-growing countries as Brazil and Korea. If "graduation" succeeded, countries of this sort could foresee the day on which they no longer were entitled to the special rights and exemptions of a developing country, and might even

---

[2]*World Bank Annual Report 1982* (Washington, D.C., 1982), p. 35.

[3]E. S. Mason and R. E. Asher, *The World Bank Since Bretton Woods* (Washington, D.C.: Brookings Institution, 1973), p. 402.

[4]Isaiah Frank, "The 'Graduation' Issue for LDCs," *Journal of World Trade Law* 13 (1979): 289–302.

be asked to contribute to the support of other countries still in that category.[5]

The efforts of the rapidly growing countries to resist graduation have, of course, affected the interests of countries that ranked below them in the development pecking order. If some countries were to give up the label of developing country, the available resources of the international lending agencies and the right to preferential trade treatment would be targeted to a smaller group of recipients. One might suppose, therefore, that the pressures from the poorest countries would be added to those of the richest group to persuade those in the middle to accept modifications of their rights as developing countries.

However, differences within the community of developing countries on this critical issue have not been allowed to surface very widely. The countries that were entitled to be regarded as "developing" or "less developed" in the 1950s and 1960s have clung to the designation in the 1980s, maintaining an unchanging coalition against the richer industrialized countries. Whatever resentments the poorest countries of Africa and Asia may have harbored against the countries earmarked for graduation—the so-called NICs (newly industrialized countries)—have been carefully contained within the family. Solidarity has been institutionalized through organizations such as the Group of 77 and through caucuses of various sorts in the different international organizations, thus relieving the NICs of some of the political pressures for graduation that they might otherwise face.

Some Measurement Problems

Comparing the economic conditions and economic needs of different countries has always entailed great difficulties.[6] To be sure, there is not the slightest doubt that the people of Mali are poorer than those of Portugal, or that the people of Portugal are poorer than those of Sweden. Nor is there any question that the economic condition of the people of Chad over the last two decades has improved more slowly than that of the Brazilians. For comparisons such as these, the differences are too stark to require actual data. But many important questions about the trend and level of economic well-being in poor countries entail much less obvious comparisons.

---

[5] A discussion of the implications of graduation in the context of the World Bank's activities appears in *World Bank Annual Report 1982*, p. 35.

[6] For a systematic review of many of the problems, see *Measurement and Interpretation of Productivity* (Washington, D.C.: National Academy of Sciences, 1979), especially pp. 19–34, 206–210.

The statistical measure that has the widest currency as an index of the economic well-being of a country is, of course, the country's gross national product (GNP) expressed in per capita terms. Although the major limitations of that figure are well enough known, one is so obvious that it is often overlooked: Per capita figures suppress an important distinction between a population with a heavy component of children and a population with few children. For instance, in 1980 only 48 percent of the Syrian population fell between the ages of 15 and 64, that is, the usual working years; by contrast, the population in the 15–64 age group in Chile came to 68 percent and in Japan to 68 percent.[7] With such wide demographic differences, per capita figures can easily produce misleading impressions.

Less obvious problems, however, are to be found in the measure of GNP itself. Though such a measure can be estimated in more than one way, as a practical matter it usually requires the technician to develop an estimate of the output of a country's goods and services. Where developing countries are compared, it is necessary to distinguish activities that lead to economic output from activities that have other purposes. This differentiation can be critical in identifying the poorest of the poor countries, where the output of subsistence agriculture, self-constructed dwellings, and housework are of paramount importance, and where the infrastructure of communities is commonly maintained by the unpaid labor of its members. The general rules that international agencies lay down with regard to the treatment of such items are fairly specific. For instance, they propose excluding the value of housework, while including the unpaid masonry work of those who are masons. But the rules are likely to be differently applied in different countries; and, even if uniformly applied, they will have different effects on national coverage. My guess is that problems such as these help to explain, for instance, why the per capita GNP of Bangladesh for the year 1979 is reported as $90, an income that by itself probably would not command enough food, shelter, and infrastructure to sustain human life, even at the price levels prevailing inside Bangladesh.

The problem of defining an economic output is matched in difficulty by the problem of distinguishing between outputs and inputs. In a world that lavishes much of its resources on weapons and fighting men, for instance, it is no trivial question whether military expenditures are to be thought of as an input—the cost of maintaining peace— or as an output. And as those expenditures rise and fall in any country, the question whether such changes should be thought of as affecting the

[7]*World Development Report 1981*, published for World Bank by Oxford University Press, New York, Appendix Table 19, pp. 170–171.

country's per capita level of output can take on real significance. In the event, governments conventionally count these expenditures as output—guns are counted as if they were butter.

A third set of problems arises out of the special difficulties associated with collecting data on output in the developing countries. Facilities for the collection of data are scarce, especially when the producers are many and scattered. In view of the overwhelming importance of agricultural production in such countries, governments cannot fail to make a stab at estimating the output of that sector; yet the resulting statistics are inherently subject to wide margins of error. Outside of agriculture, the authorities tend to rely to an inordinate degree on the output of a few industries, namely, industries whose output is capable of being more readily measured. Accordingly, measures like electric power production, railroad carloadings, cement production, textile cloth production, and so on, acquire considerable weight in the estimates. This means that major changes in the composition of the country's output can sometimes escape the country's statistical net for considerable periods, especially if the changes take the form of new products or services and even more particularly if those changes are dispersed among many producers. Factors such as these account for the familiar fact that the GNP of various countries, when revised some years after the period being measured, commonly exhibit a higher level and a higher rate of GNP increase than the original estimates.[8]

As important as any of these factors is the question of how to place a value on the various outputs. In many cases, that choice is predetermined by the fact that the only available measure of output is a money value expressed in the national currency of the country concerned. In such cases, the market price prevailing in the country is usually the price that determines the reported value. In other instances, where the output is expressed in physical units such as tons of cement, the technicians are obliged to apply a price to the output; and once again, governments tend to use their national prices for that purpose. The introduction of prices in the calculation, it is evident, raises the usual problems of intertemporal comparisons: As prices and outputs change, how is one to compare the real value of the output of goods and services between any two periods? This is a familiar problem that requires no special comment in the context of GNP data.

[8]Studies that reflect such a tendency include: on Malaysia, J. J. Stern, "An Analysis of the New National Accounts Data," Harvard Institute for International Development, Cambridge, November 15, 1977; on Bangladesh, W. I. Abraham, "Macroeconomic Indicators of Industrial Activity," Harvard Institute for International Development, Cambridge, September 21, 1983; and on Egypt, Richard S. Eckhaus, "Interactions of Economics and Political Change," *World Development* 7 (1980):783–797.

When the gross products of different countries have to be compared, however, a distinctive problem of valuation must be faced, namely, finding a common unit of currency in which to state the various national figures. For that purpose, international agencies typically convert national figures into U.S. dollars, using the market rate that exists for exchange between the national currency and the U.S. dollar.

Various scholars have pointed out the problems that are involved in using the going exchange rate to compare the real incomes of any pair of countries.[9] For one thing, the prices of basic commodities in developing countries are often grossly distorted; although there is a general tendency for governments to hold down the prices of basic commodities with subsidies and to elevate the prices of other products with protection, the size of these interventions varies from one country to the next.[10] For another, the rate of exchange that is determined by the market for the currencies of the two countries is commonly quite different from the levels that would express parity in purchasing power between the currencies.

The size of the exchange rate distortion can be illustrated by comparing the estimates of GNP derived from two different approaches: One approach uses the rate of exchange of the country's currency with the U.S. dollar in order to measure the output of the country by a common *numeraire*; the other approach applies an exchange rate that is derived by comparing the relative purchasing power of national currencies for a wide range of goods and services in the various countries. The most ambitious effort of that kind was undertaken in a so-called International Comparison Project (ICP). Unfortunately, the complex calculations were undertaken for only two years, 1975 and 1980, and only for a limited group of countries. But the data were sufficient to provide a basis for estimating the per capita GNP of all countries in 1980.

Table 1.1 compares the conventional GNP figures with the figures that are generated from the rates that were inferred from purchasing power comparisons. As the table indicates, the biggest adjustments are found in the incomes of the poorest countries, including notably Pakistan, India, and Sri Lanka. For countries in this category, per capita income figures are more than tripled.[11]

[9]One of the most extensive treatments of the problem is contained in Irving Kravis and others, *World Product and Income: International Comparisons of Real Gross Product* (Baltimore: Johns Hopkins University Press, 1982).

[10]For some remarkable work on the degree of similarity in prices between pairs of countries, see Kravis and others, *World Product and Income*, especially pp. 106–107. Although strong similarities exist across many countries, marked dissimilarities are reported when comparing the price structures of, say, Hungary with Mexico or Syria with Thailand.

[11]Kravis and others, *World Product and Income*, p. 10.

TABLE 1.1

Two Measures of GNP per Capita, 1980, U.S. Dollars

	Using Dollar Exchange Rate	Using Purchasing Power Relationships
ALL DEVELOPING COUNTRIES	850	1,790
Oil importers	$ 790	$1,700
Low-income	220	730
Middle-income	1,710	2,690
Oil exporters	1,060	2,080
INDUSTRIAL COUNTRIES	10,660	8,960

SOURCE: *World Development Report 1981,* published for the World Bank by Oxford University Press, New York, 1981, p. 17.

Having raised so many questions about the reliability of national GNP data—and, by inference, of national income data as well—it may seem almost redundant to raise a series of questions of another sort. From the viewpoint of the international community, the object of such measures is presumably to record the level of human needs in the various countries, largely in order to determine where special help should be targeted to those countries by the international community. A number of analysts have made the point, however, that although the per capita income of a country says something about the size of its needs, the distribution of that income within the country is a major factor determining the extent of those needs.[12] Others have pointed out still other limitations in the GNP data as a measure of human needs, such as the fact that such data are a poor reflection of the physical quality of life in the countries they purport to represent.[13]

In sum, the principal yardstick by which the economic condition of developing countries is commonly gauged is distorted by numerous factors. Its capacity for measuring what it purports to measure, namely, the relative poverty of nations, is quite limited. Yet it continues to function as the principal calibrator of need in international circles.

The Interplay Between Statistics and Politics

Obviously, the authority of the figures on per capita output has managed with remarkable success to survive the criticisms of the academics. It is true that data generated by the ICP, addressing one

[12]The subject is extensively developed in Hollis Chenery, *Structural Change and Development Policy* (New York: Oxford University Press, 1979), pp. 456–495.

[13]See, for instance, Morris D. Morris, *Measuring the Condition of the World's Poor* (New York: Pergamon Press, 1979), pp. 52–56.

significant source of error, have managed to insinuate themselves into some of the publications of the World Bank. But the support of the international community for a continuation and extension of the ICP's work is less than enthusiastic. Far better, from the viewpoint of the poor governments concerned, to rely on data that the governments themselves have produced in the first instance, notwithstanding the distortions and errors that they may contain.

That widespread reaction of governments raises the question whether governments manipulate the data they collect in order to achieve some desired objective, such as increasing their financial support from other governments and international institutions or resisting pressures for graduation. How much manipulation actually goes on is not easy to determine. Some governments have shown no hestitation about suppressing various statistical series that they had previously published, whenever they thought that continued publication might be harmful to their interests. Official figures that measure foreign indebtedness, for instance, have a tendency to disappear from public sources whenever governments run into balance-of-payment difficulties. Governments have also been suspected of tinkering with their price indexes when these were recording especially rapid increases, by changing the weights or identities of commodities covered in the index. Governments also have been known to announce a set of official price ceilings on basic commodities in such circumstances, and thereafter to disregard the black market prices that developed in those commodities. There have even been cases in which poor governments have been thought to understate their agricultural output, in order to qualify for increased grain shipments at concessional terms.

If governments have manipulated their data substantially, however, it is not at all clear what the manipulation has achieved. It is almost impossible to say, for example, whether the distortions that governments introduce have tended to increase the errors already embodied in the data or whether the two sets of errors have worked in opposite directions. When unintended errors understate the real rate of growth, as sometimes appears to be the case, a government that distorts the figures upward may be the inadvertent agent for a more accurate estimate. Besides, when considering how they would like to see their performance recorded, governments in developing countries are often torn between competing objectives. In many cases, they would like to appear efficient and successful to their own constituencies while appearing poor and needy to international agencies; accordingly, their efforts to influence the data may prove inconsistent in direction over the course of time.

Another reason for being uncertain regarding the effects of official manipulations is the complexity of the statistical consequences that such manipulations can produce. At one point, political leaders may feel that they would be helped if the official price indexes did not register quite so large a rise. If the price index is adjusted, however, it is likely to produce unintended consequences for GNP estimates, consequences that could be hostile at times to the subsequent goals of the policymakers. By applying the official ceiling prices to estimates of physical output of agricultural products, for instance, policymakers could inadvertently be understating the real value of such output.

The example just presented is intended to do no more than illustrate the complexity of the consequences of data manipulation, not to contend for the special importance of the particular case that has been cited. Indeed, the story could just as well have had a different ending. After officials had fixed the price index to establish a record of more stable prices, they could as readily have discovered that their alteration of the price index was giving an unintended fillip to the real growth rates of GNP in the succeeding year. That result could come about because estimates of real growth in GNP from one period to the next usually require a price deflator, an index that will remove the influence of price changes upon money measures of the goods and services produced in the country. But if the price index has been artificially restrained, the deflated measure of real growth will be overstated. That could be a boon or a loss, depending on what the officials feel they need at the particular moment in the evolution of their political strategies; in either case, the result could be unanticipated and unintended.

All told, the policymakers of developing countries cannot fail to link GNP estimates with the political process. But the linkages are sufficiently complex that the policymakers' control over the estimates may prove to be fairly weak. Indeed, it is almost as plausible to think of the important causal flows as running in the other direction: The technicians, operating by the book to the extent that circumstances permit, do their objective best to measure GNP; their objective best produces the illusion of reality in the form of a number; even if the number is subject to wide margins of error that are well known to the international community, its existence becomes a political fact of some importance; and its importance is a fact that politicians must acknowledge and to which they must adapt.

Is American Productivity Declining?
The Issues

The political process has also become entangled in the cross-national comparisons that are made to substantiate arguments about relative decline of the U.S. economy. Critics contend that the productivity of U.S. labor has fallen since the banner 1960s, in relation to both past American performance and the recent performance of the country's principal competitors.

Table 1.2 presents a typical set of data purporting to illustrate the trend. To produce these figures, the GNP values of each country have been deflated to remove the effects of price changes, and thus to generate a measure of the "real" output of each country in each indicated year. The output so adjusted is divided by the number of workers, to produce a measure of output per worker, shown in index form to permit easy comparison of the trends in different countries. In one variant or another, data of this sort have been widely circulated both in the United States and abroad.

The dissemination of such data greatly stimulated ongoing discussion over the purported eclipse of the U.S. economy. The disputes have been mainly over causes and remedies, not over whether relative slippage has occurred. Supply-siders, for instance, have concentrated on the hypothesis that the decline stemmed from the inability of enterprises to earn an adequate profit, a situation that they generally attributed to the interference of government and labor. Advocates of a more aggressive national industrial policy hypothesized that the decline resulted from the U.S. government's unwillingness to address the special problems of specific industries, such as the steel industry's hesitations in phasing out obsolete capital facilities and the aircraft industry's difficulties in financing large-scale research undertakings.

To be sure, there have also been some queries, demurrers, and dissents over the interpretation of the facts, as well as some basic questions about the reliability of the underlying data.[14] But these queries have come mainly from scholarly sources. For the most part, political adversaries have accepted the general view that, over the course of time, the growth of U.S. labor productivity has been disappointing by historical standards and compared to competing countries. Yet the quantitative basis for that conclusion is remarkably vulnerable.

[14]George Terborgh, "A Quizzical Look at Productivity Statistics," *Capital Goods Review*, Machinery and Allied Products Institute, no. 110, August 1979; Michael R. Darby, "The U.S. Productivity Slowdown: A Case of Statistical Myopia," National Bureau of Economic Research, Working Paper no. 1018, 1982; *Measurement and Interpretation of Productivity*, prepared under the chairmanship of Albert Rees by a National Research Council panel (Washington, D.C.: National Academy of Sciences, 1979); E. F. Denison, *Accounting for Slower Growth: The United States in the 1970s* (Washington, D.C.: Brookings Institution, 1979), especially pp. 122–144; Frank R. Lichtenberg and Zvi Griliches, "Errors of Measurement in Output Deflators," Discussion Paper no. 1267, September 1986, Harvard Institute of Economic Research, Harvard University; and Clint Bourdon, "Is Construction Productivity Declining?," Joint Center for Urban Studies Working Paper no. 68, Cambridge, Mass., April 1981.

TABLE 1.2

Changes in Output per Head in Five Countries, 1972 = 100

	1972–1975	1983
United States	100.4	102.5
Japan	104.9	135.2
Germany	105.2	128.9
France	104.7	128.6
United Kingdom	103.0	120.4

SOURCE: Adapted from *Economic Outlook*, publication of the OECD, Paris, no. 32, December 1982, p. 45.

Measurement Problems Again

The concept of productivity is a tricky one, as academics have repeatedly observed. Output is a function of various factors acting in combination, including capital, knowledge, labor, and public infrastructure. Measuring all variations in output on a per capita basis can prove grossly misleading.

That critical point is occasionally acknowledged by one party or another in political discussions. What is much less often recognized, however, is that the available measure of national output may contain large margins of error. The calculation of annual estimates of output per worker or per unit of input entails all the difficulties that are associated with estimates of GNP. Reducing such estimates to a series that describes productivity in "real" terms can involve all the issues of pricing and exchange rates that were encountered earlier in our discussion of measures for the identification of poor countries.

Unlike the poor countries, however, the United States and its principal competitors are relatively rich. They have reasonably open markets for their products and services and reasonably unimpeded markets for the exchange of their respective currencies. Are the prices these products generate still so distorted as to represent an unreliable and inconsistent measure of value? A number of different studies suggest that the problems of measurement remain quite large—indeed, so large, according to some analysts, as to raise in question whether the data can support any statement about relative productivity trends in the United States when compared with other advanced industrialized countries.

Recall that when measuring the output of poor countries, the ICP analysis attributed one major source of error to the choice of the exchange rate. The ICP analysis comes to a similar conclusion with respect to comparisons of output among the richer countries. According to that analysis, the exchange rates that prevailed between the currencies of the advanced developed countries in 1975 and 1980 differed significantly from their respective purchasing power parities, enough to require considerable changes in the various estimates of GNP. The effect of that adjustment in 1980 was to reduce the per capita GNP of the industrialized countries relative to the United States by 16 percent. Moreover, the ICP data offer an indication—albeit an indication subject to some major statistical weaknesses—of what the trend in GNP would have been from 1970 to 1975 if exchange rates based on purchasing power rather than the conventional exchange rates had been used. According to those data, the principal countries of Europe and Japan continue to show gains in gross domestic product per capita when compared with the United States; but the gains are considerably less than those calculated on the basis of market exchange rates.[15]

The problem of developing the right price deflators to measure productivity trends in the advanced industrialized countries during the 1970s is exacerbated by the rapid changes that were taking place in those countries in products and processes. The profound effects of changes in process on the measurement of productivity are illustrated by the construction industry, a sector that has been identified as one of the principal contributors to the decline of U.S. productivity in the latter half of the 1970s. One interesting study attributes the statistical trend to an obvious bias in the calculation of the construction industry's "real" output.[16]

Once again, the bias is said to arise in the price index that is used to deflate the annual figures representing the value of construction in the United States. In this case, the price index was constructed by tracing the changes in the prices of inputs, such as union labor, nonunion labor, machinery, power, and materials; but the relative weight of each of the inputs was established by their importance in 1975. According to the study, the bias arose from the fact that after 1975, some substantial changes occurred in the inputs of the construction industry: There was a rapid movement toward mechanization and a shift from union to nonunion labor. After adjusting for these changes, according to the analysis, the productivity declines disappear.

Changes in product prove as difficult to handle as changes in process. It is a daunting challenge to measure the trend in the price of automobiles in a period when the quality of automobiles is undergoing a transformation; yet such pricing will affect the measure of automobile output, which in turn will determine the productivity of the industry's

---

[15]Kravis et al., *World Product and Income*, pp. 12–13.

[16]Clint Bourdon, "Is Construction Productivity Declining?," Joint Center for Urban Studies, Working Paper no. 68, Cambridge, Mass., April 1981.

labor force. That problem is compounded when the changes in output represent a shift from products to services, especially if the services are of a kind that is delivered without charge by the public sector. When an auto worker turns traffic policeman, his work effort may not change, but the statistical measure used to reflect his output will change dramatically. As long as he is an automobile worker, his productivity will be measured by the estimated value of his output; when he turns policeman, however, his productivity will be measured by the cost of the inputs, including notably his wages. The very considerable shifts in the patterns of final demand in the United States during the 1970s offer grounds for speculation whether factors such as these had some effect on output measures; and if so, to what extent the effect was paralleled by similar tendencies abroad.

In addition to the problems of finding an appropriate way to measure real output from one year to the next, the analyst also encounters the ubiquitous problem of deciding what is an input and what is an output in the advanced industrialized countries. Expenditures to prevent the degradation of the environment, for instance, are counted as an input, a cost of production of the goods and services to which they relate; the effects that those expenditures have on the environment are not included as output. If all countries were equally affected by changes in the levels of those expenditures, that factor might not weaken the validity of comparisons; but it is unlikely that the expenditures were so distributed.

There are numerous other problems that threaten the validity of comparisons of productivity between countries. One in particular deserves mention because it almost surely had an effect in the United States that differed from its effect on other countries. In the United States from 1965 to 1978, an influx into the labor force of young people, immigrants, members of minority groups, and women substantially altered the U.S. work force. One study concludes that these alterations alone can entirely "explain" an apparent lowering of U.S. labor's productivity for the period after 1965 as compared with earlier periods.[17]

In offering this inventory of statistical booby traps, I do not mean to suggest that comparative studies of national productivity are incapable of shedding any light on the subject. For instance, anyone who still harbored doubts that Japan's total productivity increased faster than that of the United States in the years from 1960 to 1979 would find his doubts reduced as the result of several painstaking studies of the question.[18]

[17]Michael Darby, "The U.S. Productivity Slowdown," National Bureau of Economic Research, Working Paper no. 1018, November 1982, pp. 3–10.

[18]See, for instance, Dale W. Jorgenson, Masahiro Kuroda, and Mieko Nishimizu, "Japan-U.S. Industry-Level Productivity Comparisons, 1960–1979," Working Paper, Harvard Institute of Economic Research, Cambridge, Mass., 1983.

But even studies of such high caliber, although undertaken with a thorough understanding of the issues reviewed here, fail to free themselves of some of the fundamental weaknesses of the data they employ. For cases less overwhelmingly obvious than those of Japan, the observer would be entitled to cling to the Scotch verdict, "not proved."

Politics and Statistics

In this case, as in the development of criteria for identifying poor countries, the weaknesses of the underlying data have played a very limited role in the debate. Technicians in national governments and international agencies have ground out the numbers that served as grist for the political mill, impervious to the uses to which the data would be put. Whatever misgivings the technicians may have had regarding the validity of the numbers were never loudly voiced; their task was largely confined to producing data pursuant to a common format that appeared to prepare the ground for comparisons. Politicians and policymakers picked up the data, using them—wherever they seemed useful—for a variety of ends. In some cases, the various ends to which the data were put were flatly in conflict, as when proponents for unfettered private enterprise and proponents for an active industrial policy both invoked the alleged decline in productivity in support of their recommendations.

In at least one major respect, this case seems to suggest a pattern similar to that suggested in the case of the poor countries. In both cases, the technicians produced according to their requirements; and their needs for continuity, consistency, and comparability in the data limited the extent to which they were prepared to be responsive to criticisms of the data. The politicians used the data if they could fit the material to their arguments, and disregarded the data if they could not. In any event, there was little impetus from political quarters to improve the usefulness of the data for analytical purposes. All told, therefore, the data on productivity were making an uncertain contribution to the formulation of better public policy.

Comparing U.S. and U.S.S.R. Military Expenditures

In the debate over U.S. policies toward the Soviet Union, protagonists in the United States have repeatedly raised the question of how much each country spends on military programs. The interest of U.S. policymakers and military strategists in the size and nature of Soviet military expenditures is easy enough to understand; such expenditures may offer some clues to the nature of Soviet military intentions and to the level of their capabilities. Much less clear is why the expenditures of the U.S.S.R. can appropriately be compared in amount with those of the United States; and more obscure still is why those expenditures should be compared as a proportion of the GNP of their respective economies.[19]

Those in the United States who seek to compare the absolute level of military expenditures in the two countries usually are trying to make the point that the U.S. military effort is inadequate to meet the Soviet threat. However, using relative military expenditures to bolster that view is vulnerable on a number of well-known counts. To begin with, expenditures represent inputs, not outputs; at best, therefore, they represent a measure of the country's effort, not a measure of its military capabilities. Moreover, the strategic position of the United States is wholly different from that of the U.S.S.R., suggesting totally different needs for arms and manpower. The armed forces of the U.S.S.R. are pointed at Chinese, Afghans, Poles, Europeans, and perhaps even Uzbeks and Georgians, not at Americans alone. If Soviet expenditures should be compared, the comparison should be with Europe, China, and the United States, not with the United States alone.

The argument for comparing the military expenditures of each country as a proportion of their respective GNPs is even weaker, approaching blatant absurdity. Equality in those ratios says practically nothing about either the relative effort or the relative capabilities of the adversaries. Yet U.S. debaters, especially those who are on the side of higher military expenditures, have repeatedly invoked such ratios in the debate. The conventional view of this group is that the U.S.S.R. spends between 10 and 15 percent of its GNP on military expenditures, as compared with 7 or 8 percent for the United States.[20]

It may seem redundant to observe that even if such comparisons were justified in principle, the figures available for making the comparisons are subject to the grossest kind of error. Suppose for the moment that the expenditures of the two countries were being compared in order to measure their relative efforts rather than their capabilities. In that case, one might be justified in asking how much the Soviet Union had spent on its military establishment, measured in terms of its

---

[19]A careful exploration of the conceptual and statistical problems of comparing military expenditures—in this instance, without introducing the special problems posed by a command economy such as the U.S.S.R.—appears in *Measuring Price Changes of Military Expenditures*, a study prepared by the Bureau of Economic Analysis, U.S. Department of Commerce, for the U.S. Arms Control and Disarmament Agency, G.P.O., Washington, D.C., June 1975. The study concludes that all the price indicators then existing in the United States and elsewhere were "inadequate and possibly misleading" (p. 267).

[20]*World Military Expenditures and Arms Transfers 1969–1978*, U.S. Arms Control and Disarmament Agency, Publication 108, December 1980, pp. 66, 71.

home resources. And if the ruble prices and wages that were prevailing in the Soviet Union conveyed a solid hint of the relative value of different human and physical resources to that economy, one might be justified in adding up the ruble value of the various items in the Soviet military budget.

U.S. scholars are divided on the question how useful ruble prices are as a guide to value in the U.S.S.R. That they are substantially imperfect measures goes without saying; the price-setting practices of the U.S.S.R. create shortages, rationing, bartering, and black markets on a vast scale, a sure sign of the limitation of official prices as a measure of internal value. Besides, if there is any bargaining within the Soviet Union between the producing entity and the acquiring entity over the prices of military goods, it is bargaining in a bilateral monopoly, a situation that produces notoriously unpredictable results. Finally, the U.S. intelligence sources that claim to know something about ruble prices in the U.S.S.R. can hardly be expected to know very much; even in an open society like the United States, it usually takes a full-scale congressional study to pry out of procurement agencies the approximate costs of a substantial piece of military hardware.

If Soviet military expenditures do not serve very well as a measure of effort, can they be used to develop some rough measure of the country's fighting resources as compared with those of the United States? For that purpose, statisticians might make a case that comparability could be achieved by applying U.S. prices to Soviet hardware and applying U.S. military wages to Soviet manpower; indeed, that is just what the analysts of the Central Intelligence Agency regularly do, concluding that the "dollar cost of Soviet defense activities exceeded U.S. outlays by almost 30 percent" in the decade of the 1970s.[21]

The use of U.S. prices to measure the Soviet Union's acquisitions of fighting resources is no less vulnerable than the use of Soviet prices to measure its military effort. The validity of using U.S. prices rests on two wobbly assumptions: that any dollar which the United States spends for military men and machines buys more or less the same amount of fighting resources, whether spent on men or on machines, on aircraft or on tracked vehicles; and that the utility of any item bought by the military establishment in the United States bears some predictable relationship to the utility of an item with a similar label acquired by the armed forces of the other country. These, of course, are altogether improbable assumptions; but the assumptions are implicit in the many comparisons of military expenditures that are made with the use of U.S. dollar prices.

---

[21]Central Intelligence Agency, *Soviet and U.S. Defense Activities, 1970–79: A Dollar Cost Comparison* (Washington, D.C.: National Foreign Assessment Center, 1980), p. 3.

Some analysts have proposed that, in comparing the records of the two countries, the distortions from pricing errors can be reduced by combining the two kinds of estimates, namely, the estimates based on ruble prices and the estimates based on dollar prices.[22] The proposal, however, seems of very limited value. When the figures of the two countries are used to measure relative effort, the introduction of the prices of another country may actually reduce the reliability of the data rather than increase it; the prices of a foreign country may provide a poorer measure of opportunity cost than the prices of the home country. And when the figures of the two countries are used to measure relative fighting capability, the effect of using the prices of a foreign country is equally uncertain; pricing the services of a Soviet soldier by the pay scale of the U.S. army, for instance, may create an impression of relative fighting capability that is as misleading as an estimate that begins with expenditures denominated in home currencies.

Academics have made assiduous efforts to overcome the various statistical difficulties entailed in these comparisons, hoping to develop a defensible set of standards.[23] In a few cases, their efforts have been helped by analyses from U.S. agencies operating at arm's length from the policymaking centers.[24] None of these analysts supported the CIA view that the U.S.S.R. was outspending the United States by 15 to 40 percent. In fact, some scholars concluded that the United States may have been outspending the U.S.S.R.[25]

Nevertheless, the CIA analysis seemed to carry the day. A series of public opinion polls conducted between 1976 and 1983 by various polling organizations regularly recorded the fact that more Americans believe the U.S.S.R. military system is stronger than that of the United States than hold the contrary opinion.[26] To be sure, the dominant view has been much stronger in some periods than in others; the Reagan administration's energetic efforts to expand U.S. military programs, for instance, seem to have reduced the number of Americans who believe that Soviet military capabilities are superior. But the demonstration by

[22]See, for instance, F. D. Holzman, "Are the Soviets Really Outspending the U.S. on Defense?," *International Security* 4 (Spring 1980): 86–104; also his "Soviet Military Spending: Assessing the Numbers Game," *International Security* 6 (Spring 1982): 78–101.

[23]See, for instance, Abraham S. Becker, *Military Expenditure Limitation for Arms Control: Problems and Prospects* (Cambridge, Mass.: Ballinger Publishing, 1977), especially pp. 11–48; also SIPRI, *The Meaning and Measurement of Military Expenditure* (Stockholm: SIPRI, August 1973).

[24]The Department of Commerce study, *Measuring Price Changes of Military Expenditures*, is an outstanding example.

[25]One of the more extensive critiques of U.S.–U.S.S.R. comparisons is found in the Holzman article, "Are the Soviets Really Outspending the U.S. on Defense?"

[26]William Schneider, "Military Spending: The Public Seems to Say, 'We've Gone Far Enough,' " *National Journal*, April 23, 1983, no. 17, p. 866.

academics that the evidence on this score will not support the conclusion cannot have had much impact.

Envoi

It has only been a few decades since the first solid statistics served
as a basis for comparing the functioning of different national
economies. Learning the strengths and the limitations of such comparisons is a process that has only begun. It would be unreasonable to
expect that such comparisons could have contributed much to the level
of political debate and policymaking either within the countries compared or in international conclaves.

The preliminary indications suggested by the three cases in this
chapter offer no great hope that these comparisons will soon raise the
level of the analysis and the quality of the debate. One source of
difficulties is in the conceptual and statistical problems that stand in
the way of making useful cross-national comparisons. These problems
still seem formidable, leaving numerous opportunities for inadvertent
error or for advertent distortion.

Yet the conceptual difficulties and statistical problems may prove
less important roadblocks to the constructive use of such data than the
cultures of the three groups that I identified earlier. Politicians and policymakers are sometimes engaged in an earnest search for the facts,
eager to find a basis for creating more effective policy. But more often,
their positions are predetermined by their institutions and their interests; and when that is the case, they use the data as adversaries
would, calling on them to support a position and disregarding them
when they are unhelpful for that purpose.

Although academics commonly criticize the way in which politicians and policymakers use the available data, they appear to have little
immediate influence on the process. Part of the reason may be a division of interest among academics themselves. Some are interested in
the data for their own sake, without being greatly concerned about how
they affect policy. Some are interested in policy without having the interest or the expertise for dealing in detail with the quality of the data
or the nature of its manipulation. Happily, there are occasionally gifted
academics who can straddle both fields; but these are rare. The
discourse of the academics, therefore, tends to be slow to percolate into
the political arena.

One might perhaps have hoped that the technicians within national
and international public agencies might create a bridge between the political and the academic worlds. Here again, the hope is occasionally

realized. But technicians, for the most part, serve political masters. Moreover, their principal criteria are commonly those of continuity and uniformity, criteria that are often at war with the goal of providing data appropriate to the varying conditions of different countries and to changes in the needs of policymakers over time.

As a result, the vastly expanded supply of comparative national statistics over the past few decades has contributed only a little thus far to the improvement of public policymaking. To be sure, technical debates among economists over the comparative performance of national economies have been elevated somewhat in subtlety and complexity. But the debates over policy continue to rely largely on vulnerable data and to use those data mainly as weapons to beat down opposing views. We seem launched on a journey of a thousand miles, on which we have taken only the first few steps.

2

THE POLITICS OF
INCOME MEASUREMENT

CHRISTOPHER JENCKS

E VERY March since 1948 the Census Bureau's *Current Population Survey* (CPS) has included a supplement asking how much income every adult in every sample household received during the previous calendar year. Every year the bureau also publishes a summary of its findings, consisting of a short introduction and a large number of tables and currently titled "Money Income of Households, Families, and Persons in the United States."[1] The introduction to this report always begins by comparing the change in median family income over the previous year to the change in the Consumer Price Index (CPI). Following conventional practice, the bureau characterizes this difference as the change in "real" income during the relevant year. While the bureau wisely offers no interpretation of this change, the mass media faithfully report it as an indication of how much the average American family's

NOTE: An earlier version of this chapter was presented at an SSRC conference on the Political Economy of National Statistics held in Washington, D.C., on October 14–15, 1983. I am indebted to Fay Cook, Reynolds Farley, Daniel Garnick, Jack Goldstone, Frank Levy, Janet Norwood, Arthur Stinchcombe, James Wetzel, Chris Winship, and the editors for helpful suggestions. Needless to say, they are in no way responsible either for my opinions or for any errors in the data presented here.

[1] U.S. Bureau of the Census, *Current Population Reports*, Series P-60 ("Consumer Income"). These reports are issued twice annually: first in a short "Advance Report" and then in a full report. I will focus on the full report on money income in 1980, which I will refer to for brevity as "Money Income: 1980."

material standard of living rose or fell during the previous year, and the bureau makes no effort to discourage this interpretation.

The Census Bureau also emphasizes real family income in publications describing long-term changes in income. The bureau's *Statistical Abstract of the United States: 1982–83*,[2] for example, includes a 36-page section on "Income, Expenditures, and Wealth." The section begins with a chart showing changes over time in the percentage of families with "constant dollar" incomes above $5,000, $10,000, $15,000, and $25,000. Again, the bureau offers no interpretation of these figures, but both journalists and social scientists habitually cite changes in such percentages as an indication of how material well-being has changed since World War II. If they do not measure change in material well-being, they hardly deserve the emphasis that the bureau gives them.

Taken at face value, the bureau's "real family income" (RFI) series tells a familiar story. RFI rose by an average of 3.25 percent per year during the 1950s and 2.96 percent per year during the 1960s, but it rose only 0.04 percent per year during the 1970s. The RFI series thus seems to show that the economic boom which began after World War II petered out around 1970, and that since 1970 American families have had to run hard just to stand still.

Such statistics have had obvious political consequences. They have been used to explain the public's alleged disenchantment with the welfare state and with policies aimed at economic redistribution. They have also been used to argue for new political institutions, adapted to the needs of a "zero sum" rather than a "permanent growth" society. At a more mundane level they were used to demonstrate that those who held political and economic power during the 1970s must have been inept, and that a "new approach" or "new leadership" was necessary if we were to do better.

Unfortunately, the Census Bureau's RFI series does not provide a very accurate picture of trends in material well-being. As we shall see, the average American family's material standard of living rose significantly during the 1970s. Indeed, most measures suggest that the standard of living rose as much during the 1970s as during the 1950s, and a few show as large a rise during the 1970s as during the 1960s. This does not mean that the American economy as a whole was healthy during the 1970s. It was not. But despite high inflation, high unemployment, and low productivity growth, the average American family's material standard of living rose substantially during the 1970s. This was partly because prices did not rise as fast as official indicators suggest

[2]Washington, D.C., U.S. Government Printing Office, 1983, referred to hereafter simply as *Statistical Abstract, 1982–83*.

they did, partly because more women were working, partly because people had fewer children to support, and partly because personal taxes rose less rapidly during the 1970s than during the 1960s or 1950s.

The first two sections of this chapter document these claims. Not all the difficulties discussed in these two sections bias the RFI series in the same way. Some of the defects of the RFI series make the 1970s look better than they should relative to earlier decades, not worse. In other cases it is hard to say how a problem alters the story the RFI series tells. On balance, though, I will argue that the defects of the RFI series make the 1970s look considerably worse than they were.

Section 3 turns to the problem of why census publications continue to emphasize trends in RFI. Many of the problems discussed in Sections 1 and 2 are well known to the Census Bureau's professional staff. Nonetheless, bureaucratic inertia and the absence of outside criticism have interacted both to perpetuate the RFI series and to discourage the development of supplementary series. The absence of outside criticism in turn reflects the fact that conservatives, liberals, and radicals have all had political reasons for accepting the gloomy implications of the RFI series at face value.

Alternative Measures of Economic Well-Being

The Census Bureau faces both conceptual and practical problems when it tries to measure trends in real family income. At a conceptual level, it must decide what constitutes "income," what constitutes a "family," how to convert incomes reported in different years to "constant" dollars, and how to summarize trends from one year to the next. At a practical level, the bureau must devise procedures for eliciting the information it wants from respondents and for estimating the likely direction and magnitude of errors in the resulting data.

This section describes how the Census Bureau deals with each of these problems. I will begin by discussing the bureau's emphasis on the median to measure trends, then turn to its use of the CPI to measure inflation. After that I will examine the problem of defining a "family," and finally the problem of defining "income." When the bureau's solution to a problem seems questionable, I will try to present alternative solutions, so the reader can assess the direction and magnitude of the difference between the bureau's RFI series and alternative series. The discussion will focus on how the bureau's conceptual and practical decisions have affected the apparent rate of change in material well-being during the 1970s relative to the rate of change during the 1950s and 1960s.

As will become apparent, choosing between alternative measures of economic well-being often requires either empirical data that do not exist, controversial normative judgments that government agencies are rightly reluctant to make, or both. One would expect a cautious scholar or bureaucracy to respond to this situation by publishing several different statistical series, each based on different assumptions, and then spelling out the assumptions under which each series yields an accurate estimate of whatever it is supposed to measure. The Census Bureau has never adopted this approach. It emphasizes only one measure of income trends over time, and its publications say next to nothing about the circumstances under which this series provides an accurate picture of changes in material well-being. The bureau's reasons for not following conventional academic standards in this matter clearly deserve attention, but I will postpone discussing them until the final section.

Medians Versus Means

The Census Bureau's annual "Money Income" reports emphasize changes in median family income rather than mean family income. Since the mean is more statistically pliable and is widely accepted as the preferred measure of central tendency for interval scales, the bureau's preference for the median requires some explanation. The annual "Money Income" reports offer none.

So far as I have been able to discover, the bureau originally emphasized medians rather than means because medians were easy to compute from grouped data. But the bureau evidently began computing means in 1958, and it has presented both means and medians in most tables since 1967. The bureau has also estimated population means for the years from 1947 through 1958 using grouped data. For 1958, its estimate of the mean based on grouped data is only 1.4 percent higher than its estimate based on ungrouped data, so the bureau's trend estimates for mean family income are probably almost as reliable as its trend estimates for median family income.

The usual rationale for emphasizing the median rather than the mean when looking at interval scales is that the median is less sensitive to extreme values. But insensitivity to extreme values is not an obvious virtue when measuring trends in family income. If most people's incomes remain constant, for example, but the poor get poorer, the median will remain constant while the mean falls. It seems unlikely that many users would feel the median told a more important story than the mean in this situation.

Fortunately, while the choice between the mean and the median is of considerable practical importance when we compare groups such as men and women or blacks and whites, it is of little practical importance when measuring time trends during the postwar period. Rows 1 and 2 of Table 2.1 give the Census Bureau's estimates of both median and mean family income for 1950, 1960, 1970, and 1980 in current dollars. The last three columns of each row show the average annual increase in each measure during each decade. The median and the mean grew at about the same rate from 1960 to 1980. The difference looks greater in the 1950s, but this is probably because the bureau's procedure for estimating the mean from grouped data overestimates the true mean prior to 1958. As a result, Table 2.1 probably understates the annual increase in the mean during the 1950s by 0.1 or 0.2 percent. The fact that the

TABLE 2.1

Measures of Family Income and Inflation: 1950 to 1980

| | 1950 | 1960 | 1970 | 1980 | Average Annual Percent Change During the: | | |
					1950s	1960s	1970s
1. Median Family Income (current dollars)	3,319	5,620	9,867	21,023	5.4	5.7	7.8
2. Mean Family Income (current dollars)	3,815	6,227	11,106	23,974	5.0	5.9	8.0
3. Consumer Price Index (1980 = 100)	29.2	35.9	47.1	100	2.1	2.8	7.8
4. Personal Consumption Expenditures Deflator (1980 = 100)	31.8	40.1	51.6	100	2.3	2.6	6.8
5. Median Family Income (in 1980 CPI dollars)	11,366	15,655	20,949	21,023	3.3	3.0	.0
6. Median Family Income (in 1980 PCE dollars)	10,437	14,015	19,122	21,023	3.0	3.2	1.0
7. Median Income of Unrelated Individuals (in 1980 PCE dollars)	3,286	4,289	6,079	8,296	2.7	3.5	3.2

NOTE: In this and all subsequent tables, the "average annual percent change" in X between, say, 1970 and 1980 is defined as $(X_{80}/X_{70})^{1/10} - 1$.

SOURCES, *by line:*
1. *Money Income: 1980*, Table 16.
2. *Money Income: 1980*, Table 19.
3. *Money Income: 1980*, Table A-1, adjusted to make 1980 = 100.
4. *Economic Report of the President: 1983*, Table B-3, adjusted to make 1980 = 100.
5. *Money Income: 1980*, Table 17.
6. Line 1/Line 4.
7. *Money Income: 1980*, Table 16/Line 4.

mean and median have changed at about the same rate reflects the fact that the distribution of reported income was quite stable over this period.

In the remainder of this chapter I will mainly emphasize trends in mean income. This is not because I believe that mean income is necessarily a better measure of mean well-being than median income is, but because the mean is easier to manipulate statistically, and trends in the mean seem to track trends in the median quite closely. I will also refer to trends in both median and mean income as indicators of trends in the "standard of living." Readers who think of the "standard of living" as some kind of "social minimum" or "floor" below which no one should be allowed to fall, or expects to fall, may find this use of the term confusing, but I believe it is consistent with everyday language.

Converting Current to Constant Dollars

The Census Bureau has always used the Labor Department's Consumer Price Index (CPI) to convert "current" to "constant" dollars. This practice is mandated by the Office of Management and the Budget (OMB). The Bureau of Labor Statistics (BLS), which developed the CPI, did not design it to measure the cost of goods and services bought by the population as a whole. Initially, the CPI measured the cost of the goods and services bought by urban families of two or more whose heads were blue collar or clerical workers. In 1965 the BLS changed the weights it assigned to various goods and services, so as to take account of purchases by single individuals as well as families of two or more. In 1977 it again changed the weights, so as to take account of purchases by families whose heads were not employed and families whose heads held professional, managerial, or sales jobs. The BLS has never modified the CPI to take account of purchases by rural families. While I know of no evidence that these limitations in coverage significantly distort the CPI, one would expect them to encourage the OMB and the Census Bureau to consider a more comprehensive price measure whose meaning had remained the same over time. The various deflators for Personal Consumption Expenditures, developed by the Bureau of Economic Analysis for use in the National Income and Product Accounts, are obvious candidates.

The main argument against the CPI, though, is not the fact that it focuses on urban consumers but the fact that until January 1983 it treated the costs of home ownership in a very misleading way. First, the CPI assumed that all homeowners' mortgage payments were determined by the current value of their homes and by current interest rates.

Since both housing prices and interest rates rise and fall with the expected rate of inflation, the CPI made the cost of home ownership look much more volatile than it really was, and made it appear to rise more during the 1970s than it really did. Second, while the CPI counted mortgage interest as a "cost" of home ownership, it did not count either realized or unrealized capital gains from home ownership as a "benefit." During inflationary periods, when both interest costs and capital gains are high, this approach made the CPI overestimate the true cost of home ownership. Third, the CPI ignored the fact that interest payments are tax deductible. The overall result was that the CPI registered a substantial increase in the cost of home ownership during the 1970s. Had the CPI taken account of capital gains and the tax advantages of home ownership, it would almost certainly have shown a *decline* in the net cost of home ownership during the 1970s relative to earlier decades. Indeed, for many people the net cost of home ownership became negative during the 1970s, since their capital gains and tax deductions exceeded their out-of-pocket costs.

While it might in principle be possible to construct a measure of the costs of home ownership that took account of capital gains and losses, such a measure would not tell us much about changes in the amount of income a family needs to maintain a given standard of living. Home ownership serves two functions: it provides owners with a place to live and it provides them with a way of investing whatever savings they have accumulated. Like all investments, home ownership is somewhat speculative. It was very profitable during the 1970s, for example, but not during the early 1980s. No one really wants a price index to reflect speculative gains and losses from capital investment. A price index should measure the cost of *using* a house, not the average profit or loss owners realized from buying and selling houses in a given year. This suggests that the best way to measure changes in the current cost of housing is to look at changes in the *rental* cost of housing. That is what cost-of-living indices do in every other country, and it is what the CPI has done since January 1983.[3]

While the new CPI deals with the cost of home ownership in a sensible way, the published values of the CPI for years prior to 1983 have not been revised to incorporate this new approach. (Such a retrospective revision would be technically simple, since it merely involves reweighting components of the CPI whose value is already known.) In the absence of such a retrospective revision, published values of the CPI still exaggerate the amount of inflation during the 1970s. As long as the RFI

---

[3]On the problems of the CPI, see, e.g., Robert Gordon, "The Consumer Price Index: Measuring Inflation and Causing It," *The Public Interest* (Spring 1981):112–34.

series goes on using the CPI to convert current to "constant" dollars, its value as a historical record of income growth will be seriously compromised. To assess the magnitude of this bias it is instructive to compare trends in the old CPI with trends in the implicit price deflator that the Bureau of Economic Analysis (BEA) uses to convert "Personal Consumption Expenditures" (PCE) to "constant" dollars. The PCE deflator uses the same basic price data as the CPI, but it covers rural as well as urban purchases and it uses changes in rents to estimate changes in the "use value" of housing. It also uses a slightly different set of weights to aggregate price changes.[4]

Lines 3 and 4 of Table 2.1 show that the PCE deflator rose slightly more than the CPI during the 1950s, slightly less during the 1960s, and a lot less during the 1970s. These differences between the CPI and the PCE deflator have appreciable effects on the apparent trend in real family income. Measured in "CPI dollars," median income rose 3 percent per year in the 1950s and 1960s but was essentially constant during the 1970s (see line 5 of Table 2.1). Measured in "PCE dollars" the increase is still 3 percent per year during the 1950s and 1960s, but is 1 percent per year during the 1970s (see line 6). Substituting the PCE deflator for the CPI still leaves the 1970s looking worse than the 1960s or 1950s, but the difference is appreciably less than the Census Bureau's RFI series would lead unsuspecting readers to imagine.

[4]BEA now publishes three measures of change in consumer prices: the "implicit price deflator," the "fixed weight price index," and the "chain price index." Like the CPI, the "fixed-weight" price index is a Laspeyres index. It shows price changes for the market basket of goods and services that consumers bought in 1972. Because the composition of the market basket remains stable over time, this index can be used to compare prices for any two years, so long as the user bears in mind that the resulting price change is for the mix of goods bought in 1972, not for the mix of goods bought in either of the years under study. The "chain price index" is also a Laspeyres index, but it gives the change in price for each year's market basket over the course of the following year. It is ideal for comparing adjacent years, but because the composition of the market basket changes, it is hard to interpret over longer periods. The "implicit price deflator" is a Paasch index with a 1972 baseline. Its value in, say, 1980 gives the change in price between 1972 and 1980 of the market basket consumers bought in 1980. Because the market basket changes, the change in the implicit price deflator between years has no clearcut interpretation unless one of the years is 1972. (For a fuller discussion of these issues, see Jack Triplett, "Reconciling the CPI and the PCE Deflator," *Monthly Labor Review* (September 1981):3–15).

None of these three measures constitutes a "true" cost of living index (see Lawrence R. Klein and H. Rubin, "A Constant-Utility Index of the Cost of Living," *Review of Economic Studies* 15 (1947–48):84–87). Nor do I know of any evidence indicating which of these three indices most closely approximates a true cost of living index for the years 1950 to 1980. For present purposes, however, the issue is moot, since neither the fixed-weight nor the chain-price index is available before 1959. I therefore used the implicit price deflator for all three periods. During the 1960s, the implicit deflator typically rose 0.3 percent more per year than the fixed-weight index, and the chain-price index rose 0.1 percent more. During the 1970s, the pattern was reversed, with the implicit deflator rising 0.3 percent less in a typical year than the fixed-weight index and 0.2 percent less than the chain-price index.

Since 1981 the Census Bureau's annual reports on "Money Income" have alluded to the defects of the CPI, but not in such a way as to help the reader appreciate the character or magnitude of the problem. Thus, the bureau began its "Advance Report" on the March 1982 CPS (*Consumer Income*, Series P-60, #134) as follows:

> For the second year in a row, the income of American families failed to make headway against inflation according to results of the March 1982 Current Population Survey conducted by the Bureau of the Census. In 1981, the median family income was $22,390, an increase of 6.5 percent before adjusting for the change in consumer prices. After adjustment for a 10.4 percent increase in consumer prices between 1980 and 1981, however, median family income decreased by 3.5 percent.

An accompanying footnote qualifies the judgment in the text as follows:

> Changes in real income refer to comparisons after adjusting for inflation. The percentage change in prices between 1980 and 1981 was computed by dividing the annual average value of the Consumer Price Index (CPI) for 1981 by the annual average value of the CPI for 1980. Research has shown that, in recent years, the treatment of home prices and mortgage interest costs in the calculation of the CPI tended to overstate the increase in prices experienced by the average consumer.

The footnote tells the reader, in other words, that the text is wrong. It does not say *how* wrong, though, and it does not offer interested readers any guidance should they want to know what "really" happened to prices. In fact, the PCE deflator rose only 8.5 percent between 1980 and 1981. This suggests that "real" family income fell only 1.8 percent between 1980 and 1981, not 3.5 percent.

Even the PCE deflator may well exaggerate the impact of inflation on living standards, since many of the goods and services available in 1980 did not exist in 1970. If one prices these goods by asking what they "would have been worth if they had been available," the answer is sometimes that they would have been worth staggering sums. In 1978, for example, my prematurely born son's life was saved by a drug that did not exist in 1970. In order to estimate the change in my "real" level of consumption due to this invention, one must calculate the price of the consumer goods that would have been needed to compensate me for the absence of the drug in 1970. Since *no* bundle of goods would have done this, my standard of living was "infinitely" higher in 1978 than it would have been in 1970 had my son been born then. Conventional price indices cannot deal with technical innovation of this kind. Neither, as we shall see, can they deal with increases in consumer information that lead to changes in consumer preferences. The Census Bureau can hardly be expected to solve this problem, but it should perhaps mention it. I return to it in Section 2.

Defining the Family

The Census Bureau defines a "family" as any group of individuals related by blood, marriage, or adoption who live together at the time of the March survey. Individuals who live alone or with nonrelatives are covered by a separate series on "unrelated individuals," to which the bureau devotes relatively little attention. "Family income" is the sum of current family members' incomes during the previous calendar year, regardless of where they lived during that year.

This approach would pose no problem if family composition never changed. But births, children's growing up and leaving home, marriages, divorces, and deaths lead to continuous changes in family composition. As a result, the "family income" calculated by the bureau sometimes describes a family that did not actually exist during the relevant year. If a man abandons his wife and children in February, for example, the March survey will define the wife and children as a family, ask about each member's income for the previous year, and sum those incomes to determine the family's total income for the previous year. If neither the wife nor the children had any income during the previous year because they depended on the now absent husband, the bureau will record the family's income as zero. It will then obscure this anomaly by grouping this family with families whose incomes were negative (from business losses) or less than $1,000. The same thing will happen if two recent college graduates who had no income during the previous year get married.

The bureau's preparatory work for its new Survey of Income and Program Participation suggested that this sort of mismatching between incomes and those they support inflated the poverty count by about one-tenth.[5] It also lowers the bureau's estimate of mean (or median) family income by 2 to 4 percent. This happens for two reasons. First, the bureau underestimates total income because it misses income received by people who die before March of the following year. Because the incomes of the aged improved faster than the national average during the 1970s, ignoring those who die probably leads to slightly more

[5] See Martin David, "Measuring Income and Program Participation," in Martin David, ed., *Technical, Conceptual, and Administrative Lessons of the Income Survey Development Program (ISDP)* (New York: Social Science Research Council, 1983), p. 6.

downward bias during the 1970s than during the 1960s or 1950s. Second, since population growth and family break-ups keep pushing up the number of families, the number of family units at the time of the March survey is always larger than the average number of families during the previous year. This biases mean family income downward by about 0.9 percent during the 1950s and 1960s and 1.0 percent during the 1970s.

A more serious problem is that what constitutes a "family" has changed over time. More mothers are raising their children without male help. Elderly parents are less likely to live with their grown children, although this decline is partly offset by the fact that those parents who do live with their children stay alive longer. At the same time, high birthrates from 1945 to 1965 meant that more families had children over 16 living with them in the 1960s and 1970s. The net result was that while the number of adults per family fell in the 1950s, it hardly changed between 1960 and 1980.

The number of children per family has been changing, though. The birthrate rose after World War II, peaked in the late 1950s, declined during the 1960s, and remains low today. Line 9 of Table 2.2 shows that families have gotten smaller as a result.

Although these shifts in family composition may not look large, they have significant economic implications. During the 1970s, for example, mean family size fell by an average of 0.9 percent per year. As a result, families' mean real income *per person* rose 2.0 percent a year, even though mean income *per family* rose only 1.1 percent a year. The Census Bureau's "Money Income" reports make no explicit reference to these trends in family size when discussing the RFI series. The 1980 report does note that the percentage of the population living in families has been falling (compare lines 3 and 4 in Table 2.2), but it does not mention that unrelated individuals' incomes have also been rising faster than family incomes (compare lines 6 and 7 of Table 2.1). The incomes of unrelated individuals have risen largely because these individuals are increasingly likely to be young, well educated, and employed. It follows that adults who live in families are a less economically select group than they were, which is one reason their incomes have lagged.

Whether these changes in family composition imply changes in material well-being depends on whose perspective we adopt. Economists often assume for convenience that all individuals have equal needs and then measure trends in material well-being by estimating trends in income per person. The Census Bureau has long published a series that at first glance appears to do the same thing, namely, its series on "Persons 14 Years Old and Over, by Total Money Income." But this series reports means and medians only for individuals who had nonzero incomes in

TABLE 2.2

Demographic Changes in the Civilian Noninstitutional Population: 1950 to 1980

| | 1950 | 1960 | 1970 | 1980 | Average Annual Percent Change During the: | | |
					1950s	1960s	1970s
TOTALS (IN MILLIONS)							
1. Persons	149.1	176.3	199.7	223.1	1.7	1.3	1.1
2. Persons over 16	105.0	117.2	137.1	167.7	1.1	1.6	2.0
3. Unrelated Individuals	9.1	11.1	15.0	26.4	2.0	3.1	5.8
4. Persons over 16 in Families	95.9	106.1	122.1	141.3	1.0	1.4	1.5
5. Persons under 16 in Families	44.1	59.1	62.6	55.4	3.0	.6	−1.2
6. Families	39.3	45.1	51.6	59.9	1.4	1.4	1.5
INDIVIDUALS PER FAMILY							
7. Over 16	2.44	2.35	2.37	2.36	−.4	.1	−.0
8. Under 16	1.12	1.31	1.21	.92	1.6	−.8	−2.7
9. Total	3.56	3.66	3.58	3.28	.3	−.2	−.9

SOURCES, by line:
1. Total Persons (from *Economic Report of the President, 1983*, p. 195) less Armed Forces (ibid., p. 196) and inmates (*Statistical Abstract, 1983*, p. 53 and *Historical Statistics of the United States*, Series A-359). These figures do not agree with the CPS population shown in the "Money Income" report for the relevant year. The CPS figure is actually for March of the following year, and in some cases it does not appear to reflect the results of the decennial census for the relevant year.
2. *Economic Report of the President, 1983*, p. 196.
3. *Statistical Abstract, 1982–3, p. 43.* Unlike the figures shown in the "Money Income" report, these figures appear to take account of the results of the decennial census for the relevant year.
4. Line 2 − Line 3. Virtually all "unrelated individuals" appear to be at least 16.
5. Line 1 − Line 2. This calculation again assumes that all individuals under 16 live in families or institutions.
6. *Statistical Abstract, 1982–3*, p. 43. To maintain consistency with earlier years, the estimate for 1980 includes unrelated subfamilies. The estimate for 1980 in *Money Income, 1980* excludes subfamilies and is not corrected to take account of the 1980 Census results.
7. Line 4/Line 6.
8. Line 5/Line 6.
9. Line 7 + Line 8. These estimates do not agree exactly with *Statistical Abstract, 1982–3*, p. 43, for reasons I have not been able to identify, but discrepancies are all less than 0.02.

the relevant year. Because the percentage of persons with income has risen over time, this series seriously underestimates the growth in per capita income for all persons. Furthermore, since the bureau's "Money Income" reports have only recently started to show the total number of persons under 14 in the CPS universe, readers who want to estimate income per person must do a fair amount of homework (see the notes to Table 2.2).

The bureau took a useful step toward resolving this problem in 1982, introducing a new series on money income per person. The bureau has only computed this series back to 1967, but it is still instructive. Whereas the bureau's RFI series shows virtually no improvement during the 1970s, this new "real per capita income" (RPCI) series shows an average increase of 1.4 percent a year during the 1970s. Yet at least in 1982 the bureau made no reference to the new series in the text of its annual report.

Line 3 of Table 2.3 presents estimates of real per capita income for 1950, 1960, 1970, and 1980. My estimates differ from those in the bureau's RPCI series largely because I have used the PCE deflator to convert "current" to "constant" dollars, but there are also some differences in population estimates (see the notes for Table 2.2). My estimates indicate that mean income per person rose 2.3 percent during the 1950s, 3.3 percent during the 1960s, and 2.2 percent during the 1970s. Using this yardstick, therefore, the 1970s look about the same as the 1950s, but both are still worse than the 1960s.

TABLE 2.3

Effects of Alternative Adjustments for Family Composition on Estimated Incomes (In 1980 PCE Dollars), 1950–1980

	1950	1960	1970	1980	Average Annual Percent Change During the:		
					1950s	1960s	1970s
1. Total Money Income (in billions)	543	805	1,264	1,754	4.0	4.6	3.3
2. Mean Family Income	11,997	15,529	21,523	23,974	2.6	3.3	1.1
3. Mean Income per Person	3,645	4,564	6,329	7,862	2.3	3.3	2.2
4. Mean Income per "BLS Adult Equivalent"	4,043	5,139	7,069	8,573	2.4	3.2	1.9
5. Mean Income per "Unrelated Adult Equivalent"	4,705	5,908	8,134	9,893	2.3	3.2	2.0
6. Mean Income per "Subjective Adult Equivalent"	4,879	6,409	8,658	9,989	2.8	3.1	1.4
7. Mean Income per Adult	5,175	6,866	9,220	10,459	2.9	3.0	1.3

SOURCES, *by line:*
1. $T = N_M Y_M + N_F Y_F$, where Y_M and Y_F are mean money incomes for males and females with income, N_M and N_F are numbers of males and females with income, and all figures come from *Money Income, 1980*, Table 43. The 1980 values of N_M and N_F in this table have been inflated to reflect the results of the 1980 Census.
2. (Line 2 of my Table 2.1)/(Line 4 of my Table 2.1).
3. (Line 1)/(Line 1 of my Table 2.2).
4. (Line 1)/N_{AE}, where N_{AE} = (Line 2, my Table 2.2) + (2/3) (Line 5, my Table 2.2).
5. (Line 1)/N_{UAE}, where N_{UAE} = (Line 3, my Table 2.2) + (Line 6, my Table 2.2) (W_F), and W_F is an adjustment for family size, calculated as $W_F = 1 + (2/3)$ (Line 9, my Table 2.2 − 1).
6. (Line 1)/$N_{AE'}$, where $N_{AE'}$ = (Line 2, my Table 2.2) + (Line 5, my Table 2.2)/7.
7. (Line 1)/(Line 2, my Table 2.2).

The fact that income per person and income per family have grown at different rates underlines the importance of adjusting family income for changes in family size, but it does not tell us how to accomplish this task. Substituting income per person for income per family would suffice if a family's material needs rose in direct proportion to its size, but that is obviously not the case. Almost everyone would agree, for example, that a family of four is better off on $30,000 a year than a family of two on $15,000 a year, even though both have the same per capita income. At the same time, almost everybody would also agree that a family of four is worse off on $15,000 a year than a family of two with the same income. These examples suggest a general rule: if all else is equal, changes in income per person and income per family set upper and lower bounds on the "true" change in family income, adjusted for family size. If all else had been equal, for example, Table 2.3 would tell us that the material standard of living rose at least 1.1 percent and no more than 2.2 percent a year during the 1970s.

In order to narrow this range of uncertainty, the Census Bureau would need a "family equivalence scale" that specified exactly how much money families of different sizes need in order to enjoy the same level of material comfort. The most obvious candidate would be the official federal poverty line. In 1980, for example, the poverty threshold for a childless couple under 65 was $5,514, while the threshold for a couple with two children was $8,315. These thresholds implied that a low-income couple with two children needed 51 percent more income than a childless couple to enjoy the same material standard of living. If we assume that differences in size and composition have analogous effects on more affluent families, we can compare the material well-being of different families by dividing each family's income by its poverty threshold to obtain its "poverty ratio" and then comparing these ratios. Nongovernment researchers, notably those associated with the Institute for Social Research at the University of Michigan, have used the poverty ratio in this way for many years.[6] The Census Bureau has never done so, however. It reports the percentage of persons whose poverty ratio is less than 1.00 (that is, the percentage who are officially poor). In recent years it has also reported the percentage whose poverty ratio is less than 1.25. But it has never published a cumulative distribution of poverty ratios or data on trends in the mean or median of this ratio.

Trends in the mean and dispersion of the poverty ratio would tell us considerably more about trends in material well-being than existing data on income per family or per person. But the poverty ratio is not

___

[6]See, e.g., James Morgan et al., *Five Thousand American Families—Patterns of Economic Progress*, vols. 1 to 10 (Ann Arbor: Institute for Social Research, University of Michigan, 1974 to 1983).

ideal for this purpose, because the poverty thresholds for families of one or two persons are almost certainly too high relative to those for larger families. Table 2.4 expresses the poverty thresholds for families of various sizes as a percentage of the threshold for a married couple with two children. In 1980, for example, the threshold for a single individual was $4,284. Table 2.4 tells us that it rose $1,230 if the individual was married and another $1,114 if the couple had a child. If the couple had a second child, however, its poverty threshold rose $1,723, and if it had a third child the threshold rose another $1,477. The notion that the fourth and fifth household members cost more than the second and third is strongly counterintuitive, especially when the fourth and fifth household members are children while the second is an adult. If this result rested on empirical evidence, we might simply conclude that intuition is an unreliable guide in such matters. But it has no empirical basis. It is simply a mistake. To see how the mistake arose, a little history is necessary.

TABLE 2.4

Family Equivalence Scales from Five Sources

	Food Based Scales			Subjective Scales	
	Poverty Line	BLS	USDA Food Budget	Judgments about Others	Judgments about Self
FAMILY TYPE					
Unrelated Individual	51	36	33	NA	58
Couple	66	60	61	81	87
Couple Plus:					
One Child	79	80	82	91	91
Two Children	100	100	100	100	100
Three Children	118	118	116	107	108
Four Children	132	NA	137	1.14	NA

SOURCES, *by column:*
1. U.S. Bureau of the Census, "Characteristics of the Population Below the Poverty Level," *Current Population Reports,* Series P-60, No. 133, p. 3.
2. U.S. Bureau of Labor Statistics, "Revised Equivalence Scale: For Estimating Equivalent Incomes or Budget Costs by Family Type," BLS Bulletin No. 1570–2, Washington, D.C., U.S. Government Printing Office, 1968. Estimates for couples with children are weighted averages for all families of the relevant size, except those with a single parent.
3. U.S. Department of Agriculture, *Family Economics Review,* January 1984, p. 31. Estimates for children are based on average costs for all children aged 0 to 18.
4. Lee Rainwater, *What Money Buys* (New York: Basic Books, 1974), Table 5–4, col. 1.
5. Stephen Dubnoff, Denton Vaughan, and Clarise Lancaster, "Income Satisfaction Measures in Equivalence Scale Applications," *Proceedings of the Business and Economics Section,* American Statistical Association, Washington, D.C., 1981.

The official federal poverty line is based on estimates developed in 1965 by Mollie Orshansky of the Social Security Administration.[7] Her poverty line consisted of thresholds that varied with the size of the family, the number of children under 18, the sex and age of the family head, and whether the family lived on a farm. Distinctions based on sex and farm residence were dropped in 1980, but the equivalence scale for families of different sizes and ages is still based on Orshansky's work.

Orshansky's family equivalence scale had two components: the U.S. Department of Agriculture's estimate of the relative cost of feeding different sorts of families equally well, and her own estimate of the incomes required to bring food expenditures up to the level required by USDA's "economy" food plan in families of different sizes. USDA's food budgets vary according to the age, number, and sex of family members. The age and sex differences are based on the National Research Council's estimates of nutritional requirements. The adjustments for family size are based on USDA's estimates of economies of scale in the purchase and consumption of food. USDA assumes, for example, that four adult men spending $100 a week can eat as well as one man spending $30 a week. Column 3 of Table 2.4 shows the "food equivalence scale" for low-income families of various sizes in 1983.[8] The values appear intuitively reasonable.

If increases in family size drove up the cost of housing, clothing, transportation, and other items at the same rate as the cost of food, poverty thresholds for families of various sizes would be directly proportional to USDA food budgets. Orshansky made this assumption for families of three or more, setting their poverty thresholds at three times the cost of the USDA "economy" food plan for all such families.[9] When family size fell below three, however, Orshansky argued that food expenditures fell more than other household expenses. To get a poverty

[7]Mollie Orshansky, "Counting the Poor: Another Look at the Poverty Profile," *Social Security Bulletin 28* (January 1965):3–29.
[8]The USDA food equivalence scale in Table 2.4 differs slightly from the one that Orshansky used because Table 2.4 is based on USDA's "low cost" food plan for 1983 rather than on its "economy" food plan for 1964. USDA made minor changes in its estimates of the economies of scale associated with family size between 1964 and 1983; the relative cost of feeding a child and an adult varies slightly across the two plans; and my estimates of relative costs assume a rectangular distribution of children's ages whereas Orshansky used the observed distribution in 1963.
[9]Readers might therefore expect Orshansky's poverty thresholds to yield the same family equivalence scale as the USDA food budgets for families of three or more. This does not quite happen, partly for reasons discussed in footnote 8 and partly because Table 2.4 uses poverty thresholds for 1980, not 1964. The percentage of families with female heads and living on farms varies by family size, so eliminating these distinctions in 1980 slightly altered the apparent effect of family size.

threshold for families of two she therefore multiplied the cost of the USDA "economy" food plan by 3.7. To get a threshold for single men she multiplied the threshold for a married couple by 0.80.[10]

Orshansky's inconsistent assumptions about the effect of family size on the ratio of income to food expenditures account for the anomalous fact that the second and third family members appear to cost a family less than the fourth and fifth. Orshansky could have eliminated this anomaly in one of two ways. One possibility would have been to use a multiplier of 3.0 for families of all sizes, lowering the poverty thresholds for single individuals and families of two relative to those for larger families. A second possibility, more consistent with Orshansky's overall argument, would have been to keep reducing the multiplier when family size increased beyond three. This would have lowered the thresholds for very large families relative to smaller ones. Orshansky rejected both alternatives. The Johnson administration was already committed to a poverty threshold of about $3,000 for a family of four, so Orshansky had little leeway in setting a threshold for these families. She had more leeway in setting the thresholds for families of other sizes, and she used this leeway to set their thresholds as high as possible relative to the threshold for a family of four. She rejected the idea that the food multiplier for very large families should be less than 3.0 on the grounds that these families currently ate inadequately. She insisted that the multiplier for very small families should be more than 3.0 on the grounds that a multiplier of only 3.0 would leave too little money for other household expenses. Compassion was thus the mother of inconsistency—an old story.

Because the "poverty ratio" embodies a faulty family equivalence scale, it is not ideal for tracing changes in material well-being over time. But a better alternative is readily available. The BLS published a widely used family equivalence scale in 1968, which the Census Bureau could easily use to construct a family income series adjusted for changes in family size. Unfortunately, BLS's theoretical rationale for its scale is not very persuasive, so the scale has not won general acceptance among scholars. But the BLS scale turns out to have a strong empirical rationale nonetheless.

The BLS scale is based on Engel's Law, first enunciated in 1857, which states that as family income rises the proportion of family income spent on food falls. This fact convinced Engel that "the proportion of the outgo used for food, other things being equal, is the best measure

[10]Combining farm with nonfarm families and males with females reduced this ratio to 0.77 after 1980.

of the material standard of living of the population."[11] The BLS scale makes the heroic assumption that Engel's caveat about "other things being equal" did not require families to be the same size. Since a family of four with $20,000 a year typically spends the same fraction of its income on food as a family of two with $12,000 a year, for example, BLS assumes that the two families have the same standard of living. Table 2.4 shows the full BLS equivalence scale for families of different sizes, based on this assumption.

Unfortunately, the BLS paper that derived this scale offered no evidence that Engel's law did, in fact, apply to families of different sizes. To see why it might be wrong, imagine that Mr. Smith has a job paying $12,000 a year after taxes, that his wife has no job, that they spend $5,000 a year on rent and $2,400 on food, and that they have no children. Now suppose that Mr. Smith gets a series of raises which bring his after-tax earnings to $20,000 and that he and his wife have two children. They move to a larger apartment that costs an extra $3,000 a year, they spend an extra $1,600 to feed their two children, and they spend another $1,400 a year on other child-related goods and services. Overall, their income has risen $8,000 while their expenses have risen $6,000, so they think they are better off. Yet Engel's Law—and the BLS family equivalence scale—tell us that they are no better off, because they are still spending 20 percent of their income on food. The problem is clear. Engel's Law only holds so long as food claims the same fraction of what is spent on both children and adults. There is no a priori reason this should be true, and it is not true in this example. Because the Smiths allocated 20 percent of what they spent on themselves to food but allocated 27 percent of what they spent on their children to food, Engel's Law does not hold for them. The question is whether they are typical.

The only way to verify Engel's Law is to measure different families' standard of living directly. The most obvious measure is the ratio of food expenditures to food "needs." USDA claims that on the average a couple with two children needs to spend 64 percent more than a childless couple of the same age in order to eat equally well (see column 3 of Table 2.4). The BLS scale tells us that if a couple with two children has 67 percent more after-tax income than a childless couple, the two families will spend the same *percentage* of their income on food. It follows that a couple with two children typically spend 67 percent more on food than a childless couple with "equivalent" income. Thus, if a couple with two children has an income "equivalent" to that of a childless

---

[11]Quoted in Bureau of Labor Statistics, *Revised Equivalence Scales for Estimating Equivalent Incomes or Budget Costs by Family Type* (Washington, D.C.: U.S. Government Printing Office, 1968).

couple, the couple with children will typically eat $1.67/1.64 - 1 = .018$ (about 2 percent) better than the childless couple. For all practical purposes, therefore, the two families eat equally well. Because the USDA food equivalence scale is very similar to the BLS income equivalence scale for families of *all* sizes (compare columns 2 and 3 in Table 2.4), all families with what BLS defines as equivalent incomes must eat about equally well by USDA standards. If eating well has about the same priority relative to other forms of consumption in families of different sizes, eating equally well will imply the same overall level of material welfare. The fact that the BLS scale implies equally satisfactory levels of food consumption as well as equal percentages of income spent on food thus tells us that Engel's Law *does* hold for families of different sizes.

Before adopting the BLS equivalence scale the Census Bureau would obviously need to verify its accuracy using more recent data on consumer expenditure patterns. (The BLS scale was based on the 1960–61 Consumer Expenditure Survey.) It would also be important to ask whether families with equivalent incomes on the BLS scale usually had comparable levels of material welfare when one looked at indicators other than food. *Any* measure of material consumption that is primarily individual rather than collective can, in principle, be used to test the validity of an income equivalence scale. Thus, we should not only ask whether couples with two children and $20,000 a year eat steak as often as couples with no children and $12,000 a year, but whether they dress equally well, drive equally good cars to work, and own equally good television sets. Any particular measure may yield the wrong answer, because changes in family size may be associated with changes in the priority that adults assign to a given item, but the problem is not intractable on that account. Pending such studies, the fact that the BLS scale appears to ensure that families of different sizes end up eating equally well gives it considerable face validity.[12]

If we accept the BLS family equivalence scale, we can compare the cost of supporting a child to the cost of supporting an adult at the same standard. Table 2.4 suggests that it costs about two-thirds as much to support a child as to support an adult at the same level. If the Census Bureau wanted to adjust trends in family income to take account of changes in family size, a first step might be to adopt the "two-thirds rule" implicit in the BLS family equivalence scale. Using this rule, the

---

[12]For a more complex approach to this problem, see Edward Lazear and Robert Michael, "Family Size and the Distribution of Real Per Capita Income," *American Economic Review* 70 (March 1980): 91–107, and Jacques van der Gaag and Eugene Smolensky, "True Household Equivalence Scales and Characteristics of the Poor in the United States, *Review of Income and Wealth* 28 (1981):17–28.

bureau could convert children to "adult equivalents." It could then divide the total income reported in a given year by the number of adult equivalents in the population. This would yield an estimate of income per adult equivalent. Row 4 of Table 2.3 shows trends in this measure of living standards. A more precise procedure would be to construct a revised version of the poverty line and calculate trends in the mean and dispersion of the resulting poverty ratio.

An alternative approach to estimating the relative cost of supporting children is to ask adults how much income they think families of various sizes need to achieve some specified level of well-being. Lee Rainwater, for example, asked respondents how much income families of various sizes needed not to be "poor," to "get along," to be "comfortable," to be "prosperous," and to be "rich." Changes in family size had about the same percentage effect on people's answers regardless of the criterion used. Column 4 of Table 2.4 shows his estimates for families of varying size. Whereas a couple needs a 67 percent income increase to maintain its material standard of living when it has two children, it only needs a 23 percent increase to maintain its position in the eyes of others.

Still another approach to estimating the relative cost of children and adults is to ask adults to choose one of several adjectives to describe *their own* standard of living, and then see how the number of children in the family affects the choice of adjectives. Dubnoff, Vaughan, and Lancaster (1981) show that family size has very little effect on the adjectives people choose to describe their standard of living. Their estimates appear in column 5 of Table 2.4. The differences between their estimates for one, two, or three children could be due to sampling error, but the difference between their estimates and the BLS estimates could not.

What do these figures mean? The BLS budgets imply that a couple with two children needs $20,000 a year to be as well off as a childless couple with $12,000. Rainwater's respondents think it takes only $14,800. Dubnoff et al.'s parents of two need only $13,800 to characterize their standard of living the same way childless couples with $12,000 do. It seems very unlikely that families of four with incomes of $13,800 to $14,800 enjoy the same level of material comfort as families of two with $12,000. The Rainwater-Dubnoff figures thus suggest that people don't *expect* to enjoy the same level of material comfort when they have children as when they don't.

The fact that people with a lot of children feel almost as well off as people without children is hardly surprising. Most parents have children because they want them. If they do not want children they use contraceptives, get abortions, place their unwanted children for adoption, or—if they are men—leave home. Adults presumably spend money on children because they get more satisfaction from such expenditures than from alternative uses of the money. (Spaghetti eaten with people you love is usually more satisfying than steak eaten alone.) If this is so, it may make no more sense to say that having children lowers an adult's standard of living than to say that owning a yacht does. Children are expensive, and having children leaves less money for other things, but that is true of a yacht, too. The fact that most people preferred children to yachts in the 1950s, whereas many chose yachts over children in the 1970s, means that the material standard of living was higher in the 1970s, but it does not necessarily mean that people *felt* better off in the 1970s than in the 1950s.

If all parents felt the same way about children that yacht owners feel about yachts, our best estimate of trends in adult living standards would be income per adult. But as Dubnoff et al. demonstrate, respondents with a lot of children are somewhat less satisfied with their standard of living than respondents with comparable incomes and fewer children. The same may, of course, also be true of yacht owners. People with expensive tastes inevitably feel worse off on any given income than people with inexpensive tastes, and children are certainly an expensive taste. But children also differ from other "consumer durables" in one crucial respect. If I buy a boat and then find that I cannot afford the upkeep, or do not like it as much as I once did, I can sell it. Selling off children who no longer give pleasure is much harder. The likelihood that people will end up with more children than they really want is therefore higher than the likelihood that they will end up with more boats, cars, or houses than they want. As a result, the dollars adults spend on their children may on the average give them less pleasure than the dollars they spend on themselves. The fact that adults with large families are less satisfied with a given income than adults with small families may reflect this fact.

All this suggests that there is no one "correct" procedure for estimating children's impact on the standard of living. If we want to estimate trends in individual consumption of material goods and services, the BLS family equivalence scale probably describes the effect of changes in family size as accurately as any available alternative. Line 4 of Table 2.3 shows that if we follow the BLS scale in assuming that children cost two-thirds of what adults cost, the annual increase in the standard of living averaged 2.4 percent in the 1950s, 3.2 percent in the 1960s, and 1.9 percent in the 1970s. In addition, some might argue that we should adjust for changes in adult living arrangements. BLS assumes, for example, that a couple needs only 67 percent more money than a single individual to enjoy an "equivalent" standard of living. This suggests applying the "two-thirds rule" to all but the first family member. Using this rule, we can calculate the number of "unrelated adult equivalents" in a given year and the trend in "income per unrelated adult equivalent." Line 5 of Table 2.3 shows, though, that this adjustment hardly alters the results obtained by adjusting for age alone in line 4. The 1970s still look marginally worse than the 1950s and considerably worse than the 1960s.

But if we are interested in how adults *feel* about their standard of living, the "two-thirds" rule exaggerates the subjective cost of children. Rainwater's data suggest substituting a "one-fourth" rule, while Dubnoff et al.'s data suggest a "one-seventh" rule, and conventional economic theory suggests ignoring children altogether. All three procedures yield roughly the same result. Line 6 shows the estimated rate of growth in adults' subjective well-being when we use the "one- seventh" rule to calculate the net cost of children. Mean income per "subjective adult equivalent" grew 2.8 percent a year during the 1950s, 3.1 percent a year during the 1960s, and 1.4 percent a year during the 1970s. Line 7 shows the estimated rate of growth if we assume that the subjective costs of children are equal to the subjective benefits and simply calculate income per adult. It is almost identical to line 6.

Because income per adult grew less during the 1970s than during the 1960s or 1950s, it is tempting to argue that adults cut back their fertility in order to maintain the traditional rate of growth in adult consumption. This argument would be quite compelling if fertility had begun to fall only when growth in income per adult slowed. In point of fact, however, fertility began to fall in the early 1960s, when income per adult was rising at an unprecedented rate. This suggests that fertility fell primarily because tastes changed. One obvious possibility is that as a result of cultural changes that began in the early 1960s young adults came to see taking emotional responsibility for children more as a burden and less as a joy, independent of its economic costs.

Lines 6 and 7 probably present a better picture of how adults feel about their standard of living than lines 4 and 5 do. Lines 6 and 7 do not, however, tell us anything about how *children* feel. Adults seem to get considerable vicarious satisfaction from spending money on their children. Children show no sign of getting comparable satisfaction from money spent on their siblings. Growing up in a family with a lot of siblings has a negative effect on children's school achievement and on their subsequent economic success. Thus, while parents probably enjoyed spending their rising incomes on big families during the 1950s, there is no reason to suppose that children enjoyed it. If we look at matters from the children's perspective, and use the BLS yardstick in lieu of anything better to assess material well-being, lines 4 and 5 suggest that children's standard of living rose almost as fast during the 1970s as during the 1950s.

While the estimated rate of income growth during the 1970s is quite sensitive to one's choice of procedures for dealing with changes in family composition, *any* adjustment for changes in family composition makes the 1970s look better than they do when one makes no adjustment. One can hardly expect the Census Bureau to decide which adjustment is "best." But one can expect the bureau to mention that adjusting for family composition would change the apparent implications of its RFI series. Indeed, one might even expect the bureau to present several possible adjustments, so that readers could see how much difference they make. While the introduction of the per capita income series is a step in this direction, the fact that the bureau has thus far made no mention of this new series in the text of its reports on money income suggests that it is still wedded to the "one best series" model of data presentation, and that its definition of the "best" series is still the oldest.

Defining and Measuring Income

The last set of potential problems in the RFI series derives from the Census Bureau's procedures for defining and measuring income. The bureau, following OMB guidelines, defines income as money income from earnings, self-employment, dividends, interest, rent, and transfer payments. The bureau does not include income "in kind," and it does not exclude taxes. CPS interviewers will accept information from any "responsible" adult who is at home when they arrive. The interviewer asks this informant to estimate each household member's money income from each possible source during the previous calendar year. If the informant does not have the required information or refuses to provide it, the bureau estimates the missing income data from whatever information the informant provides about the individual in question (for example, race, sex, age, schooling, and so forth).

In evaluating the RFI series we must ask two kinds of questions about the bureau's income measure. First, how accurately do respondents report their family's money income before taxes? Second, how closely does their "true" pretax money income correspond to their economic welfare? When we focus on income trends, as I have here, we must ask specifically whether the discrepancy between reported and actual money income has changed since 1950, and whether the discrepancy between money income and economic welfare has changed. I will take these questions up in turn.

Census Bureau respondents tend to report their wages quite accurately, but they tend to underreport income from other sources. The bureau periodically compares the total amount of income its respondents reported with BEA estimates of money income for the same year. BEA bases its estimates on data provided by government agencies, banks, corporations, and others about their payments to individuals. Census–BEA comparisons suggest that CPS respondents reported 84 percent of their money income in 1950, 87 percent in 1960, 88 percent in 1970, and 89 percent in 1980.[13] The Census Bureau does not adjust its RFI series to take account of underreporting. Nor does its annual "Money Income" report mention the fact that part of the apparent increase in money income, especially in the 1950s, is due to better reporting. Table 2.5 tries to correct this deficiency. Comparing lines 1 and 3, we see that correcting for underreporting appreciably reduces the estimated annual increase in pretax money income during the 1950s but does not have much effect after 1960.

The Census Bureau's definition of income also poses problems if we want to make inferences about trends in material well-being. Asking respondents to report household members' money income before taxes simplifies the respondent's task, but it yields a measure that does not necessarily move in tandem with the respondents' material standard of living.

The first problem is that focusing on income before taxes can be quite misleading if the tax rate is changing. Line 4 of Table 2.5 shows that personal taxes rose faster than money income throughout this period, but they rose fastest during the 1950s, somewhat slower during the 1960s, and slower yet during the 1970s. This result may surprise those who think of the 1950s as a period of fiscal conservatism. The image is correct in that governments financed almost all spending from taxes, not borrowing, during the 1950s. But it is incorrect if it implies that legislators successfully resisted pressures for higher taxes during the 1950s. Defense spending rose from 5 to 9 percent of GNP between 1950 and 1960. In addition, suburbanization and the baby boom led to enormous increases in state and local spending on highways and education during this decade. Comparing lines 3 and 5, we see that posttax income grew 0.6 percent less per year than pretax income during the 1950s, 0.4 percent less during the 1960s, and 0.3 percent less during the 1970s. Line 8, which presents the NIPA estimate of "disposable income," tells essentially the same story as line 5.

Subtracting taxes is essential from an accounting viewpoint, since otherwise government payments to individuals often get counted twice.

[13]The estimates for 1980 and 1970 come from "Money Income: 1980" and "Money Income: 1971." The estimates for 1960 and 1950 come from Herman P. Miller, *Income Distribution in the United States* (Washington, D.C.: U.S. Government Printing Office, 1966), p. 173, and apply to 1949 and 1959.

TABLE 2.5

Alternative Measures of Aggregate Income: 1950 to 1980
(In Billions of 1980 PCE Dollars)

| | 1950 | 1960 | 1970 | 1980 | Average Annual Percent Increase During the: | | |
					1950s	1960s	1970s
1. Reported Money Income	543	805	1264	1754	4.0	4.6	3.3
2. Unreported Income	106	117	172	217	1.0	3.9	2.4
3. Total Money Income before Taxes	649	922	1436	1971	3.6	4.5	3.2
4. Personal Taxes	74	149	278	425	7.2	6.4	4.3
5. Money Income after Taxes	575	773	1158	1546	3.0	4.1	2.9
6. Government Services "In Kind"	108	155	259	407	3.7	5.3	4.6
7. Adjusted After-Tax Income	683	928	1417	1953	3.1	4.3	3.3
8. Disposable Income (NIPA)	650	878	1347	1824	3.1	4.4	3.1
9. Adjusted After-Tax Income per BLS Adult Equivalent	5085	5924	7925	9546	1.5	3.0	1.9
10. Adjusted After-Tax Income per Adult	6509	7915	10336	11646	2.0	2.7	1.2

SOURCES, *by line:*
1. My Table 2.3, Line 1.
2. The estimates for 1980 and 1970 come from "Money Income: 1980" and "Money Income: 1971." The estimates for 1960 and 1950 come from Herman P. Miller, *Income Distribution in the United States* (Washington, D.C.: U.S. Government Printing Office, 1966), p. 173, and apply to 1949 and 1959.
3. Line 1 − Line 2.
4. *Economic Report of the President, 1983*, pp.189–90. Includes employee's share of social security.
5. Line 3 + Line 4.
6. Robert Eisner and David Nebhut, "An Extended Measure of Government Product: Preliminary Results for the United States, 1946–76," *Review of Income and Wealth* 27 (1981): 33–64. Eisner and Nebhut's estimates are for 1946, 1956, 1966, and 1976. I used these figures to estimate average annual growth rates for 1946–56, 1956–66, and 1966–76, used these growth rates to estimate values for 1950, 1960, 1970, and 1980, and inflated the results to 1980 dollars using the PCE deflator. The deflator for government services might (or might not) be more appropriate but it would not alter the results much.
7. Line 5 + Line 6.
8. *Economic Report of the President, 1983*, p.191.
9. (Line 7/Line 1) (Line 4, my Table 2.3).
10. (Line 7/Line 1) (Line 7, my Table 2.3).

The Census Bureau's measure of earnings, for example, includes the employee's share of Social Security taxes. Since Social Security is a "pay-as-you-go" program, Social Security taxes are almost all paid out to retired beneficiaries in the year they are received. Such taxes are therefore counted twice: first as earnings and then as transfer payments. They are spent only once: by the beneficiary. The same problem arises when the government uses income tax receipts to pay interest on government securities held by individuals.

While we must subtract personal taxes from income in order to avoid double counting, we must also add back something for the value of the free services governments provide to individuals. When higher taxes provide better schools, cleaner air, better recreation facilities, or shorter driving time to visit friends and relatives, these improvements constitute income in kind to individuals. Estimating the value of these "free" government services to individuals poses conceptual and empirical problems beyond the scope of this chapter. Line 6 of Table 2.5 does, however, present an estimate of the consumption value of government services to individuals, based on the work of Robert Eisner and David Nebhut. These estimates include both government expenditures on current consumption (public recreation facilities, for example) and government investments in individuals' "human capital" (schools and hospitals, for example).

Line 7 of Table 2.5 estimates "adjusted" income, defined as money income minus taxes plus the value of government services to individuals. Adjusted income rose 0.9 percent less per year than reported money income during the 1950s, 0.3 percent less during the 1960s, and no less during the 1970s (compare lines 1 and 7). The interested reader can also apply these percentage adjustments to trends in income per family, per person, or per adult, as shown in Tables 2.1 and 2.3. Table 2.3 shows, for example, that mean income per "BLS adult equivalent" rose 2.4 percent per year during the 1950s. After adjusting for underreporting, taxes, and the value of government services, the figure is $2.4 - 0.9 = 1.5$ percent.[14] Line 9 of Table 2.5 shows these figures for the 1960s and 1970s as well. In this case the adjustments make the 1970s look somewhat better than the 1950s, though they still look worse than the 1960s. Line 10 shows, however, that if we focus on income per adult rather than income per adult equivalent, the 1970s look somewhat worse than the 1950s, though nothing like as much worse as in the RFI series.

Government services are not the only kind of "in kind" income people receive. Anthropologists, sociologists, and economic historians usually assume that the proportion of goods and services acquired outside the market has declined over time. Indeed, the apparently relentless spread of the cash nexus has provided the starting point for much social theory over the past two centuries. If people are in fact acquiring an ever larger fraction of all goods and services through the market, in-

[14]In principle, these adjustments are multiplicative rather than additive. In order to estimate the annual change in after-tax income, therefore, one should multiply the implied ratios in Table 2.1 or 2.3 by those in Table 2.5. The annual change in after-tax income per unrelated adult equivalent for the 1950s is thus $(1.023)(1.034/1.040) - 1 = 1.71$ percent, not $1.023 + (1.034 - 1.040) - 1 = 1.70$ percent. In practice, the difference is not worth worrying about when the annual change is small.

creases in money income will inevitably exaggerate the improvement in true economic welfare.

People raise less of their own food than they used to, for example. This is partly because fewer people live on farms and partly because farmers are more inclined to concentrate on cash crops, buying their groceries in supermarkets like everyone else. Such changes obviously raise money income more than they raise living standards.

Recent changes in the banking industry have followed the same pattern. Banks used to pay depositors for the use of their money by providing "free" services. Now most banks pay interest on deposits while charging customers for the services they render. This change from barter to cash transactions raises depositors' nominal income, but it also raises their expenses by roughly the same amount. Depositors therefore experience little net change in their economic welfare. If we look only at their money income, though, they appear to be better off.

While these examples suggest that people are still buying an ever increasing percentage of their goods and services, other recent developments have worked in the opposite direction. During the 1970s the federal government expanded many of its "in kind" benefits, including Food Stamps, Medicare, Medicaid, and housing subsidies. Such benefits evidently grew as fast as home-grown food and "free" banking services shrank, since the Census Bureau's "Money Income" reports indicate that "in kind" benefits constituted about 4 percent of "personal income" in the National Income and Product Accounts in both 1970 and 1980. The 1960 "Money Income" report gives a figure of 5 percent. Neither the bureau's 1950 report nor the NIPA gives a figure for 1950, but my guess is that it was more than 5 percent. If so, even line 7 of Table 2.5 exaggerates the increase in economic well-being during the 1950s.

Lines 7 to 9 of Table 2.5 represent my best quantitative estimates of what "really" happened to income between 1950 and 1980, but they are still subject to several important limitations. First, even BEA's estimates of individual income surely underestimate actual income. Many people have strong incentives not to report their income to the government. The self-employed are particularly likely to understate their true income. Edgar Feige has argued in a series of provocative papers that the proportion of all economic activity recorded by the government peaked some time ago and is now declining.[15] If he is right, the growth in total income from 1950 to 1980 was greater than Table 2.5 indicates, and the downward bias was larger for the 1970s than for earlier decades.

[15]Edgar Feige, "How Big Is the Irregular Economy?" *Challenge* (November 1979), and "A New Perspective on Macroeconomic Phenomena: The Theory and Measurement of the Unobserved Sector of the United States Economy: Causes, Consequences, and Implications," University of Wisconsin, Madison, Department of Economics, August 1980, xerox.

Another problem is that NIPA estimates of income "in kind" do not include estimates of the value of either housework or leisure. Because of technical innovations (gas and electric stoves, refrigerators, washing machines, dishwashers, vacuum cleaners, sewing machines, and so forth), housework has become increasingly capital-intensive. Many wives who would once have done 60 hours a week of housework now find they can do better working 35 hours for pay, buying a lot of household hardware with their earnings, and spending 20 hours on housework. Partly as a result of this change and partly for other reasons, many mothers are also taking paid jobs and hiring someone else to care for their children 35 or 40 hours a week instead of caring for their children 168 hours a week themselves. While these changes have undoubtedly led to increases in net economic welfare, they have led to even larger increases in money income. When a woman takes a job paying $10,000 a year and uses the income to buy $4,000 worth of childcare, make $1,000 a year in payments on household appliances, and pay $2,000 a year in taxes, the Census Bureau records a $10,000 increase in money income, without any deduction for the cost of child care or the increased need for household hardware. A more realistic reckoning might show a $3,000 increase in net income instead of a $10,000 increase.

While ignoring housework and leisure exaggerates the growth in economic welfare since 1950, it does not greatly distort comparisons between the 1950s, 1960s, and 1970s. Among wives living with their husbands, the proportion who worked for pay was 23.8 percent in 1950, 30.5 percent in 1960, 40.8 percent in 1970, and 50.1 percent in 1980. The annual increase was thus only slightly less during the 1950s than during the 1960s and 1970s.

Some Preliminary Conclusions

1. Using the pre-1983 CPI to convert current to "constant " dollars makes the RFI series underestimate the increase in economic well-being during the 1970s.
2. The bureau's procedures for estimating money income exaggerate the growth in purchasing power since 1950, both because they ignore the decline in underreporting and because they ignore the increase in taxes. Both these sources of upward bias are especially severe for the 1950s.
3. Judgments about changes in the standard of living depend to a great extent on whether we look at income per family, per adult, per "adult equivalent," or per person. If we assume that children consume only two-thirds as much as adults, the 1970s

look almost as good as the 1950s. But if we look at parents' subjective well-being and assume that they value children as highly as other things they spend money on, the 1970s look somewhat worse than the 1950s. No matter what adjustment we make for family size, the 1960s look better than the 1950s or 1970s. No matter what adjustment we make, the 1970s also look better than they do if we ignore changes in family size altogether, as the Census Bureau does.

The Census Bureau cannot be expected to resolve all the difficult problems posed by efforts to relate trends in money income to trends in material well-being. It can, however, be expected to alert readers to the existence of such problems and to quantify discrepancies between the two trends wherever possible. While the bureau's annual reports do a somewhat better job in this regard today than in the past, their text still falls far short of the standard of excellence the bureau sets for its data collection procedures.

It would be relatively easy to improve these reports without arousing much controversy.

1.   The bureau could reestimate the CPI from 1947 to 1982, using the alternative treatment of housing adopted in 1983. With OMB's consent this revised version of the CPI could be used to construct a historical RFI series that took an internally consistent approach to inflation.
2.   The bureau could estimate a per capita income series from 1947 to the present and could give trends in per capita income as much publicity as trends in median family income. This would warn readers that conclusions about trends in economic welfare depend to a great extent on whether one counts children as a "cost" or not.
3.   The bureau could assemble and publish time series showing trends in mean and median income for specific types of families, such as married couples with two children at home, married couples with no children at home, female-headed households with two children, single individuals over 65, and so forth. These series would allow readers to see how much of the trend in median income is due to compositional shifts and how much to changes in the incomes of families with fixed composition.
4.   The bureau could adjust its estimates of mean and median family income for underreporting.
5.   The bureau could draw attention in its "Money Income" reports to its work on family income after taxes.
6.   The text of the bureau's annual report could discuss income "in kind" in more detail, giving more attention to government ser-

vices, housework, and leisure, and indicating how taking account of "in kind" income might alter apparent trends in money income.

These steps would not solve all the problems of the RFI series, but they would be a start.

Income and Living Standards: Larger Issues

The Census Bureau makes no explicit claims about what its RFI series measures, but users habitually interpret the series as measuring changes in economic welfare. If the RFI series does *not* measure economic welfare, the bureau certainly ought to warn potential users of this fact. Unfortunately, even if the bureau were to deal with the problems outlined in the previous section by publishing several alternative income series, the link between money income and economic welfare would remain problematic. The reason is that a measure of economic welfare must deal with "final" goods and services—goods and services that consumers value as ends in themselves, not as means to some other end. The goods and services on which families spend their income are not, by and large, "final" goods in this sense. They are mostly "intermediate" goods that families then use to produce "final" goods. When one tries to measure trends in the consumption of final goods, these trends do not necessarily correspond with trends in expenditures on intermediate goods. Trends in health, housing, and nutrition all illustrate the difficulty in drawing inferences about trends in economic well-being from trends in expenditures.

Medical Expenditures

People seldom value medical services as an end in themselves. Some medical services are, it is true, designed to make the sick less miserable rather than making them healthier. Hospices for the dying are an extreme example. For the most part, though, patients find medical care disagreeable, and they value it only insofar as it helps maintain or restore their health.

Table 2.6 suggests that trends in health are not very closely related to trends in medical expenditures. Lines 1 to 5 show per capita health expenditures in current and "constant" dollars from 1950 to 1980. Lines 7 and 8 show the two most widely used measures of health: infant mortality and life expectancy. Judging by these two measures, the rate of increase in "real" health expenditures had no relationship to the rate of improvement in Americans' health between 1950 and 1980. Life expec-

TABLE 2.6

Per Capita Medical Expenditures and Health: 1950 to 1980

| | 1950 | 1960 | 1970 | 1980 | Average Annual Percent Increase During the: | | |
					1950s	1960s	1970s
EXPENDITURES							
1. Medical Services (in current dollars)	76	137	332	1024	6.1	9.3	11.9
2. Medical Research and Construction (in current dollars)	6.2	9.3	26	52	4.1	10.8	7.2
3. Price Index (1980 = 100)	20.2	29.8	45.4	100	4.0	4.3	8.2
4. Medical Services (in constant dollars)	374	460	731	1024	2.1	4.7	3.4
5. Medical Research and Construction (in constant dollars)	31	31	57	52	0.0	6.3	−0.9
BURDEN							
6. Personal Medical Expenditures as a Percent of Personal Income	3.0	3.8	5.0	6.2	2.4	2.8	2.1
HEALTH							
7. Infant Mortality	29.2	26.0	20.0	12.6	−1.2	−2.7	−4.5
8. Life Expectancy	68.2	69.7	70.9	73.7	.22	.17	.38

SOURCES, *by line:*
1–2. *Statistical Abstract, 1982–3,* p. 102 and *Historical Statistics,* Series B-222 and B-233. These two series show identical values for 1960 but not for 1970. The figures in the text for 1970 are from the *Statistical Abstract.* As usual in such matters, neither publication explains the discrepancy.
3. *Statistical Abstract, 1982–3,* p. 461. The index is part of the CPI and covers only private expenditures not government expenditures.
4. Line 1/Line 3.
5. Line 2/Line 3. Note that the CPI deflator is probably not appropriate for estimating "real" expenditures on research and construction.
6. *Economic Report of the President, 1983,* pp. 179 and 190.
7. *Statistical Abstract, 1985,* p. 73. Rate per 100,000.
8. *Statistical Abstract, 1985,* p. 69.

tancy improved much faster during the 1970s than during the two previous decades.[16] Infant mortality also fell slightly faster in absolute

[16]Estimates of life expectancy for those born in, say, 1980 are based on age-specific death rates in 1980. To derive these rates, the National Center for Health Statistics divides its estimate of the number of individuals of a given age who died in 1980 by the Census Bureau's estimate of the number of individuals of that age living in the United States in 1980. Most observers assume that NCHS's death count is more complete than the Census Bureau's count of the living, especially for black males. It follows that NCHS slightly overestimates age-specific death rates and underestimates life expectancy at birth. Since the Census Bureau's count of the living appears to have become more complete with each decennial census, the downward bias in life expectancy has probably diminished over time. If so, Table 2.6 slightly overstates the true increase in life expectancy from 1950 to 1980. But when Farley and Allen reestimated life expectancy using the Census Bureau's estimates of the undercount, they still found as much improvement during the 1970s as during the 1950s and 1960s combined, so the basic point in the text still holds. See Reynolds Farley and Walter Allen, *The Color Line and the Quality of Life in America* (New York: Russell Sage Foundation, 1987).

terms and much faster in percentage terms during the 1970s than during the two previous decades. "Real" health expenditures, in contrast, appear to have increased faster during the 1960s than during the 1970s.

One possible explanation for these results is that the BLS price deflator for medical services does not try to take account of changes in the effectiveness of a service due to new knowledge. If an $8 pill that works replaces a $4 pill that does not work, BLS simply records a 100 percent increase in the price of pills. A second problem, which flows from the first, is that technical improvements in one service can reduce the need for others. The introduction of polio vaccine, for example, led to a substantial reduction in medical services to polio victims. Because BLS prices medical "services" rather than "health," a reduction in services to polio victims leads to a decline in "real" as well as nominal medical expenditures. Yet this decline in real expenditure is associated with an improvement in both health and consumer satisfaction. This seems odd, to say the least.

If we wanted to estimate the economic value of introducing polio vaccine, we would have to estimate the amount of money Americans would have been willing to spend to get such a vaccine in, say, 1950. Then we would have to calculate the amount of money Americans actually had to spend to get the vaccine once it became available and record the difference as an unmeasured price reduction. If we were to calculate medical prices in this way, we would find that they had risen far less than Table 2.6 implies. Unfortunately, there is no way of quantifying this change. As a result, there is no sensible way of saying to what extent the increase in medical expenditures has been matched by an increase in the value consumers put on the services they receive. It follows that there is no reliable way to convert expenditures in different years to "constant" dollars.

The cost of maintaining a given level of health may also have changed during the 1960s or 1970s for reasons that had nothing to do with the volume or quality of medical services. The health improvements of the 1970s could, for example, be by-products of smoking less, driving more slowly, exercising more, reduced employment in hazardous industries, or the fact that patients were better educated and hence more likely to follow medical advice. Such possibilities underline a critical point. While journalists often describe the CPI as measuring the "cost of living," it does not in fact try to do this. A cold winter, for example, drives up the amount of fuel a family needs to stay warm, independent of its effect on fuel prices. The CPI does not measure such changes in what a family has to spend to stay warm. It only measures the unit cost of fuel. The medical component of the CPI works the same way, measuring the cost of specific services, not the amount of service needed to maintain a given level of health. Yet if we are to connect trends in material well-being with trends in expenditures, we need a measure of changes in "cost," not "price." The journalist's impulse to call the CPI a "cost of living" index rather than a "price" index thus reflects a sound intuitive sense of what the public needs to know, even though it reflects badly on journalists' grasp of what government statistics actually measure.

Another possible reason why health does not change in tandem with health expenditures is that official statistics on health expenditures omit a number of important items. Official statistics do not, for example, include expenditures on workplace safety, cleaner air and water, or reduction of toxic wastes. If those were *government* expenditures, they would show up as public health measures. They would also show up as "money income," albeit money income used to pay taxes. But business expenditures mandated by government do not show up in the national income accounts. Instead, BEA treats such expenditures as an ordinary cost of doing business. When such expenditures increase, BEA treats the resulting increase in prices as "inflation," not as a service to the public. While it makes sense to say that a reduction in air pollution by steelmakers has increased the price of automobiles, one should also treat it as reducing the cost of health. Neither BEA nor BLS tries to do this.

Housing Expenditures

Table 2.7 shows trends in the estimated rental value of residential housing from 1950 to 1980. Line 1 indicates that in "constant" dollars the *per household* rental value of residential housing rose 39 percent in the 1950s, 33 percent in the 1960s, and 24 percent in the 1970s. Line 2 shows, however, that rental value *per person* rose 40 percent in the 1950s, 41 percent in the 1960s, and 41 percent during the 1970s. The discrepancy between the two sets of figures reflects the fact that household size was essentially stable in the 1950s, fell slightly in the 1960s, and fell a lot in the 1970s (see line 3).

It is not obvious which of these estimates provides a more accurate picture of trends in housing conditions. Clearly neither is ideal. Line 1, which makes no adjustment for the numbers of people living in the typical housing unit, surely underestimates the rate of improvement in housing conditions during the 1970s. But line 2 assumes that changes in household size exert proportional effects on the amount the household

TABLE 2.7

Housing Expenditures and Standards: 1950 to 1980

	1950	1960	1970	1980
RENTAL VALUE IN 1980 DOLLARS				
1. Per Household	1448	2007	2664	3296
2. Per Person	430	603	848	1144
3. Percent of Disposable Income	10.9	13.7	13.5	14.6
RENTAL PRICE INDEX				
4. NIPA (1980 = 100)	34.4	45.4	55.6	100
HOUSEHOLD SIZE				
5. Mean	3.37	3.33	3.14	2.76
HOUSING STANDARDS				
6. Rooms per Unit	—	4.9	5.0	5.1
7. Rooms per Person	—	1.47	1.59	1.85
8. Rooms per Adult Equivalent	—	1.76	1.89	2.11
9. Percent Less than 10 Years Old	—	27.0	24.0	25.0
10. Percent with Complete Plumbing	—	84.0	95.0	98.0
HOME OWNERSHIP				
11. Percent of Housing Units Occupied by Owner	55.0	61.9	62.9	64.4
12. Percent of Individuals and Families Owning Their Home	48.7	58.4	59.9	60.0

SOURCES, *by line:*
1. Total rental value from *Economic Report of the President, 1983,* p. 179. Households from *Statistical Abstract, 1985,* p. 40. Deflator from line 4.
2. Line 1/Line 5.
3. *Economic Report of the President, 1983,* pp. 179, 190.
4. U.S. Department of Commerce, *The National Income and Product Accounts of the United States, 1929–76,* U.S. Government Printing Office, 1981, Table 7.11, and *Survey of Current Business,* February 1982, p. 11, Table 7.11.
5. *Statistical Abstract, 1985,* p. 40.
6. *Statistical Abstract, 1985,* p. 731. Value shown is median, not mean.
7. Line 6/Line 5.
8. (Line 7) (Population)/(Population over 16 + Population under 16/2).
9–11. *Statistical Abstract, 1985,* p. 735.
12. (Owner occupied units, in Line 11)/(Line 3, my Table 2.2 + Line 6, my Table 2.2). This estimate assumes that only one individual or family can own a given unit. This leads to some downward bias, especially in 1980.

must spend to maintain its material standard of comfort. This seems unlikely. As with income, the truth presumably lies somewhere between these two extremes. But because households consume housing collectively rather than individually, we cannot construct a "housing equivalence scale" that tells us, say, how many rooms a family of four needs in order to be as well housed as a family of two. Living with children is different from living without them no matter how many rooms you have. How many rooms you need in order not to *feel* worse off depends on how the children behave and how you feel about their behavior. In many cases families feel better off when they have children even if they get no additional space whatever.

Nonetheless, if the BLS price index is right, housing conditions improved markedly during the 1970s. This conclusion is clearly contrary to conventional wisdom, which holds that housing costs rose so fast during the 1970s that many families were "priced out of the market." This view is far too simple. Rents rose less during the 1970s than prices in general (compare line 4 of Table 2.7 to line 4 of Table 2.1). And while the cost of *buying* a house rose faster than most other prices, the cost of *owning* a house probably fell, for reasons noted earlier.

These estimates are, of course, no better than the price indices from which they are derived. It is therefore of some interest to ask whether the steady rate of increase in the quality of housing from 1950 to 1980 was accompanied by an equally steady increase in direct measures of the quality of housing. Lines 6 to 8 measure spaciousness. The number of rooms per unit rose at the same rate during the 1970s as during the 1960s. But the number of people per unit fell faster during the 1970s than during the 1960s, so the number of rooms per person rose more in the later period. Line 8 shows that this remains true if we estimate rooms per "adult equivalent" instead of rooms per person. In principle it would be desirable to make a further adjustment for the increase in people living alone or with nonrelatives, since two people living separately are often thought to need more rooms than two people living together. I doubt, however, that such an adjustment would alter the basic trends in lines 6 through 8. It would also be desirable to correct for changes in room size, but I have not tried to do this.

A building's age is another proxy for its quality. Line 9 shows that the percentage of all housing that was less than ten years old rose slightly during the 1970s, though the striking thing about these figures is really their stability over time.

Line 10 measures the percentage of housing units with complete plumbing. Since 93.5 percent of all units had complete plumbing in 1970, this measure could not possibly have risen 6.7 percent during the 1970s, as it had during the 1960s. Nonetheless, the trend during the 1970s is instructive, because it says something about the extent to which the least adequate units improved. Line 10 shows that housing without complete plumbing almost disappeared during the 1970s. The improvement in housing standards during the 1970s thus seems to have affected the poor as well as the rich. Taken together, these direct measures seem to confirm the story told by the trends in "real" rental value per person and per household.

Another popular measure of housing conditions is the number of household appliances a home contains. Table 2.8 shows the percentage of households with various items in 1960, 1970, and 1980. Some of the figures are almost surely wrong. Personal experience makes me doubt, for example, that 99.9 percent of American households own either a vacuum cleaner or an electric coffee maker. Indeed, a significant fraction of American households do not even contain a coffee drinker. Nonetheless, the figures are of some interest.

Note, first, that every item listed in Table 2.8 was more widely diffused in 1980 than in 1970. This includes items that were already owned by more than 90 percent of all families in 1970 and could only become more widely diffused by becoming "standard equipment" even among the poor. This apparently happened for television sets,

TABLE 2.8

Percentage of Households with Various Kinds of Equipment:
1960 to 1980

	1960	1970	1980
1. Television	87	95	98
2. Telephone	79	91	96
3. Vacuum Cleaner	74.3	92.0	99.9
4. Electric Toaster	72.0	92.6	99.9
5. Electric Coffee Maker	58.3	88.6	99.9
6. Electric Clothes Washer	55.4	62.1	77.3
7. Electric Blanket	23.6	49.5	64.2
8. Electric or Gas Clothes Dryer	19.6	44.6	61.5
9. Air Conditioner	12.4	36.7	57.3
10. Electric Dishwasher	7.1	26.5	43.0
11. Electric Can Opener	4.8	45.5	63.6

SOURCES, *by line:*
1. *Statistical Abstract, 1982–3*, p. 555. Industry estimate.
2. *Statistical Abstract, 1982–3*, p. 555. Industry estimate. The Census of Housing (*Statistical Abstract, 1982–3*, p. 751) reports lower levels of telephone service in 1970 and 1980, though not in 1960.
3 to 8, 10, and 11. *Statistical Abstract, 1982–3*, p. 758. These are industry estimates, covering only homes with electricity. By 1960 this bias should be negligible, but the data are still suspect (see text).
9. *Statistical Abstract, 1982–3*, p. 751.

telephones, vacuum cleaners, electric toasters, and electric coffee makers.

Lines 6 through 11 cover items that were not so widely diffused in 1970. For these items the gains of the 1970s were only marginally smaller than those of the 1960s. The two exceptions were electric blankets and electric can openers. Since some people actively dislike electric blankets, slow diffusion after 1970 may well have reflected consumer resistance rather than budget constraints. Similar factors may have been at work with electric can openers.

Table 2.8 does not include items introduced after 1960, but there is no reason to suppose that including such items would make the 1970s look worse than the 1960s. There was, for example, no increase in the ownership of microwave ovens or food processors during the 1960s, because these items were not commercially available at that time. By 1980, 10 to 15 percent of all households owned each of these items. Home video recorders had a slightly later start, but had reached 1.5 percent of all homes by 1980 and were expected to reach 10 percent by the end of 1983, despite the worst recession since World War II. Home computers were not far behind.

Tables 2.7 and 2.8 show steady improvement in the quality of the average American family's housing. The improvement during the 1970s appears to have been about as rapid as the improvement during the 1960s and 1950s. This is quite reassuring, since the increase in "real" rental values was also about the same during the 1970s as during the 1960s. It seems reasonable to conclude that BLS price deflators based on rental values work pretty well for housing, and that trends in the "constant dollar" rental value of housing provide a reasonable proxy for trends in the quality of housing.

Food Expenditures

Table 2.9 estimates food expenditures from 1950 to 1980. Line 1 shows the NIPA estimate of food purchases per capita in current dollars. If we inflate expenditures for earlier years to 1980 prices using the BLS food price deflator, we get the estimates in line 2. Since USDA food budgets suggest that children under 16 typically need to eat about three quarters as much as adults, line 3 estimates expenditure per "adult equivalent" on this assumption. Lines 2 and 3 tell essentially the same story, suggesting that people ate better and better during the 1950s and 1960s, but that there was no further improvement after

TABLE 2.9

Food Expenditures and Consumption: 1950 to 1980

	1950	1960	1970	1980
EXPENDITURE PER YEAR PER PERSON				
1. Current Dollars	354	449	677	1510
2. 1980 Dollars	1208	1298	1501	1510
PER ADULT EQUIVALENT				
3. 1980 Dollars	1305	1417	1629	1610
AS PERCENT OF DISPOSABLE INCOME				
4. Current Dollars	26.1	23.0	20.0	18.8
PRICE INDEX				
5. CPI (1980 = 100)	29.3	34.6	45.1	100
CONSUMPTION PER ADULT EQUIVALENT				
6. Calories	3510	3482	3624	3645
7. Protein (in Grams)	102	105	110	108

SOURCES, *by line:*
1. *Economic Report of the President, 1983,* p. 178.
2. Line 1/Line 5.
3. (Line 2) (Adult Equivalent Ratio), where the Adult Equivalent Ratio is equal to (Population)/(Population over 16 + [0.75] [Population under 16]).
4. *Economic Report of the President, 1983,* pp. 178 and 190.
5. Same as in note 4, Table 2.7.
6 and 7. (*Statistical Abstract, 1982–3,* p. 128) (Adult Equivalent Ratio).

1970.[17] Taken at face value these figures seem to contradict my argument that the material standard of living rose significantly during the 1970s. Instead, they suggest that the material standard of living stagnated, just as the RFI series implies.

[17]Unlike the BEA expenditure measure, the U.S. Department of Agriculture's food consumption index shows a slight rise between 1970 and 1980. Since this index weights items by price, it should in principle move in tandem with "real" expenditures. I have not tried to unravel the reasons for this apparent contradiction, but it must reflect differences in the weighting procedures employed by USDA and BEA. The USDA series appears in the *Statistical Abstract, 1982–3,* p. 127.
  To check the validity of the USDA and BEA series, I also looked at responses to a Gallup question about family food expenditures per week. For reasons I do not understand, responses to this question imply that Americans spent more on food in 1950 and less in 1980 than the BEA thought they did. Gallup responses imply that "real" food expenditures fell steadily from 1950 to 1980. The Gallup data appear in the *Gallup Report* for April 1983, p. 11. For another series with a still different trend, see the U.S. Department of Agriculture estimate of per capita food expenditures in the *Statistical Abstract, 1982–3,* p. 671.

The apparent leveling off of food expenditures represents a sharp break with the past. Cross-sectional surveys typically show that among families of any given size a 1.0 percent increase in after-tax income is associated with an increase of 0.5 percent in mean food expenditure. [18] Changes in mean income had analogous effects on mean food expenditure during the 1950s and 1960s. During the 1950s, for example, real after-tax income per "adult equivalent" rose by an average of 1.5 percent a year, while real food expenditure per adult equivalent rose by an average of 0.8 percent a year. During the 1960s the annual increases averaged 3.0 percent for real income and 1.4 percent for real food expenditure. The 1970s look completely different. Real after-tax income per adult equivalent rose 1.9 percent a year, but real food expenditure per adult equivalent fell 0.1 percent a year. Part of the change in the traditional relationship between income and food expenditure is presumably attributable to the fact that food prices rose somewhat faster than other prices (compare line 5 of Table 2.9 to line 4 of Table 2.1), but this cannot be the whole story. Other factors must also be at work.

The most plausible explanation for this puzzling development is, I believe, that Table 2.9 exaggerates the true increase in food prices during the 1970s and therefore underestimates the increase in the value shoppers assigned to their food purchases. Table 2.9 uses the BLS food price index to measure changes in food prices. This index measures the price of the market basket American shoppers bought in 1972. This 1972 market basket was essentially the same as the 1970 market basket. The fact that "real" expenditures look almost constant from 1970 to 1980 therefore tells us that shoppers spent enough in 1980 to buy the same market basket they were buying in 1970. But shoppers did not, in fact, buy the same market basket in 1980 as in 1970. Since they could afford the old market basket, but chose a new one in its place, they must have preferred the new one. In theory, we could estimate the monetary value of this change by seeing how much more shoppers were prepared to pay in 1980 for what they bought in 1980 than for what they bought in 1970. No one has done this, but the difference could be substantial. If we could take this difference into account we might well find that the value consumers placed on what they ate increased as much during the 1970s as during the 1960s or 1950s.

One reason shoppers bought a different mix of foods in 1980 than in 1970 was that relative prices had changed. All food prices rose during the 1970s, but some rose more than others. As relative prices changed, shoppers inevitably found that they could increase the amount of satis-faction they bought per dollar by allocating more of their budget to items whose price had risen slowly and less to items whose price had risen rapidly. This source of upward bias in food price indices was not new, of course. But if, as appears to be the case, relative prices changed more during the 1970s than during the 1960s or 1950s, the upward bias in conventional price indices is likely to be larger for the 1970s.[19]

A second reason why shoppers bought a different mix of foods in 1980 than in 1970 was that their tastes changed. Economists habitually assume that changes in taste have no effect on the utility that shoppers derive from their expenditures. In this case, however, changes in taste were partly due to increased knowledge about the effect of various foods on health and longevity. There is no reason to suppose that shoppers' underlying preference for health or longevity changed. What changed was their conviction that their diet would affect their health and longevity. In conventional economic terms this is not a true taste change. Instead, it is a change in people's ability to achieve fixed goals. In 1970, for example, most Americans still equated good nutrition with eating a lot of expensive meat. By 1980 many Americans had become convinced that cheaper foods were nutritionally superior to meat. As a result, the price of adequate nutrition rose less than the BLS food price index.

There is, of course, no universal rule ensuring that the price of ade-quate nutrition will always rise more slowly than the BLS food price in-dex. If Americans had become convinced that fish was the only healthy substitute for meat, for example, the price of adequate nutrition would have risen faster than the BLS food price index during the 1970s, not more slowly. In general, however, new knowledge about nutrition seems to increase demand for low-cost foods as much as demand for high-cost foods. Since new knowledge about nutrition also makes shoppers put more weight on nutritional considerations and less on traditional notions of palatability, and since the latter are highly corre-lated with price, new knowledge about nutrition usually makes it possi-ble to construct a new menu that costs no more than the old one and is superior in terms of overall consumer satisfaction.

Information about the way different foods affect health has, of course, been increasing since the 1920s, when knowledge about vita-mins became widespread. As a result, traditional price indices probably

[19]Laurits Christensen and Marilyn Manser, "Cost of Living Indexes for U.S. Meat and Produce, 1947–71," in Nestor E. Terleckyj, ed., *Household Production and Consumption*, Studies in Income and Wealth, No 40, National Bureau of Economic Research, 1975, con-clude that the bias is negligible. But their results are for a period of low inflation and they assume an atomized model of preference formation that seems unrealistic.

exaggerate the cost of improved nutrition throughout the past sixty years. In order to show that this bias was more severe during the 1970s than during the 1960s or 1950s, we must show that nutritional considerations exerted more effect on changes in food consumption during the 1970s than during the 1960s or 1950s. Testing this hypothesis rigorously would be a major undertaking, but published evidence seems to support it. The foods that health-conscious consumers seemed most anxious to avoid during the 1970s were meat, eggs, milk, butter, sugar, and coffee. Consumption of all these items fell.[20] Poultry, fish, fresh fruit, and fresh vegetables were preferred alternatives among the health-conscious. Consumption of all these items rose during the 1970s. Some of these changes could also be explained by budgetary considerations. Chicken is cheaper than meat, for example, and margarine is cheaper than butter. But fish is more expensive than meat, so the shift from meat to fish can hardly have reflected budgetary pressure. Likewise, the fact that people replaced canned fruit and vegetables with fresh fruit and vegetables can hardly have been a response to budgetary considerations, since canned goods are usually cheaper than fresh ones. When we turn back to the 1960s, the pattern of change in the typical shopping basket is quite different. Chicken and fish consumption rose, but so did meat consumption. Milk and butter consumption fell, but so did consumption of fresh fruit and vegetables. Coffee consumption fell, but sugar consumption rose. If we had asked health-conscious consumers in 1980 to choose between the typical diet of 1970 and the typical diet of 1960, it is not clear which they would have chosen. Thus, it seems fair to conclude that from the vantage point of 1980 the nutritional value of what Americans ate improved more during the 1970s than during the 1960s.

Analogous issues arise when we shift our attention from food expenditures to direct measures of food consumption, such as caloric and protein intake. Table 2.9 shows that both these measures rose during the 1950s and 1960s but were almost stable during the 1970s. By traditional standards this implies that improvement in American nutritional standards stopped around 1970. But traditional standards are not really applicable to either mean caloric intake or mean protein intake. Even in 1950 there were almost certainly more Americans who ate too much than who ate too little. During the 1970s a growing fraction of the population came to accept this medical judgment. The best seller lists were filled with books about the perils of eating too much, and especially about the perils of many traditional sources of protein, such as meat, milk, and eggs. As a result, consumers no longer believed that more was

[20]*Statistical Abstract, 1985*, p. 121.

necessarily better. Using caloric or protein intake to measure material well-being makes no more sense in late twentieth-century America than using alcohol or cigarette consumption for this purpose.

If we want to measure trends in the nutritional adequacy of what Americans ate, we need data on the distribution of caloric and protein intake, not data on the mean. Specifically, we need data on the percentage of the population eating less than some specified minimum and the percentage eating more than some specified maximum. Without such data we cannot tell whether increases in mean consumption during the 1950s and 1960s imply that more people ate adequately or that more people ate excessively. Conversely, we cannot tell whether mean consumption leveled off in the 1970s because overeating diminished or because more people were going hungry.

I know no published data that speak directly to these issues, but indirect evidence suggests that reductions in caloric and protein consumption during the 1970s were probably concentrated among overeaters. The Health and Nutrition Examination Survey (HANES) found that among the poor caloric intake per person *rose* slightly between 1971–74 and 1976–80. Among those above the poverty line, caloric intake fell slightly. The HANES data also show that while protein intake fell slightly among the poor, it fell even more among the nonpoor.[21] The HANES data thus suggest that food consumption fell among those most likely to be overeating. They are inconclusive with regard to trends among those most likely to eat too little.

Expenditures and Welfare

Taken as a group, Tables 2.6 to 2.9 suggest that because of technical innovation and increased knowledge the cost of "final" goods such as health and nutrition tends to rise less rapidly than the cost of "intermediate" goods such as medical services and steak. The case is clearest for health. "Constant dollar" medical expenditures grew slower during the 1970s than during the 1960s, but health improved faster. In the case of food, the standard measure of inflation suggests that shoppers' expenditures rose no faster than prices, but distributional evidence suggests that nutrition probably improved both among the poor and among the affluent. In the case of housing, there is no reason to suppose that conventional price indices yield biased results.[22] Overall, however, the evi-

[21] *Statistical Abstract*, 1985, p. 122.
[22] Jack Triplett provides an excellent review of research on this and related issues in "The Measurement of Inflation: A Survey of Research on the Accuracy of Price Indexes," in Paul Earl, ed., *Analysis of Inflation* (Lexington, Mass.: Lexington Books, 1975), pp. 19–82. Triplett's discussion does not deal with consumer services, however.

dence suggests that even the PCE deflator probably exaggerates inflation, and that this upward bias is probably greater in the 1970s than in the 1960s or 1950s. Neither the Census Bureau nor any other government agency can hope to construct price indices that solve this problem fully. They could, however, report them more candidly.

Bureaucracy, Ideology, and Social Statistics

The initial purpose of the Current Population Survey was to implement the Employment Act of 1946 by determining how many people were looking for work and unable to find it. The discovery that only 4 percent of those who wanted a job had not found one was therefore good news in 1948. But it did not remain news for long. By 1949 the "news" was that the unemployment rate had risen from 4 to 6 percent. If the initial figure had been 6 percent, it would probably have been greeted with the same huzzahs as 4 percent, since both figures were a marked improvement over the 1930s. But with 4 percent as a baseline, 6 percent was clearly a turn for the worse. The emphasis on trends rather than on absolute levels has continued to the present day. When unemployment falls from 10 to 9 percent, this is greeted with cheers. An increase from 6 to 9 percent is seen as a catastrophe. Thus, while the CPS was originally intended to measure the incidence of unemployment, its main political use is now to measure change.

Using the CPS to measure change poses few problems so long as we are concerned mainly with short-term changes. When the CPS showed that unemployment had risen from 4 percent in 1948 to 6 percent in 1949, the public was surely right to conclude that it had gotten harder to find work. And when the CPS showed that unemployment had fallen to 3 percent during the Korean War, it was right to conclude that finding work had gotten easier.

But while the CPS provides a good guide to short-run changes in the difficulty of finding work, it is a less certain guide to longer-term trends. Unemployment averaged 4.5 percent during the 1950s, 4.8 percent during the 1960s, 5.4 percent during the first half of the 1970s, and 7.0 percent during the second half of the 1970s. This long-term increase is comparable to the "peak to trough" swings during the recessions of 1949, 1958, and 1975. But it does not follow that it was harder to find a job in 1980, when unemployment averaged 7.1 percent, than in 1950, when it averaged 5.3 percent. If we look at *who* was unemployed, we find that among married men the unemployment rate actually fell, from 4.6 percent in 1950 to 4.2 percent in 1980. Unemployment increased only among unmarried men and among women. This could mean that employers discriminated against women and unmarried men more in 1980 than in 1950, but there is no obvious reason for such a change. Alternatively, the change could mean that women and unmarried men have raised their expectations and therefore have to spend longer looking for a job that meets these expectations. They may want a "good" job, not just "any" job, and may be willing to keep looking until they get what they want or until they get discouraged and drop out of the labor force. I know of no direct evidence for such attitudinal shifts among women or unmarried men. My point is merely that one must take such possibilities seriously when looking at thirty-year trends, whereas one need not pay much attention to them when looking at short-term changes.

Similar issues recur for virtually every kind of data available from the CPS, including family income. The problems with the RFI series are relatively minor when one is looking at change over a single year. But when one tries to assess income trends from 1970 to 1980, the problems multiply tenfold. And when one compares income growth during the 1970s to income growth during earlier decades, when many biases had opposite effects, one can easily end up drawing seriously misleading conclusions.

The Census Bureau's staff is certainly aware of these problems.[23] Yet it keeps publicizing the RFI series, not just as a measure of short-term change but also as a measure of long-term change. This practice raises three questions.

1. Why doesn't the Census Bureau draw more attention to what everyone knows are errors in the series, notably the use of the old CPI to convert "current" to "constant" dollars?
2. Why doesn't the bureau publicize other possible trend measures such as money income per person, money income per adult, or the median ratio of families' incomes to, say, the BLS "intermediate" budget for families of a given size and composition?
3. Why doesn't the bureau say more in its annual "Money Income" report about likely discrepancies between trends in real family income and trends in the standard of living?

My first hypothesis is that the Census Bureau has gone on publicizing the RFI series because it knows the series is widely accepted as a valid measure of change in the standard of living, even though no one on the professional staff would defend this interpretation. The Census

---

[23]For a Census Bureau publication dealing with some of the issues discussed here, see Gordon Green and Edward Welniak, "Changing Family Composition and Income Differentials," Bureau of the Census, Special Demographic Analyses, CDS-80-7 (Washington, D.C.: U.S. Government Printing Office, 1982).

Bureau's budget depends on its ability to convince OMB, the White House, and Congress that it serves a vital function. The claim that the bureau provides accurate, impartial, and timely information about changes in material well-being has become one of the primary rationales for Census surveys. The RFI series is a widely publicized, easily interpreted example of what such surveys seem able to tell us. No controversy now rages around the RFI series. Whereas BLS has been subject to a great deal of adverse criticism for the way it constructs the CPI, and had to "take sides" first with organized labor and then with management on this sensitive issue, no one has made a comparable fuss about the RFI series. From the Census Bureau's viewpoint, therefore, there is no compelling reason to alter the RFI series. Indeed, there is every reason not to rock the boat.

The Census Bureau's desire to avoid controversy has made it reluctant to say much of anything about the statistics it collects and publishes. The bureau has employed a number of distinguished scholars over the years, and it still does today. These scholars have turned out valuable research papers and have greatly improved the quality of the data the bureau collects and the tables it publishes. They have done far less to improve the text of the Census Bureau's regular reports. Bureau publications offer hundreds of millions of numbers, but they offer readers little guidance in interpreting these numbers. Helping readers interpret numbers—or even helping them avoid the most common misinterpretations—evidently threatens the "objective" image that the bureau cultivates. The text accompanying CPS reports usually reads like a "public information" handout, not a serious analysis of evidence. Even the technical appendices, which are supposed to describe the sources and limitations of the data, are remarkably skimpy. It is as if any shift from numbers to prose spelled danger, even when the prose is largely technical. In the case of technical appendices, though, the danger is not that the prose will be controversial but that by enumerating the many ambiguities surrounding the interpretation of its findings the bureau will encourage nonspecialists to dismiss the findings altogether.

The bureau's impulse to let its data "speak for themselves" means that it can only communicate with the public using "everyday language" categories and assumptions. The RFI series illustrates the results of this approach. To the average reader—and, indeed, to many rather sophisticated readers—its meaning is "obvious." Readers make a series of simplifying assumptions about the world that eliminate most of the ambiguities discussed earlier, and the bureau makes the same assumptions—or at least encourages readers to make them—when it reports its findings.

When the bureau begins a report by saying, "The average American family experienced a significant decline in real income between 1979 and 1980," readers imagine an "average" family, composed of a mother, a father, two children, and a Golden Retriever. Then they assume that this particular family's income rose less between 1979 and 1980 than the price of the things it had bought in 1979. As a result, they imagine that the family had to give up consuming some goods and services.

As I have indicated, the reality behind the bureau's opening sentence is far more complicated than the one readers conjure up. This is always true in social science. Sentences of finite length can never describe reality fully. The question is not whether the bureau has simplified reality but whether it has simplified reality in ways that are likely to mislead the reader. It seems to me perfectly reasonable for the bureau to speak of changes in the income of "the average family," even though it did not in fact follow families over time and did not correct its estimates for the fact that the members of any specific family would inevitably have been a year older in 1980 than in 1979. Indeed, it seems reasonable to speak of the experience of "the average family" even though this hypothetical family was slightly smaller in 1980 than 1979, and therefore needed less money to maintain its standard of living.

I have more trouble with the second sentence of the same report, which says that "a 13.5 percent increase in consumer prices between 1979 and 1980 caused a 5.5 percent decline in real median family income." Consumer prices did not, in fact, rise 13.5 percent between 1979 and 1980. Only the Consumer Price Index rose by that amount, and the bureau knew perfectly well by the time this sentence appeared that the CPI exaggerated inflation. (The Appendix to this particular Census report concedes this point, though without acknowledging its implications.) The PCE deflator rose only 10.3 percent between 1979 and 1980, suggesting that purchasing power fell 2.7 percent, not 5.5 percent.

My second general hypothesis is that while the RFI series would never have survived in its present form if it had been subjected to serious outside criticism, it escaped outside criticism because it told a story most outsiders already accepted for other reasons. As I noted at the outset, the RFI series seems to show that the postwar economic boom petered out in the 1970s. This belief is almost universally accepted, for at least five reasons. First, while the CPI exaggerates the rate of inflation, *any* index would show more inflation during the 1970s than ever before in America's peacetime history. This created the impression that the economy was "out of control." Second, while the unemployment statistics cited earlier cannot be taken completely at face value, new labor market entrants clearly had a harder time finding the kinds of jobs they wanted in the late 1970s than in the 1960s or 1950s. This was especially true for college graduates, whose fate exerts a disproportionate influence on opinion leaders. Third, the economic situation of college professors deteriorated relative to that of the general population, so they were especially inclined to assume that the economy had turned sour. And college professors are the main group likely to engage in serious criticism of the RFI series. Fourth, America's ability to compete in international markets deteriorated. Fifth, worker productivity rose less during the 1970s than during the 1960s or 1950s, and completely stagnated after 1977. Part of this apparent problem may also be attributable to poor measurement, but that was not the whole story.

Taken together, these developments convinced many people that hard times had arrived. This judgment was probably correct. There were sound reasons for questioning America's ability to improve its standard of living as much during the last quarter of the twentieth century as it had during the third quarter of the century. But it does not follow that the standard of living was stagnant or falling, as many imagined. This illusion rested on our collective readiness to "hear" evidence that sounded bad, while ignoring evidence that sounded good.

Had there been a lot of scholars eager to show that the American economy was still capable of "delivering the goods," the gloomy implications of the RFI series might have gotten more critical scrutiny. But by the late 1970s virtually nobody was trying to show that the American economy was a success. Radicals had never wanted to believe this, even in the 1960s. Conservatives, who had traditionally argued that the economy was basically healthy and just needed to be left free from government intervention, went on the attack in the 1970s, arguing that government intervention should be reduced. To justify this argument they needed to show that we "couldn't afford" the kinds of well-intentioned interventions that had taken place over the previous seventy years. Liberals, who had traditionally argued that the economy was healthy enough to support a steadily growing welfare state, were increasingly pessimistic about government's capacity to patch up the damage done by the private sector. Skepticism about the welfare state led many liberals to look for a "new relationship" between the public and private sectors, in which private firms would take more responsibility both for their employees' welfare and for the public welfare, and the public sector would therefore be freed from many of its responsibilities. To make this argument, liberals needed to argue that the traditional mores of American private enterprise were no longer capable of motivating workers. If one wanted to argue, for example, that major American corporations should emulate their Japanese competitors by offering permanent employment to blue collar workers, it was very helpful to be able to assert that American firms were less efficient than their Japanese competitors.

As a result of these ideological shifts, virtually everyone had a stake in showing that the American economy was in a shambles. Since the RFI series seemed to support this view, nobody questioned it. This is not to say that *all* gloomy statistics were accepted at face value. Unemployment statistics, for example, came in for a lot of criticism from conservatives, because conservatives had a stake in minimizing the perceived cost of restrictive fiscal and monetary policies and the perceived need to help those who could not find work. Inflation statistics were also subject to a lot of criticism, for while some conservatives were happy to overestimate inflation in order to justify more stringent fiscal and monetary policies, many businessmen wanted to underestimate it, in order to justify giving their employees smaller annual pay increases. Productivity statistics, in contrast, got relatively little attention. Management blamed lagging productivity on labor, while labor blamed it on management. A few economists argued that the problem was a statistical illusion, but almost nobody listened.

Overall, one must conclude that both ideology and self-interest helped shape the statistical climate of the late 1970s and early 1980s, determining which statistical series would be carefully examined and which series would be accepted at face value. In many cases ideology and self-interest conflicted. In the case of the RFI series, though, ideology was critical and self-interest relatively unimportant. No private interest group had a direct stake in what the RFI series showed. The Ford and Carter administrations had a stake in making their own performance look better, but this stake was not great enough to make anyone in the White House look carefully at the series and ask how it could be made to tell a more encouraging story. Perhaps nobody whose primary loyalty was to the party in power realized that the RFI series could be legitimately faulted for making things look worse than they were. Or perhaps no political appointee wanted to challenge the bureau's traditional procedures, since the political risks of appearing to tamper with the federal statistical apparatus outweighed the likely gains. This certainly seems to have been the case in the battle over the Consumer Price Index. The CPI made the Nixon, Ford, and Carter administrations look bad, and it exacerbated inflation by increasing the cost-of-living allowances given many workers. Yet even after the Carter administration realized all this, it refused to change the CPI, because it knew any such change would be widely interpreted as an effort to "lie about inflation."

When a statistical procedure has been in place for many years, *any* change will be carefully scrutinized for partisan motives. Perhaps the most troubling implication of the RFI story is that we have created a political system in which federal statistical agencies often find it safer to go on doing something wrong year after year than to make improvements.

3

POLITICAL PURPOSE
AND THE NATIONAL ACCOUNTS

MARK PERLMAN

ECONOMIC data are constantly used in the interpretation of economic events and the formulation of economic policies by both
government and the private sector. But which data are collected
and how they are manipulated and analyzed depend on the underlying
objectives of a statistical system. If and when the purposes of a system
are redefined, new objectives may require different choices in data collection and analysis.

This chapter takes as a case study the growth of national income
accounting in the United States from 1933 to the present, focusing on
its intellectual origins and changes in objectives during the formative
period 1933 to 1948. It is not presented as a comprehensive history of
the construction of the national accounts since several excellent his-

NOTE: This chapter is part of a larger project on the American contribution to
modern empirical economics. That project has been supported by grants given by The Institute for Advanced Study, where I was a Member during the 1981–82 academic year, and
by the Rockefeller Foundation's research program at the Villa Serbelloni (Bellagio, Lake
Como, Italy), where I was a Resident Scholar during April–May 1983. It is a pleasant duty
to acknowledge their interest and help.

tories are already available.[1] I stress as my theme the several shifts in the main uses for which our accounting system has been designed. My interest is to identify changes in the socioeconomic philosophical choices underlying the measurement of national income.

My point of departure is the recognition that those who participated in designing the national accounts, beginning in 1933, have had, at different times, distinct and partially conflicting objectives. Economists have wanted variously to use the national accounts to measure or identify: (1) the distribution of income and of the costs of government; (2) the extent of unused capacity in various sectors of the economy; (3) the sources of economic growth; (4) pecuniary well-being; and (5) the fluctuations of the business cycle so as to design economic stabilization policies.

This discussion of the changes in the principal purposes of national accounting aims to bring out the choices that were faced, the alternatives accepted and rejected, and what the cost of the decisions may have been.

[1]In 1980 the U.S. Department of Commerce published *Reflections of America: Commemorating the Statistical Abstract Centennial.* Within it there are several short chapters dealing with various aspects of economic materials as they emerged in the Statistical Abstracts; in particular, see John Kenneth Galbraith, "The National Accounts: Arrival and Impact," pp. 75–80.
There are several excellent histories of the development of the American government's interest in statistical material. Among the best is the one by Joseph W. Duncan and William C. Shelton, *Revolution in United States Government Statistics, 1926–1976* (Washington, D.C.: U.S. Department of Commerce, Office of Federal Statistical Policy and Standards, 1978), which covers in detail and with apparent accuracy much of the material I summarize here. What it does not do, and what I shall undertake, is to discuss the foregone choices made by the designers of our national account system. But it goes far beyond my efforts in describing the variety of social, including economic, statistics that the federal government has undertaken. It was followed by a second volume, intended to peer into the future, Duncan and Shelton, *A Framework for Planning U.S. Federal Statistics for the 1980's Government Statistics, 1926–1976* (Washington, D.C.: U.S. Department of Commerce, Office of Federal Statistical Policy and Standards, 1978).
There are also two indispensable summary histories of the American experience in the development of its present national accounting institutions. The first is by Carol S. Carson, "The History of the United States National and Product Accounts: The Development of an Analytical Tool," *Review of Income and Wealth* 21 (June 1975):153–81. A second is by John W. Kendrick, "The Historical Development of National Income Accounts," *History of Political Economy* 2 (Fall 1970):284–315, which goes back to before the period covered by Carson. But I have found no historic treatment, particularly with the fascinating early English experiments, that begins to touch the quality of "The Use of National Income Statistics in English Economic Thought in the Seventeenth and Eighteenth Centuries," chap. 2 of George Jaszi, "The Concept of National Income and National Product with Special Reference to Government Transactions" (Ph.D. diss., Harvard University, 1946). Another useful account is by Richard Ruggles, "The United States National Income Accounts, 1947–1977: Their Conceptual Basis and Evolution," in Murray F. Foss, ed., *The U.S. National Income and Product Accounts: Selected Topics* (Chicago: University of Chicago Press, 1983).

Origins of National Income Measurement in the United States

Although a few studies of national income and wealth appeared in the mid-nineteenth century, the first modern study was published in 1896 by Charles B. Spahr, a writer on economic topics. Socialism and the distribution of income and taxation were timely topics, and Spahr's approach carries the appropriate hallmarks. In estimating the distribution of American income and wealth during the 1880s and 1890s, he wanted to determine whether the working classes bore the heaviest burden in financing government. On the basis of his findings he argues that because of regressive taxation, a large and growing share of the cost of the federal government was borne by the laboring class. [2]

Spahr's pro-working class, if not actually socialist, conclusions helped to stimulate a lengthy 1915 study for the period 1850–1910 by Willford Isbell King at the University of Wisconsin. Although King was primarily interested in measuring changes in the distribution of income and wealth, his work reflected the prewar concern that the shift in origins of immigrants to the United States meant the defeat of the Jeffersonian ideal of economic equality. King's conclusions, as I read them, were simultaneously antimonopolist and Malthusian. First, he noted the tremendous growth of manufacturing and other economic output. Second, he concluded that concentration of income was even greater than when Spahr had written, but that much of the change had come at the expense not of the poor but of the middle classes. However, the propensity of the poor (and I interpret this to mean particularly the immigrant poor) to have excessively large families was likely to keep them impoverished, even as average incomes rose.

King's interest in economic class structure continued after he moved to New York University, and when the National Bureau of Economic Research (NBER) was established in 1920, he became one of its earliest professional associates. He undertook to measure national income and its distribution, using estimates from the sources of production. Oswald W. Knauth, another of the early NBER associates, undertook similar measurements, using distributed and undistributed incomes. As the results from the two methods for the period 1909–19 appeared to be the same (within about 7 percent), King and Knauth were satisfied that their findings were correct. Published in 1921–22, these findings stressed that concentration of wealth had diminished during

---

[2]This is discussed rather fully in Paul Studenski, *The Income of Nations*, vol. 1 (New York: New York University Press, 1961), pp. 132–34.

the wartime period. King found that the top 5 percent of the population were receiving less of the total national dividend than at the time of his 1915 study. The middle classes seemed to be moving toward greater equality of income.

In an effort to extend his conclusions, King decided to include estimates of unrealized capital gains as an element of income. This decision led to a conflict with several other economists working on the measurement of national income; among these was Sir Josiah Stamp, an English economist. In the exchanges between them, King lost the capital gains battle and apparently much of his professional standing in the subfield of national accounts. In any event, the NBER decided to reform its approach to national income accounting. At this point Simon Kuznets entered the scene. Lest we lose sight too soon of King and his interest, it is worth stressing that his approach to national accounts, unlike Spahr's, focused on the size distribution of income (even more than wealth). What reduced King's influence were his limitations as a statistician, specifically, his reliance upon too-fragile data and his apparent inability to conceptualize alternative approaches to his problem.[3] By 1931, when Kuznets took over the national income work of the NBER, he was already a recognized and, for his age, seasoned scholar. Like Spahr, he had a strong interest in the economics of social class relations.[4] He had by this time written several major works. In the most important, *Seasonal Variations in Industry and Trade* (1933), Kuznets thoroughly analyzed the reliability of available data as well as the problem of choosing the optimal techniques of statistical manipulation. The study provides an imaginative discussion of the underlying political question about which social classes bore the costs and gained the benefits of seasonality in manufacturing.

In his work on national accounts, Kuznets was initially concerned with the same questions that had interested both Spahr and King: (1) whether the poor and the wage workers were bearing a disproportionate (and possibly growing) share of the costs of an industrial society; and (2) whether workers' incomes were rising in relative or in absolute terms. But Kuznets's interests went beyond theirs to the causes of economic growth. Briefly put, as much as he was interested in the old socialist questions about the burdens of the working class, Kuznets was equally and even more interested in the Schumpeterian problem of the triggers of economic growth.

[3]King continued his work in the area, even under NBER sponsorship. See Willford Isbell King, *The National Income and Its Purchasing Power* (New York: National Bureau of Economic Research, 1930).

[4]See Mark Perlman, "Jews and Contributions to Economics: A Bicentennial Review," *Judaism* 25 (Summer 1976):301–311.

Kuznets's initial explicit work in national accounts is to be found in his article, "National Income." His opening statement is worth quoting because it illustrates the breadth of his ultimate objective:

> National Income may be defined *provisionally* as the net total of commodities and services (economic goods) produced by the people comprising a nation; as the total of such goods received by the nation's individual members in return for their assistance in producing commodities and services; as the total of goods consumed by these individuals out of the receipts thus earned; or, finally as the net total of desirable events enjoyed by the same individuals in their double capacity as producers and consumers. Defined in any one of these fashions national income is the end product of a country's economic activity, reflecting the combined play of economic forces and serving to appraise the prevailing economic organization in terms of its returns.[5]

Kuznets then turns his attention to the uses of such information. These include measuring: (1) the comparative productivity of nations; (2) per capita welfare; (3) the constancy of income flow (another per capita welfare consideration); (4) the rate of growth of the nation's economy, if the analysis were maintained over sufficient time; (5) the distribution of income among social classes; and (6) the division of income between consumption and other uses.

Pointing out some difficulties in using available figures, Kuznets accepted as a necessary compromise the idea that national income accounting nets to cruder approximations of income received or consumed. He then asks where the summary of "the combined play of economic forces" might best be seen. Is it at the levels of production, distribution, or consumption? This became his principal operative question. True, each level allows for measurement, but what best measures our objective? Is it mostly an effort merely to summarize the production process, or to appraise its organization, possibly for reasons of augmenting output? Kuznets apparently concluded that income received by individuals "after it leaves the productive units proper and before it has been diverted into the various channels of consumption" provides the best and most versatile measure for the analysis of both welfare and growth.

Among the measurement problems Kuznets faced, none was more difficult than measuring the value of the multifarious activities of government. The economy can be perceived as an interplay of production and consumption forces. On the consumption side are things

---

[5]Simon Kuznets, "National Income," *Encyclopedia of the Social Sciences*, vol. 11, pp. 205–224 (New York: Macmillan, 1933), p. 205.

directly consumed (final product), indirectly consumed (intermediate product), and deferred for later consumption (inventories, consumer durables, or consumption hoards). On the production side, the evaluation is more or less straightforward in the private sector; the price paid by the buyer is the value of the product or the service. But the question becomes thornier when dealing with such complex institutional realities as the government and the banking system. How does one price those services of the government for which no payment seems to be made? The technique has been to argue that they are worth what is paid for them; but what is paid for them is not for the output but for the input. As the economic role of government expands, the assumption that the value of the output is defined by the cost of the input affects an increasingly important part of our totals.

Ultimately, Kuznets gets to the accounting problem in differentiating between physical and human capital (of course, the latter term was then not in current use). The value of the output of the former is affected by depreciation (even by obsolescence), but it is not easy to find a comparable method for evaluating the changes in the "remaining productive value" of the individual. One can see the value of one's physical capital being diminished as it is being transferred to output. Can one say the same for labor? To Kuznets, as I read his 1933 work, the answer is clearly *no*. But Kuznets's answer, as I understand it, does not satisfy him.

Two additional points should be stressed: Kuznets was critically concerned about the role of economic organization and the societal importance of the distribution of family income. He wanted most to stress his interests in income distribution, economic growth, and the roles played by banking and particularly government institutions in stimulating economic growth. Kuznets did not focus on economic stabilization as an area of comparable importance.

National Accounting Becomes a Government Function

In June 1932 the U.S. Senate passed a resolution requesting the secretary of commerce "to report . . . estimates of the total national income of the United States for each of the calendar years of 1929, 1930, and 1931." The resolution specified that the work was to be done by the Bureau of Foreign and Domestic Commerce (BFDC). It soon became clear that the bureau's personnel was inadequate to the task. The secretary turned for help to Wesley Clair Mitchell, head of the NBER, who asked Kuznets, now professor of statistics at the University of Pennsylvania, to oversee the establishment of a cadre to organize the new statistical system. Thus, for about two years after January 1933 he was in weekly contact with the department's statistical data-processing unit. In January 1934 Kuznets submitted a 261-page report, which included material for the unasked-for year 1932 as well.

Thus the first set of governmental accounts came out. Kuznets, however, left the BFDC, returning to the National Bureau where he maintained his interest in national accounts. After an internal struggle, the BFDC did get the national accounting program operationally established.[6] It was Robert F. Martin who stressed that regular and prompt publication of these accounts permitted their use for multiple purposes. He argued that the administration needed accurate and adequately classified national income data in order to design appropriate welfare and economic recovery programs; that the Internal Revenue Service needed such data for making projections, based on a variety of changes in the tax laws; that these data were invaluable to business for market analysis and to scholars for research; and that only the federal government had the resources essential to the checking (thereby insuring the reliability) of the vast amount of data involved. Thus developed an identifiable new objective for national income accounting, namely, an equitable, efficient, reliable, and speedy numbers supply, essential to the experimental functions associated with economic reform through legislative action.

Martin left the BFDC shortly after the report came out and was replaced by one of Kuznets's University of Pennsylvania graduate students, Robert R. Nathan.[7] Nathan's staff, again very small, produced two bulletins: *National Income in the United States 1929–35* (1936), and *National Income in the United States 1929–1936* (1937). The previous format and emphases remained, the only major innovation being revision of some of the earlier estimates. One of the major problems of any government statistical agency is the necessity of getting its data out

---

[6]Duncan and Shelton, *Revolution*, quote Carol S. Carson, "The History of the United States Income and Products Accounts," as the basis for a lengthy account of bureaucratic in-fighting about the regularization of the national accounts research work in the Department of Commerce. The problems were apparently legion: (1) Congress had not appropriated funds; (2) Kuznets and those whom he had brought into the effort did not remain with the Commerce Department's Bureau of Foreign and Domestic Commerce (BFDC); (3) the secretary had little sympathy for the effort and refused to allocate funds for printing an updated version (including data for 1933). These 1933 data did appear in the department's *Survey of Current Business*, in the January, August, and November 1935 issues and in the July 1936 issue. The BFDC, largely under the leadership of Willard Thorp and Robert F. Martin, and aided by Winfield Riefler, chairman of the Central Statistical Board, did get the program institutionalized and congressionally funded.

[7]Martin went to the National Industrial Conference Board ". . . where he was a frequent critic of the Department of Commerce figures." Duncan and Shelton, *Revolution*, p. 80.

quickly; speed and accuracy are basically trade-offs, and the obvious solution is not to hold up publication but to publish later revised figures when the corrections become available. By 1937, national income figures began to be published in preliminary *monthly* form. The monthly data were regarded as essential for estimating current and near-future purchasing power and for inferring near-future levels of business output, including the demand for employment.

In retrospect, we see that three somewhat unrelated developments occurred during this period. Together they shifted the national accounts system significantly from the broad outlines of Kuznets's 1933 blueprint and from the contextual composition of the 1934 publication. The first was the passage in 1935 of the Social Security Act, which called for massive employee and employer contributions to retirement funds. Combined with welfare (relief) payments and the one-time payment of World War I bonuses to veterans, these transfers put a strain on the simplicity of Kuznets's 1933 definition of payments to business firms and individuals for goods and services provided. The Kuznets definition was accordingly modified, this being the first of several major movements away from his 1933 architectural blueprint.

The second was the publication in 1936 of Maynard Keynes's *The General Theory of Employment, Interest, and Money*, which triggered a major professional effort at redesigning macroeconomic (a word then all but unknown) policies for full-employment stabilization. Looking back, we see clearly that the Keynesian formulation offered a theoretical system, and thereafter many, indeed most, of those who worked on the national accounts wanted their work to reflect and to be integratable with what the Keynesian analysis offered. Kuznets's blueprint did not begin to offer a well-knit theoretical system; indeed, anyone familiar with Kuznets's work recognized his preference for empirical rather than *a priori* research.[8] Thus, with the appearance of a *theory*, certainly something easier to grasp than an endless literature of historical generalizations, the Kuznets-NBER influence among the national-income specialists first acquired a rival in Keynes and later lost considerable ground.

The third major factor entering the stage in this period was the obvious failure of the 1936 business revival, signaled by the business recession of 1937–38, an event that seemed to confirm the fear that the country faced a period of indefinite economic stagnation and large-scale unemployment. This fear so dominated the thinking of the period that

[8]There was an exchange of correspondence (April through August 1936) between Kuznets and Keynes after the publication of Keynes's *The General Theory of Employment, Interest and Money*. The letters dealt with Keynes's mishandling of data on capital formation. (*The Collected Writings of John Maynard Keynes*, XXIX pp. 188–206).

the principal focus of the whole accounting system fastened on measuring consumer purchasing power as the means to economic recovery.

Federal peacetime deficit financing, though known to and employed by President Herbert Hoover, had also been well advertised as the principal hallmark of the New Deal recovery program, even before Keynes's book appeared. In Washington, "pump-priming" had become by 1937 a regular if not exactly a successful policy. This perception, later synthesized by Abba Lerner and others as a program of "functional finance," was at the time being touted in Washington by Professor Alvin Hansen of Harvard and Lauchlin Currie, assistant director of research and statistics at the Federal Reserve Board. In any case, the kind of economy for which Kuznets's 1933 blueprint had been drawn was less and less the actual case. By the mid- and late 1930s, the federal government's role in the economy had expanded, and whether the Kuznets 1933 perception could have been implemented is now a moot question. In practice, the government's various roles in the economy were held to be *sui generis*, and all its economic activities were segregated for accounting purposes.

As already mentioned, by 1937 monthly national income estimates were being made and published. Another change occurring during this same period was the disaggregation of national accounts by state. Duncan and Shelton report that this series attracted immediate and vast business interest, and by October 1938 the estimates included: (1) the addition of direct relief payments and the veterans' bonus; (2) the deduction of the workers' contribution to the Social Security funds; and (3) the addition of payments from these same funds.[9] What was now being emphasized was the frequent measurement of short-period changes of potential purchasing power by local area.

Emphasis on measuring purchasing power, the principal Keynesian key to unlocking the door to economic recovery, took other forms as well. After several somewhat unsuccessful efforts, the Commerce Department in 1941 began to publish reports on retail sales, manufacturers' inventories, orders, and shipments. The department also took into account Kuznets's own post-1934 work on commodity flows and capital formation. The goal here was further to improve the quality of the consumer expenditure data.

At this point two shifts could clearly be seen. The first was the rapid emergence of a wholly new set of economic problems. The characteristic Depression crisis of overproduction was replaced rapidly by the 1938–40 rearmament crisis of underproduction; chronic unemployment

---

[9]Duncan and Shelton, *Revolution*.

was giving way to the specter of price inflation. The other shift was more personal. Kuznets's one-time student, Milton Gilbert, took over the leadership of the whole national economic account effort.

For expository purposes I discuss the Gilbertian influence first. Gilbert, unlike his immediate predecessors, not only felt thoroughly qualified to take charge of the national accounts program; he also decided to change the focus of its presentation to make it readily adaptable to the incoming Keynesian macroeconomic mode. In brief, the new format was a standardized report meant to mirror at short intervals (not impeded by delayed preparation) the economy as it was actually operating, from the standpoint of both its immediate past and the quickly developing inflationary pressures. With the *tour d'horizon* offered by the mirror, policies could be quickly modified as their shortcomings became evident.

It is important to stress that at about this time the British, under the leadership of James Meade and Richard Stone, were compiling for Churchill's war cabinet an accounts system that would reveal any possible slack areas that could be filled with orders for war material. In his biography of Maynard Keynes, Roy Harrod describes the origins of this wartime attempt to assess the economic capabilities of the British economy.[10] These origins, in Harrod's view, lay with E. A. G. Robinson's efforts to implement Keynes's *How to Pay for the War*. Robinson brought together Meade and Lionel Robbins, the former something of a Keynesian (although in truth many of the so-called Keynesian principles Meade had anticipated before 1936). Meade was then paired with Stone, and in the winter of 1940–41 the two rushed through an analysis of income and expenditure, published at the time of the 1941 budget.[11] The English developments influenced American events, but what was happening on the American side proceeded almost completely independently.

The American events of the period 1940–42 are remarkable for many reasons. Talent was quickly identified and employed; new concepts were quickly developed and discussed; and the national accounts system as we know it seemed to emerge almost overnight. True, in a general academic way, the British in some sense were leading the way; the publication in 1940 of John R. Hicks's "The Valuation of the Social

---

[10]Roy Forbes Harrod, *The Life of John Maynard Keynes* (New York: Kelley, 1969).

[11]Stone (now Sir Richard) and Meade have individually recounted to me the skimpiness of the resources allocated to them by the Treasury in the first stages of their efforts. Initially denied even a calculator, they were able to proceed only because Stone, very much the junior of the two, owned a hand-operated model. Their stories of Meade's looking up the numbers and Stone's pushing the buttons and turning the crank, only to discover empirically that comparative advantage lay in the reversal of the assignments, emphasizes more than anything else the magnificence of their achievement.

Income" opened the eyes of the profession to the wholly new set of wartime "overconsumption" problems. Hicks's terminology was not completely new, although his use of the term *gross national product* (initially used in a slightly different sense by Clark Warburton in 1934) gave a completely different slant to the national income analysis routine. GNP was defined as national income plus business taxes plus depreciation and other capital charges. It included not only civilian economic activity but also government expenditures, which in wartime were particularly important. Hicks's paper introduced the basic equation:

$$GNP = C + I + G$$

where C stands for consumption, I for investment, and G for government expenditure.

While the British were making these innovations, developments in the United States led to the formation of the now-familiar national accounts system. Robert R. Nathan and Simon Kuznets, at that time both employed at the War Production Board, were responsible for estimating how quickly and to what levels the economy would be able to switch to war production.[12] The accomplishments of the Kuznets-Nathan group during the less than two years between 1941 and 1943 are awe-inspiring. The board had informed the White House that the maximum

---

[12]On January 16, 1942, the president created the War Production Board, with Donald M. Nelson as its chairman. Nelson set up several staff (advisory) bodies that reported directly to him and whose duties were to advise him with regard to the actual orders his office was issuing concerning production allocation priorities. One of these advisory committees was the Office of Progress Reports, headed by Stacy May. Another, set up in February 1942, was the Planning Committee; its chairman was Robert Nathan. In May 1942 Nathan asked Kuznets to join him. Kuznets had previously been working with the statistical group, an association he managed to continue. Somewhat earlier (before the Japanese attack on Pearl Harbor), the administration had felt the pressure, largely focused by a French refugee, Jean Monnet (who was an official on the joint Anglo-French purchasing commission), to formulate an overall production program designed to achieve military victory in Europe. By the end of September 1941, even before the United States was formally at war, the administration established a $150 billion Victory Program, which was targeted for achievement of its goal and invasion of the European continent by mid-1943. The Victory Program gave rise to the feasibility and the inflationary gap questions. The events of Pearl Harbor, of course, changed the previous plans. The goals were revised upward, thus exacerbating the twin problems of feasibility and inflation. In due course, Kuznets prepared and Nathan sent several memoranda to Nelson regarding the achievable limits. These memoranda were subjected to what eventually was harsh criticism. The history of the bureaucratic skirmishing is well detailed in John F. Brigante, "The Feasibility Dispute: Determination of War Production Objectives for 1942 and 1943" (Washington, D.C.: Committee on Public Administration Cases, 1950). In the end, there were several historically important results; the critical one was that the Kuznets-Nathan approach was accepted by the military not only for the prosecution of World War II but also for its future military planning.

output goals for 1942 would amount to about 40,000 tanks and about 50,000 airplanes. The day after receiving these estimates, President Roosevelt informed the Congress that his goal was 60,000 planes for 1942 and no less than 125,000 for 1943. He "upped" the tank promise for 1942 from 40,000 to 45,000 and for 1943 he "promised" 75,000. And he revised the output of merchant shipping, which the board had thought would amount to 7 million tons in 1942, to 8 million tons for that year and an all but unbelievable 20 million tons in 1943. Such promises gave rise to two related problems: Were the plans *feasible*, and what would be their *inflationary* impact?

The effort by Nathan and Kuznets to work out the principles of American military procurement planning was to become one of the great technical triumphs in the history of the economics discipline. The Nathan-Kuznets group estimated how and where the American economy could summon the resources to meet the new targets. In effect, it was telling the armed forces that military procurement was a "science." To ask for too little was to prolong the conflict; to ask for too much was to inflate costs without producing significantly more. To look to the wrong sectors was to hamper technological innovation; to look to the right sectors was to minimize the pecuniary and nonpecuniary costs of the war. Anyone who thinks that the armed forces, particularly the army, were willing students has only to look at the narrative of John Brigante. But anyone who concludes that the lesson cannot be successfully taught has only to look at the record. The War Production Board, over violent opposition and at the cost of the physical and emotional exhaustion of Nathan and Kuznets, managed to show how the goals could be achieved. This they did by relying on the national accounts system, as then produced by the Commerce Department, and on the accounts for capital formation that Kuznets had developed. What they helped to accomplish for 1942 was the expansion of national output by $17 billion through (1) more intensive use of the existing plant (for example, lengthening the work week by eliminating overtime pay for anything less than forty-five hours per week); (2) the transfer to war-related purposes of $7 billion worth of resources normally devoted to civilian capital formation (for example, residential or commercial construction); (3) depleting accumulated inventories (mostly consumer goods) in the amount of $4.5 billion; (4) reducing consumer demand by $7 billion by increasing taxation (not a signal success) and by consumer goods rationing; and (5) a variety of other, somewhat smaller, shifts designed to release resources.

As mentioned, Gilbert had taken charge of the national income accounts program in 1941. His acknowledgment of Kuznets's ideas, added to his grasp of what Meade and Stone were doing in Britain, led to the development of a new blueprint. His plan reflected not only the omnipresent specter of American defense preparations but also the Keynesian macroeconomic theoretical system, with its emphasis on postwar full-employment, compensatory government investment if necessary, and a federal program of income redistribution. In 1942 Gilbert published two critically important expository articles, using the national income/gross national product approach to explain both the wartime production allocation problem and the likely impact of the proposed solutions. His "War Expenditure and National Production" is an educational *tour de force,* including a projection of gross national product to fiscal 1943 in 1941 prices. In December 1941, he had laid out much of this analysis in a paper read before the American Statistical Association. Both works drew heavily on "The Construction of Tables of National Income, Expenditure, Savings, and Investment," published by Meade and Stone in 1941. Gilbert made two major contributions to the program. First, he was integrating actual recent numerical estimates with a Keynesian theoretical analysis to answer such timely questions as (1) how the peacetime economy could be converted to war purposes with the least inflationary impact; and (2) how the essential needs of the civilian economy could be successfully protected from wartime demands. Second, he was using the *Survey of Current Business,* with its fast printing turnaround time, to explain immediately the economics of the current war-production effort.[13]

National income accounting during these wartime years had as its avowed purpose the reallocation of productive resources and encouragement of certain areas of economic growth needed to win the war. But scarcely concealed by this purpose was Gilbert's continuing pedagogical effort to provide a set of national accounts mirroring the economy to show what government policy was doing and what, perhaps, it could do. War exigencies led the national accounts far from the types of objectives that either Spahr or King had had in mind.

One point should be added, indeed, stressed. The Commerce Department officials were greatly influenced by the English macroeconom-

---

[13]In all, the *Survey of Current Business* published the new research results including articles on changes in consumer income and expenditure (Bangs, 1942); on the gross flow of finished commodities and new construction (Shaw, 1942); on surveying the gross national product, 1929–41 (Gilbert and Bangs, 1942); on quarterly estimates of construction (Klein, 1942); on corporate profits and national income by quarters, 1938–42 (Smith and Merwin, 1942); on the distributive costs of consumption commodities (Fowler and Shaw, 1942); on the distribution of income payments by state, 1929–41 (Creamer and Merwin, 1942); on reviewing the national income and the war effort for the first half of 1942 (Gilbert and Bangs, 1942b); on estimating national business inventories, 1928–41 (Hance, 1942); on consumer expenditures for selected groups of services, 1929–41 (Denison, 1942); on monthly dividend payments, 1941–42 (Smith, 1942); and a general recapitulation of the 1942 national income and national product (Gilbert and Jaszi, 1943).

ic theory formulated largely by Keynes and the social accounting system worked out first by Meade and Stone and then largely refined by Stone. Hicks's *The Social Framework*, first published in 1942, helped to popularize national accounting. In 1945 the publication of an American edition under the adapted title, *The Social Framework of the American Economy*, capped the transformation of the discipline, which had so recently depended on Marshall's *Principles of Economics* plus the modifications regarding deviations from competition introduced by Edward Chamberlin and Joan Robinson.

The postwar growth of the American economy reinforced the economics profession's great confidence in the scientific basis of its discipline. That confidence reflected a well-grounded satisfaction that the newly developed expertise displayed by economists, achieved at forced draft, could make it not only possible but also almost easy to avert the economic disaster of the 1930s. The war experience had shown that economists like Gilbert and his associates, to say nothing of the more senior architects like Kuznets and Nathan, apparently could bring order out of chaos and organize quickly the material requirements for victory. If the war gave the medical profession antibiotics, it gave economists new tools and techniques and comparable optimism about what their future role would be. Immediately at the war's end, the American group on national income accounting turned to preparing an integrated set of accounts. It appeared in a supplement to the July 1947 *Survey of Current Business* under the title, "National Income and Product Statistics of the United States, 1929–46." Its publication seemed like the keystone to the economists' arch—theory and observation now fit neatly together.

The 1947 publication drew heavily on Richard Stone's systematizing of social accounts. Using the form of traditional double-entry bookkeeping, it introduced several elements that were not strictly a debit–asset comparison. The supplement was a lengthy document with forty-two annual tables (covering more or less completely the data for the years 1929–46), five quarterly tables for 1939–46, and a monthly table for 1929–46. An industry breakdown included twenty tables in manufacturing and an additional thirty-seven in other areas. Care was taken to explain thoroughly the sources of the data. In addition, the data were presented so that for the first time it was possible "to compare corporate profits with wages, salaries and supplements paid by corporations." The whole was displayed in six basic tables, called (in the tradition of double-entry bookkeeping) "T-accounts": National Income and Product Account; Consolidated Business Income and Product Account; Consolidated Government Receipts and Expenditures Account;

Rest of the World Account; Personal Income and Expenditure Account; and Gross Saving and Investment Account.

The 1947 study was widely hailed and extensively reviewed. But it met with serious criticism from the original architect, Kuznets. In a lengthy critique published in 1948, Kuznets repeated his position that any "view of national income as a *net* product total . . . can be defined only in relation to *some end-goal of economic activity*." But the Commerce Department did not clearly define the end-goal.

Kuznets's approach is characteristically historical. From the time of Quesnay the conventional approach had been to perceive a country's economy as an aggregation of component sectors connected by continuous flow relationships. Kuznets writes:

> One may therefore ask, what is the specific advantage of the approach via a system of economic or social accounts? How does it help a student who is already aware of the desirability of presenting not merely single national totals but of articulating them by significant components at different stages of economic circulation? Does a system of accounts help the student deal with the vexing problems of scope, netness, and consistency of valuation that must be resolved when national income is defined as a measure of an economy's *net product?*[14]

Having thus put the question, Kuznets finds that a simple answer, given what the group has done, is improbable. The difficulty is the ambiguity of their use of the term "account." On some occasions they have used it in the conventional, narrow sense of debits contrasted with assets; on other occasions, they have used it to "connect" two separate estimates of some entity like gross national product. In the end he concludes:

> There is little in the technique of the system of accounts in and of itself to help us determine the proper scope of national income and the observable flows that represent net yields and those which, from the standpoint of the national economy, represent costs; . . . and the significant sectors to be distinguished at any level of economic circulation. Indeed, examination of the report fails to convey the impression that the setting up of the accounts assisted in any way in solving these problems of definition and distribution. On the contrary, the impression is that these problems were solved without benefit of the system of accounts, and that the system of accounts was constructed to fit the solutions. Consequently, the statement in the report that "the accounts . . . show . . . how the whole is derived as the sum of the

[14]Kuznets, *Income*, pp. 151–152.

parts" . . . cannot be intended to imply that the cast of the accounts determined in any way either the parts or the whole.[15]

Kuznets is clearly not overwhelmed by the technique of setting up T-accounts. They are at best a neutral means to illustrate what one wants to show:

> Providing one exercises full freedom in deciding what is a transactor group, what is a transaction, and what the economic meaning of a transaction is from the viewpoint of the economy at large, a set of accounts is like a blank notebook: One can write in it anything one wishes. And this is in fact what the report does: It recognizes families living in their own houses as transactor groups, although it excludes illegal firms which are more obviously a group of transactors; it classifies retention of product by farmers as a transaction, but does not classify tax collection by government as a transaction representing charges for services rendered. One may agree with these decisions or not; there is no sign that the system of accounts affected them in any way.[16]

I read the Kuznets review principally as the assessment by an economic institutionalist about the Procrustean effect that economic theory seems always to have had. And it is precisely this point that must not be buried as the data collection and data presentation processes proceed.

> My conclusion would be different were the system of accounts to stand not for merely another way of casting statistical tables, but for something more substantial—the corpus of accounts as they are *in fact* formulated and used by business enterprises and other economic institutions. If one were willing to accept the judgments of the various economic units as to what they think their net income or product is, as expressed in their accounts, one could resolve many conceptual and classification problems. *But obviously no such acceptance is feasible when the definition and distribution of national income is governed by some theoretical concept of the operation of the economy.*[17]

Withal, however, Kuznets has to admit that the national income experts cannot in fact accept the businessmen's estimates; they have, instead, to try to fashion more stable measures than the latter would give them. What seems to bother him is that what these experts have

[15]Kuznets, *Income*, p. 153.
[16]Kuznets, *Income*, p. 153.
[17]Kuznets, *Income*, p. 153. Emphasis added.

fashioned relied too heavily on the Keynesian *a priorism*, and too little on their own independent work. This is a matter of judgment. Kuznets's unchanging essential definition remains:

> The final goal of economic activity is provision of goods to consumers, that final products are those turned out during the year to flow either to consumers or to capital stock (for the ultimate benefit of future consumers), and that everything else, by the nature of the case, is intermediate product whose inclusion in the output total would constitute duplication.[18]

But Kuznets makes his complaint most strongly about the way that Gilbert et al. have handled the governmental account, something so complicated that it should not be swept under a single rubric (or carpet). He argues that inclusion of government goods "that are to be consumed either by business enterprises or by society at large for shoring up its own organizational structure . . . involves duplication. . . . The total we are seeking is that of *product*, of the end-result of activity—not of the volume of *activity* itself."[19]

Kuznets's review then treats in detail the handling of product totals and the national income total. He stresses the changes that this report introduces from his earlier 1934 Commerce Department work. He notes his differences from the English group's work and also takes care to identify how much of the deviation of the 1947 practice was introduced to handle the special case of a war economy. Both of the factors had, he allows, their one-time reasons. His point is, however, that those reasons impede rather than contribute to the understanding of the growth and operation of the economy under more normal conditions. In the end, Kuznets's position is that many of the changes are matters of arbitrary judgment, and what has been lost is the connective link with the history of the efforts to measure the dynamic qualities of national economic growth; who bears the burdens and why; and the many efforts made in the 1920s at the NBER to determine whether different approaches would lead to substantially different answers. In his assessment, the new system veiled the real pecuniary transactions in the economy. The institutionalization of the accounting system was purchased at the expense of considering the ever-changing philosophical underpinnings that constituted the essential purpose for the exercise.

Thereafter, Kuznets turns to discussing the impact of the group's revisions from the figures he had earlier derived in order "to show the changes in the magnitudes of major components of the national totals

---

[18]Kuznets, *Income*, p. 156.
[19]Kuznets, *Income*, p. 156–157.

both on the income flow and the final product approaches" and to make some comments about the margins of error associated with the new figures.

And what was their reply? Gilbert and his associates open by agreeing with Kuznets that no system of accounts will in itself answer all of the questions that rightly should be asked. But they go on immediately to assert that what they have produced is superior to anything previous (including specifically Kuznets's own 1941 *National Income and Its Composition*). They justify their work on pragmatic grounds, which they appear to believe is a criterion that Kuznets would accept. There are five reasons for what they have done: (1) their system reveals clearly the structure of the economy; (2) it forces consistency and thus aids in the handling of socioeconomic policy problems; (3) it parallels pedagogical material currently in use; (4) its framework is sufficiently flexible to permit further improvements; (5) it provides material in such a way that most conclusions can be achieved by alternative routes, thus making checking possible.

From the standpoint of our original question, the Commerce group's objectives seem far more short-run and ahistorical than the kinds of things that had earlier attracted Spahr, King, and Kuznets. Specifically, Gilbert and his colleagues, as Gilbert wrote in 1945, were "not trying to measure welfare but the value of production from a business point of view." And while there have been many changes in the national accounting system since 1948, the changes have occurred within the framework of the 1940s.

Kuznets's criticism reflected an articulated doubt about the implicitly Procrustean nature of the Keynesian theoretical system. Most economists, trained along Keynesian lines, would not have shared Kuznets's reservations, at least not until the early 1970s, when the era of fine-tuning was over along with the general belief that the Keynesian system contained the solution to all important macroeconomic problems.

But it is not the loss of supreme confidence in the perfection of macroeconomic theory, as worked out since the 1936 Keynes formulation, that explains the shifts in the national accounts since 1947. In the ensuing years, the accounts underwent refinements as well as extensions into new areas, or, more precisely put, began to include the careful measurement of additional national economic phenomena, such as income distribution by size of share and changes in labor and total factor productivity.

While several committees from time to time have advised the national income unit on how and why it ought to change its procedures, the unit has largely pursued its 1948 pattern. From the standpoint of the set of questions put at the beginning of this chapter, the point is clear.

We have institutionalized and expanded a national accounting system to offer us answers to many of the various questions that prompted work in national income measurement. We have surely improved the coverage of data as well as their quality, but whether the project can ever be properly finished remains a moot point. Kuznets's original view, that the end-goals essentially determined the statistical means, remains viable. Surely the failure in recent years of our capacities to measure the benefits of pollution control, affirmative action, and better occupational safety standards, to say nothing of controlling the costs of entitlement programs, suggests that we know a good deal less than we thought. The loss of confidence in macroeconomic forecasting, even in the relevance of macroeconomic descriptions, is evidence of this judgment. On the other hand, there are those like Richard and Nancy Ruggles who are confident that a unique social accounting system will produce answers to all of the questions:

> It is now generally recognized that national accounts have three major functions: They serve as the coordinating and integrating framework for all economic statistics; they give timely and reliable key indicators on the performance of the economy; and they illuminate the relationships among the sectors of the economy that are fundamental to an understanding of its functioning. During the past two decades, both the availability of data for national accounting systems and the uses of these systems have grown. . . . At the same time, the increasing complexity of economic and social problems has led to more sophisticated types of analysis. . . . The emphasis of policy and analytic interest has changed for an exclusive focus on aggregate output to questions of distribution, and to social, as well as purely economic concerns. This changing emphasis has significantly broadened the range of data for which national accounts can serve as a framework, while the rapidly increasing and complexity of the data have intensified the need for a broader framework.[20]

In sum, if there is a lesson to the history of the national accounts, it is that much is to be gained by looking not only at the finished product but also at the original architectural plans. The building process, by its very nature, modifies the original vision. Whether these modifications, created by choice or by the exigencies of the moment, should remain as dominant decisions may be the real question. If so, it can be answered only by the appearance of a new master architect, conscious and capable of perceiving and designing new answers not only to the old questions but also to those that are emerging.

[20]Richard Ruggles and Nancy D. Ruggles, "Integrated Economic Accounts for the United States, 1947–80," *Survey of Current Business* (May 1982), vol. 62.

PART II
The Politics of Population Measurement

4

THE 1980 CENSUS
IN HISTORICAL PERSPECTIVE

MARGO A. CONK

T HE 1980 census was marked by controversy from beginning to end, from its initial planning phase to its final reporting period. Some critics claimed that it cost too much, invaded people's privacy, or collected too much information. Others charged that the census undercounted the population, missing people in poor, urban, and minority neighborhoods, or that it did not ask the right questions, that it reported too little, too late. Fifty-four lawsuits were filed by cities, states, private citizens, and lobbying groups against the Census Bureau charging that the bureau inadequately or improperly counted the population. Many of the knotty technical, political, and constitutional issues raised by these suits have yet to be fully solved.[1]

The controversies have inevitably tarnished the Census Bureau's morale and its image for peerless statistical competence. During 1981 and 1982 the bureau struggled with budget cuts which slowed the processing and publication of the data. The final 1980 population count

NOTE: I would like to thank Conrad Taeuber and Harvey Choldin for their comments on this paper.

[1]See, for example, Andrew Hacker, "The No-Account Census: Attempting the Impossible," *Harper's*, March 1980, pp. 28–32; Ian Mitroff, Richard O. Mason, and Vincent Barabba, *The 1980 Census: Policymaking Amid Turbulence* (Lexington, Mass.: Lexington Books, 1983); B. Robey, "American Out of Focus," *American Demographics* 3 (April 1981): 16–21; "Embattled U.S. Census Is Facing Its First Major Test This Month," *New York Times*, July 6, 1980, pp. 1, 16.

came in over 4 million above the bureau's own estimates. The numbers rightly or wrongly provided ammunition to those who charged the bureau with undercounting. And over the past few years, many career statisticians have taken early retirement or left to work in other capacities rather than continue to work in the increasingly contentious setting of the Census Bureau.[2]

Moreover, the 1980 census reported momentous changes in the U.S. population. Population shifted to the South and West. Many of our older eastern and midwestern industrial cities experienced radical population declines. The exurban population grew dramatically. Household size shrank; the occupational structure continued to shift more toward service and white collar jobs. Though it only confirmed trends that social scientists have long discussed, the census nonetheless makes the changes "official." The census publicizes the changes to the broader populace and triggers the revision of apportionment and allocation formulas to take cognizance of the new demographic realities.[3]

The Changing Sources of Controversy

Most commentators agree that the 1980 census was controversial because so much was at stake. The numbers translate into political power and tax dollars, and local governments worried that their populations would not be adequately or accurately counted. Further, everyone could see that the demographic changes of the 1970s would lead to shifts of political power and possibly public money to growing areas—and away from regions that were declining or stable.

But none of this is new; every census has had such an effect. The census was established in the first place as a mechanism for political and economic apportionment. The United States population has always been demographically dynamic. This may well have been more the case in the past than it is now. Over the past twenty years there has been a vast expansion in the amount of money allocated by census-based formulas to state and local governments. Still, the fact that more money rode on the outcome of the count did not inevitably mean that state and local governments should distrust the census results.

----

[2]Cf. the estimates issued in *Data User News*, August 1980, p. 1, with the final census results. The Census Bureau estimated the 1980 population at 221.7 million. It counted 226.5 million. It estimated the Hispanic population to be 12.1 million in 1979. It counted 14.6 million in April 1980. On the retirements, see *Washington Post*, February 6, 1979; *New York Times*, February 2, 1979; February 6, 1979.

[3]See *Data User News*, January 1981; *New York Times*, December 17, 1980; December 25, 1980; January 1, 1981; February 24, 1981; March 1, 1981; March 3, 1981.

Different trends made the 1980 census controversial. The first were the reapportionment decisions of the 1960s that articulated and implemented the one man-one vote principle of representation. These decisions reversed the patterns of most of the twentieth century, when political apportionment mechanisms were consciously or unconsciously allowed to atrophy. Prior to these decisions, on the federal level, congressional districts represented radically different-sized populations. For example, under the 1930 apportionment, the largest congressional district in New York contained 799,407 people, the smallest, 90,671. Before the *Baker* v. *Carr* decision of 1962, 14 of Michigan's 19 districts, 14 of Ohio's 24, and 20 of Texas's 23 were malapportioned. On the state level, many state legislatures simply stopped redistricting altogether. Illinois and Tennessee did not redistrict after 1901 despite massive population growth, until forced by the *Baker* v. *Carr* decision. These malapportioned legislatures overrepresented the rural areas of the country and underrepresented the urban and suburban areas. Only with the spate of court decisions that began in the 1960s did Americans inquire into the nature of popular representation in Congress, state legislatures, and local government and reverse a half-century-long tendency toward malapportionment of our representative bodies. And the one man-one vote principle depended on the accurate data of the census-takers. [4]

Second, the civil rights court decisions and legislation of the postwar era drew attention to data on minorities and required still further statistics. Though the census has always been concerned with counting the minority populations of the nation, the civil rights revolution added new demands on those data. The statistics were to serve the needs of the minorities themselves in their push for equal opportunity and social justice. [5]

Third, policymakers have at their disposal much more statistical information than they did in earlier decades. Developments in the field of statistics and survey research have enabled the census to collect much more accurate and useful information about the population than was possible fifty years ago. These data improvements have allowed, perhaps even encouraged, lawmakers to write complex pieces of legislation for allocating government funds. The revenue-sharing legislation of the early 1970s, for example, aimed at developing uniform, national, au-

---

[4]See, for example, "History of Reapportionment and Redistricting," *Guide to US Elections* (Washington, D.C.: Congressional Quarterly, 1975), pp. 519–541; Gene Graham, *One Man, One Vote* (Boston: Little, Brown, 1972); Robert Dixon, *Democratic Representation: Reapportionment in Law and Politics* (New York: Oxford University Press, 1968); Robert McKay, *Reapportionment: The Law and Politics of Equal Representation* (New York: Twentieth Century Fund, 1965).

[5]See, for example, Margo A. Conk, "The Census, Political Power and Social Change," *Social Science History* 8 (Winter 1984).

tomatic, and precise mechanisms for allocating federal funds to state and local governments. Several of the measures in that legislation employed census data.

Even the discovery of the census undercount by officials at the 1940 census should be seen in this light. Bureau statisticians pioneered in the measurement, analysis, and correction of all kinds of errors in the census, and should be credited with bringing the issue to public consciousness in the first place. The new statistical techniques tested the accuracy of the data of the census-takers, and facilitated their use.[6]

Finally, though, the aftermath of the 1970 census cast a cloud over the reputation of the Census Bureau and made policymakers and political leaders worry about whether the data really were as good as they should be. For example, despite increased efforts to reduce the differential undercount of minorities, the 1970 census missed 7.7 percent of the black population but only 1.9 percent of the whites. The data on Hispanics were incomplete and unreliable. And when the first revenue-sharing checks were mailed in December 1972, everyone discovered that the revision of the data base for the calculations in light of more complete census data had changed the allocations significantly for 13,000 local communities. The "objective" data were not so perfect after all. For the rest of the 1970s the census and the Census Bureau came under increasing scrutiny by Congress and the public. By the time the 1980 census approached, it was apparent that the bureau had not calmed its critics.[7]

Thus, several kinds of pressures came to bear on the 1980 census at once. On the political side, the court decisions called for relevant, precise, accurate local area data for drawing legislative and congressional districts. On the fiscal side, grant-in-aid programs called for good local area data to distribute funds. Yet events of the 1970s undermined the faith of those calling for the data. A brief history of the census and its uses in the nineteenth and twentieth centuries provides the background for the more recent developments.

Broadly speaking, Americans have used the census in two basic ways. First, the census has been an apportionment mechanism. Second,

---

[6]Joseph Duncan and William Shelton, *Revolution in United States Government Statistics, 1926–1976* (Washington, D.C.: Government Printing Office, 1978); Robert Jenkins, *The 1940 Census of Population and Housing Procedural History* (Madison, Wisc.: Center for Demography and Ecology, 1983).

[7]Mitroff et al., *The 1980 Census*, pp. 20ff.; Paul Dommel, *The Politics of Revenue Sharing* (Bloomington: Indiana University Press, 1974), pp. 175ff. See also Congressional Research Service, Library of Congress, "The Decennial Census: An Analysis and Review," prepared for the Subcommittee on Energy, Nuclear Proliferation and Federal Services of the Committee on Governmental Affairs, United States Senate (Washington, D.C.: Government Printing Office, 1980).

the census has been an instrument to observe, define, monitor, and analyze the changes in the society as a whole. During most of the nineteenth century the demands of the apportionment system played the primary role in determining the character of the census. The particular form the census took, the questions asked, and the data reported all were initially designed and justified as a means to facilitate the apportionment process. As the nation grew and industrialized, though, the "monitoring" or "stock-taking" function of the census assumed increasing importance and prompted expansion of both the data produced and the administrative structure of the Census Bureau. Congress and the public pressed for the increased data because they wanted to understand how and why political power was shifting in the country and they wanted to address entirely new issues of urbanization, industrialization, economic development, and social welfare. These two uses of the census for apportionment and as a monitoring mechanism have somewhat different histories. It is useful to separate them analytically and explore each in turn.

Nineteenth-century Americans saw the census develop with the country as a whole. The Founding Fathers had created the census as a means to apportion political representation in the House of Representatives. Article 1, Section 2 of the Constitution mandated a decennial count of the population and directed that the census separate the free, slave, and untaxed Indian populations to determine the apportionment. During the Constitutional Convention of 1787, the delegates debated whether population, wealth, or some other measure would provide the most appropriate yardstick for apportioning House seats. They decided that for all practical purposes population was highly correlated with wealth and that population was much simpler to measure. The issue was partially prompted by the question of whether slaves were to be counted as people or property. The Three-Fifths Compromise provided a rather awkward solution to the problem by allocating lesser representation to states for their slave populations.[8]

Designed to remedy one of the long-standing grievances of the American Revolution, the census became the mechanism for apportioning political representation to geographic areas, and for changing the apportionment of legislative seats as the population grew. The Constitution, though, did not specify exactly how the census was to be taken, or how the apportionment would be made. These matters were left to Congress and the executive branch to work out in practice. Historians

[8]Bernard Bailyn, *The Origins of American Politics* (New York: Vintage, 1968), pp. 80–83; James Madison, *Journal of the Federal Convention*, ed. E. H. Scott (Chicago: Albert, Scott & Co., 1893).

generally suggest that the reason for this situation was that the science of statistics was itself in its infancy, and that in the absence of experience the technical problems of census-taking and apportionment had simply not occurred to anyone.[9]

The census mechanism worked well. During the nineteenth century, the federal government counted the population, reported the figures, and Congress was reapportioned and redistricted. Over the years there were several major changes in apportionment methods as well as furious debates about the meaning and impact of each reapportionment.

After the first few censuses, Americans became increasingly interested in the census results. They began to see the patterns that made the United States one of the most demographically dynamic and diverse nations in the history of the world. The census showed that the population was growing steadily and extremely rapidly. Each decade, new areas of the country were settled; new states and cities and towns sprang up from the frontier. And they saw the differential patterns of growth between regions, and between racial and ethnic groups. Over time Americans came to recognize that even a simple reporting of relative population changes for regions or demographic subgroups of the population had implications for political reapportionment and thus for the trajectory of social and political change for the nation as a whole.[10]

It is not surprising therefore that nineteenth-century Americans who were pleased with the overall thrust of population change claimed that the census proved the virtue of the American way of life or the American system of government. Conversely, those who felt shortchanged by reapportionment or were concerned about the tendencies of population change challenged both the census and the apportionment system. A review of some of these discussions should illustrate the contemporary debates.

During the first half of the nineteenth century, the census was a very simple affair. The population was counted by household by assistant U.S. marshals. They totaled up the answers to a few simple questions for their districts and reported them to the secretary of state. The State Department checked the figures and then published them so

[9]Patricia Cline Cohen, *A Calculating People: The Spread of Numeracy in Early America* (Chicago: University of Chicago Press, 1982); James Davis, "The Beginnings of American Social Research," in George Daniels, ed., *Nineteenth Century American Science: A Reappraisal* (Evanston, Ill.: Northwestern University Press, 1972), pp. 152–178.

[10]Congressional Quarterly, "History of Reapportionment and Redistricting"; Carroll Wright and William Hunt, *The History and Growth of the United States Census* (Washington, D.C.: Government Printing Office, 1900). On the early interpretation of census results, see Cohen, *A Calculating People*, pp. 150–174, or such contemporary works as George Tucker, *Progress of the United States in Population and Wealth in Fifty Years as Exhibited in the Decennial Census* (New York, 1843).

Congress could be reapportioned. The most significant result of the census during these years was rapid population growth. Total population grew at the remarkable rate of 30–35 percent a decade and prompted dramatic changes in the character of Congress. The size of the House grew from the original 65 in 1790 to 233 in 1850, and the balance of power shifted away from the original thirteen states. Virginia, Massachusetts, Connecticut, Vermont, New Hampshire, and Maryland reached their peak congressional delegations in 1820. Even Kentucky and Tennessee reached their peaks (thirteen members each) in 1830. Americans came to be keenly aware of differential population growth, and they searched for explanations why some parts of the country or some subgroups grew faster than others. They concluded, a bit crudely, that the fastest growing populations were the most "vital," virtuous, and advanced. Yet even the residents of the slower-growing older thirteen states suggested that faster-growing western states were populated by the sons and daughters of the original thirteen colonies, and thus the differential growth rates were no threat to the future of the Republic. In the relatively underpopulated antebellum United States, all population growth was considered good. More people meant more labor to clear new lands, settle farms, and build cities.[11]

But Americans soon discovered that it was a treacherous business to pin one's claim to political and social virtue on population growth rates. The South was the first to feel the problem in the context of the sectional crisis over slavery. By 1850 the South had lost its ability to win its positions in the House of Representatives because the anti-slavery regions of the country were growing faster and hence were increasing their relative representation. The 1850 and 1860 censuses showed the South slipping further in political power. Historian Roy Nichols has even suggested that the 1860 census results published on the heels of the Lincoln election victory in the secession winter of 1860–61 prompted Southerners to secede rather than accede to increasing northern population dominance.[12]

Ironically, Southerners had a hard time accepting the fact of slower growth, because they had themselves been using the comparisons of black and white population growth rates to defend slavery. The slave population grew more slowly than the free white; and the free colored grew more slowly than both. Southerners therefore argued both that whites were more "vital" than blacks, and that blacks would not survive the competition with whites if given freedom. Though these no-

[11]Walter Nugent, *Structures of American Social History* (Bloomington: Indiana University Press, 1981); Conk, "The Census, Political Power and Social Change."
[12]Roy Nichols, *The Disruption of American Democracy* (New York: Macmillan, 1948), pp. 460–461.

tions seem absurd today, the research of George Frederickson and others has shown that these views were widely held among nineteenth-century race theorists and influenced social policy toward black Americans into the twentieth century.[13]

In fact, the notion that the fastest growing populations were the most virtuous and vital was not seriously challenged until it became obvious that old-stock native Americans were losing out in "competition" with immigrants in the late nineteenth century. Statisticians in New England were the first to discover the decline in native birth rate in the mid-nineteenth century. Birth rates and growth rates were highest on the frontier, and New England was the first region of the country to experience the "closing" of its frontier, industrialization, and significant European immigration. Postbellum New Englanders discovered that the native population was stable or declining while the foreign-stock population of industrial workers was growing rapidly from both immigration and births.[14]

Francis Walker was the Gilded Age census director and statistician who popularized these developments and warned native Americans that they were being overrun by hordes of "degraded" immigrants from Southern and Eastern Europe: "beaten men from beaten races," as he so eloquently put it. Walker was the intellectual founder of the immigration restriction movement; he developed the theory of the differences between old immigrants and new immigrants which was so crucial in the passage of the National Origins Act. Walker also improved the census because he saw the need to collect more data to monitor the monumental changes in the American economy and population. For example, he developed the center of population maps and the population density maps, which provided clear, intelligible evidence of both the movement of the population and the urbanization and industrialization of the nation.[15]

Walker and many of the statisticians whom he encouraged to work in the Census Bureau were still a bit ahead of their times in the late nineteenth century. Walker's efforts to restrict immigration in light of the declining native American birth rates were unsuccessful because

---

[13]George M. Fredrickson, *The Black Image in the White Mind* (New York: Harper & Row, 1971), pp. 228–255; Mark Aldrich, "Progressive Economists and Scientific Racism: Walter Willcox and Black Americans, 1895–1910," *Phylon* 40 (Spring 1979): 1–14.

[14]Nugent, *Structures of American Social History*; Jesse Chickering, *Immigration into the United States* (Boston, 1848).

[15]Francis Amasa Walker, *Discussions in Economics and Statistics*, ed. Davis R. Dewey (New York, 1899). The quotes are from Volume 2, pp. 134–135, 445, 438, 446, 448. See also James Phinney Munroe, *A Life of Francis Amasa Walker* (New York: Henry Holt, 1923); Barbara Miller Solomon, *Ancestors and Immigrants* (Cambridge, Mass.: Harvard University Press, 1956); Margo Conk, *The United States Census and Labor Force Change* (Ann Arbor, Mich.: UMI Research Press, 1980).

most of the country was still rural and frontier, and even industrial employers needed more labor. These were the years in which the Census Bureau had to watch for deliberate overcounts. Young communities competed for the fastest growth rates and eagerly awaited the results of the census. The political problems that Walker and others saw in the immigrant voting blocs were not seen to be a major problem in Congress. Even the inevitable reapportionment of Congress following the census was not terribly painful because the size of the House was increased to guarantee that older regions of the country did not lose congressional seats. Between 1880 and 1910, the size of the House was increased from 332 to 435; no state lost a seat.[16]

In 1920, though, things appeared in a different light. The 1920 census was a controversial count for a number of reasons. First, it disclosed the shift of population from majority rural to majority urban. Second, the date of the census had been pushed back to January, and rural interests argued that many farm laborers were working in the city at that time of year. Rural areas were thus allegedly undercounted. Third, the census came on the heels of the World War I mobilization and the turmoil it engendered. Immigrants from Central Power nations were seen as enemy agents. Much legitimate antiwar feeling among socialist and immigrant groups led to waves of vigilante and official violence against the foreign-born. The 1919 strike wave following the armistice led many to see the cities and their polyglot populations as destroying the fabric of American democracy.[17]

When the results of the 1920 census showed that the population growth of the previous decade would add representatives to those urban industrial states with large foreign-born populations, Congress balked at passing reapportionment legislation. There were calls to exclude unnaturalized aliens from the count (about 7 percent of the population). The old solution of increasing the size of the House failed. Congress was not reapportioned again until after the 1930 census when malapportionment of districts within the states "solved" the problems of growing urban domination.[18]

[16]Another way to view the apportionment issue is to compare the changes in the size of the House in the late nineteenth century with those of the early nineteenth century. Between 1820 and 1870 the population grew 302 percent while the size of the House increased only 14 percent (from 213 to 243). Between 1870 and 1910, the population grew 139 percent while the size of the House increased 61 percent (from 243 to 391). In the earlier period Americans let the weight of representation shift to the West; in the later period, they did not allow absolute declines in congressional delegations.

[17]"History of Reapportionment and Redistricting"; John Higham, *Strangers in the Land* (New York, 1955); P. K. Edwards, *Strikes in the United States* (New York: St. Martin's Press, 1981); William Leuchtenburg, *The Perils of Prosperity* (Chicago: University of Chicago Press, 1958), pp. 66–83; Robert Murray, *Red Scare* (Minneapolis: University of Minnesota Press, 1955).

[18]"History of Reapportionment and Redistricting."

In the 1920s the problem of the growing power of immigrants was also "solved" by immigration restriction legislation that relied upon a census apportionment mechanism, namely, the proportion of the national stocks in the United States population. The difficulty faced by the immigration restrictionists since Francis Walker's day was how to develop an effective mechanism for admitting immigrants. Literacy tests, health examinations, and the like proved ineffective. Frankly, the restrictionists wanted a means to admit immigrants from the nations of Northern Europe—particularly the British Isles—while excluding Southern and Eastern Europeans, those they thought of as racially inferior. But direct discrimination on the basis of nationality was likely to invite the wrath of the European governments affected. Again, the Census Bureau came to the rescue with a study of the "national origins" of the population, which showed that though immigrants were one of the fastest growing groups in the population in the early twentieth century, the "descendants of persons enumerated at the Second Census" actually made up over half of the 1900 white population. Since the restrictionists argued that immigration should be allowed only insofar as it did not disrupt the existing "racial" balance of the nation, and the majority of Americans in 1800 came from Northern Europe, the majority of twentieth-century immigrants would have to come from Northern Europe. With this logic, the National Origins Act of 1924 cut immigration to 150,000 a year and allocated 71 percent of the quotas to Great Britain, Germany, and Ireland.[19]

The refusal of Congress and state legislatures to reapportion and redistrict effectively after the 1920s had considerable impact on the character of the census. Studies have shown that although early-twentieth-century apportionments were far from perfect according to today's standards, they were better than those governing Congress and state legislatures from the 1920s to the 1960s. Over time, malapportionment got worse as state legislatures refused to acknowledge the continuing urbanization of the country as a whole.[20]

From the point of view of the census, these malapportionments meant that local officials did not have much interest in precise population counts. It was more important to have more information about the population counted, for example, on housing, consumer goods, etcetera, than it was to make sure that everyone was counted. The nineteenth-

[19]Higham, *Strangers in the Land;* Conk, "The Census, Political Power, and Social Change"; the study, *A Century of Population Growth* (Washington, D.C., 1909), provided the basis for the calculations. The quote is from pp. ix–x.

[20]McKay, *Reapportionment,* pp. 45ff; Paul David and Ralph Eisenberg, *Devaluation of the Urban and Suburban Vote: A Statistical Investigation of Long-Term Trends in State Legislative Representation* (University of Virginia, Bureau of Public Administration, 1961), pp. 10ff; Andrew Hacker, *Congressional Districting: The Issue of Equal Representation* (Washington, D.C.: Brookings Institution, 1964).

century local booster's concern with counting everyone did not seem so pressing if there was no legislative payoff to the numbers. The early- to mid-twentieth-century census responded by shifting gears. The monitoring function of the census became primary. The bureau concentrated on providing more data and more analysis of the census results.

Beginning in the mid-nineteenth century, the monitoring mechanism of the census had assumed increasing importance. As a result of a dispute over the accuracy of data from the 1840 census on black–white insanity differentials, and a general call for more and better information, Congress overhauled the census law in 1850 and provided for data on the individual level. A formal Census Office was set up in the Department of the Interior to tally the results of the census. The 1850 census is generally considered the first serious effort at collecting detailed data on the population. The questions on nativity, occupation, and specific age were initiated. Almost 200 clerks had tallied the census. The final quarto volume of population statistics ran to almost 1,200 pages. Statistics of mortality, manufactures, and agriculture were also published.[21]

In 1880 dissatisfaction with the results of the 1870 census again prompted an administrative overhaul of the census and authorized the collection of more data. Because of turbulent conditions after the Civil War, the southern population was inadequately covered in the 1870 census. Francis Walker convinced Congress that the improper count resulted from the use of federal marshals and their assistants as the census field force. As of 1880 the Census Bureau received authorization to hire its own local enumerators and field supervisors. Walker was also authorized to hire "special agents" to conduct the inquiries into technically difficult areas—for example, statistics on mining, public health, cities, or steam and water power.[22]

These refinements on the basic process of census-taking and the mandates to collect additional data placed an incredible burden on the hand-tallying methods of the Census Bureau. Despite the growth in the population and the expansion of the types of data compiled in the decennial census, the Census Bureau was still a temporary agency in the Department of the Interior. Each decade it was recreated a year or two before the count, brought up to full staffing during the actual count, and then disbanded two or three years into the decade. Needless to say, census officials found it very difficult to maintain administrative continuity, develop new procedures, or evaluate the performance of the census. Further, the constitutional requirement to report population

[21]Cohen, *A Calculating People*, chap. 6; Wright and Hunt, *History and Growth of the U.S. Census.*
[22]Wright and Hunt, *History and Growth of the U.S. Census.*

figures for apportionment placed a kind of lockstep pressure on the bureau to meet its deadlines.

All census superintendents after 1850 lobbied strenuously for the creation of a permanent Census Office to smooth out the workload, but during the nineteenth century Congress was unwilling to create any kind of central statistical office. Other solutions would have to be found. Most important for the future of census-taking was the introduction of machine tabulation in 1890, using the famous Hollerith cards. The bureau could tabulate and publish much more data in a shorter period of time without increasing the clerical costs of the census exorbitantly.[23]

Shortly thereafter, in 1902, the Census Bureau became a permanent agency and moved to the newly created Department of Commerce and Labor. The general pressure of the Progressive reform movement, the lobbying efforts of such groups as the American Statistical Association, the American Economic Association, and business organizations and the inherent administrative logic of staggering the bureau's heavy workload of population and economic censuses finally convinced Congress to institutionalize the Census Bureau. In the early years of the century, there was some hope that the bureau would become a true Central Statistical Office, like those of European nations. The already well-developed statistical programs of other cabinet departments—particularly the Treasury and Agriculture departments and the Bureau of Labor Statistics—frustrated those plans. Nevertheless, by the early twentieth century, the Census Bureau finally had the capability to hire statisticians and technical experts permanently. The bureau could plan and develop data improvements, prepare analytical studies of the census results, and provide continuous data to other government agencies. [24]

All these improvements in the census were prompted by the congressional and public concern with the meaning of the changes in the American population. The patterns evident in early censuses were simple ones: The population grew rapidly and moved in a westward direction. Since the population growth and expansion were accompanied by economic growth and opportunity Americans drew equally simple conclusions. Westward expansion and growth were good and provided the best guarantee of continuing progress and social equality.

---

[23]Leon Truesdell, *The Development of Punch Card Tabulation in the Bureau of the Census, 1890–1940* (Washington, D.C.: Government Printing Office, 1965); for a discussion of these innovations on the labor statistics of the census, see Margo A. Conk, "Labor Statistics in the American and English Census: Making Some Invidious Comparisons," *Journal of Social History* 16 (Summer 1983): 83–102.

[24]W. Stull Holt, *The Bureau of the Census: Its History, Activities and Organization* (Washington, D.C.: Brookings Institution, 1929); A. Ross Eckler, *The Bureau of the Census* (New York: Praeger, 1972).

As Horace Greelcy put it, "Go West, young man." Even Francis Walker initially theorized that immigrants were a "problem" not because they were racially inferior to Americans but because they did not have sufficient resources to leave the cities of the East for the rural areas of the West.[25]

In the late nineteenth century, different patterns of population growth began to challenge the previous conventional wisdom. The results of the censuses in those years illustrated the patterns outlined in Walter Nugent's *Structures of American Social History.* Population growth slowed permanently after 1870, dropping to an average of 24 percent per decade from 1870 to 1910. After 1910 growth averaged 13 percent per decade. With this demographic transition came massive urbanization in the East and a distinct slowing of the westward thrust of the population. By the turn of the century demographers and statisticians began to notice that old rural areas from New England to Iowa were losing population.[26]

These patterns were deeply disturbing to Americans concerned with the well-being of the American economy and polity. Was the American population losing its "vitality"? Was the "higher civilization" of the Gilded Age leading to an "unwholesome state of society"? Following Jefferson, nineteenth-century Americans believed they had avoided much of the social turmoil of Europe because there were few crowded cities; Americans had the opportunity to become freehold farmers. The population movements of the late nineteenth century indicated instead a growing urban and working-class population together with "a constantly increasing disinclination of our population to follow agricultural pursuits." In short, by the early twentieth century Americans faced two new patterns: (1) congested cities with large numbers of poor, exploited workers; and (2) depopulating rural areas many of which were suffering from soil erosion, overcutting of timber, or other indices of economic decay.[27]

At the same time, federal policy began to be directed toward ad-

---

[25]Conk, *The United States Census and Labor Force Change,* pp. 74ff.

[26]Nugent, *Structures of American Social History,* discusses these changes in great detail, and connects the demographic changes with the American worries about the closing of the frontier. Frederick Jackson Turner's famous essay, "The Significance of the Frontier in American History," was based almost entirely on his reading of the results of the 1890 census—especially the population density maps. These maps in turn were developed by Francis Amasa Walker to illustrate the changing character of the American population. See Gerald Nash, "The Census of 1890 and the Closing of the Frontier," *Pacific Northwest Quarterly* 71 (July 1980): 98–100, and Conk, "The Census, Political Power, and Social Change."

[27]The quotes are from Conk, "The Census, Political Power, and Social Change," and William C. Hunt, "Workers at Gainful Occupations at the Federal Censuses of 1870, 1880, and 1890," *Bulletin of the Department of Labor* 2 (July 1897): 415.

dressing these problems. In the late nineteenth and early twentieth centuries, reformers argued that government functions such as the regulation of railroads, the control of large corporations, the provision of education, or the encouragement of agriculture required national legislation and national funding. The states were either incapable of providing the requisite monies to support such efforts or they did not have sufficient reach to achieve the necessary results. Those arguing for national solutions to what traditionally had been arenas for state legislative efforts argued that historically Congress had encouraged and paid for state government functions or even private development through land grants.[28]

Congress bought the argument hesitantly and very selectively and funded a few particular functions through such grant mechanisms. Nevertheless, by the early twentieth century advocates of vocational education, agricultural extension systems, conservation, a national highway system, and public health all had argued that the federal government should pay the states to set up such programs, and had used the land-grant analogy to justify providing money grants to the states. The grants allocated to the states from these programs were relatively small, but it was this disparate set of laws passed between 1887 and 1921 that laid the foundation for the grant-in-aid system and that first made use of census allocation formulas for distributing federal funds to the states.[29]

At the time, few people saw the possibility or the need to expand such a system of tax or revenue-sharing with the states. Congress made limited use of the general welfare clause of the Constitution in the first third of the twentieth century. By 1930 the grants amounted to about 3 percent of the federal budget (about $100 million); 60 percent of that went for highway aid.[30]

In the Depression years of the 1930s, though, state and local governments could not meet the dramatic welfare demands they faced. Policymakers called for federal tax sharing and for "federalizing" many government functions. By 1936, emergency grants for unemployment relief had forced the federal expenditures of grants to the states to more than $2 billion (over a third of the federal budget). The amount dropped sharply in later years, but continued to hover around the $1 billion

[28]V. O. Key, *The Administration of Federal Grants to States* (Chicago: Public Administration Service, 1937); Committee on Federal Grants-in-Aid of the Council of State Governments, *Federal Grants-in-Aid* (Council of State Governments, 1949); William Anderson, *The Nation and the States, Rivals or Partners?* (Minneapolis: University of Minnesota Press, 1955); Jane Perry Clark, *The Rise of a New Federalism* (New York: Russell & Russell, 1965, originally published 1938).

[29]Key, *Administration of Federal Grants*, pp. 5–16.

[30]Ibid., p. 325; Dommel, *Politics of Revenue Sharing*, p. 19; Committee on Federal Grants-in-Aid, *Federal Grants-in-Aid*, pp. 30ff.

mark. The Roosevelt administration adopted the grant-in-aid mechanism initially because it was an existing device to funnel large amounts of emergency money to the state and local agencies traditionally charged with administering welfare and relief programs. With the passage of the Social Security Act in 1935, the federal government took a major step toward creating a permanent, broad-based, and comprehensive grant-in-aid system in the social welfare field. Funds were provided for public health, maternal and child health, old age assistance, aid to the blind, aid to families with dependent children, as well as for old age pensions and unemployment insurance. All these programs, with the exception of old age pensions, were administered through the states. In the 1940s the grant-in-aid was used to provide federal assistance for such functions as school lunch programs (1946); airport construction (1946); hospital construction (1946); and water pollution control (1948).[31]

As the types of federal aid proliferated, so also did the types of allocation formulas used in particular pieces of legislation. The pre-Depression grant programs had used very simple formulas, based upon such measures as population, area, or road mileage. The agricultural extension and the vocational education grants had employed slightly more complicated measures: the Census Bureau's rural population, urban population, or farm or nonfarm population. These measures had already shown themselves to be a bit troublesome in practice, since, for example, not all rural populations were farm populations. Nevertheless, they functioned well enough given the small amounts of money being allocated.[32]

With the New Deal programs, Congress began to allocate funds on the basis of such measures as per capita income, maternal mortality rates, or population density. Many of these measures were introduced because Congress recognized the differential fiscal capacity or wealth of the various states, and wanted to equalize the national impact of the programs. As they did so, the grant programs shifted from being a simple mechanism for delivering money to another, more appropriate administrative level of government to a controversial method of national income redistribution. A new set of census apportionment mechanisms—this time designed to distribute economic power—was being born. As these mechanisms developed, it became obvious that they were designed to have an impact markedly different from the census political apportionment mechanisms.

[31]Key's study was prompted by the passage of the Social Security Act; see Key, *Administration of Federal Grants*, pp. viiff. See also Committee on Federal Grants-in-Aid, *Federal Grants-in-Aid*, pp. 31ff., and chaps. 14–16.

[32]Key, *Administration of Federal Grants*, pp. 322ff.

The somewhat jerry-built character of American intergovernmental relations tends to give the impression that many of the effects of these New Deal measures were unintentional. Yet, if anything, the record of intent of the policymakers in the Roosevelt administration indicates that they had in mind much grander schemes for income and social equalization than they achieved in actual legislation. In particular, advocates of population policy—influenced by the census studies of urban congestion, rural depopulation, and migration—played a major role in convincing lawmakers and the public that policies promoting income redistribution were required to prevent further depressions.

Perhaps the most important of these was a 1938 study by the National Resources Committee, *The Problems of a Changing Population*, which examined in detail the overall character of the American population and the varied patterns of educational opportunity, income, or employment potential. The study suggested that national economic health depended upon equalizing the opportunities among regions, between urban and rural areas, and between the demographic subgroups of the population. As the committee wrote in its introduction,

> It cannot be too strongly emphasized that this report deals not merely with problems regarding the quantity, quality, and distribution of population . . . but also with the widening of opportunities for the individuals making up this population, no matter how many or where they are. In our democratic system we must progressively make available to all groups what we assume to be American standards of life. The gains of the Nation are essentially mass gains, and the birthright of the American citizen should not be lost by indifference or neglect.[33]

Economists Alvin Hansen and Harvey Perloff went even further in their 1944 study, *State and Local Finance in the National Economy*. They suggested that the federal government should "underwrite" "minimum service standards" in such matters as education, urban redevelopment, public health, national health insurance, and welfare. And they argued that the absence of such national standards already amounted to income redistribution subsidies from one part of the nation to another. By way of example they suggested that the long-term migration pattern of youth from poorer, rural areas into the cities in effect constituted an educational subsidy to the cities. It was only fair, therefore, that the declining population region receive aid to equalize the educational burden. In short, Hansen and Perloff envisioned a kind

---

[33]National Resources Committee, *The Problems of a Changing Population* (Washington, D.C.: Government Printing Office, 1938), p. 5. For the context of the report, see Otis Graham, *Toward a Planned Society: From Roosevelt to Nixon* (New York: Oxford University Press, 1976); and Marion Clawson, *New Deal Planning: The National Resources Planning Board* (Baltimore: Johns Hopkins University Press, 1981), pp. 125ff.

of Keynesian grant-in-aid policy. They advocated a streamlined, coordinated federal grant system that would both provide effective services and equalize the delivery of the services nationwide. In so doing it would become a mechanism for smoothing out the ups and downs of the business cycle by preventing the kinds of fiscal crises that state and local governments faced in the early 1930s.[34]

I would suggest that the theories developed by the National Resources Committee staff and economists such as Hansen and Perloff provided some of the philosophical rationale for increased use of grants to state and local governments in the 1950s and 1960s. Further, as cities grew while state government remained under the control of rural interests, the cities came to demand their own place under the intergovernmental sun and developed direct relationships with Washington. By 1967, thirty-eight grant programs dealt directly with cities. Programs proliferated in highway construction (the interstate highway system); housing assistance; antipoverty; employment and training; urban redevelopment; water and sewer projects. By the late 1970s, 146 categorical grant programs supplied funds to state and local governments. The amount of money distributed jumped from $10 billion in 1964 to almost $35 billion in 1972 and then to $80 billion in 1980. In percentage terms such outlays accounted for almost a quarter of the federal budget in the early 1970s; they made up a fifth of the revenues of state and local governments.[35]

Whether these grants actually had an "equalization" effect was subject to academic dispute, but it is clear from the construction of the grant formulas that Congress intended such an effect. In various laws, Congress used the unemployment rate, poverty level, per capita income, growth lag, or the proportion of substandard housing of a geographic area to distribute funds. Overall, 83 of the 146 programs counted in the late 1970s employed population or a derivative of population as a factor for distributing funds.[36]

[34]Alvin Hansen and Harvey S. Perloff, *State and Local Finance in the National Economy* (New York: Norton, 1944); see also Hansen's discussion of the implications of the slowing national population growth rate in his *Fiscal Policy and Business Cycles* (New York: Norton, 1941), pp. 42ff. Hansen had been using census population statistics to analyze the changes in the American economy as early as 1920. See Conk, *The United States Census and Labor Force Change*, pp. 77ff.

[35]Dommel, *Politics of Revenue Sharing*, pp. 127ff., 19; Herrington Bryce, "The Impact of the Undercount on State and Local Government Transfers," in U.S. Bureau of the Census, *Conference on Census Undercount: Proceedings of the 1980 Conference* (Washington, D.C.: Government Printing Office, 1980), p. 112.

[36]See, for example, Key, *Administration of Federal Grants*, pp. 3–5; U.S. Advisory Commission on Intergovernmental Relations, *The Role of Equalization in Federal Grants* (Washington, D.C.: Government Printing Office, 1964); Richard Nathan, Allen Manvel, Susannah Calkins, *Monitoring Revenue Sharing* (Washington, D. C.: Brookings Institution, 1975), pp. 37–177.

Congress could not introduce these complicated allocative devices without also upgrading the federal statistical system. The critical decade was again the 1930s. The early years of the Depression were particularly demoralizing for the Census Bureau. Congress and the public, not surprisingly, looked to the 1930 census for clues to the causes and character of the Depression, and were disappointed by what they found. The census could not provide a credible statement of the number of unemployed. Budget cuts decimated the staff of the bureau; its work force was aging. Even the new business statistics programs that Hoover had encouraged in the 1920s both as secretary of commerce and as president seemed to be completely irrelevant in the face of the Depression. [37]

The Roosevelt administration became the innovating force. The New Deal put statisticians to work in devising the statistical series that became second nature to postwar Americans. Over the next decade, the government developed the National Income and Products Account series, monthly unemployment statistics, and the Current Population Survey. The 1940 census introduced sampling into the decennial count and made it possible to add major new inquiries. Among these were questions on income, internal migration (where the person lived in 1935), and usual occupation. The Census Bureau hired a new generation of statisticians, men such as Stuart Rice, Philip Hauser, Morris Hansen, and William Hurwitz. These officials were pioneers in modern social science methodology and administration. By the late 1940s, the bureau again had the reputation of a quiet professional agency that served the needs of the national government well. [38]

In the 1950s and 1960s, the bureau introduced computers to process the census and became the arena for continuous breakthroughs in statistical theory and method. It continued to expand the amount of published data, and it searched for methods to lower costs and improve efficiency. One of the most promising was the proposal for self-enumeration by mail. Such a system would eliminate the need for the armies of local enumerators that had to be mobilized each decade. The bureau knew that the local enumerators had always been the Achilles heel of census accuracy. It had always been difficult to recruit sufficient numbers of educated, responsible, adventurous, dedicated, and patient enumerators.

If the statisticians could dispense with one layer of bureaucracy by going directly to the respondent's house by mail, they could eliminate

[37]Duncan and Shelton, *Revolution in United States Government Statistics*; Judith I. de Neufville, *Social Indicators and Public Policy* (New York: American Elsevier, 1975); Eckler, *Bureau of the Census.*
[38]Duncan and Shelton, *Revolution in United States Government Statistics*; Jenkins, *The 1940 Census of Population and Housing Procedural History.*

such problems as enumerator error, or dwellings with no one home during the day. And they could save money at the same time. The experience of the decades after World War II gave the bureau the confidence to embark on such a system. Each decade a major new innovation had been introduced: first sampling, then computerization, then the FOSDIC system. The bureau began to dream of further advances in automating the census process.[39]

The bureau did not, however, anticipate the impact of reapportionment decisions on the demand for census data. Nor should it be faulted for not anticipating the rapid turn of events. For forty years the federal courts, and particularly the Supreme Court, had refused to rule on apportionment cases. The courts had argued that legislative apportionment was strictly a legislative matter. The remedy for a group of people underrepresented because of a malapportioned legislature was through that legislature itself. In the most important case on the issue, *Colegrove* v. *Green* (1946), Justice Felix Frankfurter had ruled that congressional apportionment was a "political thicket" that the courts had no right to enter. The effect of the decision was to uphold the constitutionality of the Illinois congressional delegation. The largest district encompassed 914,053 people and the smallest only 112,116.[40]

But the issue reemerged in the 1950s in the federal courts, and slowly a series of carefully designed test cases made their way to the Supreme Court. Perhaps the relative political calm of the 1950s compared with the upheavals of the Depression and the war allowed Americans to take a look at their representative institutions and see the anomalies of malapportionment. Certainly reformers pressing the issue said as much. They pointed to two cogent reasons for reversing the trend toward malapportionment. First, they pointed out that by the 1950s malapportionment was not simply a rural versus urban issue. The exploding suburban populations of middle-class whites were also underrepresented in their state legislatures, and the discrepancies were widening. Further, commentators in the 1960s suggested that urban riots and turmoil were at least partly the result of decades of systematic underrepresentation and underfunding of poor urban areas.[41]

[39]U.S. Bureau of the Census, *The 1950 Censuses—How They Were Taken* (Washington, D.C.: Government Printing Office, 1955); U.S. Bureau of the Census, *Procedural Report on the 1960 Censuses of Population and Housing* (Washington, D.C.: Government Printing Office, 1963); U.S. Bureau of the Census, *1970 Census of Population and Housing Procedural History* (Washington, D.C.: Government Printing Office, 1976).

[40]*Colegrove* v. *Green*, 1328 U.S. 549 (1946) at 557–559. The first notation of the need to tailor census data to apportionment needs occurred in the *1970 Procedural History*, pp. 1–13.

[41]David and Eisenberg, *Devaluation of the Urban and Suburban Vote*; Graham, *One Man, One Vote.*

The Supreme Court accepted these arguments and in 1962 ruled in *Baker* v. *Carr* that the Tennessee legislature had to be reapportioned. It had last been apportioned in 1901. A series of subsequent cases overthrew apportionments in other legislatures and in Congress. By 1964 the phrase "one man, one vote" had entered the nation's political vocabulary to define the new principle of legislative apportionment. Suddenly accurate census data for local areas came to be of added importance. Not only were the Great Society programs of the mid-1960s prompting increased use of census data, but the apportionment cases suggested that the bureau had a strict constitutional duty under the equal protection clause of the Fourteenth Amendment to count everyone.[42]

The New Politics of Census Undercounts

By the late 1960s, then, the new meaning of the constitutional requirements for apportionment and the needs of the federal grant system led to major new pressures on the census. During the planning for the 1970 census the disproportionate census undercount of minorities ceased being a technical problem of census field procedures and became an explosive political issue. A 1967 conference on "Social Statistics and the City" marked the change. At that conference, census officials and prominent social scientists met in Washington to discuss the extent and cause of the undercounts. They also proposed remedies and articulated the constitutional principle that made eliminating the differential undercount imperative. "Where a group defined by racial or ethnic terms, and concentrated in special political jurisdictions," wrote David Heer in the conference report, "is significantly undercounted in relation to other groups, then individual members of that group are thereby deprived of the constitutional right to equal representation in the House of Representatives, and by inference, in other legislative bodies." They are also "deprived of their entitlement to partake in federal and other programs designed for areas and populations with their characteristics."[43]

By the time of the conference, the bureau was well into its planning for the 1970 census. The bureau had decided to use a mail census for 60

---

[42]Graham, *One Man, One Vote;* Dixon, *Democratic Representation; Baker* v. *Carr,* 369 U.S. 182 (1962); *Reynolds* v. *Sims,* 377 U.S. 533 (1964); *Wesberry* v. *Sanders,* 376 U.S. 1 (1964) was the major congressional districting case.

[43]David Heer, ed., *Social Statistics and the City* (Cambridge, Mass.: Joint Center for Urban Studies, 1968). The quotation is from p. 11.

percent of the country, primarily the large metropolitan areas. The bureau was also developing complex geographic coding systems to facilitate the mail census. The calls for detailed information on blacks and other minorities had prompted requests to increase the publication of data on minorities in the 1970 census. Officials expressed guarded optimism about their ability to move toward a mail census while improving overall coverage of the population. After all, the technical studies of census procedures and special test censuses had provided the bureau with a great deal of information about what worked and what did not, where errors crept into the data, which methods were most efficient, and so on.[44]

Nevertheless, there were some troubling signs on the horizon. First, though the bureau had known about the differential undercount for almost twenty years, they had not been terribly successful in reducing it. In 1950 11.5 percent of blacks were not counted; 9.5 percent were missed in 1960. Only 2.2 percent of whites were missed in 1960. Eli Marks and Joseph Waksberg concluded in 1966 that the techniques designed to improve coverage in 1960 "were not sufficient to deal with the extraordinary difficulties that were encountered in the slum areas." Further, social scientists worried that mail enumeration procedures would even worsen coverage if address lists were incomplete, if the local population did not read English, if people lacked that middle-class attribute of civic-mindedness that would make them voluntarily fill out and mail in a census schedule. The bureau assured its critics that it would develop major new publicity programs to advertise the census, and would work closely with local leaders and officials to make sure that everyone was counted.[45]

At the same time, other pressures also bore down on the bureau. Some congressmen objected to particular questions on the grounds of invasion of privacy, as had occurred in previous decades. In 1940, the income question became the focus of an attack on the Roosevelt administration for promoting Big Government and violating personal privacy. In the late 1960s, the questions on the number of children ever born to a woman and on bathroom facilities prompted similar objections. There were proposals to drop the penalties for refusing to answer the census. Although unsuccessful, these efforts did consume official time and ef-

[44]See, for example, the papers presented at the American Statistical Association meeting in August 1966, published as the *Proceedings of the Social Statistics Section* (Washington, D.C.: American Statistical Association, 1966), pp. 1–42.

[45]Eli Marks and Joseph Waksberg, "Evaluation of Coverage in the 1960 Census of Population Through Case-by-Case Checking," *Proceedings of the Social Statistics Section of the American Statistical Association, 1966*, p. 64.

fort. The bureau found itself condemned both for collecting too much information and for not collecting enough. As the census year approached, the pressure increased.[46]

Overall, the 1970 census proceeded well. The bureau counted 203 million people, close to its own estimate of the 1970 population. Eleven seats in Congress were reapportioned. The census showed dramatic population shifts out of cities and toward the suburbs, and toward the South and West. California's population outstripped New York's as it became the most populous state.

Nevertheless, there were complaints about the count. Before it took place, federal lawsuits filed against the bureau charged that the mail census would fail to reach the non-English-speaking urban populations and Hispanic Americans. The courts dismissed the suits on the ground that the bureau had the authority and expertise to determine the best method of enumeration; and no evidence indicated that the mail census would produce an undercount. Mayors of large cities worried that their cities would show population declines. And a coalition of civil rights groups formed a Coalition for a Black Count to encourage people to cooperate with the census and then to make sure the Census Bureau counted black Americans.[47]

The controversies over the 1980 census began the moment the 1970 census was completed. Representatives of black and Hispanic civil rights groups felt that the 1970 results confirmed their prior reservations about the accuracy and adequacy of the count. By late 1971 the *New York Times* reported that their demographic analysis of the published census results indicated that the bureau had again undercounted the black population. The bureau responded that the 1970 count was the most accurate ever taken. However, in April 1973, announcing the results of its own analysis, the bureau admitted that it had missed 2.5 percent of the population, some 5.3 million people. Again the undercount differed sharply by race. Only 1.9 percent of whites but 7.7 percent of blacks were missed. In July 1973 Dr. Robert Hill of the Urban League reported that the largest number of blacks missed were in New York City. In New York and California alone over 1 million people were overlooked in the 1970 census.[48]

The early 1970s also saw the mobilization of Hispanic Americans to

---

[46]Jenkins, *The 1940 Census of Population and Housing Procedural History*, pp. 15ff; *1970 Procedural History*, pp. 1-16–1-17; Conrad Taeuber, "Invasion of Privacy: The Case of the United States Census"; and William Petersen, "The Protection of Privacy and the United States Census," in Martin Bulmer, ed., *Censuses, Surveys and Privacy* (London: Macmillan, 1979), pp.170–183.

[47]*1970 Procedural History*, 1-13ff; *Quon* v. *Stans*, 309 F. Supp. 604 (1970); *Prieto* v. *Stans*, 321 F. Supp. 1420 (1970); *New York Times*, February 11, 1970.

[48]*New York Times*, December 26, 1971; April 26, 1973; July 24, 1973.

demand better coverage from the census. Before the 1970 census the federal Inter-Agency Committee on Mexican American Affairs had requested that the 1970 census contain a question on Spanish origin. The bureau responded that most of the schedules had already been printed but Hispanics would be identified by questions about language, birthplace, and surname in five southwestern states. The Inter-Agency Committee's further efforts produced a Spanish origin question on the 5 percent sample questionnaire. Unsatisfied Hispanic Americans and scholars charged, however, that the 1970 census undercounted Hispanics since the bureau did not routinely employ a Spanish language census form nor put much manpower into counting non-English-speaking groups.

In 1974 the U.S. Commission on Civil Rights focused on many of these complaints in a report, *Counting the Forgotten*, a major indictment of the Census Bureau and its methods. Calling census efforts to count Hispanics in 1970 "disastrous," "confusing," and "not well thought out," the commission also accused the bureau of stonewalling on reforms for 1980. The commission recommended a Spanish origin question for the 100 percent schedule and called on the bureau to "take steps to ensure that all aspects of its program, including questionnaire design and data collection, tabulation and publication, are responsive to the needs of the Spanish speaking background population."[49]

Further adverse publicity focused on the census after revenue-sharing legislation passed in 1972. This legislation, unlike many of the categorical grant programs, provided funds to all fifty states and to some 39,000 local governments. The revenue-sharing allocation formulas relied upon population and per capita income measures; to many it seemed relatively simple to calculate the effects of an undercount on federal aid. Congress and local officials learned this lesson early when the final allocations changed from those used by Congress to write the legislation some months earlier.[50]

[49]U.S. Commission on Civil Rights, *Counting the Forgotten: The 1970 Census Count of Persons of Spanish Speaking Background in the United States* (Washington, D.C.: Government Printing Office, 1974). The quotations are from pp. 99, 100, and 106.

[50]For a history of the legislation, see Dommel, *Politics of Revenue Sharing;* and Nathan et al., *Monitoring Revenue Sharing,* pp. 344–72. For Nathan's estimates of the impact of the undercounts on the allocations, see Arthur J. Maurice and Richard P. Nathan, "The Census Undercount: Effects on Federal Aid to Cities," *Urban Affairs Quarterly* 17 (March 1982): 251–284; and Richard P. Nathan, "Clarifying the Census Mess," *The Wall Street Journal,* January 2, 1981. See also Courtenay Slater's article, "The Impact of Census Undercoverage on Federal Programs," in *Conference on Census Undercount,* pp. 107ff. She points out that the "income undercoverage has a far greater impact on the distribution of revenue-sharing funds than does population undercoverage" (p. 108). Because the formulas are so complicated, it is hard to predict the impact of census undercounts on the allocations. See also Robert Strauss and Peter Harkins, *The 1970 Census Undercount and Revenue Sharing: Effect on Allocations in New Jersey and Virginia* (Washington, D.C.: Joint Center for Political Studies, 1974).

Needless to say, all this controversy unnerved officials of the Census Bureau. Bureau statisticians were proud of their achievements in producing a professional, objective census, and responded somewhat defensively to the charges of outright bias or incompetence. Pointing to their accomplishments, they insisted they were doing the best job possible, given their technical and financial resources.[51]

The Census Bureau also created several advisory committees on minority statistics. The Census Advisory Committee on the Black Population for the 1980 census was organized in 1974. The initial meetings between black leaders and Census Director Vincent Barabba were described by the *New York Times* as "tense." In 1975 the bureau established a similar committee on the Spanish origin population; a year later it convened an Asian and Pacific Americans Population Committee. All three were designed to improve communications with the affected communities and to help plan the 1980 census. The power and scope of the committees themselves soon became a further source of dispute.[52]

Since the end of World War I the bureau has had a system of advisory committees on particular phases of census work. Usually the members have been drawn from interested groups of professionals or retired bureau officials. Today committees provide advice in such areas as marketing statistics, agricultural statistics, and government statistics as well as about privacy and confidentiality of data. The minority advisory committees were official extensions of the advisory system, but their functioning soon proved to be different.[53]

They were strong advocates for changing census procedures to correct what the groups saw as inadequate coverage in the past; and when they felt that the bureau was not sufficiently responsive, they went to Congress and the media to press their case. For example, in

[51]For the bureau's responses to criticism, see *New York Times*, December 16, 1971; the testimony of George H. Brown, Census Director, at the Hearings on the "Accuracy of 1970 Census Enumeration and Related Matters," September 15, 1970. U.S. Congress, House, Committee on Post Office and Civil Service, Subcommittee on Census and Statistics, *Hearings*, 91st Cong., 2d sess., September 15, 1970, pp. 3ff; the bureau's responses to *Counting the Forgotten, passim; 1970 Procedural History*, pp. 1–17.

[52]*New York Times*, September 26, 1974. For a description of the efforts of the bureau to reach out to minority representatives in the mid-1970s, see the March 9, 1977, memorandum on the "Minority Statistics Program of the Bureau of the Census," reprinted as part of the testimony of Manuel Plotkin, Census Director, before the House Committee on Post Office and Civil Service, Subcommittee on Census and Population, *Hearings on the 1980 Census*, 95th Cong., 1st sess., June 1977, pp. 83ff.

[53]For a discussion of the role of Census Advisory Committees and their membership from the 1960s through 1976, see *1970 Census Procedural History*, pp. 1-56–1-73. Until 1960, the only standing advisory committees were those sponsored by the American Statistical Association (and the American Economic Association from 1919 to 1937), and the American Marketing Association (founded in 1946).

June 1977 Luz E. Cuadrado, chair of the Spanish Origin Advisory Committee, testified before a House subcommittee that the advisory group felt the bureau would repeat the mistakes of the 1970 census. It had declined to include a Spanish-origin item in the 100 percent schedule, and proposed field procedures were inadequate to guarantee good coverage of Hispanics.[54]

By the time Jimmy Carter took office, the planning for the 1980 census was well advanced. Public disclosures of the battles over the census raised concern in Congress; at the same time, cost estimates for coverage improvements began to escalate sharply. The bill for the 1970 census had been $221.6 million, and by 1977 David Kaplan of the Census Bureau predicted the 1980 cost at $500 million. In 1977 Census Director Manuel Plotkin predicted that the bureau would spend $75 million for coverage improvements. This was something of an underestimate. The final cost of the 1980 census came to almost $1.1 billion, which included $406 million for improvements. Of this, $203 million was spent on "obtaining a better population count."[55]

In 1978 the bureau "bowed" to the pressure of minorities and changed the race and ethnic questions for the 100 percent schedule. It expanded the list of possible responses to the race question and added a separate item on Spanish/Hispanic origin. The bureau also included a question on "ancestry" on the sample questionnaires; this question replaced the birthplace-of-parents questions initiated during the period of major European immigration in the nineteenth century. Representatives of minority groups were pleased with these changes; demographers were not so sure of their wisdom. Nevertheless, these concessions calmed some of the concerns about the 1980 census, though perhaps they only focused greater attention on adequacy of the field enumeration itself.[56]

As the census drew near, the results of the pretests added fuel to controversy about an undercount. New York City, for example, complained that the bureau's intercensal estimate of its population was too low. City officials testified before Congress that the dress rehearsal conducted in the city indicated that the 1980 methods would miss people. In early 1979, Census Director Manuel Plotkin resigned amid criticisms

[54]*Hearings on the 1980 Census*, pp. 174ff.

[55]For Kaplan's figures, see the *New York Times*, November 25, 1977; Plotkin's estimates are in his testimony at the June 1977 *Hearings on the 1980 Census*, p. 82. For an analysis of the costs of the 1980 census, see the 1982 GAO study, *A Four Billion Dollar Census in 1990?* (Washington, D.C.: Government Accounting Office, 1982), pp. 4–6. For additional discussion on the plans for the 1980 census, see U.S. Congress, House, Committee on Post Office and Civil Service, Subcommittee on Census and Population, *Hearings on the 1980 Census*, 94th Cong., 2d sess., June 1976.

[56]*New York Times*, May 14, 1978.

on his handling of the bureau, and several high-level career officials also took early retirement.[57]

President Carter replaced Plotkin with Vincent Barabba, who had been Census Director during the second Nixon and Ford administrations and had proved himself to be an effective administrator during his tenure. It was clear by 1979 that the bureau needed a leader who could successfully handle the outside pressure, build internal morale, and conduct the census effectively.[58]

By the time Barabba was appointed, most of the crucial plans for the 1980 census had been made. In the year before the count, the bureau turned its attention to publicizing the census and minimizing the barriers to a complete count of hard-to-enumerate groups. Coverage of the illegal alien population presented one of the bureau's most difficult challenges. Undocumented immigrants, those entering the country without official permission and therefore without being counted, seek to remain anonymous to avoid deportation, yet are of great interest to policymakers. In the 1970s Congress was beginning to wrestle with immigration reform legislation.[59]

Thus the Census Bureau very much wanted to count the alien population in 1980. Since most of the illegal aliens are Hispanic and live in the South, Southwest, and large cities of the Northeast and Midwest, representatives of these areas were also interested in an accurate count. The bureau sought unsuccessfully to enlist the aid of the Roman Catholic Church to convince people in the local community of the confidentiality of census records, but local officials in areas thought to have high concentrations of illegal immigrants did organize local campaigns to convince people to fill out the census. They also pressed the Immigration and Naturalization Service to curtail its efforts to round up illegal aliens during the census period.[60]

Other people thought that illegal aliens should not be part of the official census. In December 1979 the Federation for American Immigration Reform (FAIR) and several congressmen filed suit in federal

[57]*Washington Post*, February 6, 1979; *New York Times*, February 2, 1979; February 6, 1979.

[58]On the initial cool reaction to Barabba, see De Neufville, *Social Indicators and Public Policy*, p. 230. On Barabba's return to the bureau in 1979, see the *New York Times*, April 13, 1979; April 18, 1979; April 28, 1979.

[59]Simply arriving at a reasonable estimate of the illegal alien population in the country is very difficult. The Immigration and Naturalization Service estimated there were 8 million illegal aliens in the country in 1976. The *FAIR* v. *Klutznick* suit discussed below estimated 5 million. Legal immigration was about 300–450,000 a year from the late 1960s to 1970s. The foreign-born population was about 10 million in 1970.

[60]*New York Times*, May 7, 1979; June 7, 1979; August 16, 1979; September 3, 1979; October 3, 1979; November 15, 1979; November 18, 1979; December 6, 1979.

court asking that the census separate legal and illegal aliens and exclude illegal aliens for apportionment. The court dismissed the case: Whenever Congress had considered excluding aliens for the purpose of apportionment, it had always decided not to do so. Illegal aliens were to be counted for apportionment if they filled out census forms.[61]

The other major debate of late 1979 and 1980 was whether the Census Bureau should adjust the reported census figures to correct for an undercount. As the census drew near, city officials and minority leaders began to propose adjusting the count in light of the known undercount. Such an adjustment seems to many a reasonable solution to the intractable problems and huge expense of counting everyone. The bureau and private demographers began efforts to devise mechanisms to adjust the figures not only nationally but also at the state and local levels.

Such efforts raised difficult technical, legal, and political issues. And they provoked a huge barrage of arguments on all sides. Briefly, the bureau and its critics had to decide if adjustment was necessary, practical, or possible, legal, or politic. Announcing that the results would be adjusted might detract from the actual enumeration; an adjustment might also undermine the overall credibility of the census. These questions challenged some of the most deeply held beliefs about the proper conduct of the census. If the numbers were to be tinkered with because they were flawed, what did it mean for the fairness of the entire apportionment system?[62]

Sorting out these issues was no easy task. In the fall of 1980 the

[61]*FAIR* v. *Klutznick*, 486 F. Supp. 564 (1980); *New York Times*, December 21, 1979. The plaintiffs lost their appeals to higher courts.
[62]The literature on the undercount is voluminous. For an annotated bibliography of many of the most important sources, see Barbara Ginsburg and Juliette Redding, *The U.S. Census: A Checklist of References on Census-Taking Procedures, Error Estimation, and Technical and Legal Aspects of Undercount Adjustment*, Working Papers in Employment and Training Policy (DeKalb, Ill.: Northern Illinois University Center for Governmental Studies, 1983). For the bureau's positions, see *Conference on Census Undercount*; Mitroff et al., *The 1980 Census*, U.S. Bureau of the Census; *Data User News*, June 1980, October 1980, December 1980, January 1981, February 1981, December 1981. For some of the earlier studies that brought the issue to public attention, see David Heer, ed., *Social Statistics and the City*; U.S. Commission on Civil Rights, *Counting the Forgotten*; National Academy of Sciences, National Research Council, Advisory Committee on Problems of Census Enumeration, *America's Uncounted People* (Washington, D.C.: National Academy Press, 1971); Charles H. Teller, ed., *Cuantos Somos? A Demographic Study of the Mexican American Population* (Austin: Center for Mexican American Studies, University of Texas at Austin, 1977). For a discussion of the legal issue, see "Demography and Distrust: Constitutional Issues of the Federal Census," *Harvard Law Review* 94 (February 1981): 843–63. For a key statistician's analysis of the issues, see Nathan Keyfitz, "Information and Allocation: Two Uses of the 1980 Census," *The American Statistician* 33 (May 1979): 45–50.

Census Bureau announced that it would not adjust the count. This position was ultimately upheld by the courts, but only after a protracted battle that initially seemed to be going the other way.

Beginning in the spring of 1980, numerous lawsuits were filed in federal court charging that the census had undercounted the population. The best known and most legally significant of these cases were those filed by the city of Detroit *(Young* v. *Klutznick)* and the state of New York *(Carey* v. *Klutznick).* In these cases the federal district courts found for the plaintiffs in the fall of 1980 and ordered the Census Bureau to adjust the population figures for the 1980 census "at the national, state, and substate level to reflect the undercount, and to adjust the differential undercount to prevent the known undercount of blacks and Hispanics, as well as whites." These orders were stayed by the Supreme Court pending appeal. Throughout the fall and winter the cases worked their way through the courts.[63]

The plaintiffs in *Young* v. *Klutznick* argued that the bureau had the capability to make such adjustments and had done so in 1970 when it added people during the National Vacancy Check. Many of the arguments in the Detroit case were substantiated by former Census Director Philip Hauser and University of Wisconsin sociologist Karl Taeuber, who testified as expert witnesses for the plaintiffs. Judging from the court's quotations from Hauser's and Taeuber's testimony, they played a major role in explaining the difficult statistical questions to the court and in assuring the court that an adjustment would not do violence to the accuracy or reputation of the census.

The Census Bureau responded by citing its own efforts to improve coverage and assuring the court that coverage would improve in 1980. In its view, the plaintiffs had not shown any injury or harm if the census were not adjusted. The bureau also maintained that there was no generally accepted method of adjustment for state and local civil divisions. Though it might be statistically possible to calculate a national undercount rate, it did not necessarily follow that it was possible to distribute the undercount accurately below the national level. The bureau also argued that its constitutional mandate to conduct an "actual enumeration" of the population for apportionment meant that it could not legally adjust the census.[64]

While appealing the court orders to adjust, the Census Bureau attempted to sort through the issues during 1979 and 1980 in a series of

[63]*Young* v. *Klutznick,* 497 F. Supp. 1318 (1980); *Carey* v. *Klutznick,* 508 F. Supp. 420 (1980). The quote is from *Young* v. *Klutznick,* pp. 1338–39.
[64]Ibid.

workshops and conferences. During the enumeration itself, day-to-day events—snafus, minor scandals, and mistakes—further complicated the picture. The bureau, for example, was forced to cancel one phase of the "local review" process. Address lists were not available on time, and so local officials were given only one chance to check the numbers before they went to Washington. The census office in Brooklyn, New York, burned and the enumeration there had to be redone. There were reports of improperly filled out forms and mass dismissals of temporary census workers. By the summer of 1980 the bureau was falling behind schedule in completing the count. As early figures dribbled out, newspaper headlines announced that the older cities in the Northeast and Midwest were experiencing dramatic population losses. The counts for the South and West were coming in higher than bureau estimates. New York City's population, for example, was reported in September 1980 as off by almost 14 percent to 6.8 million. (The final count proved to be 7.1 million.)[65]

In December 1980 Census Director Barabba announced that the bureau would not "adjust the 1980 census population to compensate for undercount unless directed by the courts." He further reported that "the Bureau will publish the entire series of decennial census reports without adjustment for undercount." Two factors informed the decision. First, the bureau decided that the census enumeration itself was of sufficiently high quality that an adjustment was unnecessary. It was reporting over 4 million more people than expected. Second, it insisted that no means were available to measure the "number and distribution of illegal residents." Together "these two factors have the effect of negating the method currently available for estimating the undercount." In short, the bureau said that because it had covered the population more completely, its own methods of estimating coverage and undercount were flawed.[66]

In late December 1980 the Supreme Court ruled that the bureau could release the unadjusted data to Congress. The lower court rulings were stayed pending appeal. In June 1981 the Second and Sixth Circuit Courts of Appeal upheld the bureau's positions in *Carey* v. *Klutznick*

---

[65]Mitroff, Mason, and Barabba trace the decision-making process. On the plans for the local reviews, see the GAO Report to the House Committee on Post Office and Civil Service, *Programs to Reduce the Decennial Census Undercount* (Washington, D.C.: pub., pls 1976), pp. 16–17. On the cancellation of one phase, see U.S. Congress, House, Committee on Government Operations, Commerce, Consumer, and Monetary Affairs Subcommittee, *Hearing on the Problems with the 1980 Census*, 96th Cong., 2d sess., March 18, 1980. See also *New York Times*, July 18, 1980; June 14, 1980; October 28, 29, 30, 1980; September 26, 1980, September 20, 1982.

[66]*Data User News*, January 1981.

and *Young* v. *Klutznick* on the ground that the plaintiffs had not shown that a differential undercount would injure them. The Supreme Court refused to review the cases in 1982.[67]

While there still may be further legal challenges, the results of the 1980 census appear to have been sufficiently nondiscriminatory to discourage such suits. In the future the issue may become the magnitude of an undercount that would constitute malapportionment. The Supreme Court considered congressional districts with population variances of 4.1 percent to be "malapportioned," a benchmark that could provide a rule of thumb for evaluating census undercounts.[68]

The Significance of the 1980 Census

After all the controversies, the 1980 census did proceed to count the population. On December 31, 1980, Barabba reported the official count of 226.5 million people. As expected, the census confirmed some dramatic changes in the nature of the United States population. Seventeen seats were reapportioned in the House of Representatives. The losers were almost all in the Northeast and Midwest; the gainers in the South and West. The Census Bureau reported that overall the population grew at the rate of 11.4 percent between 1970 and 1980, the slowest rate in the nation's history except for the decade of the Great Depression.[69]

The census also showed that the black population grew 17 percent and the Spanish population 61 percent since 1970. Clearly some of this increase was an artifact of the new questions and commitment to avoid a minority undercount. There were 14.6 million Hispanics, and 26.6 million blacks in the United States in 1980.[70]

Some dramatic changes also were evident in migration patterns and living arrangements of Americans. For the first time since 1820, the ex-urban regions of the country were population gainers. New York State, a highly urbanized state by contrast, experienced an absolute population loss of almost 700,000 people, the largest ever for any state. The size of the average household shrank to 2.75 people, and the number of households grew radically—up 27 percent during the 1970s. Nonfamily households grew 72 percent; female-headed family households grew 51

[67] *Carey* v. *Klutznick*, 653 F. 2d 732 (2d Cir. 1981), cert. denied March 8, 1981; *Young* v. *Klutznick*, 652 F. 2d 617 (6th Cir. 1981), cert. denied February 22, 1982, 455 U.S. 939.

[68] See "Demography and Distrust" for a discussion of possible further avenues of litigation; *Data User News*, March 1982, discusses the estimates of 1980 census undercount. The black rate reported is 4.8%.

[69] *New York Times*, January 1, 1981; *Data User News*, January 1981.

[70] *New York Times*, February 24, 1981; March 1, 1981; *Data User News*, April 1981.

percent.[71] In various ways, the 1980 census proved to be a major demographic watershed. During the 1970s, for example, the standard twentieth-century migration pattern for blacks reversed. The 1970s saw the Sunbelt come into its own. And the nation's old industrial cities lost population to their own suburbs and the nonmetropolitan areas of the nation.[72]

These demographic changes were plainly evident in the census results, despite the efforts of urban officials who pressed for improved coverage in the 1980 census. In large measure, those pressing for better coverage won that battle, only to discover that no matter how well counted, their population base was eroding. And, unlike the rural interests who faced this dilemma in 1920, the big cities will not prevent reapportionment and redistricting in their own self-interest.

The controversies surrounding the census have also led to other achievements that may make the 1980 census a statistical as well as demographic watershed. The data on Hispanics are more complete than before. We still may not know very much about the illegal alien population, but at least the issue is before the statistical community and general public. Minority groups who became involved in the census advisory committees saw their recommendations accepted and have grappled with the logistical problems of taking a national census. Congress has become more conscious of the implications of its myriad allocation formulas. And the response of the Census Bureau to the undercount issues indicates that it survived its ordeal by fire and developed new administrative techniques to cope with the increased demands on its data and expertise.[73]

The future is not altogether rosy, though. These data improvements were very costly, and the grant programs using census data have come under increasing attack. As the 1980 census was being completed, the election of Ronald Reagan signaled a major shift in federal spending and in the political priorities of the nation. During 1981 and 1982 the Census Bureau suffered from budget cuts and furloughs, a delay in the appointment of a new director, more retirements, and a further decline in agency morale. The General Accounting Office issued several reports urging the bureau to plan new procedures to cut costs in 1990. The Reagan administration disbanded the Office of Federal Statistical Policy

[71]*New York Times*, March 3, 1981, May 23, 1981; Bryant Robey and Cheryl Russell, "How America Is Changing: 1980 Census Trends Analyzed," *American Demographics* 4 (July/August 1982): 16–27.

[72]Ibid.; *Data User News*, March 1982.

[73]Cheryl Russell, "The News About Hispanics," *American Demographics* 5 (March 1983): 14–25. "Demography and Distrust" discusses the new sensitivity of Congress to the census and the bills and resolutions introduced in Congress that would allow data adjustments to remedy an undercount. See notes 12, 82, and 145.

and Standards and moved toward cutting the funds available for statistical programs generally. Observers of statistical policy suggest that President Reagan considers the current elaborate census "an invasion of privacy and a waste of money."[74]

Given these developments, it is not at all clear how we will ultimately evaluate the 1980 census. It may well mark the beginning of a new era of statistical service, characterized by closer ties between the Census Bureau and social groups and census users. Or perhaps the 1980 census will be seen as an expensive white elephant, which did a good job of "counting the forgotten," but at too great an economic—and political—cost.

[74]*New York Times*, July 13, 1981; November 25, 1981, January 31, 1982; *Washington Post*, August 2, 1982; *Wall Street Journal*, March 9, 1982; GAO Report to the Congress, *A $4 Billion Census in 1990?*; GAO Report to the Subcommittee on Census and Population, Committee on Post Office and Civil Service, H. Rep., *The Census Bureau Needs to Plan Now for a More Automated 1990 Decennial Census* (Washington, D.C.: Government Accounting Office, 1983); James T. Bonnen, "The Government Statistical Muddle," *American Demographics* 4 (July/August 1982): 28–31; Bryant Robey, "More Than One Bathtub," *American Demographics* 5 (April 1983): 2.

5

POLITICS AND THE
MEASUREMENT OF ETHNICITY

WILLIAM PETERSEN

Is Ethnicity Mensurable?

AGE AND SEX, the two characteristics of a population about which
almost every census or survey asks, exemplify so-called hard
data. The interviewer does not even need a response to specify a
person's sex. Age is frequently misstated, but whether or not the
respondent gives it accurately, various techniques can be used to approximate the single true figure. Other attributes frequently included in
census or survey schedules, however, are decidedly softer. In classifying
persons by marital status, one must decide whether to designate
common-law marriages as the equivalent of those that the state has
sanctioned, or whether a divorced person who has not remarried is to be
counted as single. As another example, the number and diversity of
types of work recorded in statistics have lagged decades behind those in
the real world, and in the United States definitions of occupations were
so greatly altered in the 1980 census that a commission had to be instituted to align the new data with those of 1970. Before counting persons

NOTE: Sections on particular groups in an earlier draft were reviewed by experts on those
populations. I am grateful for the criticisms from Reynolds Farley on blacks, Russell
Thornton on Indians, and A. J. Jaffe on Hispanics. Jacob Siegel and Conrad Taeuber commented on the whole essay. However, I alone am responsible for the final product.

with characteristics associated with soft data, one must set certain conventions to define each such attribute, which is thus moved partway from the population to statisticians' concept of it.

Where in the hard–soft dichotomy should one place ethnicity? According to some analysts, any imprecision or ambiguity is due to distortions brought about by political pressures; and the misclassification most often cited in recent criticisms of ethnic counts, the underenumeration of particular minorities, might be used to support this view. That some blacks or Hispanics are not included, however, need have nothing to do with their racial or ethnic identity, and in any case such selective underenumeration is only one of the faults of ethnic counts. Over the history of the American census, enumerations have helped create groups, moved persons from one group to another by a revised definition, and through new procedures changed the size of groups.[1] Though some of the resultant anomalies have probably never been discerned, others are so patently clear that the census volumes themselves pointed them out. Such deviations from a simple classification may lead one to conclude that essentially race and ethnicity cannot be measured accurately. Or, with a lower standard of precision, one must nevertheless aver that these characteristics differ from age and sex not merely in degree of mensurability but in kind.

Any enumeration depends essentially on three factors—how members of the population regard the particular attribute, the methods used by the statistical agency, and the political or fiscal influences on one or both of these. Let us consider these overall influences in turn.

1.   Most subnations consist of a core population, an intermediate sector with some but less than full participation in the subculture, and a marginal sector that, depending on the criterion used, can be classified as either in or out of the group. Whether it is a census enumerator or, as presently in the United States, the respondent who specifies the

---

[1]One should not suppose that the American census is unusual in these respects. The international range of such lacks and errors is evident, for example, from a booklet by Marzio Strassoldo, published by the faculty of political science of Trieste, *Language and Nationality in the Compilation of Demographic Data*. This work is particularly interesting when one compares it with an earlier one, a paper on nationality statistics that Alajos Kovács presented to the 1928 meeting of the International Statistical Institute. The tone of this earlier presentation can be inferred from its peroration—to collect better ethnic statistics "would do more than serve the interests of science; it would help ensure a durable peace by silencing the accusations and counter-accusations based on the imperfections of nationality statistics and the impossibility of checking on them." Strassoldo used many of the examples that Kovács had gathered, but Strassoldo's analysis was rather about how statistics could be shaped to political ends. What had been a difficult but technical problem became, in a view reflecting more recent trends, a means of manipulation that the author deplored. See Alajos Kovács, "La connaissance des langues comme contrôle de la statistique des nationalités," *Bulletin de l'Institut International de Statistique*, 23 (1928), Part 2, 246–346; Marzio Strassoldo, *Lingue e Nazionalità nelle Rilevazioni Demografiche*, Contributi e Ricerche Scienze Politiche Trieste, no. 8 (Trieste: CLUET, 1977).

identification, neither precision nor consistency can be assured. When either the same or matched persons were asked their ethnic origin in Current Population Surveys of successive years, one out of every three gave different responses from one survey to the next. The percentage of consistent replies ranged from 96.5 for Puerto Ricans down to 32.0 for "Other Spanish."[2] According to Tom Smith of the National Opinion Research Center (NORC), survey organizations, the U.S. Bureau of the Census, and NORC itself have all found that half or less of the white population is both able and willing to answer a question on national origin, which "of all the kinds of basic background variables about a person, is the most difficult of all to measure and to measure reliably." Some 10–15 percent of adult white Americans can give no ethnic identity, he pointed out, for they do not know their heritage, and 35–40 percent cite two or more ethnic strains (and of these, 11–12 percent cannot choose among them).[3]

Not only is the size of an ethnic group indeterminate at any particular count but it may change over time in one direction or the other. In his analysis of traditional Hindu India, M. N. Srinivas coined a term, sanskritization, to denote lower castes' conscious adoption of certain of the customs, associations, and beliefs of a higher caste, for by such a closer identification over a generation or two, they could sometimes raise their own level in the caste hierarchy.[4] If we generalize this concept to mean a group's social mobility by the manipulation of symbols, the statistical reclassification of marginal populations can be denoted as one type of sanskritization. Upward mobility in terms of such "real" differences as occupational status or income may be easier after a group has effected such a shift in symbols. Several decades ago some small groups with Negro-Indian-white forebears successfully protested against their classification as "Negro" and were reclassified as "Indian," which in the American South of that time was a step up.[5] In Hawaii the "Portuguese" and "Spanish" virtually began their ascent into middle class life by inducing local census officials to redefine them in 1940 as "Cau-

[2]Charles E. Johnson, Jr., "Consistency of Reporting of Ethnic Origin in the Current Population Survey," U.S. Bureau of the Census, *Technical Papers*, no. 31 (Washington, D.C., 1974).

[3]Illinois Department of Human Rights, "Report of Public Hearings on the Department's Proposed Rules Governing Equal Employment Opportunity and Affirmative Action by State Executive Agencies" (Chicago: mimeographed, 1982). Cf. Tom W. Smith, "Problems of Ethnic Measurement, Over-, Under-, and Misidentification," General Social Survey Project, *Technical Report*, no. 29 (Washington, D.C.: mimeographed, 1982). See also Michael J. Levin and Reynolds Farley, "Historical Comparability of Ethnic Designations in the United States," American Statistical Association, Social Statistics Section, *Proceedings of the Annual Meeting, 1982* (Washington, D.C., 1982).

[4]M. N. Srinivas, *Caste in Modern India and Other Essays* (Bombay: Asia Publishing House, 1962).

[5]Brewton Berry, *Almost White* (New York: Macmillan, 1965).

casian," for in local usage the two nationality tags were known to denote racially mixed populations.[6]

2. Since the civil status of the several sectors of the Republic's founding population set a basic differentiation between "race" and "ethnicity," the Bureau of the Census and its predecessors have classified subnations by one of two principles. Those of European origin have been specified as the "foreign stock" if they or one or both of their parents were born abroad; but from the third generation on, whites of any nationality disappear statistically into the native population. For non-whites, however, a separate category has been maintained, irrespective of how many generations lived in this country. At the margin this difference between race and ethnicity has been blurred, particularly since the statistical agency never developed an adequate and consistent definition of either term.

From 1790 to 1860 no instructions were given defining racial terms, and each enumerator was free to determine the race of each person in his district. Later, Negroes (or sometimes subcategories within the race) were defined by their supposed quanta of blood, hardly a criterion that could be readily used in a census operation. At all times classification of marginal persons undoubtedly reflected local opinion, which for those of mixed blood would depend in large part on the respondent's social position. Thus, the association between social class and race was sometimes set not by the generalization that blacks were typically in the lower classes but, on the contrary, by the postulate that a person in the middle class generally was not black.[7]

The country of birth of respondents has been asked in every United States census since 1850, and the countries of birth of the respondents' two parents from 1870 to 1970 (but not in 1980). These are seemingly straightforward questions that would yield unambiguous and meaningful data, but in fact most of those statistics have what Oskar Morgenstern termed "specious accuracy": "data are given which even when they have only a very small margin of error are nevertheless useless."[8] Even when it was correctly reported, the country of birth has been a very poor indicator of the ethnicity of emigrants from the multilingual

[6]Robert C. Schmitt, *Demographic Statistics of Hawaii: 1778–1965* (Honolulu: University of Hawaii Press, 1968), p. 94. See also William Petersen, "The Classification of Subnations in Hawaii: An Essay in the Sociology of Knowledge," *American Sociological Review*, 34 (1969):863–877.

[7]In Mexico this reverse definition has been written into enumerators' manuals. As defined, an Indian is a person who speaks an Indian language and wears huaraches; if he learns Spanish and wears shoes, he is redefined as a mestizo. The allegation that an "Indian" is incapable of fitting into a highly technical society, thus, is made a "fact" by the definition of the term.

[8]Oskar Morgenstern, *On the Accuracy of Economic Observations*, 2nd ed. (Princeton, N.J.: Princeton University Press, 1963), chap. 3.

empires of Central and Eastern Europe, who comprised the majority of newcomers from the 1870s to the 1920s. If we can assume that for certain periods data on various foreign stocks are adequate, that does not at all mean that each ethnic component reacts in the same way to the general American culture. Some minorities are highly concentrated in a Chinatown, for instance, where they make up a sharply distinguished group. At the other extreme, anglophone Canadian Americans are diffused over the whole country, cannot be readily differentiated from the native population, have no important ethnic organizations, and probably in many cases are unaware of one another's existence. The distinction between the first "group" and the second "category," a sine qua non in the interpretation of ethnic data, cannot be made directly from census counts.

3. Both ethnic leaders and the general community used to pressure alien groups to acculturate, and until very recently most whites that could be distinguished as different not only aspired to disappear into the broader population but, to a significant degree, actually did so. With the present emphasis on searching for one's roots, on bilingual education and multilingual census schedules, on civil rights defined in racial or ethnic terms, on affirmative action to compensate for the prior deprivation of whole groups, it is easy to forget how recently this official encouragement of differentiation came into being. The procedure of counting various subpopulations can be interpreted adequately only against a background of this sharp reversal in public attitudes and expectations.

The Special Characteristics of American Ethnicity

The populations of the thirteen colonies that evolved into the United States lacked the characteristics ordinarily associated with a nation. Their inhabitants were not all descended from a single putative ancestor; they spoke different languages; many had migrated in order to practice freely their separate religions. J. Hector de Crèvecoeur (1735–1813), a Frenchman who traveled widely and eventually settled in New York State, wrote a series of essays later assembled as *Letters from an American Farmer*, which became internationally popular as an authentic picture of America in the late eighteenth century. The American, he wrote, is "a European or the descendant of a European, . . . whose grandfather was an Englishman, whose wife was Dutch, whose son married a French woman, and whose present four sons now have four wives of different nations."[9]

[9]J. Hector St. John de Crèvecoeur, *Letters from an American Farmer* (London, 1782; reprinted, New York: Albert and Charles Boni, 1925), pp. 54–55.

Yet these diverse elements not only fused into a single nation but, over the following two centuries, absorbed more immigrants than any other country in the world. Though English became the language of the new country and such other institutions as English common law were incorporated into American civilization, the country was too diverse to become a "nation" in the conventional sense. Lacking a natural unity based on biology or a common history from some mythical past, Americans—in the words of George Bancroft (1800–1891)—"seized as their particular inheritance the tradition of liberty."[10] A conglomerate population unified by civil rights and personal liberty was so novel a concept of a "nation," however, that it was difficult to bring the colonies together and overcome their jealousies.

The instrument of this unification was the Constitution, and the delegates who assembled in Philadelphia in 1787 to write it were among America's most distinguished men. The country that had been fashioned by the Articles of Confederation was on the point of collapse; Britain and Spain had troops at the borders, ready to absorb the pieces if it did fall apart. Whenever differences among the delegates threatened to disrupt the convention, they would remind one another of the urgency of their work. In the existing Confederation each state had equal power, but the delegates from larger states wanted to give equal weight to each person. The compromise effected was to balance power by establishing a bicameral Congress; in the Senate, with equal representation from each member of the Union, the less populous states had relatively more weight; and in the House, with representation proportionate to the population, those with more inhabitants dominated. To maintain this balance the number in the lower house had to be adjusted periodically to population growth, and the first link between politics and enumeration was thus inscribed in the Constitution itself. The North and the South were divided on several issues but most sharply, of course, on slavery; several delegates from the North aggressively denounced the institution and especially the slave trade, but to have

[10]Hans Kohn emphasized this point by contrasting historians' views of the American revolution and the one that followed in France. Both were based on universal slogans, the Declaration of Independence and the Declaration of the Rights of Man, but the struggle to establish *liberté, égalité, fraternité* never catalyzed the consolidation of revolutionary Europe's heterogeneous population into one people. On the contrary, in postrevolutionary writings French virtues were discovered also in prerevolutionary France, attributes of Frenchmen rather than of democrats. In the works of Jules Michelet (1798–1874), the overseas counterpart of George Bancroft and a prototype for later French interpretations, the glorious climax to which French civilization rose in 1789 was inevitable, given the excellence of France's people. See Hans Kohn, *American Nationalism: An Interpretative Essay* (New York: Macmillan, 1957). To this day French intellectuals—or, for that matter, intellectuals of any nationality—are puzzled by the designation "un-American," for they have not understood that a nation built on political principles rather than biological uniformity can have political opponents within itself.

called for abolition would have brought the convention to an immediate end. In a second major compromise, apportionment was based on all free persons except Indians "not taxed" (that is, not living in the general population), plus three-fifths of "all other persons." For each 100 slaves in a congressional district, that is to say, it received representation equivalent to that for 60 free persons.[11] Up to the Civil War, slaves were probably counted more or less accurately, but with only partial data on even their basic demographic characteristics.

The enumeration in 1790 followed the constitutional provisions regarding the census. The population in each district set its representation in Congress, and the national total was printed in a pamphlet of 56 pages. Since slaves and Indians had a special relation to apportionment, they were distinguished from whites, all of whom were classified together. Before the 1800 census was started, two learned societies sent memorials to Congress recommending that questions be added on, among other topics, the numbers of native citizens, citizens of foreign birth, and resident aliens; but no move into ethnic statistics was taken at that time. In the fourth census, in 1820, a question was asked to determine the number of unnaturalized foreigners. In 1840 the first effort to go much beyond the classification in force since 1790 produced a result notably deficient in many of its details. The first six censuses, in sum, were limited mainly to a count of the population classified by age groups, sex, and race (subdivided between slave and free); and the attempts to include such other topics as occupations were admitted fiascos.[12]

As a consequence of "the manifest and palpable, not to say gross, errors" in the 1840 census, as a Senate bill put it, a central control was established to set uniform practices for the marshals who supervised the count in each district. In 1850 and 1860, six separate questionnaires were used to make a complete inventory of the nation, with items (in 1860) covering population, health, mortality, literacy, pauperism, occupation, income, wealth, agriculture, manufactures, mining, fisheries, commerce, banking, insurance, transportation, schools, libraries, newspapers, crime, taxes, and religion. So many data, compiled by marshals as one of their subsidiary duties and tallied by hand, were hardly useful. Much of the information was not published until it was well out of date, and census officials themselves testified to the many weaknesses in their operation. Yet it is remarkable how few items in that vast mass

---

[11]Edmund S. Morgan, *The Birth of the Republic, 1763–89* (Chicago: University of Chicago Press, 1977). See also Forrest McDonald, *Novus Ordo Seclorum: The Intellectual Origins of the Constitution* (Lawrence: University Press of Kansas, 1985).

[12]Carroll D. Wright, *The History and Growth of the United States Census* (56th Cong., 1st sess., Senate Document no. 194, 1900; reprinted, New York: Johnson Reprint Corp., 1966).

pertained to ethnicity (apart from race), which up to the mid-century had little or no place in American law or, thus, in the country's censuses.

America as a Melting Pot

Apart from the two anomalies, Indians and Negro slaves, the population was seen as unitary or, at worst, in the process of becoming homogeneous. The expectation that all whites would assimilate into a single new nation was countered by opposition, usually temporary, to the various European nationalities. During the middle decades of the nineteenth century prejudice was strong against Germans and especially Irish, but only for a time. Many of the immigrants' leaders tried to preserve their native languages in the new country, but over the longer term generally with little success. For until recently the dominant impetus from both sides was to foster acculturation, and this peculiar feature was a typical leitmotif of writings on American ethnicity. In Europe the aim of an ethnic minority had been to maintain its language or religion or way of life, but in the United States any group that was defined as distinctive tried to hasten its consolidation into the general population.

The American theory of ethnicity evolved in the context of two debates on policy issues: whether to restrict immigration and what the Negro's proper place was in American society. The questions were whether differences between immigrants and natives, and between blacks and whites, were more or less permanent and thus significant, or merely transitory and therefore to be discounted for the long run.

Though it has become routine to deride the metaphor, at the time the melting pot accurately represented the desire of the insecure immigrant generation to disappear totally, to merge into indistinguishable sameness with "real" Americans. Assimilation was taking place while the country was debating whether "New Immigrants" from Southern and Eastern Europe should be allowed to come in such large numbers, for they were allegedly unassimilable into American society. Their exclusion was first sought indirectly, by banning the immigration of illiterates, and then in a series of new laws.[13] Many in academia opposed

[13]In 1921 European immigration was limited to 3 percent of the number of foreign-born of each nationality residing in the United States at the time of the last available census figures, those of 1910. A second law, passed in 1924, set up another temporary system, more restrictive than its predecessor in two respects: the 3 percent was reduced to 2 percent, and the base population was changed from the 1910 to the 1890 census, when the proportion from Southern and Eastern Europe was smaller. The 1924 act also provided that eventually immigration quotas would be based on the national origins of the total population, rather than merely of the foreign-born.

the thesis behind these statutes and argued that the melting pot was indeed working. Robert E. Park, perhaps the most important American sociologist of the 1920s, offered a model in which the association of diverse peoples would lead inevitably to assimilation, and many of his students and disciples followed this lead. According to a typical statement of the period, "Assimilation . . . goes on wherever contact and communication exist between groups. . . . It is as inevitable as it is desirable. The process may be hastened or delayed; it cannot be stopped."[14]

In *An American Dilemma*, a synthesis of a generation's writings on race relations, the Swedish sociologist–economist Gunnar Myrdal expounded at length the similar thesis that all but the most superficial differences between the races derived from whites' prejudices and the discriminatory institutions in which they were embedded. He forecast a kind of vicious circle in reverse, which he called the "principle of cumulation," setting an interaction between changing attitudes and improving social conditions. As the quality of blacks' education, for example, got better, whites would be less likely to believe that blacks are innately less intelligent and therefore would be more willing to foster other improvements in their schooling, and so on. The work ended on a note of high optimism: "The driving force behind social study" is "the faith that institutions can be improved and strengthened and that people are good enough to live a happier life."[15] Prejudice and discrimination did indeed decline markedly over the next generation, but without giving rise to the rapprochement between blacks and whites that many students of race relations anticipated.

For several decades the actual assimilation of minority groups was sometimes exaggerated by a systematic effort to blur remaining differences. For if all significant ethnic variation was disappearing (in fact, had not disappeared only because of racists' last-ditch efforts to maintain it), then it was incumbent on every person of good will to move a bit ahead of the trend and act as though the distinctions had already become obsolete. As recently as 1950 an American academic who voiced a phrase like "the Jewish vote" or "the Negro vote" would have put himself beyond the pale, for in relation to federal elections American citizens were expected to act as individuals in an ethnically undifferentiated population. The American Civil Liberties Union tried to get the question on race deleted from the 1960 census schedule, and New Jersey did omit race and color from its birth and death certificates for the

---

[14]Maurice R. Davie, *World Immigration, with Special Reference to the United States* (New York: Macmillan, 1949), pp. 498–499.

[15]Gunnar Myrdal, *An American Dilemma: The Negro Problem and Modern Democracy* (New York: Harper, 1944), p. 1024.

year 1962 (restoring them, however, one year later). Following the example of the prestigious *New York Times*, many newspapers omitted for a decade or so all racial identifications of persons in the news. Many local jurisdictions in the United States stipulated that employment applications, applications for entrance to college, and similar forms might not require an ethnic identification or—what was regarded as an approximate equivalent—a photograph.

Censuses taken during the era of the melting pot reflected concern about newcomers' supposed characteristics and their rate of Americanization. In 1870, as we have noted, two questions were added to determine whether either of the respondent's parents had been born abroad. In 1890 foreign-born males aged 21 or over were asked how many years they had resided in the United States, whether they were naturalized, and, if not, whether they had taken out naturalization papers. Also in that year the entire population was asked whether they were able to speak English and, if not, what language or dialect they spoke. After the restrictive immigration laws of the 1920s were passed, interest in ethnic composition waned somewhat, and from the depression decade of the 1930s onward censuses reflected the growing interest in economic well-being.

From Cultural Pluralism to Ethnic Competition

In one generation, as we can now see, spokesmen for European immigrants went from a joyful anticipation of their disappearance into general American society to a demand for full corporate equality with the earliest settlers. According to a thesis first enunciated by Marcus Lee Hansen, this change of attitude might have been anticipated when immigrants were replaced by their sons and then their grandsons as the dominant sector of the European stock. While immigrants were linked to their native countries by childhood memories and recurrent nostalgia, as well as by immigrant-aid societies, national churches, and other ethnic organizations, their acculturation was not usually impeded by a conscious reluctance to give up most old-country remnants. The aspiration of many immigrants to be more American than a Mayflower descendant was taken over a little more realistically by the second generation, which typically attempted to learn nothing of the language and other culture traits of its European forebears. The third generation, however, often tried to organize a revival of their grandparents' native way of life. Thus, the procession of nationalities that came to the United States was often followed by a succession two generations later of amateur historical societies, folklore associations, and other organized efforts to keep alive or revivify or invent elements of the various overseas cultures. As Hansen put it, it was an "almost universal phenomenon that what the son wishes to forget the grandson wishes to remember."[16]

Such aspirations of the third generation were legitimized by, among others, Horace Kallen, who developed the concept of "cultural pluralism" in a series of influential papers.[17] The maintenance of American democracy, he held, did not require that immigrants be totally assimilated; one could distinguish those alien attributes that had to be forgone (in particular, loyalty to a foreign state) from those that could well be retained in a pluralistic society, such as, for example, language and religion. Critics pointed out that precisely those characteristics—language and religion—have been proximate causes of conflict the world over. Moreover, even insignificant remnants of minority cultures would encourage each ethnic population both to maintain a certain coherence and to continue its links to the home country, and the most abrasive charge against immigrants had typically been that their loyalty to the United States was compromised by enduring ties of any sort to the country of birth.

In spite of such seeming flaws, cultural pluralism soon supplanted the melting pot as the typical symbol of social policy, and the list of acceptable characteristics of the alien stock was repeatedly expanded. Indeed, it soon included the one attitude that, according to Kallen, had to disappear—a vestigial political (rather than merely cultural) adherence to another country. According to the often-cited thesis of Samuel Lubell, both the "interventionists" who wanted the United States to support the Allies in World War II and the "isolationists" who wanted to stay out of Europe's troubles were expressing half-hidden nationalist sentiments. Since it was politically impossible to advocate directly that the United States back Germany, isolationist descendants of Germans in the Midwest voiced this wish indirectly. And when Britain's need was dire enough, New England Yankees voted to help her even though they were half a dozen generations removed from immigrant status. In scholarly circles Lubell's work helped establish a link between ethnic blocs and American foreign policy as a routine element of most anal-

[16]Marcus Lee Hansen, *The Problem of the Third Generation Immigrant* (Rock Island, Ill.: Augustana Historical Society, 1938; reprinted in *Commentary*, November 1952, pp. 492–500).

[17]See, for example, Horace M. Kallen et al., *Cultural Pluralism and the American Idea: An Essay in Social Philosophy* (Philadelphia: University of Pennsylvania Press, 1956), reporting a symposium in which Kallen defended his fully elaborated thesis against several critics. See also Philip Gleason, "American Identity and Americanization," *Harvard Encyclopedia of American Ethnic Groups* (Cambridge, Mass.: Harvard University Press, 1980).

yses, and thus to carry out the promise of its title, predicting "the future of American politics."[18]

The works of Hansen, Kallen, and Lubell typified a broader discussion among descendants of European immigrants pertaining to the white population. During the same years the melting pot, to the degree that it ever applied to Negroes, was also rejected by them. The Martiniquan poet Aimé Césaire coined the word *négritude*, the essential quality of black people, and his work was fulsomely praised by such Paris intellectuals as Jean-Paul Sartre and André Breton. Césaire tried to resolve "the dilemma of a victim forced to free himself from the shackles of his oppressor by the use of those very shackles."[19] That is, though reason and the technology of white civilization were to be exorcised and replaced by blacks' vitality and "soul," the advance of black people had to come about in part by making use of the very instruments that they were rejecting. The ferment among black writers over *négritude* was broadened by the "search for roots" popularized by the novelist Alex Haley, who claimed to have traced his ancestry through 200 years of slavery and oppression. For eight consecutive nights during January 1977 an estimated 80 million persons watched a television version of Haley's work. According to a check by two professional genealogists, the roots that Haley had claimed to uncover were largely fictional: Some of his presumed ancestors did not exist, others were too young or too old to have contributed to the family tree, others lived in the wrong place. The cited records "contradict each and every pre–Civil War statement of Afro-American lineage in *Roots*."[20] This refutation, published in an obscure journal, was generally ignored even by professional historians; certainly it did not disturb the extension of the search for roots from a European to an African context.

Earlier, ethnicity had had no legitimate place in *national* politics, though in any metropolis ethnic blocs manifestly and unashamedly

---

[18]Samuel Lubell, *The Future of American Politics*, 2nd ed. (Garden City, N.Y.: Doubleday-Anchor, 1956). The thesis linking national origins with political attitudes is dubious or, at best, unprovable. Adequate statistics on nationality beyond the second generation or on religion at all did not exist, and linking such data as existed with secret votes involved all the well-known faults of ecological correlations. Concerning specifically the 1940 election, the one that Lubell used most to substantiate this argument, so distinguished a political scientist as V. O. Key concluded from an intensive study that "foreign policy seemed to have far less bearing on the vote than did questions of domestic policy. . . . The data indicate a comparatively mild relation between attitudes on foreign policy and vote shifting." See V. O. Key, Jr., *The Responsible Electorate: Rationality in Presidential Voting, 1936–1960* (Cambridge, Mass.: Belknap Press, 1960), p. 50.

[19]Anon., "Twilight of a Dark Myth," *Times Literary Supplement* (September 16, 1965), pp. 805–806. See Aimé Césaire, *Cahier d'un Retour au Pays Natal*, with "Un grand poète noir," by André Breton (New York: Brentano's, 1947).

[20]Gary B. Mills and Elizabeth Shown Mills, "Roots and the New 'Faction': A Legitimate Tool for Clio?" *Virginia Magazine of History and Biography*, 89 (1981):3–25.

constituted interest groups. This was partly because the "hyphenated" identity of immigrants and their children once would have been regarded as a far more sensitive issue in elections linked to international relations, but principally because the local governments distributed jobs, contracts, licenses, access to facilities, and other benefits. In order to get preferential treatment from a ward boss, a voter had to join with others into a less blunt wedge than one of the heterogeneous American parties; and associations for mustering such power were ready-made in the quasi-political ethnically based social clubs and churches. After President Roosevelt's New Deal coalition was amplified in President Johnson's subsequent War on Poverty, the standard municipal pattern of distributing preferments became the prototype for a new kind of federal patronage, with the consequence that ethnic blocs began to compete also in Washington. The search for one's roots would hardly have become so fashionable an element of American culture without the material advantages associated with that quest. In combination, ideological and monetary forces were irresistible.

During these same decades, finally, the concept of "equality" was revised, with momentous effects on ethnic relations and thus on the significance of how ethnic groups are classified. The moral equality guaranteed in the Declaration of Independence, half-compromised by the Founders' acceptance of slavery, was given legal force in the Thirteenth, Fourteenth, and Fifteenth Amendments to the Constitution, which abolished slavery, guaranteed all citizens equal protection under the law, and safeguarded the right to vote from racial discrimination. As one can see from the debate in Congress on those amendments, those who framed them wanted to outlaw all legal distinctions based on race, but the U.S. Supreme Court ignored this intent. The separate-but-equal doctrine, which it laid down in 1896, was not reversed until 1954, in *Brown* v. *Board of Education*. During the following decades the Court consistently denounced racial distinctions as, in Chief Justice Harlan F. Stone's words, "by their very nature odious to a free people whose institutions are founded upon the doctrine of equality" (*Loving* v. *Virginia*, 388 U.S. 1, 11, 1966).

Congress also repeatedly insisted that the government remain neutral with respect to race, enacting the Civil Rights Acts of 1957, 1960, and 1964, the Voting Rights Act of 1965, and the Civil Rights Act of 1968. That these laws were intended to establish a colorblind standard is clear not only from their language but, even more obviously, from the debates in Congress. Opponents of the Civil Rights Act of 1964, for example, worried about the possible effects of Title VII: prohibiting discrimination in employment, they feared, might lead to new racially determined preferences. The bill's sponsors adamantly rejected this interpretation, and finally Senator Hubert Humphrey, who was shepherding the bill through the upper house, became so exasperated with the continued skepticism that he declared, "If . . . in Title VII . . . any language [can be found] which provides that an employer will have to hire on the basis of percentage or quota related to color, . . . I will start eating the pages [of the bill] one after another." Similarly, Title IV of the same act plainly stated that " 'desegregation' shall not mean the assignment of students to public schools in order to overcome racial imbalance," and that the act would not "empower any official or court of the United States to issue any order seeking to achieve a racial balance" in public schools.[21] Those who abhor racial distinctions in employment or in access to other kinds of benefits happily joined what seemed to be a national consensus in, at long last, establishing a colorblind society in the United States.

However clear the mandate of Congress, it was ignored by federal agencies and federal courts, which once again frustrated the will to establish laws that did not differentiate by race or ethnic affinity. The attempt to equalize education moved from securing equivalent schooling to the peripheral issue of busing children away from their neighborhoods in order to balance the number of white and black pupils. Affirmative action in employment went from equal opportunity as a goal, to using quotas to test the efficacy of programs set up to achieve that goal, to many instances of reverse discrimination.[22] As implemented, the laws were not what their proponents had intended them to be; on the contrary, in many cases nothing mattered so much about a person applying for various types of preferment as race or nationality or sex. Class-action suits, increasingly common from the 1960s on, helped the move toward a restructuring of American society, with previously private groupings given a new public identity. The size of ethnic groups thus acquired a new salience: It was no longer the native stock checking on whether immigrants were being assimilated on schedule but rather certain minorities making demands on the public purse in proportion to their numbers.

[21]Cf. William Bradford Reynolds, "Legitimizing Race as a Decision-Making Criterion: Where Are We Going?" Forum on Law and Social Justice, Amherst College, Amherst, Mass., 1983 (unpublished manuscript).

[22]Nathan Glazer, *Affirmative Discrimination: Ethnic Inequality and Public Policy* (New York: Basic Books, 1975). On so contentious an issue as affirmative action, no single work suffices to represent the range of opinion. Glazer can be recommended for his detailed differentiation between the original law and the subsequent interpretation; R. A. Rossum is a good analysis of its topic, *Reverse Discrimination: The Constitutional Debate* (New York: Marcel Dekker, 1980); and C. J. Livingston gives a spirited defense of "affirmative action" against "equality of opportunity" in his *Fair Game? Inequality and Affirmative Action* (San Francisco: W. H. Freeman, 1979).

The speed with which federal agencies and federal courts reversed the will of Congress is suggested by the fact that in several contexts the legal stipulation that race or ethnicity must be ignored overlapped with the subsequent one setting de facto quotas for the admission of students or the hiring or promotion of workers. For a period, thus, universities and business firms were both prohibited from taking cognizance of race or ethnicity and required to report on the assigned balance among designated groups.

From Race to Ethnicity

The two categories—Negroes and Indians—that the Republic distinguished during the first half-century or so were counted differently mainly because of their anomalous civil status; but this distinction helped set the contrast among races as the fundamental ethnic characteristic in the censuses and eventually also in other works. It has been argued with some plausibility that the defenders of slavery did much to exaggerate the significance of race, and one can presume that one consequence of this perspective was that in American statistics the various Asian peoples were also classified differently from Europeans. Reformers trying to remedy the country's social ills also stressed the special disadvantages of being black, and the vast expansion of writings on minorities focused, at least initially, on the same group. As one index of this emphasis, of the 482 articles on ethnic groups that appeared in the *American Journal of Sociology,* the *American Sociological Review,* and *Social Forces* from 1900 to 1974, 71 percent dealt with blacks, 29 percent with all others.[23]

This extraordinary focus on blacks has been challenged in a number of ways. Some anthropologists, most prominently Ashley Montagu, tried to combat racism by deleting the word "race" from scholarly and genteel language, and the proposed substitution of "ethnic group" would seemingly blur what others saw as the special handicap of blacks.[24] Others pointed out that that handicap, however specified, was shared by other components of the population. In his work on the his-

---

[23]Abraham D. Lavender and John M. Forsyth, "The Sociological Study of Minority Groups as Reflected by Leading Sociological Journals: Who Gets Studied and Who Gets Neglected?" *Ethnicity,* 3 (1976):388–398. One might object that the result of this survey was in part the factitious consequence of the choice of journals; many papers on Jews, for instance, appear in specialized journals, but there are also such serials as *Phylon,* devoted almost entirely to blacks. Lavender and Forsyth cited a number of other studies that came to the same conclusion that they did.

[24]Ashley Montagu, *Man's Most Dangerous Myth: The Fallacy of Race* (New York: World, 1964), Appendix B.

tory of ethnic differentiation, Thomas Sowell, a black economist, was obviously fascinated by the discrimination and humiliations long suffered by Irish immigrants; the many parallels that he pointed out cut across the race line.[25] The broader analysis of America's minorities began to transcend earlier filiopietism and to acquire a far wider hearing. Andrew Greeley, who began with Irish Americans in Chicago and then in the whole country, expanded his view to "the rediscovery of diversity" and the importance of ethnic identity in itself, not simply as a function of social class. "We know less about Polish Americans," Greeley wrote, "than about some African tribes," and he joined others in trying to repair that gap.[26]

The shift from race to ethnicity was stimulated not only by piety but also by politics. One of the most influential works in documenting, and thus fostering, this shift was Nathan Glazer and Daniel P. Moynihan's *Beyond the Melting Pot*. As a study of politics in New York City, it started with a milieu in which ethnic blocs were traditional, but the interpretation included the whole of American society. The "new ethnicity" of their analysis, however, was not readily accepted. One of the funding agencies withdrew its support of the study, and some critics objected especially to the fact that racial groups like Negroes and Puerto Ricans were discussed precisely in the same way as ethnic groups like Jews, Italians, and Irish.[27]

Federal intervention in the country's ethnic structure was once limited to defending ex-slaves from discriminatory local practices, and at first laws and court decisions of the recent period also reflected a major concern with the continuing discrimination against blacks. However, the groups given preference under affirmative action have steadily grown in number, and those who watched this spread from the outside wanted to be included as well. There can be no doubt that the nationalities once labeled the New Immigration have suffered, and in many instances still suffer, from discrimination. One symptom of the resentment that is building up was provided at hearings in 1982 before

[25]Thomas Sowell, *Ethnic America: A History* (New York: Basic Books, 1981), chap. 2 and passim. See also Stanley Lieberson, *A Piece of the Pie: Blacks and White Immigrants since 1880* (Berkeley: University of California Press, 1981); Nathan Glazer, *Ethnic Dilemmas, 1964–1982* (Cambridge, Mass.: Harvard University Press, 1983), chap. 5.

[26]Andrew M. Greeley, *Ethnicity in the United States: A Preliminary Reconnaissance* (New York: Wiley, 1974); idem, "Political Participation among Ethnic Groups," *American Journal of Sociology*, 80 (1974):170–204.

[27]Nathan Glazer and Daniel Patrick Moynihan, *Beyond the Melting Pot: The Negroes, Puerto Ricans, Jews, Italians, and Irish of New York City*, 2nd ed. (Cambridge, Mass.: M.I.T. Press, 1970). See also Glazer, "*Beyond the Melting Pot* Twenty Years After," *Journal of American Ethnic History*, 1 (1981):43–55.

representatives of the Illinois Department of Human Rights on a bill concerning affirmative action and equal employment opportunities. According to Representative Robert Terzich, who had sponsored the bill in the Illinois legislature, its main purpose was to amend the laws prohibiting discrimination so as to give protection to those defined by national origin. By a threshold set in the bill, any group comprising less than 2 percent of the state's population would not be so protected, but according to Representative Terzich, "group" could be interpreted to include "umbrella groups and multiple ethnic communities . . . similar to a grouping of many national origins under the general title of Hispanics." Such "groups" he exemplified as Southeast Asians, Eastern Europeans, and persons from the Baltic states. Asked to define an ethnic group, Becir Tanovic of the United Yugoslavs noted that neither federal nor state legislation is very specific, but it is "common knowledge that the intent was to include primarily East European and South European groups because they have been discriminated [against] and that has been demonstrated well enough over many years." He listed the ones he meant: first of all Poles, well over 15 percent of the state's population, Ukrainians, Yugoslavs, Czechoslovaks, Hungarians, Greeks, and Italians. How discrimination would be proved was suggested by Roman Pucinski, local president of the Polish American Congress; he cited a recent survey showing that only an infinitesimal fraction of the executives of the 500 largest Chicago corporations were of Slavic origin.[28]

That virtually all writers on ethnicity have accepted pluralism as the norm does not mean that there is a consensus. In a review of historians' writings on the subject, John Higham divided the analysts into two types. What he called the "soft pluralists" followed in the tradition of Kallen, perceiving cultural differences as values to be cherished for their own sake. Others, the "hard pluralists," followed Herbert Gutman in linking ethnic groups with social classes, for in their view only ethnic unity enabled otherwise defenseless workers to resist industrial oppression.[29]

If group-based quotas are set for Slavs, Italians, and other nationalities not proportionately represented in high-level positions, the Bureau

[28]Illinois Department of Human Rights, "Report of Public Hearings."

[29]John Higham, "Current Trends in the Study of Ethnicity in the United States," *Journal of American Ethnic History*, 2 (1982):5–15; Herbert Gutman, *Work, Culture and Society in Industrializing America: Essays in American Working Class and Social History* (New York: Random House, 1976), pp. 3–78. See also Philip Gleason, "Pluralism and Assimilation: A Conceptual History," in John Edwards, ed., *Linguistic Minorities, Policies and Pluralism* (New York: Academic Press, 1984).

of the Census would be called on to furnish the data on which these new quotas would be based. Presumably the already complex schedule would become yet more complicated. In 1980 respondents were asked to define themselves as one of the following: "white, black or Negro, Japanese, Chinese, Filipino, Korean, Vietnamese, Indian (Amer.), Asian Indian, Hawaiian, Guamanian, Samoan, Eskimo, Aleut, or other (specify)." The list does not follow elementary rules for constructing a taxonomy—that the classes be mutually exclusive, that all the classes add up to the whole of the population, and that they be of roughly the same order of importance and magnitude.

It should be stressed, however, that this mishmash was not created by the Bureau of the Census. In a succession of directives the Office of Federal Statistical Policy and Standards designated the races and ethnic groups to be used in all federal reporting and statistics.

> These classifications [the directive warned] should not be interpreted as being scientific or anthropological in nature, nor should they be viewed as determinants of eligibility for participation in any federal program. They have been developed in response to needs expressed by both the executive branch and Congress to provide for the collection and use of compatible, nonduplicated, exchangeable racial and ethnic data by federal agencies.[30]

Ira Lowry has suggested the implicit defense of the Bureau of the Census in carrying out the procedure that this directive mandates:

> Ethnic identity cannot be established by objective criteria, at least in large-scale self-administered surveys. We therefore accept that an individual's ethnicity is whatever he says it is. The Bureau's job is to elicit self-identification and then to group the responses into recognizable categories that (a) are mandated for federal civil rights enforcement, (b) satisfy the more vocal ethnic lobbies, and (c) provide enough continuity with past census statistics to satisfy social scientists engaged in longitudinal analysis.

"However," Lowry concluded, "the Bureau's success in balancing the claims of constituencies was achieved at the expense of its fundamental mission: gathering valid and reliable information about the population of the United States."[31]

[30]U.S. Office of Federal Statistical Policy and Standards, "Race and Ethnic Standards for Federal Statistics and Administrative Reporting," Directive No. 15 (Washington, D.C., May 1978).
[31]Ira S. Lowry, *The Science and Politics of Ethnic Enumeration*, Rand Papers Series, no. P-6435-1 (Santa Monica, Calif., 1980), p. 19.

Ethnicity in the American Census

At one time most of those who wrote about race or ethnicity were interested mainly, or only, in their own forebears, with the consequence that writings on the subject usually dealt with only one group or, in composite works, one group at a time. The practice continued partly because sources are generally arranged in the same way. For someone trying to go beyond this convention, the more interesting questions concern not the culture or well-being of blacks or Jews or another grouping but, rather, how characteristics cut across ethnic boundaries. The operations of a statistical bureau, on the other hand, can be discussed chronologically (as in Carroll Wright's history of the census) or topically (as in the technical manuals on particular operations). In this presentation the emphasis is on the problems associated with the collection and presentation of ethnic data, and the discussion of particular groups is intended to highlight the conceptual ambiguities or technical difficulties that each of them exemplifies.

Ethnic "Group" versus Ethnic "Category"

Analysts of languages differentiate between bilingualism, which is a characteristic of individuals, and diglossia, which is one of populations. A simple aggregation would lead one to assume that where one exists the other must also, but in an interesting essay Joshua Fishman exemplified the distinctions to be made. There are four possible combinations: (1) A monolingual population made up of monolingual individuals, the simplest case, is restricted to very small and isolated speech communities. (2) A country with both diglossia and bilingualism is approximated in Paraguay. The rural population there once spoke only Guarani; but a substantial portion particularly of those that moved to the towns learned Spanish, which in the countryside is also the language of education, the courts, and other government institutions. As a consequence, more than half of the population uses both languages. (3) In a society with distinct social classes and little movement between them, it sometimes happens that each class has its own language. In pre-1914 Europe, for instance, the elites often spoke French and the mass of the common people another language. The small amount of low-level communication required between master and servant was likely to be in a sharply curtailed version of either language—that is, a pidgin. (4) Bilingualism without diglossia, finally, can be exemplified by the United States during the period of mass immigration from Europe. Newcomers to the country who spoke their native languages had a strong motivation to learn English, but their bilingualism was usually transitory, seldom lasting as a mass phenomenon beyond the immigrant generation or, at most, the second generation.[32] The fact that diglossia and bilingualism can be disjunctive presents a problem in the interpretation of census statistics, which are gathered from individuals who may or may not be members of speech communities. And the dilemma applies not only to languages, of course, but to any other index of ethnicity.

Whether persons are classified by some characteristic or by their self-identification, summing these persons into a race or nationality or other type of ethnic grouping passes over the problems associated with aggregation. Moreover, the confusion has been compounded by the lack of appropriate terms. *Ethnic* is an adjective; used as a noun (as in the phrase "white ethnics"), it is still sociologese or, at best, slang. Though some analysts have taken over the Greek noun *ethnos*, this is not a common usage. The lack of a convenient substantive form has induced writers to coin a number of makeshifts, of which the commonest is "ethnic group." But a crucial distinction exists between a group, which by correct definition has some degree of coherence and solidarity, and a subpopulation, category, grouping, aggregate, bracket, or sector, which denote no more than a patterning of parts. With increasing degrees of self-conscious cohesion, a subnation can constitute successively a "category," a "group," and a "community." An ethnic "group," narrowly defined, is a subnation conscious of its distinct characteristics but lacking a separate formal organization; a "community" is based not only on awareness of its different religious faith, for instance, but also on its own organizational structure.[33]

The Bureau of the Census may have helped quicken the formation of groups by granting their so-called leaders more authority than they yet exercised, as when it established nonprofessional advisory committees in an effort to improve coverage among members of minorities. Inevitably, many members of these committees were activists or mili-

---

[32]Joshua A. Fishman, *Language in Sociocultural Change: Essays* (Stanford, Calif.: Stanford University Press, 1972), chap. 5.

[33]The development of a subnation's self-awareness is similar to the rise of the same kind of cognition in a social class. It was for this reason that Marx distinguished between a "class in itself" and a "class for itself." The former, which he also termed a "stratum," constitutes all persons who share a particular relation to the means of production— owners of factories, or those who work in them, or small shopkeepers, or any similar aggregate. Because the individuals in each such category are likely to come into frequent contact and to discuss their common problems, they may (Marx would say "do") develop a "class consciousness" and become a "class for itself." Cf. Robert A. Nisbet, *The Sociological Tradition* (New York: Basic Books, 1966), chap. 5.

tants, interested not in statistical procedure as such but in how to shape the census count in order to validate their own perception of social reality. For example, the especially active Census Advisory Committee on the Spanish-Origin Population for the 1980 Census produced a large number of recommendations, some of which pertained to nomenclature and some to procedures. Seemingly it tried to raise to the maximum possible the number that would be classified as of "Spanish origin." It recommended, for instance, that the question on ethnicity appear before that on race; many Mexican Americans might designate themselves as either Hispanic or Indian, and many Puerto Ricans as either Hispanic or black, and in both cases the choice might depend on the order of the questions. As another example, the committee recommended that if a person reported himself as part-Spanish, he be classified either in one of the subordinate Spanish-origin categories or in the residual "Other Spanish." The bureau rejected this recommendation and instead asked a respondent derived from several nationalities which of them best described his own origin.

A transition from category to group is usually pioneered by a small band of intellectuals, who may propagandize for decades or perhaps generations before their arguments are accepted, if ever, by the sector of the population of which they have appointed themselves representatives. Very often such leaders, in fact, have spoken not for the whole of their supposed constituency but for one part of it, with other parts either represented by other leaders or unorganized. In the United States ethnic spokesmen have acquired their influence through wealth (German Jews in the nineteenth century), professional standing (Negro clergymen), or a place in general American politics (Irish in Eastern cities), and only occasionally through elections in an ethnic organization that is accepted by most members of the minority as truly representative (the Japanese American Citizens League in its heyday). That it is difficult to determine how many are following supposed leaders impedes the analysis of the subnations themselves, for it is mainly from the statements of alleged heads that the public can decide whether a category has become a group and, if so, what its aspirations are and how seriously its demands should be taken. Self-designated conductors always pretend that the whole of the orchestra is following their beat, even when the cacophony of divergent sections is plainly audible. The mass media and social scientists gave much more attention to such minuscule bands as the Black Panthers, to cite an egregious example, than to the Negro churches, whose totally different social programs were supported by the vast majority of the population both allegedly spoke for.

Since the line between category and group is not sharp, no indicator can distinguish between them absolutely. To ignore the difference, however, means that the statistics will often be misinterpreted not only by the general public but also by professional social scientists. Similar difficulties have arisen with various types of survey data, and polling firms have established methods of coping with them. Ira Lowry has suggested that once ethnic categories have been identified in the census by a gross characteristic, a sample of each category could be surveyed to determine the intensity of ethnic self-identification. Possible probes might include questions about family lineage, languages used, and interactions with others of the same ethnicity.[34] Until something of the sort is done, virtually the entire body of ethnic data collected is ambiguous or, worse, misleading.

Differentiation among Blacks

In the past, when blacks were much more homogeneous with respect to most characteristics, census enumerations denoted subgroups within the Negro population. Until general emancipation slaves were distinguished from freed blacks; and Negroes from the West Indies, like all other immigrants, were listed separately. In order to emphasize how important these two differentiations were, Thomas Sowell entitled an essay "Three Black Histories." Most "free persons of color," who constituted 14 percent of the Negro population in the 1830s, lived not on large plantations in the black belt but in cities or small towns. In the District of Columbia half the Negroes were free in 1830, more than three-quarters in 1860. There and elsewhere they established their own schools and reduced illiteracy sometimes to nil and always to well below that of even the most favored urban slaves. That those who escaped from slavery before the general emancipation had an enduring advantage is shown by the fact that they and their descendants were the principal leaders of the black community up to about the time of World War I.[35]

In five censuses between 1840 and 1910, an attempt was made to subclassify Negroes by skin color, usually between blacks and mulattoes but in 1890 into blacks, mulattoes, quadroons, and octoroons. According to the census report itself, the four-way classification was "of little value" or even "misleading." It is usual to dismiss these attempts to construct a taxonomy by quanta of "blood" as no more than manifestations of the nineteenth-century obsession with biologically defined race. On the other hand, one could take the black–mulatto dichotomy

[34]Lowry, *Science and Politics of Ethnic Enumeration*, pp. 22–23.

[35]Thomas Sowell, "Three Black Histories," in Sowell, ed., *Essays and Data on American Ethnic Groups* (Washington, D.C.: Urban Institute, 1978).

as a rough substitute for the slave–free one, with which there was a certain overlap. In the free Negro population of 1850, there were 581 mulattoes per 1,000 blacks, contrasted with only 83 in the slave population. Years of schooling and proportion of illiterate also differed considerably between the two subcategories.[36]

Another division within the black population has been between natives and "West Indians," or immigrants from any of the British islands together with their descendants. Though in most respects slavery was more callous in the islands than in the United States, slaves there were assigned land and time to raise their own food, and they could sell any surplus in the market to buy other things for themselves. Thus, when they were freed—a full generation before American slaves—they already had developed something of the self-reliance and resilience that their descendants later brought with them to the mainland. Though in 1980 West Indians numbered only about 1 percent of the black population, their concentration in the upper levels of the Harlem community made them important. Allegedly they differed not only in their occupations but in behavior patterns, being more frugal, hard-working, and entrepreneurial; they had smaller families and lower crime rates than other Americans, black or white.[37]

Whatever the differences in the past between slaves and the free colored, or blacks and mulattoes, or natives and West Indians, one might contend that so long as all Negroes were denigrated in law, suffrage, employment, and other major institutional settings, no distinction within the race mattered very much. It is paradoxical, now that formal segregation and discrimination have been banned, that the earlier statistical subclassifications have no significant counterpart. True, there is a large and growing immigration of blacks, who are sometimes distinguished as a component of the foreign-born (though they may choose to list themselves as Hispanics). Current data on native blacks, however, are often misleading, for along virtually every dimension Negroes are divided into two contrasting subgroups.[38] In a book whose title proclaims its subject, *The Declining Significance of Race*, William Julius Wilson contrasted the widely divergent backgrounds of the two sectors of American blacks. On the one hand, as one symptom of the general condition of the black slum, he noted that the non-white–white ratio of unemployment rates for those aged 16–19 rose from 1.37 in

---

[36]John Cummings, *Negro Population, 1790–1915* (Washington, D.C.: U.S. Bureau of the Census, 1918; reprinted, New York: Arno Press, 1968), chap. 11.

[37]Sowell, *Ethnic America*, p. 219. See also Sowell, *The Economics and Politics of Race: An International Perspective* (New York: Morrow, 1983).

[38]Reynolds Farley and Suzanne M. Bianchi, "The Growing Gap between Blacks," *American Demographics*, 5 (July 1983):15–18.

1954 to 2.35 in 1974—and it has since gone higher. On the other hand, the number of visits made by recruiters from corporations to predominantly black colleges and universities, which averaged only four in 1960, rose to 50 in 1965 and 297 in 1970. In every respect the contrast is sharp between the black unemployed, many of whom are unemployable at the minimum wage set by law, and the newly risen middle class. [39]

If blacks were given a chance in surveys by the Bureau of the Census to classify themselves into separate subgroups, would they avail themselves of that opportunity, or is the sentiment of unity so strong that it would make any such procedure nugatory? No one can say with certainty, but the past transformations of blacks' social status and life chances did bring about fundamental changes in their self-identity. As slaves they had no say in any public matter. For many years after emancipation, when it was difficult to advance or, in the worst periods, even to maintain oneself, the occasional especially talented or lucky individual who succeeded usually modeled himself on the white middle class. Once the barriers had been significantly lowered and large sectors of the race could advance in status, this widespread upward mobility was accompanied by a new emphasis on ethnic values. Elements of past history that once had been deliberately ignored or suppressed were revived to reinforce group solidarity, which it was hoped would result in a further group advance. [40]

As one indication of the change in identity, one can note the succession of official or quasi-official designations as summarized by W. Augustus Low and Virgil A. Clift. [41] For some decades after the Civil War the usual polite group name was "Colored," which avoided the connotations of both blackness and African origin. Its use declined from the 1950s, and it probably would have disappeared altogether except for

[39]William Julius Wilson, *The Declining Significance of Race: Blacks and Changing American Institutions* (Chicago: University of Chicago Press, 1978). Like any other attempt to show that discrimination against Negroes is no longer all-pervasive, Wilson's book was not well received by many other blacks. An "Association of Black Sociologists" declared itself to be "outraged over the misrepresentations of the black experience" and "extremely disturbed over the policy implications that may derive from this work." The book was also important enough to stimulate a full volume of commentary and response: Charles Vert Willie, ed., *The Caste and Class Controversy* (Bayside, N.Y.: General Hall, 1979).
[40]Belgium furnishes a parallel case in a totally different setting. During the low point of Flemings' history, individuals who moved up the social scale learned French and assimilated into the dominant Walloon sector; later, after the Flemish had overcome many of their social and cultural disabilities, the discrimination of the past was emphasized. See William Petersen, "A Comparison of a Racial and a Language Subnation: American Negroes and Flemish," *Ethnicity*, 3 (1976):145–173.
[41]W. Augustus Low and Virgil A. Clift, *Encyclopedia of Black America* (New York: McGraw-Hill, 1981), pp. 656–657.

its retention in the name of the NAACP (National Association for the Advancement of Colored People; the former Colored Methodist Episcopal Church, commonly known as the CME, changed the "Colored" to "Christian"). The designation "black" became taboo during the first decades of this century, but "negro" (which is Spanish for "black") and eventually "Negro" were coming into increasing use over the same period. During the 1960s usages began to diverge among group leaders. Roy Wilkins, long head of the NAACP, wrote in his syndicated column that he would continue to call himself a "Negro," but younger or more radical spokesmen insisted on being called "blacks" (or "Blacks"), reflecting their "black consciousness" and their desire for "black power." The substitution was widespread enough to induce the publishers of the *Negro Digest* to change the name of their magazine to *Black World*. During the same several decades the link to Africa, once regarded as especially offensive, began to be emphasized in such terms as "African American" or, more frequently, "Afro-American."

Each of such changes in designation was insisted on with great emotional fervor. When they were taboo, "negro" or "black" connoted, in Low and Clift's summary, "bad, ugly, inferior, bestial, or subhuman." Yet only a short time later many blacks and some whites used epithets just as strong to condemn those who did not immediately discard "colored" or "Negro" and substitute "black." If a person calls himself a "Negro" and refuses to be identified as a "black" or "Afro-American" (or vice versa), what is a statistical agency to do when it is trying to count all in the category irrespective of the current name? The response of the Bureau of the Census in the 1980 schedule was to offer a choice of two designations and then to coalesce the responses into a single grouping. It would have been interesting if instead the bureau had accepted the different self-identities as names of distinct subgroups rather than, as it assumed, alternative names for precisely the same sector of American society.

The group name that this minority preferred at various periods, a significant datum in itself, merely illustrates a much more general point that can be illustrated with other indicators. For example, in the 1950s the ideal Negro girl or woman had a light skin, thin lips, and "good" hair. The slogan "Black is Beautiful," often repeated over the next decades, was intended to transform not only this perception of feminine beauty. During the "colored" period, some of those light enough to pass as white shifted their racial identity by more than a change of designation. Obviously any estimate of the number who moved into the white population can be taken as only a plausible guess, but apparently the phenomenon was once relatively common, more prevalent in the United States than in countries with a recognized intermediate sector of mixed ancestry.[42] In theory it should be possible to estimate the number who moved from one racial category to another by calculating an intercensal natural increase from birth and death statistics and then comparing the figure with the growth of population shown by the two census counts. This was done to check on the number of blacks who passed[43] and, more recently, on the number of light-skinned Negroes previously counted as whites who expressed their "black pride" by changing their identity in the opposite direction. However, the vital statistics and enumerations of blacks are too imprecise to afford much confidence in a calculation that depends on both sets of data.

Who Is an Indian?

The Bureau of the Census can be faulted for adhering with remarkable persistence to a unitary classification of blacks in spite of wide differences in occupational status, income, family structure, way of life, and even language ("Black English" versus standard speech).[44] In contrast, it was never able to decide from one enumeration to the next what portion of the potential subpopulation should be classified as American Indians, who of all minorities have been counted most erratically.

Since the beginning of the nineteenth century, federal policy with respect to Indians has gone through six major phases: a continuation of the attempt to reduce the threat of Indian attacks and, through education, to prepare Indians for acculturation to American society (up to about 1850); the establishment of reservations and the removal of Indians to them (1850–85); the conversion of individual Indians into landowners and farmers by allotting to them a prorated share of tribal property (1887–1930); the reestablishment of tribal authority under the New

[42]Cf. Arna Bontemps and Jack Conroy, *Anyplace But Here* (New York: Hill & Wang, 1966). In the 1950s such popular magazines as *Ebony* and *Negro Digest* carried a series of articles depicting the psychic cost to a person leading a double life, or describing the exceptional white who passed as a Negro, arguing in sum that the phenomenon of "passing" (now generally written with quotation marks) was itself a passing fad.

[43]From one such calculation it was estimated that 25,000 blacks passed into the general community each year between 1900 and 1910; see Hornell Hart, *Selective Migration as a Factor in Child Welfare in the United States* (Iowa City: University of Iowa, 1921).

[44]A court in Michigan continued the trend toward bilingualism in schools and went one step farther. The judge required teachers to learn enough "Black English" to communicate effectively with their black pupils, who were thus officially defined as a cultural as well as a racial group. See William Labov, "Objectivity and Commitment in Linguistic Science: The Case of the Black English Trial in Ann Arbor," *Language in Society*, 11 (1982):165–201.

[45]S. Lyman Tyler, *A History of Indian Policy* (Washington, D.C.: U.S. Bureau of Indian Affairs, 1973).

Deal and continuing through World War II (1935–50); "termination," or a renewed effort to end the special political status of the tribes and to integrate their members as individuals with the rest of the citizenry (1950–70); a composite of prior goals sometimes identified as "self-determination" (1970–   ).[45] With each of these policies there was an appropriate definition of the "Indian," based essentially but only partly on whether the aim was to foster assimilation to American society or to preserve and revive tribal life.

Because of the complex relations with various jurisdictions, however, no federal policy determined a single category of "Indians." According to a 1981 brochure distributed by the U.S. Bureau of Indian Affairs, "There is no one Federal or tribal definition that establishes a person's identity as Indian. Government agencies use different criteria for determining who is an Indian. Similarly, tribal groups have varying requirements for determining tribal membership."[46] Each legal definition—enrollment in a tribe, tribal membership, adoption (for example, of a wholly white person)—has its own background of legislation and court decisions, which also varies from tribe to tribe.

The more Indians have been tied to their relatively unproductive economy, the more they have required outside assistance. The reservations, ostensibly places (somewhat like South Africa's "homelands") where Indians can develop their distinct cultures in their own settings, are maintained largely at public expense.[47] Inevitably the complexity of the law has increased with the growing number of entitlement programs, which established many new relations between individuals and either tribal institutions or those of the general community. Successful claims against one or another government for alleged past wrongs have induced many Indians to reidentify themselves with the tribes, counter-

[46]U. S. Bureau of Indian Affairs, *Information about the Indian People* (Washington, D.C., 1981).

[47]Alan L. Sorkin has written several informative works on this topic. His book on federal programs devoted to Indians in and around reservations has chapters on schools, health services, agricultural development, industrial development, manpower development, property and income management, and welfare services: Sorkin, *American Indians and Federal Aid* (Washington, D.C.: Brookings Institution, 1971). One notable program that subsidized migration from reservations to urban areas was an implicit admission that the many efforts to improve conditions in the context of reservation life were not succeeding: Sorkin, "Some Aspects of American Indian Migration," *Social Forces*, 48 (1969):243–250. Roughly half of the Indians in the United States now live in cities, where their level of living is also deplorable. Indians contribute to the slums' social ills, particularly through high rates of alcoholism; their health is poor, and the dropout rate from schools is very high: Sorkin, *The Urban American Indian* (Lexington, Mass.: Lexington Books, 1978), chap. 9 and passim. In sum, the welfare of Indians has often been inadequate no matter what their locale, and in spite of programs designed to assist them. Data from the 1980 census, however, show some recent improvement. The four main racial groups in the population broke down into two broad categories, with whites and Asians at the top by most social-economic indicators, and blacks and Indians at the bottom. Indians were sometimes better off than blacks, sometimes worse off.

ing both the pan-Indian movement and the inclination especially of younger Indians to find a place in the American culture. According to a report in the *New York Times* (March 21, 1976), a presumably authentic Mohawk commented that one consequence of federal programs had been a large-scale production of "instant Indians."

On the other hand, some of the regulations have induced tribes, contrary to the general trend, to reduce the number of persons enrolled. In 1954 a bill was offered in Congress to abolish the reservation of the Flathead Indians in Montana, for members of the tribe had become almost fully integrated into the general society. The chieftains, however, were able to forestall this threat to their prerogatives by tightening the rules for membership, so that of the 7,100 who by the earlier criteria would have been members in 1970, only 5,500 were actually enrolled. Even so, at that date no more than about 3 percent of the tribe's members were full-blooded Indians; one member in two lived off the reservation; and Indians living on it made up only a fifth of the total reservation population.[48] In short, if widespread intermarriage threatened the continued existence of Indian tribes that had signed past treaties and thus the present validity of those agreements, the solution was to bar from membership those with less than a specified quantum of Indian blood. More generally, as more and more Indians moved into American society, the preservation of treaty rights has retained special privileges for a smaller and smaller proportion of those once defined as "Indians."

As has been noted, because the Constitution specifically excluded Indians "not taxed" from the population on which the apportionment of the House of Representatives was based, they were omitted from all enumerations before that of 1890.[49] The volume of that year's census, "Report on Indians Taxed and Indians Not Taxed in the United States (except Alaska)," is a mammoth ethnographic compendium to which data on population were almost incidental.[50] No reason was given why, with no change in the constitutional provision, it was decided to institute a complete count, but one can suppose that it was because a new

[48]Ronald L. Trosper, "Native American Boundary Maintenance: The Flathead Indian Reservation, Montana, 1860–1970," *Ethnicity*, 3 (1976):275–303.

[49]The constitutional provision, however, proved to be a highly ambiguous indicator of what was intended; in fact, many of those living among the rest of the population were paupers and thus, for a different reason altogether, were not taxed. In several enumerators' manuals an attempt was made to define the exception more precisely, but these instructions were not followed consistently; cf. Wright, *History and Growth of the U.S. Census*, p. 168.

[50]U.S. Census Office, "Report on Indians Taxed and Not Taxed in the United States (except Alaska)," in *Eleventh Census of the United States, 1890* (Washington, D.C.: Government Printing Office, 1894).

and more complex relation between Indians and whites had started with the end of the prior direct conflict. The number of Indians had fallen drastically during the nineteenth century, mainly because of the ravages of infectious diseases spreading through a fresh population, but also because of wars, relocation, social disorganization, and reclassification. According to Russell Thornton, the nadir was reached in 1890, when the 600,000 estimated for 1800 was down by almost two-thirds[51] (other approximations of the depletion have been higher). The year 1890 was also the time of the nativist movement associated with the Ghost Dance, which would revive the dead and unite them with the living in a regenerated land cleansed of white intruders. This new sect spread rapidly among the Plains Indians and, as Thornton showed, especially to those tribes that had undergone the greatest losses of population.

The indicated number of all Indians, 248,253 in 1890, fell to 237,196 in 1900 and then rose again to 265,683 in 1910.[52] This decline and subsequent rise can be plausibly explained by the greater effort to include all who might be classified as Indians in 1890 and again in 1910, the years when special volumes were issued. As early as 1910 only 56.5 percent of those enumerated were described as full-bloods, and the race mixture was interpreted as a symptom that tribal life was coming to an end. The "vanishing Indian" has been a recurrent theme, one that "stained the issue of policy debate with fatalism."[53] The 1910 enumeration was seen as a last chance to make a full count.

In 1910 a special effort was made to secure a complete enumeration of persons with any perceptible amount of Indian ancestry. This probably resulted in the enumeration as Indian of a considerable number of persons who would have been reported as white in earlier censuses. There were no special efforts in 1920, and the returns showed a much smaller number of Indians than in 1910. Again in 1930 emphasis was placed on securing a complete count of Indians, with the result that the returns probably overstated the decennial increase in the number of Indians.[54]

[51]Russell Thornton, "Demographic Antecedents of a Revitalization Movement: Population Change, Population Size, and the 1890 Ghost Dance," *American Sociological Review,* 46 (1981):88–96.

[52]The 1890 records were destroyed by fire, and those from 1900 are therefore the earliest ones now available after the decision was made to include all Indians. When the enumerators' schedules for the later year were used to contrast returns from Navaho and Hopi, it was apparent that, though for different reasons, between one-fifth and one-half of both tribes evaded the count. See S. Ryan Johansson and Samuel H. Preston, "Tribal Demography: The Hopi and Navaho Populations as Seen through Manuscripts from the 1900 U.S. Census," *Social Science History,* 3 (1978):1–33.

[53]Brian W. Dippie, *The Vanishing American: White Attitudes and U.S. Indian Policy* (Middletown, Conn.: Wesleyan University Press, 1982).

[54]U.S. Bureau of the Census, *Historical Statistics of the United States: Colonial Times to 1957* (Washington, D.C., 1960), p. 3.

With these changes in procedure and definition, the population fluctuated as though suffering from recurrent disasters. In 1940, when the count was again more restrictive, the number enumerated remained almost static, presumably because the fall in those listed was canceled by the increase in actual population.

Several recent censuses have been subjected to a review by knowledgeable scholars, with disconcerting results. In 1950 the approximately 345,000 Indians counted did not include about 75,000 persons who would normally report themselves as Indians on such documents as birth and death certificates (30,000 mixed-bloods, plus almost 45,000 enrolled in federally recognized tribes). In addition, at least 25,000 persons not classified as Indians were entitled to legal benefits as members of tribes with federal treaties but did not usually report themselves as Indians.[55] From 1960 to 1970 the growth in the number of enumerated Indians was 67,000 more than the increase as measured by births and deaths. The excess was too large to be explained by errors in registration, an undercount in the 1960 census, or net immigration from Canada or Mexico. Seemingly a major part of the large difference was due to a shift in self-identification; persons who were listed as white in 1960 chose in 1970 to be classified as Indians.[56] According to provisional figures, in 1980 there were 1,418,195 Indians, Eskimos, and Aleuts, representing an increase of 71 percent over the recorded total a decade earlier.

In other words, there has been an intermittent but generally accelerating growth in the indicated population. What this means is difficult to say.[57] There are several possible components: a real growth in numbers, undoubtedly a major fraction in the most recent period; a more nearly complete enumeration, based on the readier access to remote parts of reservations and the usually easier communication with Indians; a shift in self-identification, including the creation of "instant

[55]J. Nixon Hadley, "The Demography of the American Indians," Annals of the American Academy of Political and Social Science, 311 (1957):23–30.

[56]Jeffrey S. Passel, "Provisional Evaluation of the 1970 Census Count of American Indians," Demography, 13 (1976):397–409.

[57]Even if the census population were "correct," reporting by county or state is often inappropriate for the ways the data are used. The Navaho reservation, as one example, includes parts but not all of three counties in Arizona, two in New Mexico, and one in Utah. Some Navaho live on the Hopi reservation; over 4,000 come within the jurisdiction of the United Pueblo Agency; and one Navaho subagency, Crownpoint, is off the Navaho reservation. One cannot get a reasonable approximation of the number of Navaho by counting the Indians either in particular counties or on the reservation. Yet the estimate, whatever it may be, is used as a denominator in calculating rates of which the numerator may be, for instance, the number of persons using Navaho health facilities. See Robert A. Hackenberg, "Demographic Information Systems for Transitional Populations: A Program for American Indian Studies" (unpublished manuscript, n.d.).

Indians" by various federal programs. The 282 federally recognized tribes merge into a single composite only in relation to the relatively few laws and administrative procedures regarding all "Indians." Antipathies often persist from the continual wars of the past, and suits to validate one tribe's claims have often been against not only the federal or another government but also other tribes' competing claims. If even so one attempts to aggregate all those who are in some sense affiliated with any of the tribes, there is no reason to expect consistent responses to the query, Are you an Indian? As an Indian, a person has been able to share the wealth of the tribe and acquire special access to education, employment, and medical care; and as a white he has evaded discrimination against Indians. Most writings on marginality stress the negative consequences of living in two cultures, but an individual can sometimes gain by alternately playing each of two roles.

One might believe that in the abstract the identity listed on a census schedule would remain neutral, no matter how the respondent answered the same question in other contexts. However, the Bureau of the Census itself has insistently stressed the material advantages from a full count of racial minorities. In Chicago as in other cities with a sizable Indian population, local officials of the bureau called a meeting to solicit help in improving the 1980 count.[58] In past censuses, the Indian leaders were told, the sizable underenumeration of minority groups (including Indians) had cost the cities (as well as their poorer inhabitants) federal funds allocated according to numbers. The discussion that followed, however, showed that many Indians were reluctant to be counted in the city because they were already reckoned as part of a reservation's population. When other factors are equal, tribes want to increase the number of those officially enrolled, for this figure also sets the amount of money dispensed under various federal programs. Even the slightest sentimental attachment to the tribe would induce a potential member to enroll, particularly since he would then become eligible for his share. Indians away from the reservation who avoid being counted because they are drawing benefits elsewhere would thus be recorded by the Bureau of Indian Affairs but not in a census. The bureau's campaign to improve coverage was combined, it must be emphasized, with the recently instituted self-identification. "Indians" are no longer so classified in a census enumeration because they are so regarded in their community, because they are members of a recognized tribe, or because they have a certain minimum proportion of Indian forebears. They become Indian by their own declaration, in part reacting

[58]Sol Tax, "The Impact of Urbanization on American Indians," *Annals of the American Academy of Political and Social Science*, 436 (1978):121–136.

to an often reiterated assertion that it is in their monetary interest so to classify themselves. A less satisfactory way of enumerating members of a minority would be difficult to devise.

Classification of Europeans

Few things facilitate a category's coalescence into a group so readily as its designation by an official body. Those departing from the multi-ethnic pre-1914 empires of Central and Eastern Europe had little or no consciousness of belonging to a nationality. As he saw himself, such an immigrant had four identities. He was the subject of a particular state, for example, Russia; he spoke a particular language, for example, Lithuanian; he was an adherent of one or another religion; and he regarded a certain province or village as home. Even immigrants from nations that had achieved political unity sometimes did not identify themselves as natives of those countries; an "Italian," for instance, was much more likely to look on himself as a Sicilian or a Calabrian. In many cases, thus, it was only after they had left it that migrants learned to identify themselves with "their" country, first of all by the questions put to them by immigration officials and census schedules. The technical requirement that the question on ethnicity be put in a simple form—"What was your country of birth?" or something equivalent—meant not only that superficially valid responses were in a deeper sense false but that posing them helped solidify new ethnic groups. Having learned that they belonged to a nation, some of the immigrants submerged their provincialisms into a broader patriotism, their local dialects into a language. The first Lithuanian newspaper was published in the United States; the Erse revival began in Boston; the Czechoslovak nation was launched at a meeting in Pittsburgh.

How loose an indication of ethnicity could be derived from statistics on the country of origin is suggested in a paper by Richard Böckh (1824–1907), the eminent German statistician.[59] For the years 1898–1904, when for the first time the United States classified immigrants by stock independently of their country of origin, Böckh calculated that in addition to the 151,118 "Germans" from the German Empire, there were 289,438 from such other countries as Austria-Hungary, Russia, and Switzerland. Russia provided an especially interesting case. Though Slavs (apart from Poles) made up about 70 percent of the population, they constituted only 2 percent of the 625,607 "Russian" immi-

[59]Cited in Albert Bernhardt Faust, *The German Element in the United States, with Special Reference to Its Political, Moral, Social, and Educational Influence* (New York: Steuben Society of America, 1927), vol. 2, chap. 1.

grants during those seven years. The others were:

"Hebrews".	41.9 percent
Poles	26.5
Finns	11.4
Lithuanians	10.1
Germans	6.8
Scandinavians	1.3

In short, American immigration and census statistics—or at least that portion of the data pertaining to pre-1914 Central and Eastern Europe—began to furnish a genuine clue to the newcomers' ethnic identities only shortly before the imposition of national quotas.

The statistics on the countries of birth of the foreign stock were supplanted in the 1920s by data on the national origins of the entire population, beginning with the first census. Most impressionistic accounts of the population when the Republic was founded, as typified by Crèvecoeur's work (see p. 191), pictured a polyglot people amalgamating into a new type of nation. There are no firm data to check this usual assumption, but in a census monograph W. S. Rossiter (1861–1929) estimated the national origins of the population from the surnames listed in the 1790 enumeration as follows:

English	83.5 percent
Scotch	6.7
German	5.6
Dutch	2.0
Irish	1.6
French	0.5
"Hebrew"	>0.1
All others	0.1

That is to say, the American population in 1790 was overwhelmingly of British stock.[60] However, many names are common to several nationalities, and in an English-speaking country the tendency is to assign "Martin," for instance, to the English component rather than the German, French, or Spanish. According to Rossiter, a larger proportion of non-English stock was to be found in particular areas, such as New York with 16.1 percent Dutch or Pennsylvania with 26.1 percent German. A probable reason for this finding is that residents of a Germanic community retained their Germanic names, while many of those living

---

[60]W. S. Rossiter, *A Century of Population Growth, from the First Census of the United States to the Twelfth, 1790–1900* (Washington, D.C.: Government Printing Office, 1909), chaps. 10–11.

among persons of English stock changed them to an English-sounding equivalent. Albert Faust also checked the names registered in the country's first census, but he then compared his results for particular areas with historical records of German settlements. In the predominantly German counties of Pennsylvania most of the original names had been retained, but not, for instance, in North and South Carolina, where "it was remarkable to see to what extent German names had been anglicized." The total number of German stock so derived was 375,000, which, to be conservative, he reduced to 360,000.[61] This was 18.9 percent of the 1790 white population, as contrasted with the 5.6 percent that Rossiter had estimated; and there is no reason to suppose that the false estimate was specific to Germans, for the same factors applied to all other non-English nationalities.

These calculations would be mainly of antiquarian interest except for the fact that eventually immigration policy was set by an essentially similar reckoning. The Immigration Act of 1924 called for a calculation of "the number of inhabitants in the continental United States in 1920 whose origin by birth or ancestry is attributable to [each] geographical area" designated in the immigration statistics as a separate country; this task was undertaken by the Bureau of the Census assisted by two experts paid by the American Council of Learned Societies. One of the committee's "main sources" was Rossiter's estimate, originally accepted "as furnishing the most complete information available" on the national origins of the 1790 population. However, since the committee eventually recognized that there was a "considerable element of uncertainty" in any classification based on family names, the English component was cut by a little more than a tenth, an arbitrary figure that was then prorated among other nationalities according to the (also poorly based) proportions that Rossiter had calculated. Between 1790 and 1820 no record was kept of immigration, but the allowance made for this was not, it was thought, "a factor of very great importance in the final result." Subsequent immigration was recorded, but in statistics of notorious inadequacy. The frequent and untraceable marriages across ethnic lines made it impossible to divide the 1920 population itself into distinct ethnic groups (as the 1924 act required), and the committee undertook instead to measure the proportionate contribution of various national stocks to the total gene pool of white Americans. To the base of the 1790 population were added immigration figures, such as they were, and—for lack of a breakdown by ethnic groups—an overall rate of natural increase.[62] Since the multiethnic empires of pre-1914 Europe had been broken up after the Allied victory, those born in Ger-

[61]Faust, *German Element in the United States*, vol. 2, chap. 1.
[62]U.S. Senate, "Immigration Quotas on the Basis of National Origin," *Miscellaneous Documents*, no. 65, 70th Cong., 1st sess. (Washington, D.C., 1928).

many, Austria-Hungary, or Russia were allocated to the new nations not on the basis of their birthplaces, which were not available from the record, but also according to their names.

Many of the proponents of immigration restriction, who became increasingly active from the 1870s to the 1920s, were motivated by antipathy to Jews and Roman Catholics. Some of the charges they made were obviously prejudiced, but it was impossible to test any of them against accurate data, for the United States had no useful statistics on religion.[63] For example, Jewish immigrants from Eastern Europe were listed by their country of origin in both immigration statistics and census data on the foreign stock, and it is difficult in retrospect to work out how many of the "Russians" were in fact Jews.[64] Indeed, there have been many private studies of the Jewish population; probably no American minority has shown more interest in itself. The surveys that attempted to estimate the number of Jews and their demographic characteristics, however, were generally poor substitutes for official data. Persons with "Jewish names" have been counted, but this procedure is probably even less reliable in this case than for gentiles. Counts have been made of children absent from school on Yom Kippur, the most solemn of Jewish holy days; from a comparison of their number with the average absence and an estimate of the size of Jewish families, one can guess how many Jews lived in the school district. Questions on mother tongue in the 1940 and 1970 censuses were used to extrapolate from those reporting Yiddish to the whole of the metropolitan Jewish population. Since its first volume in 1899–1900, the *American Jewish Year Book* of the American Jewish Committee has regularly published estimates of the population. Of such reports, one of the fullest and most informative was by Sidney Goldstein, a demographer who has specialized in the analysis of American Jewry.[65]

The Bureau of the Census considered including a question on religious affiliation in 1960. It conducted a preliminary survey, which resulted in a partial report.[66] Opposition was voiced by only a very

---

[63]In a survey of world Jewry in 1975, U. O. Schmelz estimated that 95 percent of the total lived in only nine countries, of which three (Israel, Canada, and South Africa) have maintained satisfactory census data on Jews, three (Argentina, Brazil, and the Soviet Union) have incomplete or otherwise inaccurate census data, and three (France, Britain, and the United States) lack any census data at all. See U. O. Schmelz, *World Jewish Population: Estimates and Projections* (Jerusalem: Institute of Contemporary Jewry, Hebrew University of Jerusalem, 1981).

[64]See, e.g., Erich Rosenthal, "The Equivalence of the United States Census Data for Persons of Russian Stock or Descent with American Jews: An Evaluation," *Demography*, 12 (1975):275–290.

[65]Sidney Goldstein, "American Jewry, 1970: A Demographic Profile," *American Jewish Year Book, 1971* (New York: American Jewish Committee, 1971).

[66]U.S. Bureau of the Census, "Religion Reported by the Civilian Population of the United States, March, 1957," *Current Population Reports*, Ser. P-20, no. 79 (1958).

small sector of the population, especially a few liberal and Jewish organizations (including the American Civil Liberties Union, American Jewish Committee, American Jewish Congress, and Anti-Defamation League), but they were so vehement that the idea was abandoned,[67] and the suggestion to include the question in the 1970 schedule never got off the ground. Most of the data collected in the one survey were made public only after demographers resorted to the Freedom of Information Act to force their release.[68] No other statistics have ever been secreted in this fashion, contradicting the norm that all of the bureau's data not pertaining to identifiable individuals are to be open to public scrutiny in full.

Hostility toward the Catholics who immigrated from Southern and Eastern Europe derived in part from the ill will built up earlier against the Irish, who had begun to leave in large numbers after the famine of the 1840s and thus became the first sizable Roman Catholic bloc in the United States. The Famine Irish, as they were called, arrived as paupers, lived in hovels, and for a generation or two helped perform the country's most menial tasks. When they climbed up, it was only—or so it was believed—to the lower middle class. According to private survey data, however, by the 1950s and 1960s the average Irish Catholic had risen to levels of education, occupational prestige, and income second only to those of Jews. That this was not recognized earlier was due to the lack of official statistics on religion: Irish Catholics, identified only by their nationality, were confounded with the so-called Scots-Irish, Protestants of whom most had immigrated earlier and remained low on the social ladder.[69] The crucial distinction between the two types of Irish was made mainly from a series of polls by the National Opinion Research Center, since this private institution did ask respondents for their religion; Andrew Greeley used its data both to demonstrate the success of the Irish Catholics and to illustrate how this was achieved.[70]

Survey data from other sources also furnish a general view of reli-

[67]Charles R. Foster, *A Question on Religion* (New York: Inter-University Case Program, no. 66; Indianapolis: Bobbs-Merrill, 1961); Dorothy Good, "Questions on Religion in the United States Census," *Population Index*, 25 (1959):3–16; William Petersen, "Religious Statistics in the United States," *Journal for the Scientific Study of Religion*, 1 (1962):165–178.

[68]Sidney Goldstein, "Socioeconomic Differentials among Religious Groups in the United States," *American Journal of Sociology*, 74 (1969):612–631; Ira Rosenwaike, "A Synthetic Estimate of American Jewish Population Movement over the Last Three Decades," in U. O. Schmelz, P. Glikson, and Sergio Della Pergola, eds., *Papers in Jewish Demography, 1977* (Jerusalem: Institute of Contemporary Jewry, Hebrew University of Jerusalem, 1980).

[69]Since these Scots-Irish were undoubtedly the major component of the "Irish" in Rossiter's reconstruction of the 1790 population, they unwittingly furnished a larger quota for people they customarily denigrated as "Papists."

[70]For example, Andrew M. Greeley, *That Most Distressful Nation: The Taming of the American Irish* (Chicago: Quadrangle Books, 1972), chap. 6.

gion in the United States. The Princeton Religious Center uses reports from the Gallup organization, which has surveyed Americans' religious affiliation since 1947. According to those statistics, the percentage who reported membership in a church or synagogue fell from a high of 76 in 1947 to 69 in 1980; the proportion responding that they had "no religious preference" rose from 2 percent in 1967 to 8 percent in 1979.[71]

The Creation of the "Hispanics"

The rather dubious results from classifying European populations by these various criteria did not deter the Bureau of the Census from applying the same types of indicators to Mexican Americans. Until 1920 that population was treated in census statistics like Europeans, classified as part of the foreign stock for two generations and then not distinguished as a separate grouping. But the procedure did not seem to fit: the Spanish-speaking minority in the Southwest, it appeared, was not acculturating to American society but rather remained distinct. In 1930, the Bureau of the Census established the classification "Mexican" and placed those in it under the broader rubric "other races" (or nonwhites). This new designation was in accord with Mexican Americans' common self-designation of "La Raza" (or "The Race"), as well as with the sentiment developing in Mexico itself that its destiny depended on the exceptional quality of its mestizo population. Both the Mexican government and the U.S. Department of State, however, objected to the new classificatory criterion as racist, and in any case it proved to be an unsatisfactory measure of the subpopulation. There was a gross undercount of the native-born of Mexican descent, particularly among those of lighter complexion or in the middle class. "Hispanos"—the population already residing in the Southwest when that territory was annexed to the United States—are not "Mexicans" or "Mexican Americans"; in 1930 they refused to accept those labels, as they still do.[72] New Mexico had an estimated 200,000 Spanish-speaking people, or about half the state's population. The census count was only 61,960 "Mexicans."

The fact that the racial criterion failed particularly in New Mexico,

---

[71]Martha Farnsworth Riche, "The Fall and Rise of Religion," *American Demographics*, 4 (May 1982):14–19, 47.

[72]A. J. Jaffe, Ruth M. Cullen, and Thomas D. Boswell, *The Changing Demography of Spanish Americans* (New York: Academic Press, 1980), chap. 5. "Hispano" is used by some analysts as a synonym for the category usually labeled "Hispanic." Thus, "the term *Hispanos* is used to include native Spanish Americans, Mexican immigrants and their descendants, Puerto Ricans in the Continental United States, and other persons of predominantly Spanish culture": William W. Winnie, Jr., "The Spanish Surname Criterion for Identifying Hispanos in the Southwestern United States: A Preliminary Evaluation," *Social Forces*, 38 (1960):363–366. This usage, however, is not in accord with the self-identification of any group.

then the only bilingual jurisdiction, may have suggested to census officials the index that was substituted for it. In 1940 a sample of the entire population was asked for its mother tongue, and the results showed that the conventional assumption that the use of foreign languages generally disappeared by the third generation did not hold across the board. Nearly 22 million whites, or 18.6 percent of the white population, reported a mother tongue other than English. Of this sizable number, moreover, some 13.5 million were native-born, and almost 3 million of those had native-born parents. Among the languages listed, the most important were, in order: German, with almost 5 million; Italian, 3.8 million; Polish, 2.4 million; Spanish, 1.9 million; Yiddish, 1.8 million; and French, 1.4 million. On the other hand, about 7 percent of the native population with one or both parents born in Mexico reported English as their mother tongue.[73]

Since the demarcation by race or language had proved to be unsatisfactory, in 1950 (and, with minor changes, again in 1960 and 1970) the same population was delineated on the basis of Spanish surnames. To the approximately 7,000 Spanish names collected earlier by the Immigration and Naturalization Service were added some 1,000 other names provided by specialists in Romance languages. When one analyst supplemented the 7,718 names then used by the bureau with 11,262 others (including some from such subcultural regions as Galicia, Catalonia, and the Basque country), the number of American respondents classified as of Iberian origin was raised by 21 percent.[74] Since the name of the head of the household, at that time typically the male, was used as the indicator, Hispanic women who married out of the group disappeared statistically, and non-Hispanic women who married in were added to it.[75] According to one standard source, Martín is the tenth commonest name in Spain, but the bureau omitted it from its list because it

<hr/>

[73]Dorothy Waggoner, "Statistics on Language Use," in Charles A. Ferguson and Shirley Brice Heath, eds., *Language in the USA* (New York: Cambridge University Press, 1981). Since the size of these ethnic minorities was not the same, the proportions retaining another language differed from this ranking, but Mexican Americans were clearly not the anomalous group they had been thought to be. According to a study in Los Angeles, Chicanos' shift to English was faster than had been anticipated, and the seemingly great loyalty to Spanish was due to the continuing large immigration; see David E. Lopez, "Chicano Language Loyalty in an Urban Setting," *Sociology and Social Research,* 62 (1978):267–278; Calvin J. Veltman, "Melting Pot USA: L'anglicisation des Hispano-américains," *Cahiers Québécois de Démographie,* 10 (1981):31–48.

[74]William E. Morton, "Demographic Redefinition of Hispanos," *Public Health Reports,* 85 (1970):617–623.

[75]A study of Spanish-surnamed Californians found that between one third and two fifths married out, with little difference by age or sex. Native-born were more likely to choose non-Spanish spouses, especially in the second or later marriage. See Robert Schoen, Verne E. Nelson, and Marion Collins, "Intermarriage among Spanish-Surnamed Californians, 1962–1974," *International Migration Review,* 12 (1978):359–369.

occurs frequently among those of English, French, or German origin. Some persons with a Spanish surname had changed it to an Anglo-Saxon equivalent. Among the natives of such countries as Chile and Argentina, as also among the small proportion of immigrants from those countries, non-Spanish names are common. On the other hand, many Filipinos, who are classified as Asians, have Spanish surnames.

In the March 1971 Current Population Survey, those of Spanish origin were matched against Spanish surnames, identified independently. In the five states of the Southwest, 81 percent of those with a Spanish surname identified themselves as of Spanish origin, and 74 percent of those who identified themselves as of Spanish origin had a Spanish surname. Outside the five states those percentages fell, respectively, to 46 and 61. By a rather relaxed standard, Spanish surname "appear[ed] to provide a fair approximation of Spanish origin" in the Southwest but not outside that area.[76]

Even if the data on the number of Mexican Americans were considerably better than in fact they are, they would be rendered almost meaningless by the large component of illegal or "undocumented" migrants. By definition, their number is unknown, and guesses vary with the politics of the person offering the figure, the stringency of control measures, and other spurious factors.[77] About 4 million people live on either side of the 1,966-mile border between Mexico and the United States. Each day an estimated 40,000 Mexicans who possess the coveted "green card" cross the border to work, and something close to an equal number go to shop, perhaps having to pay a bribe of 20 pesos in place of the tariff that they avoid. Nor is the flow back and forth across the border new. The number of illegal Mexicans apprehended and/or deported annually rose very slowly from a few thousand in the mid-1920s to well over a million in 1954, then fell to several tens of

---

[76]Edward W. Fernandez, "Comparison of Persons of Spanish Surname and Persons of Spanish Origin in the United States," U.S. Bureau of the Census, *Technical Papers*, no. 38 (Washington, D.C., 1975). See also Charlotte A. Redden, "Identification of Spanish Heritage Persons in Public Data," *Public Data Use*, 4 (1976):3–11.

[77]Cf. Charles B. Keely, "Counting the Uncountable: Estimates of Undocumented Aliens in the United States," *Population and Development Review*, 3 (1977):473–481; Jacob S. Siegel, Jeffrey S. Passel, and J. Gregory Robinson, "Preliminary Review of Existing Studies of the Number of Illegal Residents in the United States," in *U.S. Immigration Policy and the National Interest: The Staff Report of the Select Commission on Immigration and Refugee Policy* (Washington, D.C.: U.S. Government Printing Office, 1980), Appendix E; Frank D. Bean, Allan G. King, and Jeffrey S. Passel, "The Number of Illegal Migrants of Mexican Origin in the United States: Sex Ratio-Based Estimates for 1980," *Demography*, 20 (1983):99–109; Marion F. Houston, "Aliens in Irregular Status in the United States: A Review of Their Numbers, Characteristics, and Role in the U.S. Labor Market," *International Migration*, 21 (1983):372–414; Susan Ranney and Sherrie Kossoudji, "Profiles of Temporary Mexican Labor Migrants to the United States," *Population and Development Review*, 9 (1983):475–493.

thousands in the following decade, rising again from under 100,000 in 1966 to over 500,000 in 1973,[78] and to 960,000 in fiscal year 1982. Over the long run it was the demand for agricultural labor that set the number of Mexicans entering the United States, many of them more or less illegally. It is thought that undocumented migrants presently fill sizable proportions of low-level jobs also in the meat industry, furniture manufacture, and rubber and chemical plants. Whatever the size of the illegal Mexican American population, it is likely to grow more rapidly in the next decade or so, for the virtual breakdown of the Mexican economy has greatly increased the number of lower-class Mexicans who will want to cross the border to seek work.

Should illegal immigrants have been included in the 1980 enumeration? Because political representation, federal grants, and various other benefits are allocated on the basis of the enumeration in each district or state, some held that it would be impermissible to include such persons as part of the population base. An organization called the Federation for American Immigration Reform (FAIR) brought suit to prevent the Bureau of the Census from including illegal aliens in the recorded population; after a lower court ruled against the plaintiff, the U.S. Supreme Court declined to review the case. For census officials the primary objection was technical: How could those in the country illegally have been distinguished by normal enumeration procedures?[79]

One more or less fortuitous consequence of the experimentation with several indices of Mexican Americans was that a new grouping, "Hispanics," came into being, since not only Mexican Americans but also many Puerto Ricans, Cubans, and others spoke Spanish in their childhood and/or had a Spanish surname. At first, it was more or less possible to distinguish the component elements of Hispanics by geographical location, but this became less and less satisfactory with the spread of all the subgroups to new areas throughout the country. Whatever differences exist between whites and blacks, or between whites and Indians, are masked within the Hispanic category, since those so

[78]V. M. Briggs, Jr., "Mexican Workers in the United States Labour Market: A Contemporary Dilemma," *International Labour Review*, 12 (1975):351–368.

[79]Interaction between immigration regulation and the conduct of the count can be well illustrated by one incident. After about 1,500 Phoenix citizens complained that they were being denied jobs, some 800 illegal aliens were deported from that city. The reaction from the local Chicano organization was to denounce this as "a racist directive. Maybe they don't want Chicanos counted in the census." And the local affiliate of an international Spanish-language radio network stopped its broadcasts of materials promoting the coming enumeration. These protests were supported, moreover, by the local director of the census, who declared that the ten days of raids had undermined years of preparation and would make it impossible to conduct an accurate count in the area. Finally, the Immigration and Naturalization Service announced that it would conduct no more sweeps until after the count had been completed (*New York Times*, March 28–29, 1980).

classified may be of any race. The ethnic groups comprising the 14.6 million persons "of Spanish origin" in 1980 varied greatly in median age, family type, fertility, educational level, type of occupation, proportion below the poverty line, median income, and almost any other social indicator on which there are data. On the 1980 census schedule, each respondent was permitted to choose among four subgroups, which had the following 1980 populations and 1982 incomes:

Hispanic Population	Population (−000), 1980	Median Family Income, 1982
Mexican American	8,740	$16,400
Puerto Rican	2,014	11,100
Cuban	803	18,900
Other Spanish	3,051	19,100
Total Hispanic	14,608	16,200

As a group the Cubans, who arrived last, have a higher level of living than the other large Hispanic populations; they seemingly dislike being classed with them. On the other hand, in the opinion of Manuel A. Bustelo of the National Puerto Rican Forum in New York City, "The use of 'Hispanic' rather than specific ethnic groups has distorted realities. In many instances this has served to convey a more positive picture of overall advancement, while concealing the fact that Puerto Rican communities on the mainland are worse off than in previous years."[80]

The supposed unity of Hispanics is based on the fact that they all, to one degree or another, derive from Spanish culture. Even if one ignores the acculturation to English, the varieties of Spanish differ significantly among the several subgroups, as is clear from studies of the distinctive "dialect" or "language" of Chicanos.[81] Ernest Garcia quoted a passage from a 1953 manual, Pauline Baker's *Español para los Hispanos,* which noted the "lamentable decadence of Spanish in the United States. . . . Every day one feels more the necessity of correcting the errors of poor Spanish that one must avoid and to develop the good Spanish that one ought to use." However, the deviations from Castilian or standard Mexican are consistent among Chicanos and therefore, in Garcia's judgment, are acceptable as the beginning of a genuine new language.[82] One of the best known anthropological studies of Mexican Americans, Arthur Rubel's *Across the Tracks* (1966), was used to exem-

[80]Quoted in *American Demographics,* 2 (June 1980):7.
[81]Cf. E. Hernández-Chávez, A. D. Cohen, and A. F. Beltramo, eds., *El lenguaje de los chicanos* (Arlington, Va.: Center for Applied Linguistics, 1975).
[82]Ernest Garcia, "Chicano Spanish Dialects and Education," *Aztlán,* 2 (1971):67–77.

plify how someone competent in Spanish can misunderstand completely the speech of Chicanos. In describing a political campaign, Rubel translated *Hay mucha movida* as "moving the people"; as he could have found out from very few Spanish dictionaries, among Chicanos it means "There's dirty work going on."[83] Even commercial firms seeking customers among Hispanics often take care to differentiate among the several groups.[84]

Not only is the whole Hispanic population a miscellany but none of the four units within it is really homogeneous. "Other Spanish" is a very large residual category with no internal consistency. In the opening paper of Volume 1 of *Aztlán*, perhaps the best of the journals devoted to Mexican American interests, Fernando Peñalosa offered a tentative three-way classification of the population: "Americans of Mexican ancestry," who regard their forebears as of little importance one way or the other; "Mexican Americans," who are constantly conscious of their ancestry, usually with an uneasy blend of positive and negative feelings about it; and "Chicanos," who are committed to the defense of Mexican American subcultural values as they view them.[85] "Attempts to form national alliances of Mexican American organizations have failed over the question, 'What do we call ourselves?' " and selecting the proper ethnic label has postponed or interrupted important social programs.[86] As with other minorities, official agencies accommodated quickly to the demands of the more militant sector. Tino Villanueva quoted two reports of the U.S. Commission on Civil Rights, of which the first, published in 1971, referred only to "Mexican Americans," while the second, published the following year, noted that the term "Chicano" and "Mexican American" were used interchangeably.[87] Even earlier, various lower courts in the Southwest had used "Chicano" to identify an ethnic group to which the rights guaranteed by the Fourteenth Amendment and various federal statutes applied. Thus, when the Bureau of the Census offered "Chicano" as one alternative to "Mexican American" on the 1980 schedule, it was following the precedent set by

[83]Américo Paredes, "On Ethnographic Work among Minority Groups: A Folklorist's Perspective," in Ricardo Romo and Raymund Paredes, eds., *New Directions in Chicano Scholarship* (La Jolla, Calif.: Chicano Studies Program, University of California, 1979).

[84]When the Anhaeuser-Bush brewery translated its advertising slogan "This Bud's for you" into Spanish, for instance, it found it expedient to produce four versions of the jingle—a hot salsa beat for Puerto Ricans in New York, a chiranga style for the Cubans in Florida, and two different mariachi arrangements, one for the Mexican population of Texas (who had come mostly from the border regions) and the other for those in the rest of the Southwest (whose subculture derived more from the area of Mexico City).

[85]Fernando Peñalosa, "Toward an Operational Definition of the Mexican American," *Aztlán*, 1 (1970):1–11.

[86]Ralph C. Guzmán, *The Political Socialization of the Mexican American People* (New York: Arno Press, 1976), p. 187.

[87]Tino Villanueva, "Sobre el termino 'Chicano,' " *Cuadernos Hispanoamericanos*, 336 (1978):387–410.

other official bodies. The cooptation of a symbol of militancy has seldom been so rapid.

Why, in sum, has the Bureau of the Census established the category "Of Spanish origin"? Undoubtedly the main reason is that it is convenient for summary tables. As another factor, some members of Congress or other politicians may want to enhance their power by fostering a still nonexistent unity; in 1976 four Democratic members of the House of Representatives from Texas, California, and New York joined with the resident commissioner-elect of Puerto Rico to form a Congressional Hispanic Caucus.[88] That the bureau has attempted to cooperate with representatives of Chicano and other Hispanic groups has also been a factor, but a common response of such associations can be exemplified by a letter from one organization to the bureau director concerning the 1970 count of persons of Spanish origin. It was "a waste of taxpayers' money, . . . wholly without scientific basis." The alleged consequence was that Spanish Americans were underestimated by half, with a resultant loss to the community over the following decade of "at least" $10 billion in revenue from federal programs based on the enumeration.[89]

Conclusions

From this review of the national statistical agency's operations, one can conclude that each step toward keeping track of the population's ethnic composition was taken ad hoc, responding to pressures from Congress or the public. The sectors of the population specially noted in the first censuses had an exceptional relation to apportionment, which was and remains the primary purpose of the counts. During the nineteenth century and particularly its later decades, when political debate focused on immigration restriction, the schedules were amended to test how well newcomers were fitting in with their new country's culture. This proved—until very recently—to be a temporary concern, and one could have assumed that this would also be so of the subsequent measurement of discrimination and relative deprivation by race and nationality. In the 1930s and 1940s no one could have anticipated how salient an issue the counting of ethnic blocs would become, or how troublesome it would therefore be for officials supervising the operation.

As one would expect from something that developed rather haphaz-

[88]*New York Times*, December 9, 1976.
[89]Mexican-American Population Commission of California, *Mexican-American Population in California as of April, 1973, with Projections to 1980* (San Francisco, 1973), Appendix B.

ardly, ethnic counts have been far from satisfactory. Indeed, there have been very few instances when statistical data were deliberately manipulated to support a political position,[90] but many of the decisions on how a group was to be defined, or how it was to be counted, have had political consequences. Ideally an enumeration should take place in a political vacuum, for partisan passions about the results typically affect the route to those results. With the development of a welfare state, the financing of many local or private functions was shifted to the national capital and, with it, the same means of seeking preferment. It is the supreme paradox of our time that, not only in the United States but generally, the greater state control over the economy and society has brought about not the growing indifference to nationalism and ethnicity that every socialist since Marx anticipated but precisely the opposite.

By 1990, the date of the next census, the bureau's operations will almost certainly have been even more politicized. The groups given preferment under affirmative action are not the only ones who have suffered and still suffer from discrimination, and the nationalities once labeled the New Immigration have shown an increasing resentment. If group-based preferences spread, as spokesmen for these minorities demand, the Bureau of the Census presumably would be called on to furnish the data on which to base the new quotas. One can readily suppose that the small tribe of "instant Indians" would be augmented by considerably larger numbers of "instant Poles" and "instant Italians." The agency in charge of summing up the ambiguously bounded groups and thus specifying how much federal largesse each of them would receive would be in the middle of a political free-for-all that, should it so develop, would make the difficulties of the past censuses seem insignificant. Nor could the bureau officials easily defend any of their decisions on this matter. For, as Charles Price concluded in a useful review of how ethnic groups are classified, "one has to accept the reality that there is no final certainty in the matter; that estimates, no matter how well based and researched, are only estimates."[91]

It is not easy to lay down general principles by which one could de-

[90]In 1840 an enumeration of "insane and idiots" showed that the proportion of blacks in either category was markedly higher in the North than in the South, demonstrating that Negroes adjusted well to slavery but could not cope with freedom. Edward Jarvis, a Massachusetts physician, studied the census publications for more than a year and published a complete refutation; his demand for a formal correction of the many errors he found was supported by the Massachusetts Medical Society and the American Statistical Association. However, John C. Calhoun, who as secretary of state was in charge of the census, not only blocked efforts to have the data corrected but also continued to use them in his defense of slavery. See William Stanton, *The Leopard's Spots: Scientific Attitudes toward Race in America, 1815–59* (Chicago: University of Chicago Press, 1960), pp. 58–67.

[91]Charles A. Price, "Methods of Estimating the Size of Groups," *Harvard Encyclopedia of American Ethnic Groups* (Cambridge, Mass., 1980), Appendix 1.

cide which groupings are significant enough to warrant the extra cost of recording them. Understandably, census procedure has generally been to subclassify populations that are well known in America (thus, English, Scots, Welsh, and Irish, rather than merely British) but to ignore differences of equal or greater importance in less familiar nationalities—such as that between Japanese Americans who originated in the main islands (known in Japanese as *Naichi*) or in Okinawa, or Chinese Americans who derived from Canton or from Hong Kong (or, in many cases, via Hong Kong from Northern China). On the other hand, the 1980 schedule called on each American Indian to name his tribe and on Eskimos and Aleuts to designate themselves separately. When Congress renewed the Voting Rights Act in 1982, its action affected the way the enumeration in 1990 will be conducted. The Census Bureau will probably be required to include Eskimos and Aleuts as racial categories on the long form for the entire country, though these two groups are highly concentrated geographically and together total fewer than 70,000 persons. Hispanic civil-rights organizations have also argued that the revised law required the bureau to ask a question of 100 percent of the population, rather than only a sample, specifying the respondent as Cuban, Puerto Rican, Mexican, or of other Spanish origin. These are striking examples of how money is wasted not to obtain information of even possible utility, but to satisfy the demands of particular ethnic organizations or groups.

The grossest category based on race is, of course, "non-whites," which was introduced in 1960 as an economy measure. A two-category classification by color may have been defensible for national summaries, in which Negroes constitute the overwhelming majority of non-whites (92 percent in 1960), or for regions of the country with few Indians, Asians, or other non-Negro non-whites. In the West, however, the figures made no sense; the state of Hawaii incurred the additional cost of a new summation of 1960 data that gave census-tract totals by the prior racial classification. Even social analysts well aware of the limitations of the color dichotomy have sometimes been constrained to follow it, for if the denominators of rates were so given, the numerators had to be denoted in the same way. After a good deal of criticism, the Bureau of the Census responded only by abandoning the term and substituting for it "Negroes and Other Races," which (though it seems to mean the whole population) designates precisely the same sector as "non-whites." Somewhat similarly, the contrived category of "Hispanics" presents an appealingly simple view of the ethnic spectrum: all who speak any version of Spanish (though recognizably distinct for each of the three main groups), or whose forebears came from no matter which Spanish-speaking country, are lumped together irrespective of cultural or racial differences that, to many persons in the separate minorities, are a good deal more important than these characteristics.

To say that the ethnic classification has not been consistent or logical is to point to the obvious. The issue is rather why this has been so. Four major factors are involved. The first, which with some charity we can label Science,[92] denotes the effort to classify the population as accurately as possible, using all the techniques available to statisticians and demographers. The second is Law, the constitutional requirement that the Bureau of the Census count the population in order to allocate seats in the House of Representatives and, following the directives in particular pieces of legislation, to set the distribution of federal funds according to the relative numbers in each locality. A legal scholar, Thomas A. Cowan, held that Science and Law, at best complementary, are often at odds; and in their examination of the 1980 enumeration, Ian Mitroff and his associates made much of this contention.[93] Some fifty-four municipalities or other entities brought suit against the bureau, generating more litigation than any prior United States census. America has become an extraordinarily litigious nation altogether, and the new laws and regulations have invited the third factor, Politics, to participate in each count as a major contender. Some of the dubious decisions of the bureau, whether to classify Aleuts separately or to abandon the plan to count by religious affiliation, resulted from standard bureaucratic conservatism augmented by diverse interest-group pressures. The fourth factor, which can be called Expediency, is the constant effort to accommodate to fiscal and technical constraints. There was no "nonwhite" category insisting that it be classified as such; and demand for a "Hispanic" grouping was hardly more visible. Imputation, or the computer techniques the bureau uses to fill in data not gathered in the field, became the basis for many of the legal challenges to the resultant figures.[94] There is no way of achieving a classification of ethnic groups that satisfies all of these governing principles—Science, Law, Politics, and Expediency. The Bureau of the Census has been engaged in a mission impossible, and not one of its own choosing.

Congress's repeated decision to use population-based formulas to allocate federal grants means that any undercount becomes an issue between local governments and the bureau, with organizations representing minority groups helping to raise the heat of the dispute. Is

[92]This is the appellation of Ira Lowry; see Lowry, *Science and Politics of Ethnic Enumeration.*

[93]Ian I. Mitroff, Richard O. Mason, and Vincent P. Barabba, *The 1980 Census: Policymaking amid Turbulence* (Lexington, Mass.: Lexington Books, 1983), chap. 3.

[94]For a judicious critique, see Judith Banister, "Use and Abuse of Census Editing and Imputation," *Asian and Pacific Census Forum*, 6 (February 1980):1–2, 16–20.

the bureau competent? Should local governments have a say in judging the results of the count? When there is an undercount, is a compensation for inequities appropriate? How can a check be made without violating the privacy of personal information?[95] Passing over a single person could in theory deprive a state of a member in Congress and of more than $100 per year in federal funding. But the census, to put it no stronger, is hardly exact to the nearest person; the estimated under-enumerations in 1950, 1960, and 1970 were each more than 5 million.[96] Errors of this magnitude are remediable only to a slight degree, and the solution is less technical than political.

Indeed, the Bureau of the Census can do little or nothing to alter the political context of ethnic counts, nor can it escape from fiscal control by a Congress sensitive to racial and ethnic blocs. What it can do, for instance, is not to repeat the egregious error of inviting representatives of special interests to act as formal consultants supervising its operations. Instead of seeking to avoid pressures from ethnic blocs to revise definitions or enumeration procedures, the bureau invited the participation of blacks, Hispanics, Indians, and others, each of whom wanted to shape the process to its political advantage. These committees were of a type different from those made up of statisticians or typical users of census data, for their members were generally chosen less for their knowledge than for their ideology. Giving aspirant leaders this kind of quasi-official standing aggravated the disadvantages of the procedure already established—the delineation of ethnic categories by self-identification combined with promotional campaigns that stressed the monetary advantage of larger counts, thus encouraging the creation of "instant" members of the various categories.

The bureau's preparations for the 1990 enumeration and for the inevitable controversies it will engender might well be of two general types—to minimize to the degree possible its involvement in ethnic disputes, and to avoid contributing to false impressions by distributing data of "specious accuracy."

[95]For a good discussion of such questions, see Daniel Melnick, "The 1980 Census: Recalculating the Federal Equation," *Publius*, 11 (1981):39–65.

[96]When the recorded natural increase and the recorded net immigration were added to the 1970 enumerated population, the total proved to be 5.5 million under the 1980 count; but what the exercise indicated about the accuracy of the last census is difficult to surmise. See Jeffrey S. Passel, Jacob S. Siegel, and J. Gregory Robinson, "Coverage of the National Population in the 1980 Census, by Age, Sex, and Race: Preliminary Estimates by Demographic Analysis," *Current Population Reports*, Special Studies, Ser. P-23, no. 115 (1982).

6

THE SOCIAL AND POLITICAL CONTEXT OF POPULATION FORECASTING

NATHAN KEYFITZ

NUMBERS provide the rhetoric of our age. In discussing world poverty it is better to say that there are 3 billion poor people, and there will be 4 billion by the end of the century, than merely to say that there are now many poor and they are increasing; and similarly in a discussion of food, that there are 700 million hungry today, and there will be a billion twenty years from now unless we do something about it.

It is not customary, and even not courteous, for a listener to inquire into the relation of such numbers to actual censuses or other counts, to try to set bounds to them, or to ask for a definition of their concepts, in respect of either the present or the future. What rounded periods and flourishes were to Victorian eloquence, what Latin tags did for the eighteenth century, numbers contribute to eloquence now; they testify to the seriousness and trustworthiness of the speaker, as well as to his proper education. That purpose is served by predictions that have little basis in present tendencies; the listener who would not notice the difference between 3 million and 3 billion does not ask awkward questions. Ask the next few people you meet what is the world population; you will be surprised to find their answers varying by orders of magnitude. Yet all of them will trust a speaker who uses numbers more than one who does not.

To those of us who see science as measurement and forecasts as important for practical life, such use of numbers is a painful caricature of what we do at the same time as it is a tribute to our scientific work. So high a valuation of numbers, including those concerning the future, is associated with the empirical tradition in science, earliest and most prominently shown in English-speaking countries, and more recently identified with planning for the future, fully as important for a corporation as it is for a socialist state.

The eloquence that makes use of numbers in a poetic vein derives its force from the very real usefulness of numbers in their professional application. A production plan in which the elements are set out explicitly is more effective than no plan. The plan depends on what will happen in the future—what will be the size of the market, what the competition will do, how costs will change. At the very least the forecasts of these elements will expose them to professional criticism, will reveal hidden contradictions, will help ensure coordination of the various divisions of the corporation or the state. Before moving on to these points we must face a contradiction of pervasive importance, arising from the nature of time itself.

Forecasting: Impossible Yet Unavoidable

Because things are connected we cannot know the future of one variable—population—without knowing the future of every other variable. The number of people in the United States in the year 2000 depends on the condition of the economy, how our environment will hold out, what foreign demand for our goods will be, and many other circumstances, at each moment between now and the beginning of the next century.

One can of course "forecast" in the trivial sense of uttering a statement about the year 2000, but to forecast in the sense of making an estimate that will turn out to coincide with what is actually going to happen is beyond human capacity. The sentences, "He forecasts the end of the world at the next millennium," and "He forecast the present drought several months ago," are both grammatically correct. The essential distinction is not between a correct and an incorrect forecast, but between the utterance (whether or not later proven correct) and the congruence of utterance and subsequent event. It is a hindrance to clarity that the same word has two wholly different meanings, one signifying a prophetic assertion, however subjective or objective, the other genuinely anticipating an event that subsequently occurs.

The difficulty of the latter follows from a realistic view of the world's variability and its immunity to human control and prescience.

All this applies in principle to forecasts of population as of any other feature of the future. Time's arrow winging its way forward penetrates into forever new territory. Even if our knowledge base regarding the past were perfect and complete (of which there is no prospect ever), the real novelty in the world would still make genuine forecasting impossible.

Yet standing against this assertion of the absolute impossibility of knowing the future is the absolute necessity of a picture of the future if behavior is to have any sense. One cannot act purposefully in any small respect except within a picture of what the world will be like when the action produces its effects. So strong is the felt necessity of forecasting that major human institutions have no other purpose than to establish a milieu in which it is possible. Every time schedule, every stable community, every geographical arrangement enables us to foresee that some person will be present or some event will occur in a certain place at a certain time. But no set of institutions can go more than a short distance toward organizing the future. When we talk of forecasting, we refer to those items—such as whether births in the year 2000 will be above replacement—that cannot be taken for granted. When we say that forecasting is impossible, we are referring to matters on the margin of possible knowledge. It is not the population for the next five years— that essentially we know—nor that of the twenty-second century—that we have no possibility of knowing—but the population between those times that we refer to when we speak of forecasting.

The tension between the need to know the future and the impossibility of knowing it is resolved more readily in a society in which institutions change slowly. That is not the kind of society in which we live. The need to know the future increases as change accelerates, and at the same time the future becomes more opaque and impenetrable. The greater the need to know, it seems, the less the possibility of accurate knowledge.

A market economy provides one solution to the problem of knowledge and ignorance. Competing firms each make their own forecast, the accuracy of these forecasts constituting the locus of competition: The firm that can hire the best forecasters, including demographers, is the one that makes the largest profit, so that it expands while the firm with less good forecasters goes under.

It is true that forecasts are in some degree the locus of competition, but that does not lessen the advantage to the community of having official forecasts that are available to all; firms can build them into their own private models with or without modification. This public forecasting—now a part of the infrastructure of the economy—is the subject of this chapter.

Forecasts Are Everywhere

Because readers are hungry for news of the future, forecasting is pervasive, to be found implicitly in the conventions that have developed in the routine presentation of population as of other data. Expressive of this viewpoint are current rates of population increase, the net reproduction rate (which indicates what current fertility and mortality imply for the size of future generations), and the intrinsic rate of natural increase, all of which are implicit projections. Like the custom of presenting data on national income in terms of annual increase, these suggest (or threaten) that current conditions may continue through time. Showing rates invites the reader to suppose their indefinite continuance, just as a population projection invites confidence in the number given as the medium estimate. Yet in both cases the form of presentation enables the author to repudiate the invitation should he later wish to do so.

A division of responsibility develops that is natural to a society in which institutions have to protect themselves while performing needed services. The national or international statistical agency cannot take formal responsibility for performing a task that is impossible: describing the future before it occurs. Therefore, it claims only that its numbers for the future are the working out of a set of assumptions based on the present, just as it calculates rates that do not even mention the future explicitly. It allows the user to take responsibility for treating its work as forecasting.

This division of responsibility is one feature of the social context of forecasting, which I will analyze at some length in what follows. But first we need to look briefly at the data that support projections, particularly the census counts that are their necessary jumping-off points.

A Census Confirms the Nation

William Kruskal (1983) has pointed to a neglected aspect of the census, its character of ceremony and symbol: "It provides a sense of social cohesion, and a kind of non-religious communion: we enter the census apparatus as individual identities with a handful of characteristics; then later we receive from the census a group snapshot of ourselves at the ceremony date."[1] That helps to explain the worldwide census movement that began in the nineteenth century and especially since 1950 has spread around the world. Sponsored by the United Nations, it has been one of that organization's unqualified successes. At a

---

[1] W. Kruskal, "Research and the Census," paper presented to CRS Census Workshop (Jan. 1983), pp. 26–27, Xerox.

time when it was not yet permissible for international agencies to promote population control, taking censuses was an outlet for the urge to
do something about the population problem. If poor countries only
knew their populations and how fast they were growing, they would
spontaneously act to control births. By now only a few countries have
not taken at least one census.

The Western sponsor of census-taking has had a perspective very
different from that of the less developed countries that acceded to the
project. Where the sponsors expected that the poor country in question
would progress from the taking of a census to recognition of the need
for population control, the poor countries fell in with census-taking because the population count would somehow validate their nationhood.
They used the opportunity to include disputed territories in their
counts and so legitimate their claims. The emergence of the modern
state in Western Europe had been marked by the taking of national censuses, and we need not be surprised that censuses were likewise welcomed by the new nations of Asia, Africa, and Latin America.

But if the census is a symbol of the nation, then the larger the
count in comparison with other nations, the more imposing the symbol. In this perspective a large population is by no means to be deplored.
The census movement helped to make population a measure of the importance of nations and of the weight of each in the council of nations.
Poor countries made extensive reference to their large populations.

At least that was the view up to the 1960s; it is only with hardships
and grave problems associated with population and its growth during
the past fifteen years that new nations have come to see that the symbolic value of a large population can be offset by the difficulty of providing for that population. And in Africa this offset is still by no means
universally understood.

What applies to the last census count applies equally to the forecast. Nigeria is the tenth most populous country in the world today; according to World Bank projections, it promises to be the third most populous country toward the end of the twenty-first century. Nigerians and
other Africans see their increasing numbers as giving them a growing
weight in world affairs.

Vital statistics are by no means as widespread as censuses. It is true
that most countries have some provision for registration of births and
deaths, but outside of territories containing about 30 percent of the
world population there is an unknown but substantial undercoverage.

Complete registration of births requires effective government, as
does a good census. But a census can be taken with a few thousand, or a
few hundred thousand, literate and trained enumerators, while a registration system requires more than registrars; it depends on the sensitiz-

ing of virtually the entire population. In a mature system statistics for the country are obtained at the same time as proof of age and citizenship for the individuals registered. But peasants do not apply for passports and have little need to prove their age and citizenship. The social changes that will alert parents to the usefulness of registration will take long enough that we must hope the population problem will be solved before it can be measured by vital statistics.

This absence of good base material will continue for the foreseeable future to be a serious handicap to forecasts.

Population Has Long Lead Times

Whether growth is to be speeded up or slowed down, population is in most situations a question for the long term. Rarely is it argued that a country is under- or overpopulated today; rather it is feared—in Mexico, say, or China—that a crisis will occur in the next generation or two; or, in Austria or France, that the twenty-first or twenty-second century will see an undermining of the culture because too few people will carry it. The nation, like the individual family, is prepared to live with the children already born, however strong its reasons for fearing further births. Of all policy issues, population, along with the associated problem of resources, spans the longest term. No one even contemplates the 1990 discount rate; people do worry about population in 2050.

If a country is going to be unable either to produce or to buy enough food for its population in the year 2050, it must act quickly on its birth rate. What is easily done now, by control of births, might have to happen the hard way—by higher death rates—if overpopulation were to appear without warning.

Because infants do not require much food and other resources, many can be generated; only later does it become evident how substantial is the commitment that each imposes on the community—five years later for schooling, fifteen years or more later for an opportunity to work and gain an independent living and to engage in adult consumption, sixty-five years later for income in old age. It is this low initial cost, combined with the subsequent heavy obligation, that makes population a long-term matter.

A second reason is an offshoot of the first: A population that has been growing rapidly has an age distribution highly favorable to further growth. Because reproduction takes place mostly at ages under 35, and because a population that has been growing rapidly has a high proportion of its members under age 35, it is virtually impossible to put the brakes on quickly. Suppose that a country has been increasing for a long time at rate r, with birthrate b, average age at childbearing μ, expectation of life $\mathring{e}_0$, and net reproduction rate R_0. Suppose also that it now suddenly curtails its births, so that each couple from this point on produces only 2.2 children, or whatever is the number at that level of mortality that will just replace each generation. Ultimately, of course, that population will be stationary, but for the next generation or two it will increase, and when it does reach stationarity it will have

$$\left(\frac{-b}{r}\right)\left(\frac{\mathring{e}_0}{\mu}\right)\left(\frac{R_0 - 1}{R_0}\right)$$

times as many people as it had at the moment when it dropped its family size to 2.2.[2] Entering numbers appropriate to many developing countries today gives ratios as high as 1.7; the population will increase by 70 percent over the following half century, even if it immediately lowers its birth rate to 2.2 children per couple and its death rates are frozen at present levels.

Long-term forecasting is likely to be less reliable than short-term, if only because the uncovering of error is delayed. The cycle of prediction and discovery of accuracy of about twenty or thirty years for typical population forecasts is of the same order of magnitude as the length of individual careers. The sequence of cycles of forecast, check by comparison with actuality, adjustment forecast, check, etc., is a matter of months for unemployment or the prime rate, and this possibility of an early check provides a certain seriousness that is not possible when the check on one's work is a generation away.

The public may think demographers spend most of their efforts trying to determine the future population; a glance at any of the professional journals will show how wrong this perception is. Most of the country's demographers do not engage in forecasting; they have learned from the errors of the past that there are better ways to use their skills. A much larger proportion of top economists give their effort to forecasting; they are clearly attracted by the shortness of the forecast-discovery cycle and the frequent correction of methods that a short cycle permits.

Projection Versus Forecasts

The pioneer of the kind of work here described was P. K. Whelpton, who called his numbers for future population "estimates." Neither he

[2]N. Keyfitz, *Applied Mathematical Demography*, 2nd ed. (New York: Springer, 1985), p. 156.

nor others made any fine differentiation of language until the mid-1940s, when the birthrate turned unexpectedly upward, revealing a conspicuous divergence between population forecast and performance. The official agencies who put out forecasts were deeply embarrassed. This history has been described elsewhere,[3] and we refer to it only briefly here.

By the 1940s, while there was disillusionment with existing forecasts, estimates of future population had become a part of the work of national agencies in the United States, Canada, and other countries. Despite gross errors, the demand was strong, and the national agencies could not simply cease publishing them. They needed some means of differentiating their work on the future from the figures they were currently producing based on relatively solid censuses and surveys. It would be disastrous if the public came to think that all statistical series were as defective as the estimates of future population were proving to be. At that time someone came up with a distinction between projections and forecasts. The former consisted of a noncommittal working out of a set of stated assumptions and did not pretend to be an account of the future. That would protect the agency from blame for the inevitable errors.

Users, on their part, continued to seize on any set of numbers labeled with future years. They reasoned that such numbers would not be published unless they were usable, and the assumptions selected by the Census Bureau or other office were taken (usually without examination) as representing a reasonable assessment of the future—why else would they be chosen? The device by which numbers called projections (and hence in principle hypothetical) could be put out by census offices and read and used by the public as though they were the best possible forecasts seemed to cover all requirements: They protected the official agency at the same time that they provided needed material. The fiction embodying this contradiction served a valuable purpose.

It is in the shadow of the disappointments in forecasting experienced so strongly in the 1940s that the Bureau of the Census currently presents its material. The bureau says simply that "net immigration is assumed to be a constant 450,000 per year," and makes similar statements for fertility and mortality. Nothing in the entire publication refers to the use of the results as forecasts.[4]

[3]H. F. Dorn, "Pitfalls in Population Forecasts and Projections," *Journal of the American Statistical Association* (1950), vol. 45, pp. 311–334; J. Hajnal, "The Prospects for Population Forecasts," *Journal of the American Statistical Association* (1955), vol. 50, pp. 309–322; and T. Frejka, *World Population Projections: A Concise History*, Center for Policy Studies Working Paper No. 66 (New York: The Population Council, 1981).

[4]"Projections of the Population of the United States: 1982–2050," *Current Population Reports*, series P-25, no. 922 (Washington, D.C.: U.S. Government Printing Office, 1982).

The United Nations, on its part, has largely given up the fiction. The numbers in its publication of 1982 are the "results of the 1980 assessment of demographic trends. . . . They provide an assessment of plausible prospects for the population of each country." The same report states that the medium variant "represents future demographic trends that seem more likely to occur considering observed past demographic trends, expected social and economic progress."[5] I cannot be sure just what "more likely to occur" means, yet plainly the recognition that users want forecasts prevails against inhibitions dating from past gross errors.

A similar difference applies with regard to the high and low variants. The Census Bureau says only that it applies alternative assumptions, while for the United Nations the high and low variants represent the "plausible, but not exhaustive, range of future deviations from the medium variant projections."

Projection in the Planning Context

The quintessential application of forecasting is in the context of planning. A simple case is the plan of a corporation or a specialized ministry where nothing in the plan will affect the population. The decision of IBM to produce a new minicomputer will not influence the national birthrate. The demographer does his best to interpret trends and provide a forecast on which the rest of the plan can be based. Influence is in one direction only: from the population to prospective sales.

If the plan's execution does affect the size of the population, we could talk about solving equations or else iterating through a sequence of intermediate plans. But this would be mere talk, for the relation between population and economic activity is so little known that such second-order effects are drowned out in the noise of the system in which the plan is being made. We have heard much of self-fulfilling or self-defeating forecasts, but they are foreign to the subject here treated, if for no other reason than the fact that no one has a certain grasp on the mechanisms governing population growth and decline.

However great the uncertainty as to what the future population will be, the uncertainty in other variables is greater yet. The corporation's planning depends on future supplies of labor and raw materials, on demand for the product, and, most important, on what the competition will do. This applies to nations as well as firms: The Soviet planner, say, of electronics development has to forecast what the

[5]United Nations, *World Population Prospects as Assessed in 1980* (New York: United Nations, 1981).

Japanese will be doing five years ahead, and that is much harder than knowing the size of the population to which the product will be sold.

My point is that planning is a gamble on the future actions of many variables. The ante is the large amount of investment needed up front to get production going; the prize consists of billions in sales and profits. Uncertainties and errors of population forecasting may be lost in the larger errors of the other variables on which the plan depends, but this is no reason to be careless about population.

The forecast is as much a means of coordination as it is an advance statement of the future. If a telephone company accepts a certain population for the United States in the year 2000, and uses this and other assumptions in planning its output of instruments and its construction of central office facilities and lines, then whatever happens to the population its supplies of equipment will correspond to its central offices and the lines laid down. It will not have central offices lacking equipment, nor lines with no central office to connect them to.

William Alonso points out that the attainment of consistency is a little appreciated virtue of forecasts; one tries to have them approximate the subsequent performance, but even if they fail in that they can still serve to coordinate diverse elements of the production process. In declining areas, he says, industrial parks are developed by the various localities; in some instances the sum total of workers who could be accommodated by these investments is several times the total conceivable number of workers in the region, so that the strategy is wasteful and can only lead to disappointment. At least this kind of inconsistency can be avoided by explicit forecasts of population, industrial activity, and employment in relation to the size of projected industrial parks.

Demographic forecasts often run a hundred or more years into the future, while plans for the economy or for a particular concern tend to be short-run—few have a span of more than ten years. We have here a difficulty. If population projections are primarily ancillary to planning, how to account for the different time horizons of the projections and the plans they are supposed to serve?

One resolution of the seeming contradiction is that long-range projections are made to check out the method, to be sure that they are correct in their early parts. It is not entirely illogical to make a 100-year projection and, if its numbers seem reasonable, to use its first ten years. We would not want to depend on the first ten years without seeing where they were going; the long-range forecast is a test of the short-range one.

Beyond that one can fall back on models in which what to do in the next year depends on a forecast of the context of the action for the next year, but much more: What is the right thing to do next year depends on what we anticipate for the next 100 years. William Butz points out that dynamic programming is a concept that goes back through a long development in which Hicks's *Value and Capital* (1939) played an important part.[6] Howard Raiffa (1968) has shown the practical application of mathematical programming.[7]

But there is a more popular source of demand for long-term models.

Projection and Journalism

Many forecasts are produced for the lamest of reasons: they are "interesting." If they cause the newspaper reader to raise his eyes from the page and say, "That's a lot of people," they have fulfilled their purpose. Expressed more positively, forecasts are made to inform, enlighten, and surprise the public. They take their place alongside the scandals, the cooking hints, and the vagaries of movie personalities that make up the evening news.

Given the transience of messages carried by the media and the short memory span of newspaper and television audiences, the congruence of the forecast with the subsequent reality is unimportant in this application. An audience that does not notice when today's headlines say the opposite of yesterday's is not going to recall a discrepancy between a forecast made twenty years ago and the census total announced today. The criterion of success in the journalistic use of forecasts is their ability to attract attention on the day they are announced. If the well-known futurologist can make it to the front page with a catchy forecast and if his name is noticed by a businessman, so that the volume of his consultantship is increased, then the purpose of the forecast is attained. There is no further need to refer to it, and checking it against the subsequent realization is wholly superfluous.

That goes at least for the primary journalistic use. We may think of a less spectacular secondary use as a background for other stories. In Sunday-magazine accounts of the ecology of the year 2000, estimates of population are required. Standards here are higher than in the primary journalistic use, but the ultimate criterion is still whether the forecast contributes to an "interesting" story.

Projections Are Marked by Professional Caution

Professional statisticians, demographers, and planners are intellectual leaders in a number-conscious society. They may be academics,

[6] J. R. Hicks, *Value and Capital* (Oxford: Clarendon Press, 1939).
[7] H. Raiffa, *Decision Analysis* (Cambridge, Mass.: MIT Press, 1968).

government or corporation officials, or the burgeoning statistical services industry, as Starr and Corson call it (see Chapter 14). These are people who do know the difference between 3 million and 3 billion; for them numbers are something more than poetry. Their aim is to distinguish themselves from the seers and soothsayers of the past, as well as from contemporary nonprofessionals, the politicians, and journalists, whose casual forecasts fill the daily media.

Professionalism is no abstract ideology alone but is maintained by very concrete corporate bodies. In a remarkably short time professions such as statistics and demography have matured to the point where most of those entrusted with the work are officially trained and certified. In contrast to the time up to the middle of this century, there is now a formal way of becoming a statistician. One goes through college and graduate school and learns a large amount of mathematics and probability theory, most of which will not be applied in later work. What counts is the hidden agenda of the college and the graduate school, those things that are not the subject of class instruction and examination. Of all the elements of this hidden agenda the most important is the assimilation of certain attitudes toward data: a combination of respect and skepticism, and especially concern for its integrity.

One learns that the opinions of journalists and of the public do not count. People outside the profession may be in a position to make their weight felt politically, but truth is the province of one's own professional group. Galileo could stand for a while without the support of such a group, but even he ultimately gave in. Most of us need a corporate body to enable us to identify truth. Thus, the important thing that the student learns in graduate school is that on all questions within its scope the authority is the body of the initiated in statistics or demography or social science generally. While he is brooding over issues of probability and decision theory, the real lesson he is learning is that his fellow statisticians are the right people to look to for answers to questions on measurement of social phenomena and the errors of such measurement.

Canons developed in statistics and social science include repudiation of any claim to direct knowledge of the future. Such claims are for soothsayers. The world is infinitely rich in the variables that may possibly influence the future, and the most elaborate models include only an infinitesimal part of the operative variables. The professional sets out a scenario of a few elements, then another scenario, then a third. The client is offered the several scenarios, which thereby become subjects of preference and choice. The scenarios do not claim to be forecasts; they are ways of focusing discussion and judgment.

Demographers were early proponents of this outlook, in which the forecast future is subject to the choice of the client or user. The logic of this approach is that the demographer presents a few main possibilities in respect of the components of population growth, shows what population they will result in twenty or more years later, and leaves the selection to the user. It is up to the user to study the assumptions on which the components were projected forward, choose the *set of assumptions* that seems right to him, and then accept only the demographer's arithmetic to read out the resulting future population. We return later to what happens if the user does not follow this script, if he is in too much of a hurry to read the assumptions and simply chooses the *forecast* that seems right to him.

Forecasting as Persuasion

We started by saying that numbers are the rhetoric of our times. Quantitative social science has diffused to the masses, at least to the point where writers are required to present numbers at all cost.

But such embellishment of discourse is only part of the use of numbers to persuade. Numbers regarding the future can be specifically targeted to bring about the action that the writer is urging. Is one making a case for limiting immigration from Mexico? The release of a famous estimate of 12 million illegals now in the United States was of no small help in getting the budget of a protective agency through Congress. Does one want to advance measures for raising the birthrate in France? Showing that in fifty years the native French population will have diminished to less than it was a century ago helps push for increased family allowances.

The forecast need not be explicit. Malthus argued for restraint in childbearing by pointing to the properties of a geometric progression as a potential, never saying what would happen in the future. The absence of explicit forecasts in Malthus is a measure of his sophistication. He left it to the reader to see what would happen with a doubling of population every twenty-five years, the rate in the America of his time. On this point at least Malthus had the better of his opponent, Godwin, who said that eons and eons must pass before the world became overpopulated, even at the rates postulated by Malthus. Apparently Godwin never studied the exponential function.

Sometimes the strength of an argument depends on a projection into the future based on survey data. If we made contraceptives available at low cost to the Javanese peasantry, how many would accept and use them? KAP (Knowledge, Attitudes, Practices) surveys carried out by many LDC governments show that a large proportion of the population would like to limit their further progeny. But when the means to do so are made available, they do not always have the anticipated effect in limiting births.

The situation of the woman or couple being questioned is not the same as the situation of the couple making a decision on the use of contraceptives in their everyday life. To take the response given the enumerator and written down by him, and tabulated and interpreted as though it represents future behavior, can lead only to disillusionment. One can be in favor of dispensing contraceptives for population control without supporting all of the arguments used to advocate it, and certainly without accepting the statement of childbearing ideals provided by respondents to KAP surveys. Statements by couples of their individual childbearing intentions have proven an uncertain basis for overall fertility forecasts.

The 1982 population forecast of the Census Bureau showed net immigration of 450,000, implicitly placing illegal immigration at zero. Presumably the unwillingness of the bureau to charge the Department of Justice with tolerating large-scale violations of law led to this unlikely hypothesis. But imagine the effect on Congress of a census estimate of 1 million illegal immigrants a year, an error in the opposite direction to its zero estimate.

Forecasts of electric energy use in the United States provide some striking instances of forecasting as persuasion, particularly in the political debate on the energy crisis triggered in 1973 by the OPEC cartel's temporary success in establishing radically higher oil prices. Prepared in the immediate wake of the crisis, the 1975 *Statistical Abstract of the United States* reported that Americans used twice as many kilowatts per capita in 1973 as in 1960.[8] It forecast per capita "requirements" in 1990 at two and a half times the 1973 rate, or a fivefold increase from 1960. This forecast, appearing in such an august source and apparently the product of dispassionate, scientific analysis, seemed more like a fact than a guess, and made a strong argument for the urgency of expanding electric generating capacity.

But two things were wrong. The first was that the forecast did not take account of changes in behavior and technology that were adaptive to the new energy situation. When prices shot up, people and industries managed to do with less, kept their homes cooler, substituted capital for fuel in the form of insulation or better technology, or used other forms of energy, such as gas. The 1975 forecast ignored such adaptive

[8]U.S. Bureau of the Census, *Statistical Abstract of the United States: 1975*, 95th ed. (Washington, D.C.: U.S. Government Printing Office, 1975).

responses and so was wildly wrong. By 1980 per capita consumption was one third below the forecast's estimate.

The second error in the 1975 forecast is directly related to the political economy of statistics. The fine print below the *Abstract's* table indicates that the projection had not, in fact, been made by the Bureau of the Census; it merely reported a projection from another source, cited as "U.S. Federal Power Commission, *National Power Survey, 1970,* and unpublished data." A reader might be skeptical of the projection on two grounds. First, it was not produced by a detached observer but by an agency interested in the expansion of electric energy. Second, although the numbers were published in the 1975 *Statistical Abstract,* their principal source dated to 1970, well *before* the beginning of the energy crisis, and thus before any adaptive responses to the new situation could be observed.[9] Thus neither the source nor the date of the forecast are what they appear to be. The very meaning of the numbers projected is unclear. The table refers to "requirements," but requirements for what? The term suggests that the forecast was constructed with some unspecified objective or norm in mind, on the basis of undisclosed assumptions about prices and technical or economic possibilities for substitution. Offered with five-digit precision, the forecast is a perfect example of persuasion dressed as a fact.

The 1982 *Statistical Abstract,* using later data, was more circumspect in its quantitative projections, but just as ambiguous. It forecast a "production" of about 12,500 kilowatt hours per capita by 1990, about a 200 percent increase over the 1960 rate, but less than half the increase predicted in the 1975 volume.[10] While in 1975 the *Abstract* labeled its numbers as "requirements," implying that they were needs or demand, the 1982–83 *Abstract* labeled its numbers "production," implying that they were the supply needed. But the Census Bureau did not indicate whether these were forecasts of what would happen, or someone's normative notion of what had to happen to satisfy some unstated criterion. (William Alonso's words of the page or two preceding greatly improve my original statement of this example.)

No one can say exactly what per capita electric energy will actually be in the future, but one would like to be assured that forecasting errors

---

[9] It is unlikely that the unspecified "unpublished data" remedy this obsolescence: the crisis occurred in the winter of 1973–74, allowing little time to produce and incorporate data for the 1975 *Abstract,* particularly in view of the severe disarray which existed in energy statistics at this time. See Aaron Wildavsky and Ellen Tenenbaum, *The Politics of Mistrust* (Beverly Hills, CA: Sage, 1981).

[10] *Statistical Abstract of the United States: 1982–1983,* 103rd ed. (Washington, D.C.: U.S. Government Printing Office, 1982).

are innocent of any attempt to influence public policy. These examples of energy forecasts retailed by the U.S. Bureau of the Census in the *Abstract* illustrate the conflict between the Census Bureau's operational need to get information where it can and the social need for data clear in meaning and produced professionally and disinterestedly. Good statistics, in this case, would be uninfluenced by the electric energy lobby. The error in forecasts is inevitable, but it need not be compounded by bias.

Other instances where impartiality is desirable are not far to seek. The official estimates of the Social Security Administration provide the basis for determining the adequacy of provision for old-age pensions far into the next century. The number of old people for the next sixty-five years is easily calculated within a small margin of error, but this is not the main element in the future pension burden. More difficult to ascertain is the number of workers paying into the fund. The required tax in the twenty-first century is highly sensitive to the number of births starting now.

Given the key role played by population forecasts in assessing Social Security policies and the inevitable arbitrariness of those forecasts, it is strange that these are not sought from some outside source. Making up one's own forecasts is like auditing one's own books or judging one's own case in a court of law.

As William Alonso has pointed out, the disinterestedness of a source contributes to the legitimacy of both current data and forecasts.[11] Judith de Neufville indicates that statistics produced by operating agencies (for example, the FBI crime statistics) enjoy less legitimacy than do those of scientific bureaus. An operating agency, rather than publishing its own numbers, might find it advantageous to persuade an apparently disinterested statistical agency to calculate and publish them. The numbers would be better, and would be more easily believed.

The Ideological Element in Data Presentation

There is no unique way to present data. The 3.6 million births and 2.0 million deaths each year provide one basis for discussing the demographic prospects of the United States. Without counting immigrants, the population is increasing by the not negligible amount of 1.6 million per year, or about two-thirds of 1 percent. But the very same births and deaths, when used to construct a life table and age-specific rates of birth, show that the mean family size implied by the rates is only about

[11]William Alonso, Personal communication.

1.8, so that in each generation at those rates there would ultimately be a fall of over 10 percent. If the present rates of birth and death continue, deaths will rise as the population ages and births will fall as the large cohorts of the baby boom move past childbearing.

Disregarding migration, then, are we increasing or decreasing? Note that this is a much easier question than forecasting future fertility and mortality. It asks only what will happen if present conditions continue. The absolute numbers of births and deaths suggest an increase of 40 million persons per generation; age-specific rates suggest a decline of 26 million. Can the matter be decided by looking into the past record to see which has been more nearly constant—numbers or rates? My own examination has shown no preponderance one way or the other.

The range of possibilities in selecting and projecting extends far beyond population. Per capita income has long been accepted as measuring the condition of nations, and its changes as measuring their progress or decline. Plainly, per capita income is a better measure than total income, since it allows for the size of countries; yet an average composed of disparate elements is not meaningful. Suppose the world income is $9 trillion, and we divide this by the corresponding population, 4.5 billion, to find a mean income of $2,000 per year increasing at 2 percent per year per capita. That would give an average income of $4,000 within the next thirty-five years, $8,000 within the next seventy. Universal development seems in sight.

But one can extrapolate with very different results simply by recognizing two or more averages rather than one at each moment. Extrapolation that takes account of distribution shows rapid increase in the number of poor in the world well into the twenty-first century, even on the fastest likely increase in overall per capita income.

The possibilities for selecting items and modes of presentation have been enlarged with the advent of computing. A lot of data are published in machine-readable versions, for example, the bulky local data of the U.S. census; they are transmitted from machine to machine without need for human intervention. But then a human enters: perhaps a scholar who is looking for a relation between variables. By manipulating a large volume of data he stands a better chance of discovering a relation than if he had to study the original material line by line and do hand calculations.

Some of the newer ways of finding patterns in data may be too effective. The computer is apparently not as good as the human observer at seeing patterns, but it can go through much more material. Combining the strengths of computer and human observer is the technique called "projection pursuit." Such a technique may speed up the accumulation of knowledge while at the same time accepting some results that will later be found to result from chance and hence add to the errors of forecasts. No test of significance can possibly be devised to protect against nonsignificant results when a relation is found by combing through data in the way described.

The Advantage of Disinterested Forecasts

The official projections of the Bureau of the Census or the United Nations have a prestige that derives from their authoritative work in more factual spheres. Technical and administrative achievements in the gathering and publication of data lead one to believe that numbers on the future produced by these two agencies are the best possible. Yet this assertion of the trustworthiness of official forecasts is clearly too strong. Sophisticated users hardly accept that the projections of official agencies are the best possible forecasts. They fall back on a lesser commendation: The projections are a disinterested view of the future.

We have already referred to the virtue of disinterestedness. To put the matter in a slightly different way, if I am trying to make a case for some policy, it is an advantage to be able to use numbers for future population that I have not fabricated for the specific argument. The more my argument is taken from the public domain, so that its errors are at least unrelated to the view I am arguing, the stronger the case I am making. No one will accuse the Census Bureau of having conspired with me to advance my case. This indifference to particular policies is an important feature of official forecasts.

In fact, we would be better off if such standard scenarios as the Census Bureau's medium estimate of projected population existed for many other series. When the administration tells us that a given tax proposal will add $10 billion to the Treasury's take for the coming year, it is likely to base this statement on its own figures of prospective employment, income, balance of payments, etcetera, without even saying what these are. Standard scenarios on all these matters, and not only on population, would facilitate debate and increase the chance of coming to a sound decision. Far from criticizing what a disinterested official agency like the Bureau of the Census does in the field of population, one is inclined to recommend that it extend its activities to other fields. Of course, the difficulty of agreeing on a common scenario increases with the number of variables.

Such acceptance of the judgment of the official agency is in direct opposition to the theory of projections by which the user decides which is best. Some users are less trusting than the preceding paragraph supposes; they do look at the assumptions underlying the published variants and choose the one they like. If they do, they are within the official theory of the projections. But suppose the user finds that the assumptions are stated obscurely, perhaps some omitted altogether; they are published in the midst of a good deal of routine material on census definitions of the base numbers, as well as on uninteresting technical descriptions of how the calculations are done. They are part of the fine print of the publication that few readers think is meant for them.

Facing the fine print, the user is likely to stop reading and turn instead to the final numbers—to what the projections show for the year 2000, and judge how reasonable that number is. In short, the user chooses according to the outcome of the calculation in disregard of the assumptions on which that outcome is based.

The reader who exercises his judgment in such a way is not at all helped by the calculations. If he is to choose which outcome most closely corresponds to his idea of the future population, he might just as well have a set of random numbers to choose from. Looking among the projections published by the central agency until he finds his own idea of future population is a curious but not uncommon use of those publications.

The Division of Labor

That projections are subject to error by no means prevents their effective use. A large body of theory and methods on decision-making under uncertainty, by Howard Raiffa and others, is available to assist in the utilization of necessarily imperfect forecasts.[12] But with the expansion of knowledge and the difficulty of mastering more than one narrow specialty comes inevitably the problem of coordination.

The division of labor between statisticians, whose projections are merely the working out of the consequences of assumptions, and users who convert these to forecasts by judging which set of assumptions is most appropriate, is only a beginning. A more satisfactory mode of collaboration between those knowledgeable in demography and professionals in the field who will use the forecasts is due to Muhsam, and its logic is readily expounded.[13] The demographer would provide not point estimates of the future population but distributions. It suffices for such purposes that the forecast be of this nature: The population of the United States in the year 2000 will be 280 ± 20 million, the probability

[12]Raiffa, *Decision Analysis.*
[13]H. V. Muhsam, "The Utilisation of Alternative Population Forecasts in Planning," *Bulletin of the Research Council of Israel* (1956), vol. 5, pp. 133–146.

being 0.67 that the range will straddle the performance. Such a statement may be based on past variation in the inputs (*ex ante* error) or on past errors in forecasts made by similar methods (*ex post* error). We call the probability distribution of the future population $P(x)$, that is, the (subjective) probability that the true population at the future time considered will fall between x and $x + dx = P(x)dx$.

The user on his side knows nothing of population but does know the loss to which he will be subjected if the estimated population, x, departs by a given amount from the performance that subsequently appears. Call the loss function $L(\hat{x} - x)$. Then he would like to choose his particular $\hat{x}$ in such fashion that the expected value, $EL(\hat{x} - x)$, is as small as possible. If the functions are integrable, then he needs the total $R(\hat{x})$,

$$R(\hat{x}) = \int_{-\infty}^{\infty} L(\hat{x}) - x)P(x)dx,$$

to be as small as possible. In principle that is easily calculated; I have given a numerical example elsewhere.[14]

The loss function may be asymmetric—it may be much worse to have an underestimate than an overestimate of the future population. In that case the minimization would shift one toward the high estimate. Unquestionably some users apply this informally, taking the high estimate because it is "conservative" with regard to their particular risk.

Note that the collaboration between the demographer and the user in this situation does not require them to meet and discuss the problem; it can simply take place via the published probability distribution.

The preceding model brings out that we need not insist on a single forecast for all purposes: One "stakeholder," as the Census Bureau calls him, needs a maximum figure, another needs a low one. Alongside such legitimate differences of need are differences that are not acceptable, such as a social security agency wanting a forecast to assure the public that no further taxes will be needed.

Conflict of Forecasting and Policy

When I was in China in 1982, I was told a good deal about goals for population. At that time one group in the leadership argued for 700 million; nothing larger would enable the country to feed itself, provide jobs for its youth, and industrialize with its own raw materials. Another

[14]Keyfitz (1985), p. 234.

group considered the drop to 700 million within the next century intolerably distorting to the age distribution, and favored stabilization at a total of between 1.2 and 1.5 billion.

After having witnessed the strong feelings at high levels of the administration engendered by the different aims, I was asked to make a scientific forecast of what the future population would actually be. I had to explain that no science at my command would forecast which side was going to win the debate and secure the political power to put its policies into effect.

The example is not unique, though a sufficiently tight hold on the territory to determine the number of births is purely a fantasy for most governments. Even in China the current liberalization of the economy makes children useful once more, causing a rise in the birthrate. Overall it seems fair to say that policy is the enemy of forecasting. That is a troublesome conclusion to accept when we think that the purpose of forecasts is to help determine policy.

The difficulty of mixing policy and forecasting becomes apparent when any kind of statistics becomes important in the real world. When it was first proposed that the census be used for the apportionment of federal monies, the census-takers welcomed that as another use of the census that would increase its importance. Few foresaw that it would lead to innumerable court cases and other struggles that threatened to weaken public trust in the census.

The lesson, that mixing politics and statistics is harmful, was learned in other countries as well as in the United States. In China the Cultural Revolution took it that statistics, like everything else of importance, needed to engage the masses—that no narrow group of professionals should be allowed to operate their arcane techniques out of the public view. Everyone got into the act of collecting statistics, and communes competed with one another on the amount of grain production they could show statistically. After a year or two of such manipulation no one had any idea of what the grain production of China was. Now a degree of professionalism has been restored, at least with respect to the census, and hard numbers are again becoming available.

Error Is To Be Judged Quantitatively

When the use of a logistic enabled Raymond Pearl to forecast the 1930 census total with a margin of error that was smaller than the error of the census itself, it could be claimed that at last population growth was understood, and that from then on we would be able to say exactly what future numbers would be. After 50 years it is difficult to convey to readers the confidence that emerged from that virtual coincidence of forecast and performance. All that had been problematic and mysterious about population counts vanished from view, and the answer to the question, "How well can population be forecast?" seemed to be, "Perfectly."

But all this changed during the 1930s, when again and again the forecasts turned out to be wrong and had to be rejected—not twenty or thirty years after they were published, but within two or three years. There seemed no bottom to the rate of increase as births in the United States and other countries fell below replacement. The answer to the question of whether population forecasting was possible seemed to be, "No, it is impossible," and this was confirmed when births unexpectedly rose through the 1940s and 1950s, and forecasts were unaccountably and persistently too low.

By the 1980s, enriched by the successes and failures of half a century, demographers and their public need not discuss whether population can or cannot be forecast, but only the degree of accuracy that can be expected.

Ex Post Error

I have elsewhere examined the errors of some 1,000 forecasts made by what is essentially today's standard method.[15] The metric used for evaluating a forecast was the difference between the mean annual percent rate of increase of the forecast and the mean annual percent rate of increase of the performance. All we require to note here is the summary result that for populations nearing stationarity the root-mean-square departure of forecast from performance was about 0.3 percentage points. If a forecast implies 0.6 percent per year increase, the 67 percentage points on the distribution of prospective rates of increase would be 0.6 ± 0.3, or 0.3 to 0.9 percent per year. That would put the U.S. totals for 2020 at 255 to 323 million. The general conclusion is that for the next ten or twenty years estimates have moderate error; much beyond that the range is so wide as to be equivalent to saying that we simply do not know the population.

Where the Future Is Known

This chapter has placed its main emphasis on the uncertain, even mysterious, character of the future, yet there are cases where the future is known with virtual certainty. The number of people in the United

---

[15]N. Keyfitz, "The Limits of Population Forecasting," *Population and Development Review* (1981), vol. 7, no. 4, pp. 579–593.

States who will be alive and with a claim to Social Security is known for the next sixty or more years.

When the Social Security Act was passed in 1935, forecasts of claimants were available to the end of the twentieth century, and despite much higher immigration than anticipated, these have not been far off. It is true that the number of persons contributing was much less certain, yet enough was known so that the public need not have been led to believe that payment of $60 per year during working life would somehow suffice to cover an income of $1,200 per year—twenty times as much—from age 65 onwards. The working population was never 20 times as large as the number over age 65.

Since that time, Congress has repeatedly raised the contribution. We find it discouraging that Congress was prompted less by forecasts of population than by the immediate shortage of cash to cover the outgoing monthly benefit checks.

Another instance in which reasonably accurate and highly relevant forecasts were available and disregarded was in education. The birthrate started to fall in the early 1960s, and it was inevitable from about 1963 that entrants into elementary schools would diminish five years later. Clearly, the schools already in existence would more than suffice; indeed many of these would be superfluous. Yet few plans for construction of new schools were canceled until the number of children actually showing up to enroll declined in the late 1960s. Somewhat the same applied all the way to university, despite a warning eighteen years ahead.

The point at which the contraction need least have been a surprise was at the graduate-school level. Here what economists call the accelerator is operative. If we think of graduate students as future capital goods, and their teachers as existing capital, then it is the year-to-year *increase* in the number of students that determines the absolute *number* of teachers hired.

During the 1960s a major scholar in a research university would have several new graduate students each year; he would see to the dissertations and graduation of perhaps one or two a year; these would go to some other research university, where they would carry on the work into which they had been initiated in graduate school. Such was the expansion of the system that for perhaps a decade virtually all the graduating Ph.D.s could find teaching jobs and constitute the intellectual progeny of some master; and each of them expected to have a similar number of descendants. Those who were seduced by this perspective included scholars in the field of demography who did not face the fact that a birthrate of one descendant per year per member of the population, a doubling each year, could continue for only a very short time. Most of us believed in birth control for the national population as a whole but not for our own profession. Only long afterward did it occur to this writer as well as to others, that in the stationary condition to which every system must ultimately converge, each scholar can have only one student who will take up his work, that is, one successor during the course of his entire career—not one per year, but one per thirty or more years.

Such points are clearer now than they were then. A part of what obscured them was that elements other than population determined the future condition of Social Security and the schools. The former was bound to be affected by the rate of unemployment, which reduced contributions, by the generosity of Congress with respect to pensions for dependents, and other factors. The main other element for the schools was the proportion of the population that would attend, especially at higher levels. If the proportion attending college went up from 40 to 60 percent, that would be the equivalent of a 50 percent increase of population and could offset the end of the baby boom for at least a few years. Again, while the average attendance for the country was still more or less predictable, that for particular areas and types of school was less so. School populations of Sunbelt states have indeed grown. Public schools have lost to parochial and other private schools. But beyond all these obscuring elements lies a degree of inertia in public planning that delayed the response of school systems to what was an inevitable decline.

Achievement Despite Social and Political Context

A discussion of the social and political context of anything gives a superficial impression of denigrating that thing. We have said that judicial impartiality is crucial to statistical data and forecasts, at the same time admitting that it is extremely difficult to attain. That in itself is negative, but beyond it is a deeper philosophical difficulty. Statistics of the past are all we have; as such they are useless for immediate policy, which depends on what will happen in the future. What will happen is impossible to know. Should we stop collecting statistics because they refer to the past and so are irrelevant to action, and stop making forecasts because they are inevitably in error?

Quite the contrary. Given all the dilemmas and contradictions—of which this chapter has sketched only a few—the degree of objectivity and usefulness for decision-making so far attained is truly remarkable. The skills of the statistician and the demographer, together with a degree of continuity provided by nature even in these changing times, combine to generate data invaluable for decision-making. Improvements are possible, in the direction of bringing practice closer to the professional ideal of total impartiality, and such improvements will be made sooner when the hazards and dilemmas are kept in full view.

PART III
Statistics and Democratic Politics

7

PUBLIC STATISTICS
AND DEMOCRATIC POLITICS

KENNETH PREWITT

I F, TO paraphrase Harold Lasswell, politics has become how much for how many, it is clear that measurement moves toward the center of political life. The result is a politics of numbers. What is to be counted? By whom? Can the numbers be trusted? In which direction is the trend line moving? Who is at fault for the (now numerically defined) failure of a policy or program? The intrusion of numbers into politics is global, as the world's nations now endlessly debate issues couched in numerical estimates and forecasts: weapon counts, oil reserves, trade balances, North–South inequities, debt ratios.

With reason, then, scholars have quickened their attention to how numbers are generated, and then used or misused in politics. This important scholarship rests on the assumption that public statistics are not politically neutral. Decisions about what to count are influenced by

NOTE: I wrote this chapter while a Fellow at the Center for Advanced Study in the Behavioral Sciences and a Guggenheim Fellow. Financial support was provided by the National Science Foundation, under grant BNS 76–22943, and by the Exxon Educational Foundation. An early version of this chapter was presented at a symposium on "Knowledge in Social and Behavioral Science: Discoveries and Trends over Fifty Years," National Research Council, Committee on Basic Research in the Behavioral and Social Sciences, November 29–30, 1983. I appreciate critical comment from colleagues at the Center for Advanced Study, and participants in the NRC symposium, and the strong editorial attention of this volume's editors.

the dominant political ideologies, and numbers enter the political fray on behalf of social interests.

The approach adopted in this chapter accepts this assumption, but focuses it as follows: Public statistics in the United States are generated as part of democratic politics. This invites inquiry into the ways in which this particular nation's "number system" advances or retards democracy, informs or distorts civic discourse, helps or hinders political participation. For just as public statistics are not neutral with respect to the everyday politics of group interests, so they are not neutral with respect to the principles and practices of democracy. Consequently, to study constitutional democracy, as it is today practiced in the United States, requires a perspective on numerical reasoning and the nation's number system. Providing this perspective is a task for social theory.

There are, of course, unresolved issues in what does, or should, constitute democracy in the United States. We cannot here attempt to sort out the relative emphasis that contending theories of democracy give to such issues as popular participation, economic and social equalities, the protection of property, civil liberties and citizen rights, or democratic procedures. In this chapter we take the simpler route of concentrating on two central issues: accountability—how public leaders are held accountable for their performance in office—and representation—how diverse interests are represented in setting the political agenda.

Democratic Accountability

The centrality of the concept accountability in democratic theory derives from the observation that democracies no less than other forms of government have public officials with immensely more power than average citizens. Democratic theory does not deny the power advantage enjoyed by those in charge of the government, nor does it optimistically presume that democracies are free of the tendency of power-holders to expand control. Embedded in a democracy, no less than in other forms of government, is a structure of bureaucratic and political power.

The task of democratic theory is to direct us toward practices that reconcile the inclination of power-holders toward dominance with the democratic ideal of popular sovereignty. The basic terms of this reconciliation are to be found in the Constitution, especially in the provision for separating and fragmenting official power so that leaders can check and control each other, and in the companion provision that regular electoral competition will force leaders to contest with each other for the favor of the voters.

The general idea of this second provision is summarized in the phrase "theory of electoral accountability" as first adumbrated in *The Federalist Papers* and subsequently elaborated by Joseph Schumpeter and other democratic theorists. There is competition for public office. Leaders present themselves and their records to the electorate. Voters, basing their judgments on the past performance or estimates of future performance of leaders, elect, reelect, or evict accordingly. Leaders, knowing this, and wanting to gain and retain office, promote policies that will attract public support.

This theoretical formulation is a reasonably accurate though partial description of what, in fact, does happen. The empirical evidence has been most compellingly presented by Morris Fiorina, who has demonstrated the use voters make of retrospective evaluations.[1] Voters routinely reject incumbents who governed during a period marked by deterioration in social and economic conditions. Another political scientist reports that voters "clearly react in an incumbency-oriented fashion to the record of current officeholders, responding positively to success in the economic and other arenas but negatively to perceived failures."[2]

Two explanations are available. Citizens vote according to recent changes in their personal economic conditions; or, citizens vote according to the improvement or deterioration of national economic conditions. Under the first explanation, votes would be influenced by the personal experience of unemployment, the loss of purchasing power through inflation, or the need to postpone homeowning because of high interest rates. The experience of these negative economic conditions leads to votes against the political party in power.

Under the second explanation, voters punish or reward politicians depending on the performance of the national economy during the incumbents' tenure. Even citizens secure in their own employment nevertheless vote against leaders whose policies bring about high rates of unemployment. Or, citizens not themselves seriously affected by high interest rates nevertheless take into account double-digit interest rates when evaluating the performance of incumbent officials.

Somewhat counterintuitively, current research supports the second explanation. Voters in the United States give more weight to negative or positive trends in national economic conditions than to changes in their own economic circumstances. The most extensive development of this finding is offered by Roderick Kiewiet, who concludes that "changing perceptions of the national economy account for a considerably

[1]Morris Fiorina, *Retrospective Voting in American National Elections* (New Haven, Conn.: Yale University Press, 1981).
[2]D. Roderick Kiewiet, *Macroeconomics & Micropolitics: The Electoral Effects of Economic Issues* (Chicago: University of Chicago Press, 1983), p. 115.

larger proportion of the swing in support for the incumbent party from good years to bad than do changes in personal economic conditions."[3]

This research finding is of importance in the present context for what it indicates about the function of national statistics in implementing democratic accountability. If voters punish and reward officeholders less in terms of personal experience than in terms of national economic performance, they can vote responsibly only if they have reasonably accurate information about national economic performance. This information, of course, is often made accessible when it is summarized as statistical trends. Political leaders can be judged by the upward or downward movement of statistical indicators of those socially important issues for which government has assumed responsibility: unemployment, inflation, balance of trade, interest rates, test scores, poverty levels, crime rates. When economic and social indicators are moving in politically popular directions, political credit is claimed; when they are moving in unpopular directions, political blame is assigned. Here, then, is a contribution of public statistics to the workings of democracy.

This application of numbers to the purposes of democratic accountability occurs in a period when many other political developments undermine the conditions necessary for holding officeholders to account: the decline of party discipline, even of political parties themselves; the increased costs of electioneering and the related packaging of candidates by media experts; the growing political influence of single-issue interest organizations; the comparatively low rates of political participation. These trends occur as the political agenda is ever more crowded with issues difficult for the average citizen to comprehend. A weakened party-electoral system combined with a crowded and complicated issue agenda is not conducive to democratic accountability. Against this background, the improvements in information brought about by modern statistical reporting are all the more important.

This argument about the accountability of officeholders can be generalized, at least as a hypothesis. Just as a particular administration in power can be evaluated by statistical trends, so also can broad social policies. In this more generalized version, citizens continually evaluate and reevaluate broad policy commitments made by previous political generations. In modern nation-states, this retrospective public reflection is facilitated by measures of long-term trends.

Descriptive statistics offer voters before and after information about the performance of incumbents as well as of general policies. Consequently, these statistics contribute to the procedures that establish accountability in democratic politics. If we could leave matters at this

[3]Kiewiet, *Macroeconomics & Micropolitics*, p. 131.

point, the story would be a welcome one for democratic theory. But it is more complicated.

Numbers, no less than words, have the power to distort as well as enhance the reasoning capacity of the public. The greater the importance of numbers to the securing of power, the stronger the incentives to those in power to make certain that numbers present a favorable even if inaccurate picture. Across a broad front, democratic politics must contend with ways in which numbers distort and mislead.

At this point it is necessary to draw attention to an important subset of any nation's number system, the "performance indicators." Performance indicators typically serve two functions: They act as internal signals for the agency, informing it whether its goals are being achieved; and they serve as signals to those outside the agency, including, of course, those who set policy and control budgets. These two functions subject an agency to conflicting pressures. When an agency designs performance measures in a manner that maximizes internal information, it invites external attention to its failures as well as its achievements. It risks sending negative signals which those having power over the agency can use to trim budgets or punish incompetence.

It is a familiar complaint that when officials are rewarded or punished in terms of statistical evaluations, they are drawn to policies that favorably present the agency to the oversight process. The numbers become more important than progress toward the policy goals they presumably index. Krushchev is said to have lamented: "It has become the tradition to produce not beautiful chandeliers to adorn homes, but the heaviest chandeliers possible. This is because the heavier the chandeliers produced, the more a factory gets since its output is calculated in tons."[4]

Our interest lies not in this well-known flaw in command economies but in the implications for democratic accountability. If the number system is systematically manipulated so that personnel and policies are presented to the public in the most favorable light, we have little warrant for claiming that public statistics enhance democratic procedures.

We come here to a point in the discussion when the larger analysis of democratic accountability intersects with a more specific argument about the professional accountability of those who administer the nation's statistical system. This accountability is to professional peers who evaluate, against the standards of their disciplines, whether government statistical agencies are maintaining the integrity of the

[4]Cited in Charles E. Lindblom, *Politics and Markets* (New York: Basic Books, 1977), p. 71.

numbers. Professional statisticians, in and out of government, hold that proper controls and procedures can protect the public from the abuses associated with fraudulent or misleading statistics.

There is no question that in well-established statistical agencies, such as the Bureau of Labor Statistics and the Census Bureau, the production and reporting of statistics is managed by professionals. The norms of professional control are deeply rooted in the development and organization of these agencies. Perhaps no stronger testimony to the credibility of our major statistical series is needed than to note the reliance placed on them in the marketplace, where substantial amounts of money are committed on the assumption that national statistical series are trustworthy. The monthly statistical reports of the Crop Reporting Board of the Department of Agriculture, for instance, have such high credibility that hundreds of thousands of dollars change hands through the commodity markets as soon as the data are released.

But even if we accept that professional control over national statistics can largely eliminate fraud and greatly lessen bias in the most important of our social and economic indicators, other issues remain. The statistics of even the most professional agencies suffer from measurement problems for which there are no presently available solutions. When these problems lead to errors of serious magnitude and yet political leaders use the numbers to set policies and citizens use them to evaluate these policies, the accountability process is compromised.

The aptly labeled "unobserved economy" offers a telling illustration. If, as seems to be the case, the unobserved economy is growing more rapidly than the observed, that is, "counted" economy, but policy is guided by statistics only about the latter, serious policy errors can hardly be avoided.[5] This in turn, of course, distorts the process by which fault is assigned, and moves us away from democratic accountability.

The technical and conceptual errors associated with measurement are serious, but for important economic and social indicators continuous professional attention and public discussion offer safeguards. Social scientists and professional statisticians have the technical skill—and career incentives—to discern discrepancies between what the statistics purport to measure and what they actually measure.

These safeguards can operate only when the statistics are indeed public, that is, accessible to professional attention. Such is not the case for critical domains of national security policy, where secrecy prevails. Professional review of the adequacy and integrity of, say, unemployment

[5]Robert R. Alford and Edgar L. Feige, "Information Distortions in Social Systems: The Unobserved Economy and Other Observer-Subject-Policy Feedbacks," unpublished and undated paper.

or inflation measures is order of magnitudes more informed than professional review of numbers purporting to describe, for instance, the comparative weapons/systems of the United States and the Soviet Union.

A democratic society is preserved when the public has reliable ways of knowing whether policies are having the announced or promised effect. Is inflation being brought under control? Is a war of attrition being won? Are defense expenditures buying national security? Numbers, a part of this publicly available political intelligence, consequently contribute to the accountability required of a democracy. Except, of course, when flaws in the statistics, whether inadvertently or deliberately introduced, mislead citizens regarding the performance of their government, thereby diminishing accountability. But it can be plausibly argued that the wide public availability of reasonably accurate statistics about social conditions for which government is responsible enhances more than it diminishes democratic accountability. This conclusion, at best an informed guess, rests on assumptions about what is required if civic discourse is to be reasonably informed under the conditions of advanced industrial societies. It also rests on (largely untested) assumptions about the capacity of an electorate to make intelligent use of statistical information.

Representation of Diverse Interests

The genius of the Constitution, as a document in democratic political theory, lies in its provision for the representation of diverse interests in political decision circles. This commitment to political representation involved the founders in political engineering, one aspect of which established the close association between political representation and the nation's number system. In order that seats in the House of Representatives might be fairly allocated, the Constitution mandated a population count. It further directed that this count distinguish among the free citizens, the slave population, and the untaxed Indian population. This distinction arose because the founders wanted wealth as well as property to be reflected in apportionment; counting slaves as three fifths of a person was a way to recognize their property value. Representation had to be apportioned according to politically acceptable criteria. Moreover, the method chosen should allow for adjustments as the population expanded, redistributing itself among the existing states or spilling over into territories that then would achieve statehood. Thus was established the decennial census, the centerpiece of our statistical system.

The limited use of the census to apportion congressional seats did not satisfy James Madison. In early congressional debates Madison urged that the census "embrace some other objects besides the bare enumeration of the inhabitants." Madison suggested that the census describe "the several classes into which the community is divided." On this basis, continued Madison, "the Legislature might proceed to make a proper provision for the agrarian, commercial, and manufacturing interests, but without it they could never make these provisions in due proportion."[6]

We know from *The Federalist Papers* that Madison viewed society as consisting of multiple and diverse interests. To govern such a society in a democratic fashion required complex information about the composition of the public. Thus, for Madison, it was not enough that the census enumerate the population for the sole purpose of apportioning. It should be expanded to include many population characteristics, and thereby become the basis on which the legislators could allocate taxes, benefits, and services according to the "real situation of our constituents." But in anticipating a democracy in which numerical proportionality cuts much deeper than assigning congressional seats, Madison was ahead of his times.

Madison's opponents started from a different theory of politics. Reflecting eighteenth-century theories of the organic society, they "viewed the object of government as the pursuit of an undifferentiated common good; for them, politics was a sphere of virtue, and empirical investigation was irrelevant."[7] In the early days of the Republic it was Madison's opponents who prevailed. Enumeration was sufficient to serve representation.

Contemporary practice, however, is much closer to Madisonian pluralism, as reflected in the vast expansion of the national statistical system and the policy uses to which it is put. The question before us now is how these developments in the statistical system affect the political representation process.

Providing for the representation of diverse interests in political decision circles is at the core of the theoretical formulation known as democratic pluralism, the now dominant interpretation of American democracy. Democratic pluralism takes as its central problem the conditions that allow for the participation by interested parties in various

[6]James Madison, *Annals of Congress*, First Session, House of Representatives, 1790 (Washington: Gales & Seaton, 1834), cited in Steven Kelman, "The Politics of Statistical Policymaking: Justification for Public Information-Collection and Theories of the Role of Government," Conference on the Political Economy of National Statistics, Social Science Research Council, New York, October 14–15, 1983, p. 14.

[7]Paul Starr, "Measure for Measure," *The New Republic*, February 13, 1984, p. 37.

policy domains. Democracy requires that there be no barriers to the organization and expression of the full array of interests in society.

Democratic pluralism is an attractive theory, and since the early days of the Republic it has gradually gained adherents among those who have puzzled about the prospects for democracy in large-scale advanced industrial nations. But the theory has also attracted critics. In recent decades the effort to formulate a democratic theory has placed a participatory emphasis in opposition to pluralism, and in the process generated a critique of conventional pluralist theory.

This critique holds that pluralism has not offered a satisfactory account of nonparticipation in democratic politics, too readily attributing low participation levels to presumed citizen defects such as apathy or ignorance. The critics argue that since levels of participation covary with social and economic resources, pluralism functions as a justification for the representation of middle- and upper-class interests in politics rather than a description of how the full array of social interests find a political voice.

An alternative explanation of nonparticipation is suggested by E. E. Schattschneider's famous phrase, "mobilization of bias." In explaining why the socially and economically disadvantaged often fail to participate in politics, Schattschneider wrote "whoever decides what the game is about also decides who gets in the game."[8] Here is introduced the argument that whatever is on the political agenda provides a referent point that selectively mobilizes participation across different social groups and interests. Citizens participate not just to put issues on the political agenda but also, and more often, in response to the issues already there. This mobilization process, according to Schattschneider, is biased against the interests of the less well-off groups in society.

It is in this theoretical context that we consider how the analysis and political reporting of social statistics intersects the representation system. Although our emphasis is on contemporary politics, the practice we draw attention to is at least 150 years old. Starting around 1820, writes the historian Patricia Cline Cohen, "Many private agencies and volunteer groups with reformist agendas adopted the statistical approach to social facts in order to document the dimensions of the problem they were dedicated to eradicating."[9] Cohen offers several examples: the use of statistics to describe the miseries of public prisons; the effort by the temperance movement to prove quantitatively that alcohol

[8]E. E. Schattschneider, *The Semi-Sovereign People: A Realist's View of Democracy in America* (New York: Holt, Rinehart & Winston, 1960), p. 105.
[9]Patricia Cline Cohen, *A Calculating People: The Spread of Numeracy in Early America* (Chicago: University of Chicago Press, 1982), p. 169.

abuse was a growing problem; and local surveys of pauperism as a basis to challenge poor laws.

In deploying their privately collected statistics on behalf of social reform, the early-nineteenth-century activists anticipated developments surrounding publicly collected statistics which did not come fully into view for another half-century, when the federal Bureau of Labor Statistics was established in the 1880s. The 1820s reformers were signaling to later activists that statistics could mobilize political participation and inform public debate.

In the latter part of the twentieth century these possibilities are etched much more deeply in our political life. The nation's number system uncovers social conditions, and popularizes them as statistical descriptions: proportion of the population below the poverty line; incidence of child abuse; persistence of structural unemployment; addictive behavior and its social costs; the differential in infant mortality between whites and non-whites; the gap between male and female wages in similar occupations. The transformation of politically unnoticed social conditions into visible social statistics puts issues on the political agenda that would otherwise be ignored.

These statistical conditions then provide a political referent point for interested groups. This perhaps is one of the most striking aspects of twentieth-century democratic politics. Resource-poor social interests turn to a statistical description of their plight in order to generate political pressure and to mobilize adherents to their cause.

The history of the civil rights movement is suggestive in this regard. The concept of institutional racism, which held that black poverty was caused not just by racial prejudice but also by structural conditions of the economy, polity, and society, made its political appearance through statistics on residential segregation, black–white income differentials, unequal educational opportunities, inequities in access to health care, and so forth. Civil rights leaders first used the numbers to emphasize the scope of institutional discrimination. They then used them to gain political support for new social policies such as Headstart, job training, and affirmative action. Other groups have reached the conclusion that being "measured" is to be politically noticed, and to be noticed is to have a claim on the nation's resources. Thus the physically handicapped in New York initially resisted being counted, for fear that this would further stigmatize them, but then reversed their position when they realized that political visibility followed on the heels of statistical visibility.

Data presented in Michael Harrington's *The Other America* helped initiate the War on Poverty by identifying the poor as a target group for government action.[10] The consumer protection movement has made heavy use of statistical arguments, as have the environmentalists. Describing public-interest citizen groups, one commentator writes that "the quality and quantity of information and the way it is structured, presented and amplified" shapes their political choices and strategies.[11]

Harold Wilensky generalizes these observations when he writes that "facts and figures" assist those political interest organizations "weak in grass-roots political resources." Information "may give an advantage to the weak, whose case, if strong and technical, can count for something."[12] This is not a trivial observation when examined in the context of the historical effort in democracies to establish equal civil and political rights in the face of inequalities in resources which different social interests bring to the political arena.

The correction resorted to most often, both in democratic theory and in actual practice, is organization. The less wealthy but more numerous social interests combine and increase their political strength through working-class parties, social movements, and interest groups. Consequently, a resource that helps to organize the resource-poor will help to correct political imbalances and promote broader democratic participation.

This observation leads us to consider whether statistical programs can actually help establish group identity and lead to the formation of interest organizations. In his careful account of the interplay between ethnicity and the census reported in this book, William Petersen notes the role of the census in helping to solidify group identification (see chapter 5). Hispanic Americans are particularly important in this regard. More than any group in American political history, Hispanic Americans have turned to the national statistical system as an instrument for advancing their political and economic interests, by making visible the magnitude of social and economic problems they face.

In the processes by which groups are formed and diverse interests are represented in democratic politics, public statistics are not, of course, an unmixed blessing. Just as some groups can establish a political identity by being enumerated, other groups cannot escape the way they are socially classified because of this same enumeration system. For example, for two centuries we have had a statistical practice of racial classification, which undoubtedly has contributed to the continu-

[10]Michael Harrington, *The Other America* (Baltimore: Penguin Press, 1963).

[11]Hazel Henderson, "Information and the New Movements for Citizen Participation," in Thomas J. Kuehn and Alan L. Porter, eds., *Science, Technology, and National Policy* (Ithaca, N.Y.: Cornell University Press, 1981), pp. 434–48.

[12]Harold Wilensky, *Organizational Intelligence* (New York: Basic Books, 1967), p. 19.

ing salience of race in American society. Policies now being implemented could easily result in the Hispanic Americans becoming a permanent racial minority in the statistical system, with what long-term effects it is difficult to foresee. Moreover, the statistical system is not sufficiently robust to withstand the distortions accompanying severe political pressures. When political criteria are transparently used to determine what should be technical issues, such as the best way to count a population group, statistics lose their credibility.

Racially sensitive measurement policies are not likely soon to be reversed now that so many government services are allocated according to race and ethnicity. The brief period during which it was thought wrong to identify race, gender, or national origins on employment or school applications was swept away by the emergence of affirmative action and statistical parity in the 1970s. The nation has entered a period in which "proportionate allocation" is carried to ever greater extremes. There is a contagion effect. Once statistical proportionality is elevated to a principle of government, there is great pressure from various racial and ethnic groups to be fully counted.

From the perspective of democratic theory these developments are troubling in at least three respects. First, to assign to the statistical system responsibility for group classification and resource allocation is to transform the thing being measured—segregation, hunger, poverty— into its statistical indicator. Always in tension with the judgmental in politics is an insistent search for objective rules to reduce the element of arbitrariness in subjective judgment. The legal code is one set of such objective rules, formalized bureaucratic procedures another, and now we have statistical formulas. This of course does not eliminate politics; it simply pushes politics back one step, to disputes about methods. Arguments about numerical quotas, availability pools and demographic imbalance become a substitute for democratic discussion of the principles of equity and justice.

Second, if statistical identification facilitates political consciousness among some resource-poor groups, these same statistics make invisible to the policy process other groups at the margins of social and economic life, where measurement often fails—the undocumented workers, the illegal aliens, and the vagrant, homeless populations. With respect to many government programs, persons not counted are not there. Another difficulty stems from the inertia of statistical systems. For technical as well as bureaucratic reasons, statistics lag behind the dynamic patterns of group formation and change resulting from immigration, internal migration, transformation in the occupational structure, and new levels of social consciousness. Insofar as politics is organized by the numbers, there will be a tendency to overlook more recently established social conditions in favor of those already reflected through the statistical system.

The third and most troubling danger is the shift away from a system of representation and public policy based on the individual citizen toward one based on the representation of demographic aggregates: ethnic, racial, income, gender groups. This shift invites, even mandates, the allocation of benefits and rights in terms of group membership rather than individual accomplishment or need.

To many observers of American democracy this tilt toward group representation undermines the fundamental premise of liberal democracy. Nathan Glazer laments the drift toward numbering and dividing up the population into racial and ethnic groups. "This has meant that we abandon the first principle of liberal society, that the individual and individual's interests and good and welfare are the test of a good society, for we now attach benefits and penalties to individuals simply on the basis of their race, color, and national origin.[13] Glazer, of course, does not attribute the rise of quota politics and group-based representation to the availability of statistical information. But if statistical information has not caused, it has certainly abetted the emergence of demographically defined groups as a category in public policy.

The formal system of political representation itself has not escaped the insistent pressure for demographically defined proportionality. As Abigail Thernstrom so artfully traces elsewhere in this volume, the 1965 Voting Rights Act was transformed in two decades from a law to protect black voting rights to one that appears to require the "correct" number of minority seats in legislative bodies (see chapter 9). Demands for proportional representation, in which the legislature is to mirror the characteristics of the population from which it is selected, are not new. Until recently, however, group politics intersecting with the electoral process was the preferred avenue for achieving this political end. Legal remedies were, appropriately, limited to insuring fair procedures, not particular outcomes. Now, buttressed with statistics, we begin to see laws affecting the very composition of legislative bodies.

As was the case in our discussion of accountability, we see in this discussion of representation that countertendencies are at work. On the one hand, statistical description can bring social conditions to public attention, mobilize disadvantaged groups, and broaden the political agenda in ways that lessen the bias inherent in an electoral-representation system based largely on the resources of wealth and political organization. On the other hand, these statistics introduce practices and policies

---

[13]Nathan Glazer, *Affirmative Discrimination: Ethnic Inequality and Public Policy* (New York: Basic Books, 1975), p. 220.

inconsistent with our traditional understanding of democracy: the objectification of politics; the assumption that what is not counted is not there; the temptation to substitute group membership for individual merit or need as the basis for public policy; the allocation of legislative seats according to designated racial or ethnic criteria.

We are far from having the evidence that would allow us to sort out the relative strength of these contrary tendencies, and again must resort to an informed guess. With respect to democratic accountability I suggested that the benefits of statistical descriptions outweighed the harms. With respect to the representation of diverse interests I am less sanguine. The distortions of the representational process seem to me every bit as strong as the improvements. Moreover, the negative tendencies are not of the sort that can be corrected with greater professional scrutiny of statistical information. They are much more political than technical in nature, and in fact become stronger as statistics become more precise and reliable.

Because of, and notwithstanding, the various problems and risks identified in this chapter, those who care about democracy have a large task before them. The task involves analysis of the political role of numbers, as well as a professional commitment to making the numbers perform according to the burden that a democracy places upon them.

8

THE POLITICAL FOUNDATIONS
OF AMERICAN STATISTICAL POLICY

STEVEN KELMAN

IN NINETEENTH-CENTURY America, federal spending ran at less than 3 percent of the GNP—and most of that was spent on interest payments for debts incurred during wars and on pensions to disabled war veterans.[1] Most Americans saw government's role in society as very limited.

Yet one thing a government that saw itself as doing very little did do was gather statistics. The Constitution mandated that the federal government undertake a "decennial enumeration" to determine representation in the House, making the United States the first country in the world to take a regular census.[2] As early as 1810 the federal government attempted a census of manufacturers in addition to population. No nation had previously made such an effort.[3] In 1840 the government added a census of agriculture and expanded the population census to count the number of insane and mentally retarded, schools, and illit-

[1]M. Slade Kendrick, *A Century and a Half of Federal Expenditures* (New York: National Bureau of Economic Research, Occasional Paper 48, 1955), pp. 10, 38.

[2]Carroll D. Wright and William C. Hunt, *The History and Growth of the United States Census*, Committee on the Census, U.S. Senate, 56th Congress, 1st sess., no. 194, 1900, p. 13.

[3]Ibid., p. 23. See also W. Stull Holt, *The Bureau of the Census: Its History, Activities, and Organization* (Washington, D.C.: Brookings Institution, 1929), p. 6. The Holt volume, along with Wright and Hunt, which is somewhat more detailed, provides excellent overviews of the changes in questions asked in the census during the nineteenth century.

erates over twenty years of age.[4] In 1850 it began to collect data on public libraries, crime, and the number of people who had died the previous year, together with their age, occupation, and residence.[5] By 1880 the volume of statistics gathered in the census was stupendous: The census by then included no less than 215 schedules and over 13,000 discrete questions, up from 156 questions a decade earlier.[6]

By this time census questions sought a level of detail that calls to mind recent complaints about the paperwork burdens of twentieth-century "big government." Ranchers were asked whether their cattle were corralled, and cotton manufacturers had to indicate whether there had been improvement "in the dwelling houses of the operatives" and whether sanitary arrangements in worker's homes were "better or worse than at former periods." Insurance companies were required to report on the total amount of the company's stock owned by directors, and the company's total assets and liabilities (including separate listings of the value of bonds and securities). Public schools were asked to report on the qualifications and salaries of teachers; on whether textbooks were provided free to pupils; on whether instruction was given, *inter alia*, in botany, geography, drawing, music, and civics; and on whether pupils were "regularly exercised in calisthenics, gymnastics, or military drill." Museums were asked to report how many "ancient busts" and "copies of busts" they possessed, with separate listings for marble, bronze, metal, ivory, wood, terra cotta, and plaster, and how many exhibits of weapons, domestic utensils, articles of clothing, ornaments, and models of houses or boats they had.[7]

How could all this data-gathering be justified as a function of government during an era when proposals for government activity needed to meet an especially strong burden of justification? That is the puzzle this chapter attempts to solve.

I take as my starting point an influential solution provided by neoclassical microeconomic theory. Microeconomic theory regards the functions of government as quite limited, just as most Americans of this period did. It sees production of things that people value as generally best occurring through the market. Information is something of value. Individuals may use it to help them make decisions, for example, about what products to buy or produce. More information about the quality of a product gives a consumer a better idea of how to satisfy his

[4]Holt, *Bureau of the Census*, p. 11.
[5]Ibid., p. 15.
[6]Wright and Hunt, *History and Growth of the U.S. Census*, pp. 86–87.
[7]These examples are culled from the lengthy listings of census schedules for 1880 appearing in Wright and Hunt, *History and Growth of the U.S. Census*, pp. 264, 330, 691, 653–55, 679, 681.

or her preferences; more information about customers in a market gives a firm a better idea of what customers want. To take an example relevant to government-provided information from the nineteenth century, information about the yields of different crops in different growing areas can help a farmer decide which crops to produce.[8]

Although information has value, neoclassical microeconomics regards it as an exception to the rule that things of value should be produced by the market and not by government. Much information constitutes what economists call a "public good" that is underproduced by market processes alone. When an economist says that the market "underproduces" information, he is *not* arguing that the benighted multitude fails sufficiently to appreciate the wonders of knowledge. He is instead suggesting that information is underproduced in the sense that the quantity produced is less than people themselves would be willing to pay for.

A good explanation of the concept "public good" appears in Walter Nicholson's introductory test on microeconomic theory. Public goods are goods whose consumption has a "nonrival nature."

> Once the good is provided, additional persons may use the good without reducing the benefits that those currently using the good are receiving. A private good, say, a pork chop, is consumed by either Smith or Jones. Consumption of the pork chop by Smith precludes its consumption by Jones. On the other hand, public goods do not have this property. For example, Smith may enjoy the prevailing level of public health without detracting from the level Jones enjoys. The incremental cost of Smith's enjoying public health is zero.

Why will such goods be underproduced in the marketplace?

> In the case of a private good, the purchaser of that good can expropriate benefits of the good entirely for himself. Smith's pork chop, for example, yields no benefits to Jones. The resources that were used to produce the pork chop can be seen as contributing only to Smith's utility, and he is willing to pay whatever this is worth to him. The resource cost of a private good, then, can be "attributed" to a single individual. For a public good, this will not be the case. An individual in buying a public good would not be able to appropriate all the benefits of the good. *Since others cannot be excluded from benefiting from the good, society's utility obtained from the resources devoted to the good will exceed the utility that accrues to the single individual who pays for the good.* . . . However, the potential purchaser will not take the benefits

[8]See, for example, Jack Hirschleifer and John Riley, "Analytics of Uncertainty and Information: An Exposition and Survey," *Journal of Economic Literature* 17 (December 1979).

that his purchase has to others into account in his expenditure decisions. Consequently, private markets will tend to underallocate resources to public goods.[9]

To avoid this problem, people who value a public good can band together to agree to purchase it collectively and simply to let everyone consume it, without further charge. Such an agreement conveniently occurs through government. Public provision can bring about production of levels corresponding to people's preferences, in a way that private provision will not. "Since everyone in society can benefit from efficiency," concludes Nicholson, provision of public goods "is a proper governmental function."[10]

Those who study the economics of information have noted that information is often (though not always) a public good. Perhaps the most straightforward example is information about the price and quality of competing consumer products. Information about competing brands of dishwashers has value to a consumer choosing which to buy. The information is of a nonrival nature: Other consumers can use the information without reducing the benefits of the information to the consumer who gathered it. Yet in deciding what resources to devote to such information-gathering, any single consumer will only consider the value of the information to himself, not to others who could benefit from the same information. Individual decisions will tend, therefore, to lead to an underproduction of such information.[11]

Microeconomic theory provides an influential general account of the role of government in society, particularly of a limited government role. How, then, does this justification for a governmental role in provision of statistics compare with arguments people actually gave during an age of self-styled "limited government"? To answer that question, I examined congressional debates, reports, and other available materials for the period from 1790, when the first Congress discussed the first census, through the end of the nineteenth century. Since there existed at the time no permanent census bureau or enabling legislation, Con-

---

[9]Walter Nicholson, *Microeconomic Theory*, 2nd ed. (Hinsdale, Ill.: Dryden Press, 1978), pp. 612–613.

[10]Ibid., p. 614.

[11]To make the discussion slightly more technical, a private information gatherer could capture gains to others by charging others for the information he has gathered. Given the price elasticity of demand, charging for the information will make the demand from others less than it otherwise would be, and since the marginal cost of information dissemination is essentially zero—that is another way of stating the principle of nonrivalry—any such charge would be inefficient, and produce an inefficiently low level of information production.

gress debated the matter every decade. Furthermore, these were days when details such as specific census questions were debated on the floors of Congress, not simply delegated to the executive branch, so there is rich material not only on justifications for the general enterprise but also on specific items.

Bewilderment and disorientation will be the lot of anyone who sits down with these hoary materials intellectually armed only with the view that government gets involved in provision of information because the private market will not produce an optimal quantity, or that information is valuable mainly as a tool to help individuals make better private decisions about what to produce or buy. For the materials contain scant reference at all to anything like these views. Instead, the debates are filled with arguments that bespeak a completely different set of concerns. One comes upon widespread embarrassment, after the first census of 1790, that the census showed the United States had fewer than 4 million inhabitants.[12] One comes upon the observation by a chronicler of American census history that "the 1880 census was designed as a great 'centennial contribution of facts' in the spirit of enthusiasm over the nation's hundredth anniversary."[13] One comes upon groups asking to have information collected about them as a token of regard for their endeavors. And, repeatedly, one comes across the view that government should gather statistics because statistics are needed for public, legislative decisions, rather than because individuals need them for private use.

In short, the justification economists give for a government role in information provision bears little resemblance to justifications contemporaries gave during the century or so following the founding of the Republic. And it is not convincing to reply that political actors need be no more aware of the theory of public goods in order to follow it than consumers need to be aware of indifference curves for the concept to explain consumer behavior. It is correct that the theory of public goods can explain the failure of data-gathering to emerge in the market without any necessity that actors be aware of the theory. But the view that government is *justified* in providing public goods is a normative conclusion. And one needs to understand the theoretical account, at least approximately, to justify public provision, because it is this account that allows one to distinguish between information and private goods some people might like the government to provide (say, govern-

---

[12]Hyman Alterman, *Counting People: The Census in History* (New York: Harcourt, Brace & World, 1969), pp. 204–205.
[13]Ann H. Scott, *Census U.S.A.: Fact Finding for the American Republic 1790–1970* (New York: Seabury Press, 1968), p. 33.

ment-produced gasoline sold at below market price).[14] So the disjunction between the justifications actually offered for government statistics and the justification provided by the theory of public goods is significant.

Although they believed in limited government, our forebears nonetheless had a broader vision than do microeconomists of the functions government serves. This vision has been lost in the theory of the role of government inspired by microeconomics, and it needs to be remembered to see what that theory is lacking.

Why Government Statistics?

In this section, I present the most important arguments encountered through the end of the nineteenth century on government information-gathering. The arguments to be discussed are: (1) information as an aid to legislation; (2) information as a source of patriotic pride for all citizens; (3) information as a signal from society of recognition to individual groups; and (4) information-gathering as a statement by society about the special value of knowledge. Finally, the scant references in the materials to information as an aid to private decision-making will be noted.

Information as an Aid to Legislation

Probably the dominant justification for government information-gathering, especially in the earlier debates, was that statistical information was needed to help public officials determine what legislation government should enact. Legislators were attempting conscientiously to decide what laws best served the people, and statistics, by revealing more about the conditions of the people, would aid in that task.

In the congressional debates in 1790 on the first census, James Madison, as a member of the House, urged that the census be expanded beyond the constitutional requirement. His main argument was that it would aid legislation. According to Madison, Congress

> had now an opportunity of obtaining the most useful information for
> those who should hereafter be called upon to legislate for their country,
> if [the census] was extended so as to embrace some other objects be-

---

[14]Nicholson is explicit on the normative character of the theory of public goods as a justification for government activity; see *Microeconomic Theory*, p. 608.

sides the bare enumeration of the inhabitants. . . . In order to know the various interests of the United States, it was necessary that the description of the several classes into which the community is divided should be accurately known. On this knowledge the Legislature might proceed to make a proper provision for the agrarian, commercial and manufacturing interests, but without it they could never make these provisions in due proportion.[15]

Madison's suggestion for an expanded census was referred to a select committee, which reported back a plan to include a question about occupations as well as a division of returns by sex and gross age category (over and under 16 years old). The question about occupation was defeated in the Senate, but the 1790 census did provide returns by age and sex.

The surviving congressional records for censuses between 1800 and 1840 contain no appreciable information on the content of congressional discussion, suggesting that little substantive debate took place. The 1810 census of manufacturers, the first major addition to the population count, resulted from an amendment proposed by Representative Bacon of Massachusetts, after the enabling legislation for the census had already been passed.[16] No details are provided on any debate on the resolution, and the resolution itself provides no justification for introducing the change. But Representative Bacon had one year earlier moved that the secretary of the treasury report to the House "a plan for the application of such means as are within the power of Congress, for the purpose of protecting and fostering the manufactures of the United States."[17] It would appear that Bacon proposed a census of manufacturers to provide information for legislation (such as tariff protection) to help industry.

The impetus for the first major expansion of the census in 1840 came from Joseph Worcester, a compiler of dictionaries, atlases, and almanacs. In the preface to the 1838 edition of his almanac, Worcester wrote that "all intelligent and judicious legislation must be founded, in a great measure, on statistical knowledge." If statistics on population, manufacturers and agriculture, crime and pauperism, and education and religion "were collected regularly," it would "greatly increase the ability of the national and state governments, as well as of societies and in-

---

[15]*Annals of Congress,* First Congress, House of Representatives, January 25, 1790 (Washington, D.C.: Gales & Seaton, 1834), p. 1077.

[16]Ibid., 11th Congress, 2nd sess., April 25, 1810 (Washington, D.C.: Gales & Seaton, 1853), p. 1954.

[17]Ibid., 11th Congress, 1st sess., May 31, 1809, p. 162.

dividuals to promote the interest, and advance the moral civilization and improvement, of the people."[18]

Worcester persuaded President Martin Van Buren, who as secretary of state had been in charge of conducting the census of 1830, that his ideas were sound.[19] Van Buren recommended census expansion in his 1838 state of the union message. The census might profitably, he argued, "embrace authentic statistical returns of the great interests especially entrusted to, or necessarily affected by, the legislation of Congress."[20] The new questions asked in the 1840 census were those Worcester had urged.

The most impassioned (and by far the lengthiest) debates prior to the Civil War on the government's role in statistics-gathering concerned the 1850 census. Some of the proceedings occurred in the midst of the wrenching disputes over the fate of slavery in the territories that were later in the year to produce the Compromise of 1850. The expansion of the census hence became embroiled in debates over strict construction of the Constitution, with Southerners arguing that there was no constitutional sanction for statistics-gathering beyond the enumeration the Constitution mandated.

The answer proponents gave centered on the role the information would play in helping produce better legislation. Statistics were "necessary to inform the legislator," Representative Thompson, who presented the bill on the House floor, told his colleagues.[21] Senator Hunter stated that it was especially important "for the American statesman to obtain a full and accurate view of all the parts of that vast society whose machinery he directs."[22]

Participants in the debate were specific. It was necessary to know the "extent and condition" of industries and of agriculture, so that Congress would know the significance for the country of various industries for which tariff protection was being proposed.[23] Proper legislation regarding "the amount of currency which the wants of the country required" was dependent on information about the value of property in

[18]Joseph E. Worcester, *The American Almanac and Repository of Useful Knowledge* (Boston, Mass.: Charles Bowen, 1838), pp. iii–iv.

[19]For an account, see Patricia Cline Cohen, *A Calculating People: The Spread of Numeracy in Early America* (Chicago: University of Chicago Press, 1982), p. 179.

[20]"Message of the President of the United States to the Two Houses of Congress," *Public Documents Printed by Order of the Senate of the United States*, 25th Congress, 3rd sess., v. 1, December 4, 1838 (Washington, D.C.: Blair & Rives), p. 14.

[21]*Congressional Globe*, April 24, 1850 (Washington, D.C.: Blair & Rives, 1850), p. 812.

[22]Ibid., 30th Congress, 2nd sess., March 1, 1849, p. 628.

[23]Ibid., 31st Congress, 1st sess., April 24, 1850, p. 810.

the country.[24] Information on the number of illiterates could lead to legislation "to remedy such an evil."[25]

Post–Civil War congressional debates on the census, particularly those of 1870 and 1880, were extensive. In 1869 the House passed a bill dramatically increasing the scope of census questions, based on a lengthy study by a special committee chaired by Representative (later President) James Garfield. The bill called for a great increase in social statistics, as well as statistics of cities, wage statistics, and special censuses of the railroad and insurance industries. The bill failed in the Senate that year but ten years later became law.

Debates over the 1870 and 1880 censuses are rich in various justifications for a government role in statistics-gathering. Although continuing to appear, the view that census data were needed for legislation no longer had a unique place among the plethora of arguments. The report of the House Committee in 1870 noted that "healthy legislation can only flow from an exact knowledge of the condition and wants of the people," and added that "public statistics . . . have become more and more the basis of the enactment and administration of laws."[26] In introducing the 1880 census to his House colleagues, Representative Cox argued that a census was "indispensable . . . for the proper conduct of government" and that "a country without a census cannot be well-governed."[27]

If statistics were gathered to provide information needed to evaluate legislation, it becomes clearer why some questions were included and not others. Questions reflected contemporary demands for legislation. The introduction of questions on manufacturers in the 1810 census reflected a new interest in the industries of the industrial revolution and demands for legislative action to aid them. The dramatic expansion of statistics about social problems such as illiteracy, ill health, insanity, pauperism, crime, and so forth, that began in an important way with the censuses of 1840 and 1850, mirrored a growing concern that the large wave of immigration of poor people was creating social problems. The collection of wage statistics and detailed information about the railroad and insurance industries, introduced after the Civil War, was a sign of the growing legislative interest in labor relations and big business.

During debates congressmen sometimes referred to the relationship

[24]Ibid., p. 813.
[25]Ibid., April 29, 1850, p. 837.
[26]*Report of the Committee on the Ninth Census*, U.S. Congress, House of Representatives, 41st Congress, 2nd sess., 1870, pp. 7, 9.
[27]*Congressional Record*, 45th Congress, 3rd sess., February 18, 1879, p. 1534.

of census questions to current social concerns. In his opening remarks to the House in 1850, Representative Thompson noted that the census sought for the first time to ascertain the number of paupers and their place of birth. "It is said and believed," he stated, "that Europe is pouring out upon our shores the paupers that would be, and should be, a charge upon themselves." He noted that "legislation has been solicited to prevent this" and argued that a census question was necessary to discover whether such legislation was appropriate.[28] Another congressman that year proposed an amendment to add an enumeration of Indians. (The Constitution stipulated that "Indians not taxed" not be counted for purposes of congressional representation, and the census did not count them.) He wanted such an enumeration to establish a baseline for determining whether the number of Indians was decreasing. Should this be so, he argued, it would give force for an inquiry "as to the cause of this distressing fatality." He continued that the

> wretched and forlorn condition of the remaining tribes is to be ascribed entirely to the unsympathizing and cruel policy of the Government towards them. . . . It is evident that no beneficial action can be taken by Congress, with reference to the condition of the Indians, without such information about their number and physical condition.[29]

Inclusion of Chinese as a separate racial category was proposed for the census of 1870 "so as to throw some light on the grave questions" Chinese immigration raised.[30]

One of the major innovations proposed for the 1870 census was a series of detailed questions about railroads. The proposed questions ranged from queries about rates and profits to interrogatories on accidents to railroad workers and the public. The committee report was quite explicit about the justification for gathering this new information:

> Now that the great question of human slavery is removed from the arena of American politics, the committee are persuaded that the new great question to be confronted will be that of corporations and their relationship to the interests of the people and to the national life. . . . [We seek to] demand from these corporations a statement of the elements of their power and an exhibit of their transactions.[31]

Floor amendments were adopted during House debate to collect similarly detailed information about insurance companies and banks.

[28] *Congressional Globe*, April 24, 1850, p. 810.
[29] Ibid., April 30, 1850, p. 855.
[30] Ibid., December 9, 1869, p. 180.
[31] *Ninth Census*, pp. 56–57.

Another floor amendment that year in the House called for collecting wage statistics on an individual level, rather than using the previous method of asking firms about average wages paid. Representative Haldeman, who moved the amendment, argued that many people believed that the country's economic system "whether wittingly or unwittingly, is calculated for the benefit of the capitalists and the injury of the laboring people."[32] He wanted the census therefore "to ascertain what progress has been made towards the building up of distinctive poor and rich classes in this country."[33] The amendment passed. In arguing that the old census schedules from 1850 gave insufficient information to guide the legislator of 1870, Senator Sumner noted that at the time of the 1850 census

> such questions as those relating to wages and profits, the hours of labor, the employment of women, and conditions of health to the laboring man, commanded little attention. At the present time . . . they are of overwhelming interest. . . . [This] demands that the inquiries of our census shall be so framed as to secure the information necessary to guide legislation on these subjects.[34]

Agrarian unrest spread through the 1880s, and in connection with the 1890 census there were sixty-six petitions to the House from farmers' groups requesting inclusion of questions about agricultural indebtedness. Such data would presumably show the extent of the farmer's plight and encourage legislation to ameliorate it. An item was added.[35]

Of course, citizens concerned about politics also might be interested in information as an aid to legislation. In fact, the growth of the scope of statistics-gathering from 1840 through the remainder of the century cannot be understood apart from the humanitarian social reform movements of the time—prison, educational, and public health reform, temperance, and abolitionism.[36]

The reformers, often advocates of a "scientific" view of society, introduced greater sophistication into discussions of the legislative value

---

[32]*Congressional Globe*, December 14, 1869, p. 128.

[33]Ibid., p. 158.

[34]Ibid., February 7, 1870, p. 1108.

[35]"Memorial of William G. Moody and Other Citizens," *Senate Miscellaneous Documents*, 50th Congress, 2nd sess. (1888), no. 19.

[36]A good general account of these movements appears in Alice Felt Tyler, *Freedom's Ferment* (Minneapolis: University of Minnesota Press, 1944), Part 3. See also David J. Rothman, *The Discovery of the Asylum* (Boston, Mass.: Little, Brown, 1971). On public health, see Gerald N. Grob, *Edward Jarvis and the Medical World of Nineteenth-Century America* (Knoxville: University of Tennessee Press, 1978). On abolitionism, see Ronald G. Walters, *The Antislavery Appeal: American Abolitionism after 1830* (Baltimore: Johns Hopkins University Press, 1976).

of statistics. The traditional view was that statistics gave a simple expository account of the situation of the country—how large an interest, say, textile manufacturing represented—so as to provide a basis for deciding whether textiles were important enough to the country to deserve tariff protection. The new conception was to use statistics to discover regularities in the connection between what today are termed independent demographic variables (such as race, occupation, or region of residence) and dependent life circumstances variables (such as insanity or disease).

In seeking to discover these regularities—or "laws of society," as they were frequently called—social reformers were motivated by the view that problems individuals suffered were not simply the will of God but the result of bad environments that wise legislation might remedy.[37] The best example in the first part of the nineteenth century was the diligent effort by Dr. Edward Jarvis, one of the founders of the American Statistical Association, to include mortality statistics in the census. If mortality was compared among people of different occupations and regions, Jarvis believed that the data would disclose what society needed to do to curtail premature death.[38]

Information as a Source of Patriotic Pride

From the very beginnings of governmental statistics-gathering in the United States, an important justification for government's role was that the good tidings brought by the information would instill pride in Americans as a people. Foreigners as well, beholding our progress, would have greater respect. The valued thing people obtained from information would, therefore, be a stronger pride of common identity.

Initially, this use of information was more to defend Americans against detractors than to trumpet our wonders. At the time many believed that the larger a country's population, the more influential it would be. And a growing population was seen as a sign of a thriving economy and a well-ordered polity. The very first census in American history was held by the Virginia colonists in 1624–25 to show sponsors in London that the colony was not dying out, as some had alleged.[39] So when the census of 1790 showed that the United States had under 4

---

[37]See Rothman, *Discovery of the Asylum*, chaps. 5 and 7; and Walters, *Antislavery Appeal*, chap. 4.

[38]See Grob, *Edward Jarvis*.

[39]Walter F. Willcox, *Studies in American Demography* (Ithaca, N.Y.: Cornell University Press, 1940), p. 68.

million people—previous guesses had ranged up to 5 million—there was some embarrassment. Secretary of State Thomas Jefferson was "concerned about the effect of the size of the population upon foreign opinion" and sent American diplomats copies of the census, "with explanations as to why, in his opinion, the totals were seriously in error."[40] President Washington wrote an American in Europe that, corrected of errors, the true population of the United States was "far greater . . . than has ever been allowed in Europe," and that "this fact will have no small influence in enabling [Europeans] to form a more just opinion of our present growing importance than has yet been entertained there."[41]

Nineteenth-century Americans had a special reason to feel pride at signs that their country was flourishing. These signs spoke of the success of the unique American experiment in popular government. In 1800 the American Philosophical Society, in a communication signed by Thomas Jefferson, petitioned Congress for various additions to the census. The petition emphasized the patriotic value of the information. The "duration of human life in this portion of the earth will be found at least equal to what it is in any other" and "its population increases with a rapidity unequalled in all other."[42] When in 1850 critics asked what possible legislative purpose might be served by gathering information on membership in religious denomination, since the Bill of Rights prohibited legislation regarding religion, Representative Thompson replied that the information would allow Americans to show how well religion flourished in the United States, even without the government support received in Europe.[43]

That information about America should be gathered in ever greater quantities because it would display the grandeur of American society became perhaps the dominant theme in justifications for governmental statistics-gathering in debates over the censuses of 1870 and 1880, held in the aftermath of the salvation of the Union and in the context of the nation's centennial. "The next census should furnish a muster-roll of the American people, showing . . . their vital, physical, intellectual, and moral power," Representative Garfield told his colleagues in 1869.[44] Debates over the 1880 census gushed with patriotism. Representative Cox commended the expanded census as "the great picture of our social and physical freedom . . . displayed for the judgement of mankind, . . . so that our development upon this continent can be justly ap-

---

[40]Alterman, *Counting People*, p. 204.
[41]Ibid., p. 205.
[42]Quoted in *Ninth Census*, p. 36.
[43]*Congressional Globe*, April 24, 1850, p. 813.
[44]Ibid., December 9, 1869, p. 183.

preciated.''[45] Another representative exclaimed:

> When the whole world knows . . . the extent of [our] boundless contri-
> butions to the support of man, . . . then for the first time will we . . .
> attain that rank in the family of peoples to which we are entitled. . . .
> Let us know what all of our institutions are doing, and the record will
> soon be such that we can point to it with pride. . . . Gather all these
> things, garner them up in one capacious storehouse of knowledge, and
> invite not merely our own people, but those of other countries, to learn
> what we really are.[46]

The sources of pride were not only economic growth but also
American social conditions. Referring to a proposal to add statistics
about housing to the census, the Garfield committee stated, "Few
things indicate more fully the condition of a people than the houses
they occupy. The census ought to show us how comfortable a place is
the average American home."[47] In connection with debates over the
census of 1870, Representative Garfield noted that the British historian
Francis Macauley had argued that the historian of the future should not
write solely of kings and lords but of ordinary people as well. A census
made that possible, because it enabled the observer to go "into the hovels, homes, workshops, mines, fields, prisons, hospitals, and all places
where human nature displays its weakness and its strength."[48] It was,
therefore, fitting that the census should be most developed in the United States, where popular government had raised the common man to a
status unknown in Europe.

Information as a Signal of Social Recognition

There are glimpses in the historical material of a different way the
collection of information was justified as providing a source of pride.
Congressmen suggested that gathering information about some particular group of Americans dignified the group and its pursuits. Patriotic
pride belongs to all. Social recognition, by contrast, comes when the
community singles out some groups or individuals as worthy of a special accolade.

This theme appeared less frequently and less obviously than the
other two justifications discussed above. In presenting plans for the
1870 census to the House, Representative Garfield noted the addition of

[45]*Congressional Record*, 45th Congress, 3rd sess., February 18, 1879, p. 1543.
[46]Ibid., p. 1552.
[47]*Ninth Census*, p. 52.
[48]*Congressional Globe*, December 16, 1869, p. 179.

mining statistics, arguing that mining was *"worthy* of a place" in the census. He used similar language regarding the addition of statistics of fisheries and of commerce.[49]

In the same debate, Senator Sumner repeatedly referred to pursuits that had not been counted separately in the census of 1850, suggesting that this failure was an insult. Speaking of the fishing industry, Sumner exlaimed that it was

> once the commanding interest of this Republic, the interest which oc-cupied more of the attention of our early plenipotentiaries in Europe than any question except that of independence itself—the interest which entered into the debate that ended in the acknowledgement of independence. . . . And yet—would you believe it, sir?—the law of 1850 has no provision for them.[50]

As for the limitation of the manufacturing census of 1850 to merchant-able articles, with a consequent exclusion of information regarding con-struction of railways, bridges, factories, and homes, Sumner stated: "The labor of [these] men . . . who make the grand, the permanent, al-most the only real addition to the capital of the country, is treated as of no account, while the production of articles for immediate, it may even be for mischievous, consumption is carefully recorded."[51] And while agriculture had been included in 1850, Sumner argued that there were not enough questions to show sufficient regard for it.[52]

In response, Senator Conkling, who led the opposition to the expan-sion of the census, accused Sumner of appealing for the vote of senators from Nevada with this call for a separate mining census. Conkling clearly understood the nature of the appeal Sumner was making. It was to the "pride of locality" of representatives of that state, newly admit-ted to the Union, to the self-respect that would come from the recogni-tion accorded them. And his words to the senators from Nevada, drip-ping with sarcasm, were in the same vein.

> How will the patriotic hearts of the Senators from Nevada swell with agonizing emotion when I point them to the place dedicated to the pre-cious metals in the schedules [passed by] the House, . . . consigned to a place side by side with "women's corsets" and "ready-made cloth-ing." Oh, that I could bind up the gashed bosoms of the Senators from Nevada.[53]

[49]Ibid., December 9, 1869, pp. 37–38 (emphasis added).
[50]Ibid., 41st Congress, 2nd sess., February 7, 1870, p. 1107.
[51]Ibid.
[52]Ibid.
[53]Ibid., pp. 1145–1146.

There appear to have been only three petitions from private organizations during the nineteenth century requesting that the government gather statistics about the group the organizations represented. The full texts of two of these survive, one from the New York Chamber of Commerce in 1860 requesting inclusion of statistics of domestic trade, and one from the National Electric Light Association in 1888 requesting a special census of the electrical industry. Although both petitions mentioned use that individuals in the business in question could make of the statistics, both, and especially the National Electric Light Association document, also appeared to be requesting the statement of social approval of their endeavors that the collection of government statistics would imply.

The petition of the New York Chamber of Commerce noted that "there are those who believe that commerce is unproductive. They perceive that it neither produces commodities nor changes their forms, and thence infer that instead of adding to the volume of wealth it diminishes it, by drawing its sustenance from other industrial interests."[54] But, the petition went on,

> They forget that a change in locality and a change of ownership are just as essential to the ultimate usefulness of commodities as their production or change of form. . . . Therefore an interest of such magnitude and usefulness should not be overlooked in a professed inventory of the wealth and productive resources of the country.[55]

The petition of the National Electric Light Association emphasized heavily the statement of social appreciation that a special census would provide a new industry. Electricity, the petition argued, had accomplished miracles. Yet it was under attack from critics for charging monopoly prices and for electricity-related accidents. A census would provide a sign of public appreciation.[56]

Information-Gathering as a Social Statement About the Special Value of Knowledge

Some enthusiasm for promoting government statistics-gathering rested on a belief in knowledge and the wish that the pursuit of knowledge receive a social accolade in the form of special government

[54]"Memorial of the Chamber of Commerce of New York Praying That Provision Be Made for Collecting Commerce Statistics in Taking the Census," *Senate Miscellaneous Documents*, 36th Congress, 1st sess., no. 14, February 2, 1860, p. 2.
[55]Ibid.
[56]"Memorial to Congress and Statement of the National Electric Light Association," *Senate Miscellaneous Documents*, 51st Congress, 1st sess., vol. 4, no. 197 (1888), p. 7.

efforts on its behalf. Like the concern for social recognition, this interest in statistics represented a singling out of something—in this case, knowledge, and perhaps, as well, those who seek knowledge—as being especially worthy.

The first efforts at "outside pressure" on the government to expand the census came from petitions in 1800 of the American Philosophical Society and the Connecticut Academy of Arts and Sciences. Many of those who supported census expansion throughout the century, from political leaders such as John Quincy Adams to academic social reformers, were people especially attached to the value of knowledge for its own sake.

Yet such attachment was not universal. Government did not become much involved during the nineteenth century in support of knowledge, and many people ridiculed the idea of knowledge for its own sake.[57] In debates over the 1850 census, critics referred on several occasions to questions added to the 1840 census simply as "gratifying an idle curiosity." Probably because the mere satisfaction of curiosity was not enough to persuade a majority of Congress, increasingly frequent statements about the importance of knowledge in post–Civil War debates about the census were generally tied into other arguments.

One argument was that failure to show an interest in knowledge would reflect badly on Americans as a people. It was a matter of patriotic pride that Americans cared about something as noble as knowledge. Representative Garfield told the House in 1870 that important questions needed to be answered about the effect of the Civil War on aspects of American society, such as the ratio between the sexes, and the state of education and religion. If the census failed to answer such questions, he continued, "the failure will reflect deep disgrace on the American name."[58] The 1870 debates saw frequent criticism of the 1850 census law; Senator Sumner referred to it as "antediluvian."[59] The most dramatic expression of that view came during debates over the 1880 census, when Representative Cox stated to the House:

> The footman gave way to the coach, the coach to the locomotive; the carrier pigeon even drooped his wings before the telegraph; the wooden sailing ship is giving way to the iron steamer. . . . As well go back to these obsolete methods of labor and vehicles of transport as return to the law of 1850.[60]

In opposing an expanded census in 1870, Senator Conkling took

[57]See Hunter Dupree, *Science in the Federal Government* (Cambridge, Mass.: Harvard University Press, 1957).

[58]*Congressional Globe*, December 9, 1869, p. 183.

[59]Ibid., February 7, 1870, p. 1107.

[60]*Congressional Record*, February 18, 1879, p. 1535.

this argument seriously enough to devote to it a long rebuttal. The 1850 census was nothing to be ashamed about. "Its equal was never attempted in history." And Conkling proceeded to read to the Senate a letter of praise for earlier censuses by the "French philosopher and scholar," Guizot.[61]

Congressmen also lauded statistical information for its contributions to scientific understanding of human behavior. Here their tone was especially grandiose. In the peroration of his address supporting an expanded 1870 census, Garfield proclaimed:

> The scientific spirit has cast out the demons, and presented us with nature clothed and in her right mind and living under the reign of law. It has given us, for the sorceries of the alchemist, the beautiful laws of chemistry; for the dreams of the astrologer, the sublime truths of astronomy; for the wild visions of cosmogony, the laws of God. But more stubborn still has been the resistance against every attempt to assert the reign of law in the realm of society. In that struggle, statistics has been the handmaid of science, and has poured a flood of light upon the dark questions of famine and pestilence, ignorance and crime, disease and death.[62]

Information as an Aid to Private Decision Makers

Even by a generous interpretation, none of the congressional discussion can be construed as making the argument that government should become involved in statistics-gathering because the marketplace would fail to produce an optimal quantity of information. The closest is an occasional reference to the immensity of the task, too large for private parties to undertake. (But the simple immensity of a task need not make it too large for the private sector or else the transcontinental railroad and the electrification of cities would never have been undertaken.)

Nor could any reader of these materials conclude that the conception of information as an aid to private individuals was an important justification for the gathering of statistics by government. Such allusions are there, scattered through the materials, sandwiched between the more prominent arguments. They appear more frequently toward the end of the century. The following is, I believe, a complete list of such references through 1900.

1. In connection with the House debates over the 1870 census,

[61] *Congressional Globe*, February 7, 1870, p. 1082.
[62] Ibid., December 16, 1869, pp. 178–179.

Representative Strong of Hartford, Connecticut, where many insurance companies were headquartered, supported the proposal to collect information on insurance firms, but for a somewhat different reason than the more widely presented one of gathering information for possible legislation. Such information, Strong argued, would help consumers choose solid companies.[63]

2. In the House debates over the 1880 census, Representative Cox, as a member of the Select Committee on the Census, argued that the business information in the census would "allay industrial anxiety and give hope and buoyancy to trade." He also argued that mortality statistics, which could be used to show the effects of different occupations on life expectancy, have "practical applications as to life insurance."[64]

3. The two extant petitions for census coverage from private organizations both referred to such statistics as helpful to them. The Chamber of Commerce petition inserted such a reference in a statement that the statistics "will serve as data of the highest value for the guidance of statesmen and merchants; and at the same time essentially aid the students of social science."[65] The National Electric Light Association argued that data about the industry would encourage decisions by foreigners to purchase American electrical products.[66]

Government Statistics and the Limits of Economic Theory

Let us return to the question of how microeconomic theory views the role of government. That view is a direct outgrowth of a view of individual behavior and of the role of the market in satisfying wants.

Economic theory sees human behavior as self-interested: people act so as to get themselves as much as possible of the things they value. The supreme achievement of microeconomics is to demonstrate that without central direction a free market will enable consumers to get the largest possible bundle of goods they want, given the money available to them. Since the market so well satisfies people's wants, it leaves a limited role for government. Economists agree that the marketplace may produce an unjust distribution of wealth, and economic theory therefore leaves open the possibility that government may legitimately redistrib-

[63]Ibid., February 14, 1869, p. 128.
[64]*Congressional Record*, February 18, 1879, pp. 1534, 1540.
[65]"Chamber of Commerce," p. 1.
[66]"Electric Light," p. 7.

ute income, while noting that nothing in the theory allows one to conclude whether government should do so. But insofar as the production of valued things is concerned, economists believe that government's role should be limited to cases of public goods (and conceptually related cases of "external effects" not discussed here) where market mechanisms fail to assure that people succeed in maximizing satisfaction of their preferences.

Government's role in the production of public goods is not only small (because few things we choose to purchase happen to have the property of being public goods) but also matter-of-fact. There is nothing special about public goods besides the nonrivality feature that prevents them from being optimally produced through market mechanisms. Public goods are valued things, like cars or Caribbean cruises. In demanding public goods from government, people are still behaving self-interestedly; they are seeking the same type of thing from government as when they go to the supermarket to buy food. All government is really doing is to provide an economic service that, but for certain accidental features of the goods in question, would be better provided by private firms. Government is a firm for the production of public goods, no more special than any firm producing things we want.

The theory of public choice, the positive (as opposed to normative) theory of government developed by economists, expresses a different view of what government ends up doing. At the center of the public choice theory lies the homey observation that once government has been established and can use force to collect taxes, people will try to use government to "get something for nothing." Public choice theory does not assume that government will in fact limit itself to production of public goods. It may provide consumers with benefits they could have secured in the marketplace but were not willing to pay for, or provide producers with favors such as tariff protection that consumers would not have been willing to grant. In this view, government's role depends on the skill and organization of interest groups pressuring for benefits. The government arena is described as a "political marketplace," and government decisions are seen as a resultant of the strength of private, self-interested forces.

The important thing is not differences between the normative and positive theories of government in microeconomics but their similarities. Both assume no discontinuity between individuals' behavior in the marketplace and vis-à-vis government or between the kinds of things individuals seek in the marketplace and from government.

What is wrong with the views of economists on the role of government? Nothing as far as they go. Problems appear only if that *is* as far as they go. For the evidence regarding the role of government in statistics suggests that the economic conception is incomplete and impoverished.

The historical materials on the justifications for government involvement in information-gathering first become comprehensible if we see them as growing out of a broader vision of the role government can play in people's lives. This vision emphasizes the distinctiveness of government and the special functions it serves, conceives the public world as a separate sphere from the marketplace. On the other hand, theories of government inspired by microeconomics suggest the fungibility of public and private, or even worse, the reduction of public into private.[67]

In an alternate vision, public behavior is an arena for the display of concern for others and for doing what is right, while the marketplace is a sphere for self-interest. A second element of the vision is that government is an arena for the provision of valued things whose provision in the marketplace would be not merely technically difficult, but above all simply inappropriate or unfitting.

The most prominent nineteenth-century argument for a government role in statistics-gathering was that political participants needed data to help them reach conclusions about legislation. In contrast, economists emphasize the use of information to aid *private* decision-making. To be sure, the difference is partly one of emphasis; information to aid *public* decisions can also be seen as a public good that will be underproduced absent government provision.

More fundamentally, though, the view that statistics should be gathered to aid decisions about legislation bespeaks a different conception of what people do when they behave politically. In this alternative conception, legislators were attempting conscientiously to determine what laws best served the people; and statistics, by revealing more about the conditions of the people, would aid in that task. Indeed, the view that information would be useful for determining what legislation should be enacted is incompatible with the premise that all participants in politics seek only to obtain through government valued things for themselves. People generally know what they want for themselves, and if they all go into the political process self-interestedly, statistics should have little role. That statistics can influence the results of a political process requires that there be at least some participants whose minds may be changed by new information and that judgments about govern-

---

[67]A similar argument, made for somewhat different contexts and in somewhat different ways from what follows, appears in Michael Walzer, *Spheres of Justice* (New York: Basic Books, 1983).

ment policy can be influenced by disinterested consideration of evidence in the light of general views of what is right and wrong. This does not contradict, of course, the observation that self-interested partisans employ only statistics that support their cause.[68] But statistics can succeed in supporting such a cause only if there are others in the process who are not self-interested partisans, and who are subject to persuasion with the help of statistics. The desire for statistics to help determine which laws should be adopted is thus an affirmation of the role of ethical concerns in public behavior.

Statistics can influence the course of government decisions not only prospectively (in helping people form judgments about what legislation should be enacted) but also retrospectively by helping people form judgments of government performance. If citizens believe that statistics on inflation, unemployment, the number of people in poverty, or whatever show unsatisfactory government performance, they can decide to vote against incumbent officials in favor of new ones, who advocate different policies. Note again, though, that the operation of this mechanism assumes that the voting behavior of at least some citizens is motivated by factors other than self-interest. For, if one's voting behavior is motivated only by one's personal situation, one hardly needs statistics, which provide information about the situation of people in general, to decide one's vote. One does not care particularly about the unemployment *rate*, only about whether one is unemployed oneself; one does not care about how many are in poverty, only about whether one is in poverty oneself. Such personal information can be obtained without recourse to statistics. It has been widely noted that the electoral prospects of the majority party in the United States vary quite dramatically depending on the state of the economy. But analysis of survey data on voting behavior shows that this does not arise from any tendency by those personally hit by bad economic conditions to be especially likely to desert the incumbents. Instead, desertions come from those who believe that the economy *in general* is in bad shape, or that the party out of power is best capable of managing the economy. This relationship remains after controlling for effects of one's personal economic situation on views on the overall economy.[69] In making political decisions, many people care about more than themselves, and statistics are necessary to make it possible to translate that concern into political choice.

[68]See, for example, David Seidman, "The Politics of Policy Analysis," *Regulation,* vol. 1 (July 1977).

[69]Donald R. Kinder and D. Roderick Kiewiet, "Economic Discontent and Political Behavior: The Role of Personal Grievances and Collective Economic Judgments in Congressional Voting," *American Journal of Political Science* 23 (August 1979).

A second element of the overall vision of the public world as a separate sphere is that government plays a role in obtaining for people valued things they do not want to obtain through the marketplace. When Americans justified government statistics-gathering as a source of patriotic pride, recognition for individual groups, or out of a belief in the value of knowledge, they were viewing government as a source of something valuable. But the valuable things government was providing were not ordinary material goods but valued feelings.

Again, the difference here with economic theory is partly one of emphasis. It is true that nothing in economic theory implies that all valued things need be material. Valued feelings can be included as well. And if group-associated valued feelings cannot be produced in the marketplace, an economist could dub this a market failure just as the failure to produce public goods.

Although, in principle, there is no reason to exclude nonmaterial things from those giving satisfaction, economists in practice generally give them short shrift. Beyond that, once more, is something more fundamental. A feature of many of these feelings is that they cannot be produced through the market mechanism because the very definition of what produces satisfaction includes their not being for sale. Although one could imagine community recognition being produced for sale, recognition purchased (or praise or friendship or love purchased) is different from recognition, praise, or friendship that is not for sale.[70]

If what I want is "recognition that has not been purchased," I cannot obtain it through a mechanism that calls forth production only in response to a willingness to pay. The presence of such wants places an inevitable limit on the ability of the market to produce valued things and suggests a role for nonmarket institutions.

The vision of government and marketplace as distinct spheres should be seen in the context of a view of human motivation richer than that provided in economic theory. Just as there is a time to be born and a time to die, a time to cast away stones and a time to gather them together, so too is there a time to care about one's self and a time to care about others. To deny the very powerful role self-interest plays in motivating behavior would be foolish. But to deny motivations to help others, to do what one believes is right, would be incorrect as well. And just as there are fitting forums for many other activities we wish to undertake on different occasions—we dance at parties, not in the classroom; we contemplate art in museums, not in garbage dumps; we make love in our homes, not on the street—so, too, can there be fitting

---

[70]For a further discussion, see Steven Kelman, *What Price Incentives?: Economists and the Environment* (Boston: Auburn House, 1981), chap. 2.

forums for self-interested and altruistic behavior. Just as features of weekend parties make them appropriate for dancing, so too features of public behavior make it appropriate for displaying altruism. These include most obviously the fact that when one makes decisions about what to do in one's private life, the decisions are of largely personal scope, which encourages one to think mainly of oneself in making them. When making a decision about what government should do, the decision involves many others as well, which encourages one to think about others in making it. This obviously does not imply that there is no self-interested behavior in government—there is, obviously, lots of it—but it does suggest that concern for others has a role in public behavior it does not have in the marketplace. Without government, one forum for displaying altruism would disappear.

Some additional points ought to be discussed regarding the view of government presented here. The argument has been couched in terms of wants (or preferences) people have. Some critics might concede that people do want an opportunity to display concern for others and to obtain valued things through nonmarket means, but still deny that government need become involved in information provision to satisfy those wants. Privately gathered information could be used in deliberations over public policy, and citizens and legislators would still have the opportunity to display concern for others in those deliberations. Feelings of pride can come from membership in communities other than the nation, and recognition can be granted by other bodies besides government. Private methods of satisfying these wants, it might be argued, have the advantage of not forcing unwilling citizens to contribute to such want-satisfaction through their tax dollars.

In the case, though, of information as an aid to deliberation over legislation, private provision would endanger the role it is being asked to fill as a guide for those trying to determine what policy is right. Private information would frequently be seen as biased and partisan. And it is certainly true that many institutions besides government, ranging from families to honorary societies, can provide recognition and other valued feelings. But only government represents the community as a whole, and to the extent that people wish to feel proud of being members of the national community or to receive recognition from it, government has no substitute.

There is another potential problem with an argument that justifies governmental activity in an area based on people's wants. For not everyone has the wants described in what I have called a more complete vision of the role of government. Doubtless many have no particular desire to behave altruistically, much less to have government available for some to display concern for others. As long as most people do have the wants, the presence of a minority of dissenters creates little problem; the government's role may still be justified from the standpoint of majority-rule theories or even the mainstream of microeconomic theory (which does not enjoin wealth redistribution). The presence of dissenters does raise a problem, though, for libertarians and others concerned about forcing a minority to support financially the wants of the majority. Certainly, the situation is different from government provision of public goods, which libertarians can accept on the grounds that everyone may be presumed to want them.

However, government activities providing people a forum for displaying concern for others or satisfying desires for nonmarket valued feelings can be justified on grounds quite apart from individual wants. It is not simply that people may want the opportunity for displaying altruism. It is *right* for people in their decisions to take account of the effects of alternative acts on others. Institutions that encourage people to take such account are justified on the bases of the encouragement they provide for ethical behavior. As for provision of nonmarket valued feelings, it might be justified even absent current desires for such feelings based on a view growing out of the Aristotelian tradition that one of government's roles is to educate people about what things individuals should value for themselves. With its hint of paternalism, this justification is difficult to sustain. But it clearly has rich roots in our traditions. All societies seek to educate young people, at least, about which values are best. The justification is based on a view of human nature that maintains that people have strong needs for such feelings even if they do not recognize them at a given time, that they are likely to look back on a life where they ignored pursuit of such feelings in favor of pursuit of material things alone as a life that was in some significant way empty.

The Case for Government Statistics Today

I will conclude by briefly getting out of the time machine and returning to the present. The Bureau of the Census is now, of course, only one of many agencies collecting statistics. During the Reagan administration, a number of cutbacks in federal statistics programs have been made. Some data-gathering has been eliminated, and in other cases sample sizes or the frequency of collection has been reduced.

These cutbacks provide a valuable opportunity to examine current justifications for the role of government in this area. When something previously taken for granted comes under attack, one sees arguments marshaled for why the activity is important. It is thus useful to look at two hearings held by Democratic-controlled House committees on the statistics cutbacks in 1982, both of which gave critics of the cutbacks ample opportunity to justify their positions.[71]

Someone emerging from the time machine of the earlier pages of this chapter will recognize some arguments that appear in these hearings. In particular, a number of the witnesses at both hearings emphasized quite strongly the importance of good statistics for legislation. Representative Robert Garcia, who chaired one of the hearings, asked a panel of witnesses what they believed were "the implications of these cutbacks . . . as it relates to Congress and Congress' ability to have the information necessary to make sound judgment."[72] Stephen Feinberg, chairman of the Committee on National Statistics of the National Academy of Science, noted that "the executive branch and Congress use statistical data to aid the preparation of legislation. . . . Statistics . . . provide the infrastructure used for governmental decisionmaking. . . . Statistical information [is] required for our central national debates."[73] A witness from the Bureau of Social Science Research argued that "at a time when concerns about the status of the poor, minorities and women are increasing in this society, it is unbelievable that the Government would discontinue research that would increase its understanding of how to deal more effectively with them."[74]

Missing from the 1982 hearings was any reference to other themes common in the earlier materials—patriotic pride, social recognition, the special value of knowledge. Instead, a large number of witnesses from the private sector explained how reductions in statistical information would hurt their ability to make good business decisions. They cited decisions about production levels (using data on macroeconomic trends); production schedules for agricultural equipment manufacturers (using timely farm income statistics); targeting of promotional campaigns in the tourism industry (using the Department of Commerce National Travel Survey); and location of new retail outlets (using timely census data.)[75]

Why the new justifications for a government role? For one thing, as

---

[71]The hearings are *Impact of Budget Cuts on Federal Statistical Programs*, Hearings before the Subcommittee on Census and Population of the Committee on Post Office and Civil Service, U.S. House of Representatives, 97th Congress, 2nd sess. (March 16, 1982), and *Federal Government Statistics and Statistical Policy*, Hearing before the Legislation and National Security Subcommittee of the Committee on Government Operations, 97th Congress, 2nd sess. (June 3, 1982).

[72]*Impact of Budget Cuts*, p. 241.

[73]*Federal Government Statistics*, pp. 5, 12.

[74]*Impact of Budget Cuts*, p. 124.

[75]Ibid., pp. 47–48. See also the testimony of the editor of the magazine *American Demographics* in *Federal Government Statistics*, particularly pp. 85–86.

economic life became more complicated, the value of information for private decision makers rose, presumably increasing pressures for public provision. For another, one gets a clear picture reading the earlier materials of the excitement surrounding the fact that the United States was the world's first experiment in popular government. As this excitement faded, so might one expect interest in information as a source of patriotic pride in republican institutions to fade. Perhaps more important, the twentieth century has seen the increasing organization of interest groups seeking to obtain benefits for themselves through government and the dramatic growth within government of agencies that see themselves as advocates for constituencies. As such impulses have become better organized in and around government, the kind of demands for private benefits that public-choice economists regard as constituting the whole of political activity have become, at any rate, a more legitimate feature of political activity.

Even in the nineteenth century, one sees evidence of a view of information as an aid to private decision makers from those few bureaus of government that did see themselves as advocates of specific interests, although such views left little trace in broader debates about government statistical policy. During the nineteenth century the Department of the Treasury, among its other functions, acted as an advocate for industry and trade. As early as 1845 the secretary of the treasury unsuccessfully recommended to Congress establishment of an ongoing statistical bureau within the federal government. He made perhaps the first reference to the use of information produced by government for the benefit of private decision makers:

> Agricultural, manufacturing, and commercial . . . interests are deeply concerned in having the best attainable information of all that relates to our own soil and its products, natural and artificial, the products of industry, our surplus and our wants, as well as the products of foreign soils and climates, foreign industry, foreign wants, foreign surpluses, and the annual consumption of foreign nations of those articles not the growth or product of their respective territories. An accurate knowledge of those will enable our merchants to pursue their commercial enterprises more advantageously.[76]

The Department of Agriculture, established in 1862, was set up specifically to help agriculture, making it the first agency of its kind. And it saw provision of statistics to farmers as a way to help them

---

[76]"Letter from the Secretary of the Treasury transmitting a report, with results of statistical information, etc.," *House Documents*, 28th Congress, 2nd sess., no. 35 (January 7, 1845), p. 2.

make better agricultural decisions. In his call for the establishment of such an agency, the secretary of the interior, in 1861, emphasized its statistical functions.[77]

The most dramatic, and conscious, expansion of statistics-gathering as an aid to private decision makers occurred in the early 1920s in the newly established Department of Commerce. In expanding the frequency and scope of business-related statistics, particularly production statistics, the primary goal Secretary Herbert Hoover had in mind was to even out the business cycle by combating extremes of optimism and pessimism encouraged for want of good data. During the early 1920s the government regularized the process of gathering frequent statistics on production in a large number of industries. In many cases, the statistics were first gathered during World War I for war production. Trade associations, however, requested they be continued after the war.[78]

That government-gathered statistics are now also seen as an aid to private decision makers in making better economic decisions is not itself regrettable. There would appear to be little objection to government taking steps that can be demonstrated to increase national wealth. The important question is not whether there is anything wrong with looking at the role of government in statistics-gathering the way economists do. The question is whether, in the words of the song, that's all there is. The evidence presented here argues that government became deeply involved in information-gathering for reasons that had little to do with any assistance that such information could provide private individuals. That evidence merits consideration, because it suggests that isn't all there is. Even in the hard-bitten 1980s, the continued prevalence of the argument that statistics are needed to help evaluate legislation suggests that many still assume that those involved in such deliberations are not simply self-interested. If that is true, then the economist's view of government as merely an alternate marketplace cuts off our understanding of part of ourselves. We need to recall a more complete view.

[77]"Report of the Secretary of the Interior for 1861," *Senate Executive Documents,* 37th Congress, 2nd sess., vol. 1 (1861), p. 452.
[78]See Holt, op. cit., pp. 78–79.

9

STATISTICS AND THE POLITICS OF MINORITY REPRESENTATION: THE EVOLUTION OF THE VOTING RIGHTS ACT SINCE 1965

ABIGAIL THERNSTROM

THE CHANGING, expanding use of national statistics runs like a leitmotif throughout the history of the 1965 Voting Rights Act. It was precisely the point of the act to substitute a statistical rule of thumb for the extended and complex judicial process by which Fifteenth Amendment questions were traditionally decided. The act identified a violation wherever voter registration or turnout in the presidential election of 1964 fell below 50 percent and a literacy test was used to screen potential registrants.[1] All states or counties fitting those criteria were "covered" and thus subject to a set of stringent remedies.

Numbers have a seeming objectivity. In fact, the 50 percent turnout mark worked only with the 1964 figures. That is, those who wrote the legislation knew which states had been systematically, persistently infringing the right of blacks to vote, and they designed a test to single out those states. Yet, once established, that carefully selected numerical criterion took on a life of its own. In 1970 the registration and turnout

NOTE: This chapter has been drawn from Abigail Thernstrom, *Whose Votes Count? Affirmative Action and Minority Voting Rights* (New York: The Twentieth Century Fund, 1987).

[1] By the terms of the original act, jurisdictions were "covered" that employed a literacy test and in which less than 50 percent of persons of voting age were registered or in which less than 50 percent of such persons actually voted in 1964. In future references to this "trigger," I have dropped the reference to registration. Since a 50 percent voter turnout rate is required to escape coverage, the registration rate is, in fact, irrelevant.

figures for 1968 were added to the statistical "trigger" and the act was instantly and substantially changed. The statute and the statistical test that it contains have had, in fact, a symbiotic relationship. A change in the method by which electoral discrimination was measured helped reshape the meaning of disfranchisement, and the revised definition both further changed the means by which voting rights violations were assessed and stimulated additional amendments to the act.

The new definition of disfranchisement assumed a right to a voice as well as a vote. Not simply black ballots, but blacks in office became the entitlement. And with that change other statistical rules of thumb surfaced. Population data on the proportion of minorities in a jurisdiction and their residential dispersal, as well as statistical analyses of racial and ethnic voting patterns, came to determine the legality of redistricting plans; a plan that did not "fairly reflect" the minority population was not likely to survive judicial or Justice Department review. The fate of an at-large method of voting now hinged on census findings on the racial and ethnic makeup of a city before and after an annexation. The Voting Rights Act, in short, emerged as an instrument to promote the election of minorities to office, and national statistics came to play an important role in the allocation of political power among whites, blacks, and (after 1975) Hispanics.

The Voting Rights Act in 1965

"To play with complicated formulas, to measure justice by percentages, and to aim punitive laws at some states, not only violates both the spirit and letter of the Constitution, but buries the real moral question in sophistry," the *Wall Street Journal* complained in 1965.[2] On the House Judiciary Committee that year, few Republican members supported the bill that eventually became law. "[F]air and effective enforcement of the 15th amendment," they argued, "calls for precise identification of offenders, not the indiscriminate scattergun technique evident in the 50 percent test."[3] Four years later southerners were still complaining. "The absurdity of the trigger device," Senator Sam Ervin said,

> is demonstrated by comparing the 1964 voting statistics in my state of North Carolina with those in New York, both of which have literacy tests. Hyde County, N.C., had 49.7 per cent of eligible voters voting in

[2]March 22, 1965, quoted in U.S. House of Representatives, 89th Cong., 1st sess., Committee of the Judiciary, Report #439, "The Voting Rights Act of 1965," views of Hon. Wm. M. Tuck, p. 74.
[3]House Report #439, Republican views, p. 45.

1964. New York county voted 51.3 percent. Hyde County is condemned under the act for three-tenths of 1 percent. New York County is innocent for 1.3 percent.[4]

Appearances to the contrary notwithstanding, though, there was nothing arbitrary, absurd, indiscriminate, or excessively reliant on numerical indicators about the 1965 Voting Rights Act. Framed with meticulous care, informed by years of litigation experience, it swiftly accomplished what no previous law had achieved: the enfranchisement of the southern black, ninety-five years after the passage of the Fifteenth Amendment. Senator Ervin could complain that Hyde County, North Carolina, had been "condemned" for three-tenths of one percent, while New York County (Manhattan) was "innocent" for 1.3 percent. But nothing in the history of New York spoke of a need for federal protection against local efforts to disfranchise blacks, while the record of North Carolina told quite a different story. One of the most impressive aspects of the 1965 act, in fact, was the precision of its aim.

The statistical test was, in effect, an economizing measure, and, as such, a familiar feature of the law. It allowed the finding of vote denial by a simple formula, eliminating the need to ferret out Fifteenth Amendment violations in states with abominable records with respect to black voting rights. By 1965 the excessive cost and limited effectiveness of the traditional judicial route had become abundantly clear. The 1957 Civil Rights Act had created a Civil Rights Division within the Department of Justice and gave federal attorneys new power to bring voting rights suits. Both the 1960 and 1964 acts had further enhanced that power. But such case-by-case adjudication had proved arduous, expensive, and limited in impact. Preparation for a trial often demanded examining hundreds of witnesses and scouring thousands of pages of registration records. In one case involving Montgomery, Alabama, for instance, the federal government introduced sixty-nine exhibits, one of which consisted of 10,000 documents filling five filing cabinets.[5] The effort, of course, was to show that white illiteracy was no bar to registration and black literacy no aid. Whites who could not read were put on the rolls, while educated blacks were not.

The government was invariably rewarded in its efforts, winning every suit it brought. But it sued only those counties most vulnerable to attack, and its victories were often neither swift nor complete. As

[4]U.S. Senate, Subcommittee on Constitutional Rights of the Committee on the Judiciary, Hearings on Amendments to the Voting Rights Act of 1965, 91st Cong., 1st and 2nd sess., 1969–1970, statement of Sam J. Ervin, Jr., chairman, p. 2.

[5]Carl M. Brauer, *John F. Kennedy and the Second Reconstruction* (New York: Columbia University Press, 1977), pp. 118–19.

John Doar, in charge of voting rights litigation under John F. Kennedy later put it, the Justice Department "faced tough judges"—some of whom Kennedy himself had appointed.[6] Eager to find for the defendants, Doar meant, not tough in the sense of rigorous or exacting. Too often, access to public records was reluctantly conceded, trials were delayed, cases improperly dismissed, rulings inadequate, and enforcement half-hearted.

The litigation experience paid off handsomely, however, for it laid the groundwork for the subsequent legislation. From their tribulations in southern courts, federal attorneys drew several lessons. The first was the necessity of eliminating the literacy test; its fraudulent administration was the chief means by which southern whites kept blacks from the polls. Impartial administration was no solution: Often the tests devised could not be objectively scored, and even a minimal literacy requirement penalized blacks for an inadequacy for which the state was, in great part, to blame. The importance of circumventing southern federal district courts was the second lesson that litigators learned. Southern judges could not be trusted. In fact, the question of electoral discrimination should not be litigated at all. This was the third lesson. To prove the obvious was both expensive and time-consuming, and victories were too often transient or incomplete. And finally: banishing literacy tests might not be enough. Unless prophylactic steps were taken, old methods of disfranchisement, once eliminated, might simply be replaced by new ones.

What the litigators learned in the field, the framers of the act wrote into law. Thus the central provision of the statute was the statistical test for electoral discrimination that required no judicial findings but implicitly acknowledged the established link between southern literacy tests and low levels of voter participation. States or counties where a literacy test had been employed in November 1964 and where voter turnout was below 50 percent were assumed to be engaged in electoral discrimination, with the burden on the jurisdiction to prove otherwise. From the inferred presence of constitutional violations, several consequences followed. In "covered" jurisdictions, literacy tests were suspended, initially for five years. Federal registrars ("examiners") and election observers could be dispatched to these areas whenever necessary. Moreover, "covered" states and counties could institute no new "voting qualification or prerequisite to voting" without "preclearance" (approval) by the U.S. attorney general or the District Court of the District of Columbia. No southern court was given jurisdiction.

---

[6] John Doar and Dorothy Landsberg, "The performance of the FBI in Investigating Violations of Federal Law Protecting the Right to Vote—1960–1967" (Photocopy; copyright, 1971), pp. 17–17a, quoted in Brauer, *Kennedy and Second Reconstruction*, p. 118.

Why the figure of 50 percent? Because those who wrote the legislation knew the states they wanted to "cover" and, by a process of trial and error, determined the participation level that would single them out. Those central, temporary provisions of the 1965 act—suspension of the literacy test chief among them—applied to six southern states in their entirety, a seventh in substantial part, and scattered counties elsewhere.

And why not an outright ban on all literacy tests without the intervening, indirect test for Fifteenth Amendment violations? Because it was assumed that such a ban would not survive a constitutional challenge. As recently as 1959, the right of states to screen potential registrants for their ability to read and write had, in principle, been upheld.[7]

Knowing literacy tests to be the chief means of disfranchising southern blacks, then, and using voter registration and turnout figures, the framers of the act devised a statistical test to identify their discriminatory use. They took a proven relationship between the impact of black disfranchisement on the general level of political participation in the heavily black southern states, on the one hand, and the fraudulent use of literacy tests, on the other, and used the first to identify the second.

The Amendments of 1970

In August 1970, when the central, temporary sections of the act (its "special" provisions) were due to expire, they were both renewed for five years and in seemingly small, though significant ways, also altered. Literacy tests were everywhere suspended, and the 1968 figures for registration and turnout were incorporated into the statistical "trigger" that determined coverage by the act. Thus states where voting had dropped below the 50 percent mark in the 1968 presidential election lost their traditional prerogative to restructure their electoral processes without prior federal approval. Both changes were a concession to the Nixon administration and southern conservatives. With their eyes on the 1970 and 1972 elections, the Republicans were pursuing a "southern strategy." They hoped to tap the conservative Democratic vote, particularly that which had gone to Wallace in 1968. What the South really wanted, of course, was to let the "special" provisions die. But while remarkable progress in voting rights had been made in five years, it was clearly insufficient, and a good many congressmen from both parties were committed to extension. The fall-back position was (as one southerner put it) to "spread the misery"—to extend the geographical reach of the act.[8]

---

[7]*Lassiter* v. *Northhampton County Bd. of Elections*, 360 U.S. 45 (1959).
[8]*New York Times*, June 11, 1969, p. 18.

With literacy tests everywhere banned, clearly the statistical trigger (the use of such a test in conjunction with less than 50 percent turnout) no longer served to target those states and counties in which suspension was necessary. It no longer identified jurisdictions using literacy tests for discriminatory ends. Yet it had a continuing purpose: selecting additional jurisdictions that would henceforth be required to preclear all proposed changes in their method of voting, as well as those to which federal examiners and observers could be sent.

Literacy tests were thus everywhere suspended, but the preclearance provision (which had been included only to reinforce their initially selective suspension) was not likewise everywhere made applicable. And the consequence of this use of the statistical trigger *solely* to establish preclearance coverage was to sever irrevocably the initially intimate connection between suspension and preclearance. It was a process begun by the Supreme Court, but Congress further separated those two initially inseparable provisions.[9] The preclearance provision thus acquired an independent validity that permitted its emergence as an instrument to promote the election of blacks to office. In 1965 the Department of Justice or the District Court of the District of Columbia had been expected to ask: Was the change in electoral procedure submitted for review a literacy test in disguise—different in form, not in impact? Five years later, the question became: Will the proposed change "dilute" the strength of the black vote? If a method of election had been altered to promote the election of black city councilmen, and if blacks have indeed been elected in numbers proportional to the black population, can the city retain a majority vote requirement, or is that requirement an impermissible potential impediment to future black electoral success?[10]

The use of the 1968 turnout figures had another, no less significant, consequence. In 1965 the act had one aim—the enfranchisement of the southern black—and almost every part fit the overall design. But after 1970 the aim was confused and the construction no longer clean. And once the outlines of the original act had been partially obscured, further distortions became less apparent.

In 1965, those who wrote the Voting Rights Act knew the states they wanted to cover and designed a "trigger" to accomplish the desired end. Applying the same statistical rule to the 1968 figures, however,

---

[9]The process had begun with *Allen* v. *Board of Elections*, 393 U.S. 544 (1969), which, in holding that at-large systems of voting, districting changes, and other alterations in the electoral method in "covered" jurisdictions were subject to Justice Department review, implicitly gave the preclearance provision independent status. See the dissenting opinion of Justice Harlan in *Allen*.

[10]There were, in fact, the facts in *City of Port Arthur* v. *United States*, 459 U.S. 159 (1982).

had quite a different result. An assorted collection of counties with no history of black disfranchisement were brought under coverage. *None* of these counties was in the South, and no other evidence suggested that these were counties in which minority voters were at a *distinctive* disadvantage.

The evidence, in fact, pointed in quite a different direction. Three counties in New York City were among those covered after 1970. But turnout for the presidential election of 1968 had been low across the nation, and participation in New York, reflecting the national trend, had dropped slightly to just under the determining 50 percent mark. The city had not changed; the doors of political opportunity had not been suddenly closed to blacks and Puerto Ricans. Rather, facing a choice between Nixon and Humphrey, a few more New Yorkers than before had stayed home.

The ban on literacy tests was not likely to change the level of minority electoral opportunity in New York and other such counties. In 1965 those who wrote the legislation designed the statistical trigger to bring under coverage states known to have *intentionally* barred blacks from the polls. It was reasonable to assume that those states, deprived of the opportunity to use literacy tests for purposes of disfranchisement, would *deliberately* search for other means to accomplish the same end. But there was no cause to similarly suspect those places that had been brought under coverage in 1970, all of them outside the South, and none with a record of official hostility to black participation.

If, indeed, there were northern counties in which the extraordinary requirement of preclearance was needed, some new test was required to identify them. The discovery that a jurisdiction used a literacy test and that voter participation had dropped a few percentage points in the last presidential election was not revealing. And if a new trigger were to be designed, those at the drawing boards would have to proceed as the framers of the original legislation had: by first selecting those counties likely to adjust electoral procedure to keep black officeholding down, and then ascertaining the characteristics they had in common. Perhaps a statistical measure would once again allow a short-cut to avoid the laborious judicial process that the identification of discriminatory communities otherwise required, but the level of voter turnout was not likely to be it.

As a consequence of the use of the 1968 figures, without evidence of distinctive need, the most stringent remedies contained in the act thus came into play in counties scattered across the nation but outside the South. These were, in general, extraordinary remedies, it will be recalled, to meet an extraordinary need. The act was originally intended to deal with the distinctive and shocking problem of black disfranchisement in the South; the contrast implicitly made was precisely between places like New York and Neshoba County, Mississippi, where in the summer of 1964 three civil rights workers were murdered for their participation in a black voter registration drive. Yet, in 1970 three New York City boroughs and Neshoba County came to be equally restricted in their freedom to structure their own electoral arrangements. In 1966, well before the preclearance provision acquired its subsequent greatly enlarged meaning, the Supreme Court had made clear the constitutional irregularity of the remedies, justified by the magnitude of the need.[11] Had the act in 1965 been less precise in its aim—had it upset the normal balance in federal–state relations in both North and South—it would not have stood up to constitutional scrutiny.

It can be argued that the statutory net continued to catch only culpable jurisdictions, since the law allowed those counties that had not actually used a literacy test for discriminatory ends to "bail out." Indeed, New York did briefly extricate itself by proving its racial neutrality to the satisfaction of a three-judge panel of the U.S. District Court of the District of Columbia.[12] But coverage was reinstated on the basis of another lawsuit arguing that the use of English ballots in a city with a large Puerto Rican population constituted, in effect, a discriminatory literacy test. Had the city's failure to provide election material in Spanish truly disfranchised minority voters?[13]

Ironically, it was probably the political strength of New York's minority community that prevented the city from permanently bailing out. Both blacks and Hispanics had long participated in the city's political process, and numerous minority organizations were ready and able to fight for the benefits that the Voting Rights Act conferred. Hispanics succeeded in reinstating coverage by equating a fraudulent literacy test that acted as an outright bar to black suffrage in the Jim Crow South with ballots printed in English in a city with a large Hispanic population. That Congress was later to accept this equation illustrates the basic point. The amendments of 1970 furthered a process of change that slowly but effectively obscured the original purpose of the act. Alterations made to serve the political ends of Republicans pursuing a southern strategy had left the act vulnerable to civil rights groups with their own agenda.

I have focused on three New York counties as the most blatant example of jurisdictions covered in 1970 but clearly outside the sphere of

---

[11]*South Carolina* v. *Katzenbach*, 383 U.S. 301 (1966).

[12]*New York State* v. *United States*, D.D.C. Civ. No. 2419–71, April 13, 1972.

[13]*New York* v. *United States*, 419 U.S. 888 (1974). A local court had found in *Torres* v. *Sachs* (381 F. Supp. 309 [1974]) that the conduct of elections in English deprived Spanish-speaking citizens of rights protected by the Voting Rights Act. The Department of Justice then moved to reopen the case, and on January 10, 1974, the D.C. court rescinded its initial exemption.

congressional concern five years earlier. New York had originally been the implicit standard against which the racism of southern politics was judged. It was with *distinctive* regional problems—not nationwide ones—that the act was designed to deal; hence its (never explicitly acknowledged) southern focus. But the coverage of New York and other nonsouthern jurisdictions in 1970 injected precisely that element of arbitrariness into the act that Senator Ervin had erroneously found before. The point, in other words, was just the opposite of the one he had made. Covering New York was arbitrary; the initial line was rational. Blurring the difference between the provision of protection for racial and ethnic minorities in localities with well-documented histories of blatant Fifteenth Amendment violations, and protection where the barriers to political opportunity were either linguistic or socioeconomic, was to destroy the clean lines and logical construction of the act. And once minorities in New York qualified for the extraordinary benefits of the Voting Rights Act, there was no logical place to stop. If New York, then why not Chicago? The changes in the legislation in 1970 were the opening wedge to those in 1975 and 1982, when the act was revised, first to extend even further the geographical reach of preclearance protection and then to give black and Hispanic voters more leverage in challenging at-large and other methods of voting across the nation.

Numerical Evidence of Vote "Dilution"

In 1965 the preclearance provision seemed a minor section of the act, but by the early 1970s it had become the centerpiece of the legislation. The Supreme Court had interpreted it to require the submission to the Justice Department not only of proposed procedures affecting the right of blacks to register and vote but of new electoral district lines, switches from ward to at-large voting, annexations by municipalities of surrounding areas (potentially altering the racial balance of the city's electorate), and other changes with an impact on the weight of the black ballots cast. The review of changes in electoral procedure submitted by covered jurisdictions to the Justice Department for preclearance thus became the main business of the voting section of the Civil Rights Division.[14]

As initially conceived, the result of an objection to a planned

---

[14]With the publication in the Federal Register of the first section 5 guidelines in 1971 the enforcement of that provision really took off. The guidelines had been prompted by a series of decisions, beginning with *Allen* v. *Bd. of Elections* in 1969, in which the Supreme Court held that annexations, new districting schemes, and other changes in the method of voting required preclearance when adopted in "covered" jurisdictions. By 1975 the importance of section 5 was an accepted fact.

change was expected to be simply the continued use of existing electoral practice, but a reversal to the *status quo ante* is frequently not an option. Old district lines, for instance, are usually unconstitutional, violating the equal population rule. And since blacks also benefit from the broader tax base that an expanded city creates, deannexation is regarded as an unacceptable cure. Not even the location of a polling place, once changed, can always be restored; the building where the old one was housed may be unavailable for public use. Thus the task of the Justice Department (or the D.C. court as an alternative) is not only to judge the purpose and impact of a proposed change in electoral procedure but also to preside over often complicated remedial processes.

At both stages, that of judging the impact of a proposed change and that of assessing alternative plans, numerical evidence has come to play a vital role. Attorneys in the Department of Justice or judges on the federal bench need to know the racial composition of the jurisdiction as a whole, the distribution of racial and ethnic groups within that jurisdiction, who votes for whom, and the success rate of minority candidates.

Thus, in 1982 when Sumter County, South Carolina, belatedly submitted for preclearance a much earlier change from a county commission appointed by the state legislature to one elected at-large, the Justice Department objected. The result of continuing elections at-large, the Department argued, would be the maintenance of a largely all-white legislative body. Yet more than 40 percent of the voting-age population in Sumter County was black, black registration was higher than white, and the black vote was obviously crucial to the outcome of every election. But, in the view of the Justice Department, more important were certain statistical facts: The number of blacks holding county office was disproportionately low in relation to the black population, the success rate of black candidates suggested voting along racial lines, and the residential concentration of blacks gave promise of a larger number of black county commissioners if elections were held in single-member districts drawn to reflect the racial composition of the county.[15]

Likewise, approval of a polling place change in covered jurisdictions depends, in part, on census findings on the residential distribution of racial and ethnic groups. For instance, on November 26, 1985, Hidalgo County, Texas, submitted such a change for preclearance.[16] The approval of that change would depend exclusively on the impact that it was expected to have on minority turnout in the heavily Mexican American

[15]*County Council of Sumter County, South Carolina* v. *United States,* civil action No. 82–0912, slip opinion (D.D.C. May 25, 1984) (per curiam).
[16]U.S. Department of Justice, notice of submissions (DJ 166–012–3), December 18, 1985.

county. In part, that impact would be gauged from interviews with interested parties in the community; in part, from population data. If the census showed the move to have been from a Hispanic to a white neighborhood, and Mexican American voting thus presumably discouraged, and if local observers confirmed these findings, an objection would follow—unless, that is, the county could show that whites had previously been shortchanged and Mexican Americans unduly advantaged.

Preclearance of a districting plan hinges, as well, on statistical findings. In fact, at the heart of a disagreement over the impact of a redistricting plan is frequently a dispute over how to count minority voters, how to measure white and minority voting patterns, how to determine the level of minority voter turnout, and where to draw the line between a "safe" minority district and one that wastes minority votes by excessively dispersing or concentrating them. And often, only if the state or political subdivision (city or county) can persuade the attorney general that the rules by which such statistical questions have been resolved by spokesmen for minority voters are wrong, will the alteration in the electoral environment that the jurisdiction proposes be accepted.

The Example of New York

The negotiations between the Justice Department and New York over the district lines for the City Council offer an excellent example of the role that statistics play in resolving districting disputes, and indirectly, in changing the distribution of power between racial and ethnic groups.[17] The City Council of New York is large—forty-five members in all, two from each of the five boroughs (counties), elected at-large, and thirty-five from single-members districts. Prior to redistricting in 1981 there were forty-three members. But between 1970 and 1980, the city suffered a serious loss of population (a drain of approximately 10 percent), and the redistricting commission, meeting after the 1980 census, expanded the size of the council to protect incumbents, especially those who were black and Hispanic. Not only had the city as a whole lost population in the decade, but districts once considered "safe" for minority councilmen were now more heavily white as a consequence of gentrification. One solution was a contraction of their

---

[17]I owe my knowledge of the New York City case to Lewis Liman, who graciously shared with me the material that he gathered in preparation for his excellent senior honors thesis, written for the Committee on Degrees in Social Studies, Harvard College, 1983. The documents all come from the firm of Paul, Weiss, Rifkind, Wharton, and Garrison, retained by the city as counsel.

boundaries, which could be accomplished only by increasing the total number of electoral districts, and that was precisely what was done. The council was expanded, in great part to preserve its minority membership. At the same time, district lines were redrawn to comply with the constitutional prohibition against population disparities.

When the plan was submitted to the Justice Department for pre-clearance, it was challenged not by incumbent minority councilmen (whom it pleased) but by civil rights groups.[18] Although the eight minority incumbents were virtually certain of retaining their seats, the size of the council was now slightly larger, and thus the minority share would drop from 18.6 to 17.8 percent, even though the minority population in the city had grown. Nevertheless, the city contended, the plan was not "retrogressive," but actually ameliorative. (In theory, only "retrogressive" plans could be denied preclearance.) Civil rights groups were both counting minority residents incorrectly and demanding an excessive concentration of minority voters to make minority districts "safe." By New York City's calculation, its plan contained fifteen such districts, nine of which had a minority concentration of over 65 percent.[19]

With census findings in hand, counting minority residents would seem straightforward. But a serious dispute arose between civil rights groups and the city over how to measure the minority population. The 1980 census had asked respondents if they were "of Spanish/Hispanic

---

[18]That incumbent minorities had been satisfied with the plan was generally acknowledged. As the *New York Times* explained, "[b]lack and Hispanic incumbents, having the same instinct for self-preservation as their white colleagues, went along with the Council plan" (September 10, 1981, p. A30). Congressman Charles B. Rangel (black) and Kenneth B. Clark, a noted black social scientist, had both publicly urged Mayor Koch to sign the reapportionment bill. Memo entitled "Summary of 1981 Reapportionment: New York City Council" submitted by Fabian G. Palomino, Counsel, The Council of the City of New York Redistricting Committee, undated. The lone voice of dissent appears to have been Councilman Gilberto Gerena-Valentin, who stated that he "would not have voted for the plan if [he] had known for sure that more minority districts could have been created," and that he believed that the redistricting commission would have placed his residence outside his current district had he voiced public opposition. Affidavit, undated.

[19]Letter from Paul, Weiss et al. to Wm. Bradford Reynolds, Assistant Attorney General for Civil Rights, September 21, 1981, p. 19. "We are satisfied that at least 15 such districts exist, that all of them exceed 53% minority population, that 9 of them exceed 75%, and that the number of minority districts on any standard has been increased from 9 to 15." Press release, undated. The city reiterates the point in many of its documents. The civil rights groups, on the other hand, predicted that whites would continue to win all ten at-large seats, and that from districts the same number of blacks and Hispanics (eight) would be returned as before; that number, they said, would represent a proportionate drop in their officeholding, given the expansion of the council. "It is shocking and inexcusable," a spokesman for the Citizens Union argued, "for minority representation to be reduced at the same time as the minority population has so substantially increased." Press release, Citizens Union of the City of New York, June 23, 1981.

origin or descent," and then, in a separate question, their race. Some Hispanics identified themselves as white, others (though far fewer) as black, and still others as "other." The question was how many in each category. In the summer and fall of 1981, when the city submitted its new districting plan to the Justice Department, the responses to the two questions had not yet been broken down, leaving unclear how many safe minority districts had been created. The number of Hispanics in each district could be readily ascertained; so too could the number of persons who identified themselves as non-white. But the two figures could not be simply added together to obtain the minority total, because an undetermined number of Hispanics reported themselves as non-white. To the extent to which such people were double-counted, the minority total would be inflated. Civil rights organizations charged that a high proportion of Hispanics identified themselves as non-white, and that the city's estimates of the total minority population in various districts was thus too high.[20]

To deal with this problem, New York City relied upon national figures supplied by the Census Bureau, which showed that 55.6 percent of all Hispanics considered themselves white, 40 percent "other," and the rest black, American Indian, Eskimo, Aleut, Asian, or Pacific Islander.[21] In coming up with the fifteen minority districts, the city had relied upon the 55.6 percent figure, the only one available at the time. As it turned out, the estimate was somewhat off for New York. A census tabulation made available on the eve of the Justice Department's objection to the plan put the proportion of New York Hispanics who identified themselves as white at 39.9 percent. Using this figure reduced the minority total in the fifteen districts significantly, though not dramatically. In any case, neither the city nor the minority spokesmen could agree on how significant these new numbers were, since they disagreed on the minority concentration required to create equal electoral opportunity.

[20]New York City Council Redistricting Commission, "Memorandum on Increase of Council Districts from Thirty-Three to Thirty-Five," June 3, 1981. "In 1970," the city's attorneys said, "over 86% of Puerto Ricans identified themselves as white." (Undated, unsigned memo in Q & A format.) Again, the point is that a great many "whites" were actually Hispanic. In fact, the number of whites, the city charged, was inflated in two ways. Not only was a certain proportion of the Hispanic population being counted as white, but groups normally identified as "minority" had been arbitrarily listed as white. Thus the Civil Liberties Union plan treated Chinese, Japanese, Koreans, South Asians, and American Indians as white. Letter, Edward N. Costikian (legal counsel to the New York City Council) to Wm. Bradford Reynolds, October 19, 1981.

[21]Memorandum to Hon. Thomas J. Cuite and Hon. Edward L. Sadowsky from Edward N. Costikian, September 16, 1981. "The Bureau of the Census," he said, "has informally advised that they know of no reason why the use of the national averages is inappropriate for the New York numbers."

There was disagreement, as well, over how to categorize those classified as "others." New York had substantial numbers of Chinese, Japanese, Koreans, South Asians, and American Indians. The size of these groups was not in dispute, but their classification was. Were these voters "white" or "minority"? The New York Civil Liberties Union placed them in the former category, the city in the latter. "[O]ne can draw no conclusions about the way 'non-Hispanic others' will vote . . . ," the NYCLU argued. "It, therefore, follows that the inclusion of 'non-Hispanic others' in calculating the total minority population within each district is unjustified and deceptive.[22] As the city pointed out, "the law is clear that the 'other' racial and language minority groups residing in New York are properly classified as non-white for purposes of the Voting Rights Act." Asian Americans and American Indians were among the minority groups specifically named in the statute as entitled to protection, and if those groups did not vote predictably, neither did blacks and Hispanics.[23] It was not a dispute that was confined to New York, alone: In a case involving Norfolk, Virginia, civil rights groups also counted Asian Americans, Native Americans, and other minorities as white.[24]

It is not the raw minority count but the number registered or voting that usually determines both the count of "minority" districts and the weight given the defendant's claim of equal electoral opportunity. Some states record the race of those who register, but they are the exception.[25] Registration and turnout figures are usually, at best, rough estimates. Even the data base may be a matter of contention. Norfolk, for instance, is a city with a major naval base, and naval personnel (77 percent white) were included in the census, could vote in municipal elections, and were counted for the purpose of state legislative redistricting. Yet in gauging relative participation rates the civil rights groups omitted consideration of that group, arguing that it did not constitute an "active electorate." Black and white registration and turnout estimates were obviously affected; in fact, had the military personnel been included, the city argued, black participation rates would have been shown to have been substantially higher than those of whites[26]—a finding that would have seriously weakened the plaintiffs' case.

In the case of New York, however, both sides skirted these complex

---

[22]"Comment Submitted by the New York Civil Liberties Union in response to the September 21, 1981 submission by Paul, Weiss, Rifkind, Wharton & Garrison Regarding the 1981 New York City Council Reapportionment Plan," October 15, 1981, pp. 19–20.

[23]Letter, Costikian to Wm. Bradford Reynolds, October 19, 1981, pp. 2–4.

[24]*Collins* v. *City of Norfolk*, 605 F. Supp. 377 (E.D. Va. 1984) Defendant's Post-Trial Brief Containing Proposed Findings of Fact and Conclusions of Law, June 20, 1984, p. 58.

[25]Georgia, Louisiana, North Carolina, and South Carolina compile voter registration data by race.

[26]*Collins* v. *City of Norfolk*, Defendant's Post-Trial Brief, p. 25; 61–64.

methodological issues. A "minority" district, the city assumed, was simply one where more than half the residents (by the census count) were non-white; that was the premise upon which its count of fifteen rested. And in such districts minority candidates could win, it argued. The prime example was a district shown in the 1970 census to be only 54 percent minority, from which, in 1977, a black had been elected to the City Council.[27] But the example impressed only the city; by 1977 blacks and Hispanics far outnumbered whites in that district, the civil rights groups argued. In any case, a fight on that front was particularly hopeless; the 54 percent figure was 11 points below the Justice Department standard. In 1981, questioned on this score, a department spokesman denied any interest in getting into a "numbers game."[28] But ten years earlier, following a challenge to the New York State legislative lines, the suggested goal for minority districts had been 65 percent, and that figure was known to be the one to which the department was committed.[29] Following that lead, civil rights groups counted as minority districts only those with at least 65 percent minority concentration, and arrived at a total much smaller than that of the city.

Of course, the number of minority districts a city can draw depends not only on the number of "minority" voters and the required level of minority concentration but on where those voters reside. The black and Hispanic population in a municipality can double, but its electoral weight will depend on how that population is distributed. The charge of "retrogression" assumed that New York could draw more minority districts; the city argued that while the minority population had grown, the number of potential minority districts had not. "[P]ervasive integration on a scale never experienced before ha[s] taken place over the decade since the prior census," a memo stated.[30] It was not the view of the civil rights groups. "New York City is no more integrated in 1981

[27]The elected black councilman was Wendell Foster. The point is made in an undated memo written by Peter W. Schneider and addressed to Edward N. Costikian, as well as elsewhere.

[28]The statement was made by James W. Turner, Acting Assistant Attorney General for Civil Rights, and was reported in the *New York Times,* September 17, 1981, p. B4.

[29]That figure made its first public appearance in *United Jewish Organization* v. *Carey,* 430 U.S. 144 (1977). Asked by New York to define an acceptably black district, the Department of Justice had mentioned 65 percent as the goal. That 65 percent districts are a "rule of thumb" is now frequently acknowledged by the department.

[30]"Harlem decreased from 32% of the black population in 1970 to 25% of the black population in 1980," the city argued. "In contrast, other widespread areas in Manhattan outside of Harlem . . . showed significant increases in the black populations" (Palomino memo, "Summary of . . ."). "In this city in the last 10 years minority population has been dispersing itself into what were formally lily-white districts," an undated press release asserted. "Every district," it went on, "except three saw an increase in the minority population. The most startling change was in Queens County. . . .In Queens, seven 1970 lily-white districts with an average 7.8% minority population had a 1980 average of 25.6% minority population."

than it was in 1970," the New York Civil Liberties Union reported.[31]
From different perspectives, the same maps apparently told different
stories.

There was, finally, the difficult issue of racial and ethnic polarization, of who voted for whom. Were whites in New York bloc-voting
against minority candidates? There was no iron law, the city argued,
that blacks could only win in safe black districts, and that black voters
were consequently unequal participants in the electoral process in every
district in which they were a numerical minority.[32] The question of racial polarization is central to any voting rights dispute, but there is no
consensus on how to measure it.[33] Statistical methods can only *estimate* the percentage of a racial or ethnic group in a particular precinct
that voted for a particular candidate. Direct information as to how individuals have voted is generally not available, and techniques that use
census data to analyze election returns at the precinct level often draw
unreliable inferences about individual voter behavior. Turnout by race
may be inaccurately gauged on the basis of voting-age population data.
Calculations must assume that voting patterns evident in some pre-

[31]"New York Civil Liberties Union Report in Opposition to the 1981 City Council
Reapportionment Plan," submitted to the U.S. Department of Justice, July, 1981, p. 7. Ce-
sar A. Perales, president and general counsel of the Puerto Rican Legal Defense & Education Fund stated that "[c]ity representatives in claiming that additional minority seats
could not be created, have attempted to deliberately mislead the Federal officials reviewing the proposed reapportionment plan. We can clearly show, that by drawing compact and
contiguous districts in the Bronx, there would result three minority Council districts, and
not the two established in the City's plan." PRLDEF press release, undated. The Citizens
Union of New York asserted that "at least 2 additional minority districts (one in Brooklyn
and one in the Bronx)" could be created. Letter addressed to James Turner, Acting Assistant Attorney General for Civil Rights, June 22, 1981.
[32]The city rested its case on that election in 1977 of Mr. Foster, the black councilman
who had been elected from a district that had a total minority population of approximately
54 percent (blacks and Puerto Ricans together). Letter from the firm to Wm. Bradford Reynolds, the Assistant Attorney General for Civil Rights, dated September 21, 1981. Likewise, in 1979 Judge Bruce Wright, a black, had received almost 60 percent of the vote in
Manhattan, although the black population for that borough was less than 22 percent. And
Mr. David Dinkins, running for Manhattan Borough President, had received 48 percent of
the vote, although the Manhattan black population had dropped a dramatic 24 percent
over the decade. (The reference to Dinkins is contained in a press release, undated; the
black population figures are contained in the Palomino memo, "Summary of . . .") There
was, as well, no iron law that blacks were always elected from black districts, the city argued. In the 1977 Democratic mayoral primary, the sole black candidate, Percy Sutton, obtained only about 50 percent of the vote in election districts that were more than 90 percent black. "[W]e do not know," Costikian wrote, "of any statistical basis for asserting
that the election of a minority candidate in this city requires a minority population in excess of any number. Whatever voting patterns may exist elsewhere, it is clear that in New
York minority members have repeatedly been elected from constituencies in which the
minority was a true minority." Memo, Costikian to Cuite and Sadowsky, September 16,
1981.
[33]The best discussion of the problem of assessing racial bloc voting is contained in
Paul W. Jacobs II and Timothy G. O'Rourke, "Racial Polarization in Vote Dilution Cases
under Section 2 of the Voting Rights Act," *Journal of Law and Politics* (forthcoming).

cincts will hold for all precincts—that black and white voters residing in different demographic and socioeconomic contexts will nevertheless behave the same at the polls. Moreover, mathematical calculations may inadequately reveal *why* voters cast their ballots as they did. As one federal judge has put it, "A healthy dose of common sense and intuitive assessment remain powerful components to this factual inquiry. For example, a token candidacy of a minority unknown outside his minority voting area may attract little non-minority support and produce a high statistical correspondence of race to loss." Yet, one truly familiar with politics in the locality "may know that race played little role at all."[34] Black candidates (like those who are white) may lose elections for a variety of reasons, including insufficient support from black constituents, the power of incumbency, inadequate name recognition, age, experience, reputation, and political orientation.

Deceptive Rhetoric

Statistics are often the language of argumentation in voting rights cases. But if statistical questions frame the debate, they also hide its substance. Behind the statistical facade lie fundamental, deeply divisive judgments. For instance, racial bloc voting may seem to be a technical question: How can we best estimate who has voted for whom? But such complex questions of methodology are, in fact, secondary. The central issue is what to do with the results, how to interpret the findings.

In a South Carolina Senate redistricting case, an expert witness for the Department of Justice argued that elections were polarized "when the black community and the white community voted differently." The test for bloc voting had been met when 50.1 percent of whites gave their support to a white whom the majority of blacks opposed.[35] Thus black exclusion would characterize every election in which, for instance, a Republican had won (since blacks are predominantly Democratic). In a case involving state legislative redistricting in North Carolina, the court found polarization in one multimember district despite the fact that two black candidates had received more than 40 percent of the white vote and had *won*. The *majority* of whites, the court observed, voted for unsuccessful whites.[36] Were elections in these two southern states in fact infected with racism, such that blacks and whites stood on unequal electoral footing? One's view of American society determines the answer. To those who see it as fundamentally racist, white victories

---

[34]*Jones* v. *City of Lubbock*, 730 F.2d 233,234 (5th Cir. 1984).
[35]*State of South Carolina* v. *U.S.*, Civil Action 83–2636, U.S. District Court for the District of Columbia, Deposition of Bernard Grofman, June 19, 1984, p. 43.
[36]*Gingles* v. *Edmisten*, 590 F. Supp. 345,370 (E.D.N.C. 1984).

over a black always contain an element of race, and 40 percent white crossover voting is only 40 percent. Moreover, blacks remain politically dependent on whites, since blacks need white support to win. To those who take a more sanguine view, a *full* 40 percent of the white electorate have backed two black candidates and ensured their victory.

In the case of New York, the issue was much the same: not the extent of white solidarity but solidarity as a sign of racial hostility. The protestations of New York to the contrary notwithstanding, the two sides did not fundamentally disagree about the likely election of a white in a district more than half white. The question was the meaning of that likely result. Disputes over the extent of racial bloc voting and the record of minority electoral success disguise the real question: how much weight to give to the fact that most whites tend to vote for whites, and blacks for blacks, in designing an electoral system?

To those who believe that American society is deeply divided racially, and that only blacks can represent black citizens, the exceptions to the general rule of racial and ethnic solidarity are insignificant. The risk of leaving minorities without a voice in the political system is too high to permit less racially conscious line-drawing. But to those impressed with the danger of classifying citizens by color, and with that of promoting racial separation, the record of sporadic minority success in majority-white districts appears full of promise. And different perspectives mean a different ordering of priorities. For instance, the New York Civil Liberties Union characterized concern about incumbents a "selfish, inappropriate consideration."[37] But the city, less impressed with the urgency of blacks and Hispanics holding office roughly in proportion to the minority population, stressed the continuity in government that the reelection of incumbents promoted.[38]

[37]"New York Civil Liberties Union Report," p. 10.
[38]"[R]etention of existing councilmanic districts is necessary to preserve both continuity within the electorate, and the historic and traditional councilmanic districts. This continuity permits a district population to develop the political mechanisms and community groups which insure that their interests are adequately considered by their council representative." Section on incumbency in memo to Edward N. Costikian from Peter W. Schneider, written in preparation for a press conference, no date. The city firmly maintained, however, that the "claim (Citizens Union) that new district Councilmanic lines were drawn to protect white incumbents [was] *unfounded* and *unfair*." Other considerations, including maximizing minority representation, came into play. Letter to James Turner from Fabian Palomino, July 22, 1981. (Other documents made this same point.) Maintaining, to the extent possible, existing district lines made sense on other grounds as well, the city argued. "The existing district lines had met the requirement of compactness, contiguity and convenience . . . [They] had the benefit of and withstood the test of time insofar as lines of communication, representation and providing such services and support as possible to communities, groups, organizations and individuals . . . Minimal alteration of existing lines would also place the least burden on the Boards of Election in the various counties of the City. Such boards have the responsibility of creating, describing and map-

Where the line is drawn between excessive concentration and undue dispersal of minority voters within and between districts also depends not on statistical information regarding voter turnout but on the weight given minority officeholding. To the civil rights groups, the risk of wasting minority voters by creating districts 65 or 75 percent minority in population appeared more acceptable than losing seats. But the city began with a different premise: that the number of black officeholders could rise, and yet real black power could nevertheless decrease. Black interests are served to the degree that representatives—black *or* white—speaking for the black community hold office. To assume, as an attorney for the city suggested, that concentrating the black and Hispanic population benefits those voters "fails to recognize that minority access to the political process can also be enhanced by placing minority voters in largely white constituencies. That way, the minorities will have a political foothold in more than one district. Otherwise, the pure white districts are free to ignore the interests of minorities with impunity."[39]

Both the city and civil rights groups laboriously pored over census figures in an effort to determine the number of "minority" districts, but they came to that required exercise with different degrees of commitment. It wasn't just that the city found ethnic and racial solidarity both less solid than alleged and less telling, or that it saw the promise of minority influence as more important than that of guaranteed control. It questioned the entitlement of blacks and Hispanics to compensation when minority leaders failed to get out the vote; that is, it doubted the justice of the 65 percent rule. And it believed the term "minority" was itself deceptive. The tendency of civil rights groups was to blur the difference between blacks and Hispanics, to see the great divide in American society as between whites, on the one hand, and minorities, on the other. Districts were thus labeled either "minority" or "white." Yet almost 40 percent of New York's Hispanics (Puerto Ricans, for the most part) classified themselves as "white" on the census questionnaire, whereas almost none checked "black." The city wondered why civil rights advocates looked at a "minority" section of the Bronx and

---

ping new election districts . . ., as well as establishing new polling places, notifying voters of changes in election districts, preparing registration lists, and transferring poll registration cards to new election districts. Further, most of these changes have to be completed prior to the first day for the circulation of designating petitions—June 16, 1981." Palomino memo. Lines that seemed well-established, legitimized over time, appeared racially gerrymandered, however, to the Puerto Rican Legal Defense & Education Fund. In fact, it accused the city of ignoring the requirements of compactness, contiguity, and convenience, and of destroying natural communities and boundaries. Press release, undated.

[39]Memo of Edward Costikian addressed to Paul Hancock, U.S. Department of Justice, January 27, 1982.

assumed a community of interest, a natural political unit. Why were minority citizens considered "fungible"?[40]

Equally questionable was the notion that all blacks (and all Hispanics) had the same interests. That they gave the same answers to the census taker did not demonstrate group cohesion on political matters. Figures on the racial and ethnic makeup of the population, the city contended, did not mark the boundaries of distinct political interest groups.

It is tempting to side with the civil rights groups and the Justice Department, and to argue that the numbers speak for themselves: that discrimination is unmistakable, for instance, when a given distribution of blacks and Hispanics reveals a potential for more minority districts than planned. But such a view would be a tribute not to the truth of the statistical assertion but rather to the success of professional civil rights spokesmen and the Department of Justice in obscuring the difference between the numbers that told all—the figures for black registration in the South in 1965—and those that are usually suggestive but never definitive. The data upon which the outcome of a preclearance review will often depend are frequently of questionable worth. Equally important, the seeming objectivity of numbers works to conceal subjective judgment; allegedly simple statistical questions obscure complex normative issues.

Further Amendments

In August 1975, the special (temporary) sections of the statute were again due to expire, and the process of renewal was once more an occasion for revision. There was initially little expectation that the act would be further strengthened. With the Republicans in the White House, black organizations set their sights on a straight five-year exten-

---

[40]Letter, Palomino to Turner, August 5, 1981. Palomino argued, in fact, that there were "distinctly identifiable minorities such as Hispanic" for whom "separate districts" had to be created. "They may not be homogenized with other minorities, as suggested by the CLU, merely to create additional 'minority districts,'" he wrote. "That would be as discriminatory as homogenizing them into white districts and denied separate representation" [sic]. See also letter of February 8, 1982, from Costikian to Paul Hancock: "It is simply inaccurate and misleading to describe the so-called 'minority concentration' outlined by the Citizens Union as a single, homogeneous 'community.' In fact, the rather large geographical area identified by the Citizens Union is characterized by diverse and rapidly changing types of residential and commercial development, and contains persons of widely varying national, ethnic and socioeconomic origin and status. To describe this area as a 'community' simply because a majority of its residents are either black or Hispanic is to rob the term of any useful meaning, and indeed to adopt a view of minority persons that smacks of racial stereotyping."

sion. But the new definition of enfranchisement—the commitment to ensuring not just a vote but a voice—had an unexpected effect. It mobilized the Mexican American community to demand the same extraordinary protection accorded blacks. As the 1965 act and 1970 amendments had been interpreted, Mississippi cities could annex no territory, move no polling place, without federal approval. San Antonio, Texas, however, could freely alter its municipal boundaries (with a consequent change in the city's ethnic balance) without abandoning its at-large method of voting. Most important, redistricting in Texas following each decennial census was not subject to federal oversight.

Yet providing protection for Southwest Hispanics posed a number of problems. Coverage required not only the cooperation of reluctant black organizations, who feared for the life of the entire act were alterations to be proposed, but different statutory language as well. Texas was the state Mexican American spokesmen most wanted covered, yet it had never had a literacy test. The chief means used to disfranchise blacks in the South had never been employed in Texas. The presence of a literacy test had been an essential component in the "trigger" for coverage designed in 1965. Turnout figures were included only as a means of identifying its fraudulent use. The link between Fifteenth Amendment violations, low turnout, and a literacy test was viewed as well-established, while that between disfranchisement and low turnout, alone, was seen as speculative. A low level of political participation, the framers of the Voting Rights Act understood, could have many causes; whites, after all, often went to the polls in low numbers. Absent a device by which registrants could be screened by race, black disfranchisement could not be inferred. Covering Mexican Americans in Texas thus required different assumptions and different statutory language.

There was an additional problem. Were Mexican Americans a racial group? The statute secured Fifteenth Amendment rights, protecting against denial or abridgment of the right to vote on account of "race or color." If Mexican Americans were white, they were ineligible for protection. A history of discrimination suggested that they had been treated as a racial group, it could have been argued, and, in fact, the Justice Department indicated that in implementing the act, it had assumed Mexican Americans in already covered jurisdictions to be non-white.[41] Yet Congressman Herman Badillo of New York objected to the racial designation, the Census Bureau had historically (with the exception of

[41]Hearings on Extension of the Voting Rights Act Before the Subcommittee on Constitutional Rights of the Committee on the Judiciary, U.S. Senate, 94th Congress, 1st sess., 1975, p. 698.

1930) classified Mexican Americans as white, and a substantial number of Hispanics continued to think of themselves as white. Just how many was of course an issue in the New York case.

In solving this cluster of difficulties, Congress again substantially altered the act. It simply skirted the problem of having to designate Mexican Americans a racial group. A new term was found: "language minority." And because the Fifteenth Amendment could not be stretched to protect against disfranchisement on account of linguistic identity, the base of the act was broadened to include the Fourteenth as well.

But how to cover states that did not use a "test or device" to screen potential registrants? That problem was solved by redefining such a test—by equating the provision of ballots or other voting materials only in English with the fraudulent southern literacy test used to bar blacks from the polls. Thus the act was amended to apply to states or counties that met the traditional low turnout test, and in which (in addition) elections were conducted only in English and more than 5 percent of the voting-age citizenry were members of a single "language minority" group. The entire states of Texas, Arizona, and Alaska, as well as scattered counties in California, Colorado, Florida, New Mexico, and South Dakota, among others, were henceforth required to submit for federal review annexations, redistricting, and all other changes in electoral procedure.

The list of covered jurisdictions would have been considerably longer had not the term "language minority" been carefully defined. The principle was denial or abridgment of the right to vote on account of language. But lest that principle be interpreted literally—lest anyone think that Italians or French, in sufficient concentrations, were eligible for protection—four groups were specifically named: Asian Americans, Alaskan Natives, American Indians, and persons of Spanish heritage. Why these groups and no others? Or why not just Mexican Americans? The act provided extensive protection for certain groups whose distinctive characteristics were never explained.

Other important changes were made in 1975. The national ban on literacy tests was made permanent. The trigger was once again updated to include the turnout figures for November 1972. In addition, bilingual election materials were required in every state or county that met the criteria of the new trigger: English-only ballots and a language minority concentration in the context of low voter turnout. Bilingual ballots and other material were also obligatory in every county (whatever the level of electoral participation) where the minority-language citizens had an illiteracy rate higher than the national average. Illiteracy was defined as "failure to complete the fifth primary grade."

The Use of Statistics as a Subterfuge

After 1975, in the Southwest and elsewhere, the continuing freedom of states and counties to shape their electoral procedures to meet their particular needs obviously depended heavily on what the census revealed. The census determined whether more than 5 percent of the citizens of voting age in a jurisdiction were members of one of the four named language minority groups. The registration and turnout figures for 1972 were collected and reported by the Census Bureau. And for information on the illiteracy rate of the sufficiently concentrated language minorities, the Justice Department also turned to the census. These determinations were not subject to judicial review, yet the counts of citizens of "Spanish heritage," particularly, were far from conclusive. The census did collect data on persons of Spanish surname, but only for the Southwest. For New York, New Jersey, and Pennsylvania, the census counted only citizens of Puerto Rican birth and parentage. For third-generation Puerto Ricans and other Hispanics outside the Southwest, it used data on mother tongue—data, that is, on the language spoken in the household in which the person grew up, and based on a 15 percent sample which included aliens as well as citizens.

The count was more accurate for other groups. Specific census questions identified American Indians, Alaskan Natives, Koreans, Japanese, Chinese, and Filipinos. Yet there remained a serious problem. A concentration of Koreans or Japanese did not indicate the presence of citizens whose status as members of a "language minority" placed them at a disadvantage in the electoral process. The 1965 act had permitted an inference of discrimination from the joint presence of literacy tests and low levels of voter participation. Now, the act permitted an inference of discrimination where registration or voting was below the 50 percent mark and the state provided no bilingual ballots for Filipinos, Japanese, and other designated language minorities.

The original act had used an impact test (low turnout as determined by the director of the census) to identify the intentionally fraudulent use of literacy tests. Such tests were assumed to have been purposefully manipulated to accomplish a desired end: black disfranchisement. But that crucial element of implicit intention was entirely absent from the amended 1975 trigger. There was no suggestion that where language minorities were concentrated, election materials had been printed exclusively in English for the purpose of keeping otherwise qualified voters from the polls.

The point is not that requiring bilingual ballots is unwarranted absent a showing that their omission was purposefully discriminatory. If limited English discourages Mexican Americans from voting, the interest of the state in maximizing political participation perhaps suggests a need for election materials in Spanish. The provision of such materials, however, would appear to solve the problem. In 1965, framers of the legislation feared that suspending literacy tests might not be enough; southern states would invent new methods of disfranchisement—hence the preclearance requirement, as a prophylactic measure. But it was precisely the historic commitment of these states to keep blacks from the polls that was the source of concern, and no equivalent commitment had been shown to underlie the use of election materials exclusively in English in the Southwest and elsewhere. There was, in other words, no reason to assume that the provision of ballots in Spanish and a consequent rise in Mexican American registration would trigger new disfranchising efforts. And thus the absence of bilingual ballots (in conjunction with low voter participation) could not justify, as the presence of a traditional literacy test had, the imposition of the preclearance requirement on those newly covered jurisdictions.

The traditional logic did not work, but it was not meant to be closely examined. The coverage formula was devised as a means of reaching districting plans and other aspects of the electoral environment that the Mexican American groups believed to be discriminatory. That is, no one ever believed the primary problem in the Southwest and elsewhere to be the disfranchising effect of English-only election material. The equation with the southern literacy test was legally satisfying but not otherwise convincing. The point of the 1975 amendments—unlike that of the 1965 act—was not access to the polls for citizens disfranchised in clear violation of the Fifteenth Amendment but increased protection for minority candidates by means of advantageously drawn single-member districts. In 1965 the preclearance provision was a means of reinforcing the suspension of literacy tests; in 1975 the definition of literacy tests was amended to secure the benefits that preclearance brought.

The act was again amended in 1982, but the trigger was, for the first time, not revised. No additional groups were identified as in need of protection; there was no new reliance on voting and registration figures from elections subsequent to the last statutory revisions (those of 1976 and 1980); and the number of jurisdictions covered therefore remained the same.

A little-used provision in the act was altered, however, enabling plaintiffs in covered and noncovered jurisdictions alike to prevail if the method of voting in question, whatever its purpose, was discriminatory in "result."[42] The logical question that followed the revision of the stat-

---

[42]The revised provision was section 2 of the act.

ute in 1970, in other words, had finally surfaced: if New York, then why not Chicago? If federal protection against disadvantageous districting plans is provided for blacks and Hispanics in some cities, then why not for minority voters in all others?

The new amendment heightened the relevance of statistics on the number and location of the minority population, minority officeholders, and racial and ethnic voting patterns. Where the number of black and Hispanic legislators is disproportionately low; where whites, blacks, and Hispanics tend to vote for their own; and where the geographical distribution of the minority population suggests a potential for more minority seats, district lines that disadvantage minority candidates and at-large methods of voting are now unlikely to survive.

The distance traveled since 1965 has obviously been great. National statistics were initially used, and with remarkable accuracy, to identify jurisdictions systematically violating voting rights. Already by 1970, however, quite a different destination had been selected. The end became not increased access to the polls for blacks long barred but the redistribution of political power. Alterations in the statistical test that identified discriminatory jurisdictions furthered that goal, and the use of numerical data both to establish the discriminatory purpose or impact of a change in the method of voting and to guide the design of a remedial plan became the means of attaining it. But while the initial aim of the act was precisely as stated—securing the right to vote for long-disfranchised southern blacks—that which replaced it was buried in distracting statistical rhetoric. Numbers had become the means of both implementing and concealing a fundamental legislative change.

Alterations in the statistical "trigger" in 1970 and 1975 first put jurisdictions with no history of denying voting rights under the extraordinary federal control which the Voting Rights Act allowed. The changes also extended protection to groups whose experience had not been comparable to that of blacks. The 1982 amendment was a culmination of that process. If promise and performance match, it will largely obliterate the distinction between North and South—between those states and counties that deserved to lose their traditional right to set their own electoral rules, and those in which blacks and Hispanics had long been influential political participants. If so, then national statistics will be used nationally to ensure the "fair and effective" representation of certain, specifically designated racial and ethnic groups. And the move from the conviction that no citizen should be denied the right to vote on account of race or color to a belief in a legally protected "just" distribution of legislative seats, skillfully packaged in statistical rhetoric, will be complete.

PART IV
Statistics and American Federalism

10

THE POLITICS OF PRINTOUTS: THE USE OF OFFICIAL NUMBERS TO ALLOCATE FEDERAL GRANTS-IN-AID

RICHARD P. NATHAN

FEDERAL grants-in-aid to state and local governments, expressed as a percentage of the general revenue raised by state and local governments, tripled from 10 percent in the mid-1950s to 30 percent in the mid-1980s. This growth substantially outpaced inflation. Based on federal budget data, federal grants to states and localities rose from $10 billion in 1964 to nearly $100 billion in 1984. In the process, not surprisingly, the form of federal aid also changed. In the 1970s, there was a shift to larger, more flexible, and more automatic programs as expressed in "the revenue sharing idea." These new forms of intergovernmental fiscal subvention are the focus of this chapter. Large amounts of federal funds under these programs (both revenue-sharing and block grants) have been distributed to state and local governmental jurisdictions on the basis of formulas that use official data from the U.S. Bureau of the Census. This shift to broader grants has had an important behavioral impact that can be described as a movement from pork barrel politics to printout politics.

The growth of broad formula grants and the emergence of printout politics in domestic policymaking have three main causes. One is a function of the sheer size of federal grants. As this aid stream grew, logistics alone required larger and more easily managed grants. The role of federal grants as a major revenue source in domestic public finances simply outgrew the capacity of federal agency officials to make project-by-project awards and then oversee these projects individually.

Technology also played a role in this shift to broader, less conditional, and more automatic federal aid flows. Computers came of age and allowed policymakers to develop more elaborate formulas and then modify and test them quickly in the political cauldron.

Politics, too, had a role in the rise of these newer grant forms. Nixon's New Federalism program featuring revenue-sharing and block grants grew out of the frustrations of the 1960s with the "proliferation" of federal grants. Walter Heller, chairman of President Johnson's Council of Economic Advisers, referred to this problem as "the hardening of the categories." An anecdote helps make the point.

Late in 1966, Senator Edmund S. Muskie, chairman of the U.S. Senate Subcommittee on Intergovernmental Relations, held a well-publicized series of hearings on the problems of managing federal grants. Robert F. Kennedy, then a senator from New York, was on this subcommittee, and on the final day of hearings, John T. Connor, the secretary of commerce, was a witness. Kennedy observed that "the proliferation of these grant programs over a period really of thirty years has created tremendous difficulties of administration."[1] He spoke of a mayor whose community he visited, telling "the people how marvelous we have been to them in passing all these glorious programs, you know, 30 more education programs, 14 more health programs, 17 more sewer programs, or whatever they are. But the local official cannot find out what they are and where in heaven's name can he go to learn more about them or how they can benefit his community."[2] Secretary Connor responded by describing a new computerized information system being developed to centralize information about federal grants, but the senator was not satisfied. Yes, said Kennedy, after identifying all of the ingredients of a program, the mayor would "stick it in a machine and out of it [would come] something saying, '*Vote Republican.*'"[3]

The complexities of categorical grant programs stimulated support for automatic federal aid that would give states and localities greater discretion. President Johnson was at first intrigued by the revenue-sharing idea when Walter Heller, chairman of the Council of Economic Advisors, proposed it to him, but soon afterward shifted his ground. Revenue-sharing and block grants then became "Republican alternatives" to the Great Society. As president in the early 1970s, Richard Nixon championed and won enactment of a large "general revenue-

[1]Committee on Governmental Operations, Subcommittee on Intergovernmental Relations, *Creative Federalism*, 89th Congress, 2nd sess., p. 368.

[2]Ibid., p. 370.

[3]Ibid., p. 371. Emphasis added.

sharing program" ($7 billion per year at the outset) and a number of what he called "special revenue-sharing programs," now referred to as block grants. The community development and the manpower block grants were the two main block grants enacted as a result of Nixon's efforts.

The remainder of this chapter explores the way in which data collected by the Bureau of the Census are used in decisions about the allocation of federal grants-in-aid to state and local governments under revenue-sharing and the community development block grant (CDBG). The revenue-sharing program ended in 1986; the CDBG program continues in existence. The two programs are important for understanding the major changes that occurred in federal grant-making in the 1970s.

Both of these programs provide aid from the federal government *directly* to local governments (cities, counties, townships). As a class, direct federal-local grants are relatively new; they began in the post–World War II period. Previously almost all federal funds were paid to the states. However, computers facilitated direct federal-local grants, which for tactical and political reasons as well, grew substantially in the Republican years of the 1970s. The revenue-sharing program enacted under Nixon provided 70 percent of its funds directly to local units when initiated in 1972. Under President Carter, state governments were removed from revenue-sharing, and all funds ($4.5 billion in fiscal year 1984) were provided directly from Washington to localities. Three quarters of the funds distributed under the community development block grant ($3.5 billion in fiscal 1984) went to local governments.

The federal-local link creates extraordinary problems. Although federal funds under both programs flow directly to local subdivisions, the boundaries, functions, and finances of these units are not centrally determined. In 1977 there were 38,726 general-purpose units of local government in the United States, according to the Census Bureau's quinquennial canvass, which is the ultimate authority for the political geography on which federal allocations are based. Moreover, these multitudinous local subdivisions do different things and have highly varied fiscal systems.

Another major characteristic of modern American federalism poses a formidable challenge. Local governments overlap, and they overlap in different ways. Sometimes there are as many as four layers (town, city, county, and school and special districts) in a community. In other, less frequent cases, there are no overlying local governments. New York City has only two overlying special-district governments; by contrast, the 1977 Census of Governments shows 520 local governments serving the people who live in the city of Chicago.

The role of policymakers in writing formulas involves more than overcoming these technical challenges. The formulas express values—beliefs about a just distribution—through special factors that differentiate among types of local governments. Some local governments get *more* on a per capita basis than others. Some are awarded larger per capita funds because they do more; some because they exert greater effort; and some because they have greater need. Measuring need involves "equalization" or what is often called "targeting," that is, targeting federal resources on the most needy individuals and communities.

We now turn to the two programs—general revenue-sharing and CDBG—before addressing more basic political issues. Much of the discussion is based on personal experience working on these programs in and out of government.

Revenue-Sharing

When the U.S. House Ways and Means Committee reported its version of the revenue-sharing bill that was eventually enacted in 1972, one dissatisfied member, after describing the committee's effort to develop an acceptable allocation formula, concluded: "We finally quit, not because we hit on a rational formula but because we were exhausted. And finally we got one that almost none of us could understand at the moment."[4]

Two decisions made by Nixon and others were responsible for the difficulty in devising a formula: First, all local governments were to be aided, and second, the formula was to include a needs or targeting factor. It would have been possible to take the opposite position on both issues. The original revenue-sharing proposal made to President Johnson by Walter Heller and Joseph Pechman, director of economic studies at The Brookings Institution, called for allocations exclusively to the states. The states, in turn, were to decide how to apportion these funds within their borders. This was the view of many experts on American federalism, who cited "Dillon's rule"[5] that local governments are

[4]Rep. James C. Corman (D-Calif.), cited in *Monitoring Revenue Sharing* by Richard P. Nathan, Allen D. Manvel, Susannah E. Calkins, and Associates (Washington, D.C.: Brookings Institution, 1975), p. 135. Much of the analysis in this chapter is based on this book, which contains detailed information on the history and operation of the formula for allocating revenue-sharing funds. I am indebted to Allen D. Manvel, my colleague at The Brookings Institution, who played the lead role in this part of our analysis and who provided helpful comments on an earlier draft of this chapter.

[5]John F. Dillon, an Iowa Supreme Court justice and the author of a standard treatise on municipal law, said in a decision in 1868 that municipal corporations "owe their origin to, and derive their powers and rights wholly from, the state legislature." *City of Clinton* v. *Cedar Rapids and Missouri RR. Co.*, 24 Iowa 475 (1868).

creatures of the states and that the federal government therefore should not enter into direct relations with them.

The argument to include localities was both technical and political. It was technical in the sense that the newly available data processing technology made it easier to do. It was political in the sense that including the localities made the legislation easier to pass. Nixon faced a Democratic Congress that was, to say the least, highly receptive to the arguments of the mayors for including the cities in revenue-sharing. Revenue-sharing thereby became the first grant program that covers all local governments in the nation. Previous grant programs tended to provide aid to localities on a project (as opposed to a formula) basis, and then only for some special purpose, such as public housing, airports, urban renewal, or model cities.

The second major decision—to include equalization features in the formula—could also have gone the other way. Shared revenue might have been allocated on a straight per capita basis.[6] However, Nixon, his advisers, and other participants in the decision process believed it necessary to incorporate measures of need and tax effort. Not everyone agreed. Caspar Weinberger, then deputy director of the Office of Management and Budget (OMB), objected to the tax-effort factor on the grounds that jurisdictions ought not to be rewarded for their high taxes. Weinberger's argument did not prevail, and from quite another vantage point, it was a good thing it did not. The tax-effort factor prevents areas with many overlying governments from getting a disproportionately large share of aid compared to areas where local governments are not "layered."

When the dust settled, there were over 38,000 jurisdictions—states, counties, cities, and Indian tribes—eligible to receive federal shared revenue. Some of the units to be aided were so small that the only statistic that could be used with confidence was their decennial population.[7]

Revenue-Sharing Data Needs

Three main types of official numbers are needed to operate the revenue-sharing formula: population, income, and revenue. The latter requires that taxes, intergovernmental revenue, and public school ex-

---

[6]Strictly speaking, this, too, is an equalization approach, that is, in relation to the sources of revenue raised.

[7]All governments eligible for more than $200 in revenue-sharing payments per annum were given funds. In the final analysis, Congress decided that, for small governments, the secretary of the treasury should have authority to use income and financial data of the overlying county on a per capita basis as a proxy for local statistics.

penditures be known for each locality to arrive at the figure the formula requires—"own-raised nonschool" revenue. Although one special canvass was conducted in 1972, the basic data came from U.S. Census of Governments. These numbers were not collected to serve the revenue-sharing program.

Revenue-sharing began in 1972. Population and income figures from the 1970 decennial census were still fresh and could be used with reasonable confidence. In later years, the Census Bureau updated these figures by estimates from birth, death, and other local records. These updated estimates posed problems. The data demands of the revenue-sharing formula and the tight time schedule for its implementation placed a strain on the Census Bureau's system for collecting information about local governments. Revenue-sharing also increased the need for accuracy. Figures collected by the federal government for descriptive purposes—mainly by mail questionnaires and on a voluntary basis from officials of thousands of local governments—were now being called upon in the allocation of large amounts of money.

To make matters more complicated, the allocation formula was in flux throughout the original legislative deliberations. The Senate and House passed different formulas for allocating shared revenue to state areas. The Senate adopted a three-factor formula that favored rural and smaller states; the House, a five-factor formula more favorable to urban states. The Solomon-like compromise struck at the last minute consisted of having each state receive its allocation under whatever formula was more favorable to that state, with total allocations prorated down to fit the total amount of money authorized. The original act provided funds for five years; however, revenue-sharing was extended in 1976, 1980, and 1983 without modifications in the allocation formula.[8]

"An Old Formula Is a Good Formula"

The problems and anomalies of the distribution formula—for example, defects in the measurement of fiscal capacity and tax effort and in the treatment of county governments—received close scrutiny from experts. But despite the consensus among experts that serious (though not overwhelming) problems needed attention, the formula *status quo* was maintained. This point merits comment.

Although technicians persuaded the interested political officials in the executive branch and on Capitol Hill that there were problems of some consequence with the formula, the problems were not seen as serious enough. The political system had labored and produced a work-

[8]As noted earlier, the revenue-sharing program expired in 1986.

able, widely accepted allocation formula; Congress was not willing to reopen the debate. The defects were never repaired.

It is interesting that the most serious challenges to the revenue-sharing allocation system arose in the courts when population data from the 1980 decennial census were introduced into the system. Complaints came from big-city governments about the undercount of their residents, particularly members of minority groups. Highly exaggerated (in fact, inaccurate) claims were made of losses of as much as $200 per uncounted citizen. A number of court cases ensued, but no adjustment was made for the census undercount.[9]

The Community Development Block Grant

Enacted in 1974, CDBG, like revenue-sharing, was a Nixon New Federalism initiative proposed as means of furthering decentralization.[10] The act consolidated into one block grant several programs administered by the U.S. Department of Housing and Urban Development (HUD) and provided discretionary grant funds for smaller communities. The programs consolidated into CDBG were urban renewal, the neighborhood development program (successor to urban renewal), model cities, water and sewer grants, neighborhood facilities, open spaces, and loans for public facilities.

This block grant legislation authorized $2.5 billion in the first year and $3 billion in the second and third years for a wide variety of eligible community development activities. It emphasized physical development projects, although public service spending was also permitted. The program was extended in 1977, 1980, and 1983, each time for an ad-

---

[9]Such undercount adjustments had been computed, but not used, in the recent census. Some experts tried to show that an adjustment in 1980 would not have had the effects claimed. In fact, in some protesting cities, it would have resulted in less federal aid. See Arthur V. Maurice and Richard P. Nathan, "The Census Undercount: Effects on Federal Aid to Cities," *Urban Affairs Quarterly* 17 (March 1982):251–284.

The only time the decennial population census has been adjusted was in 1870 after the Civil War because the figures seemed out of line and it was argued that the impact of the Civil War had affected the completeness of the count. I am indebted to Conrad Taeuber for correcting an error in this footnote in an earlier version of this chapter and for providing additional information used above.

When this chapter was completed, the New York City case seeking an adjustment of the 1980 population census was pending. The author, along with many others, entered the discussion with an affidavit; I argued against an adjustment on the grounds that its allocation effects cannot be known and are likely to be surprising, diverse, and counterintuitive.

[10]I am indebted to my former Brookings colleague, Paul R. Dommel, for his substantial assistance on this section. For more information on this program, see Paul R. Dommel and Associates, *Decentralizing Urban Policy: Case Studies in Community Development* (Washington, D.C.: Brookings Institution, 1982).

ditional three years. In 1981 funding for the CDBG program was reduced under President Reagan by 13 percent, and the funds for small cities were allocated to state governments for distribution, rather than having them distributed by the secretary of HUD.[11]

Understanding the CDBG allocation system requires a knowledge of some formula-writing jargon. One term is *hold harmless*, which refers to the idea that a jurisdiction should not lose when a new grant allocation system comes into effect. A second concept is *folded-in* programs—those consolidated into a block grant. A third is the *lumpiness* of grants. Capital grants are lumpy in the sense that they are received by jurisdictions in spurts rather than in an even flow. Now, we can put all of our jargon together in one statement: The conclusion of many participants in the CDBG policymaking process was that, because of the *lumpiness* of many of the categorical grants *folded into* the new CDBG program, it was decided that recipient jurisdictions should be *held harmless* for a time—but not indefinitely.

Based on this analysis, formula writers involved in the CDBG decision process in 1974 devised what they called a "declining hold-harmless provision" for the CDBG formula. Recipient governments in the first three years of the CDBG program would receive either an amount set in the new formula or the average of the amounts received under the grants folded into the new block grant over the five-year period, 1968 to 1972, whichever was higher.[12] The hold-harmless provision was to be phased out, beginning in the fourth year of the CDBG program, by one-third each year. The goal was that, by the sixth year, the program would be operating fully under the new allocation system established in the original 1974 law. Communities receiving hold-harmless grants, but without formula entitlements, would then shift over to the discretionary part of the CDBG fund to compete with other small communities for block grant money.

Steps in the Allocation Process

The new CDBG formula allocation system when fully effective is best understood as a series of steps. The first step is the division of

---

[11]See John William Ellwood, ed., *Reductions in U.S. Domestic Spending: How They Affect State and Local Governments* (New Brunswick, N.J.: Transaction Books, 1982), p. 168. Further cuts have been proposed by Reagan since 1981; a 10 percent reduction was proposed for fiscal year 1986.

[12]For a full explanation of the operation of the formula, see Richard P. Nathan, Paul R. Dommel, Sarah F. Liebschutz, Milton D. Morris, and Associates, *Block Grants for Community Development* (Washington, D.C.: U.S. Department of Housing and Urban Development, 1977).

funds between metropolitan and nonmetropolitan areas. The second step is the allocation of funds for each type of jurisdiction (cities and urban counties), after setting aside some funds to be distributed by the secretary of HUD on a discretionary basis. A crucial point in the operation of the original system is that, as the hold-harmless provision was phased out, a large part of that money was designated to go into the discretionary fund for distribution to small communities in metropolitan areas.

For the central cities of standard metropolitan statistical areas, all of which are entitled to aid under CDBG, the formula in the 1974 act used three main factors: population, overcrowded housing, and poverty (double weighted). The housing and poverty data were drawn from the 1970 census; initially, the population data also came from the 1970 census, but annual updating based on estimates was subsequently employed.

As in revenue-sharing, the formula was built on the existing official numbers and political geography. In particular, the concept of a "central city" (clearly an artifact) now came to be a matter of big money. This increased the importance after 1974 of OMB's designation of standard metropolitan statistical areas. However, no new numbers or census geography came into being for the CDBG program. An "urban county" eligible for aid is simply a large county, that is, one over 200,000 in population. The inclusion of urban counties was a victory for the National Association of Counties, which also made sure that county governments—all 3,042 of them—received revenue-sharing payments.

The Impact of the Formula

On close examination, the new CDBG formula was found to have a decidedly different allocational pattern from that implied in the speeches and commentaries of the people involved in its adoption. The situation was unusual. Because of the declining hold-harmless arrangement, the new act expired before the new formula took effect fully in the sixth year of the program. Moreover, there were indications that the framers of the act felt that the formula "was not quite right" but that there would be an opportunity to fix it later on. The original law specifically directed HUD to study the formula to determine how well it distributed the money relative to community development needs (Sec. 106[1]).

It was in this setting that The Brookings Institution entered into a contract with HUD to undertake an evaluation of the CDBG program, which included a study of the allocation system. We concluded that when fully in effect the formula would lack what we referred to as "urban focus." The formula shifted funds from large cities and distressed cities to smaller and better-off jurisdictions, many of which had received very little or no aid under the folded-in programs. By law, the share of funds to metropolitan areas (SMSAs) declined immediately from 87.4 percent in the hold-harmless base to 80 percent, with the other 20 percent being earmarked for nonmetropolitan areas.[13] The share received by central cities declined from 71.8 percent in the hold-harmless base to 42.2 percent under full formula funding.[14] We stressed that the standard used—"urban focus"—was derived from what many of the authors of the law had said about its goals when it was debated.

Previously, we had experimented with various statistical index techniques designed to show the relative socioeconomic condition of cities. We used these techniques to analyze the CDBG formula and concluded that the original formula did not reflect the physical development needs of old industrial cities, which have problems associated with aging infrastructure and industries not easily captured in census data. To deal with this problem, we suggested the use of an available census statistic—age of housing—as a proxy for the age of cities and the conditions of their infrastructure. Our judgment was that the results generated by using age-of-housing data as a proxy indicator was a feasible one for taking into account this widely perceived physical dimension of "urban focus." After reviewing a number of possible formulas, we recommended one alternative, a "dual formula" that seemed to us to correct the lack of "urban focus."

The Dual Formula

The dual approach that we suggested in our report retained the original formula for all jurisdictions that would be better off under that formula. These tend to be growing cities, particularly in the South, many with high levels of poverty. At the same time, we suggested a second formula, including the number of pre-1940 housing units, that would more strongly reflect physical development needs. Jurisdictions would receive their CDBG allocation on the basis of the second formula if it was more favorable to them. To prevent any jurisdiction from losing as a result, it was necessary to provide additional money—in effect, to "buy" the new formula. We suggested that most of the additional money be taken from the metropolitan discretionary fund.

Although skepticism initially greeted the idea of a dual formula, the Ford administration endorsed it in 1977. We expected (as did others)

[13]Nathan et al., *Block Grants for Community Development*, p. 179.
[14]Ibid., p. 180.

that President Ford's defeat in the 1976 election would doom this proposal, but the Carter administration made minor changes and claimed the idea, with the modest revisions, as its own. Despite strong protests by members of Congress from newer cities that the existence of old (for example, "Georgetown") housing was a bad test of urban need, the dual formula remains in effect.

The CDBG case was unusual. While it violates the earlier maxim that "an old formula is a good formula," the changes made in this instance reflected the seriousness of the problems. The purposes of the original legislation were not being served by the original formula. The system was modified, but in a manner that drew on the available supply of official numbers, and new money was provided to prevent any losses to existing recipients.

The two major cases studied here are significantly different, but their implications for domestic policy are similar; I turn now to this final subject.

Conclusion

A new form of political discourse and action emerged in domestic policymaking in the 1970s—the politics of printouts. No member of Congress today would vote on an important grant-in-aid formula without a printout to see who wins and who loses. Of course, negotiating about who wins and who loses is not new. But it was speeded up (in a sense, made more productive) by the new information-processing technology—a technology ideally suited to formula writing under conditions where the stakes involved warrant the costs of high-speed data.

What has been the result of printout politics? The technology may have made the outcomes more "distributive," to use Theodore Lowi's term[15]; that is, it may have reduced the targeting effect, since legislators now have better information about how to spread benefits to their districts. But one needs to be cautious on this point. Federal aid payments have never been highly targeted. Moreover, the rapid growth of Sunbelt cities and suburban jurisdictions undoubtedly was a strong underlying reason for the allocation patterns that occurred under the new grant programs of the 1970s.

To summarize, the technology may have facilitated the use of direct federal-local formula grants, and it may have influenced the outcome in the direction of being more broadly distributed than would otherwise have been the case. But we are not in a position to know the

---

[15]Theodore J. Lowi, *The End of Liberalism* (New York: Norton, 1969), part III.

counterfactual, that is, what would have happened if computers had not been invented and large and direct federal formula grants to localities had not emerged.

Did policy and institutional changes affect the form and format of official numbers? In this case, the underlying data—the official numbers—were not changed because of the establishment of direct federal-local formula grant programs and the politics of printouts. Old numbers were simply used for new jobs. There was a modest amount of updating, but no basic revision of the Census of Governments or, as far as I know, of any other Census Bureau concepts and data series. The use of the age-of-housing data as a proxy for city age in the CDBG formula illustrates this point. These data were used for lack of better numbers and tested in the cauldron of printout politics. Once their use had been legitimized, it was not easy—or apparently desirable—to change this element of the formula. New data are rarely needed because so many ways are available to work out formulas with existing data that do what policymakers want to do. Moreover, the decision process moves rapidly once serious formula writing gets underway. It is not easy to stop this train and lay new tracks once it has left the station.

But there is no question that the use of statistical formulas for distributing revenue put statistical policy under a political spotlight. The legal challenges to the 1980 census reflected the increased fiscal importance of the data. The official designation of standard metropolitan statistical areas became a point of political conflict because money began to ride on the designations. The politics of printouts did not generate new data, but it did generate a new politics of statistics and statistical geography.

11

FEDERAL STATISTICS IN LOCAL GOVERNMENTS

JUDITH INNES DE NEUFVILLE

FOR DECADES the federal government has used statistics to carry out policy at the local level. Accordingly, much of the local statistical enterprise has evolved in response to federal statistical requirements. Federal programs provided the original impetus and funding, and the changing forms of federalism have left their stamp on local institutions, attitudes, and statistical practices.

Two important periods in the federal grant system since World War II may be distinguished, each of which had significant, but different, impacts on local statistical activity. The first, from 1946 to 1970, involved predominantly categorical grants; the second, since 1970, involved mainly block grants and revenue-sharing. Categorical grants were awarded to local entities for programs defined by the federal agencies. Local agencies wrote proposals that were judged competitively, with the amount of funding depending on the project. The grants of the 1970s, on the other hand, went to jurisdictions automatically on the basis of sta-

NOTE: The research for this chapter was done with the assistance of Anne Winchester. Associates on an earlier project, Vicki Elmer, formerly of HUD's Region IX office, and Diane Laufman also contributed to the research and ideas. I am grateful to the following persons who read and commented on versions of this chapter: Duncan MacRae, Richard Rockwell, Peter Groat, Dennis Barry, Linda Moulton, Walter Postle, William Schooling, Ray Brady, Andrew Isserman, Michael Teitz, Judith Gruber, and Michele Solloway, in addition to the editors of this volume. Finally I want to thank the many busy data analysts and data users who took time to talk with us.

tistical formulas and provided only rough guidelines, if any, about the activities that could be supported by the funds.

These grants shaped local institutions and programs and became central to local policymaking. Grants have had such influence because revenue sources available to local governments have always been highly limited. Local taxes are visible, and increases are strongly resisted. Only a tiny percentage of locally raised funds have traditionally been available for discretionary spending, and federal funds provided the opportunity for innovation and for new programs benefiting many local groups. The statistics required for the grants accordingly gained considerable visibility and affected local expectations and norms for the application of statistics. The markedly different local effects of the two types of grant programs reflect fundamental differences in the role statistics had in each.

The Categorical Programs: Building Local Capacity and Statistics as Ritual

The statistical requirements embedded in categorical programs had two oddly contradictory consequences. On the one hand, they were largely responsible for the creation and institutionalization of data management activities in local governments. Thus they made possible the use of statistics in decisions and created spokesmen in local government for statistics. On the other hand, the particular statistics required by the grant proposals and reports were almost entirely ineffectual. The consequence was the evolution of two coexisting norms: one that statistics were important and should be used, and the other that they were useless forms of window dressing. The contradiction still affects local governments as they try to determine for themselves the appropriate role for statistics in governance.

The early categorical programs included urban renewal, public housing, area redevelopment, and hospital construction. Later programs extended into education, transportation, social services, and almost every other area of domestic policy. Many grants were concentrated in the larger, older urban areas. This historical pattern of funding is a major cause of the substantial variations in analytic capability now found among local jurisdictions.

Statistics, and in particular population data, played several parts in these programs. First they were used to demonstrate eligibility. In the case of urban renewal, for example, a community would have to demonstrate statistically that its housing was substantially deteriorated. Income and poverty criteria were also frequently used, as programs were largely designed to aid the disadvantaged. Second, statistical data were required as part of plans and proposals, typically in a community statistical profile or a needs assessment. Third, statistics were designed to aid in federal program monitoring. Though the statistics were required, the important point is that they were not *central* to the funding decisions. Grant approval depended on bureaucratic discretion and was influenced both by the quality of the proposal and the political importance of the jurisdiction.

While the statistical requirements did provide some rough controls on who received funding, by far their most significant consequence was to assure that local governments hired professional staff capable of manipulating data, who in turn would influence local decision processes. This result was a major objective of federal program designers, who viewed local government as neither particularly competent nor very likely to share federal policy objectives. While some jurisdictions hired consultants, others created a data management staff to aid in preparing proposals and reports. This staff then maintained census and other statistics in a form accessible for use in other local activities. The data managers became the experts whom others in local government consulted about statistics. In many localities data management and statistical advice became government functions—though often not sufficiently accepted to be routinely funded from local revenues. The statistics justified the employment of other professionals: planners, engineers, and others who could make use of the data. Indeed, by providing jobs, the requirements helped encourage the growth of some of these professions. This kind of staff came to the task with ideologies and values more likely to be in sympathy with federal policies than others in local government, and they had, by virtue of the statistics, their presumed expertise, and their role in preparing proposals, a strong voice in local governance.

Historical accident determined the location of data management in local agencies, and as a result, it tends to vary among jurisdictions. The group doing population data analysis was most often located in the planning department. Planners usually administered grants from the Department of Housing and Urban Development (HUD) and its predecessors, which consistently demanded community statistics for most of their programs. HUD also gave out "701" planning grants even to the smaller and more affluent communities ineligible for most other funds, and these also supported a great deal of statistical analysis. However, the data management function could well be located in other local agencies. For example, to get federal funding, regional transportation agencies were often required to build land use projection models, which depended heavily on population data. Accordingly, these agencies became the keepers of data for some jurisdictions.

Thus statistical requirements were used to professionalize local government, influence its policies, increase the accessibility of the data, and promote a norm that statistical information ought to be used in decisions. It became necessary to justify requests for grants through statistical descriptions of community characteristics, rather than simply through pork barrel procedures. The use of statistics began subtly to change the terms of discourse and to delegitimize blatantly political choices. The participation of the professionals, moreover, made local compliance with the spirit of federal legislation far more likely. [1]

The required statistics seldom genuinely informed or directly affected program decisions by what they showed. Rather, they were assemblages of numbers tacked onto proposals. Indeed, the preparation of the statistics was often delegated to a junior staff member or data analyst and done independently of the rest of the planning. Funding agencies often dictated that out-of-date census statistics be used. Moreover, not only were the statistics often outdated or loosely related to programs: Local governments had little incentive or occasion to use them in any analytic or informative way. The task, as seen by local governments, was to get whatever funding they could in whatever programmatic form it was available. The broad policymaking and priority setting that might have been informed by statistics were unnecessary. Nor was it essential to use statistics to match and scale programs to particular populations when the goal was to maximize funding and when programs were, in any case, designed in Washington.

Thus the required statistics became merely window dressing—part of the ritual of grant getting. As such they were not particularly accurate, but they were accepted. Few bothered to point out their limitations. It simply did not matter. The continuing, anachronistic use of similar statistical requirements in the block grants of the 1970s highlights this ritual function and illustrates the institutional logic that protects meaningless data. For Community Development Block Grant (CDBG) funding, cities had to submit a Housing Assistance Plan (HAP)—a large compendium of statistics in defined form, showing such things as the mix of families by size in substandard housing, the composition of the subsidized housing stock, and its population. Standard census data were to be used wherever possible, but many items required local estimates. The ostensi-

---

[1]Similarly, in *The Influence of Federal Grants: Public Assistance in Massachusetts* (Cambridge, Mass.: Harvard University Press, 1970), Martha Derthick found that federal requirements ostensibly designed to rationalize procedures and introduce professionals into the local welfare departments made them more sympathetic to federal goals.

ble object was to determine the exact nature of the housing need and to shape local programs to match this need. Since funding was never adequate, however, the objective was meaningless.

The task of preparing the HAP was onerous, and many detailed bits of information had to be collected or guessed at.[2] By the late 1970s it was well recognized that census data had become highly inaccurate, particularly as a source of detail on housing occupancy and quality. While HUD officials were aware of the data inadequacies, they required comparable numbers across the nation, and could, in any case, check local tabulations only by such mechanical methods as adding rows and columns. Though most data managers did their best to provide honest estimates, some discovered that invented statistics were neater and therefore more acceptable to HUD. Though none of the actors believed in these statistics, there was no incentive for anyone to explode the myth. The standardized numbers were essential to HUD's reports to Congress, and the HAPs provided the appearance that the programs were in accord with national goals. From the communities' view, statistics acceptable to HUD allowed them to conduct their programs without federal interference. The use of the statistics helped absolve each level of the bureaucracy from substantive responsibility for judging the program and reduced the need for conflict or negotiation. The numbers were not just without meaning, they actually operated as a smokescreen.

Despite the ritualistic use of statistics in the federal grant applications and the skepticism over the value of data associated with it, some locally motivated data analysis had begun in the 1960s. Creative analysts, sophisticated city managers, agency heads, and county supervisors found ways to use the statistics made available for federal grants to learn about the community, identify needy areas, evaluate proposals, or focus attention on local issues. At times they ordered their own surveys or conducted special studies. In California many growing counties found it worth the cost to conduct a mid-decade census under state supervision, as this could significantly increase funding allocations. But such efforts were rare. Even a large city might conduct a survey only once in four or five years.

A second major outgrowth of local data management was service to the community. Data managers began to help citizens and public officials to find, interpret, and use data. This happened spontaneously rather than by design, but it became a nearly universal practice. While

[2]A study of the HAPs outlines this process in more detail. See Berkeley Planning Associates, *Evaluation of Housing Assistance Plans in Meeting the Statutory Objectives of Linking Housing and Community Development* (Berkeley, Calif., 1977 and 1978).

the bureaucratic superiors of these analysts often saw this activity as diversionary, many data managers came to see aiding the public as one of their primary missions, in the spirit of education and of improving the quality of participation in governance. Moreover, data managers discovered that the effort gave them an effective constituency. Today in many localities, data managers spend 30 to 40 percent of their time working with citizen activists, businessmen, marketing analysts, students, and teachers.

Block Grants and Pressures on Methodology

The two primary consequences of the block grants, like the categorical programs, operated in opposite directions, one encouraging growth of statistics use and the other discouraging it. On the one hand, block grants involved reduced requirements for statistical reporting, and, as a result, many local data analysis units were cut or eliminated. On the other hand, the use of statistical formulas for allocation fostered the growth of local skills in data collection and population estimation and widened the politics of statistics to lay and professional groups. These groups, in turn, put pressure both on the Census Bureau and on their own data managers as they challenged figures and demanded explanations. Finally, because the formulas were annually updated, a local expectation grew that statistics should be kept current and used for local purposes.

Three interlinked objectives of the shift to block grants depended for their implementation on statistics. One was to decentralize decision-making to the states and localities, a second to reduce government expenditures, and a third to spread federal resources more widely among geographic and income groups. To achieve these ends, categorical programs were collapsed into block funding for entire classes of problems, with localities expected to set their own priorities and design their own programs. Statistical formulas based on census data on population, income, and housing characteristics dictated how much each locality would get. The formulas permitted overall cuts to be made at the national level, by displacing the onus for cutting particular programs onto localities. Statistics permitted the redistribution of funds from older cities with large needy populations to smaller suburban and rural areas by eliminating explicit consideration of need and focusing attention on numbers that could be conveniently assumed to measure need. The use of numbers also helped to spread funds by guaranteeing benefits to a constituency at the time its representative voted on legislation. Such guarantees would be impossible in a program that allowed bureaucratic discretion in dispensing funds.

Statistics in the block grants were used to implement federal programs with a minimum of human discretion and federal effort and to provide simple forms of reporting. Their use lent a superficial appearance that congressional goals were being met. Communities in the CDBG program were expected to demonstrate by statistical criteria that funds were targeted to needy neighborhoods. Unemployment levels and average length of unemployment were established as statistical triggers to activate programs and benefits automatically in other programs. Simple statistics were used for monitoring, and qualitative evaluation became uncommon. All these applications used statistics as means of control rather than as ways of knowing.

The use of statistics as the single criterion for funding has changed local expectations and statistical efforts in ways that are likely to be permanent. Most important, local attention focused on the methods and procedures of the Census Bureau, and a spate of legal challenges to the 1980 results ensued. Though congressional representation did depend on census data, the allocation formulas added significantly to their consequences, putting them in vivid and comprehensible form. Every person not counted would mean dollars lost from the community.

Second, because the undercount was so significantly composed of minorities, the counts became rallying points to mobilize minorities in cities who wanted funding, representation, and recognition. These groups entered not only into census politics, but also into local debates over statistics and became more sophisticated and knowledgeable as interest groups wanting to influence the numbers. The entrance of these groups into the debate contributed to doubts about the Census Bureau's integrity. New York City, for example, contended that counts in some minority areas required extra personnel. The bureau argued it had to treat all areas similarly, but became embroiled in a rather ugly public debate when city officials accused it of racism.

A third long-lasting consequence of block grants is likely to be the use of annual estimates of population and other statistics rather than decennial census figures, not only for grant allocation but also for many local purposes. Local governments now expect more current and precise data to be used in analysis than in the past. This change has encouraged the growth of local expertise in population modeling and the improvement of local statistical sources.

None of these uses of statistics for block grants, however, offers an incentive for accuracy. The local interest is for figures as large as possible, to maximize funding. The federal concern is primarily that statistics be conceptually and methodologically comparable across the country to assure equity in distribution of funding. Each city fights for higher figures for itself, but cities do not challenge each other's numbers. The goal is peace, not truth. Nonetheless, the debates have resulted in learning, and local resources have been applied to developing new methods and making considerable improvements in local data.

During the late 1970s, however, federal and local budgets began to be cut, and the effects of the cuts and the funding redistributions on local statistical efforts began to be felt. With federal funds no longer earmarked for planning and statistics, operating agencies such as public works departments were powerful competitors to data management units for block grant funds. By the early 1980s, data management had been drastically cut in many cities. Many counties and smaller local jurisdictions, on the other hand, began to establish analytic capabilities for the first time because their federal funding was growing, and they had planning to do. Without experience, however, they were apt to lack a sense of how to proceed or how to justify their effort. For example, in one California county the staff began an elaborate set of studies of community needs, doing the surveys and analysis the textbooks propose. In a few months all were summarily fired by county supervisors for wasting time.

As some local governments began to recognize, however, the block grants demanded more, not less, local statistical expertise. First, to be able to challenge the methods and estimates of the Census Bureau or other agencies takes considerable skill, and up-to-date tabulations of local records as evidence. Moreover, virtually for the first time, many local jurisdictions now have primary responsibility for policy in a variety of areas. The voters will blame them for mistakes. Most local agencies must now invent decision and monitoring processes and learn by trial and error how much and what type of information they require. Data management units are experimenting with ways to support themselves—through user fees, getting agencies to share their budgets, or getting their activities into the annual budget as line items. These units continue to provide public information, but most still have little visibility, recognition, or local support.

Federal Statistics and Local Policymaking

As local governments begin to use statistics for their own purposes, they are handicapped by having relied so heavily on federal statistics and developed few sources of their own. Federal statistics were acceptable as long as they were used primarily for federal purposes, but they are unsatisfactory at local levels for three reasons. First, the level of accuracy—the limitations on detail and timeliness and the errors and bias in the census—are all greater problems for local purposes than for federal ones. Second, public acceptance of statistics is particularly difficult to achieve locally because the lay public has so many sources of direct knowledge to test the numbers. Third, federal statistical policy in the 1980s has changed the distribution of access to information at the local level. I shall take up each of these three problems in turn.

Local Dependency in Statistics Production

Local statistical efforts have been limited largely to tabulating and reorganizing data designed and gathered by other agencies for their own purposes. From an efficiency standpoint, it made little sense for thousands of small-scale governments to maintain the skills and staff to do censuses, when these must be done by the federal government. Nor have many jurisdictions chosen to support the staff and expensive computer hardware necessary to conduct regular surveys, maintain sophisticated data analysis capabilities, or track and tabulate the data that are by-products of local administrative processes. Statistics have been mostly supplied by the federal government, and the census has been the single most important source for most local jurisdictions as it offers virtually the only data on the subcity level. The Census Bureau, however, makes decisions on the questions, definitions, geographic concepts, and products. Its objective of comparability across jurisdictions and over time supersedes the interest in unique or special local conditions. Moreover, the bureau has to respond to the demands of many user groups, of which local governments are only one, and neither the most powerful nor the best organized. Thus local governments have depended on data that come in forms over which they have little control and which suit few of their needs.

The Local Demand for Accuracy

Local policymaking demands a level of accuracy and precision considerably greater than what federal statistics offer. In particular, a level of timeliness and geographic detail not demanded for federal decisions is critical to the utility of the data for local purposes. A much lower level of error can be tolerated. The reason is not that local policymakers have intrinsically higher methodological standards than federal ones, but rather that local policies have different characteristics than federal ones, and local data users have the means to check the numbers. In federal statistical sources such as the census the percentage error on a national scale is small. It is, however, concentrated in particular cities and sections of cities and in certain ethnic groups. Errors effectively random for the nation as a whole are nonrandom in a small city or neighborhood. A missed housing project, or the assignment of a series of blocks to the wrong census tract can make a big difference in local analyses and in policies based on them.

Local policies can be distinguished from many federal ones which establish guidelines for the nation as a whole or set up programs that are to be used only in some areas. Local policies, however, tend to be singular in form and specific in operation. A federal program may subsidize housing for the elderly across the country while a local program identifies a particular elderly population, designing and siting a project for this group. Furthermore, urban areas are highly differentiated spatially in their social characteristics, housing types, patterns of blight, and demands for services. The success of local programs often depends on the characteristics of the population in the immediate vicinity. Census tract data are often not fine-grained enough to provide this information. Moreover, tract borders do not correspond to local planning areas, administrative districts, catchment areas for services, or impact areas for projects. While local analysts sometimes make rough estimates from tract data, they seldom consider the results satisfactory— ironically, since the bureau compiles tract data primarily on the rationale that they are locally useful.[3] In any case, it may suffice for national statistics to be correct on the average, but local statistics have to be correct in particular.

The demand for timeliness in the statistics is partly supply driven. Current estimates are available because of formulas, and therefore there is an expectation that they will be used. But also, dramatic and visible changes can occur in local populations in short periods of time. Because of long delays in the dissemination of census data many localities seldom directly use the decennial statistics. Rather, they rely on estimates, revising them when they get the census figures. The census becomes primarily a benchmark and a way of correcting estimates.

Demands for accuracy have arisen partly also because data users at the local level can evaluate the data directly. Local staff can check the census against records of address listings, housing permits, school enrollment, and so on. Even citizens may be able to tell when small-area

---

[3]A Census Bureau program to provide cities with statistics tabulated according to locally designed neighborhood boundaries may help to meet the demand for spatially detailed data.

data are incorrect because of their familiarity with the community. This direct and phenomenological awareness of the population's characteristics accounts in great part for the discrepancy in the demands for statistical accuracy and precision between national and local actors.

Legitimizing the Numbers

The consequences of many local policies are apt to be direct, immediate, and predictable. Individuals or businesses will lose or benefit from the construction of a highway off-ramp, a shopping center, or condominium project, or from a new library or a tax measure. A policy or project can alter the social character of a neighborhood or threaten its quality of life. Therefore, statistics that are prime criteria in arguments for or against local public action must achieve a high degree of public acceptability. The many lawsuits challenging the 1980 census both reflect and feed a public skepticism over statistics that extends even to that most careful of enumerations. To complicate the task, the estimates on which local jurisdictions now rely present a far greater challenge for getting public acceptance.

Political acceptability normally implies that statistics are at least viewed as accurate by opposing sides in a debate and taken as fact for the time being. Such legitimacy is achieved and protected through processes that reassure the users that the numbers are professionally produced and without deliberate bias—processes that lay out methods and evidence for public scrutiny. The Census Bureau has long recognized the importance of such processes and has begun to work with local actors in the hope of assuring acceptance of its statistics in local governments. The results thus far are only partly successful.

THE 1980 CENSUS: BUILDING LOCAL ACCEPTANCE

While the Census Bureau has long worked with local users to explain its methods, it decided to consult local governments about the 1980 census in a systematic way. While greater accuracy was one goal, building local confidence in the results was clearly another. Before the census, the bureau established Local Review Committees and designated local and regional liaison staff to discuss methods and potential problems. Since 1980 was to be a mailback census and enumerators would no longer visit each home, correct prior addresses would be the key to an accurate count. Thus it was planned that local staff would review the bureau's address listings before the census and check early counts to identify where obvious errors had occurred, so that immediate recounts could be done. In addition, the bureau encouraged the formation of community organizations to assure a higher degree of cooperation among minorities.

The effort was a valiant attempt to design a social process to produce an accurate and accepted census. Bureau staff would educate local officials on the logistics and methods of the census and the rationale, and make use of their direct knowledge of local population and housing. The bureau would maintain its professional standards and its control of the decisions, but, at the same time, would work cooperatively with local staff. Criticisms would be met or explained early on. The numbers that emerged would, at least to some degree, be a product of a mutually accepted set of methods. In addition, the strategy was a public relations effort to create local support to defend the bureau's methods if they were later challenged.

The idea was only partially successful though some of the failures were beyond the bureau's control.[4] Census counts were higher than predicted, and the undercount was substantially reduced. New ties with local agencies were established, and old ones were firmly institutionalized. The bureau, however, suffered from unexpected budget reductions and extended delays. Local committees often found that census address listings were inaccurate and could not be changed. They did not review early counts because the bureau had sent figures back to their central processing office, where delays were so long that field offices were dismantled by the time the figures were returned, and improved counts could not be made. The bureau's concerns about privacy regulations meant that they did not allow much direct local checking of returns in any case. Then a fire destroyed all the records in a minority district of New York City, increasing suspicions in that already tense situation. So while local review did produce some cooperation and mutual learning, local officials' expectations were raised and disappointed. Many began to view the bureau with a mixture of contempt and distrust.[5] The effort was not sufficient to prevent the rash of lawsuits, but the bureau did build bridges and establish strategies that could be useful in 1990.

[4] The story of the many problems in preparation of the 1980 census is told in U.S. General Accounting Office, "The Census Bureau Needs to Plan Now for a More Automated 1990 Decennial Census: Report to the Subcommittee on Census and Population Committee on Post Office and Civil Service, House of Representatives," GAO 166D-83-10, 1983.

[5] A typical expression of the hopes and disappointments is expressed by San Francisco's data manager, M. F. Groat, in "The Census and the Cities," *American Demographics* (July/August 1981):32-37.

LOCAL POPULATION ESTIMATES AND PROJECTIONS

In California, population estimates and projections are the most visible and influential of statistics. It is testimony to the success of their legitimation that the statistics are so widely used in conflictual situations where substantial funding is involved. As a result of the state's high growth rate, estimates and projections have come to be crucial in many physical planning decisions, such as determining the demand for major public and private investments in highways, shopping malls, and schools. They are used in market studies and public agency analyses to plan the location, size, and phasing of projects. Projections are part of the justification for plans and environmental regulations, and they are central to such ubiquitous work as assessing environmental impacts of proposed developments and predicting their fiscal consequences. Such studies can often lead to reduced project sizes, growth-limiting land use regulations, and limits on housing construction.

The consequences of these decisions may be considerable, and the statistics may be pivotal in them. Population projections were central, for example, to a hard-fought battle over whether to build a rapid transit line in the Wilshire corridor of Los Angeles. The figures chosen will, in turn, influence revenue and ridership projections that will be used to justify the system. In Contra Costa County a bitter public debate over building a new prison facility was settled when staff used a cohort projection model to predict prison population in twenty years. The Environmental Protection Agency requires that official population projections be used for regional air and water quality planning. As a result, these figures influence whether and where sewer hookups can be made in countless rural areas and thus set constraints on industrial or housing growth.

So much hinges on what the statistics show, and yet there is no single correct way to make local population estimates. Hence methods become a political issue in themselves. The choice of methods, from a technical standpoint, depends on whether an area is presumed to be growing or declining, on whether its growth is in natural increase or migration, and on what types of current data are available. One approach is simple trend extrapolation from benchmark data; another involves a more complex cohort projection; a third estimates population in relation to employment. The most common at the local level is a method for determining population as a multiple of housing units. Judgment must be used in any of these, and multipliers may be tinkered with to approximate changing fertility rates and ethnic or age mixes affecting average family size. The leeway is enough that more than one data manager has told me that the "population estimate is a policy decision."

Projections have all the methodological complexities of estimates, plus assumptions about the future, which, once applied, can be self-fulfilling. A high-growth image for a community can contribute to growth, while an image of decline can hasten that process.[6] I have argued that the design of any policy indicator is appropriately, at least in part, a political process, but the rationale for mixing politics with measurement is even clearer for projections.[7]

At the state level in California, local estimates and projections are produced by the Population Research Unit (PRU) in the Department of Finance. It was started in the 1950s to help reconcile competing estimates made by different agencies. The unit played a more powerful role in the 1960s, when it provided the detailed projections on which California's complex, linked system of universities and colleges was designed. It also began to make the official population estimates to be used for the allocations of gasoline and liquor taxes to localities.

The PRU was staffed by professionals and for many years headed by a demographer trained at the University of Chicago. From the outset they were under pressure from many interests, localities, and legislators, but they made clear that they would adhere to their professional judgments. The PRU was open to discussions with local staff and assessed evidence they provided on local growth. For the most part in the early years, PRU staff patiently explained why local methods were inadequate. They maintained their professional standards even under the pressure of a local tax limitation measure, which required the unit to provide annual population figures for localities. Staff did so, but refused to certify estimates they considered to be based on inadequate information; without certification these estimates could not be used for distributing state funds. Needless to say, this tactic provided a strong incentive for growing communities to improve their own data.

The PRU established a reputation for high methodological standards and detachment from daily politics and could defy even direct requests from powerful legislative leaders. It was able to develop this independence not only because of the determined professionalism of its staff but also because of its location in the state's Department of Finance, where there was no operating responsibility for particular pro-

[6]Andrew M. Isserman and Peter S. Fischer, "Population Forecasting and Local Economic Planning: The Limits on Community Control over Uncertainty," *Population Research and Policy Review* 3 (1), (1984): 27–50.

[7]Judith Innes de Neufville, *Social Indicators and Public Policy: Interactive Processes of Design and Application* (New York: Elsevier, 1975); and "Validating Policy Indicators," *Policy Sciences* 10 (1978):177-78.

grams, and the unit was not likely to be suspected of bias. Moreover, its policy of openness of method and willingness to discuss estimates helped deflect criticism as well as to educate local staff. In the 1970s outreach was broadened; workshops and public hearings were held; and PRU staff traveled through the state, consulting with local staff and gathering information. The system bears many resemblances to the Census Bureau's own program of outreach.

Professionalism, high methodological standards, and avoidance of personal or institutional bias are all important factors in the legitimation of statistics for public policy debates. But this professionalism does not require discounting the knowledge of users and those less technically skilled, nor does it demand ignorance of policy agendas. On the contrary, the legitimacy of statistics for policy use and, in some cases, its accuracy depend on the cooperative development of meanings and methods between statisticians and those who intend to use the statistics.

Local Access to the Census

Local governments in the 1980s have weak and widely varying capabilities for data management. In this context, the Census Bureau's policy of disseminating the 1980 data primarily in the form of computer tapes has created pressures on local data management institutions. Perhaps most significantly, it resulted in redistributing access to the census among jurisdictions and between the public and private sector, as well as between those who can pay and those who cannot. The consequences are particularly acute for the ordinary citizen. To the extent that information lends power to those participating in the political process, power at the local level is being redistributed.

The story, told in more detail in Chapter 14, is that the bureau decided, with the 1980 census, to supply tapes and tabulation software at nominal prices to all comers as soon as they were ready. States were encouraged to establish Data Centers, which would prepare printouts, disseminate data, train users, and provide technical assistance. Printed reports would still be published, but much later. The purposes were, in keeping with other federal policies, to decentralize policymaking, to cut federal expenditures, to encourage private sector involvement, and to get users to pay their own way. Moreover, from a technical viewpoint, tapes had the advantage of offering more information and more flexibility in the organization of the data than printed reports.

The first inequalities of access arose because there were wide variations in the capabilities of the states. California's Population Research

Unit took over State Data Center responsibility, but some states had difficulty finding any agency to take on the role. Since there were long delays at the bureau in preparation of the tapes, and even longer ones in publication of the reports, and since census tabulation software turned out to have many bugs, the technical capacity of an agency determined its access to the census. It took some states years to prepare printouts and become capable of performing other analytic tasks on the data. The tapes themselves are effectively inaccessible to all but the largest cities and some counties, as most jurisdictions lack the necessary expertise and computer capability. Most jurisdictions purchase printouts or order special tabulations from public or private agencies.

The various actors have responded in different ways. In California the Regional Councils of Government have filled some of the gap, preparing their own tabulation software and providing printouts and technical assistance to public and private census users. On the other hand, libraries, the traditional source of much census information for the ordinary citizen, teacher, and student, for the most part did not effectively cope with the changes. Many ordered the awkward microfiche version of the census, while others waited for the long-delayed, but familiar printed reports. A few librarians discovered, almost by accident, the availability of standard printouts from one or another local agency, but they often had difficulty in cataloguing or making usable the information from mountains of printout. The private sector, however, was better prepared and was first to offer printouts of standard tabulations and tailor-made analyses and first to produce multicolor census maps and graphs. Thus a significant consequence in the local context of the bureau's policy of "do it yourself" census tabulations was to alter the mix of actors and responsibilities involved in local data management. States, regional councils, and private firms were brought in as important and often new participants, and small jurisdictions had to rely on them. A second consequence was that agencies began to charge for producing the data and in amounts considerably higher than the cost of printed reports. For example, for a medium-size jurisdiction a printout of data taken from just one of the summary data tapes was priced by a typical public agency in 1982 at $75 to $100, though a few made printouts available at reproduction cost. These agencies charged by the hour for consulting advice, and special tabulations sometimes cost hundreds of dollars. The private sector charged prices many times higher.

As a result, tremendous disparities in access to census data have emerged. While printed reports are limited in their content and flexibility, at least reliance on them gave all roughly equivalent access to the census. Now, some jurisdictions get more complete and timely census data than others. The richer and growing jurisdictions tend to have better statistics than older, declining, or smaller places. The flexibility and specialization of private data firms have allowed them to innovate, but they have not primarily designed their products for the public sector nor marketed to it.[8] Accordingly, the public sector has been left behind technologically, and those who can afford to pay—the large corporations—have the best data. Small businesses have fared relatively poorly too, as they relied heavily on local data managers. The growing use of user fees and the slow adaptation of the libraries have meant that citizens, teachers, and students have fared worst of all.

The systems of statistical production at the local level are in a state of flux. Who gets statistics and how quickly and who pays and how much are all issues in question. Private firms produce public statistics, while public agencies charge for services and products as if they were private firms. Some public agencies purchase statistics about their own communities from private firms, while others behave as entrepreneurs, seeking out the business of other public agencies and private firms. As they do so, threats of lawsuits for unfair competition come from the private sector. And public agencies are caught in dilemmas over pricing their services. High fees would help support their development costs and satisfy their private competitors, but they are not justified if data are primarily for public purposes. Moreover, even low fees can disqualify entire groups of public users. Nor does a sliding scale have much promise. Profit-making users contribute to community development and citizens to local democracy. Some in each category have resources and some do not. No simple pricing principle for equity, efficiency, or public good is applicable.

At a time when statistics are beginning to be central to local public debates, such differences in access raise troubling issues, even beyond the obvious one that they redistribute the capacity to participate in governance. If the public acceptability of statistics is indeed a prerequisite to their being used in policy controversies, then privately produced data may not be acceptable. Public data production, unlike private, can be open and accountable. Its statisticians do not serve par-

---

[8]The explanation offered by private firm managers was that the elaborate proposal writing and bidding requirements of governments, the cumbersome decision-making process, and the slow payment process made marketing to the public sector much less profitable than targeting private business. Another part of the explanation for the difficulty of getting innovative technology integrated into local government activity on a large scale through the private market may be illuminated by Kenneth L. Kraemer's study, "A Requiem for USAC," *Policy Analysis* 5 (1979):313-49. Evaluating a major federal demonstration project, Kraemer found that the effort to develop model urban data banks was doomed to failure because each government's structure and objectives were so unique. The cities involved developed useful systems, but few were transferable to other jurisdictions in any simple form.

ticular interests. They can work cooperatively with all users to develop a shared understanding of the methods and concepts. Without open access and public acceptance, statistics offer the political process only confusion and mistrust.

Predictions

In the next decade local governments will increase their capacity to produce and use statistics in sophisticated ways. This change will be fueled both by the need for "defensive" statistics to fight the battles for state and federal funding and by the growing self-awareness of local governments as autonomous policymaking bodies. It is harder to predict what institutional forms will evolve to fill these responsibilities, though undoubtedly county and regional agencies will become increasingly important as suppliers of data to at least the smaller governments.

It is too early to tell where the dividing line will be established between the activities of the public and private data providers. It may well be that, as local agencies develop their expertise and improve their technology, they will crowd the private data firms out of many of their markets for basic census analysis. Whatever the case, however, there seem certain to be legal challenges to many current practices by both private firms and public interest groups. The current set of conflicting arrangements will not be stable enough to continue indefinitely.

Local governments in the next few years will place growing pressure on the Census Bureau. After the bureau decided it could not prepare printed reports of the 1980 tract data, local data managers mobilized a massive letter-writing campaign, which gave the bureau enough leverage to get funding restored. As that case suggests, local governments will become a much stronger lobbying force, demanding that census content and products respond to their needs. If the bureau is not more successful in its cooperative efforts at conducting the 1990 census than it was in 1980, legal challenges to the numbers may even increase.

Federal policies will continue to influence local institutions, whether they do so deliberately, or through the unintended by-products of policies that do not focus on the local consequences. Two possible paths seem open. Either federal agencies will find ways to incorporate local knowledge into the data they produce and ways to respond to the demands of localities for current estimates and fine-grained data, or a dual system of population and housing data may evolve—one set of federal statistics and another of local statistics. Under those conditions, federal–local conflict over statistics could be permanent.

End Note

The analysis in this chapter grows out of several of my prior studies and professional contacts with many local governments, primarily in California. In addition, for the present chapter in-depth interviews were conducted with data managers and data users from both public and private sectors in California, Vermont, New Hampshire, Massachusetts, and New York in the spring and summer of 1983. Information was gathered, in these and earlier interviews, on major and small cities, suburban jurisdictions, and county and state agencies. The sample was designed to reflect a range of experiences in growing and declining communities; well-to-do and poor ones; Eastern, older bureaucracies and the newer, more professionalized Western ones. No pattern emerged to link data analysis capability to any of the obvious factors such as city size, age, or wealth, though some limited correlation with the last variable may exist without being a determining factor.

Since the arguments in this chapter are heavily influenced by the California experience, it is worth commenting on the ways this is or is not typical. While there is much diversity within the state in terms of statistical competence, on the whole one finds more developed statistics and applications in California than elsewhere. It has a high growth rate, and localities have vested interests in accurate population counts at frequent intervals. Moreover, until recently the state has been relatively well off compared to other states, allowing more resources for the development of statistics. It also has a strong tradition of professional public administration, in sharp contrast to many other states. There has been more acceptance of the idea of formal planning, as the state itself mandates that localities prepare and follow General Plans. Thus California's experience is likely to reflect more technical sophistication than that of many other states, but by the same token it may reflect some of what the future may be as localities in other states assign a greater role to statistics.

Relevant work by the author on local statistics includes: Judith Innes de Neufville, *Federal Requirements and Local Planning Capacity: The Case of CDBG*, Institute of Urban and Regional Development Working Paper No. 365 (Berkeley: University of California, 1981); *Social Indicators in Local Government* (Washington, D.C.: Proceedings of the American Statistical Association, August 1979); and *Data and Planning in Local Government*, Department of Housing and Urban Development (San Francisco, August 1981).

There has been comparatively little empirical study of local government practices and institutions for the use of information and computer technology. The studies informing this chapter include: Janet R. Pack,

Urban Models: Diffusion and Policy Application, Regional Science Research Institute, Monograph Series No. 7 (Philadelphia: University of Pennsylvania, 1978); James N. Danziger et al., *Computers and Politics: High Technology in American Local Governments* (New York: Columbia University Press, 1982); Kenneth L. Kraemer et al., *The Management of Information Systems* (New York: Columbia University Press, 1981); idem, "A Requiem for USAC," *Policy Analysis* 5 (1979):313-49; J. D. Eveland, *Innovation as Specification: Issues and Implications,* National Science Foundation, Innovation Processes Research Section, Division of Industrial Science and Technological Innovation, unpublished; Everett M. Rogers et al., *Final Report, NSF Grant RDA 75-17952. Executive Summary: The Innovation Process in Public Organizations—Some Elements of a Preliminary Model,* Department of Journalism, University of Michigan, Ann Arbor, March 1977; and *Computers in Local Government* (Pennsauken, N.J.: Auerbach Publishers, Inc., 1980), a useful compendium of how-to articles for local data managers.

12

THE MANAGED IRRELEVANCE OF FEDERAL EDUCATION STATISTICS

JANET A. WEISS AND JUDITH E. GRUBER

IN THE perennial debates over the appropriate role of the federal government in education policy, the usual fierce controversy occasionally gives way to tranquil pockets of agreement.[1] One island of apparent consensus is education statistics. Nearly everyone agrees that the federal government appropriately collects and keeps data about the national condition of education.[2] One federal agency or another has been doing so since 1869. But agreement at this global level—that there should exist national education statistics—does not necessarily mean agreement about *which* education statistics to collect. Of all the questions policymakers might ask about schools, schooling, teaching, and learning, which are important enough to include in a permanent statistical system? This chapter examines how such choices are made by an

[1]This chapter is based on research funded by the National Institute of Education, Grants NIE-G-81-0037, NIE-G-81-0038, and NIE-G-83-0008. We are grateful for this generous support. We are also grateful to Stanley Harris for research assistance, to numerous state and federal education officials who provided the data that we report, and to Martha Feldman, Edie Goldenberg, Joseph Houska, and Donald R. Kinder for discerning advice.

[2]Even the Reagan administration's proposals for drastic reductions in the federal role in education and the abolition of the Department of Education included continued funding for statistics and research. See Congressional Research Service, *Education: FY83 and FY84 Funding Issues.* Issue Brief 83024, June 1983; Department of Education, *Justifications of Appropriations Estimates FY83: Foundation for Education Assistance.* Internal Memo, 1982.

analysis of the Common Core of Data, the primary set of general purpose statistics about elementary and secondary education (kindergarten
through grade twelve) collected by the federal government.[3]

Two distinctly political forces have shaped the ability and willingness of the federal government to collect systematic data about education on a regular basis. First is the fragmentation of control and authority over education among federal, state, and local governments and
between the public and private sectors. This fragmentation has placed
the federal government in a weak political and bureaucratic position to
impose standards for rigorous data collection or to require other institutions to report about controversial issues. The fragmentation might
have been less of a problem if there existed in the United States genuine
consensus about appropriate indicators of educational variables. But a
second force shaping the development of education statistics has been
the lack of consensus about how to measure critical pieces of the educational process, extending to vigorous controversy about which pieces
are in fact critical. When people do not agree about what is useful to
know, it becomes difficult to define a central core of information that
obviously merits regular measurement.

These two forces have combined to push federal statistics on education away from controversial policy questions and toward easy if less informative measures of resource availability. The result is a long-term
statistical record that purports to tell us about education in the United
States, but reveals remarkably little about the educational issues that
have dominated the policy agenda for a generation. Since politics, like
nature, abhors a vacuum, policy-relevant data have emerged from other
sources to influence educational choices; federal policymaking has not
been starved for information. But these ad hoc injections of data almost
never have the most attractive properties of a national statistical system: standardized data collected at regular intervals, national samples
or populations, attention to archiving and time series to permit comparisons over time, design and analysis geared to multiple users, and
universal public access.[4] Although considerable data are available, they

---

[3]In 1985, after this chapter was drafted, the Department of Education reorganized its
research and information functions. The agency that is the focus of this chapter, the National Center for Education Statistics, has become the Center for Statistics. The Common
Core of Data is scheduled for major redesign and perhaps a new name over the next few
years.

[4]For a comparison of relative federal expenditures for social statistics compared to
other types of knowledge production, see Mark Abramson, *The Funding of Social
Knowledge Production and Application: A Survey of Federal Agencies* (Washington, D.C.:
National Academy of Sciences, 1978). This report of the Study Project on Social Research
and Development defines the distinguishing property of statistics as the potential for multiple uses and users, many of them unknown at the time data are collected.

usually come from a nonrepresentative set of school districts or states, or are collected once with no capacity to examine trends over time, or, if collected more often, change definitions or questions year to year in response to changing legal or political concerns, are collected with one purpose in mind and then discarded, or are not available to other users or made part of the public record. Given these properties of alternate data collection strategies, the strengths and weaknesses of the national statistical system in education are a matter of some moment. Pressures that limit the depth and breadth of education statistics limit the possibility of ever having comprehensive national data over time to illuminate critical policy problems.

After a whirlwind tour of the history of federal education statistics, we turn to an analysis of these pressures. We focus our analysis on the Common Core of Data (CCD) and the ways in which it has been designed, collected, and distributed by the National Center for Education Statistics (NCES), a unit of the federal Department of Education. CCD is the product of a mix of political influences, historical precedents, bureaucratic pressures, financial constraints, and technical developments. Its story illustrates how turbulent debates about governance and policy have spilled over into apparently apolitical choices about statistical systems.

Our analysis is based on approximately one hundred semistructured interviews we conducted with the staff of the National Center for Education Statistics, officials in five states who collect and report data to federal education officials, the staff of the Council of Chief State School Officers, and consumers of education statistics in analytic offices within the federal Department of Education, in Congress and its staff agencies, and in the major educational interest groups. The interviews were supplemented by extensive archival research in published and unpublished federal documents.[5]

The Common Core of Data does not just happen to include some items but not others. Like other official records, CCD emerges from social and political interests that create records to serve particular purposes.[6] The purposes are not random. Nor are they strictly scientific or technical. The CCD case illustrates the complex machinery underneath official decisions about what to count, how to count, and what to do with the results.

---

[5]A detailed description of the research and its findings is available in J. A. Weiss and J. E. Gruber, *Education Data as Control in a Federal System*, Final Report to the National Institute of Education (Ann Arbor: University of Michigan, 1984).

[6]Thoughtful analysis of this general point may be found in Nancy Cochran, Andrew Gordon, and Morton Krause, "Proactive Records: Reflections on the Village Watchman," *Knowledge* 2 (1980):5–18; Aaron Wildavsky and Ellen Tenenbaum, *The Politics of Mistrust* (Beverly Hills, Calif.: Sage, 1981).

Federal Education Statistics in Institutional Context
Historical Development

In 1869 the federal education bureaucracy, in the first of its many incarnations, began collecting and publishing systematic data about schools, attendance, staffing, finance, and transportation aggregated by state.[7] These early collections set a pattern that continues to this day: Each state voluntarily responded to federal requests with whatever data it had collected for its own purposes. The resulting statistical system did not change very much until the early 1950s, in spite of persistent major flaws. Because data were aggregated by state, they told policymakers little about local conditions at a time when local districts were making most of the decisions and paying most of the cost of elementary and secondary education. Because state participation was voluntary, some states chose not to participate at all, leaving large gaps in the data. Because the states collected their own data as they saw fit, the states did not use common definitions of basic terms. As a result, the published tables had to be based on numbers that bore the same label (school attendance, for example), but did not count the same thing (for example, every student present in school on October 10 versus every student who ever attended a given school for a single day in the course of the school year).

Dissatisfaction over this sorry state of affairs finally led to activity in the early 1950s. In 1953 state and federal statisticians together designed a handbook of common definitions for 500 data items "that every state department of education should have available."[8] In 1954 the Office of Education asked states to use these handbook categories in their reports. Use of the handbook (which became the first of a series of handbooks on various categories of education data) was voluntary and therefore uneven across states. So the handbook did not solve all the problems. But it was a significant effort to introduce some standardization into state data collection, and was warmly welcomed by some state officials.

In 1965 Congress created the National Center for Education Statistics (NCES) within the Department of Health, Education, and Welfare. Its mandate was "to collect and disseminate statistics and other data re-

---

[7]Descriptions of these early statistics are included in many federal publications. See, for example, the introduction and appendices in Carol J. Hobson and Samuel Schloss, *Statistics of State School Systems 1959–1960* (Washington, D.C.: U.S. Department of Health, Education, and Welfare, 1962).

[8]*The Common Core of State Educational Information*, Office of Education Bulletin 1953, no. 8, usually referred to as Handbook I.

lated to education in the United States. . . . "[9] Bolstered by their newly enhanced visibility, the statisticians from NCES embarked on new adventures in data collection. A few years later, they cooperated (as always) with the states to launch the Elementary and Secondary Education General Information Survey (ELSEGIS), the first major federal survey to use local school districts as the unit of analysis, rather than states. NCES drew a nationally representative sample of local districts, stratified by district size. Then NCES contracted with the state education agencies to collect and edit the data from the local districts. NCES used the resulting data, combined with data on finance from the Census Bureau and on civil rights from other federal agencies, to create a data base capable of producing national estimates.

But this did not prove to be a stable answer to NCES's needs. Congress, the executive branch, and the major interest groups complained about the absence of policy-relevant data and the excruciating delays (typically two to three years) in publication of routine data. Meanwhile the states were moaning about the crushing burden of federal paperwork, and Congress was listening sympathetically. Caught in the midst of external squabbles, NCES also confronted formidable internal problems, including erratic support from the Commissioners of Education (who seldom lasted more than one year in the job), no regular budget line item (resulting in consistent mid-year reallocations away from NCES), a tight ceiling on authorized personnel slots, no guaranteed access to the HEW computer, and a relatively poor reputation in the federal statistical community.[10] According to the NCES administrators whom we interviewed, NCES had to salvage its deteriorating position by staking out new directions that would attract broader support.

The new direction proved to be the Common Core of Data, a single, comprehensive data base to serve state and federal needs for general purpose statistics and data required to administer categorical programs. In 1971 and 1972, NCES officials conducted studies to determine who had what needs for education data. A wildly ambitious proposal was drafted to include an annual collection of all education data necessary for all federal purposes from all local school districts (rather than a sample), all states, and all institutions of higher education, plus the capabil-

[9]20 U.S.C. 1221e-1.

[10]A sympathetic account of NCES's woes may be found in Gerald E. Calderone, *Statistics about Society: The Production and Use of Federal Data,* Sage Professional Papers in Administrative and Policy Studies, 03-020 (Beverly Hills, Calif.: Sage, 1974). As one of our respondents commented on the staff: "They really are good professionals. But they're the creature of one of the many educational special interests, [so] unlike the Census Bureau they do not have the sacred shell of professionalism recognized outside."

ity to do one-shot, "fast response" surveys on special issues and high-powered statistical analyses. A set of matrices depicted the data that had to be collected from various sources to address each of the policy issues identified by the user communities. It rapidly became clear that NCES staff could not possibly handle the mountains of data being considered. The delays they already encountered in processing a fraction of that amount were likely to stretch into many years, further undermining their credibility as a source of policy-relevant data.

Although the notion of a comprehensive CCD collapsed of its own weight within NCES, it also became clear that NCES did not have the political resources to assume control over data collection then being done by other agencies in HEW or the states. Program managers in other federal education bureaus had no intention of relinquishing control over data they were collecting to establish eligibility for federal funding, to monitor state and local compliance with federal regulations, and to justify their programs to Congress. The states, too, were suspicious of NCES's claims that the new, improved CCD would satisfy state as well as federal information needs. The chief state school officers' organization set up a Committee on Evaluation and Information Systems (with the acronym CEIS, pronounced "cease") to insist that NCES and the rest of the federal government leave the states alone to satisfy their own information needs. State officials also expressed concerns about the volume of data being contemplated. The chief state school officers had supported the idea of an NCES-run consolidated system in the hope that it would reduce federal requests for data from the states. The vast data matrices in the CCD proposal appalled them, causing an outbreak of cold feet.

Thus NCES found itself with a CCD proposal that appealed to statisticians and archivists but not to the education policy community it had hoped to please. By 1975 the proposed CCD had to be drastically modified. The frills were lopped off. Postsecondary education was excluded. Program-related data were left in the program offices. Gone were the analytic and policy innovations. The proposed budget shrank from $100 million to $10–14 million. Each data element was scrutinized for feasibility and cost of collection. The upshot was that new policy issues simply could not be addressed. The proposed CCD that emerged in 1976 for field testing looked suspiciously like the data collection that NCES had been doing all along, and operated at a budget under $2 million. The one major change was to collect information on local district enrollment, staffing, and facilities from all 16,000 local districts, rather than the sample that ELSEGIS used.

CCD was begun in the 1977–78 school year and fully implemented over the next few years. It included data on enrollment and attendance broken out by grade level, a census of local districts adjusted for mergers and consolidations, revenues and expenditures by category, staff by job assignments, and physical plants from all local districts (some in the form of state totals; the rest district by district) as well as data about the activities of the fifty states including revenues, expenditures, programs, and staff of state education agencies and state-operated schools. All state and local data were supplied by the state education agencies on a voluntary basis. NCES reimbursed the states for editing and preparing the data for federal use. Very little of CCD did not grow directly out of earlier federal surveys.

Intense pressures for budget reductions and paperwork control in the early 1980s resulted in substantial reductions in the number and complexity of questions in CCD surveys, and in the publications resulting from CCD. The total NCES budget for statistical activities decreased in constant dollars from $14.9 million in 1980 to $10.8 million in 1984, a 28 percent decline over a period when the overall Department of Education budget decreased very slightly in constant dollars.[11] Fiscal scarcity took its toll on CCD. Forty percent of the nonfiscal data items were eliminated from the data base during the period from 1981 to 1983. For example, questions about the gender mix of school teachers, specialists, and administrators that had been added in 1974 because of concern about the implementation of Title IX (forbidding sex discrimination in educational programs that receive or benefit from federal funds) were eliminated in 1981 because they were no longer deemed necessary.

If this is roughly the story of CCD, it is not even close to the story of education policy during the same period. While NCES was valiantly struggling with incompatible state reporting systems and primitive computing capacity, the nation was in the throes of enormous changes in educational standards and aspirations. During the last twenty-five years, the federal role in education expanded dramatically in a few critical areas—the search for educational excellence, equity for disadvantaged, minority, and female students, and special assistance to handicapped students and students with limited command of the English language. But CCD did not add questions about academic performance or equity. Courts and advocacy groups directed attention to inequitable financing of schools, illiteracy, unfair disciplinary practices, and student

[11]Eleanor Chelimsky, "Statement on the Condition of Information on Education before the Select Education Subcommittee, Committee on Education and Labor, House of Representatives," February 19, 1986. Many federal statistical programs sustained cuts during this period, but the average cut was 8 percent. U.S. House of Representatives, Committee on Government Operations, *The Federal Statistics System: 1980 to 1985* (Washington, D.C.: Government Printing Office, 1984).

rights. CCD did not add questions about literacy, discipline, or student treatment, although it did provide baseline data about funding. Increasingly militant teachers' organizations raised questions about the working conditions of school staff. CCD did not. Blue ribbon commissions and elite academic groups wondered about declining test scores, the acceptance of mediocrity, and the impact of television and video games on what children learn. CCD had no pertinent data. In a period of high technology and global competition, business leaders pressed for more and better teachers of mathematics and science. From CCD, one could not assess the supply or quality of teaching in math and science. The relationships among school, work, and life chances came under critical scrutiny. CCD data could not contribute to the scrutiny.

These controversies raged almost entirely outside the purview of federal education statistics. The statistical system took little account of them, and thus the political debates were largely uninformed by federal statistics. Huge quantities of policy-relevant data appeared from other sources—data collected, analyzed, and distributed by advocates, academics, and interest groups, by analytic or program offices within the federal bureaucracy or the Congress, and even by special units within NCES. But CCD, the "primary" federal data base, has played a distinctly secondary role in informing federal education policy. When the General Accounting Office looked at information about education in 1985 and 1986, it concluded that gaps in the core data collection systems and poor quality of data have brought us "to the point at which program management, departmental policymaking, and congressional oversight may have become extremely difficult. . . . [E]ducation information is inadequate for some of the decisions that face the Congress. [12]

One example of the distance between CCD and national policy concerns can be found in the widely publicized report of the National Commission on Excellence in Education. Concluding that "our nation is at risk . . . [having] lost sight of the basic purposes of schooling," the commission report documented its allegation with a series of statistics.[13] For example, 23 million American adults are functionally illiterate; average achievement of high school students is now lower than it was when the first Sputnik was launched; over half the gifted students do not achieve at levels commensurate with their ability. None of the data that the commission regarded as an indication of risk came from CCD and none could have come from CCD. CCD never asked such

[12]Eleanor Chelimsky, "Statement on the Condition of Information on Education," p. 16.

[13]National Commission on Excellence in Education, A Nation at Risk: The Imperative for Educational Reform (Washington, D.C.: U.S. Department of Education, 1983), p. 5.

questions. Of the commission's twenty-four findings about the reasons for the national decline in performance, only one was based in part on CCD data about teacher salaries.

We do not mean to suggest that CCD has had no value. Our research identified many uses of CCD data by many users in the federal government and out.[14] Almost always, however, would-be users have had to combine CCD data with data from other sources to construct a policy-relevant argument. In one representative example, a congressional staffer described his use of CCD's state average per-pupil expenditures: "I can't advise the Congress on different Chapter 1 formulas without them and if I had to contact each state I would have to worry about the comparability of responses." Note that the state averages themselves do not directly inform choices about the Chapter 1 (or any other) formula; they are an ingredient in an argument about a federal program that requires data from multiple sources. Without someone to build the bridges to other pertinent information, CCD data are often beside the point. Supplemented by other contextual data, CCD can be useful, even invaluable. The charge that CCD is largely irrelevant to policymaking is based more on what data are omitted than on the merits of the data included.

Two dynamics appear to have led to the narrowing of what started out to be a comprehensive data base. One is the fragmentation of authority and control over educational policies and institutions. The other is the lack of consensus over appropriate indicators of important educational variables. In the next two sections, we discuss the effects of these political forces on the development of CCD.

CCD and the Fragmentation of Control

No neat metaphor can fully convey the incongruous mix of fragmentation and interdependence that characterizes the governance of public education. Authority is widely dispersed across the federal government; fifty state legislatures and education agencies; 16,000 local school boards and their respective electorates, public officials, and tax codes; and 87,000 public schools. Resources are also widely dispersed; for example, most local districts draw upon a mix of formula-based aid and special purpose funds from local, state, and federal sources. Privately funded and controlled schools educate about 11 percent of school-aged children, and a shocking number of children do not go to

[14]Weiss and Gruber, *Education Data as Control.*

school at all.[15] Local district operations are constrained by state laws and funding patterns, by contracts with their professional staff, and by parent and student responses to school offerings. State policies are shaped by federally mandated requirements and opportunities as well as by state politics and local pressures. Throughout the entire system runs a strong ideological commitment to local control over public education, which is sometimes, but only sometimes, translated into practice.

This genre of fragmentation, in which no one is entirely sure who has authority to do what but no one submits meekly to anyone else, has far-reaching consequences for the collection of national statistics. Three sorts of fragmentation are especially important to our story: dispersion of control across the levels of government, scattering of control among agencies within the federal government, and the existence of powerful policy actors who operate outside of government altogether.

Intergovernmental Fragmentation

The messy division of control among local, state, and federal governments has historically meant that national statistics have been compiled in two ways. Either Congress and federal officials invested large sums of money in direct data collection from citizens, groups, or organizations, as they do in the case of the census or the Internal Revenue Service, or they asked state and local governments to share data that these governments had already collected from citizens, groups, or organizations. If federal officials know exactly what they want to know, and are willing to pay what it takes to get the data, the first route is likely to yield the desired results. If they are not sure what they need to know, are not willing to pay the cost of direct collection, or cannot collect data directly because of political sensitivities, then the second route is preferable. But the second route has its own price. If federal officials seek the cooperation of state and local officials, then federal goals for the data must be compromised with the goals of the state and local governments that actually do the work and pay the bills.

As we have seen, most education statistics have been collected in the second way, and federal officials have had to accept stiff compromises. Because federal officials have been generally unwilling to go to 87,000 schools for information, they have been forced to depend on

---

[15]The high school drop-out rate was stable at about 25 percent during the 1960s and early 1970s. Between 1972 and 1982 it actually increased 5.5 percent. In major cities it is far worse, averaging 40–50 percent. Harold Howe II, "Giving Equity a Chance in the Excellence Game," in B. Gross and R. Gross (eds.), *The Great School Debate* (New York: Simon & Schuster, 1985).

whatever state education officials choose to ask when *they* gather data from those 87,000 schools. Because the states have traditionally had somewhat different interests and priorities for schools than the federal government, this dependence on state discretion has led to a statistical system quite different from the education data base that federal officials might have designed if left to their own devices.

Both technical and political differences between state and federal actors have influenced the development of CCD. On the technical side, one dominant federal goal over at least forty years has been the standardization of data elements and definitions across states. If all states used the same operational definitions and collected data in the same way, then adding up the state numbers would give an internally consistent national total that could be interpreted with confidence. Significant variation in state definitions and collection procedures yields a national total of uncertain value. Variation also interferes with comparisons among the states, making it harder to understand the effects of federal action on different states or to see the results of different state policies. To increase standardization and comparability, NCES has periodically devoted substantial effort to building consensus around definitions. The series of handbooks of common definitions has been a major step in this direction. Until 1983 NCES also provided small grants and limited technical assistance to state education agencies to improve their data collection systems. Workshops in the ten federal regions offered instruction in the use of handbook definitions and access to training materials.

But because data collection has long been a state activity, administered by state officials and funded by state legislatures, NCES has never had much impact on state collection practices.[16] Certain state officials have been embarrassed into doing a better job from time to time. But if Idaho or Massachusetts (or any other state) decided not to collect any staffing data in a given year, there is little that anyone at NCES could do except to threaten to publish tables with no entry for the delinquent state. NCES is even more helpless when state legislatures require state agencies to collect education data in a way that does not comply with the handbook categories in order to satisfy some idiosyncratic state formula or legislative objective.

Thus no matter how hard NCES works (and it has never had the resources to work very hard), every year NCES publications sing the same refrain: "National data collection efforts in education continue

[16]Because NCES has so little money to offer state officials, it has not had the influence on state practices that other federal agencies have achieved. See, for example, Martha Derthick, *The Influence of Federal Grants* (Cambridge, Mass.: Harvard University Press, 1970).

to be seriously restricted by delays in reporting, missing data, nonresponse, and ambiguous information, which result inevitably and directly from the lack of standardization in educational data elements, record keeping, definitions, reporting procedures, and educational practices. Data needed for federal policy purposes cannot be collected on a comparable basis until state, local, and institutional data sources are assisted in adhering to common standards through comprehensive and integrated data collection systems."[17]

The trouble is that the federal objective of standardization competes with the dominant state technical objective for federal data collection, which is to limit the work required. The people in the states who provide data for CCD spend most of their time collecting data from local school districts to comply with sundry state mandates. In our interviews with them, it was clear that CCD and NCES do not loom very large in their lives. State and local procedures do. Although there are exceptions, most states run their data collection on a shoestring. Statistical coordinators are desperate for competent staff and up-to-date equipment. They are up to their ears in state-mandated work and local intransigence about reporting. They do not have the slack to accommodate changes in definitions and collection schedules to suit the convenience of some bureaucrat in Washington. Their technical objective is to limit the work necessary to convert their existing data into the format requested for CCD. State CCD coordinators warmly support the notion of a national data base. They are technical people for the most part and they believe in good clean numbers. But given the daily pressures they face, a national data base is a luxury. Their anxiety shoots up when federal statisticians pressure them to collect or submit data in new ways. To overgeneralize only slightly, their agenda can be summed up as "no changes." In this light it is less surprising that progress toward national standardization has been so painfully slow.

The gap between state and federal perspectives is also apparent when it comes to political agendas. The major political objectives for statistics at the federal level are to inform Congress, the White House, and top executive officials about national developments in education, to allow comparisons among the states that may point up problems or progress, and to develop a respectable national archive of data that satisfies research, planning, and forecasting needs in and out of government. CCD does not shoulder the entire burden of these objectives. Federal program offices elsewhere in the bureaucracy collect education data related to their missions, as we will discuss in the next section.

---

[17]National Center for Education Statistics, *The Condition of Education: A Statistical Report on the Condition of American Education 1975* (Washington, D.C.: NCES, 1975).

NCES collects other data, too, in the course of its special studies. But no other agency offers the systematic monitoring of national trends in elementary and secondary education that CCD can produce. One of the basic reasons to have national education statistics is to keep federal policymakers knowledgeable enough so that they can intervene in state and local practice if national need becomes evident. The mere existence of time series data on a national basis can frame issues in ways that seem to demand a national response. For example, the downward march of SAT scores seems to have focused dissatisfaction about high school standards in ways that might have been less pointed without the provocation of those vivid graphs. Accurate knowledge about the reach and depth of certain problems (such as one room schools or science teacher shortages) can make federal intervention more effective than scattered anecdotal evidence such as that usually produced at public hearings. [18]

But the states' agenda is just the reverse. State officials such as the Council of Chief State School Officers seek to limit outside intrusion into what they regard as state business. Constitutionally, the states, not the national government, have principal responsibility to provide education. Practically, they pay the largest fraction of the cost of schools. The less information the federal government has, the better state education agencies like it. Their goals are to contain the disruption caused by federal requirements, to limit the capability of the federal government to intervene by restricting access to detailed information about state practices, and to eliminate the possibility for politically damaging comparisons to be made among the states or local districts. As state people told us, the more federal officials and Congress know about what is going on in schools in Ohio or Arizona, the more likely they are to try to tinker. And, if the federal government makes available public data about how Ohio and Arizona compare, that provides fodder for disaffected state legislators or irate taxpayers to make life difficult for state education officials. Therefore, when NCES consults with state people about including more policy-relevant data on CCD, both sides confirm that the usual response is a chorus of opposition. Items that have been excluded from CCD because of state opposition include student withdrawal rates and private school enrollments; both lend themselves to unwelcome evaluation of public school performance. [19]

In line with this pattern, the states have not opposed all federal

---

[18]An elaboration of this argument is presented in Janet A. Weiss and Judith E. Gruber, "Using Knowledge for Control in Fragmented Policy Arenas," *Journal of Policy Analysis and Management* 3 (1984): 225–47.

[19]Data about school drop-out rates were collected by the federal Bureau of Education during the decade of the 1910s when expectations for high school completion were considerably lower.

education statistics, only those that increase their vulnerability to external attack. Indeed, CCD in its present form enjoys substantial moral, logistical, and political support from state officials. Our interviews with state and federal officials suggest that CCD's principal attractions to state data collectors are the ability to make realistic comparisons to other states on questions of size and resources (but not performance), and the implicit endorsement and explicit assistance of the federal government and other states for improving the technical quality of data (and thereby resisting local political pressure to manipulate data). In contrast, other federal education statistics that we studied, notably surveys of civil rights compliance, received no cooperation from state data collectors, for they exposed state vulnerability to legal and administrative intervention.

In these negotiations, the states have held nearly all the cards. NCES can only include CCD data that the states voluntarily provide. Collaboration among the states through the Council of Chief State School Officers has further strengthened the hand of state officials. Partly because of its relatively powerless location in the intergovernmental division of labor in education and partly because of a lack of effective leadership, the federal government has not been very effective in mobilizing political arguments or technical claims in support of education statistics. A strong case might be made on behalf of national data that can inform public policy. But so far there has been no influential voice to make it.

Fragmentation at the Federal Level

The second type of fragmentation that has consequences for CCD is the dispersion of data collection responsibility across many separate units of the federal education bureaucracy. NCES is the official home of education statistics. But most data about education that are collected by the federal government never even cross the desk of an NCES staffer. The program bureaus in the Department of Education collect data for planning, administration, and evaluation about the populations served by federal education programs and the recipients of federal benefits (for example, handicapped students or students in vocational education). The Office for Civil Rights collects data about civil rights compliance in schools. The planning, budget, and evaluation office collects data to evaluate the effectiveness of federal programs. The National Institute of Education collects data on educational innovation and service delivery. The National Science Foundation collects data about science education. The Bureau of the Census collects data on school attendance and levels of educational attainment in its Current Population Surveys and the decennial census. The Bureau of Labor Statistics collects data on vocational education. The Department of Agriculture collects data on school lunch programs. The Department of Defense collects data on schools serving children living on military bases. The Equal Employment Opportunity Commission collects data on school teachers. The Office of Child Development collects data about children in Head Start and other preschool programs. The National Center for Health Statistics collects data on the intelligence and achievement of children aged 6 to 17. This is by no means a comprehensive list, but it suggests the level of competition that NCES faces even within the federal government for authority, expertise, and funds in support of its data collection programs. [20]

This level of fragmentation has forced NCES to define and defend its distinctive competence within the bureaucracy in order to sustain the flow of funds and support to its programs.[21] NCES needed to protect itself against two sources of political pressure and competition. First, NCES had to justify its unique contribution to knowledge about education. Second, NCES had to protect its capacity for data collection against pressures from Congress and the White House to reduce the paperwork burden on respondents. Within the Office of Education (and after 1980 the Department of Education), the niche that NCES claimed is the educational counterpart to the Census Bureau or the Bureau of Labor Statistics—a professional, nonpolitical, impartial source of numbers equally accessible to users of all persuasions.

NCES has differentiated its data collection from program-related data collection by its emphasis on basic statistics, the importance placed on preserving and ordering data as an archive, the collection of data year after year for the sake of the archive, and careful editing to ensure internal consistency within a set of data. High standards for the statistical integrity of the CCD data have been a continuing ambition of NCES staff (albeit an ambition thwarted by the lack of standard state reporting systems). NCES staff have historically placed their first emphasis on clean data, not on timely data, not on policy relevant data, and not on satisfying requests from data users.

NCES staff members think of themselves as specialists in statistics, not in education. They often have little personal experience or background in educational issues. They do not display the level of commitment to specific educational policies characteristic of many program

[20]A similar list appears in Office for Federal Statistical Policy and Standards, *A Framework for Planning U.S. Federal Statistics for the 1980's* (Washington, D.C.: U.S. Government Printing Office, 1978).

[21]We use "distinctive competence" in the sense articulated by Philip Selznick, *Leadership in Administration* (Berkeley: University of California Press, 1957).

staff. Thus, they are less willing than program staff to defend particular data elements because they are important for policy. For example, since 1968 NCES has not collected data about student race and ethnicity, leaving the job to the Office for Civil Rights in the Department of Education. NCES has allowed questions pertinent to civil rights to be eliminated from its surveys when pressured to do so. For example, in 1981 and 1982 NCES omitted from CCD questions about school busing and gender of school staff when forced to reduce the size of the CCD surveys. But the Office for Civil Rights was (and is) full of people who cared about civil rights data, sought control over the data, were active in justifying and defending the legal and policy importance of the data, and therefore protected their continuing collection in the face of significant opposition. NCES chose to stand its ground on other parts of CCD that were essential to statistical goals of forecasting or preserving critical time series. Given such choices, NCES naturally ends up with data that are not especially relevant to current policy concerns.

This pattern has often put NCES at odds with other federal education officials, and has made those officials reluctant to rely on NCES for their data.[22] The program offices and mission agencies collect data to monitor state and local compliance, to allocate funds to eligible beneficiaries, and to assess the implementation of federal programs. Understandably, program administrators design their data collection to satisfy the specific legal and administrative requirements of their programs, and collect data on a time schedule that coincides with decisions they have to make. Thus, the program offices produce a great deal of data about federal programs. Of course these data have their own limitations: They come only from recipients of federal funds (a sample that underrepresents small school districts); they use categories and definitions that change every time the law changes; they are collected on irregular time schedules; they are seldom available to data users outside the program office for validation or independent analysis; they are

---

[22]An incident recounted by one of our respondents illustrates the point: "Marie Eldridge [the NCES Administrator] wanted to run the data collection for the handicapped and it was a classic power showdown in the bureaucracy. . . . She said [in a 1976 meeting with the assistant secretary of education], 'Well we have taken a major role. Look at this report here we have on the handicapped.' And she picked up this thing; it was this big. And Ed Martin [director of the Bureau for the Education of the Handicapped] said, 'Of course this illustrates the real problem we have, Marie, with your organization. Look at the date inside that report.' And she looked at it and said 'It says 1974.' He said, 'Well when was the data collected?' And she didn't know. And he said, '1969. You have data that's nearly ten years old. You've barely got the Civil Rights Act operating. You have nothing that's been collected since the passage of the Rehab Act [in 1973].' So that was the end of the meeting. We took it over. NCES lost. . . . So I say in terms of program operators, they're useless. Worse than useless, they get in the way."

designed to satisfy the needs of the program offices, not to describe the educational problem or prospect. For these reasons, program data do not paint an accurate picture of the national educational system, but then program offices were not designed to play that role. NCES was.

Several agencies within the education bureaucracy have poached on NCES turf, resulting in a further constriction of NCES's focus. The establishment of the National Institute of Education to conduct policy-relevant research and the expansion of the analytic capability of the Office of Planning, Budget, and Evaluation both created significant centers of expertise and data within the Department (HEW, then Education) that competed with NCES's claims to expertise about the condition of education.[23] The Bureau of Elementary and Secondary Education attempted in the late 1960s to create a comprehensive reporting system of program information to satisfy a wide range of federal evaluation mandates. When this project collapsed (for much the same reasons that the original plan for CCD collapsed), the leftover staff and budget were scooped up by an entrepreneurial director of research and planning, not by NCES. Since then, data and analysis for evaluating the effectiveness of federal education policies have been the purview of the research, planning, and budget staff rather than NCES.[24] NCES has lost a number of similar bureaucratic battles, with the resulting loss of control over data important to the development of educational policy. As policy-oriented pieces have been given or taken away by other federal agencies, NCES is left to ask the descriptive questions with no immediate policy implications—questions about the numbers of students or school buildings, administrators or teachers, state or local revenues. In this way the fragmentation within the federal education establishment has kept CCD on the fringes of the policy action.

NCES has had to defend its budget and programs from attack from outside the Department of Education as well as from within. In the last ten years, Congress and the Office of Management and Budget have worked to restrict the reporting and data collection done by the federal bureaucracy. Proposals to collect data from schools are now required to run through a gamut of stringent clearance and approval procedures in the Department, as well as external reviews by state (and occasional local) officials organized by CEIS, and by the Office of Management and Budget. Only after all parties have been convinced that the data collection is legally required, nonredundant with other federal data, and sure

[23]See Lee Sproull, Stephen Weiner, and D. Wolf, *Organizing an Anarchy* (Chicago: University of Chicago Press, 1978).

[24]One version of this experience is offered by Milbrey W. McLaughlin, *Evaluation and Reform* (Cambridge, Mass.: Ballinger, 1975).

to be used by the collecting agency, is NCES (or any other agency) allowed to proceed with data collection. This persistent, rigorous review has forced NCES to reduce the amount of data collected by CCD.

The easiest way to pass these clearances is to show that the collection of specific data has been explicitly mandated by law. But CCD is not explicitly mandated by law. Only "education statistics," without further specification, are required "from time to time." So, to survive the reviews, NCES, like other agencies, constructs a case to show that CCD data are valuable to a broad spectrum of users and that the people who provide the data (in this case the state data coordinators and the chief state school officers) support the continued collection. Because CCD does not include many policy- or program-relevant data, NCES cannot rely on the support of an active community of policy or program users. NCES has thus become dependent on state officials for political support in its struggle to collect data from the states. As we have already discussed, NCES needs state cooperation in the logistics of data collection and the adoption of national standards. The staff's reliance on the states to take the NCES side in battles with the Office of Management and Budget and Congress is yet another tie that binds the fate of CCD to the approval of the states. It is another reason not to include anything in CCD that might jeopardize the support of state education officials.

Fragmentation within the federal government has led NCES to define the purposes of CCD narrowly, in ways that make policy relevance a secondary priority. It has also forced NCES to seek a powerful constituency to defend CCD against charges that it is unnecessary red tape. The only white knights to appear have been the state data coordinators and the chief state school officers, who have been willing to defend CCD so long as it does not include embarrassing or intrusive questions. Construed in less generous terms, the states defend CCD so long as it remains largely irrelevant to controversial policy issues.

Fragmentation Between Public and Private Sectors

The third sort of fragmentation that affects NCES and CCD is the involvement of powerful, nongovernmental actors in education policy. These actors include private schools, organizations of teachers and administrators, researchers and scholars in schools of education, public interest groups, business and industry groups with a stake in the results of public education, and children's advocacy groups. Many of these private interests choose to collect their own data about education in order to promote and inform their particular policy concerns. This has created further competition for CCD.

In some cases, these outside groups have collected far more comprehensive and systematic data than CCD or any other NCES survey. For example, the Research Department of the National Education Association, which represents a large fraction of the nation's teachers, collects annual data about teachers and school districts that surpass CCD in scope and detail on key questions about teacher working conditions. Moreover, these data are compiled and released within a few months of their collection, whereas CCD, in its painstaking fashion, does not publish data for one to three years. Another example is the College Entrance Examination Board, which annually collects and analyzes data about the academic achievement and aptitude of nearly every college-bound student in the country.

These external sources of data stimulate and direct policy debate in the education community, exposing and exploring new trends and initiatives. Congress is an eager consumer of such data; so are the analytic offices throughout the federal bureaucracy. As education practice and policy evolve and change, issues facing federal policymakers come to seem different. New kinds of data assume more importance; older issues and data fade from the agenda. So long as the criteria for selection of data for CCD do not include policy relevance, CCD can remain untouched by this process. However, the result is that CCD remains isolated from the ebb and flow of policy discussion. Because policymakers can and do get data elsewhere to support their discussion, they do not bring pressure on CCD to be more relevant. Its isolation is thereby preserved.

But even if the architects of CCD sought to increase the policy content of their data base, the established mechanisms for collecting CCD data would not make it easy. Powerful groups that affect the course of public education exist outside traditional education agencies. NCES gets CCD data from state education agencies, and they get theirs from local school districts. When policy-relevant data lie outside those institutions with whom NCES has established relationships, NCES has no procedure to include them in CCD. Thus, for example, CCD contains no data on private schools or children who do not attend school, and no data on education conducted by private vocational schools or employers. While NCES can and does conduct special studies to collect data from private actors, seldom are the data collected on a regular, recurrent basis necessary to detect trends over time.

The existence of relevant data outside the networks on which NCES relies has meant that CCD is further driven into simple description. When other people collect and analyze data at their own expense, policymakers in Congress have access to policy-relevant data without having to ask for it from NCES. That lowers their expectations for CCD. Having low expectations, they are unwilling to pump the extra resources into CCD that would permit NCES to include more policy-oriented data. It is a vicious circle, within which NCES is boxed into a limited role with little prospect of escape.

The three kinds of fragmentation—among governments, within the federal level of government, and between public and private sectors—have all served to limit CCD's development as a source of policy-relevant data. The broad consensus around the principle of a national set of education statistics has repeatedly disintegrated as the groups involved battle over the details. As a consequence, NCES has been trapped into a dependent position, confined to a sliver of turf, deprived of resources necessary to strengthen its operations, and able to defend itself only on technocratic grounds. CCD has evolved according to the strengths and weaknesses of its parent agency with limited ambition, a narrow scope, a horror of political controversy, high technical standards, and inadequate resources to be all that it could be.

CCD and Lack of Consensus

In some policy arenas, the detrimental effects of institutional incoherence have been counterbalanced by technical agreement about appropriate (or at least adequate) indicators of institutional performance. For example, certain economic statistics (such as the unemployment rate or the consumer price index) are widely accepted and used (not without controversy, but used nonetheless) in spite of great fragmentation of control over economic policy. No one finds them ideal measures of the underlying policy variables, but most policymakers prefer the approximation to the feasible alternatives. This basic acceptance among diverse partisans permits the continued collection and use of data even in controversial areas.

Unfortunately, education is not an arena in which such basic consensus has lowered the obstacles to a useful statistical system. In the first place, the educational process itself is not well understood and is suffused with value conflict. Fundamental disagreements about the definition of a "good" education, the ingredients of educational performance, and the functions of schooling in society make it difficult to specify outcomes or processes that CCD should measure. But even when most people do agree about what is important (for example, can children read and write?), a second problem arises: It has proved difficult to develop technically sound indicators of many important educational variables. A hundred years of education research has produced remarkably little technical convergence on critical process and outcome measures. Consequently, CCD has not been able to build on the agreement of experts about what should be counted and how. The result has been that CCD devotes disproportionate attention to things that are easy to count—primarily inputs in the educational process that can be counted in bodies or dollars—and ignores things that are not measurable in widely accepted terms, such as services delivered to students or the effects of participation in varying types of education.[25]

Disagreements About What to Measure

Examination of the scientific literature on school effectiveness, program evaluation, standardized testing, and other educational controversies reveals a great deal about the investigation of process, outcome, and alternative treatments. It is far easier said than done.

The initial hurdle is disagreement about what students should get out of school. Possible indicators of a school's performance include students' scores on standardized aptitude or achievement tests, levels of school attendance, students' attitudes toward school, drop-out rates (or graduation rates), school grades, student success in finding paid employment after leaving school, teacher evaluations of student progress, proportion of students who go on to further education, severity and extensiveness of disciplinary problems, student participation in extracurricular activities, freedom from discrimination, student access to appropriate courses and programs of study, community support for school activities, the premium on housing prices that parents are willing to pay to live in that school district, and so forth (each reader will no doubt have additional candidates). This list reflects a variety of social aspirations and goals for schooling. Any single indicator emphasizes some valued dimensions of education (learning, socialization, preparation for the world of work, freedom of choice, safety and security, responsiveness to student and parent needs, equal treatment, enjoyment, etcetera) at the expense of others.

Any single indicator captures performance that is important to some segments of the community but not to others. The selection of performance measures is politically charged. School administrators do not care to make the choice, and higher levels of administration are

---

[25]See a similar conclusion by the Office of Federal Statistical Policy and Standards, *A Framework for Planning U.S. Federal Statistics for the 1980s* (Washington, D.C.: U.S. Government Printing Office, 1978), p. 80.

even less enthusiastic about wandering into the minefield. Given the vulnerability of the federal position, NCES is especially reluctant to identify outcome or performance criteria and enforce their measurement.[26] Without the protection of broad political or technical consensus around the choice of measures, NCES would invite howls of protest about the inappropriate intrusion of federal standards. Therefore, CCD includes no such data.[27]

Many examples of the controversy that surrounds choice of variables can be found in the states that have adopted minimum competency tests to identify those students who have attained the minimum academic or life skills necessary for graduation or promotion to the next grade. After an early burst of enthusiasm for setting and enforcing higher standards for students, educators became mired in legal, philosophical, moral, and political debates about the definitions of "minimal" and "competency" and the further problems of measuring it—whatever it was. The establishment of statewide standards raised questions like: What is the relationship between what is taught in the schools and what skills are tested for? How can a *minimum* level of competence be determined along a continuum of skill mastery? What happens to students who do not attain that minimum standard? To what extent do minimum competency tests place unfair disadvantage on minority students, handicapped students, or students whose first language is not English?[28] Different sets of competencies turn out to have quite different implications for curriculum, teaching methods, remedial instruction, and community support. Thus they elicit very different coalitions of support and opposition from educators, politicians, parents, and students.[29]

---

[26]NCES did commission a study of outcome measures when the original proposal for CCD was being prepared. They received a survey of *fifty-eight* outcome variables to consider. National Center for Education Statistics, *Indicators of Educational Outcome* (Washington, D.C.: U.S. Government Printing Office, 1973), DHEW Publication OE-73-11110). A more recent effort is underway by a task force of the Educational Leaders Consortium in response to NCES request.

[27]The closest thing to federal standards of performance is the National Assessment of Educational Progress, a federally funded program which includes regular standardized tests given to national samples of school children in selected academic subjects. But great pains have been taken to keep the development and administration of the National Assessment out of the hands of federal officials. See, for example, John Evans and David Schoemaker, "State and Federal Roles in Testing as Viewed by USOE Officers," in Richard M. Bossone (ed.), *Proceedings, Second National Conference on Testing* (New York: Center for Advanced Study in Education, City University of New York, 1978).

[28]George F. Madaus (ed.), *The Courts, Validity, and Minimum Competency Testing* (Boston: Kluwer-Nijhoff, 1983).

[29]Barbara Lerner, "The Minimum Competency Testing Movement," *American Psychologist* 36 (1981): 1057–1066.

Uncertainty about which outcomes to measure has been matched by uncertainty about which process and program variables are most important. If we knew which school processes were most directly linked to learning (or other important student outcomes), then those would be the logical candidates for routine measurement and inclusion in CCD. Extensive research on the determinants of student performance has turned up contradictory results. Beginning with the Coleman Report's stunningly counterintuitive conclusion that students' achievement was not related to the resources or programs of the schools they attended, many researchers have attempted to estimate the relationship between what schools do and what happens to students.[30] The dismaying result of much excellent research is that such factors as teacher–student ratio, teacher qualifications, teacher experience, quality of facilities, or expenditures per student have no consistent relationship to student outcomes. Nor does teacher style, internal classroom management, or school organization have strong or reliable consequences.[31] Given our impoverished understanding of the things about schools that make a difference to students, it is hard to identify a manageable set of school characteristics for routine measurement.

The results of occasional federal forays into the realm of performance and process measurement give one pause about the value of future expeditions. For example, compensatory education programs for disadvantaged students have received federal funds since 1965. Both Congress and federal education officials have wanted to know whether the federal investment in disadvantaged students had any effects on academic performance. Federal policymakers tried several ways to extract these data from local school districts.[32] First, the law simply required that local projects make "appropriate objective measurements . . . for evaluation at least annually of the effectiveness of the programs."[33] This produced thousands of anecdotal, impressionistic ac-

---

[30]James S. Coleman, Ernest Q. Campbell, Carol J. Hobson, James McPartland, Alexander Mood, Frederick D. Weinfeld, and Robert L. York, *Equality of Educational Opportunity* (Washington, D.C.: U.S. Government Printing Office, 1966). For a thoughtful review of more recent work, see Eric A. Hanushek, "Throwing Money at Schools," *Journal of Policy Analysis and Management* 1 (1981):19–41.

[31]Ann Lieberman, "Practice Makes Policy: The Tensions of School Improvement," in A. Lieberman and M. McLaughlin (eds.), *Policy Making in Education: 81st Yearbook of the National Society for the Study of Education* (Chicago: University of Chicago Press, 1982); Michael Rutter, "School Effects on Pupil Progress: Research Findings and Policy Implications," in L. Schulman and G. Sykes (eds.), *Handbook of Teaching and Policy* (New York: Longmans, 1983).

[32]This account is drawn from Milbrey McLaughlin, *Evaluation and Reform* (Cambridge, Mass.: Ballinger, 1975).

[33]Ibid., p. 18.

counts of wild successes, supported by little or no data. Next, the federal government commissioned a large-scale cost-benefit analysis of the effects of compensatory education "by comparing results on achievement tests and attendance rates prior to and after exposure to compensatory programs."[34] The contractors could not get the data they needed, and their results were uninterpretable. Next, the Office of Education decided to conduct a national survey of compensatory education. Although 93 percent of the school districts and 88 percent of the schools returned their survey questionnaires, only 5 percent of the sample answered the questions about student achievement.[35] Without systematic achievement data, federal officials were unable to draw conclusions about the impact of national policy on student test scores. Next, the Office of Education commissioned a series of thirty-one case studies of exemplary compensatory education projects called "It Works." Unfortunately only a fraction of the exemplary projects were still "working" a year or two later.[36]

With remarkable persistence, federal officials continued to press local districts to do a better job of evaluating outcomes and reporting them in a standardized format. After ten years of frustration, the Office of Education tried yet another approach—developing uniform procedures or models to be used by local evaluators for test selection, administration, scoring, data analysis, aggregation, and reporting. These models were widely implemented in local districts, but, as usual, with varying degrees of care and success.[37] Additional national studies have been done, and work continues to assess the impact of federally funded compensatory programs. The point is not whether compensatory education works, but that finding out whether it works on a national scale has been a remarkably arduous process.

These cautionary tales about experience elsewhere in the education bureaucracy have not been lost on NCES. The ideology of local control combined with substantial local variation in curriculum and instructional priorities means that local districts do not all teach the same things. Sensible testing must somehow relate to what has been taught. If there is local variation in what is taught, there must be variation in testing. But if tests vary, then there is little hope for nationally compar-

---

[34]Ibid., p. 36.
[35]Ibid., p. 56.
[36]Ibid., p. 88.
[37]Janice K. Anderson, Richard T. Johnson, Ronald L. Fishbein, Robert M. Stonehill, and Judith C. Burnes, *The U.S. Office of Education Models to Evaluate ESEA Title I* (Washington, D.C.: Office of Planning, Budgeting, and Evaluation, U.S. Office of Education, 1978). They report that of 182 evaluation reports that they examined, only 32 (18 percent) had no obvious errors.

able data about student achievement. Local discretion in use of standardized tests may make good educational sense. But it does not produce usable national statistics.

Disagreements about Measuring Educational Process and Outcomes

Even when consensus has been achieved on some minimal criterion, the state of the art of educational measurement still leaves many questions unresolved in ways that threaten the viability of national statistics. Education policy is largely preoccupied with things that are hard to measure in a standardized fashion. This by no means makes it unique among policy arenas, but it does pose quandaries for statisticians. Take, for example, equality of educational opportunity. It might be measured in dollars as equality of a community's input to the schools by way of resources, facilities, or equipment; in proportions as the racial composition of the school, as courts are wont to measure it; in attitudes as the values, spirit, or morale of the school resulting in equally high expectations of all students; in test scores or attitudes as equality of outcomes in school for students with equal backgrounds or abilities; or in test scores or attitudes as equality of outcomes in school for students of unequal backgrounds or abilities.[38] Depending on which measurement we accept, we are likely to reach quite different conclusions about equality in any given district. A similar problem arises in the effort to assess the adequacy of school finance reform. How can we tell whether school districts within a state (or across states) are equitably funded? The answer depends on how we measure equalization. Different measures lead to different conclusions.[39] How desegregated are a district's schools? Once again, the answer hinges on the choice of measure. Desegregation can be measured by the proportion of schools that enroll students in precisely the racial proportions of the community, that enroll students of approximately the racial composition of the community such that no racial group is more than twice or less than half its proportion in the community, that have less than 90 percent black or other minority students, that have no more than the degree of residential segregation in the community, or that provide the average black student

[38]James S. Coleman, "The Concept of Equality of Educational Opportunity," Harvard Educational Review (ed.), *Equal Educational Opportunity* (Cambridge, Mass.: Harvard University Press, 1969).

[39]See the compelling analysis by Robert Berne and Leanna Stiefel, "Measuring the Equality of School Finance Policies," *Policy Analysis* 7 (1981):47–69.

with a given proportion of schoolmates who are white. All are defensible measures of desegregation, but they do not all lead to the same assessments.

Even the well-worked terrain of reading raises serious measurement questions. Standardized, nationally normed tests of reading achievement are in nearly universal use across the United States. Nevertheless, these tests are constructed by different publishers, for different uses, of uncertain reliability for specific subgroups, are validated on different criteria, are surprisingly sensitive to subtle variations in the conditions under which they are administered, are very sensitive to timing in the academic year, have been charged with cultural bias, are vulnerable to practice effects and "teaching to the test."[40] As one prominent researcher concludes, reading tests "tell us whether or not the same people do best [across tests] but not whether anyone does as well as they [sic] ought to. The fact of the matter is that the district achievement test mean may be a very poor indicator of how well the curriculum has been chosen, how well it has been taught, and how well it has been learned."[41] Of course, standardized tests do a better job of assessing some skills (for example, reading) than others of equal importance (for example, writing or listening).[42]

Given the level of controversy and disagreement, it is no wonder that NCES has avoided injecting measures of such sensitive factors as student performance, equality, or school process into their delicately balanced political environment. In the absence of consensus, federal statisticians find it impossible to make a defensible case for including in CCD any particular indicators of process or outcome, even though many users of CCD would be eager to have such data. To preserve an aura of neutrality and professionalism, NCES staff prefer data items that do not raise red flags. They have enough trouble getting local districts to categorize grade levels and instructional staff in comparable ways, without getting into emotionally laden items like desegregation or achievement. Thus the lack of consensus around standard indicators has served to limit the scope of CCD. It has focused data collection on items that are not controversial, and, perhaps, not very informative

[40]See, for example, the series of volumes, *New Directions for Testing and Measurement*, published quarterly by Jossey-Bass since 1978; R. F. Baglin, "Does Nationally Normed Really Mean Nationally?" *Journal of Education Measurement* 18 (1981):97–108; the special issue "Testing: Concepts, Policy, Practice, and Research," of *American Psychologist*, October 1981, edited by Robert Glaser and Lloyd Bond.

[41]Robert Stake, "The Validity of District-Wide Test Means," in R. M. Bossone (ed.), *Proceedings of the Second National Conference on Testing* (New York: Center for Advanced Study in Education, City University of New York, 1978), p. 42.

[42]Norman Frederiksen, "The Real Test Bias: Influences of Testing on Teaching and Learning," *American Psychologist* 39 (1984):193–202.

when policymakers face controversial policy choices about those conceptually fuzzy but nonetheless critical questions about performance and equality.

Pressures Toward Irrelevance

The simultaneous pressures of political fragmentation and conceptual discord have pushed NCES to adopt a desiccated vision of what federal education statistics can or should be. Vital data about what happens in schools must be found elsewhere. State and local governments that control access to most data about public education often do not exercise or share that access. Some things they would rather not know. Others they would rather that no one else know. Federal education officials are not in a position to force anyone to provide data and, discretion being the better part of valor, choose not to ask for what they will not be given. But they cannot get nationally comparable data by asking states and localities simply to pass on data from the standard indicators, because those "standard indicators" do not exist. Thus NCES is left with a small set of easy-to-collect, nonthreatening items that everyone consents to include in CCD. This process dictates the content of federal education statistics.

The two forces reinforce each other to strengthen the trend to irrelevance. Neither by itself would be so influential as they are in concert. Fragmentation, for example, might be overcome with a technocratic fix if the contending parties were willing to go along with the expert consensus. However, in the case of CCD we find no expert consensus to mediate the fragmentation. Disagreement among experts is not, by itself, fatal to the development of workable statistical indicators, so long as there are other grounds for common action among those who collect and report data. But in the CCD case the data collectors have incentives and authority to refuse to participate in distasteful compromises. They prefer no national data about critical variables to the collection of misleading data that may expose them to damaging comparisons. The resulting federally sponsored body of national statistics is constructed with very large holes.

Given the institutional, political, legal, and financial environment that we have described, CCD's continued existence may be more cause for wonderment than its shortcomings are cause for criticism. If NCES staff have come to see irrelevance as the least of the dangers confronting them, that choice is not very hard to understand. The alternative may well have been extinction. NCES has protected CCD's survival by garbing it in neutrality and rationality, focusing on its statistical properties, and downplaying its connections to policy users. NCES publications take pains to present CCD data without analysis, minimizing the reader's ability to make comparisons or inferences with action implications.[43]

The strategy has worked on its own terms. CCD continues to operate without kicking up much fuss, even during a Reagan administration with little sympathy for federal activity in either education or data collection. It has been a sensible strategy from the perspective of NCES, if not from the perspectives of those who seek information about the likely consequences of policy alternatives. It protects NCES's niche in the bureaucracy, insulates CCD from political attack, and contributes to widespread confidence in the objectivity of the numbers that CCD does produce. It also results in a statistical system that is not very useful to the policymaking community, in data that are outdated and do not illuminate vexing policy choices, in limited user involvement in the design of data collection, and in lukewarm enthusiasm in Congress or the higher reaches of the Department of Education for investment in educational statistics.

If our analysis is correct, the prospects for change in the contents of CCD depend on the prospects for reducing political fragmentation or increasing technical and conceptual consensus. From an extreme structuralist position, a limited set of national statistics is a peripheral cost we pay for our choice to share authority over education among so diverse a group of actors and institutions. Given the broader political and ideological commitments represented by that dispersion of authority, it would be lunacy to alter it merely for the sake of a more policy-relevant set of statistics. From an extreme technocratic position, increasing the policy relevance of CCD would be equally misguided. If expert participants disagree about what to measure and how, then any addition of new variables will necessarily be arbitrary, incomplete, and to some degree misleading about the "true" state of affairs.

Although both of these positions have merit, we suspect that there is room for some flexibility in statistical design within the structural and technical constraints we have described. Such complex bureaucratic arrangements are seldom locked irrevocably into a single course of action. With adroit use of some additional resources, some political bridge-building, and some technical flair, NCES staff might orient CCD toward more policy-oriented variables. For the reasons we have discussed, this would be a risky strategy. But NCES's approach to statistics

[43]Calderone, *Statistics about Society,* p. 56, cites the report of the President's Commission on School Finance: "One gets the impression from the Office of Education that the absence of analytic content in NCES publications reflects a clear policy originating in the upper levels of the Office." Many users of NCES data whom we interviewed made the same complaint.

has been so cautious for so long that change might be less risky than it appears. Our research turned up a broad spectrum of data users, including some in the states, who would cheer a move to collect more policy-relevant data.[44]

The central premise of scholarship on the sociology of knowledge is that social organization shapes the production of official records and other carriers of information. This case fits squarely in that tradition. The story of CCD shows not only that CCD is a product of the interests of educational institutions at the local, state, and federal levels but also how actively and self-consciously policy actors in these institutions have struggled to shape that product. CCD is not an ideal representation of what policymakers want to know about the condition of education, or of what researchers or historians want to know. It is much closer to a representation of what powerful education officials can be persuaded to let the federal government find out. Participants in the policy process prefer the collection and distribution of statistics that show them to their relative advantage. This preference is not venal or malicious, and any voluntary statistical system must take it into account. It is naturally important to public officials to arrange national statistics to suit their tastes. The rest of us simply must remember that what we know about schools and schooling in the United States is a product of that high-stakes political process. For CCD, as for other social statistics, *caveat emptor.*

[44]Weiss and Gruber, *Education Data as Control,* pp. 73–81.

PART V
The New Political Economy of Statistics

13

TECHNOLOGY, COSTS, AND
THE NEW ECONOMICS OF STATISTICS

JOSEPH W. DUNCAN

T HE COLLECTION, processing, and distribution of statistics are changing dramatically as a result of the deregulation of telecommunications, sharply declining costs of computer processing and online mass storage, and the advent of decentralized computing power in the form of minicomputers and even microcomputers in the office and home.[1] This chapter describes some of the forces, especially technical changes, that will affect the basic costs and economics of federal statistical activities. I do not intend to make forecasts or predictions of technical change or to provide a comprehensive review of the technical "state of the art." Rather, I cite developments now on the horizon to indicate how statistical procedures are likely to evolve during the latter half of the 1980s. Inevitably, these technical developments (with attendant lower costs and other changes such as new methods for information dissemination) will have a major impact on the procedures of federal statistical agencies. Hence, a portion of this chapter focuses on the federal statistical and information policy issues arising as a result of the availability and use of new technology. Of special interest are the policy needs for relating public sector and private sector roles in the information industry.

---

[1]The views presented in this paper are the personal views of the author.

Adaptation of New Technology by Civilian Agencies of Government

Technical Leadership at the Census Bureau

As of the 1940s the Census Bureau was a leader in the new technology of automated analysis of statistics. This position resulted from the use of punch card equipment developed earlier by Herman Hollerith, a former employee of the Census Bureau. The initial impetus to develop punch card equipment was time and cost savings, but the equipment also improved the capacity for providing cross-tabulations efficiently.[2]

Punch card tabulation had other effects on statistics. For example, it improved the timeliness of data production. The Census Bureau estimates that if the hand methods in use for the 1880 census had been continued, the bureau would not have gotten very far into the twentieth century before it was spending the entire decade tabulating the decennial census results.[3]

In the 1940s the Census Bureau played a major role in developing the earliest electronic digital computers. The first ENIAC (the acronym for Electronic Numerical Integrater and Computer) was completed near the end of World War II at the Moore School of Electrical Engineering, a part of the University of Pennsylvania in Philadelphia. Though ENIAC was produced for military and scientific purposes, its ability to do routine calculations had obvious value for statistical applications. In 1944 Morris Hansen, assistant to the director of the Census Bureau, met with ENIAC's developer, John W. Mauchly, to discuss adapting ENIAC for statistical work. In September 1946 the National Bureau of Standards awarded a study contract to Eckert-Mauchly Computer Corporation to draw plans and specifications for a digital computer for census use. In June 1948 the company received a second contract to build UNIVAC I in time to do a modest amount of the tabulation for the 1950 census of population and housing.

UNIVAC I—the first electronic digital computer to be used for statistical processing on a sizable scale—was a pioneering effort in transferring digital computer technology from defense to civilian uses.

Technical improvements followed rapidly. The Census Bureau developed card-to-tape converters to speed up data input for the use of

[2]Leon E. Truesdell, *The Development of Punch Card Tabulation in the Bureau of the Census, 1890–1940* (Washington, D.C.: Census Bureau, 1965).

[3]"Scientific and Technological Development of Activities of the Bureau of the Census," U.S. Bureau of the Census Technical Paper 29, 1973, p. 3.

UNIVAC I. The bureau also realized that automation of input was becoming the most significant data processing bottleneck. This led to the development of FOSDIC (Film Optical Sensing Device for Input to Computers). This device provided for microfilming of census records so that spots of light recorded on negative film could be optically recognized by a photoelectric cell. Throughout the late 1950s and 1960s the Census Bureau was a leader in devising new information technology for civilian applications.[4]

Unfortunately, by the 1970s government statistical agencies were no longer in the forefront. The earlier achievements had solved the most pressing needs of federal statistical production. Refinements in the 1970s focused mainly on data base management and the development of specialized software. One noteworthy example is TPL (Table Producing Language), which was conceived and developed at the Bureau of Labor Statistics.

A more fundamental reason for the lag in census technology, however, was the general lack of aggressiveness among federal executive agencies in developing frontline computer capabilities. While the Department of Defense continued to be a major source of innovation in computer design for large-scale and powerful systems, the computer systems of civilian agencies were fragmented. Once a computer installation was available and working, civilian agencies had little interest in upgrading and improving the systems. Throughout the 1970s many computer systems in civilian agencies grew significantly out of date. Agencies increasingly turned to private service bureaus and to other private computer installations to achieve improvements in data processing capacity.

For example, when I joined the Office of Management and Budget (OMB) in 1974, I was distressed to learn that the Census Bureau was still operating with vacuum tube magnetic tape drives—devices at that time already two generations behind current technology. OMB budget examiners thwarted repeated attempts to gain approval for an upgraded computer system on the ground that processing demands for new surveys and analysis did not justify the investments.[5] Furthermore, each

[4]For a more complete discussion of the mechanization of the Census Bureau, see Joseph W. Duncan and William C. Shelton, *Revolution in U.S. Government Statistics, 1926–1976* (Washington, D.C.: U.S. Government Printing Office, October 1978), pp. 116–45.

[5]Tabulation of the 1980 census has suffered a series of delays and difficulties. However, the computing capability was upgraded significantly as a result of an inadvertent flooding of the census computer facility, which required replacement of obsolete and time-worn equipment. If the flood of the facility had not occurred in August 1979, it is likely that processing would have been delayed even further as a result of equipment breakdowns.

budget season yielded new proposals—proposals that contradicted earlier efforts and added to the confusion about needs, priorities, and strategies.

Why Government Lags in Innovation

Difficulties in upgrading the computer facilities at the Census Bureau are not unique within the federal government. Despite pressures for cost control, the budget process and the political judgments surrounding action on the budget actually discourage efficiencies available from new technology. One factor retarding innovation is the long lead time in the budget process. Budget decisions typically start at least two years before the beginning of a fiscal year. After OMB sets budget targets, each department reviews its priorities and prepares specific budget requests, which are then reviewed in the context of overall governmental policy by cabinet departments, OMB, and, occasionally, the White House. The administration submits its proposals to Congress in January before the beginning of a fiscal year. The budget is then reviewed by appropriations committees and subcommittees in the House and the Senate, which then negotiate a final appropriation. In recent years Congress has not approved appropriations for most civilian agencies until well after the beginning of the fiscal year, further lengthening the process.

For areas that have rapidly changing technology, the time lag between developing an initial proposal and gaining authority to spend money on the proposal is so long that new and even better technology is often available by the time funds are authorized. However, budget authorizations are often so specific that it is difficult to change to an improved level of technology without a re-review of the budget request.

A second factor delaying the introduction of new technology is the procurement process. Legitimate procurement requests cannot be initiated until Congress has appropriated the funds. Once funds are available, the agency must frame a specification statement for bids by alternative vendors. The proposal process is long and tedious, involving several layers of technical review before a contract can be awarded. After the contract award there is usually a substantial wait for the actual delivery of the equipment. Even "off the shelf" equipment for large and complex systems can take several months or even years to be installed. The General Services Administration estimates that the federal acquisition process takes an average of three to four years to complete. (The steps involved are shown in Table 13.1.) As a result, it takes at least five years for budget approval and procurement of upgraded tech-

TABLE 13.1

Typical Steps in the Federal Acquisition Process

Task	Probable Range
I. Requirements Definition/System Justification	1.5–2 years
A. Identify Requirements	
B. Complete Conversation Study	
C. Complete Cost-Benefit Study	
D. Obtain OMB Approval	
E. Obtain GSA Approval	
F. Complete Request for Proposal (RFP)	
G. Complete Benchmark Package	
II. Procurement Process	1–2 years
A. Advertise in *Commerce Business Daily*	
B. Release RFP and Benchmark Package	
C. Review Proposals	
D. Conduct Benchmark Tests	
E. Request Best and Final Bids	
F. Complete Evaluations	
G. Award Contract	
H. Settle Protests	
I. Install New Equipment	

SOURCE: General Services Administration

nology. And since the first proposal frequently does not survive either the administration's budget process or the congressional review, repeated proposals are necessary and the time required is even longer than five years.

The time lag described in this section is an understatement of the delays. For highly innovative proposals it often requires several years of convincing career budget and administrative staff before the proposal reaches the desk of the political leadership within a cabinet department.

Some Recent Evaluations

In June 1983 a task force of the President's Private Sector Survey on Cost Control in the Federal Government estimated that the federal agencies have over 19,000 computers and a work force of more than 250,000 federal employees in data processing activities. "During the early 1960s," the task force noted, "the federal government was the acknowledged leader in using state of the art computer hardware and software. From the mid-1960's, however, government fell farther and farther behind the private sector. *Approximately 50% of the govern-*

ment's ADP inventory is so old that it is no longer supported by the manufacturer and must be maintained by specially trained federal personnel."[6]

The average age of government ADP hardware is nearly seven years, compared with approximately 2½ years for the private sector.[7] The task force estimated that upgrading information systems could result in a cumulative net savings of over $4 billion in the next three years.

The procurement policies described in Table 13.1 include several steps such as benchmark testing and settlement of protests from other bidders that are unique to the federal government. The task force noted: "These tasks reflect policies of the federal government which are designed to assure fair competition and greater involvement of the private sector in systems development and acquisition efforts."[8] But the remaining steps in the procurement process are very similar to tasks carried out by the private sector. However, in the private sector the tasks are completed faster. The task force noted that a major factor in the length of the acquisition process is the review cycle, which is fundamentally a check on the fulfillment of numerous regulations, especially in anticipation of possible review by the GSA or inquiries by the Congress.[9]

Today the pace of technological change for information processing is quickening. It is difficult to see how the federal statistical agencies will be able to adapt new technology quickly in response to new opportunities without more flexible procedures for the design and funding of innovative approaches.

Technological Change in the Information Industry
The Context of Technological Change

Computing power is now available inexpensively in offices, schools, and even homes. Whereas in the mid-1960s forecasts expected that massive central processing systems would serve remote terminals, today's technology encompasses both powerful stand-alone computers and networks of individual work stations. Computer technology should advance significantly in the future, too.

---

[6]President's Private Sector Survey on Cost Control, "Task Force Report on Automated Data Processing/Office Automation," submitted to the Subcommittee on June 13, 1983, p. i. Emphasis in original.
[7]Ibid., p. v.
[8]Ibid., p. 27.
[9]Ibid., p. 29.

Data Collection

Traditionally, the government has collected data through special surveys or from forms used to administer benefit programs. In a majority of cases, respondents directly complete the forms; in others, enumerators interview respondents and fill out the form. By the late 1970s some information was also gathered by telephone.

Telephone interviewing has become increasingly sophisticated. Computer-supported interview schedules permit the scripting of an interview so that a respondent's answers to early questions direct the interviewer to related items. Computer-aided telephone interviews have several important attributes. First, they remove much of the responsibility from the interviewer who no longer must follow a complex questionnaire design. Second, the keyboard entry of responses received over the telephone simplifies data input and tabulation and data analysis at later stages. Further, real-time checks by the computer make it possible for the interviewer to identify answers outside preset limits or answers that vary substantially from independently provided information. Finally, the computer assistance in initial and repeated dialing of the phone number reduces the falloff of completions that might otherwise occur because of frustration.

A number of recent innovations are likely to influence future government surveys. For example, price surveys have been conducted by field observation of sample items on display. The recent development of lightweight computers with light pens makes it possible for field reporters to read the standard product code used by retail outlets for inventory control and speedier checkout. Cable television systems permit immediate feedback to televised material. Tests in Columbus, Ohio, have demonstrated the feasibility of this approach for survey data, although much work needs to be done to calibrate the samples and control for nonresponse. Consumer marketing panels with special "credit cards" to record individual purchases are also yielding interesting results. Similar identity cards could be used in federal benefit programs to collect information from sample participants.

Federal agencies have recently begun to use advanced techniques of data collection from businesses by accepting information on computer tapes. The increased availability of electronic networks suggests that direct telecommunications of required reports will soon be possible, a concept now entering test mode at the Securities and Exchange Commission. Currently, individual companies have standardized reporting formats to obtain internal data. Adaptation of data processing standards to major reporting requirements such as social security, unemployment compensation, and related reporting is on the horizon.

Optical scanning techniques have improved considerably in recent years. Optical character recognition will soon be used on a wide basis by the post office and is suitable for reading many standard forms that presently require data conversion through key-to-tape devices. Currently, however, electronic data transfers are not widely implemented.

Data Dissemination

In my view, data dissemination is the area of statistical activity that will be most dramatically influenced by the current revolution in telecommunications and computing capabilities. Further, when one considers the political consequence of statistical reporting and statistical analysis, changes in dissemination merit particular attention.

The advent of the microcomputer means that users of statistics will have increased capabilities to analyze government data. A major issue relating to dissemination is the media that will be used for distribution of raw data and summary tabulations. Mass storage capabilities for the microcomputer are especially noteworthy.

Early microcomputers used floppy disks with an initial storage of 180,000 bytes of information; now diskettes typically hold 360,000 bytes of information and megabyte densities (1 million bytes) are under development.[10]

For statistical users a read-only capability is satisfactory for initial availability of the data. A new form of read-only mass storage was recently announced. This is the laser card, which has a storage capacity of two megabytes for a cost of approximately $6. At that price the laser card will be less expensive to distribute than today's floppy disks.[11] The low cost will not represent a barrier to frequent data base updates.

A technique that promises to increase data density greatly is "perpendicular magnetic recording." Perpendicular magnetic recording magnetizes the disk surface at right angles in contrast to conventional longitudinal recording, which creates magnetized zones along the surface. With the perpendicular recording it is possible to squeeze the width rather than the length of magnetized regions to create higher recording densities. Perpendicular recording can give a theoretical performance of 100,000 flex reversals per inch versus 15,000 flex reversals

[10]NEC has introduced a half-height, eight-inch floppy disk drive (the FD 1165) with a storage capacity of 1.6 megabytes.

[11]The label laser card derives from the fact that lasers are required to write data to the cards. Some experts believe that the peripheral technology necessary to read laser cards will not require significant changes to personal computers. Information about the laser card is available from Drexler Technology Corp., 2557 Charleston Road, Mountain View, California 94043. See *Byte* 8 (March 1983):8.

per inch on a longitudinal recording. It is expected that floppy disks using this technique will offer three to five times the capacity of today's longitudinal systems.[12]

Another technology now under development is optical memory media such as laser video disks. Currently no clear standards are being developed; nevertheless, the capabilities of optical laser disks for data storage are impressive. Optical media can contain up to one hundred times the storage capacity of the same size of magnetic media. Thus, they will provide storage at a small fraction of the cost per megabyte. While it is currently difficult to erase and reuse an optical disk, the laser optical disk is especially suitable as an archive with one disk able to store the equivalent of 50,000 pages of information. Think of the possibilities of distributing the *Statistical Abstract* including alternative graphic presentations on a disk costing $12!

A development in the hard disk area is the removable hard disk. This will facilitate data transfer among machines at different locations without the risk of introducing telecommunication errors.

In the long run mass storage may include not only the famous bubble memory but also three-dimensional holograms. Holography would offer a new way to store information using optical rather than mechanical, magnetic, or electronic techniques. Holography uses a laser beam encoded with information to write into the crystal a three-dimensional holographic image. This image, in turn, is read from the crystal by a laser beam of another wave length. According to Lynn A. Boatner, a research physicist involved with the holographic crystal project, "Literally billions of holograms could be stored with this technology."[13] Both current and developing technology suggest that online data storage capabilities will expand dramatically, not only for mainframe computers but also for compact mini- and microcomputers at or near the work location of the analyst.

Implications for Electronic Data Delivery

These emerging technologies are expected to change dramatically the interface between the governmental statistical office and users inside and outside of government.

The new technology is making it possible to replace traditional data dissemination techniques with electronic data delivery. The gov-

[12]The Japanese are especially active in perpendicular recording. The first international symposium on perpendicular recording was sponsored by Tohoku University in March 1983 in Sendai, Japan. See *Byte* 8 (March 1983):64.

[13]"Holography Offers Promise of Massive Data Storage," *Infoworld* 5 (September 1983):11.

ernment has long been a pioneer in preparing machine-readable data tapes to assist those with large computing capacities to simplify data entry and data analysis. The government, however, has been slow to create data banks that can be accessed online.

During the past decade the private sector has developed a number of online time-sharing services, many of which simply repackage government data. The DataPro catalog of "On-Line Data Services" lists over 400 vendors with 1,046 identified data products.[14]

In addition to developing time-sharing services, a number of private sector corporations are developing new approaches to data delivery using electronic media. Nearly 60 percent of the credit reports obtained from the Dun & Bradstreet Corporation are now delivered through phone calls to operators with real-time access to the data base, or by direct delivery via telecommunications to printers at the user's site. Other companies also are using electronic delivery. McGraw-Hill has a program for telecommunicating data from large computers to personal computers at the user's location. Dow Jones Corporation has a series of software packages for assisting stock analysts in downloading current securities data.

Electronic data delivery is in the infant stage of development. The concept is now proven, but the true efficiencies are yet to be realized since much of the current activity is specialized. Just as the Gutenberg press revolutionized the printed word, the satellite may dramatically replace the computer tape or disk library with efficient central sources of general information.

These efficient central sources of information will not be used in the time-sharing mode that characterizes current practice. Rather, the central sources of information, using low-cost telecommunications, will be data servers. That is, they will concentrate on data base maintenance, emphasizing the consistency and quality of data. The user will download the data via telecommunications into his local storage for on-the-spot analysis and revision.

Current projections indicate that the costs of digital data communications will be reduced by a factor of ten within three years and by a factor of one hundred within a decade (probably much sooner).

As voice communications also become digital, the overall communications networks will focus on information centers that have broad demand. Hence, value added will increasingly be related to the bringing together of related data bases. Government generated statistical information will be placed in new data utilities that seek to provide

---

[14]Statistics provided by DataPro information specialists.

data availability and analysis as part of an overall service. The costs of distributing the data will be nominal; the key factor will be the availability and comparability of statistical information.

Thus data dissemination will take place via electronic transmission and through new distribution media ranging from floppy disks and laser cards to larger-capacity bubble memories and optical disks.

These cost trends contrast sharply with recent trends in conventional print media, which have been the mainstay of the statistical agencies. I recently compiled prices for representative federal statistical publications. Between 1973 and 1983 these prices increased 129 percent. In contrast, data storage, data communications, and data processing costs declined dramatically in this same decade.

Policy Issues

User Fees and Costs of Government Information Products and Services

Questions of federal data dissemination, including electronic data delivery, are embedded in the larger issue of user fees for government information products and services. Federal law, as interpreted through the courts, provides that government agencies should make a reasonable charge to each identifiable recipient for the measurable amount of government services or projects that convey a special benefit upon the recipient. Costs may be recovered from private beneficiaries even if the products or services in question also benefit the general public. Under the law, government products and services are to be financially self-sustaining to the extent possible, but the self-sustaining purpose must be weighed against the overall public policy purpose of the government agency in question. Agency heads can prescribe fees, charges, or prices that are fair and equitable.

With regard to federal statistical agencies, the policy issue arises when an agency collects information for public purposes and this information is also of value to nonfederal parties. For example, a survey is carried out within a federal agency's legislatively approved program and, as part of the survey activities, the agency itself produces computer-based information resources (CBIRs, meaning machine-readable data files, software files, and online data bases). Then private sector parties request copies of, or access to, the agency's CBIRs. Then the question arises concerning the cost recovery basis, if any, by which the federal agency should determine charges against the private sector.

Federal statistical agencies have generally followed the practice of charging only "costs of reproduction" for governmentally produced CBIRs. This practice is currently subject to debate within the federal government. Many argue that the government should recover more than the cost of reproduction. CBIRs produced by federal statistical agencies are widely used in the flourishing information industry and are of substantial commercial value. In the present restrictive budgetary climate, some critics argue that more of the commercial value should be returned to the government through user fees that would recover more of the original program costs and better reflect the market value of the products or services.

In conflict are two public purposes: that of making government services self-sustaining through user fees, and that of making governmentally produced information available to the public in a manner consistent with agency missions. The counterargument to the demand for increased user fees is that federal statistical agencies bear a responsibility to make information available to the public under the least restrictive conditions and that this responsibility extends to pricing information products and services at a level that members of the public can afford to pay.

A related policy issue centers on competition between government agencies and the private sector. It is generally accepted in the United States that the government should not compete with private business in the provision of goods and services. Certain public-use CBIRs are made available at artificially low prices because the government is subsidizing the prices by not charging users the cost of original information collection or generation. Private firms selling products and services similar to those offered by the government cannot do otherwise than to charge for information generation because the generation represents substantial costs to the firms. Government agencies maintain that the information generation activities are integral to the public purposes for which they were established; costs associated with such activities ought properly to be borne by the agencies themselves and not recovered from users of the information products and services. The private sector argues that adherence to this line of reasoning results in low prices that are anticompetitive, stifling development of private information industry initiatives.

Data Quality

Providing users with data is an expensive undertaking. Statistical agencies cannot simply prepare a computer tape and announce its availability. To assure a minimum "quality of use," the agencies have to prepare documentation about the contents of the tape and how to use the information. Personnel must be employed and trained to respond to user queries.

In addition, statistical agencies must take on some responsibility for ensuring the quality of data released. It is not uncommon for the statistical agencies or the users to discover errors in the data; many of these discoveries occur only after release to users when internal inconsistencies reveal errors that escaped earlier detection procedures. Agencies must then face the responsibility of issuing new machine-readable data files to replace the previous releases. Since there are few controls placed on copying public use machine-readable data files, agencies are frequently unable to trace all of the parties who are using error-laden machine-readable data files.

As some governmental statistical agencies have already found, an inevitable next step is to provide training for users. Communication with the users is necessary to ensure "quality of use" and to detect errors in the data. Seminars, conferences, and workshops between data producers and users follow. Surveys of users' needs and problems must be conducted.

Although these developments take time and money and cause headaches to statistical agencies, they are generally recognized as healthy developments. Agencies are beginning to recognize that data access functions must be incorporated into the basic design of statistical programs. Yet the new technology described earlier will make it virtually impossible for statistical agencies to serve all types of users. This means that it will be essential to develop careful strategies for "wholesaling" the raw data so that it can be efficiently repackaged and redistributed by the private sector, with careful attention to issues of quality.

Data Comparability

The growing number of data users, particularly those who employ sophisticated computer techniques, has led to greater demand for data comparability. As users acquire machine-readable data files from a variety of statistical agencies and attempt to integrate them into a single data base, they encounter the problem of comparability.

Oddly enough, the desire for greater data comparability also gains strength from declining budgets. If statistical agencies were collecting more highly comparable data, several agencies might share data bases and consequently save money. Statutory barriers now often prevent interagency data sharing, but efforts are currently underway to devise new legislation that would protect the confidentiality of federal statistical data bases while still allowing greater interagency sharing of data.[15]

Problems of comparability are more subtle and complex than the problems of quality discussed above. The user (or wholesaler) must understand the details of classification systems and coding procedures. As use becomes more widespread, it is increasingly likely that users will inadvertently mix apples and oranges, with results being both misleading and erroneous.

Federal Statistical Policy Issues

Federal statistical agencies adopt common statistical standards more as a result of voluntary compliance with conclusions consensually arrived at than as a result of central enforcement, although limited central direction and standards are propagated by OMB. In a decentralized system that achieves change by coordinated consensus, change is slow and major elements of the system can successfully resist proposed improvements. Ultimately, the movement of the federal statistical system toward adoption of new developments and technologies relating to electronic data delivery depends upon the sense of professionalism of the staff and the agreement of the legislative branch.

The implications for the central statistical office are pervasive. Several key issues are important:

1. Once government data are in a private data bank there is no control over the use of the data to assure that consistent applications and interpretations are employed.

2. Distribution of government data by a private organization means that the user may not be aware of the role of the government in developing the original data. This could further erode support for the government's role as collector and developer of the data.

3. Growing use of electronic media for the storage of private data means that the central statistical office could employ electronic techniques for data collection. This will require work on developing standard classifications and concepts that will be used in the private sector. It will also require new auditing and editing techniques to assure the accuracy and coverage of data collection.

---

[15]For further information on this legislation see the papers from the 1983 American Statistical Institute annual meeting. The papers from the session entitled "Disclosure and Confidentiality Issues in the Federal Statistical Environment" will be available from the Internal Revenue Service. See *Statistics of Income & Administrative Record Research*, 1983.

4. A set of policies must be developed to assure efficient dissemination through electronic means and yet to assure that all citizens have access to fundamental information. The printed media will long remain in use, yet the high cost of printed media will force trade-offs between conventional media and electronic media.

5. Given the lag in adopting new technology that is evident in the domestic (or administrative) side of government, there are difficult problems in defining the role of government in: (a) stimulating innovation; (b) implementing standards and procedures that will minimize social cost; and (c) adapting innovation at the correct time, that is, before sound technical and market decisions have been made.[16]

The Political Economy of New Technological Development

The rapid change of technology is redefining many roles and functions between the private and public sectors. In addition to the move during the Carter and Reagan administrations to reduce the size of the federal bureaucracy and to deregulate the private sector, the changing technology is redefining many of the ground rules. For example, electronic delivery of messages is creating an entirely new industry that sends voice communications by digital impulse (previously reserved for data communications) and is replacing standard mail with electronic delivery of documents.

With respect to the federal statistical agencies, new technology has been rapidly assimilated by private sector companies, who in turn oppose efforts by the government to upgrade its capabilities. This was particularly evident in the resistance of organizations such as Data Resources, Incorporated to government efforts to create data banks that would be available electronically. The argument of DRI and others was that a move by the government in this area would unfairly compete with an ongoing private sector activity.

Trade associations such as the Information Industry Association (IIA) have been concerned about issues such as the role of the Government Printing Office in competition with private sector printing. The dilemma was recently stated well by Paul G. Zurkowski of the association when he noted that "Over the years, IIA has sought to curb the growth and avert the start of government information activities that we felt were more appropriately performed by the market driven private

[16]Joseph W. Duncan and J. Timothy Sprehe, "Central Statistical Offices and Electronic Data Delivery," paper delivered at the International Statistical Institute, Madrid, Spain, September 1983.

sector. We also strongly called for the use of private sector contractors to perform government information activities that the market would not support."[17] The industry's representatives maintain that "where the private sector is meeting or can meet an information need, the government should not compete."

Many analysts of this private sector/public sector relationship would agree that fundamental information activities such as the conduct of a national census for political reapportionment and the measurement of national income are statistical functions that should appropriately be undertaken by the government, but it is not clear in many other cases where the appropriate division of responsibility is between private sector information activities, which collect, for example, statistics on industries or trade groups, and similar federal activities. The issue was highlighted in the 1970s when congressional distrust of industry sources led to the establishment of the Energy Information Administration in the newly created Department of Energy with a specific charter to duplicate private information-gathering. Estimates of oil and gas reserves had been provided by organizations such as the American Gas Association. Government efforts were ultimately designed to collect information from the very same companies that participated in trade association groups; the resulting estimates were not significantly different. Yet public distrust of the private sector information sources must be recognized as an important ingredient of evolving energy policy in the mid-1970s and even today. Thus, implementation of the principle outlined by the Information Industry Association is subject to considerable controversy.

In its policy statement the IIA set forth several suggestions. In addition to the view that government should not develop and disseminate new information products or services that compete with those already available from or planned by the private sector, the association is concerned about existing federal information activities. It believes that government information products or services currently being offered should be carefully reviewed periodically to make sure that continued production and dissemination serve a need that still exists and that is not being met or cannot be readily met by private sector sources.

The IIA suggests that where there is a genuine, demonstrable and critical need for an information product or service not currently provided (or likely to be provided) by the private sector, government should take the following steps in order of priority:

1. Encourage the private sector to meet the need.

---

[17]IIA policy statement on "Meeting Information Needs in the New Information Age." Letter to the membership of IIA, August 16, 1983.

2. Provide secondary inducements for the private sector to meet the need through such mechanisms as subsidies, loans, grants, and tax credits.

3. If the private sector cannot fulfill a demonstrable and significant information need, contract out to the private sector the development of the needed product or service.

4. When as a last resort to meet the need the government does produce such an information product or service, make it available in a way and at a price that diminishes potential competition with the private sector. That price should, with rare exceptions, be sufficient to recover all costs incurred in the development, production, and dissemination of the particular information product.

The brief principles outlined by the IIA are similar to those developed by a special task force of the National Commission on Libraries and Information Science.[18]

Conclusion

The advance of technology is evident. More cost-effective methods for collecting, processing, and disseminating government statistics are already available. Sharply reduced costs of mass storage and telecommunications will revolutionize data dissemination. In this dynamic context the definition of appropriate goals and strategies for federal statistics will be the subject of far-ranging debates.

---

[18]The public/private sector task force of the National Commission reviewed many of the current concerns both within the government and within the private sector to develop a series of principles that should be followed. Their work represented one of the early efforts to set forth the proper relationships. A brief excerpt from the report is contained in the appendix to this chapter. The full report provides an excellent background concerning the public/private sector issues discussed in this chapter. See National Commission on Libraries and Information Science, "Public Sector/Private Sector Interaction in Providing Information Services," 75 pages, 1982.

Appendix

Public Sector/Private Sector Interaction in Providing Information Services

Findings of the Task Force

The members of the Task Force reached near-unanimous agreement on each of a set of principles that should guide federal government involvement in information activities. The members of the Task Force also reached substantial, and in most cases near-unanimous, agreement on a set of recommendations for steps to be taken in implementation of those principles.

In general, these principles and recommendations are:

In favor of open access to information generated by the federal government.

> The view of the Task Force is that it is in the national interest for information in general to be widely and readily available to the public. Information generated (with emphasis on "generated") by the federal government represents a valuable resource. The principles are intended to reinforce the importance of ensuring public access to it.

In favor of reliance upon libraries and private sector organizations (both for-profit and not-for-profit), to make readily available information that can be distributed by the federal government.

> The view of the Task Force is that these two groups of institutions, taken together, provide the best means for ensuring public access to such information. On the one hand, use of libraries, especially public and academic libraries, ensures that "ability to pay" does not raise barriers that effectively and discriminatively deny access to information. On the other hand, the use of private sector organizations, in the business of providing information services, ensures individual freedom to develop and market a multiplicity of information services whose value is determined by the purchasers rather than by the government. The principles and recommendations emphasize the importance of using this balance of means for access, in contrast to creating new agencies to do so.

In favor of a leadership role for government, rather than a management role.

> The federal government has an opportunity to play a significant role in fostering the use of information as an economic and social resource. The key, though, is leadership, not management, so as to encourage development by the private sector of information resources, products, and services that will meet the needs of the public.

<u>In favor of limiting direct government intervention in the marketplace.</u>

While the Task Force recommends against arbitrary exclusion of the federal government from providing services that the political process identifies as needed, it does recommend that the government not enter the marketplace unless there are clearly defined, compelling reasons for doing so. Further more, any such decision should be subject to periodic review to ensure that circumstances continue to warrant such activity. The view of the Task Force is that the entry of the federal government into the marketplace must be subject to checks and balances.

SOURCE: National Commission on Libraries and Information Science, "Public Sector/ Private Sector Interaction in Providing Information Services," 1982, pp. x and xi.

14

WHO WILL HAVE THE NUMBERS? THE RISE OF THE STATISTICAL SERVICES INDUSTRY AND THE POLITICS OF PUBLIC DATA

PAUL STARR AND ROSS CORSON

SOMETHING new has happened to social and economic statistics, and the implications for the production and availability of knowledge about society are not widely and fully appreciated. As a governmental activity, statistics is centuries old. As a popular interest and amateur form of social research, it dates from the early 1800s and as a profession from the late 1800s.[1] But as a business, it is a phenomenon of the mid-twentieth century. And only with the technological and economic changes of the 1970s did there emerge a substantial industry of private firms selling repackaged public data and privately collected statistics, statistical models, and analytical skills.

Statistical information, of course, has long been thought to have commercial value. Governments have gathered statistics partly to regulate, guide, and encourage economic development, but they have typically not produced the information for sale. Private firms, particularly in insurance and finance, have long produced data relevant to their businesses from their own operations and cooperatively in trade associations, but they have sought the data mostly as an adjunct or intermediate good. Now, for the first time on a large scale, the statistics themselves are being bought and sold. As an independent commodity, they

---

[1]On early popular interest, see Patricia Cline Cohen, *A Calculating People: The Spread of Numeracy in Early America* (Chicago: University of Chicago Press, 1982).

have become a foundation of a growing statistical services industry that is rapidly becoming a force in its own right in the economy and in public policymaking, not simply in the United States but throughout the world.

This new industry has a complex relationship with the state. The federal government is, at one and the same time, a supplier of cheap and plentiful raw materials; a regulator and subsidizer; a competitor in some areas and a customer in others. Much of the statistical services industry probably would not exist if it were not for the long history of public investment in information technology and statistics, but the industry chafes at government competition and would prefer that the government get out of any area of information service that might yield a profit to a private firm.

Like much of the growing information industry, statistical services are primarily a business information business: The major clients are large corporations and, to a lesser extent, small businesses, investors, financial planners, lawyers, and others who need data for business use. The main products and services use econometric forecasting and financial data and, for somewhat different purposes, data about demographic patterns, consumer tastes, audience size, and public opinion. The principal uses are for financial decisions and corporate "decision support" in such areas as planning and marketing. The statistical services industry furnishes information about an organization's environment, and the industry's growth reflects a shift in the organizational uses of information technology over the past decade. The early applications of computers were to routine internal operations, such as payroll; gradually computers have worked their way up organizations to high-level decision-making (as well as down to ground-level operations). It is no longer the data processing department alone but managers throughout the contemporary corporation that work with computers.

In several ways, the statistical services industry represents a significant development in the social production of knowledge. As Hayek and Machlup have pointed out, a distinction may readily and usefully be made between ephemeral knowledge of fluctuating variables tied to time and place (for example, knowing that the price of pork bellies suddenly dropped this morning in Chicago) and intellectual knowledge of long-term relationships.[2] Knowledge of the first kind is fleeting but vital to economic life, and it can often command a higher price than knowledge of more lasting intellectual and social value. The increased speed of both data analysis and transmission due to computers and

[2]Friedrich A. Hayek, "The Use of Knowledge in Society," *American Economic Review* 35 (1945):519–30; Fritz Machlup, *The Production and Distribution of Knowledge in the United States* (Princeton, N.J.: Princeton University Press, 1962), pp. 18–19.

telecommunications has made it possible to put to everyday business use much knowledge of statistics and statistical methods originally developed primarily for purposes of long-range understanding and planning. As formerly professional or governmental concerns are turned into a business, however, a further change necessarily takes place. It is an essential requirement of any business that it be able to withhold the benefits of its products from those who do not pay for them. A concomitant of the growth of the statistical services industry, therefore, is that information formerly treated as public becomes proprietary.

Simultaneous developments in politics now also encourage the privatization of information. The Reagan administration came into office committed to cutting back the functions of government, including its statistical activities, not only for budgetary reasons but also because of a deep faith in the superior performance of the private sector and discipline of the marketplace. In the field of information services, however, privatization raises some special problems. The free flow of information is a foundation of democratic politics and of modern science and intellectual life. Information also has some unique economic characteristics that distinguish it from nearly all other commodities and that raise questions about the efficiency as well as the equity of market allocations. Our task, therefore, will be not only to give an account of the development of the statistical services industry but also to explore its wider political and economic ramifications.

The Emergence of the Statistical Services Industry
Data Bases

The businesses we are describing as statistical services provide quantitative information or the capacity to manipulate and apply it. The boundaries of the industry are difficult to draw. Statistical services overlap with computer services, management consulting, and market research, but the core is a subset of what is generally called the data base (or data base publishing) industry. Indeed, "statistical data base industry" is almost a synonym for statistical services.

The term data base came into currency with computers, but it is now used to describe any structured collection of uniquely defined elements of information, regardless of whether the information consists of words or numbers or whether it is presented in print or electronically. In this broad sense, an encyclopedia or even a newspaper is a data base. Though potentially so elastic as to encompass all organized knowledge, the broad definition calls attention to the increasing interchangeability of formats: the same information can often now be presented in print, on a computer tape or disk, or through online access from a remote terminal to a central computer.

The development of online systems has played a particularly important part in creating and shaping the new data base industry. Many data bases, once available only in print, have been converted to electronic form and made available online. This is not simply a change in the medium of communication. The shift from print to computers turns a mute product into an interactive service. Online systems can be electronically searched. They can be continually updated, a major advantage if the data refer to rapidly changing information. In addition, through computer time-sharing, online systems permit the use of the large, centralized computer processing capacities and software belonging to many data base vendors. This last feature has been particularly important for statistical services.

From the standpoint of their content, data bases are customarily divided into two types: reference data bases identify where to find information, while source data bases provide it in full in either textual or numerical form. Bibliographic data bases giving citations (and sometimes abstracts) of published material are the chief example of the first kind. Online bibliographic systems, developed initially under government sponsorship in the 1960s, were put on the market commercially in the mid-1970s and have been especially important for research in scientific and technical fields. With advances in mass data storage and transmission, online systems are increasingly able to provide access to the sources themselves rather than just citations or abstracts. Online source data bases can now provide the full text of legal documents, newspapers, and scientific and technical journals, reports, and conference proceedings.[3]

The clients of bibliographic and text retrieval, however, have been somewhat different, at least during the early stages of development that have thus far unfolded. Whereas researchers and librarians have been the primary users of bibliographic services, the early users of text retrieval have been lawyers and journalists (in financially strong organizations). The high cost of text retrieval is undoubtedly a factor in limiting

[3]See Editors of Knowledge Industry Publications, *The Business Information Markets, 1982–87* (White Plains, N.Y.: Knowledge Industry Publications, 1982); Walter Kiechel III, "Everything You Always Wanted to Know May Soon Be On-Line," *Fortune*, May 5, 1980, pp. 226–40; Charles P. Bourne, "On-Line Systems: History, Technology, and Economics," *Journal of the American Society for Information Science* 31 (1980):155–60; Judith Wanger and Ruth N. Landau, "Nonbibliographic On-Line Data Base Services," *Journal of the American Society for Information Science* 31 (1980):171–80.

its academic and popular use, but as the publishing industry adjusts to the new technologies for dissemination, online text retrieval may be opened to a wider consumer market and become the largest part of the data base industry.

Two types of data bases are relevant to statistical services. The first are source data bases with statistical information, such as are gathered from surveys and censuses. The second are administrative registers, such as mailing lists and credit information systems, that hold volumes of information about individuals or organizations. Such registers can be turned to statistical purposes, especially when they are stored electronically. For example, the Dun & Bradstreet Corporation has since 1841 produced reports on the credit-worthiness of businesses. In its early days customers came to its offices to consult handwritten reports. Now the company makes its reports available not only by mail and over the telephone but also online. And since its online system holds credit information on 4.5 million business establishments, it can also use the data to produce statistical reports on specific industries and profiles comparing a particular company's financial health with others in its industry.

Some of the data bases in the private sector are of staggering proportions. As of 1983 Data Resources, Inc. (DRI), the econometrics firm, carried about 15 million time series in its computers.[4] DRI's time series include not only macroeconomic information but also immense volumes of data about specific items in many industries in the United States and other countries—from international trade and national income accounts to the price history of a particular steel product on the East Coast. Probably the largest private register of the American population—rivaling the Census Bureau—belongs to Donnelley Marketing, a subsidiary of Dun & Bradstreet, which has computerized names and addresses for 87 percent of the households in the United States. TRW's Information Services Division has credit information on 86 million consumers.[5]

Some of the more specialized statistical services have data bases that are remarkable less for their size than for the velocity with which they carry statistical information. A. C. Nielsen, famous for its network television ratings, also tracks sales and market trends in grocery products. As it produces the weekly ratings that so greatly influence the fate of television programs, so, too, it produces weekly indexes for food, drugs, tobacco, and other mass merchandise. To do so the company (now a subsidiary of Dun & Bradstreet) has become something of a pioneer in the automation of unobtrusive measurement. While its electronic meters on television sets record viewing habits in 3,300 house-

[4]Interview with Joseph Kasputys, president of DRI, August 3, 1983, Lexington, Mass.
[5]*Business Information Markets.*

holds, the bar code scanning devices on cash registers at one hundred supermarkets transmit data about the sale of different grocery products—data then correlated with local economic conditions to produce statistical reports sold to manufacturers and wholesalers. Time, Inc., has a similar service that generates a continuous stream of statistics on the sale of retail products, analyzed by geographic area and ethnicity. McGraw-Hill Information Systems tracks a variety of industries; for example, it offers an online service with data on construction activity analyzed by geography and economic and demographic variables.

As a result of their high price, online statistical services, like online text retrieval, have thus far had a limited market. The clients have been mainly corporate and financial, though some government agencies also subscribe to the econometric services. The spread of personal computers, however, may increase the number of potential subscribers and lead to a fall in prices, but given the nature of the services, the market is likely to remain much smaller than for online text retrieval. In any event, despite the relatively small number of subscribers so far, the statistical data bases have generated substantial revenues and impressive profits.

In 1983, the data base industry as a whole (reference and source data bases, print and electronic, combined) brought in an estimated $3.4 billion in revenue, according to the editors of Knowledge Industry Publications, whose survey counts data bases as the largest single component of the $9 billion business information market. (The other components include trade magazines, newsletters, business books and market research reports, and "face-to-face" services, such as seminars and conventions.) Online data bases are undergoing the kind of dizzying growth typically associated with the infant stages of an industry. Their revenues, estimated at $1.07 billion in 1983, have been growing 30 percent annually. Between 1975 and 1982 the number of data base subscribers increased from 5,000 to 200,000, and to 675,000 by the start of 1984. The proliferation of personal computers virtually ensures rapid expansion. Moreover, as paper, printing, and postage costs rise, information producers and users both have incentives to switch from print to electronic formats. In 1975 there were only some 300 online data bases, by early 1981 there were about 700, and by 1984 over 2,000. About two-fifths are numerical data bases.[6]

The statistical service companies do more than provide data. Their resources include not only data bases but also data processing capacity, software incorporating statistical models, and professional skills in data base management and social and economic analysis. They sell a variety

[6]Figures for 1983 and 1984 courtesy of Janet Bailey, Knowledge Industry Publications.

of different products and services. Some companies, such as DRI, offer online access to their data bases, proprietary software, and data processing capacities, charging by the hour of time shared on its computers in addition to an initial subscription fee. Time-sharing provided a major source of growth for DRI in the 1970s, at one point accounting for two-thirds of its revenues. But in the 1980s, corporate economists have shifted work from DRI's mainframes to their own smaller computers. Hence companies like DRI now depend increasingly on their ability to develop products for use on their clients' own computers, such as proprietary software packages or sets of data that may be sold by disk or by the number of items of information downloaded via computer communication networks. Statistical service firms sometimes supplement their data and software packages with magazines, newsletters, and seminars, and consequently deal not merely in electronic but also in print and face-to-face services. Some companies also offer their professional consulting services in the solution of their clients' problems in marketing or planning or in managing and coordinating information resources. Statistical services necessarily shade into general information and professional services because of the forces shaping their growth.

Sources of Growth

Though technological advances and cost reductions in computers and telecommunications are not the entire explanation, they have obviously played a central part in the growth of statistical services. Computers have made it possible to collect, retrieve, and analyze statistical information on a scale previously unimaginable. Data entry and compilation, data storage and manipulation, data retrieval and distribution—all of these procedures essential to information services have been improved and reduced in cost. In addition, the increased use of computers inside organizations has encouraged a demand for externally developed computer-based information about the business environment. Hence the early, money-saving uses of computers for automating internal operations helped to prepare the way for the independent data suppliers.

Growth in demand for statistical services also stems from changes in the style of American management and the successful marketing efforts of the information companies themselves. The enthusiasm for computer-based management information and decision support systems reflects the increasing influence of quantitative techniques and the growing employment of MBAs and Ph.D. economists in American business. Parallel changes have occurred in public-sector organizations. However, even in the 1980s, the top echelons of American business and public administration still come predominantly from a generation that is uncomfortable with computers and quantitative methods. Data base companies have had to devote considerable effort to making their clients "comfortable" with computers, according to a senior vice president for marketing at Chase Econometrics/Interactive Data, a leading firm in econometric and financial information.[7] Similarly, the president of DRI observes that his firm did "a lot of missionary work" to convince businessmen they would benefit from its econometric forecasting services.[8]

It is difficult to say how much of the new demand for data stems from a rational need for exact information to improve organizational performance and how much comes from the symbolic value of numbers in the competition for influence within organizations. No doubt, there has been much conspicuous consumption of statistics; numbers offer seemingly objective corroboration for all sorts of shaky decisions (the technical term is "covering one's ass," though we are trying to avoid jargon). And the malfunctions of management information systems and mistakes of forecasters have been so numerous and well documented as to raise good grounds for skepticism about the practical value of the services, at least during the years when demand for them was emerging. Reviewers of the record of macroeconomic forecasting in the 1970s have found that the huge models of the economy assembled by DRI and other firms did no better than much simpler models or even the guesses of economists relying on their own personal judgment.[9]

The fundamental source of difficulty, according to James Henry, was the sharp discontinuity in economic trends in the 1970s; yet the very uncertainty that gave the forecasters such a poor record probably also increased the demand for their services.[10] A stable, steadily growing economy is a poor business climate for companies selling prophecy. The rapid changes in inflation and interest rates, fluctuations in the energy market, a succession of stiff recessions in the 1970s—all these contributed to the demand for forecasting as well as to its failures. However, now that the business has been launched, it can probably survive prolonged economic stabilization, though that may not be a risk to which it will be exposed in our time.

[7]Interview with William Nelson, August 2, 1983, Waltham, Mass.
[8]Kasputys interview.
[9]See James Henry, "The Future Hustle," *The New Republic*, February 4, 1978, pp. 16–20; J. Scott Armstrong, *Long-Range Forecasting: From Crystal Ball to Computer* (New York: Wiley, 1978); William Ascher, *Forecasting: An Appraisal for Policy-makers and Planners* (Baltimore: Johns Hopkins University Press, 1978); and W. Allen Spivey and William J. Wrobleski, *Surveying Recent Econometric Forecasting Performance* (Washington, D.C.: American Enterprise Institute, 1980).
[10]Henry, "Future Hustle."

Economic uncertainty was not the only specific historical factor in the last decade that helped the statistical services business. A gap opened up between public data and its potential users. Computers began to make it feasible to tailor government statistics to the needs of particular businesses. New technology also permitted online dissemination, but the federal government was not investing in such a system for public data; indeed, its data processing facilities began to fall seriously behind as new generations of computers appeared. With no central facility for dissemination, even federal officials could not easily lay their hands on existing public data. Since many organizations could benefit from government statistics but lacked the necessary technology and skills, private middlemen with the knowledge and resources sprung up to provide public data to those able and willing to pay their price.

Adding Value to Public Data

In the United States, public data have an almost irresistible appeal for private business use since they come at negligible cost. The government makes data available on computer tape at the cost of making a copy. The value of these public resources has, if anything, increased in recent years. While the costs of storing and manipulating information have been falling, the costs of collecting it in the first place have been growing. The 1980 census cost a billion dollars, and it is safe to say no private firm wants to undertake one at its own expense.

Some private vendors simply obtain information in the public domain and repackage it for sale with little modification. An entire industry called "secondary publishing" or "repackaging" has grown up around the marketing of government reports, documents, and data. In the statistical field, an extreme example is the publisher who several years ago simply reproduced the *Statistical Abstracts of the United States* and sold it in bookstores for more than the Government Printing Office was charging.

However, since competitors and large corporate clients can also obtain the same public information, statistical service companies typically look for ways to "add value" to government data and software. At least four ways are of signal importance:

1. Customizing data, software, or other products developed by government agencies to make them specifically applicable to the needs of a client.
2. Combining public data with data from private or international sources.
3. Providing online access to public data, together with data pro-

cessing facilities and superior software to enable clients to do their own analysis from their own desks.

4. Offering consulting services to help clients understand how to use the data and the system for their own purposes.

DRI illustrates all of these methods for adding value. Founded in 1968 by the Harvard economist Otto Eckstein, the company originally offered macroeconomic forecasts based on government data. The basic techniques for forecasting were not new; Eckstein's innovation was to make the numbers and his model accessible on a time-sharing computer. The initial clients were leading banks, other large corporations, and government agencies. Although even today its macroeconomic forecasts continue to attract the most public notice, DRI has grown mainly by developing a business in customized forecasts for specific industries and corporations. "As we got into the corporate world," recalls Joseph Kasputys of DRI, "we began to demonstrate to people how you could take certain variables out of a macroforecast and incorporate it into a model which would be able to do product-line forecasting or cost forecasting or just forecasting the overall growth in market size." To serve its clients, DRI fielded a network of consultants available for instruction in the use of DRI's computers, the use of its models, and the tailoring of the data and forecasts to the needs of the client organization. The business has become increasingly customer-oriented. Kasputys explains, "Instead of saying, 'How can we model the chemical industry and to whom can we sell that model?' we try to look the other way now and say, 'What is the full range of their information needs?' "[11]

The tailoring of data, consulting services, and customer-orientation—in addition to online access to DRI's models and computers—plainly distinguish what DRI offers from what its clients could secure from government statistical agencies. Chase Econometrics/Interactive Data went through much the same evolution in the 1970s, starting out with macroeconomic forecasting and becoming progressively involved in the information problems of specific companies. The company's field representatives began to analyze specific jobs and increasingly asked what information a particular manager—say, a vice-president for finance or for marketing—would need. The company also became involved in coordinating information resources for organizations through the establishment of "decision support systems."[12]

Decision support systems involve the interactive use of computers by managers in their decision-making. They are different in several ways from management information systems, which have automated data collection, storage, and retrieval inside firms. Management infor-

[11]Kasputys interview.
[12]Nelson interview.

mation systems are generally used for tasks with clearly defined procedures and standards, and their primary benefit is supposed to be lower costs. Widely heralded as a revolution in management, they have often generated streams of data that have little relevance for decision-making and, as a result, become isolated in data processing departments. Decision support systems, on the other hand, are organized specifically to improve the effectiveness of managerial decision-making, not to increase operating efficiency. A decision support system, its advocates argue, "shifts attention from the level of operations (an information system for job order status or accounts receivable) toward the issues of managerial problem solving."[13] Building such a system requires collaboration between a firm's technical staff and its management. Firms that cannot achieve the necessary cooperation or lack the technical resources turn to consultants with the combined computer and management skills to set up decision support systems for them.

Decision support systems provide the technological and organizational means for using outside statistical services. The designers are supposed to bring together the varied sources of data, reconciling differences in definitions and overcoming other obstacles to an integrated supply of relevant information. The data and analytical tools obtained online from independent services may then be combined with the firm's own information resources. Naturally, as more decision support systems are established, customers for statistical services companies multiply. So decision support systems go hand in hand with the growing business in statistical services.

The Case of "Demographics"

Demographic analysis is another type of statistical service that illustrates the private uses of government statistical resources and the new methods for adding value to public data. Like the econometric services, the demographics industry is also a comparatively recent phenomenon. The demographics firm widely regarded as the most ancient, Market Statistics, dates back only to 1951. Business use of the census tremendously increased over the past decade.[14] Many demographics companies started during the 1970s, and in 1979 a new magazine, *American Demographics,* was founded that serves as both a trade magazine and a popular survey of population trends.

The growth of demographics as of other statistical services owes much to technical advances, but two factors specific to the demograph-

[13]Peter G. W. Keen and Michael S. Scott Morton, *Decision Support Systems: An Organizational Perspective* (Reading, Mass.: Addison-Wesley, 1978), pp. 57–58.
[14]"Businesses Capitalize on Data from Census," *New York Times,* March 31, 1980, IV, p. 1.

ics business have also been significant stimuli. One was the growing interest of corporations in market segmentation and targeted marketing, that is, in selling different products, or selling them in different ways, to different groups of consumers. The other development was a new technology—developed largely at public expense—for associating demographic characteristics with address lists. In preparation for the 1970 census, the Census Bureau developed at a cost of $22 million a system called Dual Integrated Map Encoding (DIME) to code every mailbox in the United States by its location in geographic coordinates on a small-area map. The DIME file's original purpose was to assist in the mailing of census forms, but private firms soon obtained it at the usual bargain price—the cost of a copy of the computer tapes. The file has enabled them to identify the probable demographic characteristics of a household knowing only its address.

The expression "demographics industry" is somewhat of a misnomer—or, at least, not as precise as it could be. It is really a geodemographics industry, matching demographic data and geographic areas. The companies use socioeconomic and population data on small areas—data acquired almost exclusively from public sources, mainly the Census Bureau—to give their clients a more precise understanding of the relationship of people and places. Site evaluation and targeted marketing are the two main, bread-and-butter services offered by the demographics firms.

Site location is a traditional problem in industrial economics. Firms continually need to decide where to locate a production plant, a branch office, a new retail outlet. To make the best choice, they may need to know about social and demographic factors that affect, among other things, the local demand for their products, the supply of labor, and potential competitors. The services offered by demographics firms can provide specifics on the population, income, spending habits, and other characteristics of potential business areas of almost any conceivable shape (rings, sectors, travel contours, zip code areas). The data may be presented on full-color maps, graphs, and charts—in print, online, or on computer tape. Geodemographic site evaluation systems allow a retailer to target the areas with demographic characteristics that correspond to their best customers. Usually, the business must define for itself who its best customers are. Demographic companies, however, can also analyze the current locations of a business to determine what "demographics" produce the best commercial results.[15]

[15]See Martha Farnsworth Riche, "Data Companies 1983," *American Demographics*, February 1983, pp. 28–39; "Mellon's MAX System Helps Clients Find Right Location," *American Banker*, August 19, 1981, pp. 2, 10; "Selecting a Store Site, the Computerized Way," *Chain Store Age Executive*, March 1981, pp. 45–48; and the bimonthly *Industrial Development* and quarterly *Site Selection Handbook*, both published by Conway Publications.

Demographic data have long been used for marketing purposes. For example, census data on housing characteristics, such as ownership of household appliances, have for decades been used by companies selling durable consumer goods to determine potential growth areas. Segmented marketing, however, requires more sophisticated demographic intelligence because of the need to divide populations according to characteristics that indicate their receptiveness to a product or message.

Direct mail is the exemplary segmented marketing technique. A firm can use geodemographics to screen mailing lists, assigning each address to a small area for which the demographic characteristics are known. Households with unfavorable "demographics" can then be eliminated from the mailing list. A demographics company can also analyze the demographic traits of respondents to a direct-mail campaign, identifying what kind of people responded best. The company can then pick out new areas and new addresses with the same favorable characteristics to be hit in the next rounds of mail. By using these techniques to reach only those households predisposed to their product or message, businesses can economize on their resources. Geodemographics, as its advocates say, can offer a "rifle" to marketers and provide an alternative to the "shotgun" of mass marketing.[16]

"Cluster demographics" represents a further development of the same techniques. Cluster systems define geographic areas according to consumption styles. "The basic objective," says Matthew Goldstein, a statistician, "is to classify each of the 82 million households in the 50 states by the probability of consumption of a set of product categories and brands within them, knowing only the households' addresses."[17] Firms that do clustering supplement demographic data with survey research that correlates demographic characteristics and consumer tastes. Consumption styles may then be inferred for geographic areas with fairly homogeneous demographics. One company, Claritas, assigns each of the ZIP codes in the United States to one of its forty Lifestyle Clusters, to which it has given such colorful names as Blue Blood Estates and Bunker's Neighbors. Another firm, C.A.C.I., has assigned to one of forty-four clusters each of the nation's 256,000 census blocks, averaging only 280 households.

Like businesses, political organizations have turned to demographic techniques to help find the people most receptive to their messages. By correlating opinion poll data with demographic characteristics, the demographic specialists can help political campaigns target undecided

[16]See Riche, "Data Companies 1983"; "Finding Markets in Census Data," *New York Times*, June 25, 1981, IV, p. 1; "A New 'Rifle' for Marketers," *New York Times*, November 19, 1981, IV, p. 2; and "Census Is Eagerly Awaited by Marketers," *Wall Street Journal*, March 26, 1980, p. 48.

[17]Quoted in Doris Walsh, "Cluster Demographics," *American Demographics*, November 1982, p. 21.

voters for intensive contact. For example, to fight a 1978 "right-to-work" initiative in Missouri, labor organizations hired a pollster and a demographics firm. The pollster determined what demographic groups were uncommitted and persuadable; the demographics firm determined where those groups lived in Missouri. A company matched lists of registered voters with the telephone directory and eliminated all those identified as beyond persuasion. The campaign then bombarded 595,000 voters in 2,300 targeted block groups with home visits, telephone calls, and direct mail. The messages directed at each group reflected the pollster's findings about that group's concerns. The campaign spent little money on advertising in the mass media, and a public that, according to opinion polls, had earlier overwhelmingly favored the initiative ended up voting 60 to 40 percent against it in the November elections.[18]

Even the federal government itself may become a client of the demographics industry. The Internal Revenue Service is prohibited by law from receiving data on individual households from the Bureau of the Census. But that restriction did not prevent the IRS from developing a plan in 1983 to buy estimates of individual incomes from private firms that, in turn, use census data on small areas. In an experimental program, the IRS sought to use this procedure to identify people who had failed to pay any taxes.[19] The program appears, however, not to have been a success.

Religious institutions have also taken an interest in demographic services. Churches, facing declining membership, have begun to obtain demographic profiles of their neighborhoods to determine which programs and services might best attract parishioners. The United Church of Christ, for example, has employed the National Planning Data Corporation, a leading repackager of public demographic data, to provide each of its 6,400 congregations with an eleven-page report about the population in its area. "Each church has a specific market area," says a representative of the company. "What they need is a market profile of the area they serve." Bypassing private data companies, more than two dozen other denominations have joined together in a project called Census Access for Planning in the Church. With the help of census data, the churches can decide where they need bilingual ministers or programs for the handicapped, or find out if low enrollment in a Sunday school program is in fact due to growing numbers of singles in the local community.[20]

[18]Larry J. Sabato, *The Rise of Political Consultants* (New York: Basic Books, 1981), pp. 202–203.

[19]David Burnham, "Private Computers' Income Data to Aid I.R.S. in Hunt for Evaders," *New York Times*, August 29, 1983, p. 1.

[20]Charles Austin, "Churches See Computer as a Tool to Lure Flock," *New York Times*, October 23, 1982, p. 6.

To the demographics industry, the marketing and targeting problems of commerce, politics, and religion are fundamentally the same. Some critics, however, think distinctions need to be made. They are disturbed about the impact on politics of methods that put a premium on unequally distributed technological capacities and that manipulate the public by hypocritically appealing to its various segments with separately conveyed, custom-tailored messages. Of course, unequally distributed resources are not new in politics, nor is hypocrisy. The new, capital-intensive styles of political campaigning are only the most recent way in which money has influenced democratic politics. The new techniques promise to increase the efficiency of any kind of campaign, whatever its intentions. So, no matter what their beliefs, political organizations are likely to make increasing use of computers and demographic analysis because of their value in economizing on resources.

Statistical Services and the Information Industry

The growth of private statistical services and their implications for knowledge and society need to be seen in the context of the contemporary upheaval in the economics and politics of information. Statistical services are part of the information industry, and they are subject to the same underlying forces. Basic changes in technology, for example, affect all information businesses. The linkages are also organizational. Some of the leading econometric and demographics firms are owned by diversified information companies; and many firms engaged in statistical services are members of the Information Industry Association, which lobbies for commercial information interests in Washington.

Expansion, technological innovation, deregulation, economic and political turbulence and uncertainty—these are some of the forces shaping the information sector. In the last decade they have produced a blurring of boundaries between industries and a blurring of roles within them; the emergence of larger and more diversified information companies through a spate of acquisitions and mergers; an intensification of competition; and the rise of new entrepreneurial firms out of the technological, economic, and political ferment.

Twenty years ago relatively clear boundaries separated computer services; broadcast communications; telephone service; publishing; and data collection, analysis, and distribution. The technologies involved in each industry were distinct, and few companies overlapped any two. (In fact, the last grouping—statistical services—was still mostly in the public and nonprofit sector, scarcely recognized as an industry at all.) Today the boundaries are less clear. Computers and communications have become so intertwined that Anthony Oettinger has suggested the term "compunications" for the hybrid.[21] Publishing has now become so en-meshed with computers and data base services that some say publishers should stop thinking of themselves as producers of books or periodicals and recognize that they are information suppliers, not bound to any particular medium.[22]

The breakdown of traditional boundaries has been evident in the assortment of companies that have converged on the business of statistical services. They come from banking (Chase Manhattan and Citicorp), publishing (McGraw-Hill), credit reporting (Dun & Bradstreet), computer services (Control Data), market research (A. C. Nielsen), and other commercial fields as well as from the nonprofit sector (Wharton Econometric Forecasting). The confluence of computers and communications is particularly striking among the online vendors of statistical data, who tend to have entered the business through one of two routes. Some, such as McGraw-Hill and Dun & Bradstreet, began as producers of information that had traditionally been sold in printed formats; advances in computers and telecommunications enabled them to create new products and services out of the same information resources. Other firms, such as General Electric and Control Data, were in the computer time-sharing business and sought additional ways to encourage customers to use their computers. They purchased the rights to offer online access to data bases developed by other firms. These initial interests then led each kind of company into the other's territory: information producers acquired computer service companies, and vice versa. On the one hand, in 1979 Dun & Bradstreet bought National CSS, a computer time-sharing company; shortly thereafter, McGraw-Hill acquired DRI, which had developed expertise in data bases and computer time-sharing. Chase Manhattan had similar reasons for buying Interactive Data and merging it with its Chase Econometrics subsidiary. On the other hand, Control Data purchased Economic Information Systems, which collects data from the census and private sources for use in industrial marketing.[23]

As a result of these and other developments, individual companies cannot be unambiguously associated with specific roles in statistical services. In the data base industry, roles are located at various points along the path that stretches from production to distribution and use of information. However, the data base producers or providers, as they are

[21] Anthony G. Oettinger, Paul J. Berman, and William Read, *High and Low Politics: Information Resources for the 80s* (Cambridge, Mass.: Ballinger, 1977).

[22] Kiechel, "Everything You Wanted to Know," p. 236.

[23] See *Business Information Markets;* Kiechel, "Everything You Wanted to Know"; Edwin McDowell, "A Data Conglomerate," *New York Times,* September 9, 1979, III, p. 1.

called, are not always distinct from the distributors. The distribution function itself has given rise to at least three related roles: vendor, broker, and carrier. Here, too, one role shades into another. Vendors market information, but they often also produce it. Brokers provide access to a number of different data bases; they are vendors who do not produce most of the information they sell. (The largest brokers are called data base supermarkets.) Carriers provide telecommunications services linking users and online data base vendors, but, as we have noted, some of the companies operating time-sharing networks have used their resources to move into data base vending. To add to this confusing picture, the so-called end-users of data are often information producers themselves—and so the cycle begins again.

There is a logic to the blurring of boundaries and roles. By acquiring firms strong in the storage, manipulation, and delivery of computerized data bases, McGraw-Hill and Dun & Bradstreet were gearing up to become integrated information service companies. When McGraw-Hill acquired DRI in 1979, it paid a price much higher than industry analysts considered wise; until the decline in DRI's time-sharing business, the gamble seemed to have paid off. McGraw-Hill added DRI's data to its own and acquired DRI's expertise for computerizing its previously inert print data bases. McGraw-Hill's Oilgram services, its Standard & Poor's Compustat financial data, and its Dodge construction activity reports became available for online interactive use.

Similarly, Dun & Bradstreet acquired a time-sharing company, National CSS, at an unusually high price and has used its computer expertise for integrating its various information services. With Donnelley and Nielsen also under its umbrella, Dun & Bradstreet, like McGraw-Hill, is now involved in nearly every segment of the business information market, from trade magazines and newsletters to online statistical services.

There are a number of reasons for these tendencies toward integration. To provide "value-added" information services rapidly and reliably in a computerized society requires an array of resources and skills that were previously dispersed. Some companies, such as McGraw-Hill, Dow-Jones, and Dun & Bradstreet, were traditionally strong in collecting data. Other companies, such as Data Resources and Chase Econometrics, developed expertise for adding value to data. Still others, such as Control Data and General Electric, were strong in computer communications. Rather than build up the capacities they lacked, the larger firms have used acquisitions as a shortcut to secure complementary strengths.

The integration of various services within the information industry has also been encouraged by the prevalence of economies of scale and economies of scope. Scale economies—declining marginal costs with increases in volume—tend to be substantial in information because of its special characteristics. Once information is produced, the cost of supplying another buyer is typically small. As a result of its nondepletable character, information remains in the hands of the seller no matter how many sales are made. The costs of producing information are mostly the costs of producing the "first copy"; by the second copy marginal costs typically take a nosedive.

Economies of scope involve lower costs in the joint production of two or more commodities, and they, too, are pervasive in information because of its distinctive character and the effects of new technology. Once information is produced today, the cost of supplying it in another format is relatively small. Print data bases are now usually produced electronically anyway, allowing for easy conversion to electronic forms for distribution. And because computer technology permits such flexible rearrangement of information, the same data base can sometimes be turned at low cost into a variety of different products and services. Moreover, once an information system such as an online data base service is in operation, the cost of adding another data base may be small, compared to setting up a separate system. Thus substantial combined economies of scale and scope often result from the changeover from print to computers.[24]

Finally, some users of information want "one-stop shopping" for information services. A chief advantage of electronic data bases is that they save time; indeed, in some cases speed is primarily what is being paid for. However, the proliferation of suppliers may increase the time needed to find a specific item or source of information. For customers that would rather economize on transaction costs than invest in knowledge of the information market, the data base supermarkets and statistical brokerage services serve to reduce search time. And insofar as clients want not simply data or software packages but advice and instruction about the use of models and information systems, they will look to firms that have the array of services of McGraw-Hill or Dun & Bradstreet.

Those various factors give large, integrated firms definite advantages, but they have by no means blocked small firms from entering statistical services. In demographics, for example, although a number of firms are subsidiaries of larger corporations, there are also independent companies, such as Urban Decision Systems, Claritas, and C.A.C.I. Various small entrepreneurial firms have also emerged, usually by finding a highly specialized niche based on technological expertise.

---

[24]Yale M. Braunstein, "The Functioning of Information Markets," in Jane H. Yurew et al., *Issues in Information Policy* (Washington, D.C.: Government Printing Office, 1981), p. 59.

The diminishing advantages of centralized data processing should also increase the opportunities for small firms. Data base vendors and computer service companies became intertwined because many clients wanting to use large data bases also needed more computing power. However, with the spread of more powerful mini- and microcomputers, the users now have greater processing capacity in their own organizations and even at their own desks. Increasingly, data base companies will sell data and software on disks, transmit them via unused portions of broadcast wavelengths, or else download them via computer networks and data base supermarkets. Time-sharing may continue to be used only for large-scale undertakings. This change may reduce the capital needed to enter some areas of statistical services.

Despite the looming presence of large companies, competition in information has intensified. Early leaders in statistical services have met new competition as financial service and communications companies have diversified into data bases. The deregulation of the telephone industry has permitted AT&T to move into information services, and new competition will also come from cable television, videodisc, and other technologies. In addition, partly as a result of satellite telecommunications, information services have become a global market, with firms from different continents thrown into competition with each other. Many statistical service companies are now extensively engaged in work around the world for both foreign companies and foreign governments. Even the government statistics of some European countries are now processed in the United States. This kind of transborder data flow has given rise to fears of lost confidentiality, lost sovereignty, and, not least of all, lost jobs. However, despite some protectionist measures, American firms' international business continues to grow rapidly. There has also been some movement in the reverse direction. In 1983, Wharton Econometric Forecasting was purchased by Compagnie Internationale de Service en Informatique (CISI), a computer time-sharing company 90 percent owned by the French atomic energy agency.[25] And when the Thatcher government, as part of its crusade to shift state functions to the private sector, decided to contract out online distribution of British vital statistics, the winning bid ironically came from Service in Informatics and Analysis (SIA), also a French state enterprise. "Accuse the British government of inconsistency," declared *The Economist*, "but do not accuse it of nationalism."[26] Which brings us to our final blurry boundary—that between the public and private sectors.

---

[25]"A Forecaster for France," *Business Week*, March 28, 1983, p. 46; see also "A Squabble Stalls the Wharton Deal," *Business Week*, February 21, 1983, p. 49.

[26]"Government Data: French Connection," *The Economist*, February 12, 1983, p. 56.

The Statistical Services Industry and the State
Public Investment and Information

Earlier we said that technology played a central role in the growth of the statistical services industry, but it would have been just as accurate—and probably more informative—to say that the central role was played by government. For a great many of the key technical innovations were underwritten by public investment. It was the Bureau of the Census in the late nineteenth century that financed the development of the first electronic tabulating machines by its former employee, Herman Hollerith, whose company later evolved into IBM.[27] In the 1940s and 1950s the armed services and again the Census Bureau were the key sponsors of the development of computers and their application to social and economic data. The government subsidized the development of the information sciences when they had little commercial support, and it paid for the work in the social sciences that led to the development of macroeconomic forecasting and other techniques. Through NASA, the Defense Department, the National Science Foundation, the National Library of Medicine, and the Office of Education, the federal government played the key role in financing the development of electronic data base systems. Two of the major companies in data bases, Dialog Information Systems (part of Lockheed) and the System Development Corporation (now owned by Burroughs), got their start in the 1960s providing software to the federal government for computerized information storage and retrieval.[28] The Census Bureau's DIME file mentioned earlier is only one of many software systems developed at public expense and used freely by private companies. And then of course there is the steady stream of statistics flowing out of Washington: Government agencies irrigate the computers of private information companies as constantly and abundantly as the waters of the Colorado irrigate the corporate farms of California's Imperial Valley.

Yet, despite being long nurtured by federal funds, the information industry now vociferously protests against what its representatives say is excessive government support for free information. They would like to repackage and sell for a profit what government sometimes gives to the public for free or at prices that private firms cannot match. To them these giveaways seem a violation of the principles of a free-enterprise economy. According to Paul Zurkowski, the executive director of the Information Industry Association (IIA), free government information

[27]Geoffrey Austrian, *Herman Hollerith: Forgotten Giant of Information Processing* (New York: Columbia University Press, 1982).
[28]See Kiechel, "Everything You Wanted to Know," p. 233; Bourne, "On-Line Systems," pp. 155–57.

threatens to drive private information producers out of business, thereby limiting information to a government monopoly. "Beware, time is short!" Zurkowski warned in Churchillian tones in 1975. "From SUNY [the State University of New York] on Lake Erie to NLM [the National Library of Medicine] in Bethesda and from the Research Triangle in North Carolina to the golden triangle in Pittsburgh, an iron curtain forged out of free information is descending across the competitive marketplace of ideas. Just as surely as the Berlin Wall stands today, in the absence of a concerted industrywide effort, user choice in information one day soon will be replaced by 'free information' from one source."[29]

To save the public from this fate, the industry has urged the government to reduce or terminate programs offering free or low-cost information. It has supported cutbacks in the range of publications and number of retail outlets of the Government Printing Office (GPO) on the grounds that some activities of the GPO compete unfairly with private publishers. Traditionally, for example, the GPO has offered inexpensive publications about nutrition, infant care, health, and other personal problems. Under the Reagan administration, many such publications have been discontinued, while the prices for those remaining in stock have been substantially raised. The GPO raised to $4.75 its price for a 67-page pamphlet called "Infant Care," which used to be distributed to mothers for free as part of public health programs.[30]

There have also been efforts to dismantle the National Technical and Information Service (NTIS), which disseminates research performed by or for the federal government. The service is an enterprise of considerable proportions: its 300 employees handle about 25,000 reports and other items daily. Ever since being established in 1964, NTIS has been run on a self-sustaining basis, recovering its costs through sales of reports and charges to other government agencies for marketing their publications, but many in the industry would like its functions ceded to the private sector.[31]

Another target has been the National Library of Medicine, which pioneered the development of online bibliographic services in the biomedical sciences. In addition to offering direct service to physicians and

[29]Quoted in John Berry, "Free Information and IIA," *Library Journal* 100 (1975):795; see also Paul Zurkowski, "Information and the Economy," *Library Journal* 104 (1979):1800–1807; and idem, "The Library Context and the Information Context: Bridging the Theoretical Gap," *Library Journal* 106 (1981):1381–84.

[30]Dorothy Wickenden, "Rebel Without a Case: The Public Printer Goes Private," *The New Republic*, January 31, 1983, pp. 11–13; Daniel W. Gottlieb, "Notice to Federal Publication Users: Supply Is Down and Prices Are Up," *National Journal* 15 (1983):1634–37.

[31]John Berry, "Libraries and the 'Fourth Debate,'" *Library Journal* 107 (1982):121; "NTIS Takeover by Private Sector Stirs Lively Debate," *Library Journal* 107 (1982):382.

scientists, the NLM leases its tapes to data base vendors. However, a firm called Excerpta Medica, a subsidiary of the Dutch publishing house Elsevier, operates a competing online retrieval system that overlaps about 40 percent, and in recent years it has lobbied Congress to force the NLM to charge higher prices for its services and leased tapes.[32]

Some information industry spokesmen have also suggested that the government take a more restrictive view of its functions in statistical services. In 1980, for example, Kasputys of DRI declared that while the federal government should continue to produce data for its internal purposes—regulation, program operation, and policy analysis—it no longer needed to concern itself as much with programs of public information.

> Prior to the extensive development of publishing, media, and information industries, the government indeed fulfilled an important need by supplying information that facilitated commerce and industry that would not otherwise be available. However in 1980, we find a highly developed information industry, utilizing the latest technology, that has a strong capability to identify information needs, collect data, deliver results frequently tailored to the needs of specific clients and even provide special analysis on the meaning of information for business decisions. In lieu of unilateral governmental determinations on the nature of private sector information requirements, market demand and the profit motive can now be used more extensively to govern statistical collection. . . . The efforts of a strengthened central statistical policy office should focus on transferring data collection and distribution of this nature to the private sector while improving and rationalizing statistical operations in support of regulation, program operation, and policy analysis.[33]

In an interview, Kasputys recalled that he had fought successfully against the development in NTIS of a facility for online dissemination of government statistics to the public. In his 1980 paper, he opposed any government effort of this kind, but explained what he thought government should do:

> The government can encourage private sector innovation in the on-line database industry through the ready availability of public data in

[32]Constance Holden, "Library of Medicine Versus Private Enterprise," *Science* 212 (1981):1125–26; Nicholas E. Davies, "The Health-Sciences Information Struggle," *The New England Journal of Medicine* 307 (1982):201–204; and Martin M. Cummings, "Medical Information Services: For Public Good or Private Profit?" *The Information Society* 1 (1982):249–60.

[33]"Remarks by Joseph Kasputys," in Joseph W. Duncan et al., "Private Versus Public Sector Responsibility for the Collection, Distribution, and Analysis of Statistical Data," *Review of Public Data Use* 8 (1980):319.

machines readable form on magnetic tape. I support the role of NTIS as a 'one-stop' wholesaler of such government tapes by private sector vendors. Again, I would caution against NTIS acting as a retailer of these data, except where a clear and definite need exists in society that, for some reason, is not being met by the private sector.[34]

Some members of the Reagan administration apparently agree with Kasputys that the government should limit its statistical activities primarily to information it needs to operate programs and make policy. Between 1981 and 1983, the administration cut statistical services about 20 percent in real dollars. In a *New York Times* interview in 1982, Christopher Demuth, head of information and regulatory affairs at the Office of Management and Budget, explained that federal agencies had been collecting "much greater detail than was needed for national policy-making purposes." Now "the needs of Federal agencies alone, not of states, local governments or private firms" were to be the basis for justifying statistical programs. But he offered solace to the private sector, if not to budget-squeezed local governments: "We hope in the future to make the additional information available to private firms on a user-fee basis."[35] In an unprecedented move, the administration sold the rights to part of the 1980 census to a consortium of private companies; for a while those who wanted data by zip codes had to buy it from the consortium.[36]

The cutbacks in federal statistical programs and shifting of information to the private sector are a source of concern to those who feel the American people are losing access to information they were compelled to give under penalty of law and for which they have already paid billions of dollars in taxes. In mid-1983 Andrew Hacker pointed out that the Census Bureau had still to issue publications with many of the basic findings of the 1980 census, even though tapes with the data were already in the hands of demographics companies. The problem, he suggested, was that during the 1970s the bureau became increasingly oriented to the needs of the companies: "ours is no longer a citizen's census."[37] Researchers, students, or curious citizens who wanted to see the data had to pay such firms the high prices they were demanding. One company, National Decision Systems, charged $395 for the five volumes of 1980 data it published in advance of the Census Bureau, warning readers that the arrangement of the data was proprietary, protected by copyright. Reviewing the set, Hacker noted, "In their intro-

[34]Ibid., p. 322.
[35]Quoted in Ann Crittenden, "A World with Fewer Numbers," *New York Times*, July 11, 1982, III, p. 4.
[36]Ibid.
[37]Andrew Hacker, "Lost Our Census," *Harper's*, April 1983, p. 16.

duction, the editors state that 'the U.S. government is not in the business of providing data to the public.' A more accurate explanation would be that the public will have to wait because the Census Bureau now regards its corporate customers as its prime constituency."[38]

Some fundamental questions of principle are at issue in the controversy over government statistics and other forms of public information. On the one hand, the information industry argues that the government should do nothing that can be carried on profitably in the private sector. Industry representatives say that if some service or product is—or might be—provided commercially, the government should not enter into competition with private firms. On the logic of this argument, if National Decision Systems can publish census data profitably, then the government need not bother; what price the company charges for its books is irrelevant, since the free market will drive it down.

On the other side of this question are the principles embodied in the nation's public libraries and government information programs that presume a positive advantage for society at large if information is freely and readily available. A long tradition of American thought going back to Madison and Jefferson holds that the success of democratic government depends on an informed public. Access to information is vital to the knowledge of one's own interests and of the broader life of the community. The distribution of information has long been understood as a means of social improvement; and of all the techniques available for improving welfare, the provision of information is one of the least coercive. Furthermore, in a society without an official church or central planning, the national production of certain limited kinds of information has been a modest means of promoting consensus. For example, the statistics produced by government about unemployment, inflation, and poverty provide a common point of reference for the conduct of political debate.

In addition to these political functions, which involve complex issues of justice, political equality, and civil coordination, government information serves some economic purposes. Much information has been produced by government rather than by private firms because of efficiency considerations that arise from the information's special characteristics. As even conservative economists recognize, the optimal functioning of a market depends on a variety of conditions that do not apply to information. Possession of information is not exclusive; many people can have the same item of information at the same time. The marginal costs of a second person's having the information are often

[38]Andrew Hacker, "Census Figures for Corporate Use," *New York Times Book Review*, August 21, 1983, p. 7.

negligible. Since competitive markets are, in theory, supposed to drive prices down to marginal costs, they should drive out much information production. Information is also hard to evaluate; often the prospective buyers cannot know the value of information without knowing the information itself. And the benefits of information are hard to control; those who invest in its production may find that others recoup some share of the rewards. As a result, self-interested economic actors underinvest in information, particularly if its benefits are likely to be distant and widely diffused in society. These are the sources of "market failure" that many believe can best be remedied by a more extensive government role.[39]

The information industry does not entirely reject a government role, for many of its firms could scarcely do business without it. But political interests within the industry vary. On the one hand, for example, the demographics companies depend on the Census Bureau's collection of statistics with great local detail. At relatively little expense the industry acquires reliable data that probably could not be obtained in any other way. Consequently, it opposes any budget cutbacks that would sacrifice local detail. Nor would it be happy if government were to charge high user-fees for census data, since the prices of demographic services would have to increase accordingly and higher prices would discourage business. Similarly, government-produced software, unpatented and easily copied, is of great value to the private information sector. The same software that helps the government manipulate its data also helps the private sector manipulate the data it gets from government.

In some instances, however, government data and software also compete with products sold by private companies. The companies worry that potential clients, instead of contracting with private firms, may acquire data and software in the public domain and establish in-house operations. One firm that produces software for census tapes sued the Census Bureau to force it to cease distributing its low-priced software: the courts, however, said the bureau was acting fully within its authority to disseminate its work.

Relationships between government agencies and firms repackaging public information vary according to several factors, particularly the extent of a firm's dependence on public data and the amount of value it adds. There is little threat to the companies that do customized forecasting and consulting. "We don't feel that we compete with the government in any sense of the word," says an executive of Chase Econometrics. "We think of them [government agencies] as a great market

---

[39]Braunstein, "Information Markets," p. 58.

and source of raw data."[40] Nor is there much threat of government competition for demographics companies that emphasize "value-added" services such as clustering. The major point of conflict comes with the companies that are offering products and services that differ little from what the government has produced. However, even the companies that face no real government competition want to keep it that way and would prefer that more government statistical activities be contracted out to them or simply left to the market to decide whether or not they should be produced. Structurally, they have an interest in the model of public–private relations hinted at earlier in the quotation from Kasputys. The information companies want government generally to act as a wholesaler of data, while they are the retailers—not simply to other private firms, but also to government agencies themselves. However, even among business-oriented reformers of information policy there are major differences about the policies needed to make the market the standard of decision-making.

The Ambiguities of Market Reform

Though they seem little conscious of it, business-oriented reformers have advocated two different and contradictory ideals or models for operating government information services. According to one model, government should be run as a business; according to the other, anything that can be run as a business should be excluded from government.

In information agencies, the first approach—putting government on a businesslike basis—emphasizes the objective of cost recovery. In its strictest form, it sets the potential for recovering costs as the decisive test for determining whether government should carry on an activity. Such an ideal calls for an agency to develop and promote products and services that pay their own way so the agency is not a burden to the taxpayers.

The recent history of the GPO illustrates the aggressive practice of cost-recovery management. The Reagan administration's appointee as Public Printer, Danford L. Sawyer, Jr., arrived with the conviction that the GPO was a morass of inefficiency and that it needed to be run like a private publishing firm, although the agency was, in fact, already making back its costs from sales of documents. Nonetheless, Sawyer hired a high-paid marketing staff, launched a $2–3 million "multimedia blitz," and issued an attractive book catalog. Had it not been for Congress, he would have closed down twenty-three of the GPO's twenty-seven bookstores. But he did raise prices 10 to 50 percent for government publications, and sold off as waste paper some 7,000 back titles. "Cut out the

[40]Nelson interview.

440

losers and accentuate the winners," he explained. "That's what everybody does. If a grocer sees that his dates aren't selling, what does he do? He gets rid of them."[41] In other words, the criterion for the work of a public agency ought to be the same as for a private firm: Will the product sell?

This approach, sensible as it seems as a business proposition, potentially threatens information companies if adopted more generally. They do not like the idea of aggressive public-sector marketing, though that may well be a rational means of recovering costs. If there are economies of scale, as is common in information, marketing efforts may result in higher volume, lower costs, and consequently (under cost recovery), lower prices. The information companies generally approve of cost-recovery management, but their enthusiasm has a limit. They do not exactly want it to be practiced upon them; for they would find it a considerable burden to pay the costs of the public data so vital to their businesses. So they have another approach to the management of government information.

The central principle commonly advocated by the information industry is that the government should do nothing that can be done in the private sector. In this view, the private sector should have a first and last option on all information products and services. The role of government, therefore, is to do what is commercially unprofitable—what does not sell. Whereas the test of cost recovery says that government should operate only self-sustaining services, the second view says that these are precisely the services that ought to be turned over to the private sector.

For an exposition of this viewpoint, one may turn to the 1981 report of a task force on public and private sector relationships set up by the National Commission on Libraries and Information Science (NCLIS). Although the task force had some internal differences, its report basically reflects the thinking of the information industry. The federal government, according to the task force, should provide leadership in information, but it "should not provide information products and services in commerce except when there are compelling reasons to do so, and then only when it protects the private sector's every opportunity to assume the function(s) commercially."[42]

The task force's concern to protect the information industry's "every opportunity" is evident in its discussion of access to public data,

[41]Wickenden, "Rebel Without a Case."

[42]Public Sector/Private Sector Task Force, *Public Sector/Private Sector Interaction in Providing Information Services* (Washington, D.C.: U.S. National Commission on Libraries and Information Science, 1981), p. 43. For critical perspectives, see Patricia Glass Schuman, "Information Justice," *Library Journal* 107 (1982):1060–66; and Anita R. Schiller and Herbert I. Schiller, "Who Can Own What America Knows?" *The Nation*, April 17, 1982, pp. 461–63.

particularly online access. The development of online systems by public institutions is particularly threatening to the information industry because such systems, if interactive, enable their users to extract and rearrange information according to their specific needs. This is, of course, precisely the function assumed by many of the private firms. In a revealing passage, the task force reports that it interpreted access as "including retrieval of prespecified (not user-specified) packages of information. It would include an ability to communicate online, but only with limited interaction with the user."[43] In general, the task force recommended that the federal government "make governmentally distributable information openly available in readily reproducible form." Note that it did not recommend that the information be readily available—which would suggest active government distribution—but only "openly available" in a form "readily reproducible." In a note about the committee's deliberations, the report explains,

> The term "readily reproducible" was substituted for the original phrase "readily usable" to avoid having this principle authorize directly a variety of services to augment the usability of governmentally generated information, including translating information from one format to another. The phrase "readily reproducible" was interpreted as including machine-readable forms in standard formats, but user specific retrieval and online access would be involved only if specifically authorized [presumably by Congress].[44]

To appreciate the implications of this position, one must look at the task force's position on pricing policies. In its view, the government should price information to reflect only the cost of "access and/or reproduction," not the costs of "creating the data in the first place." Of course, as the task force itself noted, the major cost is creating the information, while reproduction costs are "relatively minor."[45] A cost-recovery policy that recovers only the cost of access does not recover much from electronic forms of data dissemination. But by limiting electronic distribution to machine-readable tapes and generally excluding interactive online services, the report ensures that the beneficiaries of its pricing policies will be the information companies rather than the public at large.

In the industry's view of the handling of public data, therefore, the government should primarily serve as a wholesaler of information, delivering data on machine-readable magnetic tape, while the industry serves as the online retailer, with the price charged to retailers being set

---

[43]Ibid., p. 49.
[44]Ibid.
[45]Ibid., pp. 51, 17.

at the negligible cost of transferring public data to them. It is difficult to imagine a position more convenient to the interests of the information companies—or a form of distribution of public data less convenient to the public.

Yet, favorable as these pricing policies are to information companies, they have not advocated them consistently. Or rather, there has been little consistency of principle, only a consistency of self-interest. Public investment and public services that complement their business are admirable; public services that compete with them threaten to impose an "iron curtain."

In criticizing the second of these two approaches, we do not mean to recommend the first. Cost recovery suffers from its own inescapable ambiguities and limitations. Economies of scale make it impossible to determine a cost-recovery price for an information product or service without knowing the price-elasticity of demand. If demand is elastic, low prices may actually yield a better return because a high volume of production will mean lower costs, whereas high prices may depress demand, reducing volume and raising unit costs. Economies of scope make the problem even more complex. In a data base system with combined economies of scale and scope, Yale Braunstein notes, "the average cost of using any one data base on the system will depend on the levels of usage of the other data bases." Consequently, "average costs of any one product are not defined"; they "depend on the level of output of that good or service *and* on the levels of output of all other goods and services produced by the firm."[46] Such ambiguities make it impossible to determine cost-recovery prices on an item-by-item basis. There may, in fact, be many sets of prices that would recover costs for the agency as a whole; the prices chosen, therefore, necessarily involve a host of policy considerations beyond the strictly economic ones.

There are also more fundamental difficulties with the application of cost-recovery management to public information. The cost-recovery test assumes that the benefit of a government information program can be measured by its revenue. None of the broader benefits of public information are given any weight. Cost-recovery management rules out of consideration the positive externalities of a pamphlet on infant care that may contribute to healthier children and lower costs for medical care and social services; the social benefits of an online bibliographic service in making available biomedical research, 65 percent of which is publicly financed; or the value of social and economic statistics in informing the public about the performance of government.

The problem with these market reforms of information policy lies partly in the effort to put public information on the same footing as

[46]Braunstein, "Information Markets," pp. 59–60.

private information, that is, to treat it as a commodity instead of a public good, to measure its value only by its revenue rather than by its broader impact. Such policies tend to diminish public access to public data, to obstruct the turning of government information into public information, and to deny to the public the broader advantages for which public resources have been invested. A reasonable and fair policy for the distribution of government-produced information would adjust prices to take account of its nonmarket value. Services that may not meet the test of cost recovery may be justified on the grounds that they are needed for political debate and public decision-making. Even if the private sector can provide such services, it may not be able to achieve as wide a distribution. But this is, in part, an empirical matter. In a mixed economy, as we have in information, the functions of the public and private sectors can be adapted to changing circumstances and changing records of performance.[47]

The Future of Public Access

Like other revolutionary technologies before it, the computer conjures up new visions of utopia and new nightmares of terror. In one utopian dream, the acquisition of knowledge ceases to be a struggle; all the world's information emerges from its hidden abode in libraries, ar-

---

[47]In 1985 the Office of Management and Budget published guidelines for "management of federal information resources" (Circular A-130). The initial draft emphasized relatively narrow economic considerations and gave scant mention to the role of government information in sustaining a democratic society. The draft drew extensive criticism in Congress and elsewhere. (For the draft, see *Federal Register* 50 [March 15, 1985]: 10734–10747; for the criticism, see "Librarians, Others Protest OMB Proposal to Change Policy for Government Information," Bureau of National Affairs, Daily Reporter System, Washington, D.C., June 12, 1985.) The final version was more balanced. Its statement of basic assumptions declared that government information helps to "ensure the accountability of government" and that "the free flow of information" between government and the public is "essential to a democratic society." Its key market-oriented provisions are also carefully qualified. The circular says that "the expected public and private benefits derived from government information, insofar as they are calculable, should exceed the public and private costs of the information." But since most of the benefits and some of the costs are typically not readily calculated, this requirement means little more than saying that government information management should be prudent. The circular also states, "Although certain functions are inherently governmental in nature, being so intimately related to the public interest as to mandate performance by Federal employees, the government should look first to private sources, where available, to provide the *commercial goods and services* needed by the government to act on the public's behalf, particularly when cost comparisons indicate that private performance will be the most economical" (italics added; see *Federal Register* 50 [December 24, 1985]:52736). By recognizing some functions as "inherently governmental" and limiting privatization to "commercial goods and services" (where available), the circular falls short of mandating revolutionary change. It reflects the Reagan administration's preference for relying on private markets, but the guidelines do not appear to have accelerated the privatization of public data.

chives, and bureaucracies and, at the touch of a few buttons, dances on the screen of an inexpensive computer. Like all visions of an end to scarcity, this one invites us to play the children's game called "What is wrong with this picture?" (The picture might be of a quiet domestic scene, but the dog would have the head of a horse and be curled up next to an armchair missing two legs.) In the picture of computer utopia, something is, indeed, missing: the relationship of information to money and power.

While no one doubts that the new technology has wondrous possibilities, there is no certainty that those possibilities will be realized. In the world today there are dramatic inequalities in the capacity to obtain and manipulate information—inequalities between rich and poor nations, between classes in our own society, and between different kinds of organizations, public and private. These inequalities primarily reflect prior differences in resources.

But they also reflect the imperatives of private enterprise in information. Any business, we said at the outset, must withhold the benefits of its products and services from those who do not pay for them. Companies that do business in public data must rely on the government not to distribute public data effectively or energetically. Proposals to use interactive technologies for the dissemination of public data are particularly threatening to the repackagers, who have developed a vested interest in keeping government from serving the public as efficiently and imaginatively as available technology allows. The protests against NTIS's development of online data services illustrate the problem. There is no persuasive reason why government should not put at the disposal of its own officials and the public advanced facilities for analyzing and communicating public data, especially since the research underlying the technology was conducted largely at public expense.

Public investment has had an enormously productive record in statistics. There is no better testimony to that success than the growth of the private information services, which have added value to public data, improved our capacity to manage information, and become a post-industrial export industry. The industry is unquestionably a national asset and will undoubtedly grow, but its short-term interests cannot be allowed to interfere with sensible public investment. Whatever profits are made from public data are an incidental by-product. They are not the reason we have given government authority to conduct statistical inquiries.

Yet the public may become confused about just what those reasons are. The privatization of public data corrodes the legitimacy of the census and other government statistical efforts. The census, in particular, may lose the public confidence that is vital to its success if, on the one hand, census findings are unavailable to the public in convenient forms, and, on the other, the public sees the census increasingly used by private companies to make money.

The transfer of statistical services from the public into the private sector also threatens to diminish the kind of public control necessary to maintain professional standards as well as confidence. Despite the aspersions frequently cast on government these days, the federal statistical bureaucracies have a record of remarkable professional accomplishment. For many purposes, they enjoy a unique combination of legal and moral authority to carry out statistical inquiries. "The quality of data gathered by most private organizations is really appalling," says John J. Casson, vice-president and chief economist of American Express. "Most people won't answer private surveys the way they will for government. And most private-sector statistics, say from trade associations, is [sic] not that good. Those people are not judged on the quality of their numbers, but on something else, like their lobbying successes."[48]

Probably the most serious risk in privatization is diminished public access. The price of private information services puts them beyond the reach of most community organizations, inquisitive citizens, or academic researchers. In 1980, when DRI was charging $16,000 as a subscription fee for its macroeconomic service (not including computer time), Joseph Kasputys, then a vice-president, said:

> Questions have been raised from time to time over whether the needs of the small organization or the individual researcher in the university are being adequately met and whether the Government should not step in, using the latest available technology. . . . If such needs are not being met now by the private sector, it is likely that they cannot be met economically on a full cost recovery basis.[49] At such time as the technology would permit such needs to be met economically, I am certain that the private sector would step in.

In the meantime, Kasputys continued, "if the government makes information available through depositories and through statistical publications and reports, the small business or small individual researcher with an occasional need for information will be able to gain adequate access to the data and reports he or she seeks."[50] Naturally, the kind of access adequate for "small" researchers would scarcely be satisfactory to the corporate clients of DRI.

[48]Quoted in Crittenden, "World with Fewer Numbers."

[49]Note the invocation of "full" cost recovery as an argument against online services to the public, even though DRI does not pay full cost-recovery prices for the data it receives from government.

[50]"Remarks by Joseph Kasputys," p. 322.

In response to criticism that high prices for public data limit access to information the public has paid for, information industry representatives sometimes say that if Congress decides there is a problem, it should subsidize the deserving information-poor directly and let them buy services at market rates. But the difficulties in carrying out this proposal are evident. To determine who deserves a subsidy, the government would have to find out who uses its data and what their means are—in other words, it would have to introduce new forms of surveillance. In addition, the choice of which groups to subsidize would give the government greater power over the use of public data than it now has when subsidizing statistical information for all. Thus the attempt to correct unequal access while preserving a free market in public data would reduce freedom rather than enlarge it.

The privatizing of statistical information poses some specific problems for the future of the social sciences and intellectual life. Without the capacity to make use of the new information resources in private hands, the universities and other nonprofit research centers may be left as intellectual backwaters. Such a development would have wide implications. Our society maintains universities and research institutions because they create new knowledge and help introduce it into education. The rules of the academy favor open conduct of research; in this sense, all such knowledge is public. Insofar as the public domain is restricted in the sphere of knowledge, research in the university suffers; and insofar as the research in the university suffers, so does public knowledge. The more the national information base passes into the proprietary sphere, the more constricted will be our resources for public life and social inquiry.

Yet there are some grounds for hope. The advent of online technology in the public sector cannot be indefinitely forestalled. As the public sector becomes computerized, much of its information should gradually become available online and be easily convertible to print. Furthermore, as computers become cheaper and more widespread, the mass market for computerized information should grow and prices in the private sector should fall. Public interest and community organizations are now beginning to master the technology and offset the disadvantages under which they have labored in the past decade.[51] But now that information technology has made statistical data as valuable as William Petty thought they would be three centuries ago, the struggle to keep public data public will be with us for a long time.

---

[51]See David Burnham, "New Tool for Public Affairs Lobbies," *New York Times*, August 26, 1983.

Name Index

A

Abraham, W. I., 68n
Abramson, Mark, 364n
Adams, John Quincy, 291
Advisory Committee on Problems of
 Census Enumeration, 181n
Aldrich, Mark, 162n
Alford, Robert R., 266n
Allen, Walter, 113n
Alonso, William, 45n, 244, 249, 250
Alterman, Hyman, 279n
Alvey, Wendy, 32n
American Civil Liberties Union, 195, 222
American Council of Learned Societies,
 220
American Economic Association, 166
American Express, 446
American Gas Association, 410
American Jewish Committee, 221
American Jewish Congress, 222
American Philosophical Society, 287, 291
American Statistical Association, 145, 166,
 286
Anderson, Janice K., 386n
Anderson, William, 168n
Anheuser-Busch, 228n
Anti-Defamation League, 222
Arbuthnot, John, 20
Armstrong, J. Scott, 422n
Ascher, William, 422n
Asher, R. E., 65n
Asian and Pacific Americans Population
 Committee, 178
AT&T, 433
Austin, Charles, 428n
Austrian, Geoffrey, 434n
Avison, N. H., 47n
Avorn, Jerry, 48n

B

Bacon, Francis, 14, 22
Bacon, Ezekiel, congressman, 281
Badillo, Herman, 323
Baglin, R. F., 388n
Bailey, Janet, 420n
Bailyn, Bernard, 159n
Baker, Keith Michael, 22n
Bancroft, George, 192
Bangs, Robert B., 145n
Banister, Judith, 232n
Bank of England, 38
Barabba, Vincent P., 33n, 155n, 178, 180,
 183, 184, 232n
Barnett, George E., 14n
Bauer, Raymond A., 42n
BEA. *See* Bureau of Economic Analysis
Bean, Frank D., 225n
Becker, Abraham S., 80n
Becker, Howard S., 45n
Bell, Daniel, 40n, 42, 42n
Beltramo, A. F., 227n
Berger, Suzanne D., 54n
Berkeley Planning Associates, 347n
Berman, Paul J., 430n
Berne, Robert, 387n
Berry, Brewton, 189n
Berry, John, 435n
Bianchi, Suzanne M., 209n
Biderman, Albert D., 47n
BLS. *See* Bureau of Labor Statistics
Boatner, Lynn A., 403
Böckh, Richard, 218
Bodin, Jean, 11
Boltanski, Luc, 54n
Bonnen, James T., 27n, 186n
Bontemps, Arna, 212n
Boswell, Thomas D., 223n

449

Subject Index

and services: data comparability, 407–408; data quality, 406–407; interaction with private sector, 406, 409–13, 416, 434–47; local access to census and, 357–59; policy issues, 408–409; pricing of, 440–44; user fees, 358, 405–406, 439

federal government role in statistics, justifications of, 275–302; current, 299–302; legislation-aiding function, 19, 280–86, 295–96, 302; microeconomic theory and, 276–78, 293–99; patriotic-pride function, 19–20, 286–88, 297, 301; private decision-aiding function, 292–93, 295, 301–302; social-recognition function, 19, 271, 288–90, 297; special-value-of-knowledge function, 290–92, 297

federalism. *See* education statistics, federal; grants-in-aid; local government, federal statistics in

Federalist Papers, The (Madison), 18, 33, 263, 268

Fifteenth Amendment, 199, 303, 304, 305, 307, 323, 324

Filipino-Americans, 325

Filipinos, 225

Finnish immigrants, 219

"first statistical era," 23–24

fixed weight price index, 90*n*

Florida, 324

folded-in programs, 338

food budgets, USDA, 97, 98, 119

food consumption, 98, 101, 120, 123–24

food equivalence scale, 97, 98

food expenditures, 97–102, 119, 120, 121–24

Food Stamps, 109

Ford administration, 130, 340

forecasting: economic, 28, 48–49, 422, 424; population (*see* population forecasting)

foreign heritage, 190, 191

FOSDIC (Film Optical Sensing Device for Input to Computer), 173, 397

Fourteenth Amendment, 174, 199, 228, 324

Framework for Planning U.S. Statistics for the 1980's (Duncan and Shelton), 134*n*

France, 12; classification in, 53; emergence of statistical inquiry in, 17, 22; output per worker in, 74

Freedom of Information Act, 222

French language, 224

G

General Agreement on Tariffs and Trade (GATT), 65

Generalized System of Preferences, 65

General Theory of Employment, Interest, and Money, The (Keynes), 140

geodemographics industry, 426–29

geographical groupings, 45

German heritage, 219–20

German immigrants, 164, 194, 218, 219

German language, 224

Germany: classification in, 53–54; emergence of statistical inquiry in, 22; university statistics in, 13. *See also* West Germany

Ghost Dance movement, 215

government: manipulation of statistics by, 38–39, 71–72, 265–66. *See also* federal government; local government, federal statistics in

Gramm-Rudman plan, 55

grants-in-aid, 185, 331–42; automatic formulas in, 55–57; categorical, 343–48; history of, 158, 168–71; shift to broadening of, 331–32; targeting and, 334; technical challenges to administration of, 332–33; undercounts and, 232. *See also* block grants; revenue-sharing

Great Britain: emergence of statistical inquiry in, 22; political arithmetic in, 14–15; U.S. immigration quotas for, 164

Green Party, 33

gross national product (GNP), 49, 51; in comparative economic statistics, 62–63, 67–70, 72–75, 78; in national income accounting, 143, 145, 147

group-based representation, shift toward, 273

group classification, 272. *See also* ethnic classification

group identity, 19, 271, 288–90, 297. *See also* ethnic classification

grouping, 44–45

Guarani, 205

H

hard disks, 403

Harlem, New York City, 209, 317*n*

Havana Charter for an International Trade
Organization, 65
Hawaiians, 189–90, 231
Health and Nutrition Examination Survey
(HANES), 124
health statistics, 30–31, 112–15
Hebrew heritage, 219
Hebrew immigrants, 219
Hidalgo County, Texas, 312
Hispanics: census classification of, 45, 207,
223–29, 231–32; in census of 1970, 158;
population growth of, 184; self-
identification of, 207, 314–15, 321;
undercounts of, 176–77, 179, 180, 188,
223; use of national statistical system by,
271; Voting Rights Act of 1965 and,
310–17, 323–27
Hispanos, 223
hold-harmless provision, 338
holography, 403
homeless population, 272
home ownership, 88–89
Housing Assistance Plan (HAP), 346–47
housing expenditure trends, 115–19
How to Pay for the War (Keynes), 142
Hyde County, North Carolina, 304–305

I

identity cards, 401
ideology, 25; population forecasting and,
250–52; real family income (RFI) series
and, 129–30
illegal aliens, 180–81, 225–26, 272
Illinois, 157, 173, 203
illiteracy, 305, 324, 325, 370
immigrants, 104, 162–64, 167. *See also*
European immigrants
immigration, 272, 284; policy, 220;
restriction of, 162, 164, 194–95, 203–204,
220–21, 229
Immigration Act of 1924, 220
impartiality, 258
implicit price deflator, 90
income: national (*see* national income
accounting); per capita, 93–96, 251; per
family (*see* real family income (RFI)
series)
income accounting. *See* national income
accounting
income distribution: automatic formulas

in, 55–57; national income accounting
and, 135–36. *See also* grants-in-aid
income measurement, politics of. *See* real
family income (RFI) series
independent agencies, 26
indexing, 55–56
India, 69
Indians. *See* American Indians
individual noncompliance, 32
infant mortality, 50, 112–14
inflation, 53, 56, 84, 142; consumer price
index exaggeration of, 128; cost of living
adjustments and, 55; current-constant
dollar conversion and, 88–92; mean vs.
median measures of, 87
information-gathering, justifications of. *See*
federal government role in statistics,
justifications of
information products and services. *See*
federal government information products
and services; statistical services industry
information technology. *See* computers;
technological change
"in-kind" income, 105, 107–12
innovation. *See* technological change
inquiry: framing of, 41–43; periodicity of,
49–50
"instant Indians," 214, 216–17, 230
institutional racism, 270
integrated statistical services firms, 429–33
intelligence function, 10, 12, 13
interagency data sharing, 407–408
intergovernmental fragmentation of
education control, 372–76
International Comparison Project (ICP),
69–71, 74
Ireland, 164
Irish heritage, 219
Irish immigrants, 202, 222
Italian language, 224

J

Japan, 67, 74–77
Japanese-Americans, 231, 325
Jewish immigrants, 221
Jews, 42, 44, 202, 207
job classifications, 46
Johnson administration, 99
Jonas v. City of Lubbock (1984), 319n
journalistic use of forecasts, 245